W9-BGX-124

Dick Clark's

THE FIRST **25** YEARS OF

ROCK & ROLL

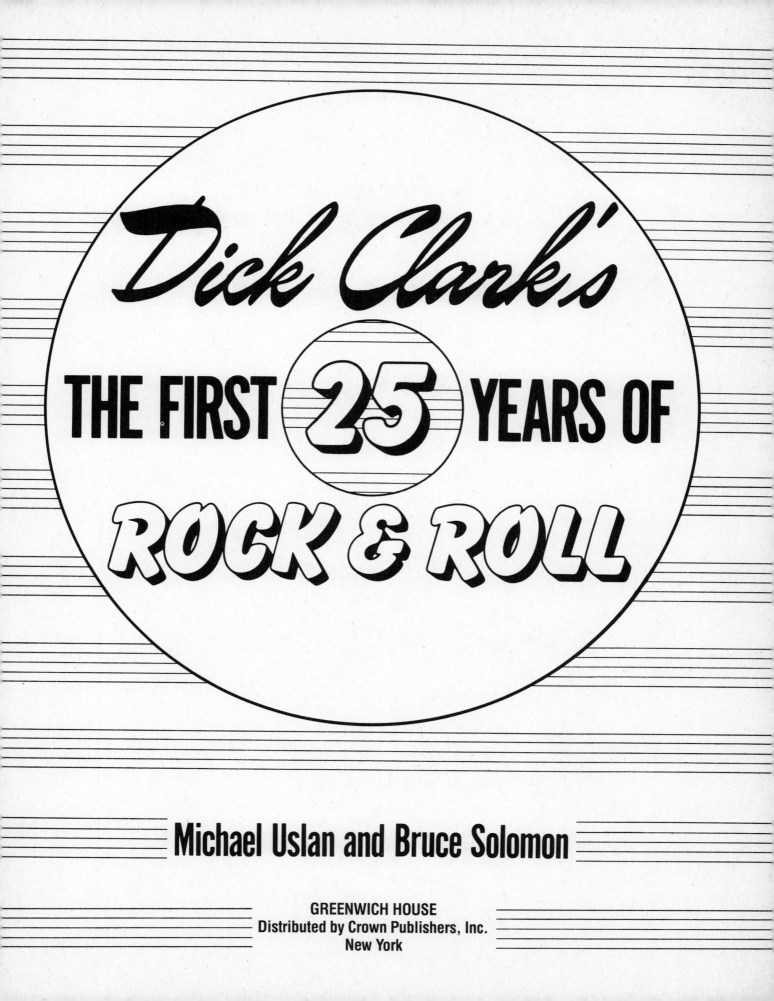

Dick Clark's

THE FIRST 25 YEARS OF ROCK & ROLL

Michael Uslan and Bruce Solomon

GREENWICH HOUSE
Distributed by Crown Publishers, Inc.
New York

To AMERICAN BANDSTAND...
it has a good beat and we can dance to it.

This 1983 edition is published by Greenwich House, a division of
Arlington House, Inc., distributed by Crown Publishers, Inc., by
arrangement with Delacorte Press.

Manufactured in the United States of America

Designed by Giorgetta Bell McRee

Library of Congress Cataloging in Publication Data

Uslan, Michael, 1951-
     Dick Clark's The first 25 years of rock & roll.
     Includes index.
     1. Rock musicians—Biography. 2. Rock groups—Biography.
I. Clark, Dick, 1929—   . II. Solomon, Bruce. III. Title. IV. Title:
First 25 years of rock & roll. V. Title: Dick Clark's The first
twenty-five years of rock & roll.
ML385.U67 1983   784.5'4'00924 [B]   83-5711
ISBN: 0-517-415976

hgfedcba

CONTENTS

1959

1960

1961

1962

1963

1964

(Courtesy of Dick Clark. Photo: Edgar S. Brinker)

FOREWORD

It's difficult for me to realize that twenty-five years have passed since the days when the most frequently asked question I was called upon to answer was, "Do you really think 'this rock and roll stuff' will last?" Those of us who were around during that musical revolution had differing opinions of rock's lasting qualities. But I really did think that the form would last, and I said so.

The old-timers who reported on the music scene in the fifties were usually big-band buffs who honestly believed that rock was "bad" music and the "good" music of their day would return. By the way, that's one argument I've always sidestepped—"good" versus "bad" music. There really is no such thing. "Good" is good to the people who enjoy it. "Bad" is bad to those who hate it for one reason or another. It became abundantly clear that rock was the music of the young and that it was looked upon by many older folks as "bad." Irving Berlin once said that popular music is popular because a lot of people like it. Obviously, a lot of people like rock and have made it an American institution. I've had my share of criticism because of my role in the development of rock and roll. I've also had my share of praise. But there's one comment of which I'm really proud: "Dick Clark was there when rock and roll needed him—he helped keep it alive."

Rock, however, wasn't the first art form to take a bum rap. "A wave of vulgar, filthy, and suggestive music has inundated the land. Our children are continually exposed to the monotonous attrition of this vulgarizing music." That's what critics said about the cakewalk in 1899! "A degenerated and demoralizing musical system has been turned loose to gnaw away the moral fiber of young people," said a prominent religious figure of swing in 1938. Frank Sinatra was categorized in 1943 as "the glorification of ignorance and musical illiteracy." According to Dr. Artur Rodzinski in 1944, "Boogie-woogie is the greatest cause of delinquency among American youth today."

By now I'm sure you've heard that rock is nothing short of harmful to your health and morals. But it has endured! In the first twenty-five years, rock's musical influences and styles have undergone several changes. There's not a single contemporary musician who hasn't been influenced by what started in the fifties. The musicians of the eighties often refer to the "roots" of their music. The Beatles were influenced by Chuck Berry, Buddy Holly, Elvis, and others. Elvis was influenced by black gospel and blues singers Arthur Crudup, Bo Diddley, and others. The big wheel just keeps on turning, and the music we still call rock sometimes bears little

1

resemblance to its beginnings. But the influence is there, and maybe that's why the form has lasted. Unlike the giant (but often stagnant) trends of yesteryear, rock changes almost daily. Other forms of pop music were a little more boxed in, more restricted. That ability to adapt to whatever the public demands has kept rock thriving.

It's hard to conceive of rock becoming a musical dinosaur. Rock has the ability to find new feeding grounds, new sources of life. It can also change color to confuse predators. It has become an art-form survivor. Only one thing can bring down the giant—the loss of creativity and inspiration through the computerization of the business itself. It's becoming more and more difficult for new artists to break in because it's too expensive. If that prevails, I guess new independent record companies will challenge the multimillion-dollar, multinational corporate conglomerates with newer, riskier talent, as happened in the stone age of rock.

Nevertheless, the technological advances in recording, marketing, and distribution can only help rock flourish. To be able to hear your music from a grooveless, almost indestructible, computerized credit-card-type record or to have the option to see and/or hear your favorite artist at a cost comparable to today's album prices will provide rock with more staying power. That really makes me happy. It's the kind of secret (though perhaps juvenile) glow you get from being able to say to the cynics, detractors, and potential saboteurs, "I told you so!"

I'd like to introduce the two men responsible for the hard work and research involved in putting together this volume. Michael Uslan and Bruce Solomon approached me. I'm a compulsive worker—a workaholic; however, I told them that I really couldn't sit down to cowrite such a detailed and extensive book considering the obligations I already had. I said, "You know that you've hit a soft spot. I'm truly interested in the subject material. I do have a certain amount of firsthand information and sources to which we can turn. You gentlemen will have to take the credit and obligation of writing the book. I'll spend every spare moment with you, in an editorial capacity. One thing I hope we can do is treat the subject fairly. So many books on the rock era perpetuate mistakes and improper conclusions. They were written by uninformed rewrite artists using secondhand information. In many cases alleged facts were printed as truth by young writers who had only *read* about what had happened."

We have attempted to correct previously printed errors, go to direct sources—people who were there—go for facts. I'm sure we, too, have made some mistakes. Hopefully they're not big ones. We've tried for accuracy. On the other hand, Uslan and Solomon have expressed some very personal opinions in parts of this book. I'd like to disclaim those opinions as being mine. In many cases they've commented on people I've worked with and known for years. I'm too close to the subject. I couldn't be as critical as they sometimes have been. However, I respect their right to their opinions. It was a pleasure collaborating with two bright, knowledgeable, and interested writers.

We hope you'll enjoy this look at rock and roll twenty-five years after.

—DICK CLARK

ACKNOWLEDGMENTS

We gratefully tip our hats to Dick Clark, who fathered this project; Kari Clark; Fran LaMaina; Larry Klein; Gene Shefrin; the secretaries and staff of Dick Clark Productions; Susie Breitner; the patience and sustenance of Nancy Uslan and Leah Solomon; the collections and recollections of Dr. Paul C. Uslan and Dr. Paul C. Hyman; the expertise of Dr. Glen D. Solomon; the all-around effort of Lisa Solomon, who not only shared her knowledge and hustled photographs, but even helped type in a pinch; the fantastic photography of John Wooding; Steve Huntington; Steve Kurland; Steve Falco; Bruce Ravid—one of the nicest and most knowledgeable people in the record industry; Julian Miller and St. Louis' own *Prom Magazine;* Rita Schlosky; Marc Chernoff; Anthony Bruno; The Memory Shop; Barry Milberg; Arnie Martinelli; the magic fingers of Marel Dunn; the gang from and disciples of *Bloomington Bandstand* and *Give Grease a Chance;* the hospitality of Dr. Daniel P. Schlosky; New Jersey Books; all of the record-company, artist-management, and publicity people who were kind enough to supply us with photographs and information on all the groups and singers; and our staff of typists and researchers, particularly the following:

Jeffrey Mendel of Upper Montclair, New Jersey, a fine rock musician and rock historian whose research and writing skills were the keystone to the completion of this book. Jeff is the coauthor of *The Best of Archie* (G. P. Putnam's Sons, 1980) and *The Best of Betty and Veronica* (G. P. Putnam's Sons, 1981). He has completed his first motion-picture screenplay and is hard at work on his second.

Bill Cross, the scourge of Kissimmee, Florida, gets special thanks for service above and beyond the call of rock and roll. Bill not only did yeoman's work in research, but he also added countless insights and clever phrases to this book. A former disc jockey from Madison, Wisconsin, Bill is now an advertising whiz, band promoter, radio producer, fledgling author, and all-around master of mass media in central Florida.

Dr. Lawrence Hoffman of St. Louis, Missouri, a student of ethno-musicology at Indiana University who became the cocreator and co-DJ of a radio show called *Bloomington Bandstand,* which began as a program of oldies and rock trivia and blossomed into an entertaining history of rock and roll and its disc jockeys.

Tim Brahney of Union, New Jersey, began his association with rock and roll in Youngstown, Ohio, promoting local bands. His writing and promotional skills led him to jobs with the Tomorrow Club of the Agora

3

Night Club chain, Jam Sound, and Special Light, and writing assignments for the trade magazine *Performance.* Tim is an account executive for the *Star-Ledger* in Newark, New Jersey.

Louis Phillips of New York City, New York has done behind-the-scenes work on the road for groups as diverse as the Beach Boys and Led Zeppelin. He attends Franklin and Marshall College, where he is honing his research and writing skills. Louis has worked as a motion-picture production assistant, most recently on the Orion Pictures release *Arthur.*

Every one of them is a true rock and roll all-star and we salute them.

INTRODUCTION

When we set out on the noble task of capturing on paper rock and roll's first twenty-five years, we had thoughts of conquering the world. We would cover every big-name group and singer; we would feature anyone who ever had a gold record or number-one song; we would include even those obscure one-hit artists if they had an interesting story or some anecdote worth relating. And our finished product would have amounted to a twenty-four-volume encyclopedia. Noble—but impractical.

We were then faced with the gut-wrenching decision as to who should stay in and who should be cast aside for some future tome. The agony of eliminating rock-and-roll stars cannot be conveyed here. Suffice it to say that by no means will everyone agree with all of our choices. Some selections were included simply for their unique story, while others, just as popular, were excluded because they gave us little to write about outside of listing their hits. Also, if we hadn't struck a balance for each year, we could have found ourselves with two entries for each of the years 1957 and 1962, eighty each for 1964 to 1968, and so on. So, in advance, we offer our apologies if you can't find your favorite group or singer in this book.

Another problem was assigning each group or singer to a particular year. For some it was a piece of cake: Bill Haley belongs in 1955; the Beatles belong in 1964. The Bee Gees or Led Zeppelin, on the other hand, could easily fit into any of five years. We tried to balance the scales by weighing the year the group debuted with the year of its biggest record(s) or the year of some milestone in its career. Again, it wasn't easy, and if we've offended the fans of the 1968/1969 Bee Gees by placing the group in 1978, we beg forgiveness.

A lot of the information within has been culled from the *American Bandstand* files and extensive interview tapes we made with Dick Clark, and we take this opportunity to thank him for his support, his time, and his invaluable contributions. He also supplied us with our top-ten information, and so, if we talk about a number-one song or a top-ten hit that you can't seem to recall from local radio station charts, it may be because the source is the weekly or yearly *American Bandstand* chart.

Whether your favorite rock-and-roll memories are centered around dancing to the Platters, screaming "yeah-yeah-yeah" with the Beatles, getting high to the strains of "Ina Gadda Da Vida," discoing with Donna Summer, or overturning cars to the beat of the Sex Pistols, we are certain that you'll find your tastes represented in the pages that follow. We wish you, the reader, a memorable journey through the pages of rock and roll's rich history. May the second twenty-five years be as thrilling as the first.

1955

The reason kids like rock and roll is because their parents don't.

—MITCH MILLER

Nineteen fifty-five was a year of beginnings. It was the year Disneyland opened its magical gates amidst the fervor of a Davy Crockett fad that put a coonskin cap on the head of every kid in America. The Salk polio vaccine was administered nationally for the first time, ending one of youth's greatest health nightmares. The AFL merged with the CIO to form a single, more powerful labor organization. Lawrence Welk began making champagne bubbles on television, and Sergeant Bilko played his first poker game at Fort Baxter.

Marty won the Oscar for Best Picture in 1955. The Cleveland Browns took the NFL championship by running all over the Los Angeles Rams, while the Syracuse Nationals won the NBA championship. The New York Yankees lost the World Series in seven games to the Brooklyn Dodgers. In Philadelphia the televised Phillies' baseball games showed commercials for beer and TastyKakes featuring a young disc jockey from middle-of-the-road WFIL named Dick Clark. Also on Philadelphia TV and in its third year was a show called *Bandstand,* hosted by Bob Horn and featuring kids dancing to pop tunes in the studio.

Nineteen fifty-five also saw the rise of youth gangs, teen-age vandalism, and juvenile delinquency. The youth of America appeared to be taking to the streets in defiance of their parents and teachers. Black leather jackets and greasy ducktail haircuts became the adopted symbols of teen rebellion. What was the cause? Who was to blame? Some claimed that communists were subverting our youth. Others found a cause closer to home—that new, inciting, arousing, loud, screaming tribal music called rock and roll.

Hit parade tunes like "Ko Ko Mo" by Perry Como, "Mr. Sandman" by the Chordettes, and "Sixteen Tons" by Tennessee Ernie Ford now had to share space on the charts with strange infiltrators such as "Earth Angel" by the Penguins, "Sincerely" by the Moonglows, "Pledging My Love" by Johnny Ace, and "Story Untold" by the Nutmegs. However, even though 1955 was the first year of the rock-and-roll explosion, only three songs that could qualify as either rock and roll or rhythm and blues broke into the top ten that year—"Rock Around the Clock" by Bill Haley and the Comets, the white-cover version of "Ain't That a Shame" by Pat Boone, and the cover version of "Dance with Me Henry" by Georgia Gibbs. The rest of the list consisted of "Cherry Pink and Apple Blossom White" by Perez Prado, "The Yellow Rose of Texas" by Mitch Miller, "Autumn Leaves" by Roger Williams, "Unchained Melody" by Les Baxter, "The Ballad of Davy Crockett" by Bill Hayes, "Love Is a Many-Splendored Thing" by the Four Aces, and the white-cover version of "Sincerely" by the McGuire Sisters.

Nevertheless, rock and roll found a strong and faithful audience. Dick Clark remembers what early rock was all about and why it became such a teen-age passion. "It was a rhythmic music. Kids were into dancing, and it was all theirs. It was a combination of country music and black music. For the most part it was created by southerners who had heard country and gospel music all their lives. Then, a little bit later, the street sounds of 'doo wop' came out of the Bronx, Philadelphia, Cleveland, and Akron, where young urban blacks sang rhythm and blues on street corners and white kids liked the sound, ultimately borrowing it.

"The move from rhythm and blues/rockabilly to rock and roll was partly due to Bill Haley and Elvis Presley, both of whom were white, country-oriented singers with a feel for black music. Chuck Berry and Fats Domino also had a hand in the creation of rock and roll. Chuck Berry was the flip side of the Bill Haley/Elvis Presley coin. He grew up with rhythm and blues, then 'whitified' his black music. 'Sweet Little Sixteen' has no gospel roots. Fats Domino was a New Orleans jazz musician who had that really weird sound; his lyrics were almost unintelligible to the white-music-oriented ear."

Bill Haley, Elvis, and Chuck Berry were soon followed by Little Richard's gospel brand of screaming rock and roll. Rhythm-and-blues stars like Ray Charles, LaVern Baker, Hank Ballard, and the original Drifters also contributed to the transition and would serve as the prime influences on succeeding rock-and-roll stars.

This was 1955—the first year of rock and roll.

FATS DOMINO

It's a funny thing about Antoine "Fats" Domino. Although he had hit after hit through the fifties and sixties, he never had a number-one song. He came close with "Ain't That a Shame" in 1955 and "I'm Walkin'" in 1957, but the impact of these records was diffused by "cover" versions of those hits by Pat Boone and Ricky Nelson respectively. A "cover" record was a white recording artist's version of a black artist's original record. Record charts separated "pop" and "race"—or rhythm-and-blues—music, and few white-oriented radio stations would give a black artist airplay. The white version of the record was practically guaranteed the lion's share of airplay. In addition, the wealthier "cover" record labels could promote the white copy extensively, helping it climb to the top of the charts.

Many critics have charged that those artists who covered black records and the DJ's who played only covered versions were racists. But Dick Clark is quick to refute that charge.

"All we wanted to do was get an audience. There was no racism involved. If you couldn't get your audience in Dubuque to buy Fats Domino, you played the Pat Boone version. It was the way to sugarcoat a new kind of music to get it across to an audience that wasn't used to it. It's like Mexican food—once you get a little taste of the hotness, you will begin to like it hotter. Then you'll want it pure rather than a bastardized version of it."

Perhaps the biggest contribution Fats Domino would make to the emerging music scene would be as a performer on the road. Fats' overwhelming popularity made him one of the first major black acts to break the racial barriers of many clubs and halls. His appeal stemmed from his famous rhythmic, boogie piano style, clever arrangements of first-class blues/jazz material and his tenor voice with the catchy but hard-to-decipher New Orleans accent.

Fats came out of Louisiana lucky to have a music career at all. As a young factory worker he had seriously injured his hand in an accident. But Fats practiced, exercised, and played his piano, overcoming physical limitation. In 1950 he made his first mark on show business with the rhythm-and-blues hit "The Fat Man," the song that gave him his monicker.

Between 1950 and 1955 pop music was in the doldrums. The big-band sound was out. Patti Page, Gisele MacKenzie, the Ames Brothers, and other voices of the Hit Parade were turning out endless trash. But country and western, pop, and rhythm and blues were slowly coming together. Country would spawn the rockabilly sound of Elvis, Carl Perkins, and Bill Haley and the Comets. Rhythm and blues would soften into a more polished, melodic sound that could appeal to a predominantly white audience. The end result of the musical melting pot would be rock and roll. Songs like Lloyd Price's "Lawdy Miss Clawdy" in 1952, the Chords' "Sh-Boom" in 1954, and the Crows' "Gee" in 1954 were omens of things to come.

In 1955 Fats ushered in the age of rock and roll with "Ain't That a Shame." His songs began turning up on the pop charts in addition to the rhythm-and-blues charts. But this rock-and-rollin' Fats was somewhat different from 1950's "Fat Man." The music was slower, his voice lower, his tunes simple and danceable, evoking more smiles than his blues had. The typical early rock-and-roll saxophone, which was often accused of being sexually arousing, came into prominent use. The new Fats clicked, and his rock-and-roll career quickly outdistanced his R & B successes. "Ain't That a Shame" was followed in rapid succession by "I'm in Love Again" (1956); "My Blue Heaven" (1956); "Blueberry Hill" (1956), which was Fats' arrangement of an old rhythm-and-blues song with traditionally suggestive lyrics; "Blue Monday" (1956); "I'm Walkin' " (1957); "Valley of Tears" (1957);

9

"Whole Lotta Loving" (1958); "I'm Ready" (1958); "I Want To Walk You Home" (1959); "Walking to New Orleans" (1960); and "I Hear You Knocking" (1961).

Rock and roll's first five years were glory days for Fats Domino. In 1956 he appeared in the film *The Girl Can't Help It* with Jayne Mansfield. He made numerous *American Bandstand* appearances in those years despite his fear of being on television. Many backstage pep talks from Dick Clark, along with a drink or two, were often necessary to help get him out on stage. His sound is classic and influences rock-and-roll artists to this day.

Today Fats still packs in his fans in concert, on the road, and at rock-and-roll revival shows.

RAY CHARLES

He watched his brother drown shortly before he was blinded by glaucoma at age six. Orphaned at fifteen, Ray Charles' raw, wild vocals and powerfully emotional delivery came from the depths of his own experiences. In the mid-fifties Ray Charles *was* rhythm and blues.

Born in Georgia, Ray Charles Robinson had roots in gospel, yet he drew on jazz influences in learning to play the piano. The two modes of music combined to give him a unique sound and piano style that would take him to the top of the rhythm-and-blues charts in the early fifties. He started professionally playing for Ruth Brown and Moms Mabley, and was soon discovered by Atlantic Records. His first national hit, the groanin', moanin' "I've Got a Woman," pierced both the "race" charts and the pop charts. It is one of the handful of songs in rock-and-roll history to become a hit twice—the second time in 1965. His success on both charts led to live performances for integrated audiences and stands as one of the first major achievements in breaking down racial barriers in music. "I've Got a Woman" and "Greenbacks" were chart busters in 1955.

Ray's greatest contribution was his combination of the secular, sexy blues with sanctified gospel music—a blend never heard in black music up to this time. Ray took the gospel strains of "My Jesus Is All the World to Me," and while retaining the passion of church singing, changed the topic to his crosstown girl friend waiting to share some loving—and soul music, in the form of "I've Got a Woman"—was born. An old-time blues singer, Big Bill Broonzy, bitterly complained: "He's crying sanctified. He's mixing the blues with the spirituals. He should be singing in church." Ray's potent blend of blues and gospel reached its pinnacle in 1959 in the form of the full-fledged rock-and-roll song "What'd I Say," which came complete with a gospel call-and-response, impassioned shouts, a rocking blues beat, and the longest instrumental introduction ever found on a rock single. Ray led the way for what would be called Soul, and broke new ground for future singers like Sam Cooke, Wilson Pickett, and Otis Redding.

Ray's R & B hits were given more and more airplay on "white" radio stations because of his growing acceptance by white audiences. He continued to return to the top of the pop charts with "What'd I Say" (1959), "Georgia on My Mind" (1960), and "Hit the Road Jack" (1961).

In 1962, Ray took an obscure country-western song recorded four years earlier by Don Gibson, utilized a smooth, almost middle-of-the-road sound, and wound up with a number-1 record, a new audience, and an award for best country-western performance of the year. "I Can't Stop Loving You" was Ray's attempt to reach the audience that his raw vocals and writhing, contorted movements had possibly alienated. The backup vocals on the record were rendered by the Raelettes, not the Ray Charles Singers, who were connected to a different Ray Charles entirely.

After a few years away from the hit charts, Ray bucked the British invasion of the mid-sixties with "Crying Time" (1965), "Let's Go Get Stoned" (1966), and his versions of the Beatles' "Yesterday" (1967) and "Eleanor Rigby" (1968). After overcoming a drug problem in 1965, Ray again became an active recording artist and performer, outlasting the musical onslaughts of British rock, acid rock, folk-rock, disco, and punk.

LAVERN BAKER

LaVern Baker was the queen of rhythm and blues and the first lady of Atlantic Records, the leading R & B label of the fifties. From her gospel wailing to her raspy, urban R & B, LaVern's ability to belt out different types of songs was apparent to the Atlantic people. It was this versatility that would allow her to make the successful transition into that stomping new music, rock and roll.

LaVern's release of "Tweedlee Dee" in December, 1954 quickly soared to the top of the R & B "race" charts in 1955. But when disc jockeys like Cleveland's Alan Freed began giving it airplay, "Tweedlee Dee" actually cracked the white pop charts and found a place in *Record World's* top ten, where it settled in through January, February, and March of 1955. But the ultimate success of "Tweedlee Dee" was dampened by the generous amount of airplay time given to Georgia Gibbs' white-cover version of the song, which reached number 16 on the charts that year. LaVern's version wasn't even close behind.

But LaVern continued releasing records described alternately as rhythm and blues and as rock and roll, depending on who was doing the describing. However,

with Alan Freed's growing popularity (now on radio station WINS in New York) and his regular playing of LaVern's hits on his show, her reputation as a soulful rock-and-roll singer was assured. With the 1956 release of "Jim Dandy," she unveiled a lower, gruffer voice, perhaps in an attempt to further penetrate the rock-and-roll market. The change was hailed by her teen-age audience, and from 1955 to 1962 she unloaded nine top hits, including "Bop Ting-a-Ling"; "Tra La La"; "See See Rider"; and "I Cried a Tear."

Under the management of SRO Artists, an agency formed by Dick Clark and Al Wilde, LaVern enjoyed additional success on tour. She became a regular crowd-pleaser at the great live shows produced by Dick Clark, Alan Freed, Murray the K, and others.

By the mid-sixties, however, LaVern's career had wound down. Perhaps if she had held on a little longer, she could have made another great transition in style to the new "soul" or "Motown" sound. LaVern has retired from performing and now resides in Japan. But her place as the leading lady of R & B and as one of the pioneers of rock and roll is secure in the history of the music.

HANK BALLARD AND THE MIDNIGHTERS

Hank Ballard's group was originally called the Royals. Coming out of Detroit, the same city that spawned a number of black rhythm-and-blues singers, the group had a rough, rhythmic, urban sound that appealed to singer Johnny Otis. Otis lined them up with King Records, and by 1954 the Royals were on their way. However, another singing group named the 5 Royales took legal action against Hank and his group for using a name that they claimed was too similar. The Royals quickly became the Midnighters, and their careers resumed.

In 1954 Hank's raucous "Work with Me Annie" became the first big hit for the group. His lyrics were more than suggestive, and the sexual explicitness caused the banning of the song by radio stations in numerous cities. Rhythm-and-blues tunes often had raunchy lyrics, but "Work with Me Annie" went further than most songs did prior to punk rock.

Other songwriters and singers reacted to "Work with Me Annie" as if it were a gauntlet thrown before them. A host of songs appeared, each claiming to be the response to Ballard's tune, and thus giving rise to what became widely known as answer songs. While "Work with Me Annie" extolled the sexual stamina of the singer, "Roll with Me Henry" (also known as "Wallflower") by Etta James questioned it. When Georgia Gibbs covered the James tune for the white market, she scrubbed down the song, altered the suggestive lyrics, and marketed it as "Dance with Me Henry." Ballard then retorted with "Annie Had a Baby," trying to settle the question of Henry's manhood once and for all. But Etta James returned for the last word with "Henry's Got Flat Feet."

Hank Ballard and the Midnighters found it harder to break out of the rhythm-and-blues charts than many other R&B acts had. Their sound remained too coarse and harsh to appeal to white audiences at the time. What seemed to be Hank's big chance came in 1960 when a song he wrote called "The Twist" made its debut. Written in early 1959, "The Twist" was Hank's opportunity to supplant "The Stroll" as teen-age America's latest dance craze. Hank's record company didn't see it that way, though, and released "The Twist" as the B-side of "Teardrops on Your Letter." Promotional efforts pushed "Teardrops," while "The Twist" was quickly spreading as an unheralded dance discovery among urban blacks. One day on *American Bandstand* Dick Clark spotted a couple doing an outrageously provocative dance. The Twist had arrived. But it would be Chubby Checker, not Hank Ballard, who would rocket to stardom with it.

The trauma of creating "The Twist" and not being able to cash in on it as performers could have been enough to drive Hank Ballard and the Midnighters right out of the music scene. But instead they softened their sound and plunged into the rock-and-roll charts with two big hits in 1960—"Finger Poppin' Time" and "Let's Go, Let's Go, Let's Go." Ballard finally achieved the rock-and-roll success he had sought, but it was short-lived. He was never again in the top forty of rock and roll and has since moved into record production. However, he never gave up performing, at various times playing backup for James Brown and even trying his hand at disco.

OPPOSITE PAGE:

Big, bad Bo Diddley with his maracas player, Jerome Green. (*Courtesy of Dick Clark*)

BO DIDDLEY

Bo Diddley, born Ellas McDaniels, was another victim of music's racial barriers in the mid-fifties. His work was characterized as "race" music and didn't get the kind of airplay it deserved. Yet Bo's guitar playing was legendary and would serve as a source of inspiration to Jimi Hendrix and many other guitarists in rock and roll's first quarter-century.

Bo came from Mississippi by way of Chicago and arrived at Chess Records with a song that paid homage to his own guitar playing. The song had an African tribal beat, accented by maracas and a heavy electric bass guitar, producing the kind of sound that would become the foundation of psychedelic rock some thirteen years later. The song was called

BO DIDDLEY

"Uncle John," but the folks at Chess didn't like this title, so Bo renamed the tune after himself.

Bo Diddley didn't have many successful singles; "I'm a Man" (1955) and "Say Man" (1959) were his most popular recordings. But even without twenty-five years of hits, his influence on rock-and-roll guitar is staggering.

The early seventies' animated motion picture *Fritz the Cat* incorporated "Bo Diddley" into its soundtrack. At about the same time, Bo became active on the rock-and-roll revival circuit. His genius was highlighted at a 1972 Madison Square Garden revival show in New York where he jammed with the legendary Chuck Berry and drove the crowd wild; the performance was captured on film in the 1973 release *Let the Good Times Roll.* Live on stage with an explosive chemistry, two of rock-and-roll's founding fathers played the kind of music that made rock and roll what it was then and is today. Loud, rebellious, jubilant, inciting, exciting, and provocative, their music is exactly what so many parents, teachers, and clergymen reviled and condemned in the 1950s.

Bo Diddley and Dick Clark. *(Courtesy of Dick Clark)*

The Sound of 1955

BILL HALEY AND THE COMETS

"Rock Around the Clock" was *the* sound of 1955. The song became the battle cry of the rebellious post–World War II rock-and-roll generation. The song's message to their shocked elders was simple: "Up yours!" And carrying the message of "Rock Around the Clock" were Bill Haley and the Comets.

From Chester, Pennsylvania, by way of Michigan, Haley started out as a western swing singer with his group, the Saddlemen. But by 1951 some of their songs, like "Rock the Joint," were sounding crazier, louder, and faster than country tunes. This was actually early rockabilly, a primitive rock-and-roll form. In early 1955 the Saddlemen became the Comets and recorded a song called "Rock-a-Beatin' Boogie," which some people regard as the first true rock-and-roll song. If it wasn't, it at least foreshadowed, with its silly but historic lyrics, what was soon to come: "Everybody rock, rock, rock! Everybody roll, roll, roll!" Could these lyrics have inspired Cleveland's WJW disc jockey Alan Freed to dub the emerging music "rock and roll"?

In 1953-54 Haley merged his rockabilly with rhythm and blues to create hits like "Crazy Man Crazy" and his cleaned-up cover version of Joe Turner's R & B hit "Shake, Rattle and Roll." It's interesting that Bill sang a "clean" version of "Shake, Rattle and Roll," moving the setting of the song from the bedroom to the kitchen, while his 1956 hit "Rip It Up" proclaimed that "We're gonna rip it up, and ball tonight." But in 1956 the slang verb "to ball" actually meant "to rock," and conversely "to rock" had the sexual connotation then.

Then came "Rock Around the Clock," a record that has had sales approaching the twenty-five-million mark. Its initial impact was incredible. Kids hadn't been dancing since the end of the swing era. Suddenly, this spirited tune with a bouncy, rhythmic beat had the kids clapping and dancing to the newest version of the lindy—the jitterbug. It revitalized dancing the way the twist and the hustle would in later years.

Perhaps one of the reasons "Rock Around the Clock" was associated with juvenile delinquency was its use as the theme song of two motion pictures: *Rock Around the Clock* and *Blackboard Jungle.* The former was the first of a multitude of rock-and-roll movies. It was a somewhat fictionalized account of how rock and roll came to be, starring Alan Freed

17

Bill Haley and the Comets. *(Courtesy of Dick Clark. Copyright 1957 Columbia Pictures Corp.)*

A meeting of rock-and-roll titans—
Little Richard and Bill Haley.
(Courtesy of Dick Clark)

and Bill Haley and the Comets, featuring the group's frantic, energetic stage performance.

Leaping, bending over backwards, kicking, crawling, and even climbing over the bass—their acrobatics were not equaled until the stage antics of the Who some fifteen years later. *Blackboard Jungle,* however, was serious drama about the growing juvenile delinquency problem in one high school. It starred Glenn Ford as a teacher confronting young hoodlums who are challenging his authority. "Rock Around the Clock" blared during the opening credits of the film, linking it with teen-age punks in the minds of the general public.

Shortly after the follow-up record "See You Later Alligator" was released, Bill had a mutiny on his hands. All the Comets except one walked out. Those Comets became the Jodimars and had one big tune on their own, "Let's All Rock Together," before numerous personnel changes and a final fading from the scene. The loss of the original Comets didn't stop Bill, however. He hired new people and went on to star in another movie, *Don't Knock the Rock,* in 1957. But by this time rock and roll was being infiltrated by the softer sounds of Pat Boone, Connie Francis, Frankie Avalon, and a horde of other teen idols. Bill lacked the appeal of newer, good-looking teen idols, and his age (he was now in his thirties) further alienated him from his market. He failed to hit the top of the charts again, so he packed his bags and tried touring Europe. From country to country he was a smash, heralded as the messiah of rock and roll. His tremendous popularity culminated in 1979 at London's Theatre Royal. Queen Elizabeth was present, sitting on the edge of her chair and tapping her feet in delight during Haley's set. After the show he was the one she wanted to meet.

In 1969, when promoter Richard Nader planned the very first rock-and-roll revival show at Madison Square Garden's Felt Forum, he chose Bill Haley and the Comets to be the headlining act. They brought down the house; the crowd went wild. In the last eleven years of rock and roll's first quarter-century, Bill Haley and the Comets continued to be the leaders of the rock revival circuit.

After the tumult of the early rock years Bill preferred the solitude of his home in Texas. In February 1981 Bill Haley, rock and roll's elder statesman, succumbed to a heart attack.

1956

> Not only are most [rock and roll] songs junk, but in many cases, obscene junk—pretty much on a level with dirty comic magazines!
>
> —BILLY ROSE

Eisenhower beat Stevenson. The Yankees beat the Dodgers in a Series highlighted by Don Larsen's perfect game. The Soviet Union beat Hungary. The Giants beat the Bears. In contending for the Oscar Award for Best Picture of the Year, *Around the World in 80 Days* beat *The Ten Commandments, The King and I, Friendly Persuasion,* and *Giant.* The Warriors beat the Pistons. Nineteen fifty-six was a very competitive year!

It was the year rock and roll made tremendous strides in knocking off easy-listening pop tunes from the charts. Three Elvis Presley tunes were in the year's top ten: "Heartbreak Hotel," "Don't Be Cruel," and "Hound Dog." The Platters held a spot with "My Prayer." The top ten was rounded out with such standard fare as "Lisbon Antigua" by Nelson Riddle, "Wayward Wind" by Gogi Grant, "Poor People of Paris" by Les Baxter, "Whatever Will Be, Will Be (Che Sarà Sarà)" by Doris Day, "Memories Are Made of This" by Dean Martin and "Rock and Roll Waltz" by Kay Starr.

Elvis, of course, was the man of the year, creating a mania equaled only by Frank Sinatra and the Beatles. Yet there were many other emerging rock-and-roll groups and artists pushing their songs onto the charts. There were Shirley and Lee's "Let the Good Times Roll," the Teen Queens' "Eddie My Love," Elvis' imitator Gene Vincent's "Be-Bop-a-Lula," "Tonight You Belong to Me" and "Gonna Get Along Without You Now" by the young Patience and Prudence McIntyre sisters, Bill Doggett's hot instrumental "Honky Tonk," Jim Lowe's "The Green Door," the Mello-Kings' classic "Tonight Tonight," Little Willie John's version of "Fever," and the Cadets' storytelling comedy "Stranded in the Jungle."

Television of 1956 featured hits like *I Love Lucy* and *Playhouse 90,* and a local Philadelphia teen-age dance show called *Bandstand.*

Bandstand was still seen on WFIL-TV, which was owned by *The Philadelphia Inquirer. The Inquirer* had been running a series of articles about the dangers of drinking and driving in 1956 when the M.C. of *Bandstand* was arrested for drunken driving. He was fired as a result, and a replacement was needed. They brought in the young DJ who had substituted for the host and had done the radio version of *Bandstand*— Dick Clark.

With the development of *Bandstand*, one feature on the show became the focus of both fan and record-industry attention. It was called Rate-a-Record. Dick has his own thoughts about its real importance. "It never meant anything to the success or failure of a record. We had songs that were condemned on Rate-a-Record that became big sellers, and vice versa."

Rate-a-Record scoring ranged between 35 and 98. For years many *Bandstand* viewers have wondered, "Why not less or more?" Dick explains:

"Ninety-eight made the upper limit because nothing is perfect, and 35 was the lower limit because nothing's all bad. I did that to avoid smart-ass kids who might say 'I give it a zero' just to get others in the studio to laugh. It would have gotten to be a 'thing.' I set up those artificial limits to keep it within the bounds of politeness."

It was 1956—the second year of rock and roll.

HOUND DOG - ELVIS PRESLEY
ANADIAN SUNSET - H. WINTERHALTER
BE BOP A LULA - GENE VINCENT
ASUAL LOOK - SIX TEENS
AN'T WE BE SWEETHEARTS - CLEFTONES
ANTED IN THE JUNGLE - JAY HAWKS
E PROUD ONES - BUDDY MORROW
EADY TEDDY - LITTLE RICHARD

THE PLATTERS

While many singing groups were one-hit wonders, others seemed to be blessed with longevity because of the consistent evolution of a characteristic sound, as opposed to mere trendiness, in their records. The Platters personified this successful pattern, exhibiting a unique talent and style that made them the number-1 pop music group of 1956. Many black vocal groups of the fifties were displaced by the superior sales of white-cover records. But not the Platters! They were the first black group to reach the top ten without a cover to overshadow their achievement.

The Platters were formed in Los Angeles in 1953. The original members consisted of lead singer Tony Williams from Roselle, New Jersey, tenor David Lynch from St. Louis, bass Herb Reed from Kansas City, and Alex Hodge. The group was discovered and managed by Buck Ram, a successful songwriter in his own right dating back to the early forties, who created their image and vocal style. The Platters, who at the time worked mainly as parking-lot attendants, were used by Ram to record demos of his own songs. He selected the music for the Platters' repertoire, creating a more refined sound with suitably arranged standards from the thirties and forties. These polished renditions, often simultaneously on the charts with the raucous rock and roll of their contemporaries, earned their places on playlists and in record buyers' collections.

The first major personnel change in the Platters took place when Zola Taylor was recruited from a group known as Shirley Gunter and the Queens and Paul Robi replaced Alex Hodge. Their first record company, Federal of Cincinnati (and their subsidiary label, King) had become disenchanted with them because their record sales were only moderate. Ram then negotiated with Mercury and convinced them to sign the Platters as part of a deal he was making for the Penguins, whom he also managed.

At the time, the Penguins had a blockbuster R & B hit for the Dootone label called "Earth Angel." Mercury wanted the Penguins and their projected follow-up hits so badly that they gave in to Ram's demands and signed both groups. The Platters recorded "Only You" for Mercury, and shortly after its release in July 1955 it became a national breakout hit and the group's first number-1 record. The sweet irony is that while the Platters went on to release hit after hit for Mercury, the Penguins never had another big record after "Earth Angel."

At the end of 1955 the Platters recorded another Buck Ram song, "The Great Pretender," which quickly became a number-1 disc, staying atop the charts well into 1956. It won a gold record in less than a year, becoming an international hit and an all-time rock standard. Revival songs became the Platters' mainstay. Among them were "My Prayer" (1956), a hit from 1939; "Twilight Time" (1958), coauthored by Buck Ram and a group called the Three Suns; "Harbor Lights" (1960), a 1937 Rudy Vallee ballad; "Red Sails in the Sunset" (1960); and "Ebb Tide" (1960). The Platters had a monster hit in 1958 with the Jerome Kern standard, "Smoke Gets in Your Eyes." It is said that Kern's widow attempted to obtain an injunction to prevent circulation of the new version of the song, contending that the Platters' rendition would irreparably harm the original. However, when it was explained to the complainant that the record was on its way to becoming gold and that such exposure to a new generation would probably make Kern royalties soar, all legal actions ceased.

The Platters were perhaps the most popular vocal group of the fifties, with four number-1 songs and sixteen gold records. Tony Williams continued to sing lead until June 1960, when he left to become a solo performer. He was replaced by Sonny Turner, whom

The Platters.

he himself introduced at the Copa Club in Newport, Kentucky. Following Williams' departure, the Platters' success began to fade, especially after bizarre reports of an incident involving the law in a Cincinnati hotel. This bad press, coupled with the personnel changes, spelled the end for the Platters' reign in the early sixties. The replacement of Paul Robi and Zola Taylor with New Yorkers Sandra Dawn and Nate Nelson kept the group alive and recording for the Musicor label in the mid-sixties. Various incarnations of the Platters were featured in many rock-and-roll revival shows in the early seventies, and they continued to make personal appearances for years.

Finally, a series of victories in the U.S. federal courts led to the protection of the trade name and service mark "The Platters" by The Five Platters, Incorporated, a corporation created in 1956 by Buck Ram. Although most of the Platters' performing success today occurs in Europe and Asia, they still return for sporadic U.S. tours, bringing home those sentimental love tunes that always seemed to be the last dance of the night at parties, proms, and hops of the 1950s.

In January 1981, the Platters lost the talented David Lynch after his long, hard fight against cancer.

LITTLE RICHARD

I am the beautiful Little Richard from way down in Macon, Georgia. I believe my music is the healin' music. I believe my music can make the blind see, the lame walk, the deaf and dumb hear and talk, because it inspires and uplifts people. It regenerates the heart, makes the liver quiver, the bladder splatter, and the knees freeze.

—LITTLE RICHARD

Little Richard Penniman is a rock-and-roll original. There has never been anyone who could match his manic drive, buoyant spirit, and inspired wailing. Even in 1956 Little Richard appeared in concert in a spangled outfit with his long processed hair spray-painted silver, thumping wildly at the piano. He made public appearances on a throne carried by Beefeaters who would roll out a red carpet and unfurl a flag with Richard's image on it. He would cavort, scream, explode in a frenzy, play piano with his toes, throw off his clothes, dance on top of his piano, and always leave his audience begging for more. Unlike the staged theatrics of artists like Alice Cooper and Kiss in the seventies, Little Richard was a natural, a breath of fresh air in the staid fifties.

Little Richard grew up in Macon. His grandfather and two of his uncles were preachers, but his daddy sold bootleg whiskey. His family didn't like rhythm and blues, so Little Richard grew up listening to the likes of Bing Crosby and Ella Fitzgerald. Although a church singer as a youth, Richard added his own "thang" to the gospel hymns. His father couldn't take his son's loud music, long hair, loud clothes, and bizarre behavior and threw him out of the house at age thirteen. The white couple who ran the Tick Tock Club in Macon, Ann and Johnny Johnson, took Little Richard in. They sent him back to school and encouraged his singing by letting him perform at the club. After winning a talent contest at age sixteen, he found himself in a recording studio with the Johnny Otis Band. But the usually spirited Little Richard turned solemn, trying to sing in an urban blues style that just wasn't his. Before long he found himself back in Macon, washing dishes.

While washing dishes at Macon's Greyhound bus station in 1955, Little Richard wrote his first big hit. His boss was bringing in pots and pans for Little Richard to scrub. The work was endless, but it would have meant his job if he mouthed off. Finally fed up, Richard exploded with a verbal barrage of "a wap bob a lup bop a wop bam boom!" The boss was puzzled, but Richard still had his job. That blast of gibberish became "Tutti-Frutti."

Little Richard got his first big break when Lloyd Price came to Macon. Riding the crest of his hit "Lawdy Miss Clawdy," Price was performing at a dance where Little Richard was selling drinks from a bucket. Richard barged up onto the stage and told Price that he could do what Price was doing if somebody would let him. He sneaked backstage after the show and played "Tutti Frutti" for Price, who was so impressed he told the boy to send a tape to his record company, Specialty, which Richard did. Months passed without word from Specialty, while Richard was still scrubbing pots at the bus depot. When Specialty finally did call in late 1955, they invited him out to L.A. But at the Specialty Recording Studio, Little Richard made his old mistake, unsuccessfully trying to sing the blues. Just when Specialty thought it was out its plane fare, Richard banged out "Tutti Frutti" on the piano during a break. Producer Bumps Blackwall, hearing Little Richard let loose, brought in a writer to clean up the more obscene ravings, and "Tutti Frutti" became an instant rock-and-roll classic.

Pat Boone did a cover version of "Tutti Frutti" and had a bigger hit with it in 1956. Richard felt no ill will toward Boone this time, but was determined not to let Boone beat him on a record again. He practiced "Long Tall Sally" for hours on end until he could spit out the line "ducked back in the alley" like machine-gun fire. Pat Boone's mouth wasn't quick enough, and Little Richard landed the bigger smash.

More often than not, Little Richard's tunes were made up of nonsense lyrics. His spirit and style were more important than the words he was singing. Using the same band that Fats Domino used in New Orleans, Little Richard pumped his piano, stomped out the rhythm, and wailed at breakneck speed. "Slippin' and Slidin'," "Keep A Knockin'," and "Jenny, Jenny" didn't make much sense, but their energy captured the record-buying public through 1956 and 1957.

In 1958 Little Richard was at the top, playing to packed houses on every continent. He sang in rock movies such as *The Girl Can't Help It* with Jayne Mansfield and was a sensation. Then Little Richard suddenly decided to give up show business for the pulpit. While touring Australia with Eddie Cochran and Gene Vincent, the engine of Little Richard's plane caught fire and they began to plummet. Richard swore that if the plane landed safely he would give up show business to serve God. The plane made it back to Sydney in one piece, and before Richard could change his mind, he had a fiery, prophetic dream about the recently launched satellite Sputnik. Richard threw his jewels into the ocean, renounced rock and roll as the devil's instrument, and enrolled at Oakwood College in Huntsville, Alabama, to study the gospel and become a preacher.

After he graduated, however, Little Richard decided to return to show business. His comeback in 1962 may not have been a rousing success, but he did go on to help to develop many major rock talents. Jimi Hendrix played guitar in his band for two years. Richard headlined a tour of Germany with an opening act from Liverpool, England. He took the Beatles to the Star Club in Hamburg, where he taught Paul McCartney "Long Tall Sally" and often picked up the tab when John Lennon ordered steaks that he couldn't afford. Little Richard's next European tour featured another unknown group, the Rolling Stones.

Having faded away, he came out of retirement again in 1970, appearing in the film *Let the Good Times Roll* and recording two new albums, *The Rill Thing* and *King of Rock and Roll.* As flamboyant and unpredictable as ever, Richard made the rounds of the TV talk shows and enticed a new generation of fans. But without any solid new material, his egotistical excesses became tiresome. In a lightning flash

Little Richard.

of déjà vu, Little Richard gave up show business again in the summer of 1979, ranting against the evils of rock and roll and its practitioners. Unable to serve both God and rock and roll, one of rock's wildest spirits walked away from the limelight one more time.

FRANKIE LYMON AND THE TEENAGERS

Throughout the first twenty-five years of rock and roll, unusually young stars have appeared who have shown great talent both in performing and writing. "Little" Stevie Wonder composed and recorded "Fingertips—Part 2" at age twelve, and Paul Anka wrote and performed his own music at age fourteen. But the forerunner of the prepubescent rock and rollers was Frankie Lymon, lead singer of the Teenagers.

The Teenagers were made up of several ninth graders at New York's Edward W. Stitt Junior High School. The original members included Joe Negroni and Herman Santiago, who began singing in school hallways and at neighborhood talent shows. At one of these appearances they became acquainted with a mambo percussion group that featured Howie Lymon on the congas and brother Frankie on the bongos. Frankie was accepted as a member of the Teenagers after working his way into a couple of their practice sessions. The group was known as the Coupe De Villes for a brief time, then as the Premiers. Initially Santiago was the lead singer, and their early repertoire consisted of songs copied from such groups as the Dominoes and the Valentines. They performed in backyards, on tenement rooftops, and on the sidewalks for tips.

Richard Barrett, lead singer of the Valentines and artists-and-repertoire director for Rama-Gee Records, overheard one of the Premiers' free evening serenades and offered them a studio test and a possible recording audition. One of their standards was a number called "Why Do Birds Sing So Gay." When Rama-Gee owner George Goldner heard the first few run-throughs of it, he suggested that Frankie try singing lead, since Herman Santiago seemed to have laryngitis. Goldner changed the title of the song to "Why Do Fools Fall in Love." He asked who the author was. Everyone was amazed to hear that it was

thirteen-year-old Frankie, who claimed it was his own lamentation of a shattered romance. Rama-Gee signed the group, and the song was recorded in Bell studios in the spring of 1955.

With backup by the Jimmy Wright band, the record was mastered without a written arrangement. Barrett counseled thirteen-year-old Lymon in the technical aspects of delivery—phrasing, cupping notes, and individual vocal stylizations. Jimmy Wright, the backup group leader, suggested the name change to the Teenagers. It sounded more like that of a rock-and-roll group, they felt.

"Why Do Fools Fall in Love" was withheld from release until January 10, 1956. Goldner timed its retrieval from the can to avoid conflict with the Christmas season's glutted record market. The Teenagers were featured in Alan Freed's show in Hartford, Connecticut, less than a month later, as their smash single was escalating to million-seller status despite stiff competition from covers put out by the Diamonds on Mercury and by Gale Storm on Dot. High school was left behind as the Teenagers played to sellout crowds and received standing ovations all the way from the Brooklyn Paramount to the London Palladium. Their act was choreographed by Cholly Atkins, who also directed the steps for the Cadillacs and, later, the Temptations, to name only two. The Teenagers' success was bolstered by the releases of "I Promise to Remember," "I Want You to Be My Girl," and "I'm Not a Juvenile Delinquent." They appeared on Dick Clark's *American Bandstand,* Alan Freed's TV show, and *The Ed Sullivan Show.* (When TV cameras caught Frankie dancing with a white teen-age girl on Freed's program one day, the sponsors were outraged.) Freed's TV show was suddenly canceled, and this marked the beginning of his demise. The group was also featured in Freed's movie *Rock, Rock, Rock,* which introduced "I'm Not a Juvenile Delinquent" and "Baby, Baby." Both songs were cuts from their premiere L.P. on Gee Records, *Why Do Fools Fall in Love.*

Frankie's lead billing soon caused resentment in the group. Manager Morris Levy, sensing the rift, suggested that Lymon go solo. The group's last hit together on Gee, a remake of the old tune "Goody, Goody," did quite well. The split, unfortunately, proved fatal for both careers. Frankie recorded on Roulette, but his ability to draw the crowds was reduced considerably. By 1958 such pressures as his gradual voice change had led him to a narcotics habit. He was never able to kick his heroin addiction and eventually died of an overdose in his grandmother's cold-water flat in Harlem in February 1968. Retired dancer Sam Bray had worked with him intensely in 1966, trying to restore what once was. Frankie was scheduled to record again for Roulette after a brief tour on the club circuit, all under the tutelage of Bray. He died at age twenty-six the night before his Roulette session.

Today the Teenagers are still playing, now with Frankie's sound-alike brother, Louie. Many popular groups of the seventies like the Jackson 5 attribute their styles and sounds to the influence of Frankie Lymon and the Teenagers.

THE FIVE SATINS

One of the more short-lived groups of the fifties was New Haven's Five Satins. They recorded only four single releases and one L.P. on Ember Records between 1956 and 1960, but one of those singles would be acclaimed as one of the best songs ever recorded in the history of rock and roll.

The original members of the Five Satins were lead singer Fred Parris (who was replaced by Bill Baker on "To the Aisle"), tenor Rich Freeman, second tenor West Forbes, harmony vocalist Lewis Peeples, and bass Sy Hopkins. In the early fifties Fred Parris was the leader of the Scarletts, who recorded several R&B hits for the Red Robin label, owned by Bobby Robinson, including "Dear One," "True Love," and "Love Doll." Parris teamed up with Richard Freeman, who was also with the Scarletts, and recorded "All Mine" on Standard records. He was fleetingly associated with the Velvets, supposedly the inspiration for the name of the group that would make him famous.

Fred Parris was in the Army, working the graveyard shift on guard duty, when he wrote "(I'll Remember) In the Still of the Night." When he got out of the service, the group recognized it as a potential hit song. They recorded the song with style and class, employing magnificent harmonies that combined the contrasting sounds of Parris' high-pitched vocals with the backup group's moaning, wailing, and doo-wop phrasing. The Five Satins first released the song on Standard Records, a small Connecticut label that surprisingly chose "The Jones Girl" (a response to the Mills Brothers' "The Jones Boy") for the A-side, relegating "In the Still of the Night" to the B-side. The record went nowhere. The Five Satins then made a deal with Standard, and got their music back. They made a new deal with the bigger Ember label in New York City, and the disc was released with "In the Still of the Night" as the A-side. The record charged to the top of the race music charts, and even broke into the top thirty on the national pop charts, a significant achievement for a black singing group in 1956. Eventually the disc was certified gold. But more important, it was to become the love song of teen-age steadies for years to come.

Their second hit, "To the Aisle" (which took the lovers from "In the Still of the Night" down the wedding aisle), featured Bill Baker on lead and was included on *The Five Satins Sing* album along with their previous hit and their less successful singles, "Our Anniversary" and "Wonderful Girl." Also on that album was "Oh Happy Day," a gospel standard that became a best-selling single for the Edwin Hawkins Singers in the late sixties. However, the limelight ended with "I'll Be Seeing You," a moderately popular release that got most of its radio airplay as the sign-off record for all-night disc jockeys.

Despite their lack of additional big hits, the group milked their popularity by doing many coast-to-coast tours as well as a concert sweep of Europe. In 1957 the group appeared at the Apollo Theater in Harlem and in the stage show *The Fantabulous Show of 1957*, securing their superstardom in New York City. They, too, were guests on Dick Clark's *American Bandstand.* But with no new smash tunes to maintain their audience, the Five Satins eventually disbanded.

Twelve years later promoter Richard Nader reunited the Five Satins for the Rock-and-Roll Revival Show at Madison Square Garden's Felt Forum. New York's WNEW-FM disc jockey Scott Muni, the show's M.C., explained to the overflowing crowd that the group hadn't seen each other in over a decade, and that therefore they were requesting the audience's patience with the rough edges. He then brought them out, and the tumultuous response charged the group and their fans alike. The New York crowd refused to let them offstage without additional choruses of "In the Still of the Night." They couldn't believe their reception. The Five Satins broke down and cried. Not having had many hits, they quickly ran out of material, but the crowd still yelled for more. Without any rehearsals after some twelve years, they decided to try "I'll Be Seeing You" a cappella. It was like 1957 at the Apollo again. The sound was satin smooth, harmonies blending to perfection. The concert concluded with the joyous announcement that the Five Satins had been offered a brand-new recording contract.

CARL PERKINS

Of the founding fathers of rock and roll, Cark Perkins is perhaps the most unfortunate and unsung. Born poor in Lake County, Tennessee, Carl Perkins often spins yarns about his first guitar, which was made for him by his father out of a cigar box, a broomstick, and two strands of baling wire. He was taught how to play by an old black man named John Westbrook, the reputed champion cotton picker on the plantation where his father sharecropped. Carl formed the Perkins Brothers Band with his brothers Jay on the rhythm guitar and Clayton on bass. They played in local dives two or three nights a week, "dodging beer bottles."

Filled with musical aspirations, Carl sent a tape to Sam Phillips' Sun Record Company in Memphis at the time when Phillips was caught up with the preparations for the debut of Elvis. After he was given the runaround, Perkins drove to Memphis itching for a confrontation. He barged into Phillips' office and demanded an audition. Surprisingly, Phillips gave him one on the spot. Carl recorded "Turn Around" that day and left with a promise that the side would be released. Phillips kept his word, and Perkins heard it on Bob Neal's WMPS record show from Memphis two months later. Carl was inspired. Shortly thereafter he woke up in the middle of the night and began jotting down the lyrics to "Blue Suede Shoes" on a potato sack, the only "paper" available. Phillips rushed Carl into the studio, where he recorded his new tune on the Sun label. The song was released on New Year's Day, 1956, rose to number four, remained in the top ten for nine weeks, and clung to the charts for twenty-one weeks. (Elvis later recorded the song on his first album for RCA, *Elvis Presley,* released in 1956; as a single Elvis' version only made it to number 24.)

The success of "Blue Suede Shoes" took Carl around the country. One night, after a performance in Norfolk, Virginia, Carl, his brothers, and their manager, David Stewart, began the long drive to New York for guest shots on the *Perry Como Show* and the *Ed Sullivan Show.* Outside Dover, Delaware, they crashed into a bridge abutment. Carl was in traction for weeks with multiple fractures and internal injuries. Jay eventually died of his injuries. Carl did not actually work again until 1959. All his money went toward hospital bills, and he began drinking heavily. He left Sun Records and joined Columbia, but there were no hits. After a stint on the Las Vegas circuit, he quit show business altogether until money problems forced him back.

On a 1963 tour of England with Chuck Berry, the Animals, and the Nashville Teens, Carl realized that he still had a following. During this tour he became friendly with the Beatles, who were not yet known in America, and was asked to coach them on their versions of three of his songs: "Matchbox," "Honey Don't," and "Everybody's Trying to Be My Baby." The new British groups were turning back to rock-and-roll's roots, and Carl Perkins was suddenly respected as a founding father of the music. He curtailed his drinking and headlined shows in England. Things looked up, but only for a while.

By 1965 Carl was off the wagon, had been wounded in a hunting accident, and was out of work again. Johnny Cash then helped Carl pull himself together. Until recently Carl had been working closely with the Cash troupe. He swore off alcohol as a promise to Cash before he joined the tour. Carl finally regained national exposure with his solo spots on Cash's early-seventies TV show, which triggered the rerelease of his Sun records. He remained the featured guitarist with the Cash show until 1975, content to stay out of the spotlight. Despite all his troubles, Carl Perkins has maintained a good relationship with his wife of twenty-seven years, an accomplishment worthy of applause in itself.

Carl was a key performer in the early days of rock and roll, who, like Elvis and Bill Haley, injected that all-important element of southern rockabilly into the music. Country-styled rockabilly merged with urban rhythm and blues to form pure rock and roll. Carl's influence inspired the Beatles and the British sound, and, more recently, punk rock.

The Sound of 1956

ELVIS PRESLEY

There have been a lotta tough guys. There have been pretenders. There have been contenders. But there is only one King.

—BRUCE SPRINGSTEEN

Where do you go from Elvis Presley—short of obscenity, which is against the law?

—JOHN CROSBY
New York Herald Tribune, June 1956

Elvis Presley was the king of rock and roll. He had over sixty-eight million-selling records in his career and recorded twenty number-1 singles between 1956 and 1975. Only Elvis could earn a gold record with a boxed set of fifty B-sides. In 1956 he totally dominated the record charts. "Heartbreak Hotel" landed on the number-1 spot on May 5, 1956, and at least one Presley hit sat on top of the charts for twenty-four of the remaining thirty-five weeks of 1956. Seventeen of his records made the charts in the last nine months of 1956. Presley had over 140 records make the charts in his career with over 350 million copies sold worldwide. But it wasn't just record sales that made Elvis the King.

Presley defined rock and roll in 1956. The sneer. The hair. The twisting knees. The thrusting hips. The pink Cadillac. The gold lamé suit and the leather jacket. With Elvis, rock and roll was rebellion, smoldering sexuality, and something parents were afraid to touch.

Elvis was the first rock-and-roll teen idol. Girls screamed, shrieked, fainted, tore at his clothes, and sent him teddy bears. Boys imitated his sideburns, his slicked-back hair, his leather jacket, and his tough stare. Where Elvis led, rock and roll followed. His voice was copied in every rock era from Conway Twitty, Terry Stafford, and Ral Donner in the fifties to Robert Gordon, Freddy Mercury of Queen, and occasionally even Paul McCartney today. His throaty snarl *was* rock and roll. If James Dean was a rebel without a cause to teen-agers all over the world, Elvis Presley was a rebel with a cause—rock and roll.

Elvis Aron Presley was born on the wrong side of the tracks in East Tupelo, Mississippi, on January 8, 1935. His twin brother, Jesse Garon,

The King—Elvis Presley.

died at birth, leaving Elvis an only child. The Presleys were poor, but they still doted on Elvis. Vernon and Gladys Presley somehow found a way to buy their seven-year-old son a guitar for $12.95. The Presleys belonged to the Pentecostal First Assembly of God Church, and from an early age Elvis went to revivals, camp meetings, and religious sings. When Elvis was thirteen, his family packed up in the dead of night and headed for Memphis, Tennessee, hoping for something better. There they were forced to live in a tenement in a black ghetto of Memphis.

In 1953 Elvis graduated from Humes High School and started work driving a truck for the Crown Electric Company for forty-two dollars a week. While driving around Memphis, he spotted a billboard for the Memphis Recording Service. One day that summer Elvis got up the nerve to go to the recording service to cut a record for his mother's birthday. "Well, I can't sing very well, but I'd like to try," Elvis told proprietor Sam Phillips. For four dollars, eighteen-year-old Elvis recorded "My Happiness" and "That's When Your Heartaches Begin." Phillips, who also ran Sun Records, was impressed with Presley's style and his feel for black music. Phillips' secretary, Marion Keisker, took Elvis' phone number for future reference.

In April 1954 Phillips called Presley. At a recording session with the Prisonaires at the Nashville Maximum Security Prison, Phillips found a country song that he thought suited Elvis and called to see if he would like to try to record it. Elvis is said to have made it over to Sun Records before Sam Phillips hung up the phone. The session didn't go well, with Presley trying to imitate some of the well-known crooners of the day. During a break Elvis started banging on the guitar, wailing an old blues number, "That's All Right (Mama)." Phillips came running into the studio, yelling, "What in the devil are you doing?" Embarrassed, Presley and the instrumentalists, Bill Black and Scotty Moore, mumbled that they didn't know. "Well, find out real quick and don't lose it," Phillips said. "We'll put it on tape." Sam Phillips had just discovered magic—a white man who could sing black music with a black feel. The world would never be the same again.

Sun released "That's All Right (Mama)" on July 6, 1954, and sent a copy to Memphis disc jockey Dewey Phillips (no relation to Sam) and his *Red, Hot and Blue* show. Dewey played it, and there was an immediate response. Sun got orders for five thousand copies in Memphis. Sun then released five Elvis singles over the next year, all of them blues numbers on one side backed by country tunes; but without national distribution outlets, none of them made the national charts. Still Elvis was a hot item south of the Mason-Dixon Line. Eddy Arnold's former manager, an ex-carnival man named Colonel Tom Parker, took an interest in the Memphis sensation, then managed by Memphis disc jockey Bob Neal. Parker knew Sun Records was short on cash and would welcome the chance to sell Presley's contract to a major record label. Colonel Parker worked at drumming up interest in Elvis in the North. When Bill Randle, a very influential disc jockey, started playing "Mystery Train" and "I Forgot to Remember to Forget" in Cleveland, big record companies soon became interested in Elvis. In September 1955 Colonel Parker negotiated the deal for RCA Victor Records to buy Presley's contract from Sun for thirty-five thousand dollars (a hefty sum in those days) plus six thousand dollars in back royalties that Sun owed Elvis. Elvis got a pink Cadillac in the deal, but Parker got the biggest prize of all—he became Elvis' personal manager.

In December 1955 RCA rereleased all five of Presley's Sun singles together, but nothing much happened. RCA executives began to question the deal that had bought this high-priced hillbilly. In January 1956 Elvis cut "Heartbreak Hotel," a song written by Mae Boren Axton (Hoyt's mom), at RCA's studios in Nashville. Presley's sexy growl took the record to number one by May. RCA never doubted again.

Elvis appeared on national TV for the first time on January 28, 1956, on the *Tommy and Jimmy Dorsey Stage Show* on CBS. Elvis twisted, shook, leered, and swung his pelvis at the camera. Sponsors, network executives, and parents were outraged. But the kids loved it, and so the battle lines were drawn. Steve Allen had Elvis on his show, dressed in a tuxedo and singing to a hound dog. Allen's ratings zoomed. Ed Sullivan, who initially vowed never to have Elvis on his show, offered him fifty thousand dollars to appear on three shows. Sullivan wouldn't allow the cameras to show Elvis from the waist down, which only increased Presley's mystique with America's teen-agers. His wiggle, his sound, and his style became the most hotly debated issues of 1956. Adults attacked Elvis, kids loved him, and record sales zoomed.

"I Want You, I Need You, I Love You" followed "Heartbreak Hotel" up the charts in May 1956. Presley's next single was a monster—the two-sided number-1 hit "Hound Dog," a raucous shouter penned by Jerry Leiber and Mike Stoller—and about as sensational was "Don't Be Cruel" (written by Otis Blackwell). They stayed on top of the charts for eleven weeks and became the most famous songs of the era. "Love Me Tender," based on the old folk song "Aura Lee," was the theme song of Elvis' first movie. After Elvis sang it on the Sullivan show, there were orders for one million copies the next day—and the record hadn't yet been pressed!

Elvis was the hottest name in show business. By 1958 he had starred in four films: *Love Me Tender, Loving You, Jailhouse Rock,* and *King Creole.* He caused a surge in record and guitar sales. All kinds of Elvis merchandise flooded the marketplace. And of course, he had hit after golden hit—"All Shook Up," "Teddy Bear," "Jailhouse Rock," and "Honey Don't"—all number-1 records. Then, in 1958, Elvis was drafted. Colonel Parker worked quickly. In marathon recording sessions Elvis put enough material in the can to last two years. Army private #53310761 had the most famous serial number in the armed forces. Telephone calls to Elvis on *American Bandstand* kept his name before the fans.

But when the Army shaved off Elvis' sideburns, his rebellious image disappeared with his whiskers. Colonel Parker made Private Presley a national hero, but he wasn't the kind of hero teen-agers wanted. The Army private oiling rifles in Germany just wasn't the same defiant, snarling rock and roller who had brought fear into the hearts of adult America. Elvis Presley and rock and roll were tamed by a draft notice.

The Army mellowed Elvis. When he was discharged in 1960, he no longer seemed to have his heart in rock and roll. His old rockers gave way to ballads like "It's Now or Never," "Are You Lonesome Tonight?" and "Can't Help Falling in Love With You." Except for a TV special with Frank Sinatra in 1960, Elvis made no personal appearances until 1969. He either made uninspired movies in Hollywood or cloistered himself at Graceland, his mansion. Elvis made a comeback in 1969 with an exciting televised concert, a blockbuster Las Vegas nightclub act and a string of excellent singles—"Suspicious Minds," "In the Ghetto," "Kentucky Rain," and "Burning Love." And though his impact on rock and roll had greatly diminished, his talent was still great. Elvis' old fans never deserted him— in fact, as time wore on, they grew even more fanatical. Elvis had set the course that all rock and roll would follow. When Elvis died on August 16, 1977, rock and roll truly lost its king; but though the king may have died, rock and roll gained its first "god." Diehard fans helped deify Elvis first by overwhelming Memphis for the funeral, then by buying every sort of Elvis memorabilia available. Items ranging from Elvis belt buckles to Elvis toilet seats were snapped up by adoring fans. Perhaps the best tribute to emerge from this new wave of Presleymania was *Elvis,* a made-for-TV movie produced by Dick Clark which featured a remarkable performance by Kurt Russell. The film handily defeated *Gone With the Wind* and *One Flew over the Cuckoo's Nest* in head-to-head TV ratings competition.

Elvis' later years may have been marred by alleged drug problems, health ailments, and a bizarre behavior pattern that included a proposal to go to work for the FBI, but such are eclipsed by his outstanding, ground-breaking music and the influence he had on all of us. That is the true legacy of Elvis Presley.

1957

Poison put to sound! —PABLO CASALS

In 1957 Jimmy Hoffa took over at the helm of the Teamsters. Laika, the Russian dog aboard Sputnik, became the first living creature to be sent into space. Mattel introduced the Barbie Doll, soon followed by her friend Ken, whose anatomy baffled many. (Batteries were not the only things not included!)

After two years of hard rock and roll, 1957 saw the incursion of the divisive sounds of soft rock. True, hard rockers like Jerry Lee Lewis and Chuck Berry were in their prime, but more and more Pat Boone records were sneaking onto the charts. The top ten songs of the year represented an incredibly wide range of tunes, appealing to the vast audience: "All Shook Up" by Elvis Presley; "Little Darlin'" by the Diamonds; "So Rare" by Jimmy Dorsey; "Love Letters in the Sand" by Pat Boone; "Don't Forbid Me" by Pat Boone; "Young Love" by Sonny James; "Too Much" by Elvis Presley; "Young Love" by Tab Hunter; "Round and Round" by Perry Como; and "Singing the Blues" by Guy Mitchell. Other big sellers of the year were Dale Hawkins' "Susie-Q," Harry Belafonte's "Banana Boat," the Rays' "Silhouettes," Debbie Reynolds' "Tammy," "Party Doll" by Buddy Knox and the Rhythm Orchids, "Come Go with Me" and "Whispering Bells" by the Del Vikings, "A White Sport Coat" by Marty Robbins, and "Over the Mountain, Across the Sea" by Johnnie and Joe.

Television as well seemed to be going soft in 1957, with Grandpappy Amos McCoy lecturing Pepino and Perry Mason lecturing the court. But on August 5 *American Bandstand* blossomed from a local program in Philly to an ABC network show. Its instant popularity quickly led to a nighttime version. Now with a national audience, *American Bandstand* was gaining greater appeal.

It was 1957, the third year of rock and roll.

JERRY LEE LEWIS

He rocketed out of Louisiana, grabbed rock and roll by its "Great Balls of Fire," and drove it to new heights of screaming, gyrating, and pounding insanity. And all from a former ministry student! Many parents and clergymen saw rock and roll as the tool of the devil. Well, so did Jerry Lee! To this day he still considers himself a sinner destined for hell because of his music. Nevertheless he keeps on playing.

The Killer—Jerry Lee Lewis.

Jerry Lee was discovered in 1957 by Sam Phillips of Sun Records. Sam was into rockabilly and white stars who could sing like blacks (unlike the people at Chess Records, who tried to make Chuck Berry and other black artists sound white in order to pierce music's racial barriers). Sam had found a talented kid with a feverish boogie piano and a zealous performing style that was enough to label him "obscene" by

some community standards. Sam Phillips' job was to find a way to make his boy acceptable to the public. But his fears were unnecessary. Steve Allen invited Jerry Lee on his TV show and allowed him to perform "Whole Lot of Shakin' Going On" uncensored. Overnight America had a new rock-and-roll sensation. That appearance meant so much to Jerry Lee Lewis' career that he named his first-born son Steve Allen Lewis.

If 1957 was a wild year for Jerry Lee, 1958 was a lot wilder. It began with the release of "Great Balls of Fire," which was banned by many radio stations, afraid that it *might* be "dirty." It continued to be a successful year for him, though, with "Breathless" and "High School Confidential," the latter being the theme song of the motion picture of the same name. Jerry Lee appeared in two other films, *Jamboree* and *Young and Deadly.*

In concert he played piano with his elbows, feet, and any other part of his body that would reach the keys. He often leaped onto the keyboard and danced his tunes while his backup group wailed. He rarely failed to whip the crowd into a frenzy. Once forced to go on *before* Chuck Berry, he doused his piano with gasoline and set it on fire in a total rage at the insult. It blazed away as he pounded out "Great Balls of Fire" on it.

Jerry Lee left his wife in 1958 to marry his third cousin, thirteen-year-old Myra Brown. While he was on tour in England later that year, the secret marriage hit the press, and the situation became a major incident. Never again would he have a rock-and-roll song in the top ten. He was the plague as far as DJs, promoters, and bookers were concerned. Even *American Bandstand,* which had featured Lewis on a number of occasions, was pressured by sponsors and the network to exclude him. Dick Clark believes the worst mistake of his career was reluctantly buckling under to that pressure and agreeing not to book Lewis on the show. Over the years he's tried to compensate for it by booking Lewis whenever he can, even when Lewis' career was on a downswing.

During those bleak years when his career was on the downswing, Jerry Lee faced many personal tragedies. His son, Steve Allen Lewis, drowned in their pool in 1962. His wife, Myra, divorced him in 1971. His son, Jerry Lee Lewis, Jr., was killed in a 1973 automobile accident. In 1976 Jerry Lee accidentally shot his bass player in the chest. That same year he was badly hurt himself in a car accident. From time to time Jerry Lee had problems with alcohol and/or pills, frequently ending up in a hospital for extended treatment. During one pill binge Jerry Lee's cousin, TV evangelist Reverend Jimmy Swaggart, physically pulled him off the stage in Baton Rouge, took him home, and destroyed his supply of alcohol and pills. But each time Jerry Lee was down, he was able to summon the strength to fight back.

Today Jerry Lee Lewis has found a new home in country-western, where he has produced hit after hit. Every once in a while, however, he dusts off the old rock-and-roll piano and hits the revival circuit for a frenzied night of insanity.

PAT BOONE

The color white was very important in Pat Boone's career. He made white buck shoes the craze in the 1950s, he has promoted milk on TV, and he began his rock-and-roll career doing white-cover records.

Until the late fifties it was a true rarity when a white-oriented radio station would bridge the racial barrier and play original records by black artists. Alan Freed was one of the first disc jockeys to introduce rhythm and blues to his predominantly white audience, and they loved it. Freed turned his congregation of rock and rollers on to Little Richard, Chuck Berry, Fats Domino, the Drifters, Frankie Lymon and the Teenagers, and other sensational black talent. But as was the rule in those days, as soon as a black artist released a song with potential, a white performer would release a cover version of it. Pat Boone was the leading cover artist of the day.

Charles Patrick Boone, the great-great-great-great-grandson of Daniel Boone, was well on his way up the career ladder in 1955. He had won first place on both *Ted Mack's Amateur Hour* and *Arthur Godfrey's Talent Scouts.* These appearances led to a recording contract with Dot Records.

In 1955 he covered Fats Domino's "Ain't That a Shame." In 1956 he recorded cover versions of Little Richard's "Tutti-Frutti" and "Long Tall Sally." By this time Alan Freed publicly refused to play any Pat Boone records and accused those disc jockeys who did of racial prejudice, a charge refuted by Dick Clark and others who saw Pat Boone as a way to introduce naive whites to black music. Clark did play both versions of "Ain't That a Shame," but he found that Boone's version had more commercial potential at the time. Dot eventually found that Boone was a real teen-age idol on his own, so "Long Tall Sally" became his last cover record.

In 1957 Dot gave Boone his own material to record. He was promoted as a clergyman's vision of what a rock-and-roll star should be—neatly dressed, well groomed, polite, singing a very soft sort of music debatably called rock. Many critics cite Boone's emergence as the beginning of the deterioration of the original hard rock-and-roll sound of Elvis Presley, Chuck Berry, Bill Haley, Little Richard, and Jerry Lee Lewis. Boone's success eventually led to a proliferation of soft rockers like Frankie Avalon, Fabian, Bobby Rydell, Ricky Nelson, Connie Francis, and Paul Anka. Boone's success burgeoned with the release of his first love ballad, a 1931 song entitled "Love Letters in the Sand."

Nineteen fifty-seven was also the beginning of Pat's screen career. The rock-and-roll idol became a matinee idol. Starring in *Bernadine* and *April Love,* he released hit singles of their theme songs. From 1958 to 1961 he had a dearth of hit songs but an array of motion picture successes, including *Journey to the Center of the Earth, State Fair, Mardi Gras,* and *The Main Attraction.*

"Moody River" marked Pat's return to the charts in 1961. It was followed the next year by a novelty tune that he still considers his favorite recording, "Speedy Gonzales," based on the Warner Bros. cartoon character, a Mexican mouse who moved like lightning. Mel Blanc, the cartoon voice of Speedy Gonzales, Bugs Bunny, Barney Rubble, and Porky Pig, added his voice characterizations to the song. It was a huge novelty smash and went on to rank with classics like "The Purple People Eater," "The Witch Doctor," "Beep Beep," and "The Monster Mash."

Pat Boone and his family are active performers today. Often promoting religious or moral causes, they are regulars on TV and on the concert circuit. A proud father, Pat watched his daughter Debby grab the spotlight in 1977 with the song of the year, "You Light Up My Life." They often appear as a duo in concert.

JIMMIE RODGERS

If anyone in rock and roll could spin a tale in song, it was Jimmie Rodgers. Long before the days of "Alice's Restaurant" and "Tommy," he told us the story of creation, love, and his girl friend in "Honeycomb" (1957). In "Kisses Sweeter Than Wine" (1957), he played the role of a rock-and-roll minstrel unraveling a tale about the woman he married. Following the successes of "Oh-Oh, I'm Falling in Love Again" and "Secretly" in 1958, he was back telling the story of "Bimbombey."

Jimmie came from the state of Washington with a rockabilly sound. His voice was velvety, clear, and capable of reaching falsetto notes. That voice and his talented guitar playing first brought him success on *Arthur Godfrey's Talent Scouts* and then with Roulette Records in Nashville. Almost immediately he had a hit with "Honeycomb," which prompted Roulette to search for other folk ballads Jimmie could sing in his pop style with the country coating. They found "Kisses Sweeter Than Wine," a very old Irish ballad, and it soon followed "Honeycomb" up the charts.

After "Bimbombey" in 1958 Jimmie's career unfortunately nosedived. Unable to hit the charts after four years, he was released by Roulette. He then signed with Dot, but by the end of 1964 it became apparent that no comeback was forthcoming. Then in 1967 he nearly lost his life. The details are sketchy at best, but Jimmie is said to have been driving on a Los Angeles freeway when he was stopped by the police and allegedly severely beaten, suffering a fractured skull. Recovery was uncertain. After many months Jimmie pulled through. He dropped out of public sight, only to return to do a breakfast-cereal commercial. Post was marketing a cereal called Honeycombs, and Jimmie was hired to sing a modified version of his earlier hit. Television appearances on the *Ray Stevens Show,* among others, brought him back into the limelight. He even had his own TV variety series in 1959 and again in 1969. In the 1970s he began making live appearances again, performing rockabilly, and launched a new recording career with A & M Records.

Jimmie Rodgers.

40

PAUL ANKA

The creativity of young Canadian-born Paul Anka was the substance of a career that spanned three decades and produced well over fifty recordings. He wrote most of the songs he performed, which distinguished him from the handful of prominent teen-idols in the late fifties and eventually effected the transition from teen-idol to adult entertainer which left many of his earlier contemporaries behind.

Anka, the precocious son of a successful Ottawa restaurateur, was exposed to many entertainers who came through town, such as Chuck Berry, Frankie Lymon and the Teenagers, the Platters, and Fats Domino. Anka's debut was at a high school amateur contest. He won, but *not* for his singing. He did impressions, his best being Sammy Davis, Jr. He went on to win a talent competition with a mock rendition of Johnny Ray's act. Prompted by these successes, Paul formed a high school singing group called the Bobby Soxers with fellow classmates Jerry Barbeau and Ray Carrier. They were popular in the Ottawa area, but were unable to branch out. Then one night Paul found himself backstage after a Fats Domino gig, where he met promoter Irvin Feld. Feld was so impressed by the boy's self-confidence and aggressiveness that he made a notation to contact him for possible future dealings. This meeting with Feld marked a turning point in his life. Until then Anka had still been considering a career in law or journalism.

By the summer of 1956 there had been no word yet from Feld, so Paul's father sent him to Hollywood, where he could test the waters of the music business. He met Ernie Freeman of Modern Records and penned his first tunes for that label, "Blan-Wile-Deveest-Fontaine" and "I Confess," which got limited airplay, mainly in Canada, but did serve to encourage him toward a career in music. However, there was still no word from Feld.

Paul's father pushed him to try again, giving him a hundred dollars to try his luck in New York during the ten days of his Easter vacation. When he arrived in New York, he contacted a popular group known as the Rover Boys, whom he had met while they were appearing in a Canadian club. The group recorded for ABC Paramount Records and had just had a big hit with "Graduation Day." Through the Rover Boys, Anka met ABC artists-and-repertoire man Don Costa, who arranged an audition for him. It was a big opportunity for a kid who was sleeping in a bathtub at the President Hotel. At the audition session he did four songs. Costa wanted to record him immediately. Anka attributes his early successes to this respected producer/arranger for ABC Paramount.

Paul Anka's first hit, which was released in the summer of 1957, was about a Canadian girl he had a crush on named Diana Ayoub. She was twenty years old, five years his senior. For "Diana" he used only five instruments—piano, guitar, sax, bass, and drums—plus three backup singers. It was recorded at the Capitol Studio on West Forty-Sixth Street in New York, and the finishing touches were added in Ottawa. The song launched his rock-and-roll career, and he stuck with ABC for the next five years.

Just after Anka hit it big with "Diana," impresario Irvin Feld remembered their initial contact in Fats Domino's dressing room. Feld quickly booked him to one of his upcoming rock-and-roll spectaculars and became his manager soon thereafter. But whenever Paul had an idea for a new song he would call Don Costa first to discuss it. Later in 1957 they decided to shift from the small-band sound of his first hit to a big band. The result was "You Are My Destiny," inspired by Billy Ward and the Dominoes' "Star Dust." Next came "Lonely Boy," which Anka wrote at a very emotional period of his life, when he was entrenched

41

with the trappings of success at the same time that his mother was dying.

His favorite early recording, "Put Your Head on My Shoulder," was written when, like most young boys in America, he was hung up on Annette Funicello, former member of The Mickey Mouse Club and now queen of the beach-party movies. Another Anka tune, "Puppy Love," reflected his feelings for the beach-blanket bunny whom he eventually succeeded in dating. About the same time he had a brief foray into movies himself. Though he realized that acting was not his greatest talent, he did appear in a few films, the last of which was *The Longest Day.*

By 1964 Paul had left ABC for RCA. He recorded "My Home Town," an experiment in calypso rock, somewhere between Harry Belafonte and the Diamonds. However, hits were becoming scarce now. It was an era for British rock and Motown, so Paul turned to the club circuit. He had been a regular in nightclubs since he was eighteen, and Feld now placed him in only the most prestigious clubs. In June 1960 he became the youngest performer ever to appear at the Copacabana. His string of hits had ended, but he had achieved financial stability. He attributes his continued success to his ability as a writer, having composed "My Way" for Frank Sinatra and "She's a Lady" for Tom Jones. He is still collecting royalties for the theme song he wrote for Johnny Carson's *Tonight Show.*

In 1974 Paul Anka made a recording comeback on United Artists Records when he teamed with female vocalist Odia Coates for "(You're) Having My Baby." "Times of Your Life" broke onto the charts in November 1975 and was then used by Kodak in their commercials for over a year.

Today Paul lives with his wife and five children in Monterey, California, where he continues to appear as one of Las Vegas' leading headliners.

Paul Anka.

THE DIAMONDS

Hailing from Canada, the Diamonds were one of the countless white-cover groups predominant in the early years of rock and roll. Their first cover versions of songs like the Willows' "Church Bells May Ring" and Frankie Lymon and the Teenagers' "Why Do Fools Fall In Love" never came close to duplicating the success of the originals. It was far from a promising start.

Then in 1957 the people at Mercury rushed them into the studio to cover a new tune by a rhythm-and-blues group called the Gladiolas. There was no time for any rearranging, so the Diamonds simply copied the original. The one difference was their addition of a Latin beat, a new aspect to rock and roll. The Diamonds' version of "Little Darlin'" was a monster hit and received overwhelming promotion and airplay. It absolutely buried the original by the Gladiolas, who faded into obscurity but reemerged in 1960 as Maurice Williams and the Zodiacs with the smash hit "Stay."

With "Little Darlin'" becoming one of the big hits of the year, the Diamonds were invited to appear on *American Bandstand.* They were amazed to find all the kids on *Bandstand* into a new line dance called the stroll. Dick discussed the stroll with their manager and told him that teen-agers were strolling to all sorts of slow songs, but no one had actually cut a stroll song. Within a month of that *Bandstand* appearance, the Diamonds had their second hit of 1957 with "The Stroll." The dance became an integral part of *Bandstand,* which helped propel the song to the top.

After "The Stroll" the Diamonds were hired by Alan Freed, who usually refused to play cover-version artists. Apparently Freed forgave them for burying the Gladiolas' "Little Darlin'" in light of their original "The Stroll."

The Diamonds' last single was the minor doo-wop song "She Say (Oom Dooby Doom)" in 1959. Today they have reconstructed their successful stage act for nostalgia concerts and rock revivals.

The Diamonds.

The Sound of 1957

CHUCK BERRY

No other singer, guitar player, or entertainer has had a greater influence on the evolution of rock and roll than Chuck Berry. His music was raw, with a hard rock beat. He treated his guitar as a partner, practically making love to it onstage in a style that was later matched only by Jimi Hendrix. Chuck knew how to bring his audience to its feet, and often did so with his famous duck walk. He would stoop over while playing guitar and half skip, half slink across the stage. Combined with his splits, Chuck's choreography alone could capture a crowd.

Lyrics written by Chuck Berry also played a part in his rock-and-roll success. In "School Days" (1957), which was somewhat based on his own experience, he urged kids to close their books and take to the streets— every student's dream. Chuck sang it from the heart, having served a three-year stint in reform school for attempted robbery in his hometown of St. Louis.

Originally a hairstylist, Chuck longed for a more rewarding career as a singer/guitar player. His quest took him to Chicago in 1955, where he was signed by Chess Records, a label anxious to break into the white music market. Chess felt that his careful, clear enunciation let him pass for a white performer on his records, and that's what Chess wanted the world to think.

At his first recording session Chuck did his song "Maybellene." One of the people listening in the studio was rock and roll's number-1 and only disc jockey, Alan Freed. The Chess people had brought him in to advise them on how to produce Chuck so as to reach that white audience. The legend is that Alan felt that the original lyrics to the song were too black-oriented and more suited for a real rhythm-and-blues market. He rewrote many of the words so they would appeal to the ear of the white market. As a result Alan Freed received credit as one of the writers of the song. Interestingly, another disc jockey who gave the song extensive airplay at the time also shared in the writing credit. Years later he would deny authorship. It's an odd turn of events that might be explainable in light of a practice that was popular in the industry at the time and which might be termed "subliminal payola." DJs who played the records could be given an author's credit on the song and receive a percentage of the royalties. It was a lot more subtle than offering a bag of money or a new Cadillac to a local disc jockey. Whatever the real story may have been,

Chuck Berry and Dick Clark. *(Courtesy of Dick Clark)*

Chuck's "Maybellene" was soon getting widespread radio airplay. Many radio stations assumed he was a white country or pop singer. The race music barriers that had to fall in order for rock and roll to make it big came tumbling down at last.

Before he knew it, Chuck became a movie star in the new wave of rock-and-roll films, appearing in such classics as *Rock, Rock, Rock; Mr. Rock and Roll; Go Johnny Go;* and *Jazz on a Summer's Day.* By 1958 he was on top of the world, and occasionally acted like it. He signed to do an *American Bandstand* that year, but moments before the show began, he notified Dick Clark that he wouldn't do his duck walk and refused to lip-sync "Sweet Little Sixteen." With barely any time left Dick had to get Chuck's bosses at Chess Records on the phone, and it was only after their brief but pointed conversation with Chuck that he agreed to go on. Dick and ABC breathed a collective sigh of relief. There are no hard feelings between Berry and Clark today, and Chuck has appeared on hundreds of Dick Clark's shows since.

Chuck's second major hit was "Roll Over Beethoven" (1956), a song that would become a rock-and-roll standard and a hit in 1964 for the Beatles, who were greatly influenced by Berry. "School Days" followed in 1957, and then "Rock and Roll Music." In 1958 Chuck had two huge hits with "Sweet Little Sixteen" and "Johnny B. Goode." The latter song was intentionally autobiographical, which the former would eventually also prove to be. In 1959 Chuck was arrested, then run out of Meridian, Mississippi, for dating a "sweet little" sixteen-year-old girl who happened to be white. Chuck was lucky to get out of town at all. Curiously, "Sweet Little Sixteen" was the song that the Beach Boys would one day draw from to create "Surfin' U.S.A." The songs were so similar that Chuck was eventually awarded coauthor credit for "Surfin' U.S.A."

"Johnny B. Goode" is perhaps Chuck Berry's best song. It's the story of a poor country boy who teaches himself to play guitar and becomes a rock star. It's a fast, vibrant song with a very danceable beat that became a prom favorite with jitterbuggers. It was followed by "Back in the U.S.A." in 1959, a song that the Beatles would later parody in a tune entitled "Back in the U.S.S.R."

Later, in 1959 there was more trouble for Chuck when he was charged with a Mann Act violation for transporting a fourteen-year-old New Mexico girl to St. Louis. Chuck claimed he was taking her back to give her a break in his club. The law didn't buy his story. A two-year jail term from 1962 to 1964 put his career on ice after his 1961 hit, "Nadine."

By the time Chuck was released, the British invasion was under way, and fans were more interested in the Beatles' "Roll Over Beethoven" than in Chuck's version. After "No Particular Place to Go" in 1964, Chuck vanished from the charts until 1972, when he made a comeback with his first number-1 song, "My Ding-a-Ling," which revived his career and made him a sensation in England. It was a silly tune he used in concert as a sing-along. The song was filled with sexual innuendo, and Chuck had the women in his audiences sing about how they wanted to play with their boyfriends' "ding-a-lings." Content notwithstanding, this recording took him back to the top and introduced him to a whole new generation of rock and rollers.

Chuck closed out the seventies by returning to movies as one of the stars in *Let the Good Times Roll* and *American Hot Wax.* Unfortunately his fans weren't the only ones who wanted him. Uncle Sam wanted him too, on charges of income tax evasion, for which he served time. But Chuck Berry has already come back in the eighties for his fourth decade of great contributions to rock and roll, this time in tandem with his musically talented daughter.

1958

Rock and roll—a rancid-smelling aphrodisiac.
—FRANK SINATRA

It was the year of the Boston rock-and-roll riot, in which Alan Freed was arrested for inciting a riot after local police moved into a concert hall to enforce a curfew. One person was killed and scores were injured in a melee that would only be overshadowed twenty-one years later by a Who concert in Cincinnati that would leave eleven dead.

In 1958 Khrushchev became the Soviet premier, and Explorer I rose into outer space as the U.S. entered the space race. Charles de Gaulle became the President of France, and the U.S.S. *Nautilus* became the first submarine to pass under the North Pole. Meanwhile kids were fad-crazy in America. College students were swallowing goldfish and cramming themselves into phone booths. When not in phone booths, teen-agers were twirling hula hoops around their waists.

There was great hula-hoop music in 1958. "Lollipop" by the Chordettes kept a slower pace for beginners, while Bobby Day's "Rockin' Robin" had a quicker beat for the more advanced. Other songs filling the AM radio airwaves included "Get a Job" by the Silhouettes; "26 Miles" by the Four Preps; "Little Star" by the Elegants; "Just a Dream" by the "Venus in Bluejeans" man, Jimmy Clanton; "Tears on My Pillow" by Little Anthony and the Imperials; "Summertime Blues" by Eddie Cochran; "Chantilly Lace" by the Big Bopper; and "To Know Him Is to Love Him" by the Teddy Bears. The top ten of the year were "All I Have to Do Is Dream" by the Everly Brothers; "Volare" by Domenico Modugno; "Catch a Falling Star" by Perry Como; "Don't" by Elvis Presley; "The Witch Doctor" by David Seville, the biggest of a horde of novelty records; "Patricia" by Perez Prado; "Sail Along Silvery Moon" by Billy Vaughn; "It's All in the Game" by Tommy Edwards; "Tequila" by the Champs; and "Return to Me" by Dean Martin.

The teen-age dance was the stroll, which was popularized on *American Bandstand.* The evening version of the show, *The Dick Clark Saturday Night Show,* sponsored by Beech-Nut, also premiered that year, along with *Wanted: Dead or Alive, Sea Hunt, Bat Masterson,* and *77 Sunset Strip.*

Gigi won the Oscar for Best Picture, beating *Auntie Mame, Cat on a Hot Tin Roof, The Defiant Ones,* and *Separate Tables.*

It was 1958—the fourth year of rock and roll.

47

Buddy Holly.

BUDDY HOLLY

Early in 1955, while passing through Lubbock, Texas, a new singer who called himself the "Hillbilly Cat" was hired, along with a couple of local high school kids, "Buddy and Bob," to play rockabilly from the back of a pickup truck for the grand opening of a Pontiac dealership. After they'd created a tempest at the Pontiac showroom with their mixture of country, boogie, and blues, the Hillbilly Cat shared a Coca-Cola with Buddy, the shy, bespectacled high schooler. He told Buddy how much he liked his style and encouraged him to stick with his music. Within two years the Hillbilly Cat, Elvis Presley, and the kid from Lubbock, Buddy Holly, had become the biggest stars in rock and roll, light-years away from gigs in Pontiac showrooms. Twenty-five years after playing together in the back of a truck, Presley and Holly remain two of the most enduring legends of rock and roll.

Charles Hardin Holley—"Buddy" to his family and friends—was determined to be a star. In high school Buddy hooked up with Bob Montgomery to sing country duets, blues, and West Texas rockabilly as "Buddy and Bob," assisted by Larry Welborn on bass. "Buddy and Bob" had their own local radio show on Sunday afternoons and played the dance halls, clubs, and car dealerships around Lubbock, looking for that one big break. Opportunity knocked in October 1955. On October 14, Buddy, Bob, and Larry opened the show for Bill Haley and the Comets at the Cotton Club in Lubbock. The next night they were squeezed onto a crowded bill as the opening act for Elvis Presley's return to Lubbock. Two weeks later the group played with budding country star Marty Robbins. A Nashville talent agent, Eddie Crandell, happened to catch all three shows and managed to get Buddy a record contract by himself with Decca Records. Decca was looking for another Elvis, so Bob and Larry were left behind.

In February 1956 with his '55 Oldsmobile, Buddy and his new band, the Three Tunes—drummer Jerry Allison, guitarist Sonny Curtis, and bassist Don Guess—headed for Nashville, ready to become rock-and-roll stars. There was just one problem. Decca may have wanted another Elvis, but they didn't have the slightest idea how to produce rock and roll. Nashville *was* country music, and Decca recorded Buddy more for the Grand Ole Opry than for *American Bandstand.* After all, Decca felt, what was good enough for Ernest Tubbs and Red Foley should be good enough for this hillbilly kid from West Texas. So the young, awestruck Buddy Holly—he had dropped the "e" from his last name—changed his singing style and his rhythm to please the experienced producers at Decca. The result was a disaster. Buddy's first two singles, "Blue Days, Black Nights" and "Modern Don Juan," sank like lead weights. Decca refused to release Holly's next single, "That'll Be the Day," and sent Buddy and the Three Tunes packing.

Back in Texas, Don Guess refused to buy a bass and took off for parts unknown. Discontented playing rhythm guitar to Buddy's lead and more interested in straight country music anyway, Sonny Curtis left Buddy's band to earn his fame and fortune in country music, eventually writing the theme song for *The Mary Tyler Moore Show.* But Buddy and Jerry were determined to make it in rock and roll, so they spent the rest of 1956 rockin' with just guitar and drums at the Lubbock Youth Center. When Buddy felt they were ready, he decided to cut "That'll Be the Day" again and land another record contract. They put together a new group with Niki Sullivan and Larry Welborn. Officially Buddy was still under contract to Decca, which held the rights to "That'll Be the Day." If they were going to recut the song, it couldn't be under Holly's name. They thumbed through an encyclopedia, looking for a name for their group, and

49

decided to name the band after an insect. They rejected the "Grasshoppers" and the "Beetles" but were amused by the name "Crickets" and chose it.

Hearing that a friend of a friend had a connection with Roulette Records, Buddy packed Jerry, Niki, and Larry into his Oldsmobile on February 25, 1957, and headed ninety miles west to Norman Petty's recording studio in Clovis, New Mexico, to cut a demo. Rather than charge by the hour, Petty preferred to let a group use as much time as they needed to record, and to take a share of the publishing rights as his payment. This more relaxed atmosphere was perfect for the Crickets, giving Buddy enough time to polish a song and allowing them to work through the night. The Crickets cut "That'll Be the Day" and "I'm Looking for Someone to Love" and sent it on to Roulette, but their connection fell through. Petty then tried to swing a record deal for the Crickets. After RCA, Columbia, and Atlantic turned down "That'll Be the Day," Petty sent the tape to Bob Thiele at Coral Records. Thiele flipped for the group, but his bosses at Coral thought rock and roll would hurt the label's image. Thiele finally convinced them to put out the record on their subsidiary label, Brunswick. As luck would have it, Brunswick and Coral were subsidiaries of Decca, who owned the rights to "That'll Be the Day," so even though Decca balked at Brunswick's release of the single, they realized the foolishness of trying to sue themselves to protect their rights. "That'll Be the Day" became a number-3 record. The Crickets were off and running. For good measure Bob Thiele was able to get Buddy a separate contract with Coral.

Before "That'll Be the Day" was released, Larry Welborn was replaced on bass by Joe Mauldin, and the group headed back to Petty's studio to record fifteen more songs. Because these songs were recorded before Buddy and the Crickets had separate contracts, no distinction was made between Buddy Holly songs and Crickets songs. If Petty felt a song sounded better with backup vocals, it became a Crickets song. If no backup was used, the song was released under Holly's name alone. Ironically, except for "That'll Be the Day," the Crickets never sang on any of their records. Norman Petty always used a local group, either the Picks or the Roses, to sing backup for Buddy.

With songs in the can, Buddy and the Crickets were eager to hit the road and seek a little of that rock-and-roll fame and fortune. When they landed in Washington, D.C., for their first concert, the promoters were surprised to find that the band wasn't black. The Crickets became the first white group ever to play the famed Apollo Theater in Harlem. After the Apollo engagement the Crickets signed on for eighty straight one-night stands on a tour called Biggest Show of Stars for '57 with stars like the Drifters, Chuck Berry, Fats Domino, Frankie Lymon and the Teenagers, and Paul Anka. After eighty nights on a Greyhound, Niki Sullivan quit the band and the Crickets became a threesome.

In November 1957 Coral released Buddy's biggest hit, "Peggy Sue." The song was originally called "Cindy Lou," but Jerry Allison's girl friend was named Peggy Sue and he convinced Buddy to change the title. Released as a Buddy Holly record, it rocked the top ten for nine weeks in early 1958, with its rippling drum work and Buddy's staccato vocals, peaking at number 3. Oddly enough, Buddy and the Crickets didn't have very many hit records in America. "That'll Be the Day," titled after John Wayne's pet phrase in the 1956 movie *The Searchers,* was the Crickets' biggest record, at number 3 in the fall of 1957. "Oh Boy" hit number 10 at the same time "Peggy Sue" was on the charts. In the spring of 1958 the Crickets hit again with a number cowritten by Buddy's mother called "Maybe Baby." Buddy's solo singles were less successful. The supercharged "Rave On," probably Buddy's best fast number, only stumbled to number 37 in June 1958. "Heartbeat," with its sophisticated Latin rhythm, barely made the charts at all, coming in at number 82 in January 1959. Buddy's music was some of the most innovative in rock, but he became a legend only after his death.

After a sensational tour of Britain in March 1958, where he influenced kids in the audience such as Eric Clapton and Paul McCartney, Buddy returned to America for a whirlwind romance. He met Maria Elena Santiago at his music publisher's office, arranged to have lunch with her, asked her for a date that evening, and then proposed at dinner—all within twelve hours.

Buddy split with his mentor, Norman Petty, in October 1958, while the Crickets decided to stay with him. Buddy moved to New York with Maria, determined to develop in new directions. He recorded with strings and full orchestration—a breakthrough in rock and roll. He wrote many new songs, which he sang into a tape recorder for future reference. Buddy planned to build a studio and start discovering new talent, but after his split with Petty, his funds were tied up in litigation. In need of cash, Buddy reluctantly agreed to join the Winter Dance Party tour of the Midwest in early 1959.

The Winter Dance Party tour featured Ritchie Valens, the Big Bopper, Frankie Sardo, Dion and the Belmonts, and Buddy and his new band, which consisted of Tommy Allsup on guitar, Charlie Bunch on drums, and Waylon Jennings on bass. The Midwestern winter was brutal, and the tour's unheated bus broke down often. Charlie Bunch suffered frostbite during one breakdown, so Carlo Mastrangelo of the Belmonts and Buddy took turns playing drums during performances. On February 2, 1959, the tour limped into Clear Lake, Iowa. Exhausted from sleeping in his clothes and fed up with the constant mechanical troubles that the bus was having, Buddy decided to charter a plane to take him and his band to Moorhead, Minnesota, the next stop on the tour, so they could get a decent night's sleep, do their laundry, and take care of some last-minute tour business. The Big Bopper—J. P. Richardson—whose big hit was "Chantilly Lace," had gotten sick on the bus and convinced Waylon Jennings, for whom the novelty of tour life had not yet worn off, to give up his seat on the plane. Eighteen-year-old Ritchie Valens, who had a promising career with "Donna," "La Bamba," and "Let's Go," flipped a coin with Tommy Allsup for his seat on the plane. Valens won the toss, taking the last seat on the four-passenger plane. After the Clear Lake concert Holly, Valens, and Richardson boarded the small plane piloted by Roger Peterson. At about one A.M. on February 3, 1959, the Beechcraft Bonanza crashed outside Mason City, Iowa, killing everyone on board.

After his death Buddy's home tape recordings of new songs that he planned to record were turned over to Coral Records and then Norman Petty, who spliced, reengineered, and overdubbed the tapes to construct new Buddy Holly records. Petty used a band that he managed, Jimmy Gilmer and the Fireballs ("Sugar Shack," "Bottle of Wine") to play behind Buddy's disembodied voice on one posthumous album. "New" Buddy Holly material kept showing up on the market until 1969, ten years after the plane crash.

Buddy Holly lives on through his influence on rock. Buddy enthralled English rock and rollers who made him a god. The Hollies took their name from him. John Lennon came up with the name the "Beatles" as a tribute to the Crickets. Buddy and the Crickets' lineup of lead guitar, rhythm guitar, bass, and drums became the rock group formula in Britain. Buddy's songs have become a mainstay in rock and roll—the Beatles ("Words of Love"), the Rolling Stones ("Not Fade Away"), Blind Faith ("Well All Right"), Peter and Gordon ("True Love Ways"), Blondie ("I'm Gonna Love You Too"), the Knack ("Heartbeat"), and Linda Ronstadt ("It Doesn't Matter Anymore," "That'll Be the Day," and "It's so Easy"). Interest in Buddy's music resurged in 1978 with the success of Columbia Pictures' *The Buddy Holly Story* and the Oscar nomination for its star, Gary Busey. Although well executed, the film came under attack by Buddy Holly purists for its inaccuracies, exaggerations, and fictionalizations of characters and events.

DANNY AND THE JUNIORS

Their sound was put together on the street corners of Philadelphia in 1957. As the Juvenairs, lead singer Danny Rapp, Dave ("Tricker") White, Frank Maffei, and Joe Terranova performed at school dances, weddings, bar mitzvahs, and other catered affairs until they were spotted by Artie Singer, owner of the independent label Singular Records. Singer became their vocal coach and frequent arranger. He recommended that the group change its name, and the result was "Danny and the Juniors."

In the summer of 1957 the hottest dance on *American Bandstand* was the bop. Singer wanted to cash in on it, so he had Danny and the Juniors cut a song called "Doing the Bop." He brought the tape to Dick Clark, who liked the music but hated the lyrics. Clark cautioned that the bop was on its way out, and the record would be too late to be successful. Instead, Dick suggested they save the music and rewrite the lyrics as a story about a record hop. "At the Hop" turned out to be a great debut vehicle for the group. It reached number-1 in January 1958, where it stayed for seven weeks, turning gold in the process. The song hung in the top ten for eleven weeks and clung to the charts for over five months. The record also had a fabulous love ballad on its flip-side, "Sometimes When I'm All Alone," which never received the attention it deserved.

Nineteen fifty-eight saw numerous rock-and-roll riots, notably the Boston incident at a Freed show. Rock came under attack as it never had before. One such attack was "record-breaking week," sponsored by KWK radio in St. Louis, where rock-and-roll discs were destroyed in the manner of Hitler's book burnings. As a backlash against these attacks, Dave White wrote a tune that is considered by some the theme song of all rock-and-roll music, "Rock and Roll Is Here to Stay." This 1958 release shot onto the charts and stayed there for three months.

No other Danny and the Juniors single ever made it big. A sequel to "At the Hop," entitled "Back to the Hop," was released in 1961, but no one seemed to want to go back. That same year Freddie Cannon and Frankie Valli and the Four Seasons gave the group a boost by singing with them on a record called "Twistin' All Night Long." Danny and the Juniors disbanded in 1962, each going separate ways. Nine years later David White came back to cut a solo album called *Pastel Paint, Pencil and Ink,* while Frank and Joe regrouped with Bill Carlucci to tour on the revival circuit, Las Vegas, and Reno.

THE CHAMPS

The Champs will be remembered in the history of rock and roll more for their membership than for their music. In 1957 the group was made up of Dave Burgess, Glen Alden, Dale Norris, Chuck Rio, and Ben Norman. It hardly sounds like a rock-and-roll hall of fame, but three notable musicians would later join the Champs—Jimmy Seals, Dash Crofts, and Glen Campbell.

Jimmy Seals and Dash Crofts met in junior high school. Both had country influences and joined the same local rock-and-roll band—Seals on guitar and saxophone, Crofts on drums. Their talents brought them to Challenge Records and the Champs. Meanwhile, back in Delight, Arkansas, Glen Campbell, the seventh son of a seventh son, packed up his guitar and moved to L.A. Before long he became a studio musician whose guitar and vocal talents were in great demand.

The Champs, named by Challenge Records' owner Gene Autry after his horse, Champion, had one grand hit with "Tequila" in early 1958, a gold disc that racked up over six million in sales while it perched in the top slot for five weeks, in the top ten for eleven weeks, and on the charts for four months. The raucous record had a Latin beat and the mood of a sleazy Tijuana gin joint. A grinding saxophone coughed out the melody of this powerful instrumental. At the end of each sax segment the music would halt and a voice that sounded like Donald Duck doing Pancho Villa choked out, "Tequila." It became the rock-and-roll cry of the year.

But it was a short-lived success for the Champs. Try as they would, they never could produce another hit. Of course, they did try with "Too Much Tequila" in 1959 and "Tequila Twist" in 1962. The group finally gave up in 1965 after releasing thirty more singles without any luck.

Seals and Crofts went on to a group called the Dawnbreakers before going it as a duo and chalking up winners like "Summer Breeze" (1972), "Diamond Girl" (1973), and "I'll Play for You" (1975). Glen Campbell moved on to work with an assortment of groups, the most famous of which was the Beach Boys. His solo career peaked after he won his own CBS TV show. The long list of Campbell's hits includes "Gentle on My Mind," "Wichita Lineman," "Dreams of the Everyday Housewife," "By the Time I Get to Phoenix," "Galveston," "Where's the Playground, Susie," "Rhinestone Cowboy," and "Southern Nights."

THE EVERLY BROTHERS

The Everly Brothers—Phil (left) and Don.

The Little Donnie Show came out of Shenandoah, Iowa, on radio station KMA, starring seven-year-old singing sensation Little Donnie Everly. The 1944 program gave the boy his first major public exposure, and was the start of a long career in music. By the time Donnie graduated from high school, he was performing with his younger brother, Phil. The family had moved to Tennessee, and the boys linked up with

Chet Atkins, an old family friend. Atkins, who later supervised their sessions, introduced them to Arthur Godfrey's ex-orchestra leader Archie Bleyer, who had started Cadence Records specifically to record Andy Williams.

"Let the Sun Keep Shining," an early release by the Everlys on Columbia, had not sold well. But at Cadence the duo was introduced to the husband-and-wife songwriting team of Boudleaux and Felice Bryant. The Bryants wrote the Everlys' first release on Cadence, "Bye, Bye, Love" (1957). The record climbed slowly on the charts, and though it never made number 1, it remained in the top ten for an unprecedented six months. In September 1957 "Wake Up Little Susie" made it to number 1. The song was banned in Boston, among other cities, because the lyrics intimated that Susie was sleeping with someone at a drive-in movie. The controversy over the lyrics spread and even Archie Bleyer wasn't sure about the song's title. Still, their soft, harmonious whining with the country-western coating was well received despite the censorship problems.

During the next two years there was a steady stream of hits for the Everly Brothers. Many of them climbed to the top of the charts and anchored there for amazingly prolonged periods of time. "All I Have to Do Is Dream" (1958) took a month to reach the number-1 slot, then camped on the charts for thirty-two record-breaking weeks. "Bird Dog" (1958), on the charts for four months, was about the trials and tribulations of high school teens. "Problems" (1958) was a number-2 song that lasted three months on the surveys, soon followed by "Devoted to You" (1958). "('Til) I Kissed You" (1959) was a tune the brothers recorded with the help of Buddy Holly's surviving Crickets—Jerry Allison on drums, Joe Mauldin on bass, and Sonny Curtis on guitar. It rose to number 4 and rooted in the top ten for seven weeks. "Let It Be Me" (1960) was influenced by gospel music but had a country harmony; it peaked at number 7. "When Will I Be Loved" (1960) was an original number that hit number 8 on the survey and was remade by Linda Ronstadt fifteen years later. "Cathy's Clown" (1960) was their first triumph on their new label, Warner Records. It was their all-time best-selling single, the number-1 hit for five weeks in June, nine weeks in the top ten, and 17 on the charts. "Walk Right Back" (1961), "Crying in the Rain" (1962), and "That's Old Fashioned" (1962) were the Everly Brothers' last hits on the top ten, for no future singles could match the excitement and popularity of their earlier accomplishments.

The bulk of the Everly Brothers' success afterward came from well-received albums, live performances, and network television exposure. This led to a contract for *The Everly Brothers Show* on CBS-TV, which was a replacement series during the summer of 1970.

On one Friday the thirteenth in 1973, the Everly Brothers' career together ended. They were performing at Knott's Berry Farm when they had a verbal disagreement. Phil slammed his guitar into pieces and walked offstage, leaving his brother on stage alone. They never performed together again. However, their exceptionally strong material, their country-style harmonization of rock songs, and their classic hand-clapping, high-spirited tunes provided a formidable legacy. Their work has been hailed by both Bob Dylan and the Beatles.

The Sound of 1958

NOVELTY RECORDS

A rash of novelty records took over the charts in 1958, highlighted by the multitalented and multivoiced Ross Bagdasarian, who took his professional name from one of his own fictional characters, "David Seville." He cowrote the 1951 Rosemary Clooney hit "Come On-A My House," with his cousin William Saroyan. Bagdasarian originally signed with Mercury Records in 1954, then moved to Liberty Records in 1956, where he recorded "Armen's Theme," "The Bold and the Brave," and a string of minor songs.

In 1958 Ross developed a new method of recording that resulted in a block of hits released under his pseudonym, beginning with "Witch Doctor" in March 1958. It shot to number 1 and remained in the top ten for a phenomenal three months. The song was simple, silly, and funny, with a chorus of rapid-fire nonsense syllables—"Ooo eee ooo ah ah, ting tang walla walla bing bang"—hammering away at the senses. (No one has yet succeeded in deciphering the Witch Doctor's message.) Ross's method consisted of recording his voice at one speed and varying the playback speed. This record led to the creation of a regular cast of squealing characters—the three Chipmunks: Simon, Theodore, and the dawdling Alvin. The trio made their musical debut with the smash record of the Christmas season of 1958, "The Chipmunk Song." This record was a genuine engineering feat, and one of the fastest-selling singles of the year with over 2.5 million sold. It was number 1 throughout December, and was reissued every Christmas for many years. Unlike most record novelties, the Chipmunks weren't a one-hit fluke. In 1959 they returned with another big song, "Alvin's Harmonica," which was number 3 nationally and a resident on the charts for over three months. Before the year was out they were back again with a spoof of movie westerns, "Ragtime Cowboy Joe." Each Chipmunk song wound up with Alvin and his sidekicks going out of control and David Seville screaming for order and respect. Eventually the Chipmunks became Saturday-morning cartoon stars. Unfortunately Ross Bagdasarian passed away in 1972, presumably taking his creations Theodore, Simon, and Alvin with him. However, in 1980 the Chipmunk tradition was carried on by an album called *Chipmunk Punk*, produced by Ross Bagdasarian—Jr.!

Novelty records did not begin with the Chipmunks. In June 1956 Bill

Buchanan and Dickie Goodman originated a technique in which excerpts from top chart tunes were arranged in a sound montage of sorts connected by a topical running narrative. Their first recording, "The Flying Saucer," employed current rumors about UFO sightings that year. Fans made a game out of identifying which tunes were on the record. Goodman made a career out of this kind of novelty record, picking up on personalities and trends of the time. In 1961 he produced "The Touchables" and "The Touchables in Brooklyn," takeoffs on the TV show *The Untouchables*. "Ben Crazy," released in June 1962, was about a very hairy doctor, parodying the TV series *Ben Casey*. Goodman surfaced again in '73 and '74 to take on Watergate, the energy crisis, and Jaws. Unfortunately numerous lawsuits were filed against Buchanan and Goodman, charging them with piracy of recordings, failure to obtain synchronization licenses, and copyright infringement. The problem of the plaintiffs, however, was that they could never find Buchanan and Goodman, who ran their business from a pay phone in a Manhattan drugstore. Finally, though, they surfaced. As the records soared to the top, out-of-court settlements with the publishers whose copyrights were involved ate up their profits.

Nineteen fifty-eight was a banner year for novelty records. Besides "Witch Doctor" and "The Chipmunk Song," there was "The Purple People Eater," "Beep Beep," and "Dinner With Drac." UFO sightings proliferated in the fifties, and Sheb Wooley, a country-western singer and motion picture character actor (*High Noon, Little Big Horn, Distant Drums,* etc.) penned the definitive statement on the subject of extraterrestrials, "The Purple People Eater." Described as one-eyed, one-horned, and capable of flight, this creature from outer space announced in a "Chipmunk"-style voice that he was looking for a job in a rock-and-roll band. The record blasted off, landed on the number-1 spot for six weeks, then sat for three more in the top ten.

Reflecting the love and competitive spirit shared by man and his car, "Beep Beep" by the Playmates concerned a Cadillac driver's fear of damaging his image if he allowed a little Nash Rambler with a beeping horn to pass him. The confrontation becomes a race, and as the cars speed up, so does the speed of the song. "Beep Beep" drove to number 4, where it parked for a while before it was towed off the top ten.

"Dinner With Drac" was an early horror novelty record that was narrated by John Zacherle, a popular TV horror-movie host, who worked first in Philadelphia and later in New York. It paved the way for 1962's smash Halloween dance tune, "The Monster Mash" by Bobby "Boris" Pickett and the Crypt Kickers.

Some novelty records featured funny voices—"Speedy Gonzales," "The Martian Hop," "Yogi," "Jolly Green Giant," and "Rubber Duckie"—while others told silly stories in music—"Alley Oop," "Mr. Custer," "Short Shorts," "Itsy Bitsy Teenie Weenie Yellow Polka Dot Bikini," and "Does Your Chewing Gum Lose Its Flavor on the Bedpost Overnight?" There was even a host of songs that parodied other rock-and-roll hits—"Leader of the Laundromat" (from "Leader of the Pack"), "Small Sad Sam" (from "Big Bad John"), "Mrs. Schwartz You've Got an Ugly Daughter" (from

"Mrs. Brown You've Got a Lovely Daughter"), "The Battle of Kookamonga" (from "The Battle of New Orleans"), and "A Girl Named Johnny Cash" (from "A Boy Named Sue").

By 1963 the album *My Son, the Folksinger* by Allan Sherman had sold millions upon millions of copies. His singles did equally well. The classic "Hello Mudduh, Hello Fadduh" satirized the joys and juvenile horrors of camp. Sherman became a national rage.

After Ross Bagdasarian, Ray Stevens was the most prolific of the novelty-record artists. His first big success was 1962's "Ahab, the Arab," an ode to a desert beauty who wore "rings on her fingers and bells on her toes and a bone in her nose (Ho-Ho!)." Stevens enjoyed his own network TV show in 1970, which featured a young comedian named Steve Martin. He followed up "Ahab" with "Harry the Hairy Ape," "Gitarzan," and his biggest novelty hit, "The Streak," a song about the naked races popular on college campuses at the time. In 1974 "The Streak" ran to the number-1 position on the national charts in one of the fastest advances the music industry has ever seen.

Probably the weirdest of the novelty records was recorded independently by one Jerry Samuels, who billed himself as Napoleon XIV. "They're coming to Take Me Away (Ha-Ha)" lampooned an insane asylum inmate mourning the disappearance of his dog amid the incessant beat of marching soldiers. The song was strapped down in the number-1 spot, but its glory was brief, with only six weeks on the charts, four of which were in the top ten. The reason for its quick demise was its banishment in many cities for its offensive treatment of the emotionally unstable and mentally ill. Once it sold out at record shops, many distributors and shop owners didn't reorder. By the way, in keeping with its subject matter, the flip-side of the record was the same composition recorded backwards.

1959

Nineteen fifty-nine was a black year for rock and roll. Buddy Holly, Ritchie Valens, and the Big Bopper were killed in a plane crash. The payola scandal took its toll on top DJs throughout the country, forcing the resignation, among numerous others, of Alan Freed from WINS in New York.

The rest of the world wasn't doing much better. Castro took over Cuba, and Khrushchev was beating his desk with his shoe at the United Nations to emphasize his displeasure with the proceedings. But things weren't all bad in 1959. America had two new states, Alaska and Hawaii, as well as a newly designed Lincoln penny. The Los Angeles Dodgers won the World Series crown, overcoming the Chicago White Sox. Boston was celebrating the NBA championship of the Celtics. The Baltimore Colts rolled over the New York Giants for the NFL title. And Floyd Patterson relinquished the heavyweight championship to Ingemar Johansson.

The musical champs for 1959 included "Venus" by Frankie Avalon, "Mack the Knife" by Bobby Darin, "The Battle of New Orleans" by Johnny Horton, "Personality" by Lloyd Price, "Lonely Boy" by Paul Anka, "The Three Bells" by the Browns, "Dream Lover" by Bobby Darin, "Kansas City" by Wilbert Harrison, "Come Softly to Me" by the Fleetwoods, and "Mr. Blue" by the Fleetwoods. Other big hits of 1959 included Ritchie Valens' "Donna," Annette's "Tall Paul," David Seville and the Chipmunks' "Alvin's Harmonica," Dodie Stevens' "Pink Shoelaces," Dave "Baby" Cortez' "The Happy Organ," the Impalas' "Sorry (I Ran All the Way Home)," Edd Byrnes and Connie Stevens' "Kookie, Kookie (Lend Me Your Comb)," Santo and Johnny's "Sleep Walk," and Paul Evans and the Curls' "Seven Little Girls Sitting in the Back Seat."

Popular entertainment seemed to be having a blockbuster year with the epic *Ben-Hur* as its best picture, followed by *Anatomy of a Murder, The Diary of Anne Frank, The Nun's Story,* and *Room at the Top.* On TV, NBC struck a *"Bonanza."* Other shows debuting that year included Jackie Cooper's *Hennessey, Dobie Gillis,* and *The Untouchables.* In 1959, TV bade farewell to *Your Hit Parade,* forced off the air by the onslaught of rock-and-roll tunes on the same hit parade that was once monopolized by the likes of Patti Page, Doris Day, the Mills Brothers, and Frankie Laine. But for Dick Clark, it was a year of expansion. *American Bandstand* was joined on the airwaves by the prime-time *Dick Clark's World of Talent.* Dick also organized a rock-and-roll bus tour of the U.S. called the Caravan of Stars, a tour he would successfully conduct for years. As Dick recalls:

Ronald, Rudolph, and O'Kelly Isley first hit the charts in 1959 with a rave-up on RCA, "Shout." It took the Isleys three years to follow up "Shout" with the classic "Twist and Shout," this time recording for Wand Records. Then it took a move to Motown and four more years until "This Old Heart of Mine," a Four Tops sound-alike, gave the brothers another top-ten hit. Jimi Hendrix joined up with the Isley Brothers briefly after the brothers left Motown to pursue a more progressive, funkier sound. In the late sixties the Isleys formed their own record company, T Neck, and added younger brothers Ernie on lead guitar (far left), Marvin on bass (far right), and brother-in-law Chris Jasper (center top) on keyboards. This version of the Isley Brothers earned gold records with *It's Your Thing* in 1969 and *That Lady* in 1973.

"The Caravan of Stars was originally comprised of fourteen to sixteen acts all traveling in one bus, later on a bus and truck, then on two buses and a truck as the equipment became more sophisticated. Originally we'd use whatever house amplification equipment we found. We were the first tour to send along our own gear because we played old burlesque and vaudeville houses, roller skating rinks, empty fields, and civic centers. We had to take our own equipment. The house backup band would work with all the acts.

"The show always had an intermission. The closing act of the first half could be either black or white, but the closing act of the second half was always the white teen-age idol, the one all the little girls waited for. Tickets were a buck and a half for a four-hour show.

"We did sixty to ninety days in a row and slept in a hotel every other night, but sometimes every third night in a hotel. It was an orgy of endurance, but we sold a lot of records and tied into many local radio stations. It was not very different from what's going on now, except it was in its crawling infancy stages.

"In the southeast we had to play before divided audiences—sometimes blacks upstairs and whites downstairs, sometimes split right down the middle with whites on one side and blacks on the other. Interestingly, there was equal applause for white acts and black acts. There was no prejudice despite the fact that the municipal law said you couldn't sit together. We couldn't sleep in the same hotels or eat in the same restaurants as the black artists. We had to have 'black' hotels and 'white' hotels. We finally stopped traveling the southeast because it got to be such a terrible hassle. You just couldn't travel with black people who had become your intimate friends and then have to put up with all these outside pressures.

"One of the biggest problems we ever had on tour was the night there was a riot after one of our concerts. We had been long gone when it started, but when it hit the papers I was afraid the same things that happened to Alan Freed in Boston would happen to us. We didn't incite it, though. It was an aftermath. There were a lot of young, rebellious people together there, and some got into trouble."

It was 1959—the fifth year of rock and roll.

THE COASTERS

Was it easy to be a teen-ager in 1959? All you wanted to do after dinner was meet your buddies and go cruisin' around in your automobile. But then your parents would give you the word—take out the garbage, go to the store, clean up your room, turn off that radio, do your homework, and don't talk back to your mother. And was school any better? You sit in class, minding your own business, when the class clown ambles into the room, calls the teacher Daddy-O, and starts throwing spitballs or making faces at the teacher behind his back. And what happens? The whole class gets detention. It was the same all over the country. Teen-agers just wanted to have a good time, but somebody would always get in the way. In 1959 Jerry Leiber and Mike Stoller captured that mood, and the Coasters put it on vinyl. "Yakety Yak" and "Charlie Brown" told it like it was on radios and jukeboxes all over the country.

The Coasters were rock and roll's premiere comedy singing group. They started out in Los Angeles as a rhythm-and-blues group called the Robins, one of dozens of bird groups doing blues and doo-wop in the early fifties. Following the Orioles' "Crying in the Chapel," bird groups like the Crows, the Penguins, the Wrens, the Flamingos, and the Ravens flocked to the predominantly black R&B charts. The Robins, however, became the first group ever to record a song written by Jerry Leiber and Mike Stoller, the leading songwriting team of the new musical era.

Jerry Leiber delivered groceries to his mother's ghetto customers in Baltimore before moving to Los Angeles in 1945. Mike Stoller learned piano at all-night jazz clubs in New York City before his family made the move to Los Angeles in 1949. Stoller sacrificed a career in construction to study musical composition, while Leiber quit Hebrew school to study drama and write blues lyrics. They teamed up in 1950 to write rhythm-and-blues songs.

In late 1953 Leiber and Stoller joined forces with Lester Sill to form Spark Records. They were now record producers as well as writers of three-minute musical dramas. Jerry and Mike then wrote a little ditty about a prison riot for their friends, the Robins. They brought in Richard Berry—an R&B singer who later wrote "Louie Louie"—for the deep-voiced narrator and used the sounds of machine-gun fire and police sirens to produce a hit for the group, "Riot in Cell Block #9." The record was funny, tough, and good rock and roll.

By the end of 1955 Leiber and Stoller had produced two more R&B hits for the Robins, "Framed" and "Smokey Joe's Cafe," but Spark Records was now in trouble. The small independent record company was having problems distributing its records outside California. Atlantic Records, the biggest of the R&B independent labels, was interested in acquiring the production talents of Leiber and Stoller, who were equally interested in getting out of the business end of the record company. So in 1956 Jerry and Mike sold Spark Records to Atlantic. The label also acquired the rights to the Robins and signed Leiber and Stoller to the record industry's first independent production agreement. Jerry and Mike were now free-lance record producers. However, Leiber and Stoller and Atlantic overlooked one small detail—the Robins didn't like the deal. Rather than work for Atlantic, the group dissolved.

Two members of the Robins, lead singer Carl Gardner and bass Bobby Nunn, stayed with Leiber and Stoller. Billy Guy and Leon Hughes joined Gardner and Nunn to form a group they named after their West Coast stomping grounds—the Coasters. By now Leiber and Stoller had made it big in rock and roll with a few hits recorded by Elvis Presley. They decided to move the Coasters into the mainstream of rock and roll, but keep the humorous storytelling

The Coasters appear on *American Bandstand* in August 1958. *(Courtesy of Dick Clark. Photo: Edgar S. Brinker)*

songs they had pioneered with the Robins. The Coasters' first two singles, "Down in Mexico" and "One Kiss Led to Another," failed to impress the public, but their next effort was a two-sided smash. "Young Blood" and "Searchin'" stayed on the charts for twenty-six weeks, resting comfortably in the top ten for most of the summer and fall of 1957. "Young Blood" was a ghetto version of "Standin' on the Corner Watching All the Girls Go By," with the Coasters checking out a sweet young thing, repeating "Looka there!" as she walked by. "Searchin'" was a galloping hunt for a girl friend, with the Coasters calling on Charlie Chan, Bulldog Drummond, and the Royal Canadian Northwest Mounted Police for assistance in tracking down the girl of their dreams.

Nineteen fifty-eight brought "Yakety Yak" to the top of the charts. By this time Dub Jones and Cornell Gunther had joined the group, replacing Leon Hughes. Another important addition to the Coasters' sound

was King Curtis' drilling saxophone. As 1959 approached, the Coasters' sound was complete.

Their next hit, "Charlie Brown," was about that trouble-making class clown who kept asking, "Why's everybody always picking on me?" "Along Came Jones" then chased "Charlie Brown" up the charts. Slow-walkin', slow-talkin' Jones parodied the countless television westerns that were aired in 1959.

The Coasters ended 1959 with "Poison Ivy," a tune that posed a classic romantic dilemma—you could look, but you better not touch. The group came back in 1961 with their last record, "Little Egypt," before fading from recording prominence. Ten years later they would again be a hot act on the rock-and-roll revival circuit.

JACKIE WILSON

"Mr. Excitement, Mr. Delightment," Jackie Wilson was known for his high-decibel vocals and was considered a vocal descendant of Billy Daniels and Little Richard, embodying the eroticism of the crooner and the gospel energy of the rock and roller.

Growing up in the ghetto of Detroit, Jackie is said to have wanted a boxing career. But the stories of how he lied about his age and at sixteen won the Golden Gloves and considered a professional boxing career in the late forties are all PR fairy tales, according to Billy Ward of the Dominoes. Jackie did try singing in high school shows, however, and met with an enthusiastic response. Shortly thereafter Jackie was "discovered" by singer Johnny Otis, who, upon learning of the impending departure of Clyde McPhatter from one of the top early-fifties R&B groups, Billy Ward and the Dominoes, arranged an audition for Jackie during a brief 1953 visit to Detroit. As a result Jackie became lead singer of the group when McPhatter left to form the Drifters later that year. The Dominoes were never the same after McPhatter's departure, having had their heyday in 1951–52. In 1957 Jackie followed Clyde's lead and left the group to pursue a solo career.

Jackie was quickly signed by Brunswick Records. His first single, "Reet Petite," was written by a young unknown Detroit writer named Berry Gordy, Jr., who later went on to form the black entertainment conglomerate Motown. Jackie Wilson first struck gold in March 1958 with another Gordy composition, "To Be Loved." This was followed by the classic hit "Lonely Teardrops" (1959) and "That's Why" (1959), both written by Gordy with Gwendolyn Gordy and Tyron Carlo. His biggest seller was a double-sided hit, "Doggin' Around" and "Night," released in March 1960.

At about this time in his soaring career, Jackie nearly lost his life. Coincidentally, like Billy Daniels, the man who influenced his vocal style so much, Jackie Wilson was shot by a female fan whom he had allegedly just talked out of committing suicide. Jackie was critically wounded in this bizarre incident, but he eventually recovered. However, the slug was never actually removed from his abdomen.

Jackie Wilson continued to have successful outings with Brunswick Records throughout the sixties. Among his most notable hits, typifying his style and range, are "Baby Workout," released in March 1963, "Whispers" (1966), and the raucous, rabble-rousing "Higher and Higher" (1967).

During the early seventies Wilson was one of the original members of "Dick Clark's Good Ol' Rock 'n' Roll Revue," which opened in Las Vegas in July 1974. The show featured Freddy Cannon, Cornell Gunter and the Coasters, dancers, and nostalgic film clips. Wilson continued to perform with Dick Clark until September 1975, when tragedy struck. The East Coast debut of the "Rock 'n' Roll Revue" at the Latin Casino in Cherry Hill, New Jersey, shattered all previous attendance records. Jackie went on, and his performance of "Lonely Teardrops" was charged with the energetic theatrical style that he had developed over the years. After he belted out the words "my heart is crying" and collapsed, the audience applauded and the orchestra played on for thirty seconds, thinking his fall was part of the act. Dick Clark rushed onto the stage but was unable to revive Wilson. He called for a doctor. Cornell Gunter attempted mouth-to-mouth resuscitation. The attack has left Jackie an invalid, unable to move or communicate. It's unlikely that he'll ever sing, talk, or walk again.

At that point in his twenty-five-year career, Jackie had just completed an unreleased album, the last of more than fifty L.P.'s. But at the time of his stroke he had no financial assets, no insurance coverage and no funds.

A benefit was organized for Jackie by the Spinners on October 3, 1975. It was held at the Latin Casino and featured many of Wilson's contemporaries. Sixty thousand dollars was raised, and music-industry support has continued to be strong since the benefit. Unfortunately, his doctors say his chances for recovery are slim.

(Courtesy of Rolling Stone)

LLOYD PRICE

There are two performers in rock and roll who owe their careers to commercials. Barry Manilow got his start with State Farm Insurance and McDonald's jingles. In the early fifties Lloyd Price penned a tune for a radio commercial that was received so well, he turned it into a rhythm-and-blues hit, "Lawdy Miss Clawdy."

Lloyd was from Louisiana and had a New Orleans R&B style similar to that of Fats Domino. In fact, the "Fat Man" took Lloyd under his wing and helped make "Lawdy Miss Clawdy" a hit in 1952. Besides contributing his producer and other personnel, Fats played boogie piano on the record. Lloyd suddenly had a promising rhythm-and-blues career, until Uncle Sam came calling. From 1953 through 1956 the only entertaining Lloyd did was in Army fatigues.

By the time the Army was through with him, Lloyd had to regroup and start from scratch. He was perceptive enough to see how the music market had changed, and, like his friend Fats Domino, he took advantage of it. A black rhythm-and-blues singer now had the opportunity to become a hit with white audiences by making the transition to rock and roll. He moved from Specialty Records, his former R&B label, to ABC-Paramount, a pop/rock-and-roll label. ABC set its production crew to work on Lloyd, carefully working with him on the selection of material and the development of his new sound. Lloyd's early style was replaced by a new, slick, rock-and-roll style.

"Stagger Lee," based on an old ballad, was the "new" Lloyd Price's first big hit in 1958. His music had a danceable beat, and his hits would all become prom and sock-hop favorites. Nineteen fifty-nine was a great year for Price. "Where Were You on Our Wedding Day," "I'm Gonna Get Married," and "Personality," a runaway hit, were all smashes that year. The latter song became so identified with Lloyd that he was often referred to as "Mr. Personality."

Lloyd's former label, Specialty, filled the gap he left by hiring what they must have thought would be the next best thing to Price himself—his valet. The late Larry Williams sounded quite a bit like his former boss, but Larry's specialty was in humorous songs like "Bony Moronie," "Short Fat Fannie," and his parody of Lloyd's "Lawdy Miss Clawdy"—"Dizzy Miss Lizzie."

Unable to match his earlier recording successes, Lloyd turned his talents toward producing in the sixties, working with up-and-coming talent. One of those "up and coming" was young Wilson Pickett. Today Lloyd is a record-company executive and occasionally performs in rock-and-roll revival shows.

THE CRESTS

They were like every other group of street-corner singers out of New York City in the 1950s, singing a cappella in subway stations, alleyways, and men's rooms so that their sound could reverberate. No matter how well a group sang, the sound was always twice as good with reverb.

The other unwritten law of New York street singers was that to make it to the top, you had to be black or Italian. Johnny Mastrangelo was Italian, the rest of the group all black or Puerto Rican. With Johnny on guitar and the addition of drums, their a cappella purity produced a bouncy, very danceable beat. Johnny's clear, smooth, and powerful voice belted out lyrics about the woes of teen-age love. This formula spelled success, and the boys rose to sudden but brief fame as the Crests.

Mastrangelo (who became known as Johnny Masters, then finally as Johnny Maestro) wailed a new rock-and-roll love ballad entitled "16 Candles" straight to the top of the top forty. It was, perhaps, *the* love song of the fifties generation. When Maestro called his girl friend his "teen-age queen" in that song, girls all across America responded. Most steady teen-age couples in 1958 claimed "16 Candles" as "their song." Its impact lasted an entire rock-and-roll generation, for some fifteen years later when Maestro triumphantly returned to New York's Madison Square Garden for Richard Nader's Rock N' Roll Revival Show, twenty thousand screaming, sighing ex-teen-agers wouldn't let him off the stage before receiving a string of "16 Candles" encores.

Nineteen fifty-eight was the peak year for the Crests. It was also the year of one of the biggest faux pas in rock-and-roll history when the Crests were to appear on Dick Clark's new *Saturday Night Show.* Johnny and the Crests showed up as scheduled on the afternoon of the show. It was explained to them that they would lip-sync "16 Candles" while sitting in a rowboat on a phony lake set. Their cue would be the intro from Dick, who would be in the balcony of the theater, mingling with the audience. The Crests then went backstage to dress and be made up.

Later that afternoon was the dress rehearsal where camera shots were blocked out and kinks worked out. Dick customarily let an audience in for the dress rehearsal in response to the incredible ticket demand. The live audience also permitted the staff to gauge reactions to the material. The rehearsal was soon underway, and the Crests took their places in the rowboat behind the curtain. The spotlight moved to Dick, who kibbitzed with the kids in the balcony, then introduced the smash hit "16 Candles" by The Crests. The audience went wild. The spotlight hit the parting curtain, and the Crests lip-synched the song to a tumultuous reception. The gig went smoothly, and the response was overwhelming. As the show ended, the audience filed out of the theater...and so did Johnny Maestro and the Crests! No one had told them that this was just the dress rehearsal. They saw an audience and assumed the program had already been taped for airing later that night. The Crests simply left without a word to anyone.

Almost immediately after the rehearsal came the actual taping. Once again the spotlight cut to Dick in the balcony. He built up to his introduction of the Crests. The spotlight shifted to the parting curtain, and the audience watched an empty rowboat lip sync "16 Candles" for two and a half minutes!

More unbelievably, the red-faced Crests still got bookings. In 1959 they released the chart-busting single "The Angels Listened In." It was upbeat and quick, representing a significant change from "16 Candles."

Nineteen sixty saw two more big singles. "Step by Step" was a superb dance record that featured the sound of wooden blocks imitating a syncopated clock. Maestro's voice was as powerful and appealing as ever with the teasing lyrics describing the seven steps of falling in love. By the seventh step, "We took a chance," he was titillating. But the letdown was his quick explanation of what "the chance" was. It was only a kiss. The Crests wrapped up their career with "Trouble in Paradise" and went their separate ways in 1961. The break was largely due to Johnny's wish to go solo. In the history of rock and roll, the vast majority of lead singers who split for solo careers have flopped along with their abandoned groups. The Crests were no exception. Discouraged when he could not muster any solo hits, Johnny finally consented to join a trio called the Del Satins. Ironically, the Del Satins ultimately became the backup singers for yet another lead artist who had broken off from his own group. Dion was launching his solo career apart from the Belmonts. While Johnny Maestro faded to the background, Dion had a few successful solo years supported by the Del Satins.

After a number of frustrating years Johnny made one more attempt at the limelight. He merged the Del Satins with a large orchestrated brass group, the Rhythm Method. The result was a twelve-member group similar to Blood, Sweat and Tears. He dubbed the joint venture the Brooklyn Bridge and took them to the number-1 slot in 1968 with "The Worst That Could Happen," an old Fifth Dimension number. It was a monster hit, which they followed with the less successful "Welcome Me, Love" in 1969. But the hits did not keep on coming, and it was no longer possible to carry twelve on the payroll. Johnny had to cut the group down to three. By the early seventies Johnny Mastrangelo and his threesome were playing the rock revivals under the Brooklyn Bridge banner.

FRANKIE AVALON, FABIAN, AND BOBBY RYDELL

One of the centers of independent record activity in the late fifties was Philadelphia: home of a pulsating radio market, the birthplace of *American Bandstand*, the nation's leading talent outlet; and mother of many rock-and-roll stars, particularly from South Philly. This lower-middle-class melting pot of Italians, Irish, Jews, and blacks was the home turf of Frankie Avalon, Fabian Forte, Bobby Rydell, James Darren, and Chubby Checker.

Francis Thomas Avallone was a tough ghetto kid from a poor family. At age eight Frankie was already

pursuing a boxing career, billing himself as Kid Avallone and training at the Police Athletic League gym. Then a double feature at the movies one Saturday afternoon changed his perspective on life. He saw Mickey Rooney playing a washed-up fighter in the first feature. It shook him up. *Young Man with a Horn* was the second feature, and it inspired him to turn to music. He saw the picture several times, and within a week he persuaded his father to buy him a

Frankie Avalon, Dick Clark, and Annette Funicello reminisce on the beach. *(Courtesy of Dick Clark)*

Fabian. *(Courtesy of Dick Clark)*

version of Gleason's favorite song, "Tenderly." Frankie then did a number of national TV shows, including *The Pinky Lee Show.* He played trumpet on two 1954 instrumental discs, "Trumpet Sorrento" and "Trumpet Tarantella." But the child prodigy's success soon faded. Frankie Avalon then joined a South Philly rock-and-roll group called Rocco and the Saints with his friend Bobby Ridarelli as drummer.

In 1958 songwriters Pete DeAngelis and Bob Marcucci started Chancellor Records in Philadelphia. Frankie dashed for an audition and was signed. They gave him "Cupid" and "Teacher's Pet" to record, but both tunes went nowhere. DeAngelis and Marcucci then brought him a new tune, which Frankie scorned and mocked by singing with his nose pinched, attaining a nasal, telephone-operator-type sound. But they actually liked this sound and had Frankie record it just that way. "Dede Dinah" hit the charts in January 1958 becoming his first hit as a rock-and-roll star. Its success led Chancellor to request a follow-up song done in the same style. "Gingerbread" became the young singer's second hit, but it also reinforced Frankie's novelty-record image with the public. This was not in Marcucci's game plan.

Al Marshall had written a beautiful love ballad and took it to Al Martino. Martino felt it wasn't right for himself but remembered the party crasher. Marshall showed it to Frankie at Al's suggestion. The material then got Chancellor's stamp of approval. They produced it with lots of reverb, using the echo chamber to its maximum effectiveness for the first time on a rock-and-roll recording. "Venus" was number 1 for five weeks. More importantly, it marked a change in image for the singer. Marcucci began pushing Avalon as a romantic balladeer. His handsome face soon blanketed teen magazines of the day.

Marcucci quickly followed up "Venus" with another mellow, romantic tune, the ode to female puberty "Bobby Sox to Stockings." Followed by "Just Ask Your Heart" and "Why," this progression of hits was a career plan carefully shaped by Marcucci, who was earning his title of "The Idolmaker." He was conveniently located in Philadelphia near the WFIL-TV studios where *American Bandstand* was broadcast. Frankie's frequent exposure on the show solidified his fame as a teen idol nationally.

With Avalon's popularity established, Marcucci wanted new talent to mold in a similar fashion. Frankie had a fifteen-year-old friend named Fabiano Forte whom he introduced to Marcucci. Bob thought the kid had potential and agreed to work with him. First he shortened the boy's name to "Fabian." Then he revealed that he had discovered the kid in the

thirty-five-dollar silver trumpet. He was soon playing with a neighborhood group in local talent shows. His first performance of note occurred on Talent Night, a weekly event at the President Theater in Philadelphia. This led to an appearance and a talent contest victory on the *Horn and Hardart Children's Hour.* Paul Whiteman later gave Frankie his stage name after appearing on his *TV Teen Club.* Frankie won a refrigerator and a console radio/record player for his singing efforts on that show. (Dick Clark, by the way, got his first network job in TV with the *Paul Whiteman TV Teen Club,* doing the Tootsie Roll commercials.)

In 1951 Avalon was bold enough to crash a party for Al Martino, where he performed an unsolicited trumpet medley. Martino liked what he heard and introduced Frankie to New York talent agent Jack Sobel. Sobel arranged for him to audition for Jackie Gleason, which led to a TV appearance playing his

doorway of a South Philly row house. Fabian's last name became one of rock and roll's most protected secrets. Marcucci had his work cut out for him, though, for Fabian was pudgy and had failed "chorus" in high school. They painstakingly went through the process of teen-idol manufacturing together. Fabian was given vocal and performing lessons, but his early recordings were still weak. "I'm in Love" was a 1958 bomb, as was "Be My Steady Date." It was time for some new Marcucci magic.

One Friday night Bob arrived at one of Dick Clark's sock hops with Fabian, who was sexily dressed in a sweater, tight pants, and white bucks. Fabian proceeded to lip-sync "I'm a Man," and the girls went wild, screaming and yelling for more. That hit single climbed the charts in 1959, helped along by a story in *Motion Picture Magazine* that headlined "I Blew a Fuse over Fabian." Within a few months "Turn Me Loose" was released and became one of the biggest smashes of Fabian's career, thanks to his exposure on *American Bandstand*. The tremendous upsurge of Fabian's popularity was amazing considering his lack of musical training and accomplishment. He was the target of music critics who saw him as an off-key "depraved cub scout." But despite the criticism Fabian's ability to seduce crowds of teen-age girls endured. It would be emulated by stars like Jimmy Clanton, Bobby Vee, and Bobby Vinton, and their female counterparts Sandra Dee, Annette, Connie Stevens, and Connie Francis.

Within a year after his discovery Fabian was signed to do *Hound Dog Man,* a movie whose title song became another hit single for Fabian in late 1959. But his flair for performing and his vocal ability were no better on screen than on record. Fabian said in an interview shortly after *Hound Dog Man* was released that he might never have made it if he could sing. It was quite an indication of what the business of rock and roll had become.

Fabian's last hit was "Tiger" in late 1959. In the sixties he and Frankie Avalon experienced waning popularity. By 1963 they had each moved to Los Angeles in search of renewed careers in movies and nightclubs. For Fabian it was only a shot on TV's *Bus Stop.* But Frankie teamed up with Annette Funicello for a series of trend-setting American International beach-party films. The new California surfing sound popularized in 1963 by the Beach Boys and Jan and Dean prompted such teen-age surfing musicals as *Beach Party, Bikini Beach, Muscle Beach,* and *Beach Blanket Bingo.* They all portrayed the teen-

age paradise of an endless, mindless summer. Top priorities were surfing and girls, in that order.

Bobby Ridarelli's career closely paralleled that of his friend Frankie Avalon. While still a drummer with Rocco and the Saints, Bobby was discovered by Frankie Day, the bass player for Dave Appell and the Appelljacks. Both bands had been working at the same summer resort in New Jersey. Day dug Bobby's performance and eventually became his manager. Ridarelli, now known as "Bobby Rydell," cut his first record, "Fatty, Fatty," then watched it fall on its face. But Day didn't give up. He took Rydell to one of Philadelphia's independent record labels, Cameo-Parkway, where he was signed up by Bernie Lowe. After a few less-than-immortal singles, Bobby hit it big in 1959 with "Kissin' Time," which marked the start of a recording career that would give him financial independence by age twenty-one.

With his sweeping pompadour, Rydell made numerous appearances on *American Bandstand* in

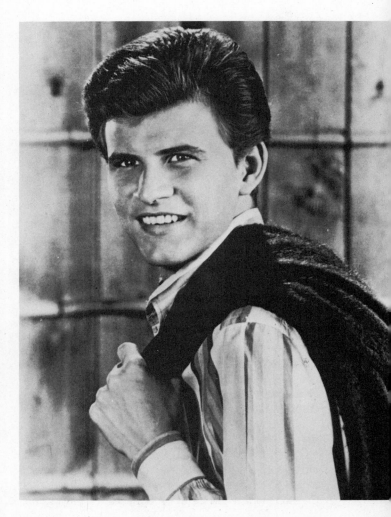

Bobby Rydell. *(Courtesy of Dick Clark)*

72

the Philadelphia teen-idol tradition. But television and media coverage was just one necessary element in the creation of a rock-and-roll star. Bobby also needed more hit records. He closed 1959 with a blockbuster single, "Wild One," and opened 1960 with "Swingin' School," followed by his popular version of the old Domenico Modugno tune "Volare." Bobby's big "dance" song was "The Fish" in 1961, a new step popularized on *Bandstand.* Putting together a nightclub act, Bobby then made his triumphant debut at New York's Copacabana. After clubs, records, and TV, Bobby looked to expand into motion pictures. He starred in *Bye Bye Birdie* with young Ann-Margret. This very successful film gave Bobby a chance to showcase his talents before millions of people who had never heard his records. One aspect of his career fed the other, and he soon racked up

new hits with "The Cha-Cha-Cha" (1962), "Wildwood Days" (1963), "Forget Him" (1963), and "A World without Love" (1964), which was simultaneously recorded by Peter and Gordon, who had the bigger hit record.

Still active in the seventies, Rydell headlined nightclub shows and performed at Knott's Berry Farm in 1972. Today he lives outside of Philadelphia with his family and performs on the East Coast nightclub circuit, while Frankie and Fabian remain on the West Coast. All three middle-age idols have recently made television appearances. *The Idolmaker,* a film about the two rock-and-roll stars and their "creator" premiered at the end of 1980 to critical, though not box-office, acclaim. Bob Marucci acted as technical advisor.

The Sound of 1959

BOBBY DARIN

One of rock's legends took his professional name from a broken neon sign on a Chinese restaurant that was missing the first three letters of the word *Mandarin.* Walden Robert Cassotto was born in 1936 in a tough section of East Harlem. He endured a sickly childhood, surviving several bouts of rheumatic fever between ages eight and eleven. He spent a great deal of time alone and taught himself to play drums, guitar, and piano. In his late teens he left Hunter College to pursue a burning desire to become a Broadway performer. Unable to find any acting jobs, he began writing radio jingles with a young publisher he happened to meet named Don Kirshner.

Endless door-knocking and pavement-pounding led to a contract with Connie Francis' manager, George Scheck, who helped set him up with Decca Records. An appearance on *The Jackie Gleason Show* failed to ignite his career. Four flops later Darin and Decca parted company. But all wasn't lost. Don Kirshner, his former jingle partner, persuaded Atco Records president Ahmet Ertegun to gamble on the ambitious singer. With Atco's R&B reputation, Bobby's first three efforts, "I Found a Million-Dollar Baby," "Don't Call My Name," and "Just in Case You Change Your Mind," were frustrating because of their slow progress. He was about to negotiate with Brunswick after having cut "Early in the Morning" for them under the group name of the Ding Dongs. Bobby, however, was still under contract to Atco, and when they threatened legal action, Brunswick turned the pressing over to Atco, which released the record under the name "Bobby Darin and the Rinky Dinks." Now without either Bobby or his record, Brunswick rushed Buddy Holly into the studio to cut "Early in the Morning." In head-to-head competition, Darin and Holly seemingly knocked each other out of the charts in the summer of 1958, with Buddy's version reaching only number 32 while Bobby's rendition peaked at number 24.

But Atco gave him time to make it. Sure enough, "Splish Splash," which was cowritten by the mother of New York disc jockey Murray the K, was Darin's first national hit, selling over a million in the summer of 1958. "Queen of the Hop," recorded during the same session as "Splish Splash," earned him a gold record that fall. Incidentally, both hits had the distinction of having been written in less than an hour.

Nineteen fifty-nine was a year of contrasting hits for Darin. First he did "Plain Jane," then "Dream Lover" (with Neil Sedaka on piano, strings, and background voices). Next came the smash hit of his career, "Mack the Knife."

Darin modeled his "Mack the Knife" after Louis Armstrong's version. With this record he gained wider acceptance from the adult audience. "Mack the Knife" is the prologue song from the *Threepenny Opera,* then in its fifth revival year off-Broadway. It scored number 1 in August 1959 and became his biggest hit, contrary to the predictions of his close friend and confidant Dick Clark. Darin sang the song on Dick's *Saturday*

Night Show, emerging from a dark stage into a misty pool of light. At age twenty-three he then became a headliner at New York's Copacabana, where he played to sellout crowds. He also had his own network TV spectacular, the youngest performer to have had one up to that time.

Darin married teen-queen Sandra Dee in December 1960, and they had a son two years later. In 1962 his movie career took off. *Too Late Blues, Hell is for Heroes, State Fair, Pressure Point,* and *If A Man Answers* were all released that year. He found the adult audience he was seeking, though several rock-and-roll hits were released between "Mack the Knife" and his switch to Capitol Records in 1962. Among them were "Multiplication," "Won't You Come Home, Bill Bailey," "You Must Have Been a Beautiful Baby," and "Things." In 1963 he was nominated for an Oscar for Best Supporting Actor in *Captain Newman, M.D.* and received the French Film Critics Award for Best Actor for that picture.

Bobby Darin had developed a brash confidence and business sense by the time he signed with Capitol. A carefully planned engagement at the Flamingo Hotel in Las Vegas marked the end of a year-long absence from the stage. His overwhelming reception floored the management, who were forced to turn away a thousand fans each night. A four-year million-dollar contract was offered. Sales of his albums and singles were good. He was close to the top in the entertainment hierarchy. But with the onslaught of the British invasion, Darin's popularity began slowly to fade. His strong image became fragmented by attempts at country-western and show tunes such as "Hello, Dolly!" He recorded his last major hit, "If I Were a Carpenter," in September 1966. This folk disc allowed him to continue on the club circuit, but his accent was strictly on folk now with new material by John Sebastian and Tim Hardin.

According to Dick Clark, Darin became a latter-day hippie in the late sixties. He sported long hair and blue jeans and moved into a trailer near Big Sur, having sold most of his possessions. He also divorced Sandra Dee in 1966 and was very unhappy at the time. In 1971 his earlier episodes with rheumatic fever caught up with him, and he had to have two heart valves replaced. His continuous battle with cardiac-related ailments seemed relentless. It was around this time, during a healthy period, that he became associated with Motown Records and returned to do club dates again. In 1972 he was delighted to host a summer replacement TV show for Dean Martin.

In late 1973 Bobby began suffering from what his longtime friend Dave Gershenson called "a general malaise and lack of functioning." He entered Cedars of Lebanon Hospital in Los Angeles with a diagnosis of septicemia. But complications led to more complications, and Darin died on the operating table at age thirty-seven.

Dick Clark, an old friend of Bobby's dating back to his hitless days on Decca, put it best: "He was the kindest, gentlest person. He had a great native intellect. If he had only been physically healthy, he probably could have gone on to be a legend."

Bobby Darin was once asked if he wanted to be as big as Frank Sinatra. Bobby replied that he wanted to be the biggest Bobby Darin he could, the best Bobby Darin in the world. He was.

1960

Nineteen sixty had a twist. Actually, it had *the* twist—a dance phenomenon that had the world swinging to the beat of several different twist records. *American Bandstand* helped popularize Chubby Checker's "The Twist," and Dick Clark sees the twist craze as one of the biggest moments in rock-and-roll history:

"Dances like the stroll, particularly in the early days of rock and roll, were all originated by black people. They were equally divided between slow dancing and fast dancing. The fast dancing was a derivative of the lindy hop or the jitterbug. The slow dancing had roots in the fox trot.

"The most significant thing that ever happened in rock and roll was the twist. I introduced Chubby Checker's song immediately. Shortly thereafter the Peppermint Lounge opened in New York with Joey Dee and the Starlighters. One of the biggest moments in rock and roll and its most socially significant period to date was when the twist hit. Adults could dance and publicly show that we weren't afraid to like this music. Rock and roll had now become socially acceptable to the sophisticated and the rich. That's why the twist was so terribly important. It didn't have so much to do with the dance itself as much as the fact that *everybody* was dancing it at clubs and gin mills. And once you can get people to admit they like rock and roll, you can forget about their previous snob attitude."

While society twisted the night away in 1960, those who stayed home listening to the radio were calling up DJs and asking them to dedicate songs to a particular boyfriend or girl friend, songs such as "Sixteen Reasons" by Connie Stevens, "Itsy Bitsy Teenie Weenie Yellow Polka Dot Bikini" by Brian Hyland, "Image Of a Girl" by the Safaris, "Tell Laura I Love Her" by Ray Peterson, "Pineapple Princess" by Annette, "Poetry in Motion" by Johnny Tillotson, "You Talk Too Much" by Joe Jones, "A Thousand Stars" by Kathy Young and the Innocents, and "You're Sixteen" by Johnny Burnette.

The top ten for the year were "He'll Have to Go" by Jim Reeves, "Theme from *The Apartment*" by Percy Faith, "Running Bear" by Johnny Preston, "Teen Angel" by Mark Dinning, "Cathy's Clown" by the Everly Brothers, "It's Now or Never" by Elvis Presley, "The Twist" by Chubby Checker, "I'm Sorry" by Brenda Lee, "Handy Man" by Jimmy Jones, and "Stuck On You" by Elvis Presley.

In 1960, Francis Gary Powers was shot down while flying over the Soviet Union in his U-2 plane. Adolf Eichmann, the infamous Nazi war criminal, was captured in Argentina. John F. Kennedy edged out Richard

Nixon for the American presidency. The Philadelphia Eagles defeated the Green Bay Packers for the NFL championship, while the Houston Oilers took the AFL title from the Los Angeles Chargers. The Pittsburgh Pirates knocked off the Yankees in the World Series, while the Boston Celtics swept to another NBA crown. At the Summer Olympics in Rome the gold medal for boxing in the light-heavyweight division was won by a young fighter named Cassius Clay. *The Apartment* grabbed the Oscar for Best Picture. And on TV, *The Roaring Twenties* replaced Dick Clark's *Saturday Night Show* and flopped.

It was 1960—the sixth year of rock and roll.

THE DRIFTERS

The Drifters' story is a long and confusing one. It's long because it spans the years from 1953 to 1980. It's confusing because there were two distinct versions of the Drifters—one a rhythm-and-blues group, the other a rock-and-roll group—and their membership underwent numerous personnel changes over the years. Consider this list of the group's members since 1953: Clyde McPhatter, David Baughan, Johnny Moore, Bobby Hendricks, Gerhart Thrasher, Andrew Thrasher, Charlie Hughes, Bill Pinckney, Tommy Evans, Jimmy Oliver, Will Anderson, Jim Johnson, Willie Ferbie, Ben E. King, Rudy Lewis, Charlie Thomas, Doc Green, Elsberry Hobbs, Johnny Lee Williams, Reggie Kimber, Bill Fredericks, James Clark, Eugene Pearson, Johnny Terry, Rock Sheppard, William Brent, Don Dandrich, Butch Leake, Milton Turner, and Don Thomas.

The Drifters began with Clyde McPhatter. As a teen-ager in the early fifties Clyde sang black gospel music. Like that of many other rock-and-roll stars, Clyde's first break came with a win on *Arthur Godfrey's Talent Scouts* TV show. He was then signed by Billy Ward to sing in his R&B group, the Dominoes. With Clyde singing lead, they plunged deeply into the rhythm-and-blues market. They had many hits, including "Sixty Minute Man," "Have Mercy Baby," and "The Bells." Yet Clyde was dissatisfied being part of someone else's group, so he left the Dominoes in 1953 and was replaced by Jackie Wilson. Clyde drifted to Ahmet Ertegun, head of Atlantic Records, and was given his own group of former gospel singers to work with, known as the Civitones. They combined to form the Drifters, turning their gospel backgrounds to classic rhythm and blues with hits like "Money Honey" (1953) and "Honey Love" (1954). By 1956 they were performing in Alan Freed's live rock-and-roll shows with their spirited stage presence, featuring a saxophone that some called obscene.

The R&B-oriented Drifters lasted until 1958, when Clyde McPhatter decided to go solo. He had hits with "A Lover's Question" in 1958 and "Lover Please" in 1962, then faded from the charts, unable to return before his untimely death in 1972. The rest of the Drifters either left the group of their own volition or were canned. George Treadwell, the manager of the group, now had a hell of a problem. He had contracts for personal appearances for the group, including a ten-year contract that called for two annual appearances at Harlem's Apollo Theater. He either had to default on his contracts or somehow get the Drifters to perform. At this time a group of street-corner singers in Harlem including Benjamin Nelson were developing a reputation. They called themselves the Five Crowns, and Treadwell caught their act one night at the bottom of the bill at the Apollo. He liked what he saw and signed them. For all intents and purposes, they would now be the Drifters. They would move from last-act status to headliners, make records and money, and keep Treadwell out of contract problems.

Atlantic Records placed the new Drifters under the tutelage of producers/composers/arrangers Jerry Leiber and Mike Stoller to mold their new sound. Leiber and Stoller took them into the realm of rock and roll. They added strings to some of their songs, full orchestrations to others, and even tried a Latin beat on occasion. From 1959 to 1964 the new Drifters had hit after hit, including "There Goes My Baby" (1959), "Dance with Me" (1959), "This Magic Moment" (1960), "Save the Last Dance for Me" (1960), "I Count the Tears" (1960), "Some Kind of Wonderful" (1961), "Up on the Roof" (1962), "On Broadway" (1963), "Under the Boardwalk" (1964), "I've Got Sand in My Shoes" (1964), and "Saturday Night at the Movies" (1964). Lead singer Benjamin Nelson, now known as Ben E. King, went solo after "Save the Last Dance for Me" with the help of

Atlantic Records, Leiber and Stoller, and Phil Spector. King, like McPhatter before him, scored quickly with "Spanish Harlem" and "Stand By Me" in 1961, returned in 1963 with "I (Who Have Nothing)," then faded from the scene.

After King departed, the Drifters continued with several other lead singers, most notably Rudy Lewis and Johnny Moore. They joined Dick Clark's popular Caravan of Stars, performing for months of one-night stands.

Perhaps the Drifters' strangest tale concerns "Under the Boardwalk." This story was created by Atlantic Records PR people at the time the disc was released. It seems that the Drifters had been working long and hard getting ready to record the song. On the morning of the "Boardwalk" recording session, lead singer Rudy Lewis was stricken by a heart attack and died. The other Drifters decided that Rudy would have wanted them to go ahead with the session, so they proceeded to the studio and recorded the song for Rudy. The Drifters supposedly used rehearsal tapes of Rudy singing the song while they recorded the backup live. Rudy was dead, but the music went on. However, "Under the Boardwalk"

One of the many lineups of the Drifters (from left: Billy Davis, Gene Pearson, Charles Thomas, Johnny Moore, and Johnny Terry). *(Courtesy of Dick Clark)*

Ben E. King of the Drifters.

was actually recorded with Johnny Moore on lead; he stepped in after Rudy's death.

"Under the Boardwalk" caused problems for the Drifters after it was released. Radio stations around the country were banning it. They could tolerate the suggestion of sexual escapades on the beach, but they could not tolerate lyrics that blatantly stated, "We'll be making love under the boardwalk." Although that version remained intact on their albums, the line was altered on the single to "We'll be falling in love under the boardwalk."

After 1964 the Drifters took a back seat to the sound of the British invasion and the new soul of Motown. During this period personnel changed rapidly. By 1970 three separate groups emerged, touring, doing concerts, and each claiming to be the Drifters. These groups often had no more than one real rhythm-and-blues Drifter or rock-and-roll Drifter, and neither Clyde McPhatter nor Ben E. King was in any of them. Although the 1980s have their ersatz Drifters, the Drifters who actually made rock-and-roll history are gone.

DION AND THE BELMONTS

Dion DiMucci and his friends were into rock and roll. They gained local fame in The Bronx as topnotch street-corner singers. They began singing doo-wop music a cappella in alleys, subways, or wherever the echo was good. The falsetto always sounded higher and the bass richer when the echo was good. It wasn't long before Jubilee Records heard about them and signed them under the name "Dion and the Timberlanes." In 1957 they released a song called "The Chosen." It wasn't, however, and Dion and the Timberlanes fell into obscurity.

That ill-fated record came to the attention of some people at Laurie Records who saw potential in Dion. They offered him a contract, but the Timberlanes had to go. Dion had to go back to The Bronx to round up some other street-corner singers on Belmont Avenue. They became Dion and the Belmonts and soon raced to the top with "I Wonder Why" in 1958.

Dion (third from the left) and the Belmonts.
(Courtesy of Dick Clark)

The song was done in classic doo-wop style with falsetto, bass, and harmony. Some great doo-wop nonsense syllables opened the tune. Studio reverb gave it a real "subway" sound.

With 1959's "A Teenager in Love," one of the great love ballads of the era (rivaled only by the Crests' "16 Candles"), Dion and the Belmonts established themselves as a major act. Their label quickly sent them out that winter on a promotional tour across the Midwest—the same fatal tour that featured Buddy Holly, Ritchie Valens, and the Big Bopper. Because one of the Belmonts was afraid to fly, Dion and the other Belmonts stayed behind and took the bus. His fear saved the group from the fatal plane crash that took the lives of three rock-and-roll legends.

After the 1960 hit "Where or When," Laurie Records agreed to let Dion go solo. He started his new career with "Lonely Teenager" in 1960, followed by a song written about the girl who would soon become his wife, "Runaround Sue" (1961); then his biggest hit, "The Wanderer" (1961); and "The Majestic" (1961). After a dry 1962 Dion came back strong with "Sandy" (1963), "Ruby Baby" (1963), and "Donna the Prima Donna" (1963). While Dion prospered, the Belmonts struggled, managing only two notable hits on their own, "Tell Me Why" (1961) and "Come On Little Angel" (1962).

The early sixties were fruitful years for Dion. He even became a film star in *Twist Around the Clock* and *Teen-Age Millionaire*. But it was during these prosperous times that Dion got into drugs, which ultimately brought him down.

Dion postponed his solo career for a while in 1964. With the coming of the British rockers, most of the old-line American rock-and-roll stars fell behind. Dion took time off to learn and experiment with his art. He was influenced by the new wave of folk-rockers like Dylan, Baez, and others. But the lull in his career also allowed him to experiment further with hard drugs. He became a heroin addict.

The road back was a long and hard one for Dion. It cost him his youth and his family, as he reported in the lyrics of his autobiographical song, "In Your Own Back Yard." As he pieced his life back together, he also reconstructed his music career with the release of "Abraham, Martin and John," one of the biggest hits of 1968. This was a different Dion from the one who had sung "I Wonder Why" ten years earlier. His hair was long and he wore wire-rim glasses. His glittery tuxedo had given way to faded jeans. His backup band and singers were gone; he preferred to strum his own guitar. His music was folk-rock and the lyrics were poignant. Dion was back, and though he never had a top-ten single again, he would cut many fine albums and draw accolades for his intimate concerts.

Perhaps the greatest moment since 1960 for fans of Dion and the Belmonts occurred in 1973 when promoter Richard Nader convinced the group to reunite for one of his Madison Square Garden rock-and-roll revival shows. For the cheering members of the S.R.O. crowd, it was a chance to relive a part of rock-and-roll history. Today Dion has turned to recording religious music.

ROY ORBISON

Mr. Orbison wanted his son, Roy, to be a geologist, but he made the mistake of buying him a guitar. By age eight the boy was singing country songs on the local radio station in Wink, Texas. Two years later Roy formed the Wink Westerners and gained new popularity through local TV appearances. From these country roots he shifted to rockabilly and finally to rock and roll. This transition was foreshadowed when he changed the name of his group from the Wink Westerners to the Teen Kings.

Roy's first big break came while he was at North Texas State University. In the right place at the right time, he was hired to back up a fellow student named Pat Boone on his initial recording endeavor, "Two Hearts." This led to a professional recording engagement at the Norman Petty Studios in New Mexico, the same studios that would record Buddy Holly just a year later.

"Ooby Dooby," written by two of Roy's fraternity brothers, was his first release on the obscure Je-Wel label. It might have disappeared completely had it not come to the attention of Sam Phillips of Sun Records in Memphis. Sam bought it from Je-Wel and re-released it. As a Sun release it sold over a quarter of a million copies.

During the second half of the fifties Sun was the kingdom of rockabilly with a court that included Elvis Presley, Carl Perkins, Jerry Lee Lewis, and Johnny Cash. Roy, however, wasn't comfortable in Sun's rockabilly mold. He felt that he wasn't being given the opportunity to explore his intense and powerful vocal skills at Sun. He began to develop an emotional ballad style. He also perfected his songwriting abilities by writing "All I Have to Do Is Dream" and "Claudette" for the Everly Brothers, as well as other tunes for Jerry Lee Lewis and Buddy Holly. By 1960 a disenchanted Orbison left Sun for Monument Records. On his way to Monument in Nashville, Roy stopped in Memphis, looking for someone to record a new song he had written. Not having recorded or performed in two years, Roy dismissed the thought of recording the song himself. But after both Elvis and the Everly Brothers rejected the material, Roy went ahead and did it on his own. The result was "Only the Lonely," his very first million seller.

The next four years saw Roy Orbison's career soar. "Crying," "Dream Baby," "Mean Woman Blues," and his monster hit "Oh, Pretty Woman" (with his famous growl) were all gold records. Pain, grief, and loneliness echoed in his voice. The clever use of strings and intimate lyrics helped secure his place in the rock-and-roll hall of fame. Roy was so big at the time that when Elvis Presley was discharged from the Army, he told the press that Roy Orbison was the biggest threat to his career. In May 1963 Roy did a concert tour of England. His opening act was the Beatles!

But by 1965 Roy's career began to crumble. The man whose trademark was a pair of dark sunglasses (they became his trademark after he forgot his regular specs at one performance, substituted prescription sunglasses, and the crowd loved it) left Monument and moved on to MGM Records. By now, only Motown artists were effectively combating the British invasion. After a few minor successes and a movie role in *The Fastest Gun Alive,* tragedy struck. In June 1966 his wife, Claudette, was killed in a motorcycle accident. Two years later his two children died in a terrible fire.

Roy returned to perform in a 1972 rock-and-roll revival show at Madison Square Garden in New York and proved that he could still hit E above high C. Although he has apparently sworn off further revival-show appearances, he does continue to tour and record. Others continue to record his songs as well; Linda Ronstadt, for instance, had her first gold single with her rendition of Roy's "Blue Bayou," while the Blues Brothers recorded Roy's "Oh, Pretty Woman." Roy remarried and now has three children. In 1979 he endured a successful coronary bypass operation and returned to his music.

Roy Orbison. (*Gary Heery*)

CONNIE FRANCIS

Like many of her rock-and-roll contemporaries, Concetta Franconero from New Jersey won first place on *Arthur Godfrey's Talent Scouts* TV show. She was signed by MGM Records under her new "Americanized" stage name, "Connie Francis," and began cutting records in 1955.

For three years fame evaded Connie Francis. But MGM had faith, and Connie broke through with "Who's Sorry Now" in 1958. The song was selected for Connie by her father, who knew nothing about rock-and-roll music and picked it for no apparent reason other than its being an old favorite of his that was originally recorded in the 1920s. She soon became first lady of rock and roll and helped usher in the new "soft" sound that many critics refused to accept as true rock and roll, calling her a "pop" singer instead. Yet her major market was rock-and-roll audiences. Connie was the female answer to the clean-cut male teen-age idols—Pat Boone, Frankie Avalon, Bobby Rydell, and Fabian. Whether pop or rock, Connie had more hits than any other solo female artist of the day.

Connie sang the motion-picture theme song for and appeared in *Where the Boys Are* and *Follow the Boys,* two early beach-party films. Connie's film career did not continue, though, and neither did her list of hits. Within a year of *Follow the Boys* the British invasion was on and Connie's rock-and-roll career was soon over.

Nevertheless, between "Who's Sorry Now" and "Follow the Boys," Connie had dozens of successes, the biggest being "Stupid Cupid" (1958), "If I Didn't Care" (1959), "Lipstick on Your Collar" (1959), "Everybody's Somebody's Fool" (1960), "My Heart Has a Mind of Its Own" (1961), and "Vacation" (1962). These were the "greaser" years, and Connie was even commissioned to record a promotional giveaway album for Brylcreem ("A little dab'll do ya!"). But with the arrival of the Beatles, the "greaser" sound was all washed up. Connie compensated by finding a loyal foreign audience and concentrating more on real pop songs.

During her rock-and-roll years Connie made numerous appearances on Dick Clark's nighttime show and on *American Bandstand,* eventually becoming a close friend of Dick's. Teen gossip magazines occasionally claimed that they were more than just friends, but Connie's actual rock-and-roll romance was with Bobby Darin.

Connie was traumatically thrust back into the public eye in the 1970s while performing at a Long Island hotel. Asleep in her room that night, she was attacked by an intruder. After suing the hotel for lack of security, she eventually won damages.

Today Connie continues to perform in the U.S. and overseas. Her audiences from 1958 to 1962 have grown up with her and still flock to her performances.

Connie Francis and Dick Clark look at Connie's collection of gold records. *(Courtesy of Dick Clark)*

BRENDA LEE

At age nine Brenda Mae Tarpley was called "Little Miss Dynamite." Despite her diminutive size, it was obvious that this little girl could belt out a tune, be it gospel or country. As she grew older, that powerful voice widened its range to include everything from a throaty, guttural growl to a falsetto. It was the kind of range that could easily excite a rock-and-roll audience.

Brenda got her first big break when Pat Boone's father-in-law, country singer Red Foley, hired her to sing on his network television show. Her country style applied to rock-and-roll material produced a rockabilly sound that appealed to both markets. Decca made a fortune on their little star, who next to Connie Francis was perhaps the most successful female artist of the early years of rock and roll. With frequent *American Bandstand* appearances to promote her releases, Brenda became a Dick Clark favorite and joined his Caravan of Stars. Unfortunately, she was the only girl on a bus filled with male rock-and-roll stars and assorted roadies. When things got too wild and the tour started to become a human endurance test, Brenda wisely bailed out and fled homeward.

As she turned out hits like "Sweet Nothin's" (1959), "I'm Sorry" (1960), "That's All You Gotta Do" (1960), "I Want to Be Wanted" (1960), "Rockin' around the Christmas Tree" (1960), and "All Alone Am I" (1962), her popularity zoomed both at home and abroad. She toured Europe and Japan, constantly met by overwhelming receptions from enthusiastic audiences. If the European and Japanese audiences were enthusiastic, however, the South American audiences were crazy, and it was not uncommon for riots to break out upon her arrival.

After "All Alone Am I," Brenda never produced another major rock-and-roll hit. Like Connie Francis, Brenda was not a rock-and-roll survivor. By 1972, however, Brenda found a new audience—the country market that had brought her initial successes. Like Jerry Lee Lewis, she has made the successful career transition from country to rock and roll and back.

The Sound of 1960

CHUBBY CHECKER
AND THE TWIST

In 1959, records by black rhythm-and-blues artists were still being covered by white artists like Pat Boone, Ricky Nelson, and others. Hank Ballard and the Midnighters had a history of having their songs covered, so they had to have been nervous when "Teardrops on Your Letter" was released. It was covered, but both the white version and Ballard's bombed. However, Ballard's record company started to get reports that urban black kids were turning on to the flip side of the record, doing some crazy dance to it. The flip side was a song Ballard wrote called "The Twist." Seeing the chance to recoup its investment, the record company adjusted the labels to make "The Twist" the A-side. Sure enough, by mid-1960 "The Twist" churned its way up the rhythm-and-blues charts, though it failed to make a dent in the pop charts.

Then, during one of Dick Clark's early summer TV shows, Dick happened to glance around the dance floor and was horrified by what he saw. A black boy and girl were gyrating their midsections at each other. Dick nearly panicked. He ordered the cameramen to avoid the couple at all costs, fearing that the show would be wiped out with one grind of the pelvis. But it started getting out of hand. Some of the white kids watched the couple and tried to imitate them. At the commercial Dick took them aside and asked them what the hell they were doing. The twist, they said, and he immediately associated it with the Hank Ballard tune.

On the next show several of the *Bandstand* regulars had picked up on the bizarre dance. After considering the situation, Dick decided to let the twist go out over the airwaves. He sensed that he was onto something very new and exciting and only hoped that he wouldn't be chastised by parents, the network, and his sponsors. Dick then called a friend of his who ran Cameo-Parkway Records in Philadelphia. He explained what was happening and suggested that they rush through a new cover version of Ballard's record. Knowing Dick's musical instincts, the company agreed that a new "Twist" should be produced, but wondered who could do it best. Again Dick had the answer.

Ernest Evans was a plump Philadelphia high school student who worked as a chicken plucker after school. Ernest had his own rock-and-roll act in which he imitated Fats Domino and other singers. But while his fellow pupils Frankie Avalon and Fabian Forte had both gone on to rock-

and-roll fame, Ernest was still plucking chickens. Then Frankie and Fabian brought him to Cameo-Parkway. It was another classic case of being in the right place at the right time.

During the winter of 1959 Dick Clark was looking for someone to cut a record that he wanted to send out as a unique Christmas card. He and his wife went to Cameo-Parkway and discovered their new artist, Ernest Evans. His imitations of rock-and-roll singers delighted Dick, and he was given the Christmas-record job. His best impression was of Fats Domino, which prompted Dick's wife, Bobbie, to remark that not only did he sound like Fats Domino, he looked like a younger version of The Fat Man. Ernest wasn't really fat, though, just chubby. He was a "chubby checker" as opposed to a "fat domino." From that day on the name stuck. Ernest Evans ceased to exist, and Chubby Checker was born.

Now Dick suggested that Cameo-Parkway use Chubby for "The Twist." The record company had been searching for material for him anyway. This would be a good start, they thought. Chubby then recorded the song exactly as Ballard had done it. This may well have been the first time that a black artist covered another black artist in head-to-head competition for airplay and sales. But Chubby held four aces in the form of Dick Clark. Dick had already given Chubby his television debut, and now he would let Chubby debut "The Twist" on *American Bandstand.*

The reaction to that show was overwhelming. The demand for "The Twist" was incredible, and to meet it Dick wound up promoting "The Twist" and Chubby Checker more than anyone. "The Twist" became synonymous with *American Bandstand,* and no radio or TV show exploited it better. But no one, not even Dick, ever imagined that it would turn into the biggest, most popular dance craze in history.

American Bandstand was *the* place to learn the twist. Chubby was on many, many times, giving lessons and explaining that the twist was like putting out a cigarette with both feet. Chubby became the dance king of the 1960s. Before long the jet set discovered the twist and made New York's Peppermint Lounge the Studio 54 of the decade. Meanwhile Chubby Checker moved on to the silver screen, starring in two awful "twist" films, *Twist Around the Clock* and *Don't Knock the Twist.*

"The Twist" was number 1 on most charts in 1960. In early 1961 Chubby's "Let's Twist Again" became number 1. By the summer of 1961 "The Twist" climbed to the number-1 spot again, gaining prestige as the only song in rock-and-roll history ever to be number 1, fade from the charts, then climb back to number 1 again. By 1962 Chubby hit once more with "Slow Twistin'." Meanwhile a proliferation of twist records saturated the market. "The Peppermint Twist," "Twistin' U.S.A.," "Twistin' the Night Away," "Twist and Shout," "Dear Lady Twist," "Oliver Twist" (by Rod McKuen of all people!), and a horde of others flooded the market.

Banned in parts of Florida and reviled by clergymen, doctors, teachers, and parents, "The Twist" became the calling card of the youth culture, the latest form of teen-age rebellion. But then adults began to accept it...and do it! It became *the* thing to do at weddings and bar mitzvahs.

Chubby Checker strikes gold on *American Bandstand. (Courtesy of Dick Clark)*

Quickly the youth of America were forced to abandon it in favor of a host of new dances. And Chubby was right there to lead the pack again. In 1960 he introduced "The Hucklebuck." In 1961 he gave us "Pony Time." Nineteen sixty-two featured his "Pop-eye the Hitchhiker" and "Limbo Rock." Limbo Rock became a sensation at teen-age make-out parties, but it quickly moved on to the catered-affair circuit. Chubby had everybody wrenching their backs attempting to bend over backward under the limbo bar. These dances were only the beginning. Next came the frug, the locomotion, the swim, the slop, the fly, the watusi, the jerk, the Continental walk, the bossa nova, the Madison, the Bristol stomp, the fish, the mashed potato, and the monkey. Yet none of these came close to the unprecedented popularity of the twist. Created by Hank Ballard and recorded by Chubby Checker, it was promoted, exploited, and forged into the most famous dance ever by Dick Clark's "sixth sense" and the influence of *American Bandstand*.

1961

Nineteen sixty-one seemed to be a great year for couples. Tony and Maria ran off with the Oscar for Best Picture with *West Side Story.* Rob and Laura Petrie arrived on CBS-TV for the award-winning *Dick Van Dyke Show,* police officers Toody and Muldoon teamed up for *Car 54 Where Are You?,* and a couple of doctors, Ben Casey and Jim Kildare, brought their bedside manners into the nation's living rooms.

Yuri Gagarin was launched into space by the Soviets and was soon followed by America's Alan B. Shepard. The Berlin Wall went up, and the Bay of Pigs invasion of Cuba collapsed. Surfing was becoming the hot new sport of 1961, but it still couldn't steal the spotlight from the Yankee's World Series triumph over the Cincinnati Reds. Roger Maris clouted sixty-one home runs to break Babe Ruth's single-season record. The Celtics claimed another NBA title, while the Green Bay Packers and Houston Oilers respectively topped the NFL and the AFL.

In 1961 teen-age eyes were on *American Bandstand,* watching the steps to the dozens of new twist-inspired dances that were sweeping the prom and sock-hop circuits. The top ten hits of the year included "Tossin' and Turnin'" by frequent *Bandstand* guest Bobby Lewis, "I Fall to Pieces" by Patsy Cline, "Michael" by the Highwaymen, "Cryin'" by Roy Orbison, "Runaway" by Del Shannon, "My True Story" by the Jive Five, "Pony Time" by Chubby Checker, "Wheels" by the String-a-Longs, "Raindrops" by Dee Clark, and "Wooden Heart" by Joe Dowell. There were dozens of other songs that scored 81 or better on *American Bandstand's* Rate-a-Record. Teen-agers were slow-dancing to "Angel Baby" by Rosie and the Originals, "There's a Moon Out Tonight" by the Capris, "Daddy's Home" by Shep and the Limelights, and "Those Oldies but Goodies" by Little Caesar and the Romans. They fast-danced to the sounds of "Blue Moon" by the Marcels, "Pretty Little Angel Eyes" by Curtis Lee, "Please Mr. Postman" by the Marvelettes, and "Let's Get Together" by Hayley Mills.

It was 1961—the seventh year of rock and roll.

Sam Cooke.

SAM COOKE

In October 1958 *Dick Clark's Saturday Night Show* was scheduled to be broadcast live on location from the forty-fourth annual Southeastern Fair in Atlanta, Georgia. Booked to appear on this special broadcast were Dave Appell and the Appelljacks, Paul Peak, Joni James, Danny and the Juniors, Conway Twitty, and Sam Cooke, a handsome black singer, best known at the time for his romantic ballads. Sam Cooke's appearance on that show would make it the first integrated performance ever held at the Atlanta Fairgrounds.

The South didn't always welcome rock and roll or black singers. In those first years after the Supreme Court's order for integration, southern tempers frequently turned nasty and violent. In 1956 Nat "King" Cole, a smooth and polished pop singer, had been brutally attacked and dragged offstage by members of the White Citizens' Council in Birmingham, Alabama. Now trouble was brewing in Atlanta. Threatening letters flooded ABC. The Ku Klux Klan announced its plans to wreak havoc upon these northerners. Dick Clark's people called for protection from the National Guard, only to be informed that the Guard was filled with KKK members. Sam Cooke already had had trouble at a motel in Atlanta that refused to accept blacks. With all this happening, Dick Clark and Sam Cooke met to discuss canceling the show. After he was warned of all the possible dangers, Sam announced, "I gotta go on, that's all there is to it." Dick smiled and nodded. Despite a bomb threat and the presence of the Ku Klux Klan and a questionable National Guard, *The Dick Clark Saturday Night Show* went on, broadcast live, without a hitch. That October night in Atlanta, Sam and Dick made rock-and-roll history.

Sam Cooke, the son of Reverend Charles Cooke of Chicago, was raised in the gospel tradition. In 1951, at age twenty, Sam replaced the popular R. H. Harris as the lead singer of the gospel group the Soul Stirrers. Articulate and handsome, he was a charismatic figure in the black community. During his six years with the Soul Stirrers, Sam also recorded gospel tunes with them for Specialty Records. But by 1957 he wanted more. Sam Cooke wanted to be a pop star.

In 1957 the religious black community wouldn't accept its gospel artists singing secular, pop songs, so Sam recorded "Lovable," his first pop release, as Dale Cooke. When they discovered that Sam was singing "worldly" songs, the Soul Stirrers forced Cooke to leave the group. When Art Rupe, the owner of Specialty Records, found out that his top gospel singer was singing pop songs with a white approach, he turned down Cooke's next single, "You Send Me," and sold his contract to producer Bumps Blackwell. Blackwell arranged a deal for Sam with a new company, Keen Records in Los Angeles. "You Send Me," Keen's very first release, sold 2.5 million copies, was number 1 for three weeks at the end of 1957, and stayed on the charts for six months.

For the next two years Sam turned out hits for Keen Records with an intentional pop and teen appeal. His clear, silky voice graced such songs as "Only Sixteen," "Everybody Likes to Cha Cha Cha" (which started a dance fad in 1959), and "Wonderful World," his last single for Keen (which he wrote with Herb Alpert and Lou Adler). The plan was to turn Sam into a teen-idol for black teen-age girls.

In 1960 Sam Cooke signed with RCA Records. He and Harry Belafonte were the only black artists on the label. After a false start with "Teenage Sonata," Sam struck gold in September 1960 with "Chain Gang." His velvety phrasing and pleasant voice enticed adults, while the single's grunts and sound effects appealed to the kids. The record shot up to number 2, staying in the top ten for two months. In 1961 Sam was back on the charts with "Cupid." Hopping on the twist bandwagon, he churned out

"Twistin' the Night Away." Sam's 1962 follow-up was "Having a Party," and for the first time Sam Cooke's voice had some grit. Halfway through "Having a Party" Sam traded in the Hugo and Luigi RCA string section for a rocking saxophone and let a rough edge show in his voice. The flip side, "Bring It on Home to Me," was a wailing, gospel-influenced duet with Lou Rawls, who was then a member of the gospel group the Pilgrim Travelers. Cook walked away with an influential two-sided hit. "Bring It on Home to Me" received more airplay than "Having a Party," and, more importantly, set the tone for the "sweet soul" sound, paving the way for singers like Smokey Robinson, Marvin Gaye, and Otis Redding.

Sam Cooke was also one of the first black music entrepreneurs. Since he wrote most of his own songs, he formed his own music-publishing firm to protect his interests. With his manager, J. W. Alexander, Sam created a management company not only to chart the course of his own career, but to develop new talent like Lou Rawls and Billy Preston.

In 1960 Cooke and Alexander organized Sar/Derby Records, a Los Angeles-based R&B outlet. While crooning "Cupid" and "Chain Gang" for RCA, Cooke was producing "Looking for a Love" by Bobby Womack and the Valentinos and "When a Boy Falls in Love" by Mel Carter for his own record company.

Sam Cooke, the image of grace and propriety, met with a sordid and bizarre end in December 1964. Cooke allegedly picked up a twenty-two-year-old woman at a party and took her to a motel in Los Angeles. While Sam was in the bathroom, the girl ran off, taking most of Cooke's clothing with her. Clad in only a sports jacket and shoes, the outraged Cooke began searching for the girl and pounded on the door of the motel manager, Mrs. Franklin. The door broke open and in the scuffle that ensued, Mrs. Franklin shot Cooke three times with a pistol, then beat the wounded singer with a club. On the morning of December 11, 1964, one of the founding fathers of soul music died from his wounds.

GARY "U.S." BONDS

Little Gary Anderson of Jacksonville, Florida, began singing in his church choir at the age of nine. A "mama's boy" by his own admission, Gary made his first break from his family and from black gospel singing when he started hanging out on street corners singing a cappella with friends. One night a man named Frank Guida heard the boys singing and was impressed with Gary's voice. He told Gary that he wanted him to record at his new studio. Gary was ecstatic, but Guida never contacted him again. The letdown was tremendous. Eventually Gary and his street-corner friends disbanded.

In 1960 Gary and his new group, the Sleepy King Band, were making the rounds on the Virginia nightclub circuit. Frank Guida showed up again one night to rave about Gary's loud, raunchy rock-and-roll style. This time, however, Gary didn't let Frank get away. He soon recorded "New Orleans" for Frank's Legrand record label. Having anxiously awaited the first copies of his single, Gary Anderson was shocked to find that his name wasn't on the disc. Instead, it credited a Gary "U.S." Bonds. Guida had decided to change Gary's name without his knowledge. Like it or not, Gary Anderson ceased to exist, and Gary "U.S." Bonds broke into the top of the rock-and-roll charts.

"Not Me" was his second release, but it failed due to a lack of airplay. The song was banned in many cities because of its sexually suggestive lyrics.

The third song Gary released emerged from a studio jam session. His studio backup band was a group called Daddy G., who had their own floundering single out called "A Night with Daddy G." During a late-night session of drinking and jamming, Daddy G. coaxed Gary to improvise some words to the music of their dying single. The jam was frenetic, and it is said that no one realized that the tape recorder was running. Whether taped accidentally or not, it was released and became the number-1 song of the summer of 1961 under the title "Quarter to Three." This would be Gary's biggest song ever, setting the sound for his future hits with lively, high-spirited vocals complemented by a wailing tenor sax, a strong rhythm section, and echoed handclapping all strung together by his frantic vocals. Reflecting on "Quarter to Three," Gary concludes, "It sounded like hell, but the kids could dance to it."

With the success of "Quarter to Three," there was a strong demand for Gary to make live appearances. But Legrand wanted him out of the public eye. Several years earlier Buddy Holly's personal appearances had shocked audiences around the country who thought he was black. The Legrand people knew that many people assumed Gary was white, and they feared a decline in record sales would result if he made personal appearances. But more rational heads prevailed, and Dick Clark managed to sign Gary up for his 1961 Caravan of Stars. And of course, Gary had no problem winning over a sometimes surprised crowd.

The hits just kept on coming for Gary "U.S." Bonds in his banner year, 1961. He teamed up again with Daddy G. to write "School Is Out" and "School Is In." He joined the twist movement with "Dear Lady Twist." By then 1961 was almost over, and so was the height of Gary's career.

Legrand insisted that all of Gary's songs follow the same formula as his previous hits, but Gary wanted to evolve. Legrand had its way, though, and record after record failed to make the charts. In the late sixties Gary left Legrand and hit the road, using local pickup bands to back him.

In addition to performing, Gary continues to write songs. His "Friend Don't Take Her She's All I Got," co-written with Johnny Paycheck, was nominated for a Grammy Award. Other artists have also come to recognize Gary as the creator of a unique, raucous soul sound. Today Bruce Springsteen often encores his live shows with a medley that includes a blistering rendition of "Quarter to Three." Springsteen proclaims that Gary "U.S." Bonds is better than seventy-five percent of the bands now performing. In 1981 he and "Miami" Steve Van Zandt, of the E Street Band, produced Orbison's *Dedication* L.P.

NEIL SEDAKA

In 1955, fifteen-year-old Neil Sedaka was sitting in Andrea's Pizza Parlor in the Brighton Beach section of Brooklyn when he was stunned by the music coming out of the jukebox. It was "Earth Angel" by the Penguins. Neil ran home to his apartment house on Coney Island Avenue to tell his songwriting buddy, Howard Greenfield, the news.

"Howie, I heard something fantastic. It's called rock and roll!"

Howard was less than excited. "I don't like it. It's offkey. It doesn't make it," he said.

Neil persisted and eventually won Howie over to rock and roll. Since that day in Brooklyn, Neil Sedaka and Howie Greenfield have written over eight hundred songs and sold millions of records. And Neil Sedaka became a worldwide star, not once, but twice.

Greenfield's mother had been instrumental in getting this songwriting team together. Mrs. Greenfield heard Neil play a classical piano piece at a hotel in the Catskills in 1953. She approached him, suggesting that he team up with her son Howie the poet to write songs. The Greenfields lived in the same apartment house as the Sedakas, but because Howie was four years older than Neil, they had never really known each other very well. Prodded by his mother, Howie eventually asked Neil if he'd like to write some songs together. After some trepidation Neil and Howie sat down to write "My Life's Devotion." It was pure pop in the tradition of Patti Page and Johnny Ray, and by Sedaka's own admission, it was awful. But it was a start for the team that would write a song a day for the next three years, always composing while Neil's mother was out shopping so she wouldn't think he wasn't practicing the piano.

Neil had been playing piano since age nine. He was named the best young classical pianist in New York City in a competition judged by famed concert pianist Artur Rubinstein. At the Juilliard School of Music he studied Brahms and Bach. At Abraham Lincoln High School in Brooklyn he formed the Tokens and sang doo-wop in the boy's room. With Neil singing lead, the Tokens had a local hit in New York with "I Love My Baby." Neil split from the Tokens after high school, and the group went on to have a number-1 record in 1961, "The Lion Sleeps Tonight."

Sedaka and Greenfield tried to sell their songs to music publishers with little success. In 1958 they heard of a new publishing company setting up shop in the famous Brill Building at 1660 Broadway in Manhattan. When Neil and Howie knocked on Aldon Music's door, Don Kirshner told the boys he was in a meeting and asked them to come back later. In reality Kirshner was only sweeping the floor, but he didn't want to tarnish his "record-exec image." Neil and Howie did come back to play some of their songs for Kirshner and Al Nevins, a former member of the pop group the Three Suns. Impressed by the music, Kirshner and Nevins wanted to know where the boys stole the songs. When they were finally convinced that Neil and Howie actually wrote the tunes themselves, Nevins and Kirshner made a contract with them and became their publishers and managers.

Aldon convinced Atlantic Records and LaVern Baker to record some of Neil's and Howie's songs. In 1958 the boys had their first smash hit when Connie Francis recorded their "Stupid Cupid." But being a successful songwriter wasn't enough for Neil. He wanted to be a singing star. Neil had sung hundreds of Aldon's songs on demo records, but no record company would consider signing him. The record companies felt his voice was too high and a little too effeminate. Finally RCA Records took a chance on him. Neil's first effort, "The Diary," reached the top twenty in early 1959. But his next two follow-ups were flops, and RCA was ready to drop him.

Neil Sedaka.

About this time Neil decided to write a song about his girl friend, Carole Klein. Carole idolized Neil, who was barely out of high school and already had songs on the charts. Neil was so in love with her that he wrote the melody for a romantic song and then asked Howie to write the lyrics about Carole. "Oh! Carol" was the result, and it went on to become a top-ten hit, securing Sedaka's singing career with RCA. "Oh! Carol" inspired Carol Klein to write a song for Sedaka entitled "Oh! Neil." It flopped, but it did start Carole's songwriting career. With lyricist Gerry Goffin, she would later crank out hit songs under her nom de plume Carole King. Like Neil Sedaka, she became one of the most successful songwriters at Aldon Music.

RCA had found a hit formula for Sedaka, and they wouldn't let him change it. For the next three years Neil wrote and sang a series of sugary but extremely popular teen-oriented songs—"Stairway to Heaven," "Calendar Girl," "Happy Birthday, Sweet Sixteen," "Breaking Up Is Hard to Do," and "Next Door to an Angel." But they all sounded pretty much the same, and by 1963 the public had grown tired of the sound. Neil had gone to the well once too often, and years later he admitted, "I blew it."

Sedaka's record-selling days were over. He toured around the world, playing the nightclub circuit in Australia, Japan, and England, then played piano on demo records for Don Kirshner and did anonymous session work with Carole King for the Monkees and the Archies. Sedaka even wrote an occasional hit for the easy-listening crowd, such as "Workin' on a Groovy Thing" for the Fifth Dimension.

Although basically retired, Neil was cajoled into doing a show at Albert Hall in London in 1971. The British audiences remembered Sedaka fondly and welcomed his new songs as well as his oldies, thus resurrecting Neil's career. Neil began turning out new hit records in England in the early seventies, working with a group called Hotlegs, who later became 10cc ("I'm Not in Love," "The Things We Do for Love"). He had his own TV show on the BBC, but he was still ignored in the United States.

In 1974 Neil was befriended by Elton John, then the most popular rock star in the world. Elton sponsored Neil's return to America, releasing a Sedaka album on his new label, Rocket Records. *"Sedaka's Back,"* a collection of the best of Neil's last three British albums, paved his way back to America. Sedaka was back with a vengeance in 1975.

"Laughter in the Rain" was Sedaka's first number-1 song in the United States since "Breaking Up Is Hard to Do" thirteen years earlier. Neil followed this with a song inspired by John Lennon's fight to stay in America, "The Immigrant"; the rocking "That's When

the Music Takes Me"; "Bad Blood," a duet with Elton John that shot to number 1; and a touching remake of "Breaking Up Is Hard to Do" that also settled in the top ten. Another Sedaka song, "Love Will Keep Us Together," recorded by the Captain and Tennille, was the biggest record of 1975. As Toni Tennille sang at the end of the record, "Sedaka is back."

A party on *Bandstand* featuring (from left) Charlie O'Donnell, Dick Clark, Fabian, Neil Sedaka, Freddy Cannon, Bobby Rydell, and Chubby Checker. *(Courtesy of Dick Clark)*

RICKY NELSON

For many kids growing up in the fifties and early sixties, conceptions of college and fraternity life were formed by television's *The Adventures of Ozzie and Harriet.* Countless episodes ended with teen-age idol Ricky Nelson strumming his guitar and singing at a frat party. The girls in their full dresses would sway to and fro while their dark-suited escorts would snap their fingers to the beat. In the background chaperones Ozzie and Harriet doled out cookies and Carnation milk to those prim toga-party rejects.

Eric Nelson was a far-from-typical American teenager. His parents were radio and TV stars, and for years he listened to a young actor play him in the show. Eventually he and his brother David decided that they wanted to portray themselves on the TV show, and Ricky, as he was now called, became the darling of America. Music did not become a part of his career until a girl walked into his life. Ricky had a real crush on her, but all she could talk about were those dreamy rock-and-roll singers. He shyly scored some points by telling her that he was a rock-and-roll singer, too. His white lie caused a love crisis when he had to prove it. He convinced his folks to let him sing on the show, and to everyone's surprise Ricky had a hell of a voice and a real guitar talent.

Although Ricky's voice and mannerisms were heavily influenced by Elvis Presley, such a look would have been counter to the Nelson apple-pie image. They settled on a smoother, more tranquilized rockabilly sound with a clean-cut Frankie Avalon-type presentation. The heavy use of "reverb" became Ricky's trademark. Even though they were promoted and packaged very differently, Ricky and Elvis stand together in rock-and-roll history as two major rock acts who never appeared on *American Bandstand.* Apparently Ricky's television contract forbade his performing on any other TV show.

With weekly exposure on national TV, Ricky turned out hit after hit. From the 1957 cover of Fats Domino's "I'm Walkin'" to 1972's "Garden Party," Ricky made the charts with "Be-Bop Baby" (1957); "Poor Little Fool" (1958); "Travelin' Man" (1961), which came to Ricky after Sam Cooke rejected it; "Hello Mary Lou" (1961), a tune penned by Gene Pitney; "Young World" (1962); "Teen-Age Idol" (1962); "It's Up to You" (1962); and "Fools Rush In" (1963).

Soon after "Fools Rush In" the combination of the British invasion and the cancellation of *Ozzie and Harriet* spelled the end of Ricky's line of top-ten hits. For the next ten years Ricky concentrated on live performances, albums, and a search for a new sound. That search led him as far adrift as country-western, but in 1970 he returned to his rock-and-roll roots with his new Stone Canyon Band. He was excited about his new direction but ironically wound up in a tug-of-war between his fans' demand for his old material and his desire to progress with his new sound and style.

In 1972 promoter Richard Nader was bringing the biggest rock stars of the fifties and the early sixties out of retirement and obscurity, reuniting groups like the Five Satins and Dion and the Belmonts for special performances at New York's Madison Square Garden. One 1972 show headlined Ricky Nelson. When he came on, the crowd went wild. They were there to hear his old hits exactly as they had sounded fifteen years earlier. At first, that's just about what they heard. But after Ricky felt he had paid enough homage to the past, he went on to his new material to show his twenty thousand plus fans how he had adapted and grown. In the middle of the biggest gig of his renewed career, the audience revolted. This was a fifties' concert, and they wanted golden oldies and nothing else. They booed and jeered his new material. It wasn't a comment on his talent; simply a

Dick Clark and Ricky Nelson on the set of the movie *Because They're Young*. (*Courtesy of Dick Clark. Copyright © 1958 Columbia Pictures Corp.*)

raucous statement that they didn't want to hear anything more recent than "Fools Rush In." Still it was a traumatic evening. Later that same year Ricky transformed that trauma into his biggest hit in ten years. "Garden Party" was Ricky's version of the events that night at Madison Square Garden. It also expressed his philosophy on his life and his music since 1963: You can't please all of the people all the time; you've got to please yourself.

THE SHIRELLES

The legions of female singing groups in the early sixties were all inspired by a group that traces its roots back to New Jersey.

With original members Beverly Lee, Addie "Micky" Harris, and Doris Kenner, and lead singer Shirley Alston, the girls first performed at school shows and friends' parties in their home town of Passaic. They called themselves "The Shirelles," combining lead singer Shirley's first name with the French feminine word *elle.* Schoolmate Mary Jane Greenberg asked them to audition for her mother Florence, who owned a small record company called Tiara. After the audition Florence Greenberg agreed to become their manager. In 1957 she arranged a talent-show appearance for them, after which they were signed by an impressed scout for Decca Records. Their first hit on Tiara, "I Met Him on a Sunday," was sold to Decca and released in March 1958.

Continuously traveling on the rock-and-roll circuit, the Shirelles were star attractions on Dick Clark's Caravan of Stars tour. They became known for shaking out their wigs from the open windows of the Caravan bus. When not on tour they were favorites on *American Bandstand.*

The two Decca singles that followed "I Met Him on a Sunday" failed to catch fire, and when the group's Decca contract expired in 1959, Florence Greenberg started Scepter Records with the Shirelles as the label's charter group. The wisdom of Greenberg's move was soon borne out. Their list of Scepter releases reads like a rock-and-roll hall of fame: "Tonight's the Night" (1960), cowritten by Shirley and Luther Dixon, marked Shirley's permanent move to lead vocals. "Will You Love Me Tomorrow," written by Carole King and Gerry Goffin, became the Shirelles' first number-1 record in early 1961. "Dedicated to the One I Love" (1961), the group's favorite tune, was another chart-topper, later remade in a much softer version by the Mamas and the Papas. "Soldier Boy" (1962), their best-selling single of all time, was a lover's lament over her boyfriend's departure for the army. "Everybody Loves a Lover" (1962) and "Foolish Little Girl" (1963) were the final big hits for the group.

During the British invasion the Shirelles cut a few more albums and went back to the road, appearing at colleges, hotels, and clubs all over the country. Doris, however, had had enough by 1968 and retired back to New Jersey.

In the early seventies the Shirelles joined both the Dick Clark and Richard Nader live oldies shows and appeared in the film *Let the Good Times Roll.* The Shirelles were the trend-setters of rock and roll's female groups, and they continue to roll with the good times in the eighties.

The Shirelles—Shirley Alston (top), Doris Kenner, and Beverley Lee (center), and Micki Harris. (*Courtesy of Dick Clark*)

The Sound of 1961

DEL SHANNON

With the dark days of the payola scandals just a memory, radio stations concentrated on making radio fun in 1961. Transistor radios had just arrived on the American scene, and everywhere you looked kids had radios "no bigger than a pack of cigarettes" glued to their ears. Stations turned to a new crop of screaming disc jockeys to put excitement back into top-forty radio. But despite their individual styles, the one thing the screamers, the shouters, the rhymers, and the speedsters of radio had in common was Del Shannon's "Runaway." "Runaway" had a wild sound with a high-pitched organ, rapid-fire rhythm, and Shannon's stuttering falsetto sliding up and down two octaves. Disc jockeys across the country loved the record, and "Runaway" held a firm grip on the top ten for nine weeks in the spring of 1961. Number 1 for four weeks in a row, "Runaway" pumped new excitement into the growing legions of transistor brothers and transistor sisters.

Del Shannon was born Charles Westover in December 1939, in Coopersville, Michigan, a little town outside Grand Rapids. Unable to play 1953's country-music classics on the ukulele he received on his thirteenth birthday, Charlie traded it in for a used guitar. Uninterested in formal music lessons, he learned to play by watching bands at the local country-and-western dance halls while ducking flying fists and bottles. Charlie developed his vocal talents when he was on the high school football team, having discovered the great acoustics of the team's shower room. The school principal let Charlie sing in the shower room during study hall as long as he agreed to entertain at pep rallies and high school assemblies.

After high school Charlie was drafted by the Army and sent to Germany, where he was assigned to the Army entertainment unit in the Get Up and Go Show, which entertained soldiers throughout Germany. When he had to accompany a flamenco dancer, Charlie learned how to strum the guitar as hard and as fast as he could.

After his tour of duty for Uncle Sam, Charlie began playing rock and roll. He hooked up with organist Max Crook and put together a band. Their first big gig was headlining at the Big High Low Club in Battle Creek, Michigan. Their act was called Charlie Johnson and the Big Little Show Band, but shortly thereafter Charlie Westover began to search for a catchier name. A member of his band wanted to become a professional wrestler and planned to call himself Mark Shannon. Charlie liked the name Shannon, but not Mark. Then, working in a carpet store one day, Charlie saw the owner pull up in a brand-new Cadillac Coup de Ville. Westover fell in love with the car and found his new first name, shortening De Ville to Del.

In 1960 Del Shannon invited Ollie McLaughlin, a black disc jockey from WGRV in Ann Arbor, to the Big High Low Club to hear him play. McLaughlin liked Del's sound, so he taped Del at the club and took the tapes to Embee Productions in Detroit. Impressed with Shannon, Embee flew him to New York for a recording session. Del, just twenty years old and very nervous, stumbled through a couple of ballads at the session. He was told that he didn't have a suitable voice for recording and was shipped back to Battle Creek. Back in Michigan, Ollie McLaughlin suggested that Del try some up-tempo material. Max Crook played some quick chord changes on the organ, and Del wrote "Runaway" on the spot. In January 1961, in the middle of a raging snowstorm, Del and Max drove to New York in an old broken-down Plymouth without a heater to record "Runaway" for Big Top Records. Three months later it was on top of the charts.

With the urgency in his falsetto voice complementing Crook's organ work, Del's "Hats Off to Larry" followed "Runaway" up the charts that summer. Despite Del's touring 250 days the next year, his record sales slumped until "Little Town Flirt" hit in early 1963.

British music polls named Shannon the Most Popular Male Vocalist of both 1962 and 1963. Del toured England in 1963 and was exposed to budding Beatlemania. Returning to America in late spring, he recorded the Lennon-McCartney tune "From Me to You." It was the first Beatles song to break onto the American charts.

"From Me to You" was also Shannon's last single for Big Top Records. Feeling that he had been treated unfairly by his record company and his manager, Del began filing lawsuits left and right. He also started his own record company, Beriee, in late 1963, but his manager threatened to sue if any radio station played any of Shannon's Beriee records. Afraid of getting entangled in lawsuits, other record companies shied away from Del Shannon. In June 1964, Del finally signed a recording contract with Amy Records. He broke into the top twenty for Amy in the summer of 1964 with a remake of Jimmy Jones's "Handy Man." In January 1965 "Keep Searchin' " became Shannon's first top-ten record since "Hats Off to Larry" in July 1961, but for all intents and purposes it was Del's swan song as a recording artist.

After his recording career faded, Shannon became a record producer and arranger. In 1969 he was floored by a performance by the house band at the Rag Doll Club in Los Angeles. The group, Smith, was fronted by Gayle McCormick, a beautiful blonde with a Janis Joplin-type voice. Shannon soon became Smith's manager and producer and even picked "Baby, It's You" to be the band's first single, only to find himself out on the street after a fight with Smith's record company. Del then took his old friend Brian Hyland into the studio and produced a haunting version of the Impressions' "Gypsy Woman." In 1970 "Gypsy Woman" was number 3. It was the first success of Del's career as a record producer.

Bobby Vinton specialized in ballads, starting with "Roses Are Red" in 1962. His list of hits includes "Blue Velvet," "Blue on Blue," "There I've Said It Again," and "Mr. Lonely." After a long dry spell Bobby was about to call it quits when "My Melody of Love" resurrected his career with a bang in 1974.

1962

James Meredith fought prejudice as he enrolled at the University of Mississippi, and *The Beverly Hillbillies* fought a similar attitude as they moved into their plush Los Angeles neighborhood. The U.S. Supreme Court ruled that children couldn't pray with their teachers in school, while America couldn't wait to *Sing Along With Mitch* on television. John Glenn orbited the earth this year and Castro, Khrushchev, and J.F.K. made the earth tremble during the Cuban missile crisis.

In 1962, the Middle East wasn't discussed in terms of oil, OPEC, or the Ayatollah Khomeini, but rather in terms of *Lawrence of Arabia,* the year's Best Picture. The Yankees were back on top that year, knocking off the San Francisco Giants in the World Series. As usual, Boston clinched the NBA title, while the powerhouse of the NFL, the Green Bay Packers, beat the New York Giants, and the Dallas Texans took the AFL crown from the Houston Oilers.

Teen-agers danced through 1962 on *American Bandstand* to the steps of the mashed potato, the locomotion, the Popeye, the watusi, and the limbo rock. Dance songs were very hot, and three of them made the top ten for the year: "The Loco-Motion" by Little Eva; "Mashed Potato Time" by Dee Dee Sharp; and a carry-over from 1961, "The Twist" by Chubby Checker. Rounding out the list was "I Can't Stop Loving You" by Ray Charles, "Stranger on the Shore" by Mr. Acker Bilk, "Roses Are Red" by Bobby Vinton, "Johnny Angel" by Shelley Fabares, "The Stripper" by David Rose, "Let Me In" by the Sensations, and "Soldier Boy" by the Shirelles.

AM radio was spinning platters like Sue Thompson's "Norman," Burl Ives' "A Little Bitty Tear," Don and Juan's "What's Your Name?," Freddy Cannon's "Palisades Park," Brian Hyland's "Sealed with a Kiss," Ray Stevens' "Ahab, the Arab," Tommy Roe's "Sheila," Claudine Clark's "Party Lights," Bobby "Boris" Pickett and the Crypt Kickers' novelty smash "Monster Mash," The Duprees' "You Belong to Me," the Contours' "Do You Love Me?," Dickie Lee's "Patches," Marcie Blane's "Bobby's Girl," and Steve Lawrence's "Go Away Little Girl." But the music was generally innocuous and bland with lots of bubblegum and teen-age laments. Rock and roll was growing soft, as if biding time for another musical messiah. It would have to wait a little while longer.

It was 1962—the eighth year of rock and roll.

THE PHIL SPECTOR SOUND

He called them "little symphonies for the kids." In those dark days of the schlock-rock, pre-Beatles sixties, they were simply the most stunning string of singles one record company ever released. "Be My Baby," "Da Doo Ron Ron," "Then He Kissed Me," and "Zip-A-Dee-Doo-Dah" burst forth from tinny car radios with an unparalleled force, sounding impossibly huge. Layer upon layer of strings, pianos, and percussion bolstered with a cavernous echo effect were forged into a thunderous roar that continually threatened to swamp the records' vocals. And the more inane the lyrics, the more apocalyptic the production. His label called it "Tomorrow's Sound, Today!" Others dubbed it "a wall of sound." With it, Phil Spector became rock's first superstar producer, his own personality and talent totally overshadowing the groups who actually sang on his records.

Most companies released records like buckshot, inundating the radio stations and record stores with dozens of new releases every week, blindly hoping that one would catch on. Most record companies were run by businessmen who sat around trying to second-guess what "those fool kids" wanted to hear. Spector never had that problem because he *was* a kid. He just made the kind of records he liked to listen to, and they caught fire.

By 1962 Phil was already an old pro in the industry, having produced a million seller with his very first try. He was eighteen when he paid forty dollars to cut a demo of a song he had written. The song had been inspired by the epitaph on his father's gravestone. "To Know Him Is to Love Him" by the Teddy Bears was released on the miniscule Dore label in 1958, and it stormed its way to number 1.

Gold records were not *that* easy to come by in those days, as Spector found out when later Teddy Bears releases met with public indifference. Now, broke, Spector left L.A. and returned to his birthplace,

New York, heading straight for the offices of songwriters/producers Leiber and Stoller. They took Phil in, assigning him to a variety of tasks. He played guitar on Drifters' sessions, cowrote Ben E. King's "Spanish Harlem," and learned all he could about making and packaging hit records.

A brief but successful career as an independent producer started in 1960. Spector produced "Corinna, Corinna" (Ray Peterson), "Pretty Little Angel Eyes" (Curtis Lee), "I Love How You Love Me" (the Paris Sisters), "Every Breath I Take" (Gene Pitney), and "Second Hand Love" (Connie Francis) all in succession. Each made the top fifty and all but one went top ten. The industry now knew that Phil Spector was a talent to be reckoned with.

In 1961 he and Lester Sills found a backer for their plan to form Philles Records, an independent label. The plan was simple. Phil would produce and Lester (the "les" of Phil-les) would handle the business end. Abandoning the buckshot method of releasing records, Philles would concentrate on one record at a time, lavishing more time and money on one single than most labels put into entire albums. Phil wasn't just after commercial success. He knew that would come. He was more interested in something that had never been associated with rock and roll before—art.

To get the sound he wanted, Spector needed anonymous singers whose voices he could mold. The girl-group craze that followed the Shirelles' success was in full swing. Spector took to the streets of New York and came back with five girls who sang under the name the Crystals. They set the pattern for most of the Philles artists who followed, including Bob B. Soxx and the Blue Jeans, Darlene Love, and the Righteous Brothers. The Crystals all had good, strong, well-trained voices, but not one of them had the ability to transcend Spector's productions, where voices were just one more instrument to add to the mix. But the Crystals did have a knack for taking the tritest lyrics and making them totally believable. Who else could have made "And when he walked me home, Da-do-ron-ron-ron, Da-do-ron-ron!" sound so urgently important?

Their first two releases, "There's No Other (Like My Baby)" and "Uptown," both cracked the top twenty, getting Philles off to a strong start and establishing the basic Spector sound—a muddy, thumping rhythm track, swirls of strings, and tons of tape echo. A shift to Hollywood's Gold Star studio with its superior echo chamber, the use of young, hipper musicians, and a Gene Pitney song about a sensitive hoodlum combined to give the Crystals and Philles their first number-1 record as 1962 drew to a close. Ironically, the lead on "He's a Rebel" wasn't even sung by a Crystal because Phil preferred the voice of his favorite session singer, Darlene Love.

The records kept getting bigger and bigger. The wall of sound had a mesmerizing, hypnotic effect. Barely aware of any individual instruments, except for the deep, punchy drums, record buyers were

The Crystals (from left) Patsy Wright, Barbara Alston, De De Henry, and Dolores "La La" Brooks). *(Courtesy of Dick Clark)*

111

grabbed by the music. It swept listeners up in its power and drive. "Da Doo Ron Ron" and "Then He Kissed Me" followed "He's a Rebel" to the top for the Crystals in 1963. Phil, now sole owner of Philles, branched out and cut records with the Alley Cats Bobb B. Soxx, and Darlene Love before finally finding his perfect girl group, the Ronettes.

Of all Spector's work, the Ronettes' singles are his most special. These girls had one thing the Crystals lacked—sex appeal! Their bee-hive hairdos and tight dresses promised forbidden delights. What red-blooded American male could resist lead singer Veronica Bennett's pleading hurt-little-girl voice when she sang "Be My Baby," "Baby, I Love You," and "Walking in the Rain"? Certainly not Spector—he married (and later divorced) Veronica.

When the British invasion had most American artists scrambling to imitate the new Mersey Beat, Phil stuck to his guns. In 1964 he decided to cut a record with the Righteous Brothers, an obscure white R & B duo who had survived for years with little chart success. Spector called in crack Brill Building songwriters Barry Mann and Cynthia Weil, and together they fashioned a song perfectly suited to the Brothers' unique high-low, call-and-response style of singing.

"You've Lost That Lovin' Feelin'" was a monster in more ways than one. Its 3:45 running time was deemed too long for most top forty stations at the time, so Spector simply changed the label time to read 3:05. The trick worked, and "Lovin' Feelin'" was soon on its way to becoming the biggest seller in Philles' remarkable history. It's easy to hear why. The wall of sound is restrained here, holding back with an ominous tension until it breaks into full orchestral fury near the end. Bobby Hatfield's desperate falsetto soars over the strings as he pleads with his

lover to bring that lovin' feeling back. Every broken heart in the sixties knew "Lovin' Feelin'" as well as the Beatles' "Yesterday."

Taking another marginally successful R & B group, Ike and Tina Turner, Spector set out to top himself. This time he went to his favorite songwriting team, Jeff Barry and Ellie Greenwich, who came up with "River Deep—Mountain High" in 1966. Spector's production was sensational. The wall of sound never sounded more majestic. George Harrison even called it one of pop's few "perfect records." In Britain it tore up the charts, but in America it did absolutely nothing. Additional publicity was pumped into it. Still nothing. Its failure devastated Spector. At the age of twenty-six he quit the music business, announced his retirement, and disappeared into the California desert.

He has been back several times since "River Deep—Mountain High," however. First, he had a hit with "Black Pearl" by Sonny Charles and the Check-mates, Ltd. on A & M in 1969. Then, after an ill-fated attempt to salvage the Beatles' "Let It Be" album, Phil stayed on at Apple to produce a number of hits for John Lennon and George Harrison, most notably "Imagine" and "My Sweet Lord." But a lot of the old fire seemed to have disappeared by now. Having influenced an entire generation of artists from the Beach Boys and ABBA to Bruce Springsteen and the Tubes, there seemed to be no new worlds for Phil to conquer. Even so, Spector today bristles at the suggestion that his best work is behind him. It wouldn't be wise to write off the man who has given us so many classics and has come back to produce an album for the Ramones in 1980. For all we know, Phil Spector is hunched over the board in some recording studio right now, twisting dials, laying down overdubs, getting ready to unleash a new masterpiece.

GENE PITNEY

Gene Pitney, one of rock and roll's most versatile singers, composers, arrangers, and instrumentalists during the first half of the sixties, was born in Rockville, Connecticut, and attended Rockville High School, the University of Connecticut, and Ward's Electronic School. This last segment of his education played an important part in changing the course of his career from songwriter to performer. Gene loved to tinker with electronic equipment, and he eventually wired his music system so that he could create multivoice tracks through constant rerecording. His sound was unique in that he could sing tenor as well as bass parts. On his first hit, "(I Wanna) Love My Life Away," released in 1961 by Musicor Records, he electronically layered all seven voices heard on the song. His voice was so proficient in the high range throughout his career that Gene always recorded his own choruses with multitracking. In late 1961 Pitney scored with his first million seller, the tearful "Town Without Pity," the theme song from the film of the same name. He followed it up in April 1962 with "(The Man Who Shot) Liberty Valance," drawing inspiration from the film of the same title. This tune, created by the famous songwriting team of Hal David and Burt Bacharach, also went gold.

Pitney himself was no slouch in the songwriting department. Ricky Nelson had released Pitney's "Hello Mary Lou," and in September 1962 he supplied the Crystals with their only number-1 song, "He's a Rebel."

As a performer, Pitney projected the sexy, romantic teen-idol image that was popular in the early sixties. He fit in well with Dick Clark's Caravan of Stars formula in which such a singer closed each show. Dick recalls paying Pitney fifteen hundred a week in 1962 to headline one such tour. While on the bus, Gene would always sleep up in the luggage rack. Intrigued, one night Dick decided to try Pitney's peculiar bus bed. The next day in Atlanta, Dick Clark was in such bad shape he had to see a doctor who recognized him from his TV shows and wondered why he couldn't afford a mattress. Pitney's touring was not limited to the U.S. He performed in Italy, Germany, France, England, Australia, New Zealand, and Canada. Moreover, his songs were recorded by a variety of other performers from Roy Orbison to Steve Lawrence. Successful as a concert performer and writer, Gene also maintained a strong recording career. In 1962 he hit again with a smash 45 written by David and Bacharach called "Only Love Can Break a Heart." That same combination made gold once more in 1963 with "Twenty-four Hours from Tulsa." Pitney hit again with the popular "Mecca" (1963) and "It Hurts to Be in Love" (1964). Throughout, his emotional, wailing voice was always his musical trademark.

Dick Clark felt Gene Pitney was not only one of the brightest stars among the teen-idols, but one of the shrewdest businessmen as well. Gene not only owned his own music-publishing company, he was one of the first rock and rollers to own his own record company, Musicor Records. Gene headed Musicor some seven years before the Beatles split from Capitol Records to form Apple Corp.

Pitney continued to release records late into the sixties, but by this time his musical sun was setting. In 1964 he was invited to play piano for the Rolling Stones on their single "Little by Little." His 1966 recording of "Just One Smile" wasn't a hit for him, but it did inspire Al Kooper to adapt it for Blood, Sweat and Tears on their first album. The seventies found Gene back in Connecticut and affiliated with Epic Records.

BOBBY VEE

Bobby Velline grew up in Fargo, North Dakota, as part of a very musical family. Both of Bobby's brothers excelled on guitar, and one of them was part of a fifteen-piece band. At age fifteen Bobby was allowed to sit in on some of their practice sessions and eventually learned the words to the band's entire repertoire. His brother taught him to play the guitar, and Bobby eventually became part of a new band, the Shadows, which was made up of his brother Bill, Jim Stillman, and Bob Korum. They soon were popular enough to get a contract and recorded "Suzie Baby" in 1959 for Soma Records.

One rock-and-roll tragedy became a boon for Bobby that winter. After the February 1959 plane crash near Clear Lake, Iowa, that claimed the lives of Buddy Holly, Ritchie Valens, and J. P. Richardson (the Big Bopper), the Shadows were quickly hired to fill in on the tour's next scheduled show in their hometown of Fargo. Bobby's extensive knowledge of popular lyrics, including most of Buddy Holly's, earned him billing as lead vocalist that night. He was overwhelmingly well received by a crowd of close to three thousand. A scout for Liberty Records who was in the crowd arranged to send him to Minneapolis for a recording session. Bobby was hired along with the Shadows, who were now his backup group. First Liberty acquired their old Soma flop and rereleased it. While not a real hit, it did well enough to keep Liberty interested in Bobby.

Bobby and his brothers then arranged a new version of the 1956 Clovers' tune, "Devil or Angel," which they recorded in July 1960. The disc sold 750,000 copies. Several more of their Liberty releases then appeared in rapid succession, and Vee was gaining national recognition as an emerging teen-idol for the sixties. He was booked on one of Dick Clark's tours, often wrapping up the shows in the closing "teen-idol" slot. Bobby recalls the Caravan of Stars and the loyalty Dick inspired from his tour family on the road: "If Dick said he wanted all of us out in front of the bus to be run over, there'd be a scramble to get there first."

Among the most memorable of Vee's hits were "Rubber Ball" (1960), "Run to Him" (1961), "The Night Has a Thousand Eyes" (1962), "Charms" (1963), and "Take Good Care of My Baby" (1961), a King-Goffin tune that was a number-1 national hit and the biggest of his career. By 1961 Bobby had signed an exclusive long-term contract with Liberty. He starred in *Swinging Along* for 20th Century-Fox and became a familiar face on network TV, while his albums continued to sell well.

But Bobby Vee, like countless other American rock-and-roll stars, was displaced by the British invasion. It took nearly five years for him to climb back onto the charts. Finally he struck gold again with a top-twenty hit in 1967, "Come Back When You Grow Up." This time, however, there were no follow-up hits. With his recording career waning, Bobby turned to club dates, and today he has a regular schedule of appearances that takes him all over the country.

Robert Thomas Velline—better known as Bobby Vee. *(Courtesy of Dick Clark)*

GENE CHANDLER

Born Eugene Dixon in Chicago, Gene Chandler's earliest recollection of singing was as a five-year-old at a July Fourth political picnic. Enjoying the day off from the steel mill, his father had him take the stage to sing "Danny Boy." A few years later a local singer who hit the bigtime—"Pookey" Hudson of the Spaniels ("Goodnite Sweetheart, Goodnite")—inspired young Gene, and by the time he turned sixteen he had joined the Gay-Tones, singing at schools, talent shows, and on a regular Illinois radio program each Sunday.

In 1957 Gene became a member of the Du-Kays, a rhythm-and-blues group with rock-and-roll leanings. After a stint in the Army he returned to Chicago in 1960 and rejoined the Du-Kays. Not long afterward Bernice Williams, a young business manager, heard the group and agreed to manage them. After an audition with Nat Records in Chicago, they were offered a recording contract. Their first professional recording session was in late 1961, at which time they cut "Nite Owl" and "Duke of Earl." Bernice received cowriting credit for both songs, but the creation of "Duke of Earl" was a bit more unusual.

The Du-Kays would warm up by singing "Do-Do-Do-Do." Gene decided it should be recorded and told them to make it "Duke" instead of "Do." Chandler "borrowed" fellow member Earl Edwards' first name to complete the phrase, then began composing lyrics on the spot. Excited and hopeful that this was a potential hit, they ran to their manager's house, and Bernice added more lyrics. Getting it released, however, was the hard part. Nat Records released "Nite Owl," but was not interested in "Duke of Earl." Bernice and the boys refused to give up. Calvin Carter, an A & R man with Vee Jay Records, loved the tune and especially liked Gene's singing style. Carter reached the president of Vee Jay in Paris and got his permission to purchase "Duke of Earl." Carter was

more interested in Gene alone than in the whole group, though. While "Nite Owl" by the Du-Kays was shooting up the national charts, Vee Jay was holding up the release of "Duke of Earl" because Gene couldn't decide whether to go solo as Carter wanted or to stay with a group that had a hit 45. In January of 1962 Eugene Dixon became Gene Chandler, taking his last name from the actor Jeff Chandler because he thought it had a romantic ring. Under this name he released solo records while still under contract with the Du-kays as Gene Dixon. "Duke of Earl" was then finally released and sold a million copies in a little over a month. It was a huge hit, number 1 for three weeks in early 1962. According to Gene, it dethroned "The Twist" from the number-1 spot. It was the only hit he had on Vee Jay. The April 1962 follow-up "Walk On with the Duke" went nowhere.

In 1964 Gene switched to Constellation Records, where Curtis Mayfield of the Impressions proved to be a fruitful collaborator. He wrote, produced, and arranged a string of hits for Chandler, including "Bless Our Love," "What Now," "Rainbow '65," and their most successful effort, "Just be True," which Constellation balked at releasing for half a year because they didn't care for the Impressions-style harmonizing and the heavy overdubbing of strings. Mayfield's songs made Chandler a first-rate ballad singer. These soft, tender, mellow songs went over well in concert with Chandler's falsetto slides sending ripples of excitement through the females in his audience.

When Constellation Records went out of business in 1966, Chess Records purchased Chandler's old material. Meanwhile Gene's manager, Carl Davis, signed him with Brunswick Records. The two companies wound up alternating their Chandler releases. But without the talents of Curtis Mayfield the hits were nowhere to be found.

Gene Chandler.

Hitless and tired of the road, Gene moved into the business end of the industry by starting two music-publishing companies and a production company and serving as president of Bamboo Records. Gene's biggest Bamboo hit was "Backfield in Motion" in 1969. He selected this song from a demo by two St. Louis bus drivers, had it cut, and released it with over a million in sales. But Gene was restless. In 1970 he produced and performed "Groovy Situation," which was a top hit that summer, selling a million. After this success most of Chandler's energy went into producing, arranging, and hyping other acts. However, he eventually dropped all his business activities, choosing to travel instead.

In 1976 Gene Chandler resurfaced to work with reggae artist Johnny Nash. In 1978 he released a disco record, "Get Down," that did very well. Today Chandler lives in Chicago and attributes his success to his faith in Jesus Christ.

117

Ferrante and Teicher.

ROCK INSTRUMENTALS

A special category of rock and roll is the instrumental recording, which often served many purposes. Some of these hits are best known as movie or TV show themes or musical beds for commercial advertisements.

Instrumentals were often reliable crossover hits from the easy listening to the rock-and-roll charts. Radio programmers employed them as segues into the up-tempo "action central" newscasts. A typical radio practice was to "even up" the hour by starting the instrumental in the middle so that it would end exactly at news time. Music and program directors used these classics seasonally in an attempt to elicit the moods and memories of the time when the tune was first popular. Such seasonal hits included "Our Winter Love" by Bill Pursell (January 1963) and "Theme From *A Summer Place*" by Percy Faith (January 1960), which was the number-1 record of 1960, as was "Stranger on the Shore" by British clarinetist Mr. Acker Bilk in 1962.

The fifties produced the memorable hit "Topsy, Part II" by former Julliard student and ace drummer, the late Cozy Cole (1958). Another memorable instrumental hit was "Honky Tonk" (1956) by one of the fathers of swing organ, Bill Doggett. It was released on the King label in July 1956 and rereleased with a slightly different arrangement as "Honky Tonk '65" nine years later. Organist Dave "Baby" Cortez popularized "The Happy Organ" in March 1959, and hit it big with "Rinky Dink" in the summer of 1962. Keyboard king Perez Prado had two number-1 mambo hits with "Cherry Pink and Apple Blossom White" in 1955 and "Patricia" in 1958. Other memorable fifties instrumentals are "Tequila" by the Champs, "The Poor People of Paris" by Les Baxter, and the jazz-inspired "Swingin' Shepherd Blues" by the Moe Koffman quartet.

A proliferation of instrumental releases came in the early sixties. Memphis' Mar-Keys did "Last Night" in June 1961, and half of that group went on to join Booker T and the MG's, who produced "Green Onions" in 1963. On the charts in 1961 were Asia Minor with their hit "Kokomo," jazz standard "Take Five" recorded by Dave Brubeck, the Oscar-winning "Moon River" by Henry Mancini, and "Bumble Boogie" by B. Bumble and the Stingers. But 1962 and 1963 seemed to have more instrumental hits than any other years before or since. Along with those hits by Bill Pursell, Percy Faith, Mr. Acker Bilk, and Dave "Baby" Cortez were "The Stripper"/"Ebb Tide" by David Rose; Nelson Riddle's *"Route 66* Theme"; "Yackety Sax" by Boots Randolph; Herb Alpert's debut, "The Lonely Bull" (which was recorded in his garage); Danish Bent Fabric's "Alley Cat"; the original *Match Game* theme song, "Swingin' Safari" by Billy Vaughn; Mongo Santamaria's "Watermelon Man"; the Dartells' "Hot Pastrami"; "Wild Weekend" by the Rockin' Rebels; Kenny Ball and his Jazz Band's "Midnight in Moscow"; bossa nova favorite "Fly Me to the Moon" by Joe Harnell; and the driving guitar sound of the Chantays' "Pipeline," their only hit release.

Two top instrumental hits of this two-year period were "Telstar" and "Out of Limits." In late 1962, London's Tornadoes did an impromptu recording of "Telstar," which rocketed to number 1 shortly after the resolution of the Cuban Missile Crisis and stayed there for three weeks. Released on Decca Records in England, "Telstar" came out on London Records in the United States. It was written by Joe Meek, a recording engineer, and performed with three guitars, a piano, an organ, and drums. Sound effects were tracked over the studio production to give it the eerie effect of a satellite in orbit. The other big song, "Out Of Limits" by the MarKetts (1963), was originally released as "Outer Limits," the same name as a popular science fiction TV show of the day. It wasn't the "Outer Limits" people who threatened suit;

rather, it was Rod Serling of "Twilight Zone." It seems that the opening bars were virtually identical to those of the "Twilight Zone" theme. That was bad enough, but linking the tune with "Twilight Zone's" biggest television competitor was too much for Serling. All reissues of the single were retitled "Out of Limits."

A silver-anniversary list of classic instrumental recordings must include many compositions by diverse artists, such as "Autumn Leaves" by Roger Williams (1955), who would return to the charts with "Born Free" (1966); "Slow Walk" by Sil Austin (1956); "Jivin' Around" by Ernie Freeman (1957); "Raunchy" by Bill Justis, which was also recorded by Ernie Freeman (1957); "Rebel-Rouser" by the twangy guitar of Duane Eddy and the Rebels (1958), who would return in 1960 with "Because They're Young" and "Shazam"; "Sleep Walk" by Santo and Johnny (1959); "Harlem Nocturne" by the Viscounts (1959); "The *Peter Gunn* Theme" by Henry Mancini (1959); the monster instrumental hit "Walk Don't Run" by the Ventures (1960), who then came back with "Walk Don't Run '64"; "Shadows" by Apache (1960); "Calcutta" by Lawrence Welk, of all people (1960); "Exodus" by Ferrante and Teicher (1960); "Hide Away" by Freddy King (1961); "Washington Square" by the Village Stompers (1963); "20-75" by Willie Mitchell (1964); "Hang on Sloopy" and "The In Crowd" by Ramsey Lewis (1965); "A Walk in the Black Forest" by Horst Jankowski; the tune from the Alka Seltzer commercial, "No Matter What Shape (Your Stomach Is In)" by the T-Bones, a group that would have greater rock-and-roll fame later as Hamilton, Joe Frank & Reynolds (1965); "Cast Your Fate to the Wind" by the Sounds Orchestral (1965); "Batman Theme" by the Mar-Keys (1966); "Summer Samba" by Walter Wanderly (1966); "Music to Watch Girls Go By," a song used for a Diet-Pepsi commercial, by the Bob Crewe Generation (1967); "Soulful Strut" by Young-Holt Unlimited (1968); "Love Is Blue," the top tune of 1968 in many polls, by Paul Mauriat; "Classical Gas" by Mason Williams (1968); "The Horse" by Cliff Nobles and Co. (1969); "Grazing in the Grass" by Hugh Masekela (1969); and "Rumble," by Link Wray and his Ray Men (1958)—the only instrumental in rock history to be banned by some radio stations because it was too suggestive—of violence, not sex! There was "Quentin's Theme," a roller-rink favorite inspired by the TV horror soap opera *Dark Shadows,* by the Charles Randolph Grean Sounde (1969); "Keem-O-Sabe" by Electric Indian (1969); "Hawaii 5-O" by the Ventures (1969); "Love Theme from Romeo and Juliet" by Henry Mancini (1969); "Joy" by Apollo 100 (1972); "Popcorn" by Hot Butter (1972); "Outa Space" by Billy Preston (1972), who returned in 1973 with "Space Race"; "Love's Theme" by Love Unlimited Orchestra (1973); "TSOP," TV's *Soul Train* theme, by MFSB (1974); "Machine Gun" by the Commodores (1974); Scott Joplin's "The Entertainer," which was the theme song of *The Sting,* recorded by Marvin Hamlisch (1974); "The Hustle" by Van McCoy (1975); "Nadia's Theme," which was also the theme song of the TV soap opera *The Young and the Restless* by Barry DeVorizon (1976); "Gonna Fly Now," the theme from *Rocky* by Bill Conti (1976); "A Fifth of Beethoven" by Walter Murphy (1976); "Theme from *Star Wars*" by Meco (1977); "Rise" by Herb Alpert (1979); and "Feels So Good" by Chuck Mangione (1979).

The Sound of 1962

THE FOUR SEASONS

Frankie Valli (born Frank Castelluccio), Nick Massi (born Nicholas Macioci), Hank Majewski, and Tommy DeVito were all friends from the Newark, New Jersey, area. In 1956 they channeled their common interests in rock and roll into a group called the Four Lovers. Playing the Jersey club circuit, they caught the attention of RCA Records and were signed to the label. They released a minor hit, "You're the Apple of My Eye," that carried them all the way to the *Ed Sullivan Show* in 1956. But they returned to obscurity just as quickly as they had left it after five follow-up singles flopped. They then spent five years back on the Jersey club circuit, trying again and again to release a hit record. As "Billy Dixon and the Topics," "Hal Miller and the Rays," "Frankie Vally and the Romans," and "Johnny Cabott," the group released songs for assorted labels that all went nowhere. They spent the rest of their time playing and singing backup for other recording artists who also went nowhere, like John Corey, Wade Felmons, Johnny Halo, Tommy Hayes, the Kokomos, Shirley Matthews, Evan Mitchell, Larry Santos, and Ken Hartford. This went on into the early sixties.

Bob Gaudio had been writing and recording hits like "Short Shorts" with the Royal Teens. Discouraged by that group's inability to cut another hit, he left them in the early sixties to join the Four Lovers, a group he believed to have untapped potential. One night when the group was working at a Newark bowling alley, they decided to start afresh with a new name and conveniently lifted one from the bowling alley's Four Seasons Cocktail Lounge. This was the start of the transformation that would soon make them one of the most popular groups in the United States. Writer and producer Bob Crewe agreed to work with the group and helped them define and develop their sound. He landed them a contract with Vee Jay records, but their first release, "Bermuda," flopped in 1962. It was back to the studio for the Four Seasons.

In September 1962 the Four Seasons were clowning with Valli's piercing falsetto in the recording studio before their serious taping. Crewe picked up on it, and Gaudio wrote some lyrics specially for Valli's falsetto. What started as horseplay ended up as a single that sold 180,000 copies in one day, went to number 1 nationally, and stayed there for five weeks. "Sherry" sold well over a million copies and established the distinctive Four Seasons sound that would sell eighty million records from 1962 to 1965.

"Sherry" startled and pleased American record buyers with its unique ultrahigh lead vocal. The Seasons proved that it was not a one-shot gimmick when they came right back with "Big Girls Don't Cry," a song that also reached the top of the charts in 1962. Gaudio and Crewe shared the writing credits on this million seller. "Walk Like a Man," also written in 1962 by Crewe and Gaudio, was released in January 1963 and became the Four Seasons' third million seller. In only half a year the Seasons had skyrocketed into the public ear from nowhere and were eclipsed only by the biggest phenomenon ever to hit the music world—the Beatles. Coincidentally, the Four Seasons had some notable connections with the Beatles. Vee Jay acquired the Beatles in 1963 and released an album called *The International Battle of the Century* that contained music by both groups in an attempt to stir up a one-on-one rivalry. Unfortunately for Vee Jay, the company was too small to handle two supergroups simultaneously, and they didn't hold on to the Beatles' contract for very long. Vee Jay would lose the Four Seasons, too, after royalty litigation. The Four Seasons were one of the very few pre-Beatles American groups to withstand the British invasion, continuing to churn out hit after hit.

The Four Seasons' first three releases for their new label, Phillips, did very well. "Dawn," "Ronnie," and the million seller "Rag Doll" were all top hits in 1964. In the fall of 1965 the group went gold again with "Let's Hang On." But Nick Massi left the group that year because of his distaste for life on the road. In an attempt to exploit the popularity of Valli's voice, Phillips encouraged the singer to record as a solo performer as well as with the Seasons. In the summer of 1967 Valli had a top-ten hit by himself with "Can't Take My Eyes Off of You," while the Four Seasons were also in the top ten with "C'mon Marianne." With the growing popularity of progressive-album-oriented music the hit-single-oriented Seasons tried to evolve in that heavier direction. But their album, *Genuine Imitation Life Gazette,* a concept L.P. with complex orchestration, practically went straight into the cut-out racks. Tommy DeVito retired in 1970, and Gaudio departed in 1971, leaving Frankie Valli and his new Four Seasons to headline on the golden-oldie circuit.

The Four Seasons might have been just another nostalgia act were it not for the November 1974 release of "My Eyes Adored You" on Private Stock Records. This million-selling chart-topper was written and produced by Bob Crewe and released as a Frankie Valli solo record. Warner/Curb Records signed Valli and the Four Seasons (with Gaudio doing occasional studio work) on the basis of this latest hit, and their first L.P. yielded the disco hit "Who Loves You." That was followed up by "December 1963 (Oh, What a Night)," the group's first national number-1 hit since "Rag Doll" in 1964. The record was released in December 1975 and sold two million copies internationally. Both of these 1975 hits were written by Bob Gaudio.

In October 1977, Frankie Valli left the group to perform solo. The following spring the RSO label released the title song from the movie

Frankie Valli (on far right) and the Four Seasons in 1977.

Grease sung by Frankie Valli. Record sales were enormous, and Valli began another chapter in his career.

While some point out that the Four Seasons' sound was not original but derivative of groups like the Diamonds and Maurice Williams and the Zodiacs, the Seasons' accomplishment was that they took that sound and created an incredible collection of screeching, intense, but still very commerical hits under Bob Crewe's guidance. Even when they covered Dylan's ''Don't Think Twice'' (1966) as the Wonder Who, the Four Seasons whipped up that infectious blend of the shrill and the sweet that gave them one of rock and roll's longest and most successful careers.

1963

In 1963 rock and roll was stuck in the doldrums. Except for the work of the Beach Boys, some early Motown rumblings, and a bit of folk music from Peter, Paul and Mary, 1963 was just a lot of the same old fluff. Top-forty radio was playing "My Dad" by Paul Peterson, "Walk Right In" by the Rooftop Singers, "Our Day Will Come" by Ruby and the Romantics, "South Street" by the Orlons, "I Will Follow Him" by Little Peggy March, "If You Wanna Be Happy" by Jimmy Soul, "Killer Joe" by the Rocky Fellers, "Sukiyaki" by Kyu Sakamoto, "Easier Said Than Done" by the Essex, "Surf City" by Jan and Dean, "So Much in Love" by the Tymes, "My Boyfriend's Back" by the Angels, "Denise" by Randy and the Rainbows, "Hello Mudduh, Hello Fadduh" by Allan Sherman, "Be My Baby" by the Ronettes, and "Deep Purple" by Nino Tempo and April Stevens.

You knew it was a strange year when the Singing Nun was able to muscle her way to the number-1 spot with "Dominique." *My Favorite Martian, The Outer Limits,* and *The Fugitive* started to invade television, while *American Bandstand* was relegated to Saturdays only from its previous daily slot, making it tougher for teen-agers to learn how to do the monkey and the bossa nova. A new prime-time show called *Hootenanny* debuted around the same time. Each week it visited a different college or university to broadcast a folk concert. By this time the music had gained a significant audience, although the top-ten tunes of the year were devoid of folk: "Surfin' U.S.A." by the Beach Boys, "Sugar Shack" by Jimmy Gilmer and the Fireballs, "Rhythm of the Rain" by the Cascades, "The End of the World" by Skeeter Davis, "Blue Velvet" by Bobby Vinton, "He's So Fine" by the Chiffons, "Hey Paula" by Paul and Paula, "Washington Square" by the Village Stompers, "Fingertips—Part II" by Little Stevie Wonder, and "It's All Right" by the Impressions.

There were some things worth celebrating in 1963. The Academy Award for Best Picture went to the ribald, racy *Tom Jones*. The Los Angeles Dodgers defeated the Yankees in the World Series. The Boston Celtics won another NBA crown. In the NFL it was the Chicago Bears and in the AFL the San Diego Chargers.

However, this was also the year that smoking was linked to cancer. Martin Luther King led two hundred thousand people in a march on Washington for equal rights. And Dick Clark's Caravan of Stars had to cancel a scheduled show in Dallas on November twenty-second as they grieved with the rest of the horrified nation over President John F. Kennedy's assassination that day.

It was 1963—the ninth year of rock and roll.

THE CHIFFONS

Judy Craig, Barbara Lee, Patricia Bennett, and Sylvia Peterson were all friends from The Bronx and Upper Manhattan. They were big fans of Little Anthony and the Imperials and the Drifters, avidly listening to AM radio and frequently catching shows at the Apollo in Harlem. They sang in the school lunchroom just for fun, except for Sylvia, who really didn't like to sing but who valued her friendship with the other girls. They probably would have dropped music for more conventional careers had Ronnie Mack not intervened.

Mack was a keyboard player and songwriter who believed in the girls' potential. While they were still in high school, Ronnie paid twenty-five dollars for an hour at a local recording studio. With just their vocals and Mack's piano, the session was a race with the clock as they tried to cut as many tracks as possible. Not expecting very much from that tape, the girls finished school and found other jobs. They also cut two flop records for the Rust label at this time under the name of the Four Pennies and did some backup singing for Little Jimmy and the Tops, but remained in relative obscurity while Ronnie peddled their tape to the major labels. No one seemed to be interested in the tape. But the Tokens, the singing group of "The Lion Sleeps Tonight" fame who were now involved in the production end of the business, liked the girls' sound. The amazed girls were soon at the Mirror Sound Studios in Manhattan putting together a song written by Mack called "He's So Fine." The Tokens produced it, and Laurie Records bought the disc. At this point the group needed a new name to launch its new career. Barbara always liked the name of the Philadelphia group, the Orlons ("Don't Hang Up," "South Street") and came up with the Chiffons.

Laurie released the tune in February 1963, and the song's catchy hook, "doo lang, doo lang, doo lang," captured the record-buying public's fancy. The record shot up to number 1 nationally and stayed there for four weeks. The Chiffons promptly quit their day jobs

and headed off to their first gig, a record hop in Springfield, Massachusetts. Unfortunately for the Chiffons, most of the royalty money from "He's So Fine" went toward paying off the record's production costs, which were enormous because of the use of a big backup band and the recording of tracks over and over in the search for perfection. This energetic tune turned out to be the group's only number-1 song.

But if you believe the courts, "He's So Fine" found itself back on top of the charts in 1970. George Harrison's first hit after the break-up of The Beatles was his tribute to Eastern religion, "My Sweet Lord." Bright Tunes Publishing, which owned the rights to "He's So Fine," didn't have anything against Eastern religion, but they did feel that if one traded in Harrison's "hare krishnas" for choruses of "doo langs," "My Sweet Lord" sounded an awful lot like the Chiffons' hit, albeit somewhat slowed down in tempo. Bright Tunes sued the ex-Beatle for infringement of its copyright, and in 1976 a judge ruled that Harrison had "subconsciously plagiarized" "He's So Fine" and awarded damages to Bright Tunes.

Turning back to 1963, Carole King and Gerry Goffin wrote a tune called "One Fine Day," which they gave to Little Eva, whose earlier hit had been "The Loco-Motion." She cut the song, but an assortment of legal and musical complications kept it from being pressed. Carole and Gerry searched for another vocalist for the song and found the Chiffons. Carole King taught the Chiffons the song, Little Eva's vocal was erased from the tape, and their vocal was recorded over the old instrumental track. Although "One Fine Day" didn't match the sales of "He's So Fine," its buoyant melody and rhythmic piano work earned the record an enormous amount of radio airplay. Carole King would sing the song herself in 1980 and turn the tune into a two-time hit.

But before long, discontent began to plague the group. The Tokens selected material for the Chiffons

125

The Chiffons.

that was aimed at the youthful pop market, material that the Chiffons did not particularly like. They found this bubblegum music distasteful to their maturing sensibilities, but the Tokens made it clear that they were calling the shots. The Chiffons rebelled, a court battle ensued, and they eventually found themselves out in the cold. Unable to write, produce, or play instruments themselves, they did what they felt they had to do and went back to Laurie Records. They had a hit with "Sweet Talkin' Guy" in May 1966, followed by their minor hit, "I Have a Boyfriend." Then, after a few subsequent failures, Laurie let their contract expire without renewal.

At their height the Chiffons toured with groups like the Four Seasons, Dion, and Jay and the Americans. But perhaps the saddest part of the Chiffons' story is the fate of the man who first dragged them into a recording studio. Ronnie Mack had Hodgkin's disease. He lasted just long enough to see them make it to the top.

The seventies found the Chiffons working day jobs again, yet on most weekends, all but Judy Craig got together to play clubs, colleges, and rock-and-roll revivals. By 1981, they were performing as actively as ever. The group that could never pick their own material and supposedly lacked fundamental creative abilities still managed to project the vibrant enthusiasm that earned them their brief moments in the rock-and-roll limelight.

LESLEY GORE

Lesley Gore was a teen heartthrob in 1963. Little boys cherished pictures of her. Little girls wanted to grow up to be just like her. When she performed at Palisades Amusement Park in New Jersey just after "It's My Party" hit number 1, the place was mobbed by devoted Lesley Gore fans. What singled her out among the other female singers of the early sixties? Connie Francis was already an "older woman" by 1963. Brenda Lee was a little kid trying to grow up fast singing teary country-and-western numbers. Lesley, however, was a teen-ager, still in high school. It was easy to imagine her having the same experiences we all had—algebra tests, high school football games, the prom, and acne. Lesley sang about the real teen-age concerns—parties, going steady, crushes, unrequited love. Lesley Gore became a star because she was one of us.

Leslie grew up in the affluent suburb of Tenafly, New Jersey. She didn't exactly go to a typical high school. She attended the exclusive Dwight Preparatory School for Girls in Englewood, New Jersey. And she didn't become a rock-and-roll star in the usual way, either.

After hearing Lesley sing with some of her cousins at a friend's birthday party, a guest with some record-business connections suggested that she cut a demo. With only five weeks of singing lessons Lesley had a private recording made, which her well-connected friend then took to Mercury Records. Mercury eventually signed her to an exclusive recording contract and teamed her with producer Quincy Jones, who later became famous for his own soft jazz recordings (and who married Peggy Lipton of TV's *Mod Squad*). Lesley and Quincy pored over a number of songs before coming up with the one they thought would be perfect for the "typical teen-ager." Lesley's first single, "It's My Party," was released nine days after she turned seventeen.

"It's My Party" was a light, upbeat record about a girl who cries all through her own party because her boyfriend dumped her for her two-faced friend Judy. The song hit the right note with American teen-agers because it was so "girl-next-door." The record zoomed to number 1 just four weeks after it was released, staying in the top ten for seven weeks.

Mercury knew a good thing when it saw one and decided that Lesley should do an answer song to "It's My Party." Answer songs were the rage in the early sixties. Diane Renay's "Navy Blue" led to "Kiss Me, Sailor." Chubby Checker followed up "The Twist" with "Let's Twist Again." Even Claude King's "Wolverton Mountain" got a reply in Jo-Ann Campbell's "I'm the Girl from Wolverton Mountain." What could be better than to give that two-timing Judy her just desserts and perhaps repeat the success of "It's My Party." "Judy's Turn to Cry" is a celebration of teen-age revenge, sexual double standards, and romantic adolescent game-playing. With so much going for it, it's no surprise that it broke into the top five during the summer of 1963.

Lesley had two more big hits that year. "She's a Fool," backed by a rousing chorus of "wack-a-doos," was another tale of teen-age trauma. In December of 1963 Lesley's ballad "You Don't Own Me" shot to number 2 as Lesley's declaration of independence. She then made excuses for devious male behavior in "That's the Way Boys Are," a number-12 song in the spring of 1964. In August 1964 Lesley was confounded in "Maybe I Know" over her cheating man. "What can I do?" she wondered. Eight years later Helen Reddy's "I Am Woman" would tell her.

By this time Lesley was at Sarah Lawrence, performing only on weekends and during semester breaks. She tried to study music at college, but her professors refused to deal with pop music, deriding Lesley's commercial success. Lesley appeared in the classic videotaped rock concert *The T.A.M.I. Show* in 1965, while still in college. Upon graduation she seemed to have given up rock and roll for more lightweight pop like "Sunshine, Lollipops, and Rainbows." Moving to California to try her hand at acting, she appeared in *Girls on the Beach, Ski Party,* and an episode of the *Batman* TV series. Unfortunately her acting career was less successful than her rock career. Lesley did, however, team up with veteran rock producer Bob Crewe in California to cut "California Nights," a fine song that reached number 16 in April 1967.

In 1980 Lesley teamed up with her brother, Michael, to write "Out Here on My Own" for the movie *Fame.* Irene Cara took "Out Here on My Own" to the upper reaches of the singles charts. Lesley was nominated for an Oscar for Best Song with "Out Here on My Own," only to lose to brother Michael and the title song from *Fame.* But with the dawn of the eighties a new career as a songwriter beckoned for the former "Queen of the Teen Weepers"—Leslie Gore.

OPPOSITE PAGE:
Jay (on far left) and the Americans

128

JAY AND THE AMERICANS

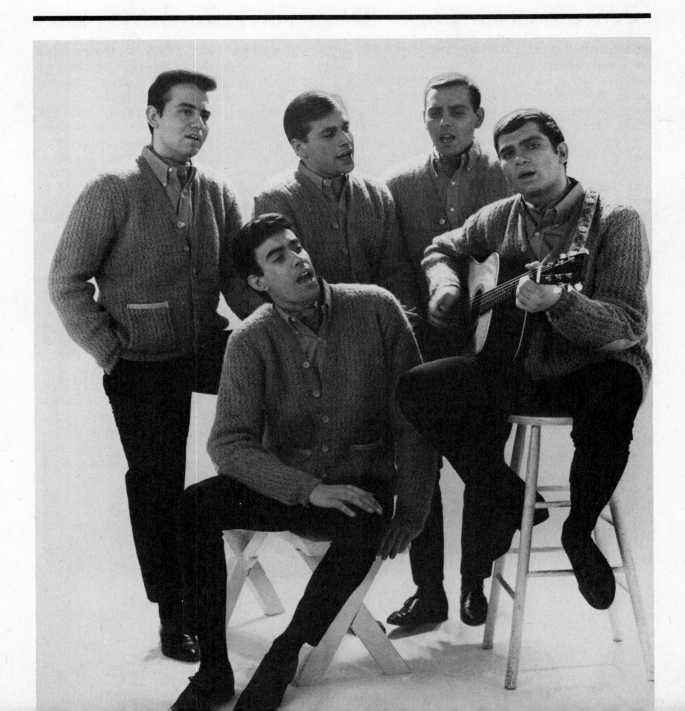

Late in 1959 John Traynor left the rock-and-roll group the Mystics after their winner "Hushabye." Searching for a group he could feel more comfortable with, he joined Kenny Vance, Sandy Yaguda, and Howie Kane to create the Harbor-Lites. After two records that went nowhere, "Angel of Love" and "What Would I Do Without You," they got the break of their careers in the form of Jerry Leiber and Mike Stoller.

The Harbor-Lites auditioned for the producing/writing duo in 1961. Leiber and Stoller liked what they heard and arranged a recording contract for the group with United Artists Records. The group's sound and style were reworked and their name was one of the first things to go. Sensing how much bigger Broadway's *West Side Story* was going to be as a motion picture, Leiber and Stoller had their nameless group cut "Tonight." Meanwhile the unofficial name-the-group contest was buzzing about Leiber and Stoller's offices, becoming something of an office joke. When someone kiddingly suggested "Binky Jones and the Americans," someone else thought it had possibilities. John Traynor's nickname was "Jay," and the group eventually became Jay and The Americans. But "Tonight" failed to become a big hit in 1961, and when "She Cried" and "This Is It" did little in 1962, Jay Traynor left the group. David Blatt was hired to replace him. But although his voice fit in well, his name didn't. They could have changed the name of the group to David and the Americans, but Leiber and Stoller felt a name change would lose them the little public identification they had already attained. Instead, they made David change *his* name to Jay. In addition, the ethnic-sounding "Blatt" was changed to "Black." It was then that success came to the Jayless Americans.

In 1963 another Leiber and Stoller group, the Drifters, were enjoying a career of smash hits. It seemed they would have another one when they recorded a song called "Only in America." But the Drifters fell victim to racial prejudice. The record company refused to release the record, fearing a public backlash against a song that talked about becoming the president of the United States sung by a black group. In 1963 the American dream was not to be dreamed by blacks. The record was cut by Jay and the Americans, in default, bringing them instant rock stardom.

The hits then came one after another. "Let's Lock the Door," "Come a Little Bit Closer," the operatic "Cara Mia," and "Some Enchanted Evening," another song from a movie based on the Broadway show *South Pacific,* kept them on top during the precarious days of the British invasion. In fact the group partially attributed their success to the Beatles. They won the honor of joining the Chiffons and the Righteous Brothers on the Beatles' first American tour. They knew they had finally made it when they appeared on the *Ed Sullivan Show,* rock and roll's superstar status symbol of the fifties and sixties.

Nineteen sixty-six and 1967 were dry years for Jay and the Americans. While other groups were maturing and branching out into new and sometimes experimental directions, Jay and the Americans weren't. Their material and their sound hadn't changed since 1963. They turned their attention to establishing their own record label, JATA (an anagram of the group's initials), and spreading out into music publishing. The new label was good luck, for their first release in late 1968 rejuvenated their careers. Turning to the Drifters for material again, they remade "This Magic Moment." Next they took a five-year-old Ronettes hit and had a success with their 1969 version of "Walkin' in the Rain."

Then acid rock came and wiped them off the charts. The older groups that managed to survive generally did so by adapting. Again, Jay and the Americans would not change. When it appeared that the end was in sight for them, the rock-and-roll revival trend started to blossom. While promoters were digging up groups that had long disbanded, trying to splice them back together, Jay and the Americans were still intact with the same old "nostalgic" sound that they had never abandoned. Billed as Jay Black and the Americans after the original group members had dropped out one by one, they became a rousing smash at oldies shows. They appeared on Dick Clark's rock-and-roll revival TV specials, and the handsome Jay Black now had to fend off a new audience of young female fans. Nearing the twenty-year mark of their erratic rock-and-roll career, Jay Black and the Americans just keep on going.

THE KINGSMEN

The organ heralded the message to the kids, and the kids got the message. The song just *had* to be about sex and partying. And their parents would never understand the words! They somehow *knew* the song was "dirty." Congress was called upon to investigate the supposedly obscene lyrics, playing the 45 at 33 1/3 rpm to root out the filthy threat to decency and morality. The governor of Indiana banned the record to protect the purity of the Hoosier State. The establishment tried, but nobody could stop "Louie Louie," the national anthem of rock and roll in 1963.

The Kingsmen. *(Courtesy of the Memory Shop)*

Teenagers gathered around record players and jukeboxes, trying to decipher the words the Kingsmen were singing in "Louie Louie." Could they really be singing "...At night and then I'll lay her again"?! In truth, "Louie Louie" was *not* obscene. Richard Berry, who had been the voice of "Henry" in Etta James' 1955 hit "The Wallflower" (a.k.a. "Roll with Me Henry") as well as the deep-voiced narrator for the Robins' "Riot In Cell Block #9," wrote "Louie Louie" back in 1956. While rhythm-and-blues songs didn't shy away from suggestive lyrics, "Louie Louie" never met the exaggerated expectations of those teenagers who struggled to make out the words. True, it was about a sailor's last night on shore, but it was really the Kingsmen's nasty stance and slurred singing that projected images of seething acts of lust.

The Kingsmen were five white musicians from Portland, Oregon, who fancied rhythm and blues and early rock and roll. Lynn Easton had formed the Kingsmen in 1957 when he was a freshman at David Douglas High School in Portland, Oregon. Easton sang lead, played saxophone, composed, and arranged. He was joined by Gary Abbott on drums and Mike Mitchell on lead guitar. As a trio, their first record, "Week End," barely edged onto the charts in September 1958 at number 84. They spent the next five years playing every possible gig in the Pacific Northwest—dances, fairs, fashion shows, TV commercials, and all kinds of one-night stands. By 1963 they had added Don Gallucci on organ and Norm Sundholm on bass.

In 1963 Portland was a growing rock-and-roll city, populated by the likes of Paul Revere and the Raiders and John Fogerty, later of Creedence Clearwater Revival. Still, the Kingsmen were Portland's undisputed leaders. They had their own float in the annual Portland Rose Festival parade and were the house band at Portland's most important teen nightclub, The Chase. "Louie Louie" put Portland on the rock-and-roll map and gave the Kingsmen national albeit fleeting recognition.

Like the Liverpool groups that invaded the American shores a few months after "Louie Louie," the Kingsmen played old R & B, Motown, blue-eyed soul, and rock and roll night after night. Finally they achieved what they wanted, becoming loud, entertaining, and professional. While the mainstream of rock had softened, the Kingsmen, much like the Beatles in Hamburg, roared through a repertoire that included "Money," "Twist and Shout," "Shout," "Do You Love Me?" and "Don't You Just Know It." With their gutsy organ, gritty soul vocals, raucous stage presence, and R & B roots, the Kingsmen paved the way for many mid-sixties American groups like the Young Rascals, the McCoys, the Strangeloves, the Standells, the Shadows of Knight, and ? and the Mysterians.

"Jolly Green Giant," a Coasters-like comedy rocker about that big green star of the TV commercials with a backup chorus calling out names of vegetables, peaked at number 4 in March 1965. Unfortunately, they soon fell off the charts for good. Still, with "Louie Louie" the Kingsmen left rock and roll quite a legacy.

THE MOTOWN SOUND

Motown Records called itself "The Sound of Young America," and it was. Not just young black America or just young white America, but everybody in the sixties was digging the sounds coming from the Motor City. Motown broke down the barriers between black rhythm and blues and white rock and roll with a smooth, glossy style of "soul" music. Motown had some of the sixties' top performers—the Supremes, the Four Tops, the Temptations, Stevie Wonder, Marvin Gaye, and the Miracles—and always seemed to have more hit records than any other record company.

The man behind Motown was Berry Gordy, Jr. Gordy grew up during the Depression in the eastside ghetto of Detroit. Having seen poverty and misery, he knew he wanted out and he had to make it big to do so. Gordy tried boxing as a way to get out of the ghetto. Fighting as a featherweight, he won ten of fourteen matches, but decided boxing wasn't for him after too many blows to the head and too few paydays. Gordy then moved into the music business, first with a jazz record store that eventually went bust, then as a songwriter in the R & B field. Songwriting was about as grueling as boxing because of the blows to the ego he had to endure from rejection slips. Then an old friend from his boxing days named Jackie Wilson gave Gordy his break in the music scene.

In 1957 Jackie recorded one of Gordy's songs, "Reet Petite," which only climbed to number 62 on the national charts. Jackie recorded another Gordy song, "Lonely Teardrops," in 1958, which resulted in a number-7 smash that stayed on the charts for almost five months. But Berry Gordy wasn't satisfied. His songwriting royalties came too slowly and he felt that his songs just weren't being produced the right way. Gordy realized that the only way to make the kind of music and money he wanted was to go into the record business himself.

In 1959 Gordy worked during the day as a chrome trimmer on the Ford assembly line to finance his venture as an independent record producer. He prowled Detroit's flourishing nightclub scene looking for new talent. Gordy signed singer Marv Johnson, worked out a leasing arrangement with United Artists Records, then set out to blend gospel, R & B, and white rock and roll into a potent commercial brew. In November 1959 Gordy and Johnson struck pay dirt with a top-ten record, "You Got What It Takes." Gordy also signed the Miracles, a group barely out of their teens. While Gordy had originally been attracted to the group by their female vocalist, it was to be the Miracles' leader, Bill "Smokey" Robinson, who would later have the greater impact on Gordy. After leasing a few Miracles tracks to Chess Records, Gordy was ready to start his own record label.

Berry's sister, Anna, had married the leader of the Moonglows, Harvey Fuqua, and they had their own small record company in Detroit. Gordy arranged a distribution deal with his sister for one of his independent productions, "Money" by Barrett Strong. Anna then lent him seven hundred dollars to start his own label. Gordy bought an old bungalow on West Grand Boulevard in Detroit and turned it into the recording studios of "Hitsville U.S.A."—Motown Records. Soon 2648 West Grand became the home of soul.

The Miracles—Smokey Robinson, Ronnie White, Pete Moore, Bobby Rogers, and Smokey's future bride, Claudette Rodgers—were the first artists signed to Gordy's Tamla label in 1960. Smokey's songwriting ability impressed his boss, and after a few lessons in song-plotting from Gordy, Robinson was set loose in the recording studio. "Shop Around," a little up-tempo motherly advice on how to find the right girl, became Motown's first million seller and a number-2 record in the early days of 1961. Led by

The Miracles without Smokey.

Smokey's cool, high-pitched vocals, the Miracles became Motown's first big act and remained consistent hit-makers over the next twelve years with a varied list of hits that included dance numbers like "Mickey's Monkey" and "Going to a Go-Go" as well as emotional love songs like "Ooo, Baby, Baby," "The Tracks of My Tears," and "You've Really Got a Hold on Me."

Smokey became the label's top songwriter, penning such classics as "My Guy" for Mary Wells, "My Girl" for the Temptations, and "Ain't That Peculiar" for Marvin Gaye. Smokey also helped to formulate the early Motown sound as a producer for the Marvelettes, Brenda Holloway, Mary Wells, Marvin Gaye, the Temptations, and his own Miracles. Smokey eventually

became a vice-president at Motown, but occasionally he steps out from behind his desk to attack the charts again as he did in 1979 with the mellow soul mover "Cruisin'" and in 1980 with "Being with You."

The Motown sound owed as much to its stable of producers—Norman Whitfield, Harvey Fuqua, Freddie Perrin, Ashford and Simpson, and Holland, Dozier, and Holland—as it did to its singers. Gordy strove for the kind of quality control that would ensure that certain feel and style that defined a Motown record. Every once in a while Gordy would pit two production teams against each other, using the same song and artist just to get the best record he could. It may have driven the producers crazy, but you couldn't argue with his successful results. In the mid-sixties, seventy percent of all Motown single releases scored on the charts.

One of Motown's leading hit-makers in the early years was Marvin Gaye, who was originally a singer with a late edition of Harvey Fuqua and the Moonglows, and then a drummer for the Miracles on the Motown Revues. Marvin was the most versatile of the Motown singers, teaming up at various times with Mary Wells, Kim Weston ("It Takes Two"), and Tammi Terrell ("Ain't No Mountain High Enough," "You're All I Need to Get By"). Marvin was also the most consistent male singer in the sixties, with nine top-twenty singles, including: "Pride and Joy" (#10, 1963); "I'll Be Doggone" (#8, 1965); "I Heard It Through the Grapevine" (his first #1, 1968); and "Too Busy Thinking About My Baby" (#4, 1969). In the seventies Marvin negotiated an independent record deal with Motown, giving him artistic freedom—a term Motown has never used lightly. The fruits of this arrangement included "What's Going On" (#1, 1971), "Mercy Mercy Me (The Ecology)" (#4, 1971), and "Let's Get It On" (#1, 1973).

Martha Reeves started out as a secretary at Motown, but was soon belting out hits in the studio as Martha and the Vandellas. The group's rockers included "Heat Wave" (1963), "Dancing in the Street" (1964), "Nowhere to Run" (1965), and "Jimmy Mack" (1967).

The Marvelettes were signed by Berry Gordy fresh out of high school in 1961. They hit the charts with "Please Mr. Postman" (Motown's first #1, 1961), "Playboy" (1962), "Beechwood 4-5789" (1962), and "Don't Mess With Bill" (1966).

The Supremes, too, spent years at Motown, from their unpolished beginnings in 1961 to superstardom, nurtured all the while by Gordy himself.

Berry Gordy has become a motion-picture mogul in recent years, leading Motown into such productions as *Lady Sings the Blues, Mahogany, The Wiz,* and *Thank God It's Friday.* Despite his other interests, Berry Gordy's hand never strays too far from the reins of the record company he built.

Motown has been synonymous with soul since it began, and rightly so. From the Four Tops and the Temptations to Stevie Wonder and the Jackson 5, it has been the premier showcase for black talent. Though it has been criticized by many for various reasons, it is one of the few record companies anywhere that can justifiably claim to have created, nurtured, and promoted a whole musical genre all by itself.

Motown Vice President
William "Smokey" Robinson.

The Sound of 1963

THE BEACH BOYS

Since 1961 the Beach Boys have been singing about summer days, the beach, surfing, girls, and hot rods. But beyond singing songs about the West Coast beach scene, the Beach Boys applied a unique style of vocal harmonizing to the basic lead, rhythm, and bass guitars with drums format and profoundly altered the direction of rock and roll with their California sound. Their music gradually evolved from their teen-age experiences and their fascination with the surfing culture.

Inspired by the Everly Brothers, Brian, Dennis and Carl, the Wilson brothers, began singing together in Hawthorne, California, calling upon their mother to complete the four-part harmony. Al Jardine, whose leg was broken by high school football teammate Brian Wilson, was eventually recruited to replace Mrs. Wilson in the group. Al played bass, Dennis wound up on drums, Brian learned the piano, Carl trained on guitar, and Wilson cousin Michael Love started on saxophone.

In September 1961 the boys formed their first band, Carl and the Passions. They were a local success, playing the tunes of Chuck Berry and the Everly Brothers, and featuring the Regents' hit "Barbara-Ann," a song they would later successfully record. Eventually they longed for original material. Dennis, the only real surfer among them, suggested they do a song about surfing. The result was "Surfin'," Mike and Brian's first collaborative effort.

The hunt for a solid recording contract led them down a few wrong paths in 1961. Brian Wilson sang backup on a forgettable tune called "Humpty Dumpty" by Bob and Sheri. Under the name of Kenny and the Cadets the group recorded "Barbie," a bomb for Rany Records. By the year's end they were calling themselves the Beach Boys, having cut "Surfin'" under their new group name for the Candix record label. This single marked the debut of this twangy-guitar, tight-harmony California sound.

In 1962 the Beach Boys experienced several setbacks. Al Jardine left the group to pursue a career in dentistry. Then Candix Records went out of business. The Wilson brothers were in trouble, and it was their father who saved the day. He took their tapes to several record companies and hit the jackpot with Capitol Records. In May 1962 "Surfin' Safari" and its popular flip-side hot-rod song "409" were released to an overwhelming reception.

The Beach Boys as they looked in 1979. Top row from left: Brian
Wilson, Al Jardine, and Dennis Wilson. Bottom row: Mike Love
(left) and Carl Wilson.

"Surfin' Safari" reached number 14 and stayed on the charts for over
four months, paving the way for a wave of hits in 1963. "Surfin' U.S.A."
made the California sound *the* big new sound of rock and roll. Obviously
influenced by "Sweet Little Sixteen," the Beach Boys eventually gave
Chuck Berry writer credit for this song by the third pressing of the 45. It
hit number 3, remaining in the top ten for six weeks. Teen-agers who
couldn't get enough of the new sound with "Surfin' U.S.A." were flipping
the record over to hear "Shut Down," the popular B-side. Flip-side record
popularity has always been a rarity in the record business, but it

happened twice more for the Beach Boys in 1963. "Surfer Girl" hit number 7 and hung on to the charts for three months, and "Be True to Your School" managed a number-6 spot, while their respective flip sides, "Little Deuce Coupe" and "In My Room," received their own extensive radio play.

The Beach Boys popularized surfer attire and the all-American image. They were tan, generally golden haired, and well groomed, all wearing neat slacks and striped, short-sleeve shirts. This image was reinforced by Mr. Wilson's strict behavior code under which violations were punished by a five-hundred-dollar fine. But when Mr. Wilson later tried to control the group's musical direction, Brian intervened and in effect demoted his father.

The Beach Boys became comfortable with success and generously supported the development of other California performers. They occasionally played behind Jan and Dean in concert and on records, and even gave them Beach Boys' songs for their albums. One of Brian Wilson's songs given to Jan and Dean was "Surf City," which hit number 1 in 1963 and stayed on the charts for over three months, making it the biggest hit the duo ever had. The Beach Boys also supported the Honeys, the three girls who provided the cheerleading on "Be True to Your School." Five flops later, the Honeys were relegated to backup singing for Jan and Dean and the Surfaris. Brian Wilson did, however, end up marrying one of the Honeys.

In 1964 Al Jardine gave up his dentistry career to return to the group just in time to record "Fun, Fun, Fun," which reached number 5 on the top ten. Three more hit singles were released that year: "I Get Around" hit number 1, "When I Grow Up (To Be a Man)" reached number 9 and stayed on the charts for over two months, and "Dance, Dance, Dance" became a number-8 record that remained in the top ten for three weeks. They appeared in two films, *Girls on the Beach* and Walt Disney's *The Monkey's Uncle,* and performed the theme song for the NBC TV series *Karen.*

The incredible pressure of the band's schedule eventually took its toll on Brian. He suffered a nervous breakdown on an airplane trip to Houston just before Christmas 1964. In addition, the loud amplification of the group in concert had caused severe damage to his hearing. When he retired at his doctor's advice, the group was dumbfounded. Eventually, Brian returned to the fold but confined his work to the studio. Dennis, Mike, and Al thought their careers were over, but Carl regrouped the family and took over as leader. Future country star Glen Campbell was Brian's first replacement. When Campbell became ill in the middle of a tour, Bruce Johnston, who would later write the Barry Manilow hit "I Write the Songs," took his place.

In 1965 the Beach Boys continued to release strong singles one after another. "Do You Wanna Dance?," the old Bobby Freeman song, peaked at number 12. "Help Me, Rhonda" climbed to number 1 and stayed in the top ten for seven weeks. Then "California Girls" hit number 3 and remained on the charts for more than three months.

Unfortunately the Beach Boys began to have differences of opinion with Capitol Records, who were not interested in having them develop and expand their music. Capitol insisted that they stick to the surfing tunes, so the Beach Boys gave them the album they wanted, *The Beach Boys' Party Album.* Dean Torrence of Jan and Dean sat in on this album. They all got drunk and began singing the Regents' "Barbara-Ann." They figured the rough but jolly sing-along would be a good filler, but Capitol had other ideas and released it as a single. It promptly nestled in at number 2 and sat in the top ten for a month.

Capitol was now more insistent than ever about wanting the old surfing material. Brian rebelled and produced a progressive album called *Pet Sounds.* He was thrilled with it, but Capitol refused to release it—until Brian threatened never to record for them again, that is. Many critics hailed the innovation of Brian's arrangements. His inspiration, he claimed, was the sandbox in his living room, where his piano stood. Apparently the sand between the toes did it for him.

In 1966 Capitol settled for "Sloop John B." from *Pet Sounds.* As a single it hit number 3 on the charts. "Wouldn't It Be Nice?" and its flip side "God Only Knows" followed "Sloop John B." as hits, both from *Pet Sounds,* finding their way to number 8 on the top-ten surveys. The climax for Brian Wilson and the new direction of the Beach Boys was reached that year with a song that was six months in the making. "Good Vibrations" was the biggest hit the group would ever have in terms of sales, the expression of their musical ability, innovation, and style. The record was number 1 in both the U.S.A. and England and almost sprouted roots at the top of the charts for an amazing seven weeks.

The Beach Boys were torn between two musical directions in 1967. Some fans preferred to revel in their early tunes, while others liked the new material that was influenced by T.M., mysticism, and mind-expanding drugs. The album *Smiley Smile* and the single "Heroes and Villains" followed the latter direction. The night they completed "Heroes and Villains," Brian was so elated that despite the fact that it was past midnight he drove to a nearby radio station and asked the DJ to play it on the air. The disc jockey refused to play the song because it wasn't slotted on his official station playlist. Brian freaked. After a few quick calls, however, the program director ordered the record to be played. "Heroes and Villains" eventually reached number 12 on the surveys.

In 1968 Dennis offered to help a new friend who thirsted for rock fame. This new friend and some of his "family" soon moved into Dennis' house. While there, he wrote a song he called "Cease to Exist," specifically designed to stop the bickering he observed among the Beach Boys. The Beach Boys rewrote some of the lyrics and cut it as "Never Learn Not to Love," the B-side to "Bluebirds over the Mountain." Dennis' friend refused credit but demanded money—and lots of it. He eventually ripped off the Beach Boys for some hundred thousand dollars and totaled Dennis' Ferrari in the process. Outraged by the failure of the record, he blamed the group and continued to press Dennis for more and more money. When Dennis refused, he threatened to kill his son. Dennis' "friend," Charles Manson, disappeared after that incident.

The rest of 1967 was bleak for the Beach Boys. "Wild Honey" failed to make it to the charts. Another single, "Darlin'," did somewhat better, barely cracking the top twenty. Remaining off the concert circuit hurt them more and more as new albums quickly faded into oblivion. The 1968 single "Do It Again" did hit number 1 in England, but stalled at number 20 in the U.S.A. "I Can Hear Music" struggled to number 24 in 1969. Finally, in 1971, the more mature Beach Boys emerged with a rebirth album, *Surf's Up.* They won back a portion of their old audience without alienating their more progressive-oriented fans. Both critics and public were receptive this time.

During the seventies the Beach Boys' greatest successes were inside the concert hall. Their tours constantly sold out, reaching audiences who spanned three decades. While there were albums such as *Endless Summer* and *Beach Boys in Concert,* and singles such as "Sail On Sailor" and "We Got Love," it was the live shows that elicited the electricity. After singing backup vocals on Chicago's single "Wishing You Were Here" in 1974, the Beach Boys went on a national tour with them. This tour was yet another triumph.

Brian returned to perform with the group in 1976. Under his guidance, *Fifteen Big Ones, The Beach Boys Love You, M.I.U. Album,* and *L.A. (Light Album)* all sold well. Their double album, *Spirit of America,* even went platinum. Never ceasing to experiment, the group remade "Here Comes the Night" as a disco hit.

By 1980, Bruce Johnston was back with the band but this time as assistant producer. Brian Wilson was back as the leader. The talent and energy are there; so is the intense need to keep moving, growing, exploring. As a result, the Beach Boys will be able to carve out a sizable market for themselves in the eighties and will continue to play to packed houses until the day they decide to pack it in.

1964

The Beatles are a passing phase. They are the symptoms of the uncertainties of the times.

—BILLY GRAHAM

Nineteen sixty-four brought the Beatles to America and rock and roll was never the same again. They spearheaded what was called the "British invasion," and as a result many U.S. artists bit the dust, one after another, with stunning rapidity. Dick Clark recalls the phenomenon and its effects on the music and the country:

"For some strange reason all of a sudden you had to be English. You had to have some sort of discernible English accent. You were even better off if your name was Ian or Derek, rather than Bill or Jim. And if you came from Liverpool—that was it! The incredible irony was that the British groups were playing the Everly Brothers, Chuck Berry, and the rest of the rock and roll that we shipped over there. They learned the music and gave it back to us with an English accent, a different style of clothing, and a snobbish attitude, and we sucked it up. We even made the Caravan of Stars as English as we could, as did every radio station, promoter, and record label."

What American singers managed to stay on the charts in 1964? Shirley Ellis ("The Nitty Gritty"), Diane Renay ("Navy Blue"), Major Lance ("Um, Um, Um, Um, Um, Um"), Terry Stafford ("Suspicion"), the Dixie Cups ("Chapel of Love"), the Reflections ("Just Like Romeo and Juliet"), Jan and Dean ("The Little Old Lady from Pasadena"), Roger Miller ("Dang Me"), Ronny and the Daytonas ("G.T.O."), and Little Anthony and the Imperials ("Goin' Out of My Head") held down the fort in a losing battle. Except for the growing Motown soul sound and the Beach Boys' California surfing sound, the charts were colonized by the British. Despite The Beatles, American artists were strong enough to dominate most of the top ten slots for the year: "She Loves You" by the Beatles, "I Want to Hold Your Hand" by the Beatles, "Hello Dolly!" by Louis Armstrong, "Oh, Pretty Woman" by Roy Orbison, "We'll Sing in the Sunshine" by Gale Garnett, "Everybody Loves Somebody" by Dean Martin, "I Get Around" by the Beach Boys, "My Guy" by Mary Wells, "Where Did Our Love Go" by the Supremes, and "Last Kiss" by J. Frank Wilson and the Cavaliers.

American Bandstand moved from Philadelphia to Los Angeles in March 1964. While the kids were doing the jerk and the swim, the show geared up for the new sounds of rock and roll. By the end of the year *Bandstand* had survived a major change in the musical taste of a fickle

Born in New York but raised in Louisiana, Johnny Ramistella won his first recording contract when Alan Freed took him under his wing. Freed also suggested that Johnny change his name to Rivers. After playing rock clubs for years, Johnny suddenly became the hottest act on the Los Angeles club scene when he headlined at the brand-new Whiskey A Go Go club in 1963. Recording success wasn't far behind. Johnny's hits include "Memphis," "Mountain of Love," "Seventh Son," "Secret Agent Man," "Poor Side of Town," "Tracks of My Tears," "Baby, I Need Your Loving," "Summer Rain," and "Slow Dancing." Johnny also became a record producer in the mid-sixties, discovering such talent as the Fifth Dimension for his Soul City record label.

public. Meanwhile, the kids just couldn't get enough rock and roll with *Bandstand,* so the networks gave them two new prime-time music shows, *Shindig* and *Hullabaloo.*

There was more to life than the Beatles in 1964, believe it or not. The U.S.S.R. gave Khrushchev the boot in favor of Brezhnev and Kosygin. Barry Goldwater lost to LBJ in the American presidential election. China exploded its first A-bomb, and a little Southeast Asian country named Vietnam came into the news with its vicious civil war. Oscar for Best Picture went to *My Fair Lady* that year and television's latest fad was *The Man from U.N.C.L.E.*

Predictably, the Boston Celtics added another NBA trophy to their crowded shelves. St. Louis surprised the Yankees by taking the World Series. It was the Cleveland Browns over the Baltimore Colts in the NFL, and the Buffalo Bills over the San Diego Chargers in the AFL. Tokyo was the site of the Summer Olympics, but the site of the action in rock and roll was halfway around the world.

It was 1964—the tenth year of rock and roll.

142

CAR-CRASH SONGS

Dick Clark interviews Jan and Dean. Life imitated art when Jan Berry crashed his car while racing on Sunset Boulevard in Los Angeles, just blocks away from the real Dead Man's Curve, not long after their single "Dead Man's Curve" hit the charts. *(Courtesy of Dick Clark. Photo: Thom Elder)*

In the late fifties and early sixties, car-crash songs became popular. All over the radio, sports cars were overturning, motorcycles were running into trucks, racers were flipping over in flames, and even your average family car was stalling in the middle of a railroad track. America's teen-age rock and rollers were captured by those morbid songs with their romantic, daringly rebellious music and lyrics. Some critics accused the artists and their audiences with being "sick" or "ghoulish." Perhaps the car-crash songs were the logical extension of rock and roll's (and America's) fascination with the automobile.

The first of car-tragedy songs was the gimmick

number called "Transfusion," released in May 1956 by Jimmy Drake, billing himself as Nervous Norvus. The song, which hit the top ten during the summer of 1956, deals with a reckless driver who ends up in traction with tubes coming out of all parts of his body, vowing that he will "never, never, never" speed again!

One of the most remembered songs of this genre is Mark Dinning's classic car-crash tearjerker, "Teen Angel." Here a train is barreling down the line toward the narrator's car, which is stalled on the railroad tracks. He gets the girl out of the car in time, but she runs back inside to search for the high school ring he had given her. He tries to stop her but fails. She is found tightly clutching his ring in her lifeless hand. Probably the most grotesque line in this song occurs when the narrator laments, "I'll never kiss your lips again, they buried you today." MGM released the smash record in late 1959 and it became an international hit, earning Dinning his only gold record in the process.

February 1964 saw the release of "Dead Man's Curve" by Jan and Dean ("Baby Talk," "The Little Old Lady from Pasadena," "The New Girl in School," "Surf City," "Honolulu Lulu"), who named the song after an actual stretch of Sunset Boulevard in Los Angeles, which, by the way, was eventually reconstructed to make it safer. The tune traces a drag race, citing actual landmarks along Sunset Boulevard. The 'Vette and the Jag slide into the curve, but only the driver of the Stingray lives to sing about it.

Ironically and tragically, Jan Berry was involved in a serious automobile accident himself in late 1965. He sustained severe head injuries, which resulted in brain damage. Suffering from dysphasia (the loss of the ability to use or understand language), Jan was a long-term patient in a rehabilitation center in Los Angeles. Jan's recovery was the subject of *Dead Man's Curve,* a made-for-TV movie of the late seventies in which Jan and Dean are portrayed making a successful comeback.

The Shangri-Las had to be the unparalleled queens of the crash songs. Their October 1964 hit "Leader of the Pack," is the story of an outcast motorcycle hood whom the lead singer met in a candy store. Wearing his ring and defying her disdainful parents and friends, she boldly declares her love for the biker. Disregarding her pleas, he speeds away on his motorcycle, cracks up, and is killed, leaving her a mourning teen-age widow with only his ring to keep

as a reminder. The song featured the wonderfully nauseating sound effects of the skidding motorcycle and a first-rate crash.

The Shangri-Las were a unique group, especially because of their provocative live performances. They were actually early punk-rockers and appeared at the time when girl groups like the Ronettes, the Chiffons, the Crystals, the Angels, and the veteran Shirelles were reaching their peak. However, the Shangri-Las were greaser girls and proud of it. They were overly made up, wore tight sweaters and leather pants, and had outlandishly teased hair. It was a "slut" look and the fans bought it.

The Shangri-Las were actually two pairs of sisters, teen-queens from Queens, New York: the Weiss girls and the Ganser twins. Their first hit, "Remember (Walkin' in the Sand)" (1964), was written by independent producer George "Shadow" Morton. Like most of their material, their first song consisted of a lot of back-and-forth nonsinging banter, both graphic and clichéd. Reverb was used heavily. Then "Leader of the Pack" became a gold disc for the girls in 1964. "Give Him a Great Big Kiss" was the third hit for the Shangri-Las that year. This one showed less punk rebellion than their others, but it was by no means a softening of their approach, for they came back in 1965, screaming in anguish, with "I Can Never Go Home Anymore." The Shangri-Las returned for the rock revival shows of the seventies but without Marge Ganser, who died of a drug overdose.

Ray Peterson of "Corinna, Corinna" fame made his own contribution to the car-crash category with his immortal "Tell Laura I Love Her" in 1960. Here Tommy enters a car race in hopes of winning the prize money so that he can buy Laura a wedding ring. His last-minute phone message to Laura's mom is to "tell Laura I love her." His car inevitably crashes, but he lives long enough to sing the song's refrain, hoping someone will tell Laura he loves her.

The record that ended the reign of car-tragedy songs was the 1964 hit "Last Kiss" by J. Frank Wilson and the Cavaliers. This time, when the narrator and his date have an accident, she is seriously injured but he is not. She requests that he just hold her for a little while and give her one last kiss before the Lord takes her away. Their future reunion in heaven is emphasized, as it was in most of the car-crash songs, renewing faith and smoothing out the romantic ending of a horribly tragic scenario.

THE SUPREMES

The Supremes (from left: Mary Wilson, Florence Ballard, and Diana Ross) and a chaperone getting ready to join Dick Clark's Caravan of Stars in 1964. *(Courtesy of Dick Clark)*

In the early sixties rock and roll was alive with the sound of the girl groups. Phil Spector gave us the Ronettes and the Crystals. The Shangri-Las and the Angels rocked forth from the streets of New York. The Marvelettes and Martha and the Vandellas wailed loud and soulfully from the Motor City. But the ultimate girl group came out of the Motown stable in 1964—a group that appealed to girls as well as boys, and whites as well as blacks. It was the group that put Motown Records on the map for good—the Supremes.

Diana Ross, Mary Wilson, and Florence Ballard came out of the Brewster-Douglass housing projects in Detroit, an urban-renewal ghetto that produced a lot of the Motown talent in the sixties. The girls would walk to school together, singing R & B and gospel on the street just for fun. When some neighborhood boys formed a singing group called the Primes, Mary, Flo, and Diana decided to call themselves the Primettes and started performing at dances and parties. The Primes later signed with Motown in the early sixties and became the Temptations. But Motown wasn't quite ready for the Primettes. Motown's Berry Gordy met the girls after they had won a talent contest in 1960. Gordy was impressed, but he insisted that they finish high school. Diana,

Mary, and Flo went back to Gordy as the Supremes in 1961 after they had graduated, and he signed them to a record deal.

Motown wasn't the place for overnight successes in the early years. Gordy concentrated on the label's bigger acts, letting the newer groups struggle on their own at Motown's "finishing school," getting polish, poise, and style. The early Supremes were anything but a success. Their first single, "Your Heart Belongs to Me," never passed number 95 on the Hot 100 in the summer of 1962. "Let Me Go the Right Way" stopped at number 90 at the start of 1963. The Supremes struggled through Motown charm school at night, while friends advised them not to give up their day jobs as clerks in record and department stores. As a favor to Berry Gordy, Dick Clark added the still unknown Supremes to his 1964 Caravan of Stars Tour for six hundred dollars a week. Diana Ross' mother went along as their chaperone on this first tour. But the Supremes were still languishing at Motown, passing from producer to producer and never finding their "sound." Finally the Supremes were turned over to Martha and the Vandellas' producers, Eddie Holland, Lamont Dozier, and Brian Holland.

Holland, Dozier, and Holland were the producers

who turned Motown into a hit-making machine on the strength of two groups, the Four Tops and the Supremes. They worked like a precision instrument, writing the songs with a constant four beats to the bar and producing them with a slick, professional finish every time. Holland, Dozier, and Holland wrote virtually every hit the Supremes ever had and turned a bunch of giggling girls just out of high school into one of the biggest-selling recording acts in the world.

In July 1964 Holland, Dozier, and Holland performed magic on the Supremes with a marching beat, a rippling piano, and Diana Ross' cooing vocal on "Where Did Our Love Go," which took the number-1 spot on the charts—the first of twelve number-1 records they would have over the next five and a half years. In fact, "Where Did Our Love Go" was the first of five number-1 hits in a row. Diana sang another galloping tale of woe with "Baby Love," taking that to the top for four weeks in November. The Supremes found their way to number 1 again with "Come See About Me" by Christmas 1964. A sliding, building organ cued the steady beat of "Stop! In the Name of Love," which was number 1 in April 1965. Holland, Dozier, and Holland just increased the tempo slightly, wrote new lyrics that had Diana question Flo and Mary's advice on a boyfriend ("...and Flo, she don't know...") and let their formula take "Back in My Arms Again" back to the top again in June 1965. But then "Nothing but Heartaches" only made it to number 11 during the summer of 1965! Was the magic gone? Hardly. They regained the number-1 slot in November with "I Hear a Symphony."

The Supremes were the superstars supreme, wearing slinky, glimmering evening gowns and elegantly coifed hairdos. Motown pushed its soul stars into nightclubs, Las Vegas casinos, and other such palaces, and the slick, glittery Supremes fit right into the scene. But the Supremes weren't ready to abandon their hit records yet. After the buzzing organ and slightly unnatural sound of "My World Is Empty Without You" and the medical implications of "Love Is Like an Itching in My Heart," the Supremes went on to record four more consecutive number-1 songs. The first three—"You Can't Hurry Love," "You Keep Me Hangin' On," and "Love Is Here and Now You're Gone"— are classics and among the best records the girls ever turned out. Their fourth number-1 hit, "The Happening," was the beginning of the end, though. This title song from a mediocre Anthony Quinn movie moved the Supremes out of soul and into the bland world of pop music.

As the Supremes moved closer to the middle of the road, Flo Ballard called it quits, leaving the group in 1967. The future was not sweet for Flo, as the elegant gowns and wigs of the sixties gave way to the welfare rolls of the seventies. A broken woman, Flo Ballard died in 1976.

The Supremes replaced Flo with Cindy Birdsong from Patty LaBelle and the Bluebelles.

In late 1967 their "Reflections" was an awful attempt to cash in on psychedelia. Not mind-expanding, the song was simply mindless. The girls' next effort was a pre-rock-and-roll pop number, "In and Out of Love." But teen-agers began to snicker as the Supremes performed for older, whiter audiences. "Love Child" and "I'm Livin' in Shame" were melo-dramatic attempts at black relevancy, but by this time Diana Ross was a long way from the ghetto, and these songs didn't really work. The Supremes had the last number-1 record of the sixties, a return to that old Motown soul, "Some Day We'll Be Together." But as soon as the record was released Diana split for a solo career, and the original Supremes were never together again.

First Jean Terrell, the sister of heavyweight boxer Ernie Terrell, and then Shari Payne tried to fill Diana's lead spot, but the Supremes floundered in the seventies, hitting only with "Up the Ladder to the Roof," and "Stoned Love." Diana Ross, of course, went on to become an actress and an international superstar. She graced the silver screen in *Lady Sings the Blues, Mahogany,* and *The Wiz.* In the seventies she recorded "Reach Out and Touch (Somebody's Hand)," "Touch Me in the Morning," and "Love Hangover." However, one must admit that when Motown moved to Los Angeles and Diana Ross went to Hollywood, rock and roll may have lost a piece of its soul.

THE BRITISH INVASION

In January 1964 the Beatles fired the first shot—a high-powered hit titled "I Want to Hold Your Hand." By the spring it was a full-scale attack! Nobody had to yell, "The British are coming!" for the airwaves were full of English invaders. By the end of 1964 Britain had captured its former colonies with rock and roll.

America was taken by surprise. The biggest British hit in America before the Beatles was "He's Got the Whole World in His Hand," a 1958 religious hand-clapper by thirteen-year-old Laurie London. The English weren't exactly bombarding the States with rock and roll in the fifties. But then, rock and roll was slow in coming to Britain. The government-controlled BBC was the only radio game in town, and it wasn't overly receptive to rock and roll. Lucky teen-agers were able to pick up rock and roll on the radio from the illegal pirate radio stations that broadcasted from ships three miles or more off Britain's shores, outside of the government's jurisdiction. But in general the British had to settle for lightweight pop and traditional jazz from the BBC, and if the children behaved nicely, they were allowed to watch the well-scrubbed teen pop stars Cliff Richard and Tommy Steele on the "telly." It was only in port towns like Liverpool, where sailors brought in American 45's, that rock and roll took hold. While rock was born in America in 1955, rock and roll didn't really come to life in England until 1961.

After the initial success of the Beatles, British acts were picked up by American record companies in the hope that lightning would strike twice. Radio stations crammed their programs with English groups, because after the Beatles had become so popular, no station wanted to miss out on the next trend. In 1964 British rock and roll was fresh, hungry, and vital, while American rock was a little tired from its early battles with the music establishment and the payola scandals. Pop producers had learned to live with rock and had

softened its fury in the process. In England they were just starting to dig that rhythm and blues. The British might have been just shipping the sounds of Chuck Berry, Carl Perkins, and the Shirelles back to America, but they were sending it with a zest and energy that American rock seemed to have lost ever since Elvis was drafted.

One of the reasons why the Beatles were so important to rock was that they opened the door for American acceptance of British rock and roll. Rock and roll became a two-way street in 1964 with British and American rockers giving each other inspirational shots in the arm whenever their music needed a boost over the years. The music of the British invasion may not have been original, classic rock and roll—it seemed that only Lennon and McCartney were writing original songs—but it was a lot of fun, and it gave America a kick in the transistor just when it needed it most.

The following are only a few of those blithe British spirits who gave rock and roll an English accent in 1964:

Gerry and the Pacemakers. Gerry Marsden, his brother Freddy, and their mates Les Chadwick and Lee Maguire had been playing in Liverpool since 1959. Gerry, an old friend of Paul McCartney, built tea chests and worked for British Railways in addition to playing music. He gave up the railway job because he claimed the trains never ran on time when he was around. Like many of the Liverpool groups, Gerry and the Pacemakers cut their rock-and-roll teeth in the clubs of Hamburg, Germany. Always one of the most popular groups on the Mersey scene, Gerry and the Pacemakers signed a recording contract soon after the Beatles. When the Beatles turned down "How Do You Do it?," a song written by Mitch Murray, the Pacemakers snapped it up and took it to number 9 on the American charts in

August 1964. The follow-up, "I Like It" (also by Mitch Murray), caught American fancies in October 1964. The Pacemakers' two biggest hits were the touching ballads "Don't Let the Sun Catch You Crying" (#4, summer 1964) and the title cut of their movie, "Ferry Cross the Mersey" (#6, February 1965).

The Swinging Blue Jeans. When it rated the top groups in Liverpool in late 1961, *Mersey Beat* magazine rated the Beatles number one, but excluded the Swinging Blue Jeans from the competition, saying, "They are beyond comparison...in a class by themselves." Unfortunately it was all downhill for the Blue Jeans from there. These early Mersey rockers had only one hit in the U.S., "Hippy Hippy Shake" in the spring of 1964.

The Tremeloes. The Tremeloes had the distinction of having been chosen over the Beatles by Decca Records in 1962. Led by Brian Poole, they had a couple of major hits in England with "Do You Love Me?" and "Twist and Shout." But they couldn't manage to break onto the American charts with the first wave of British invaders. After Poole left the band in 1966, the Tremeloes were finally able to score in America with a syncopated version of Cat Stevens' "Here Comes My Baby" in the spring of 1967 and then with a beautifully harmonized remake of the Four Seasons' "Silence Is Golden" in July 1967.

Cilla Black. Her real name was Priscilla White, and she was once the hatcheck girl at Liverpool's famous Cavern Club. Every once in a while she would forget about the coats and climb up on stage to sing with the boys. She became Cilla Black when *Mersey Beat* forgot her name (they knew it was a color but guessed wrong). Cilla was signed by the Beatles' impresario Brian Epstein, who felt she had the makings of a pop star. She sang her version of "Love of the Loved," which was the Beatles' demo that was rejected by Decca, but her only hit in the States was "You're My World," a pop love song that made it in the summer of 1964.

Peter and Gordon. Peter Asher and Gordon Waller started out singing in folk clubs and coffee houses around London. Peter was the brother of actress Jane Asher, Paul McCartney's long-time flame, and Peter and Gordon proved that it didn't hurt to be friends with a Beatle. Lennon and McCartney gave them three songs, and they took all three to the top twenty in America in 1964—"A World Without Love" (#1, June 1964), "Nobody I Know" (#12, summer 1964), and "I Don't Want to See You Again" (#16, fall 1964). They took a tune that Del Shannon originally wrote for a Motor City soul singer and hit number 9 in February 1965 with the dramatic "I Go to Pieces." In late 1966 Peter and Gordon reappeared with a novelty number, "Lady Godiva." After working as an

Cliff Richard—one of the only teen singing stars acceptable to English moms and dads in the early sixties.

exec at Apple Records for a while, Peter Asher became James Taylor's manager and most recently has managed and produced Linda Ronstadt.

Chad and Jeremy. Chad Stuart and Jeremy Clyde were always being mistaken for Peter and Gordon. In fact their own record company put Peter and Gordon's photo on their first album! Their sweet, folksy hits included "Yesterday's Gone" (#21, June 1964), "Summer Song" (#7, September 1964), and "Willow Weep for Me" (#15, December 1964).

Billy J. Kramer and the Dakotas. This group cashed in on their connection with the Beatles. In 1964 Billy, born William Ashton, was a Liverpool singer signed by Brian Epstein when his original manager felt he needed more than part-time guidance. Epstein matched Kramer with a Manchester group in his stable, the Dakotas, then got Lennon and McCartney to write them some tunes. "Do You Want to Know a Secret" was their first big hit in England, but the Beatles took it to the top of the charts on this side of the

Atlantic. After hitting number 7 in the U.S. with "Little Children," they followed up with three Lennon-McCartney songs: "Bad to Me" (#9, June 1964), "I'll Keep You Satisfied" (#30. Summer 1964), and "From a Window" (#23, Summer 1964).

Freddie and the Dreamers. This was perhaps the most peculiar band to come to America from England. Freddie Garrity looked like a wimpy version of Buddy Holly and invented an awful dance called the Freddie, where you threw your right arm and leg up into the air and then your left arm and leg, over and over again, like a puppet. Freddie, a former milkman and engineer, and his band had actually been part of the scene before Beatlemania hit. They jumped into the number-1 spot in the States for two weeks in April 1965 with "I'm Telling You Now." Even though Chubby Checker beat them to the charts by three weeks, only the original Freddie could have made "Do The Freddie" a dance sensation. The singsongy "You Were Made for Me" was the Dreamers' last success in America, reaching number 21 in June 1965.

Manfred Mann. The bearded Mr. Mann, who was born Mike Lubowitz in Johannesburg, South Africa, was not the lead singer of his group. That job went to the lisping Paul Jones. After starting out as a jazz group, Manfred Mann moved into mainstream commercial rock. The group remade an Exciters' flop, "Do Wah Diddy Diddy," and took it to number 1 for two weeks in October 1964. Following the nonsensical refrains of "Do Wah Diddy Diddy," Mann recorded "Sha La La," which was originally done by the Shirelles in early 1964. At various times Manfred Mann's band included Jack Bruce (later of Cream) and Klaus Voorman, one of the Beatles' closest associates. In 1968 Mann took an unreleased Dylan song, "The Mighty Quinn," to the top ten. The band made a comeback as Manfred Mann's Earth Band in 1977 and shot back to number 1 with Bruce Springsteen's "Blinded by the Light."

Wayne Fontana and the Mindbenders. When Wayne had an audition with Fontana records in Manchester, only one other member of his band showed up, so he quickly had to recruit two local boys, Eric Stewart and Rick Rothwell. He then made up a name for this group, borrowing from a horror movie he had just seen. The Mindbenders had a number-1 smash in April 1965 with their musical biology lesson, "Game of Love." Wayne was then asked to leave the group after a dispute over a girl friend. With Graham Gouldman added to the band, the Mindbenders took "A Groovy Kind of Love" to number 2 in April 1966.

Manfred Mann's Earth Band.

One version of the Hollies. From left to right: Tony Hicks, Terry Sylvester, Bernie Calvert, Allan Clarke, and Bobby Elliott.

Gouldman, one of England's top rock songwriters, and Eric Stewart later became founding members of 10cc ("I'm Not in Love," "The Things We Do for Love," and "Dreadlock Holiday").

The Hollies. One of the most durable British bands in the business is still with us after seventeen years, despite a frequently changing lineup that has included singers Graham Nash, Allan Clarke, and Terry Sylvester. With an infectious pop sound, The Hollies first hit the American charts in a big way in 1966 with two songs penned by Graham Gouldman: "Look Through Any Window" (#32) and "Bus Stop" (#5). A tune about a belly dancer, "Stop, Stop, Stop," went to number 7 in the fall of 1966. Before Graham Nash split in 1969, they had two more smashes, "On a Carousel" (#11, spring 1967) and the steel-drum-backed "Carrie Anne" (#9, summer 1967). Hollies' hits in the seventies included "He Ain't Heavy, He's My Brother" (#7, February 1970); "Long Cool Woman in a Black Dress" (#2, summer 1972); and "The Air That I Breathe" (#7, summer 1974).

The Animals. Eric Burdon, Alan Price, Bryan "Chas" Chandler, John Steel, and Hilton Valentine came roaring out of Newcastle-on-Tyne in 1963 as the Alan Price Combo. Playing a working-class brand of American rhythm and blues, they put on such a wild, antic stage act that they were dubbed the Animals by their fans. Led by Burdon's soulful lead vocal and Price's inventive keyboard work, the Animals reworked an old black folk song and topped the American charts in late 1964 with "House of the Rising Sun." Although beset by numerous personnel changes, Burdon remained the focal point for the Animals, who regularly broke into the top forty throughout the sixties with such hits as "It's My Life," "Don't Let Me Be Misunderstood," "We Gotta Get Outta This Place," "Sky Pilot," and "San Franciscan Nights." Alan Price left the band in mid-1965 and went on to British success with his version of Randy Newman's tune "Simon Smith and the Dancing Bear" and his musical score to the film *O Lucky Man.* Chas Chandler moved into the business end of rock, as the guiding hand of the Jimi Hendrix Experience in 1966. After the last version of the Animals split in 1969, Eric Burdon hooked up with a group of six black musicians and a Danish harmonica player and as War topped the charts in 1970 with "Spill the Wine." In 1971 Burdon departed and War, with its strong Latin influence, ran off a long string of hits, including "Slippin' into Darkness," "The World Is a Ghetto," and "Cisco Kid."

151

The Animals (from left: John Steel, Alan Price, Hilton Valentine, Eric Burdon, and Chas Chandler).

Formerly known as Nite Shift, War was supposed to back football player-turned-singer Deacon Jones at a gig in 1969. When Jones didn't show, Eric Burdon of the Animals and Lee Oskar, a studio musician, came out of the audience to join the band. The sound clicked and Eric Burdon and War had a number-3 smash in 1970, "Spill the Wine." After Eric left in 1971, War became a more improvisational group with a Latin/soul sound. The band often composed their songs on the spot in the studio. War's hits include "Gypsy Man," "Why Can't We Be Friends?" and "Low Rider."

The Kinks.

The Kinks. Two brothers who attended art school in London, Ray and Dave Davies, joined up with drummer Mick Avory and bassist Pete Quaife to form the Kinks in 1964. Aided by producer Shel Talmy, the Kinks added fuel to the British Invasion with a thumping beat, Ray's eerie vocals, and three top-ten hits—"You Really Got Me," "All Day and All of the Night," and "Tired of Waiting for You." Ray's songwriting skills grew more sophisticated over the years with satirical jabs at conservatism and Carnaby Street—"A Well Respected Man" and "Dedicated Follower of Fashion." After a run on the American charts in 1970 with "Lola," "Apeman," and "Top of the Pops," Ray and the Kinks moved in the direction of concept albums, such as *The Village Green Preservation Society, Everybody's in Show-biz,* and *Schoolboys in Disgrace.* In the late seventies Ray's fascination with rock operettas stopped and the Kinks found themselves back on the charts with "Sleep Walker" and "(Wish I Could Fly Like) Superman." Sixteen long years after they formed, the Kinks were still important recording stars on the rock scene. They enjoy a loyal following today.

The Searchers in 1980.

The Searchers. Mike Pender, John McNally, Tony Jackson, and Chris Curtis all hailed from Liverpool and first played together in 1960 as the backup band for singer Johnny Sandon. With their ringing guitars and crisp harmonies, the Searchers were one of the most respected of the Mersey bands. Their first American hit was "Needles and Pins" (#13, April 1964), written by Sonny Bono and Phil Spector's protégé, Jack Nitzsche, which had been a flop for Jackie DeShannon the year before. They remade another Jackie DeShannon tune, "When You Walk in the Room," in November 1964. Their biggest success, "Love Potion #9," was originally a hit for the Clovers in 1959. It went to number 3 in December 1964. The Searchers returned in 1979 with an album of innovative pop that brought back fond memories of the British invasion.

153

DAVE CLARK FIVE

Avis Rent-A-Car used to say "We're number two, so we try harder!" If that sentiment was true, then in 1964 the Dave Clark Five must have been the hardest-working band in the world. In a year dominated by the Beatles, the Dave Clark Five was the number-two group in the world behind the fab four from Liverpool. In 1964 they had an amazing seven hit records reach America's top fifteen when most groups would have felt lucky during any year just to have three records hit the top twenty. But 1964 was the year that the Beatles had the top five singles on the charts one week and sold millions of records, so the seven hits and the driving beat of the Dave Clark Five were only second best in 1964.

The Dave Clark Five with Julian H. Miller II of *Prom Magazine.* *(Courtesy of Julian H. Miller II)*

The Dave Clark Five was formed in 1962 by members of the Tottenham Hotspurs, an amateur soccer team from a suburb of London. They were invited to play a Dutch team in Holland, but the Hotspurs were working-class lads and didn't have enough money to get to their game. However, they did have the drive and ingenuity of one of their players, Dave Clark. Some of the Hotspurs had been playing music for years. Mike Smith had played piano in a couple of pub bands. Rick Huxley and Lenny Davidson were self-taught but accomplished guitarists, and Denis Payton had been wailing on the saxophone for about five years. With all that musical talent, Clark decided to assemble a band and run dances to make enough money for the soccer trip. A great idea except for one small detail—the band had no drummer. Dave, who had never played an instrument before, bought a drum set from the Salvation Army for ten pounds and banged away night and day to the beat of old rock-and-roll records by Elvis, Little Richard, Chuck Berry, and Bill Haley. The band now had its drummer, the Hotspurs eventually went to Holland, and the Dave Clark Five was born.

While playing these dances, the DC5 had business cards printed up. They distributed them everywhere, and one made its way to Buckingham Palace. When the Hotspurs arrived back in Tottenham after defeating their Dutch rivals, the Dave Clark Five learned that they had been invited to play at the staff Christmas ball at Buckingham Palace. The boys hadn't thought about staying together as a band, but when one is asked to play at the Palace, one plays. Too poor for fancy transportation, they lugged their equipment onto the subway, got off at the station one block from the Palace, and then hired a taxi to drive them to the Palace gate in style.

The Dave Clark Five spent the better part of 1963 playing clubs around London, learning their craft, and developing as a group. After a long engagement headlining at the Tottenham Ballroom, the DC5's hard-driving, rave-up style of rock and roll was labeled the "Tottenham Sound" to distinguish it from the more melodic "Liverpool Sound." But rock and roll remained a part-time endeavor for the Dave Clark Five, as they played only three nights a week at the clubs and worked five days a week at their regular jobs. The group didn't decide to turn professional until they already had two records in Britain's top five. Since they didn't have a formal record contract, their future in music didn't look bright; but

Dave Clark wasn't one to get discouraged. Dave was an extra and a stuntman in the movies by day, earning a hundred and twenty pounds for each car he crashed on film. With his modest wealth, he took his group to a recording studio. After producing a rousing remake of the Contours' "Do You Love Me" for the DC5, Dave swung a deal with EMI Records. In the meantime Brian Poole and the Tremeloes caught wind of the DC5 record, covered the song, and stole the hit from Dave Clark's band. But the DC5 now had a record contract, and their recording career took off. "Glad All Over," written by Mike and Dave, climbed to number 1 in Britain in December 1963. It was the first record in six months to knock the Beatles out of the top spot on the charts.

Following his ratings coup with the Beatles in early 1964, Ed Sullivan had his staff on the lookout for another big British rock group. The DC5 became the second English group to play the Sullivan show, appearing two weeks in a row. When the Beatles decided not to tour the states until that summer, the Dave Clark Five acted quickly and, in the Spring of 1964, became the first British band to tour America. For a short while the screams of American teenagers belonged to the Dave Clark Five alone.

The DC5's reputation was built on Dave Clark's pile-driver drumbeat, Mike Smith's screaming vocals, and Denis Payton's blaring sax, which was practically the only saxophone heard on any rock recordings in 1964. Their rocking beat made it impossible to sit still in your seat. "Glad All Over" roared to number 6 in the U.S.A. in March 1964 and was quickly followed up the charts by the powerful rhythm of "Bits and Pieces" in April. "Do You Love Me" and "Can't You See That She's Mine" were full-tilt rock-and-roll numbers that hit in the summer of 1964. After taking a breather with one ballad, "Because," which peaked at number 3 in September, the DC5 closed out 1964 with two more hits, "Everybody Knows" and "Any Way You Want It." By 1965, though, it became evident that the Mike Smith–Dave Clark songwriting team was no match for John Lennon and Paul McCartney. Except for "Catch Us If You Can" in the summer of 1965, all of the DC5's hits during the next two years were loud rehashes of late-fifties American rock. By 1967 Dave Clark decided to give up music and study acting, and the Dave Clark Five disbanded. Although they did not enjoy the longevity in the limelight that some other groups did, the group will be remembered as one of the first and more unique bands in the British Invasion.

The Sound of 1964

THE BEATLES

On April 4, 1964, the Beatles had the top five records in the United States. "Please Please Me," featuring a harmonica and unusual vocal harmony, was the number-5 single in the country. "I Want to Hold Your Hand," which started the Beatles explosion in January 1964 with its fresh commercial melody, was stationed in the number-4 slot. "She Loves You" was number 3 after two weeks in the top spot. Number 2 was John Lennon's raw rock-and-roll vocal on "Twist and Shout." And "Can't Buy Me Love" was the number-1 record in America after only two weeks on the charts. The next week was even more amazing. On April 11, the Beatles had fourteen of the top eighty-one singles on the charts, including five of the top ten. Fourteen singles on the charts was considered good work for a band in *two* careers' time, but the Beatles did it in one week!

In 1964 the crew-cut, buttoned-down parents of America were up in arms. They were quite vocal in their criticism of the Beatles.

"The Beatles are just another fad. In six months nobody will even remember them."

"That long hair is just a gimmick. The next thing you know, these rock-and-roll bands will be playing in the nude to get attention!"

"How can you listen to that racket? The Beatles will never last!"

In a couple of years parents would change their tune, especially after songs like "Yesterday" and "Michelle." But in 1964, with teen-age daughters shrieking, fainting, and kissing pictures of their idols, and teen-age sons growing their hair long, shopping for collarless sports jackets, and buying guitars, parents just weren't very keen on the witty, clean, but shaggy Fab Four.

In 1956 fourteen-year-old James Paul McCartney went to the Woolton Parish festival, and there he saw sixteen-year-old John Winston Lennon on stage singing the Del Vikings' "Come Go with Me." John didn't seem to know all the words. After a while Paul went backstage to meet John and taught him the rest of the lyrics to that song as well as the words to Eddie Cochran's "Twenty Flight Rock." A kid who knew all the words to a rock-and-roll song was a valuable commodity in those days, and so a friendship was formed that day between Paul McCartney and a slightly inebriated John Lennon. A couple of days later John asked Paul to join his band, the Quarrymen.

In 1958 a schoolmate of Paul's, George Harrison, left his band, the Rebels, to join the Quarrymen. John, Paul, and George made up the whole band at this time, and they began playing talent contests as Johnny and the Moondogs. Their major problem was that they were all playing guitar. There was no rhythm section—no bass and no drums. While John was attending the Liverpool Institute of Art in 1959, he became fast friends with an introverted painter, Stu Sutcliffe. John offered Sutcliffe a place in the band for the price of a bass guitar. Stu couldn't resist an offer like that, so he promptly paid sixty pounds for a bass even though he couldn't play. Now calling themselves the Silver Beatles, they picked up drummer Thomas Moore, won an audition, and got a gig backing up a second-rate singer named Johnny Gentile on a third-rate tour of Scotland. On stage they became the glamorous Johnny Silver, Paul Ramon, Carl Harrison, and Stu DeStijl, who was so frightened and self-conscious he played bass with his back to the audience.

The Beatles. *(Dezo Hoffman/Nempix)*

When they returned from Scotland, Thomas Moore went on his merry way, leaving the band without a drummer again. Pete Best, the brooding, handsome son of the owner of the Casbah Club in Liverpool, who happened to own a drum set, soon replaced Moore. After playing some of the smaller clubs in Liverpool, including an illegal strip joint where they backed Janice the Stripper, the Silver Beatles went to Hamburg, Germany, in 1960 to play at the Indra Club and the Kaiser Keller on the notorious Reeperbahn, one of the sleaziest, most debauched streets in the world. For eight hours a night, seven nights a week, the rowdy German audiences screamed for action. The Beatles quickly abandoned their reserved stage presence and expanded their repertoire. Lennon would stomp, scream, curse, play in his underwear, or appear on stage with a toilet seat around his neck. When the group tried to move to a better-paying club, the owner of the Kaiser Keller had Paul and Pete deported, charging that they had set fire to the wallpaper of their living quarters in the basement of the club. George was then thrown out of the country because he was an unchaperoned minor. When the Beatles returned to Liverpool, they were raw, raucous, and full of rock and roll. They set the town on its ear. Between engagements at the Cavern, one of Liverpool's "beat" clubs, the Beatles returned to Hamburg four more times over the next three years. In 1961 Stu Sutcliffe decided to remain in Hamburg to study art. Paul took over the bass guitar spot as the Beatles became a quartet. Stu died of a brain hemorrhage in Hamburg in April 1962, a few months after the Beatles made their first recordings under the direction of Bert Kaempfert, backing singer Tony Sheridan.

Legend has it that Brian Epstein first learned of the Beatles when a fan walked into his record store on October 28, 1961, and asked for a copy of their German record "My Bonnie." In fact, Epstein had been writing a record column for *Mersey Beat,* a Liverpool music magazine that prominently featured the Beatles. When he became the group's manager in December 1961, he cleaned the boys up, threw out their leather jackets and blue jeans, and fitted them with fashionable suits and ties. Yet he kept the long hairstyles they had brought back from Hamburg. Brian's next step was to get the band a recording contract. Armed with his record-business contacts and the Beatles' demo tape of a Lennon-McCartney tune, "Love of the Loved," Brian headed for Decca Records in London. Dick Rowe of Decca turned down the Beatles in favor of Brian Poole and the Tremeloes—probably one of the worst decisions in the history of recorded music—but Decca wasn't alone in their rejection. Columbia, Phillips, Pye, and several other English labels, both large and small, rejected the Liverpool group. Traditional pop music was firmly entrenched at the London labels, and few companies were willing to take chances on rock groups from the provinces. George Martin at Parlophone, one of the small labels of the giant E.M.I. recording group, was willing to give the Beatles a shot, signing them to a contract in May 1962. Pete Best was the heartthrob of the group, with female fans actually sleeping in his garden just to be near him. But Pete wasn't quite so well liked within the group. So in August, just two weeks before their recording

The Beatles. *(Dezo Hoffman/Nempix)*

date, Best was fired and replaced by the personable drummer from Rory Storme and the Hurricanes, Ringo Starr (né Richard Starkey).

On September 11, 1962, the Beatles had their first recording session with George Martin. Unhappy with Mitch Murray's "How Do You Do It?," the Beatles insisted on recording original songs by John and Paul, so "Love Me Do" became their first single. Ringo, who had never recorded before, was relegated to the tambourine for most of the session, with a studio drummer filling in for him. "Love Me Do" was tops in Liverpool, but only reached number 21 on the national British charts by January 1963. The group needed a big success the next time out, so John and Paul went straight to work composing. Lennon said at the time, "I tried to make it as simple as possible. Some of the stuff I've written has been a bit way out, but we did 'Please Please Me' strictly for the hit parade." His plan worked, and "Please Please Me" topped the charts in Britain in March 1963, ushering in Beatlemania with screaming, fainting fans at concerts,

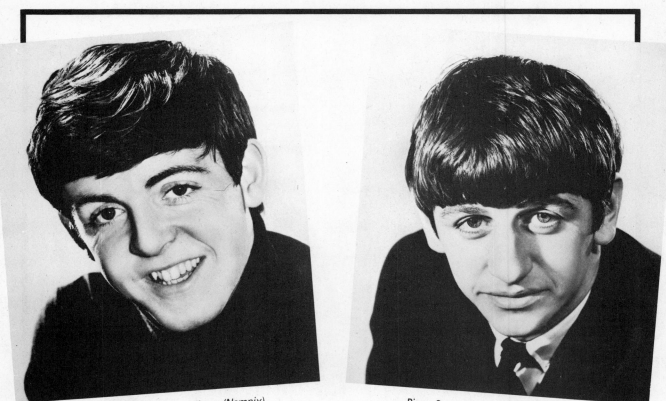

Paul McCartney. *(Dezo Hoffman/Nempix)*

Ringo Starr. *(Dezo Hoffman/Nempix)*

riotous mob scenes at airports, and a royal command performance for the Queen.

During this time the Beatles had absolutely no impact on the United States. In England they were the biggest thing since tea and crumpets, but E.M.I.'s American label, Capitol, refused to pick up its original options on the Beatles' records because no English group had ever made it big in America. Vee Jay Records picked up the option on "Please Please Me" in March 1963. It was a loser. They then tried to get an American response with "From Me to You." No reply. Next Swan Records got in on the action, releasing "She Loves You" in September. The record faltered out of the starting gate. The kids on American Bandstand's Rate-a-Record gave it only a seventy-three. It became apparent that these records needed a little help from their friends, and Capitol Records finally came through. When Epstein decided to invade America in early 1964, Capitol not only picked up its option on the Fab Four, it promised to pour fifty thousand dollars into promoting the Beatles, concentrating on New York City. "I Want to Hold Your Hand" was released by Capitol on January 13, 1964. It was number 1 by February 1. The Beatles' first American TV appearance was a film shown on the *Jack Paar Show* in January. On February 7, the group's plane landed amidst ten thousand fans in New York. They promptly charmed the American press. When they appeared live on the *Ed Sullivan Show* twice in February, seventy-five million people tuned in—over one third of the entire population of the United States. Suddenly

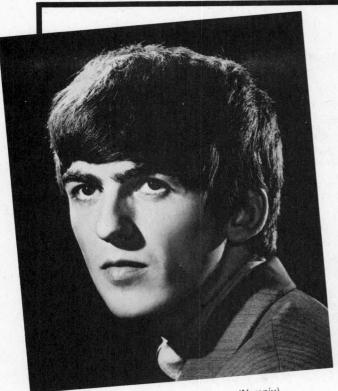

George Harrison. *(Dezo Hoffman/Nempix)*

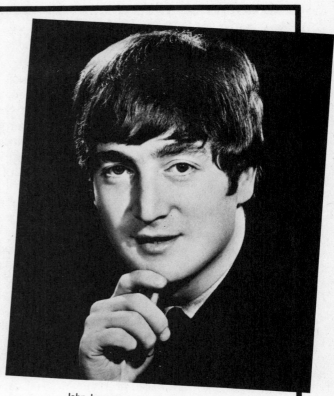

John Lennon. *(Dezo Hoffman/Nempix)*

all those Beatles singles that had stiffed months before were worth their weight in gold—and platinum.

While the press and the fans concentrated on their personalities— Paul, the cute one; George the quiet one; John, the intellectual; Ringo, the funny one—the Beatles pumped the airwaves with great music. Tasty nuggets like "All My Loving" and "I Saw Her Standing There" were on *Meet the Beatles,* their first American album on Capitol. *The Beatles' Second Album,* released in April 1964, was their hard rock-and-roll collection, with driving originals like "She Loves You," "I'll Get You," "Thank You Girl," and remakes of the classics: "Roll Over Beethoven," "Long Tall Sally," and "Money." The soundtrack to their first film, *A Hard Day's Night,* hit the record stores in late June. The rousing title cut shot to number 1 on August 1, while the love songs "If I Fell" and "And I Love Her" warmed teen-age hearts. In July, Capitol Records cashed in with the *Something New* album, which was really something old with five songs from *A Hard Day's Night* that had already been released. While Vee Jay Records kept repackaging its *Introducing the Beatles* album over and over again, Capitol had one more album ready for release in 1964. On December 15, they released *Beatles '65,* which featured the guitar buzz of "I Feel Fine," the rave-up "She's a Woman," and the eerie harmonies of "I'll Be Back." Lennon and McCartney's songs were full of melody, wit, and intelligence, but what set them apart from the competition was John and Paul's refusal to stay still, constantly growing with their music. The songs became much more complicated and varied both in terms of lyrical content and musical composition with *Beatles '65.*

When 1964 finally came to a close, the Beatles had spent an unbelievable twenty weeks of the year in the number-1 slot on the singles charts with six different releases. They had thirty songs score on the Hot 100. Three of their albums—*Meet the Beatles, The Beatles' Second Album,* and *A Hard Day's Night*—spent a total of thirty weeks at the top of the album chart. Almost singlehandedly the Beatles created a market for rock albums.

For five more years the Beatles dominated the rock scene, always innovating and changing. The baroque comment on loneliness, "Eleanor Rigby," was backed by the delightful nonsense of "Yellow Submarine" in 1966. A little slice of life in Liverpool, "Penny Lane," was on the flip side of "Strawberry Fields Forever," which practically ushered in psychedelic music in 1967 with its backward tape loops, sound effects, and stoned lyrics. Paul's "Elvis voice" and thumping piano recaptured the rock sound of the fifties with their 1968 hit "Lady Madonna." In 1969 they took a risk in releasing a seven-minute, eleven-second song that Paul composed to brighten up John's son Julian during a long car ride. "Hey Jude" (originally "Hey Jules") was number 1 for a record nine weeks, the biggest single of the year. When John married Yoko Ono in March 1969, "The Ballad of John and Yoko" soon followed. This rocker was banned on many radio stations because of his irreverent refrain about crucifixion. The Beatles even had a two-sided number-1 single at the beginning of 1970 when Lennon's surrealistic "Come Together" reached the top with Harrison's lovely "Something."

In the album market the Beatles were without peer. They had three albums from which they never released a single—*Rubber Soul, Sgt. Pepper's Lonely Hearts Club Band,* and the *White Album*—yet virtually every song was immediately recognizable to the public because of the extraordinary amount of radio airplay they got on AM as well as FM stations. Every rock radio station seemed to have stopped to play *Sgt. Pepper* through over and over again in June 1967, exploring its many textures and depths from "Lucy in the Sky with Diamonds," the song many claim was about LSD, to the ingenious proposal of "When I'm Sixty-four" to "A Day in the Life," an FM-radio instant classic. *Magical Mystery Tour* was the pinnacle of Lennon's lyrics writing, with lines like "crabalocker fishwife pornographic priestess" from "I Am the Walrus." The album *Yellow Submarine* contained the last song Lennon and McCartney really collaborated on, "Hey Bulldog."

The *White Album,* officially known as *The Beatles,* was a good barometer for the various directions in which John, Paul, George, and Ringo were heading. Paul, with his proclivity for pleasing melodies, wrote the reggae-influenced "Ob-La-Di, Ob-La-Da" and the music-hall master-piece "Honey Pie." John moved toward the abstract with his artsy and interminable "Revolution 9." George showed more than a spark of songwriting talent with "While My Guitar Gently Weeps" and "Savoy Truffle," while Ringo called out to his talented mates, "Don't Pass Me By."

Abbey Road contained some of their finest work since 1964. McCartney's "Maxwell's Silver Hammer" and Ringo's "Octopus's Garden" were snappy crowd-pleasers. "Come Together" and "Somewhere" were a two-sided number-1 smash. Paul did another tribute to Elvis with his love song "Oh! Darling," while John did a love song to Yoko, "I Want You (She's So Heavy)." And that was just side one! Side two was Paul's triumph, containing "You Never Give Me Your Money," and two medleys: "Mean Mr. Mustard" (with Lennon's "Polythene Pam") and "Golden Slumbers" — a rock tour de force.

The Beatles had become by far the most influential singing group in rock and roll, and probably the most influential artists of any single era in popular music. The Beatles seemed to have spawned a plethora of fads, giving us Beatle wigs, Beatle boots, long hair, and later mustaches and beards. Without the Beatles would the British Invasion, "Swinging London," or Carnaby Street have existed? How many people smoked marijuana, dropped LSD, or dabbled in psychedelic culture because of the Fab Four?

Not since *Rock Around the Clock* had rock movies generated such excitement and public interest as the Beatles' first film, the critically acclaimed *A Hard Day's Night.* Directed by Richard Lester, this picture brought Marx Bros.-style zaniness back to the screen, repackaged for a new generation. *Help* followed in 1965. Another Richard Lester project, the film spawned a string of hit singles and a smash album just as *Hard Day's Night* had done before. *Yellow Submarine* reflected the changing consciousness of the Beatles in 1968 in the form of a psychedelic cartoon simulating a drug "trip." Nineteen seventy gave the world *Let It Be,* the final Beatles film, which captured on celluloid the recording of the album of the same name. Would people have cared about Maharishi Mahesh Yogi, Eastern religion, sitars, Ravi Shankar, bed-ins for peace, or Yoko Ono if the Beatles hadn't? Directly or indirectly, John, Paul, George and Ringo touched almost everyone in the Western World. But what brought the Beatles to the world and made all this possible was their music. The Beatles were unquestionably the greatest rock and roll band in the world.

But the end was nearing for the Beatles after *Abbey Road.* The "Get Back" tapes, recorded before *Abbey Road,* resisted many efforts to be turned into an album. "Get Back" was recorded as an intentional rough mix without studio tricks. Unfortunately, by the time it was turned into the *Let It Be* album, Phil Spector took over the production from George Martin and tampered with Martin's previously spartan efforts. When McCartney heard how Spector had overproduced "The Long and Winding Road," he was livid. Beatle wives Yoko Ono and Linda McCartney had more influence over their husbands in matters of their careers about this time, drawing the resentment of the other Beatles. Then, amidst squabbles over management and solo projects, the Beatles separated in April 1970. They sued each other, with an army of lawyers and accountants joining in the battles. It was a sad finale for the greatest rock-and-roll band the world has ever heard. The solo careers of the four Beatles, however, comprises four additional stories.

As a teen-ager, Cher La Pierre did some backup singing for Phil Spector on a Ronettes session. There she met studio musician Sonny Bono. The rest is history. Sonny and Cher married in 1964. Their first single, as Caesar and Cleo, never made the charts, but in 1965, as Sonny and Cher, they took "I Got You Babe" to number 1 for three weeks. Dressed in bizarre fashions, they became regulars on *Where the Action Is* and struck gold with "Baby Don't Go" and "The Beat Goes On." When they found the going rough as teen idols, Sonny and Cher changed their image and aimed for an older audience with a TV variety series and songs like "All I Ever Need Is You." Cher had solo number-1 hits with "Gypsies, Tramps and Thieves" and "Half-Breed." Sonny and Cher's breakup was seen by millions on TV and Cher's marriage to Gregg Allman and fling with Gene Simmons of Kiss are legend.

1965

Astronauts were walking in space, and the country was marveling at the wonders of technology—until New York City and a large part of the Northeast corridor had a total blackout one November night. There were violent riots in the Watts district of Los Angeles, and Malcolm X was martyred in Harlem.

At times like this, escapist fare becomes a necessity, and in 1965 Americans flocked to the movies to see *The Sound of Music* (the Best Picture of 1965), *Dr. Zhivago, A Thousand Clowns, Ship of Fools,* and *Darling.* Sports fans flocked to see the Dodgers win the World Series, whipping the Minnesota Twins. The Celtics took yet another NBA title, while the Green Bay Packers beat the Cleveland Browns for the NFL title and the Buffalo Bills beat the San Diego Chargers for the AFL title.

Television was filled with comedy and fantasy, included shows like *I Dream of Jeannie, Lost in Space,* and *F Troop.* Dick Clark premiered a new afternoon show called *Where the Action Is,* which was *American Bandstand* on the beach. Featuring Paul Revere and the Raiders, Keith Allison, and Steve Alaimo, it shared with its sister-show the task of making sure America's teen-agers were learning the duck, the mouse, and the Freddie.

Rock and roll was deeply into the British sound in 1965, yet some Americans were managing to get radio airplay. Jewel Aikens' "The Birds and the Bees," Sonny and Cher's "I Got You Babe," former Dovell Len Barry's "1-2-3," and the McCoys' "Hang On Sloopy" all joined the Searchers' "Love Potion #9," Freddie and the Dreamers' "I'm Telling You Now," Tom Jones' "It's Not Unusual" and "What's New Pussycat?," and Billy Joe Royal's "Down in the Boondocks" on the U.S. charts. The top ten records of the year were "Satisfaction" by the Rolling Stones, "I Can't Help Myself" by the Four Tops, "You Were on My Mind" by the We Five, "Wooly Bully" by Sam the Sham and the Pharaohs, "You've Lost That Lovin' Feelin' " by the Righteous Brothers, "Downtown" by Petula Clark, "Help!" by the Beatles, "Crying in the Chapel" by Elvis Presley, "Can't You Hear My Heartbeat" by Herman's Hermits, and "My Girl" by the Temptations.

It was 1965—the eleventh year of rock and roll.

THE BYRDS

He was born James McGuinn in Chicago, Illinois, around the time his parents were out around the country promoting their best-selling book *Parents Can't Win.* By the time he reached his early teens, he had already taught himself to play guitar and banjo. The folksingers and musicians of the day were his inspiration. McGuinn began performing locally as Roger McGuinn. It would be the name he would make famous.

Shortly after graduation from high school McGuinn hooked up with the popular folk group the Limelighters. Within a year he was a guitarist with the Chad Mitchell Trio. (One member of that trio was a gentleman named John Denver, who would make his own mark in music one day.) His last band job before going solo on the Greenwich Village coffeehouse circuit was as lead guitarist for Bobby Darin in 1963.

In the early to mid-sixties the Village was fertile ground for young rock stars and folksingers. It was from here that Bob Dylan would emerge along with so many others. With the arrival of the Beatles, Roger began to consider the possibilities of an electric band with traditional folk-music roots. He left the Village to play the clubs and bars on the national folk circuit. Eventually he found himself playing at the Troubador, an L.A. club.

At the Troubador Roger met fellow folksingers David Crosby and Gene Clark. Crosby had a solo act that he had been doing for a few years. Gene Clark had been a guitarist with the New Christy Minstrels, the group that also spawned Barry McGuire ("The Eve of Destruction"). "McGuinn and McGuire" would also become friends and find immortality in the Mamas and the Papas' autobiographical song "Creeque Alley," which lyrically described them as "still getting higher."

But it was McGuinn, Crosby, and Clark who found that they had much in common during that summer of 1964. They agreed to form a band in order to try to realize Roger's concept of an electric "folk-rock" group. The addition of two more musicians created an amazing musical balance in the band. Chris Hillman had a country/bluegrass background. He played mandolin and bass guitar, and previously led a country group known as the Hillmen. Michael Clarke was a jazz drummer whose experience had been solely with jazz bands prior to his joining the Beefeaters, which was the name McGuinn initially gave to the Byrds.

The Byrds came to the attention of a record exec named Jim Dickson, who assisted them in their formative stages. He introduced them to Terry Melcher, Doris Day's son and A & R man for Columbia Records, and by September the Byrds had a recording contract with that label. Their first release was an electric folk-rock version of Bob Dylan's "Mr. Tambourine Man" in March 1965. The response was immediate. Within a few weeks it cracked the top ten. It has been hailed as folk-rock's first real triumph and one of the true classics of rock and roll. Dylan loved it when he heard it, and it may well have influenced him toward electric rock. That summer *The Byrds,* their debut album, turned gold faster than an alchemist could conjure.

In late 1965 the Byrds turned to another folksinger and songwriter, Pete Seeger, for the haunting "Turn, Turn, Turn." The lyrics of this number-1 song were actually a Biblical passage that Seeger set to his own original music. "Eight Miles High" followed under a cloud of controversy, for, like "Mr. Tambourine Man," it was about drugs. The Byrds ended the first chapter of their career with "Mr. Spaceman" (1966), "So You Want to Be a Rock 'n' Roll Star" (1967), and "My Back Pages" (1967).

After three albums and several hit singles, Gene Clark left the group partially because of his fear of

flying, which prevented him from touring with the others. Not long after Clark bowed out, David Crosby (who was fated for supergroup fame with Crosby, Stills, Nash and Young) and Michael Clarke left the group, citing creative differences with McGuinn and objecting to the direction the Byrds were taking. They were replaced by Gram Parsons and Kevin Kelly. The group now turned toward country rock, unleashing an L.P. entitled *Sweetheart of the Rodeo.*

But the new Byrds didn't last very long. By 1969 Chris Hillman and Gram Parsons had split to form the Flying Burrito Brothers. McGuinn wouldn't give up, however, and recruited Clarence White, Gene Parsons, and John York (later replaced by Skip Battin) into the group. These Byrds made a splash in 1969 with their *Dr. Byrds and Mr. Hyde* album and their contribution to the soundtrack of the great counter-culture movie *Easy Rider.* Their single, "Ballad of Easy Rider," netted the band an additional hit.

The seventies proved to be a miserable decade for the Byrds. Unable to repeat their earlier successes,

Three former Byrds flying together again in the eighties as McGuinn, Clark and Hillman (from left: Chris Hillman, Roger McGuinn, and Gene Clark).

the group crumbled. In 1973 McGuinn put together the *Original Byrds Reunion Album.* It attracted a lot of attention, but few raves. As a group the Byrds were never heard from again. McGuinn went solo for a few years, then regrouped with Gene Clark and Chris Hillman in 1979 for the critically acclaimed L.P. *McGuinn, Clark, and Hillman.* The album featured the hit singles "Don't You Write Her Off," "Surrender to Me," and "Stopping Traffic." Concert appearances by the trio solidified their fan support and led to a second album in January 1980.

McGuinn and his Byrds will forever be known as the catalysts of folk-rock and the first American group successfully to repel the British invasion of the U.S. charts.

167

The Temptations.

THE TEMPTATIONS

The Temptations were the crown jewels of Motown's glittering collection of soul stars in the mid-sixties. Their intricate sound with the intense vocals, adventurous harmonies, and impeccable dynamic rhythms was complemented wonderfully by their choreographed stage routines. Melvin Franklin, Otis Williams, Paul Williams, Eddie Kendricks, and David Ruffin were the pride of the Motor City. With extreme polish and finesse, these five well-dressed men, each of whom was capable of stepping in as lead singer, supplied a visual drama with each and every song they performed, mesmerizing their audiences. Over a period of twenty years with numerous personnel changes, the Temptations have remained the most durable and one of the most popular acts in the Motown stable.

The five original Temptations joined forces in Detroit, having migrated to the Motor City from the South. Mel Franklin, the booming bass, came north from Montgomery, Alabama. Paul Williams and Eddie Kendricks hailed from Birmingham, Alabama. Otis Williams was born and bred in Texarkana, Texas, while David Ruffin, the raspy baritone, moved to Detroit from Meridian, Mississippi. By the late fifties they were in Detroit singing in such groups as the Distants and the Primes.

By 1960 Franklin, Kendricks and the two Williamses had banded together as the Elgins. The group interested Berry Gordy, Jr., who signed them to his newly formed Motown organization. When David Ruffin joined the crew in the early sixties, the Elgins changed their name to the Temptations.

During the first few years at Motown, progress was slow for the Temptations. They couldn't seem to find a hit formula, and with no royalty money coming in they had to live from gig to gig. In 1964 Gordy put Smokey Robinson of the Miracles in charge as the Temptations' producer, and the hits started to come. With Smokey's "The Way You Do the Things You Do"

and Eddie Kendricks' falsetto, the Temptations made their first assault on the record charts, reaching number 11 in April 1964. Kendricks sang lead again on "Why You Wanna Make Me Blue," a number-26 record in October 1964.

When Smokey put David Ruffin's deep, full-bodied voice in the lead spot in 1965, the Temptations really began to cook. Smokey's classic love song "My Girl" gave them the number-1 record in March 1965 and introduced the Temptations to a white audience. Smokey ran the group through their paces in 1965, featuring Ruffin up front on a series of ballads and medium-tempo love songs—"It's Growing," "Since I Lost My Baby," "My Baby," and "Don't Look Back." By 1966 Smokey Robinson found himself too busy to continue charting the Temptations' career, but he bowed out as their producer with a flourish, putting Eddie Kendricks back in the lead for the up-tempo number "Get Ready."

Norman Whitfield then became the Temptations' producer. He went to work right away, replacing the ballads with a lively, raucous, more strident sound. The public welcomed the change, making "Ain't Too Proud to Beg" number 13 in July 1966. The Temptations and Whitfield worked extraordinarily well together. "Beauty's Only Skin Deep" climbed to number 3 in September. "(I Know) I'm Losing You" opened 1967 in the top ten. In September 1967 "You're My Everything" slowed their tempo, but not their sales, as David Ruffin and Eddie Kendricks shared the lead backed by a wall of violins. David Ruffin wailed "I Wish That It Would Rain" in the spring of 1968, taking the record to the top five. But big changes were in store for the Temptations in 1968.

In October of that year Motown filed a lawsuit against two New York agents, charging that they had conspired to destroy Motown's contractual relationship with David Ruffin. As a result Ruffin decided to stay with Motown, but left the Temptations for a solo career. Dennis Edwards took Ruffin's place, and producer Norman Whitfield changed the group's sound to acid-soul with "Cloud Nine." The Norman Whitfield/Barrett Strong composition, which was influenced by San Francisco's Sly and the Family Stone, was the first of a series of ghetto psychodramas—political and social statements that would change the course of soul music. In February 1969 the Temptations released "Runaway Child, Running Wild," a contrived, moralistic miniopera that answered the public's call for relevancy in the late sixties. The pulsing harmonies of "I Can't Get Next to You" then took the Temptations back to number 1 as 1969 drew to a close.

The seventies brought even more changes. Paul Williams left the group for health reasons in 1971 (and allegedly committed suicide in 1973). Eddie Kendricks reasserted himself as lead singer, and his mellow "Just My Imagination" topped the charts in April of 1971. Kendricks himself then left the group to go solo, hitting number 2 with "Keep on Truckin'" in late 1973 and number 1 with "Boogie Down" in March 1974. The Temptations proved resilient, however. Despite all the personnel shakeups, they were back on top with the sensational million seller "Papa Was a Rolling Stone" in late 1972. It won three Grammy awards that year—Best Rhythm-and-Blues Performance, Best Rhythm-and-Blues Instrumental Performance, and Best R & B Song.

The Temptations continued to record through the seventies, switching from Motown to Atlantic Records, then back to Motown in 1980. But they have yet to regain their former successful status. They were one of the top soul groups, if not *the* soul group from 1965 through 1972. Whether brilliantly interpreting Smokey Robinson tunes, spectacularly weaving sophisticated vocals with precision dance steps, or planting the musical seeds of disco with their wilder sounds of the late sixties, the Temptations demonstrated again and again a relentless capability for excellence.

JAMES BROWN

It comes as a shock to realize that the Godfather of Soul, Mr. Dynamite, The Cool Boss with The Hot Sauce, Soul Brother Number One has been around for over half a century. Born in 1928 in Pulaski, Tennessee, and brought up in Augusta, Georgia, James' was the classic rags-to-riches story. As a six-year-old shoeshine boy, he sang for nickels and quickly learned to control an audience, developing a tremendous sense of showmanship in the process. Ironically he shined shoes on the steps of radio station WDRW—a station he would later purchase.

Having overcome the trauma of three years in reform school for car theft and breaking and entering, James went on to play semipro baseball and football and even attempted professional boxing. During this period he became proficient on piano, organ, drums, and bass, and also trained his voice in various Baptist church groups and choirs. In the mid-fifties, after his athletic hopes were ended by a leg injury, he formed the Swanees, the Gospel group which later became his Famous Flames. They cut a demo that found its way to Syd Nathan, president of King Records in Ohio, who signed them to his subsidiary label, Federal Records. The group recorded James' composition "Please, Please, Please" at the studios of WDRW in Augusta in 1956, and the Federal release became the first of over twenty James Brown singles to sell over a million copies.

An emotional, preaching vocal style, a basic instrumental track, and choppy rhythm formed the sound that would sell an estimated fifty million records for Brown by 1971. In 1958 James scored with his biggest national hit up to that time, his own "Try Me (I Need You)." But it was his live shows that were the main event. James gyrated his way through each

James Brown in the fifties. *(Courtesy of Dick Clark)*

171

performance, creating buckets of sweat, contorted expressions of pain and torment, and whirling, leaping acrobatics on stage, culminating in a series of collapses and miraculous revival encores, which became James' trademark. This almost religious ritual, all planned by James down to the last drop of sweat, convinced audiences that they had just seen the eighth wonder of the world.

Despite his successes Brown was fighting an uphill battle for stylistic and creative control in 1962. A live recording of one of his Apollo Theater shows received an incredible response from the rhythm-and-blues market, convincing James that King Records didn't have the national clout or the artistic boldness to realize his potential. Ignoring his contract, he released "Out of Sight" on Smash Records, a subsidiary of Mercury, in 1964. This funky dance tune didn't impress record buyers the way James had hoped. Then a complicated legal battle with King resulted in his forced return to the label, but at least he had musical control now. In an effort to get more exposure on white pop stations, James expanded his audience in 1965. "Papa's Got a Brand New Bag," which was written by James, sold over two million copies internationally and received a Grammy for best rhythm-and-blues record of the year. "I Got You (I Feel Good)," also composed by James, went gold that same year.

After three hundred personal appearances in three hundred cities in 1964 and 1965, James returned to the recording studio. In 1967 he released the number-1 soul record of the year, "Cold Sweat."

His 1968 record, "Say It Loud—I'm Black and I'm Proud," established his role as a spokesman for many black Americans, a role that was enhanced by his legendary TV appearances in Boston and Washington on the nights following the murder of Martin Luther King, Jr. Stemming some of the mayhem and looting that followed King's death with his multihour performances, Brown won the gratitude of no less a power than LBJ.

As his career grew, so did Brown's musical empire. He hired all his musicians and assistants himself and controlled his own financial investments, buying a record production company, a music publishing company, and two radio stations. In 1971 Brown's first hit on his new label, People, was "Hot Pants." In the summer of 1972 "Good Foot" sold a million copies. His 1974 Polydor release, "The Payback," was his first disco-oriented release to go gold.

James Brown's flamboyant presence, "badass" vocals, and energetic stage manner have been imitated by many rock singers. However, the man who reportedly owns five hundred suits, three hundred pairs of shoes, and six luxurious cars was also the man who wrote "Don't Be a Drop-out" to encourage high school attendance after a tour of a San Francisco ghetto. He was the first black man to win *Cash Box* magazine's Best Male Vocalist Award. In the winter of 1979 that same man was in New York's Times Square, leading prayers and songs in support of the U.S. citizens held hostage in Iran. Without a doubt, James Brown remains Soul Brother Number One.

BOB DYLAN

By 1964 Bob Dylan had three folk albums under his belt. He was the troubadour of the folk-music world—the self-proclaimed heir to Woody Guthrie. But in April of that year, while driving across Colorado, Dylan was stunned by the fact that almost every song on his car radio was a Beatles song. The hero of folk decided that he was ready for a change.

Dylan's early songs expressed what he felt, reflecting the attitudes of awakening political activism in the early sixties. Songs like "Blowin' in the Wind," "The Lonesome Death of Hattie Carroll," and "Only a Pawn in Their Game" expressed the concerns of the civil rights movement. "A Hard Rain's Gonna Fall," "Masters of War," and "With God on Our Side" dealt with the insanity of the arms race and the threat of nuclear war. His most prophetic song, "The Times They Are A-Changin'," predicted the tumultuous social and political upheaval that would shake America in the late sixties. No one could express the new attitudes and ideas of the early sixties nearly as well as Bob Dylan.

But in 1964 Dylan was not quite ready for rock, so he filed his impressions of the Beatles away for future reference. However, he was ready to abandon social protest songs. In the summer of 1964 he recorded his fourth album, *Another Side of Bob Dylan,* and in the song "My Back Pages" he burst the idealistic bubble of his committed followers, telling them that it was ludicrous to think they could change the injustices of the world. Dylan was more honest with himself, admitting that he had acted hyprocritically in the past. He had new thoughts, new ideas of a more personal but also more complicated nature, and he needed a new sound to express them.

In early 1965 the Byrds recorded Dylan's "Mr. Tambourine Man" and "All I Really Want to Do" to a rock beat with electronic instruments. Dylan thought it was "wild!" He realized that his songs would work as rock and immediately began to work on his first rock album *Bringing It All Back Home.* Dylan seemed to be heading off in a new direction, but in fact he was returning to his roots, for before he knew anything about Woody Guthrie and the Greenwich Village folk scene, Bob Dylan had wanted to be a rock-and-roll star.

Robert Allen Zimmerman was graduated from high school in June 1959, and under his picture in the yearbook it said his goal in life was "to join Little Richard." Bob, who was to change his name from Zimmerman to Dylan in tribute to poet Dylan Thomas in 1961, grew up in the staid mining town of Hibbing, Minnesota. The only thing that ever changed in Hibbing during the 1950s was the landscape as it was ravaged by the mining companies. Attitudes and life-styles were old-fashioned and stagnant. But even

Hibbing was touched by the beginnings of rock and roll, and Dylan picked up on it.

Dylan's first idol was country-and-western star Hank Williams, but Bob was soon into rhythm and blues, listening to a black radio station that played Muddy Waters and B. B. King. Then Elvis Presley, Bill Haley, and Buddy Holly came onto the scene, and Dylan became infatuated with these early rock and rollers, especially Little Richard. Dylan formed his own rock band and banged out Little Richard tunes at his hometown high school dances, driving the Hibbing, Minnesota, kids wild. Robert Allen Zimmerman (a.k.a. Dylan) really always wanted to be a rock star. So when he plugged in his electric guitar in 1965 and unleashed the wrath of his diehard folk fans, he was really taking a step back—bringing it all back home.

Dylan now used rock to express the complex array of feelings that were swirling around inside him. His lyrics had changed. They were now more imaginative, at times surrealistic and absurd. But his message always remained clear. "You don't need a weatherman to know which way the wind blows." His music reflected a new sensibility and a new consciousness. Dylan became the guru for the growing counterculture.

Dylan caused an upheaval in rock and roll as well. As he had been affected by rock groups like the Beatles, the Byrds, and the Rolling Stones, these groups in turn responded to Dylan and the lyrical content of their songs began to expand. Dylan sat down with John Lennon and convinced him that rock could be more than teen-age love songs and vacuous moon-June-spoon rhymes. With Dylan pointing the way, rock music began to grow and evolve into something more than just pleasant pop tunes with a beat.

Dylan's pinnacle as a rock and roller was the album *Highway 61 Revisited* in August 1965. This album contained some of his finest work—"Desolation Row," "Just Like Tom Thumb Blues," "Ballad of a Thin Man," "Highway 61"—all expressing his message with the driving force of rock. The highlight of the album, "Like a Rolling Stone," captured the loneliness and alienation that was settling in on the rock generation in the sixties. Dylan asked hard questions that shook a generation. How does it feel when you have no religion and no one to look up to? How does it feel to have no purpose? How does it feel to be like a rolling stone?

In need of a backup group, Dylan signed a Canadian band in 1966 which he'd found playing bars in Somers Point, New Jersey—Levon and the Hawks. Levon Helm, Garth Hudson, Rick Danko, Richard Manuel, and Robbie Robertson changed their band

name to The Band when they toured with Dylan. On their own, they went on to become one of the most respected ensembles in rock.

Dylan recorded one more rock album, *Blonde on Blonde,* in 1966 before breaking his neck in a motorcycle accident in the summer of that year. He remained in seclusion in Woodstock, New York, for months, recovering from both the accident and his drug-filled life-style. By this time Dylan had become more than just a rock star to his fans. To many he was a messiah. With this kind of unwanted pressure, Dylan knew he needed an escape.

Dylan has a unique ability, if not a deep need, to change directions, and by 1968 the times were a-changing again for Mr. Zimmerman. Nineteen sixty-eight was one of the most tumultuous years in American history. Now Dylan got out of rock to develop a new sound and a new outlook on life. He

Dylan on stage with Van Morrison (left) and The Band's Robbie Robertson (right).

recorded *John Wesley Harding* in January 1968, an album which contained highly symbolic and religious songs set to a simple country beat. *Nashville Skyline* in 1969 was even more country-oriented, featuring a duet with Johnny Cash and a song he had originally written for the movie *Midnight Cowboy,* "Lay, Lady, Lay."

Following a separation from his wife, Sara, in 1974, Dylan's outlook changed again in *Blood on the Tracks,* his best album since *Blonde on Blonde. Blood on the Tracks* is an album of deep personal pain and discontent. Dylan's attempt to ease his pain allowed him to go back to his former protest

175

sensibilities and record a bitter tirade against the American judicial system, "Hurricane," a song about convicted murderer and ex-boxing champ Ruben "Hurricane" Carter. The soundness of his conscience was questioned, however, when he recorded a ballad on his 1975 *Desire* album that defended gangster Joey Gallo. He then went on the road with his circuslike Rolling Thunder Revue.

Street Legal was Dylan's somewhat disappointing offering of 1978, but the song "Changing of the Guard" hinted at yet another transformation. It was rumored at the time that Dylan was taking Bible study classes and converting to Christianity from Judaism. In the summer of 1979 *Slow Train Coming* reflected his apparent born-again Christian sensibilities. He took his gospel message on the road in late 1979, and as he had done at the 1965 Newport Folk Festival, Dylan shocked and offended many of his followers. But the importance of *Slow Train Coming* is the element of change. When Dylan switched from folk to rock, the world of folk cried "blasphemy!" When Dylan abandoned rock for country in 1968, the rock world was aghast.

One of Dylan's strengths has always been his ability to grow as a human being, a poet and a musician. His change in *Slow Train Coming* may not be the right one, but change is what Dylan brought to rock, and the ability to change and grow is the essence of Bob Dylan.

HERMAN'S HERMITS

It seems too easy to denigrate the musical accomplishments of Herman's Hermits, the perky pop band from Manchester that came to the United States on the second wave of the British Invasion in the mid-sixties. They were snubbed at the time by many of the so-called "serious" musicians in England and later by many musical historians, who found their records trivial at best. However, they did manage to sell over seventeen million records in the three years between 1964 and 1967. And in 1965 they outsold everyone, including the Beatles.

The story of Herman's Hermits centers around Peter Noone, the adorable lead singer and decision maker of the band. Peter was born in Manchester and educated at St. Bedde's College. His father, a musician, was responsible for his son's enrollment in singing and acting classes at the Manchester School of Music. Peter appeared in several plays and on British television before joining his first band, the Cyclones. Formed in 1961 with just one amplifier, the band evolved into Peter Novak and the Heartbeats. Peter received only eight dollars a night as the lead singer of the group in 1962. With their increased following, they decided it was time for a name change and a record contract. Some people thought Peter looked like Sherman of the TV cartoon "Mr. Peabody," and Pete's nickname eventually became Herman. It was then decided that "Hermits" went well with "Herman," and the new name was found. The record contract, however, did not come as easily. Week after week the group was turned down at each new audition. Then, in 1964, they flew in an independent record producer named Mickie Most to see one of their Manchester gigs. Mickie, who had been the force behind the Animals and who would go on to produce Donovan, Lulu, and many others, agreed to check them out. After all, the trip was free! What Most didn't know was that the group had arranged to have all their friends and fans show up

and go crazy with staged enthusiasm. Despite the ploy, Mickie said he liked Peter but felt the band was weak. Peter fired two members of the band and brought in Derek Leckenby and Barry Whitham to join Karl Greene and Keith Hopwood. This edition of Herman's Hermits would soon have young girls shrieking for them with genuine adoration. Recording with Most, they released "I'm Into Something Good" on the MGM label in October of 1964. Selected by Most and written by Carole King and Gerry Goffin, this song hit the top of the charts in England and stayed there for three weeks, selling over a million copies internationally.

In 1965 Herman's Hermits had a year that most groups would have sold their souls for. In January they released "Can't You Hear My Heartbeat," which went gold in the U.S. by May. Before they left to go on their first U.S. tour, the Hermits recorded "Silhouettes," a 1957 hit for the Rays written by Bob Crewe and Frank Slay, Jr. There were advance orders for four hundred thousand copies in the U.S. alone. In April they released "Mrs. Brown, You've Got a Lovely Daughter," a song that was originally written in 1963 for a British TV play. Initially it was just another cut on their first L.P., *Introducing Herman's Hermits,* but it received so much radio airplay that MGM released it as an American single. Advance sales surpassed six hundred thousand and went over the million mark while the group was on its first U.S. tour. The record was number 1 for four weeks, entering the charts at number 12. Within just three months Herman's Hermits had received five gold-disc awards for their first four singles and their first album. In May 1965, they struck gold again with "Wonderful World," which was credited to a "Barbara Campbell," but was actually written in 1959 by Sam Cooke, Lou Adler and Herb Alpert.

"I'm Henry the Eighth, I Am" was first made famous by a Cockney comedian in 1911. Herman's

Hermits put their version on their second L.P., *Herman's Hermits on Tour.* Again, constant radio airplay forced its release as a single, resulting in six hundred thousand orders in two days. This July release went gold, as did their September 1965 hit "Just a Little Bit Better." Later that year *The Best of Herman's Hermits* made the album charts and stayed there for an amazing 105 weeks.

The band toured from Tahiti to Cambodia. They were one of the first Western rock groups to play Japan. As was characteristic of most concerts by the British groups, almost everywhere Herman's Hermits went their fans squealed so loudly the music couldn't be heard. The Hermits were part of Dick Clark's traveling Caravan of Stars and appeared on his TV show *Where the Action Is,* as well as *The Ed Sullivan Show, The Danny Kaye Show,* and *The Dean Martin Show.* They appeared in a film called *When the Boys Meet the Girls,* which yielded their February 1966 million seller, "Listen People." February 1967 brought them their fifteenth big hit, "There's a Kind of Hush," whose flip side, "No Milk Today," also received widespread airplay.

Peter Noone (on far left) with *Herman's Hermits. (Courtesy of Dick Clark)*

By the late sixties more progressive, underground groups drove Herman's Hermits to the edge of the musical scene. A legal battle for royalties dissolved the band in the early 1970s.

Years later a Hermanless version of the Hermits surfaced but sank quickly. Peter went on as a solo singer after the breakup, then did some acting on English TV. Transplanted to California, Noone formed a new-wave band of his own in 1980, playing clubs and bars in an effort to recapture some of the musical excitement he had experienced in the early days of Herman's Hermits. Into the eighties, Noone and the group found limited success. But he was a survivor, while most other sixties' successes simply faded into obscurity.

The Sound of 1965

THE ROLLING STONES

The train was speeding toward London. It was 1960 and a boy named Mick Jagger was on his way to his studies at the London School of Economics. One of the other passengers looked very familiar to him. It was an old childhood friend from Dartford, Keith Richards. As they got reacquainted, they discovered they were both into American rhythm and blues and rock artists like Chuck Berry and Little Richard. Their friendship was renewed and they agreed to keep in touch.

Late in 1961 Mick and Keith met Brian Jones at a pub. Mick had been actively pursuing a career in music as a vocalist with Alexis Korner's Blues Incorporated. But Brian had actually studied music and could do something the other two couldn't—read music. Impressed by Brian's knowledge and talents, Mick and Keith agreed to form a band under his leadership. Hardly an overnight success, they were living in one room in 1962, hocking their furniture for grocery money.

Finally, through Mick's previous connection with Alexis Korner, the three began sitting in for his Blues Incorporated on their nights off. One night when Mick, Keith, and Brian were playing at a local club called the Marquee, they asked Korner's drummer, Charlie Watts, to sit in for their regular drummer, Tony Chapman. There was a chemical reaction among the four, and Watts was eventually persuaded to join their group. With the addition of Ian Stewart (who was a regular only briefly) and bassist Bill Wyman, later in 1962, and the selection of a name taken from an old Muddy Waters tune, "Rolling Stone Blues," they were officially in business. The Rolling Stones' first gig at a club called Crawdaddy, perhaps the premier British club of the day, drew an incredible amount of attention. They soon had a management contract with Andrew Loog Oldham, a former publicist for the Beatles' hit "Please Please Me," which led them to a Decca recording contract and their first top-twenty single, Lennon and McCartney's "I Wanna Be Your Man," in December 1963.

The Rolling Stones then took to the road, touring England as the opening act for the Everly Brothers, Little Richard, and Bo Diddley. In June 1964 and again in 1965 the Stones joined the British invasion of America with U.S. tours. For their first tour their only U.S. release had been their version of Buddy Holly's "Not Fade Away" (May 1964). But they followed this with a line of hits: "Tell Me" (July 1964), "It's All Over Now" (July 1964), "Time Is on My Side" (October 1964), "Heart of Stone"

The Rolling Stones at El Macombo.

(January 1965), "The Last Time" (March 1965), and "Play with Fire" (May 1965). By the time of their 1965 tour they had gained a reputation for being vulgar, raunchy, and sensual. Parents who had been shocked by the Beatles were absolutely repelled by the Rolling Stones. While the Beatles only wanted to hold their daughters' hands, the Stones seemed to want to do considerably more. The defiant teaser was Mick Jagger, whose raw vocals, grimaces, and suggestive body movements stoked the fires of frenzied audiences.

The Jagger and Richards rock classic "Satisfaction" then rocked the world off its feet. It hit number 1 in the U.S. in July 1965 and stayed there for six weeks. Banned by many radio stations, "Satisfaction" was scorned by some for its blatantly sexual lyrics as it sold four and one half million copies within the year. Not ones to lie back on their laurels, they followed with "Get Off of My Cloud" (October 1965) and "As Tears Go By" (December 1965), which Mick had let his girl friend Marianne Faithfull record the year before.

While their singles were hitting, so were their albums. One after another, they turned gold. At about this time wild stories of their sex practices and drug habits were spreading. Still, their record sales were unaffected. From 1966 through 1967, "19th Nervous Breakdown," "Paint It Black," "Mother's Little Helper," "Lady Jane," "Ruby Tuesday," "Let's Spend the Night Together," "Dandelion," "We Love You," and "She's a Rainbow" all hit for them. Few groups could ever match the Stones' rate of success.

In the 1950s and 1960s a spot on *The Ed Sullivan Show* was the true mark of rock-and-roll superstar status. The most famous acts hired by Ed "for all the youngsters in the audience" were the Beatles and Elvis Presley. But Sullivan was conservative, and he made it known that he would censor the raunchier, more raucous parts of an act. With Elvis he ordered the cameras to remain north of the famous grinding pelvis. With the Stones he ordered that Mick Jagger sing "Let's Spend *Some Time* Together," instead of the original lyric "Let's Spend the Night Together." The Stones begrudgingly complied, but when Ed asked them back for a second appearance and requested that they wear matching suits for a cleaner look the group was ready for revenge. They showed up for the show in rented Nazi uniforms. Sullivan threw a fit. The group had to change for the actual telecast, but they had made their point.

As the Rolling Stones moved into the psychedelic era of the late sixties, their highs were mingled with a series of lows. True, their December 1967 album *Their Satanic Majesties Request* did sell two million copies just ten days after its American release date, and their 1968 singles "Jumpin' Jack Flash" and "Street Fighting Man" did dart up the charts. But Brian Jones had to be hospitalized twice for nervous exhaustion, and a struggle for the leadership of the group ensued. Amid personal jealousies, a major fight between Keith and Brian over Anita Pallenberg, and numerous creative conflicts, the group was no longer Brian Jones' band. After three drug busts with the group and the stifling effects of his growing drug dependence, Brian quit on June 9, 1969, citing musical differences with the others as his official reason. Then on July 3, Brian

Mick Jagger with Julian H. Miller II of *Prom Magazine* in St. Louis, July 1966. *(Courtesy of Julian H. Miller II)*

Jones was found dead in his swimming pool, officially recorded as a drug-related death.

Mick Taylor, a young guitarist from John Mayall's Blues Breakers, replaced Brian and made his debut as a Stone on their first single in a year, "Honky Tonk Women." The record quickly hit number 1 during the summer of 1969. By November they had added a gold L.P. to their list of triumphs, *Let It Bleed,* a title that proved to be an omen for the group. Shortly after *Let It Bleed* was released, the Stones gave a free concert at California's Altamont Speedway.

A nightmarish murder occurred in front of the stage while the group did "Sympathy for the Devil." The crime was on celluloid in the feature film *Gimme Shelter.*

Mick Taylor left the group in December 1974 and was eventually replaced by Ron Wood, formerly of the Faces.

For a year and a half after Altamont the Rolling Stones lay low. Finally, in May 1971, they returned with "Brown Sugar," a number-1 single, *Sticky Fingers,* a new gold album, and their own Rolling Stones record label. During the remainder of the seventies the Stones continued to be hot. SRO concerts followed gold albums and chart-busting singles. Their list of seventies work includes the albums *Exile on Main Street* (1972), *Goat's Head Soup* (1973), *It's Only Rock and Roll* (1974), *Made in the Shade* (1975), *Black and Blue* (1976), *Some Girls* (1978), and *Emotional Rescue* (1980); and hit singles like "Angie" (1973), "Ain't Too Proud to Beg" (1974), "It's Only Rock and Roll" (1974), "Miss You" (1978), "Shattered" (1978), and "Emotional Rescue" (1980).

The Stones' supposed escapades with Canada's Margaret Trudeau, Mick's split with his wife, Bianca, the group's legal brawl with manager Allen Klein, and Keith Richards' drug bust in 1977 kept them in the headlines. Yet as the eighties unfold, this troubled yet brilliant musical corporation rolls on and on, gathering no moss but plenty of gold records and notoriety.

1966

The Vietnam War began to escalate with the U.S. bombing of the demilitarized zone between North and South Vietnam. The first strains of public protest were softly heard on college campuses in the "radical" Northeast and California. Yet the war was still a "popular" one with the vast majority of Americans, as evidenced by Staff Sergeant Barry Sadler's song "The Ballad of the Green Berets," the number-1 song of the year.

The rest of the top ten shunned politics and demonstrated the variety of rock-and-roll sounds: "Monday, Monday" by the Mamas and the Papas, "Soul and Inspiration" by the Righteous Brothers, "Reach Out, I'll Be There" by the Four Tops, "You Can't Hurry Love" by the Supremes, "96 Tears" by ? and the Mysterians, "Cherish" by the Association, "Last Train to Clarksville" by the Monkees, "Poor Side of Town" by Johnny Rivers, and "California Dreamin'" by the Mamas and the Papas. Other top hits of the

(Courtesy of Dick Clark)

year included the off-beat throwback to the roaring twenties, "Winchester Cathedral," by the New Vaudeville Band; the mournful, soulful "When a Man Loves a Woman" by Percy Sledge; "My Love" by Petula Clark; the fashion-inspired "These Boots Are Made for Walkin'" by Nancy Sinatra; the very danceable "Devil with a Blue Dress On" by Mitch Ryder and the Detroit Wheels; the comical Peanuts-inspired tune "Snoopy vs. the Red Baron" by the Royal Guardsmen; "Kicks" by Paul Revere and the Raiders; "Five O'Clock World" by the Vogues; "Wild Thing" by the Troggs; "See You in September" by the Happenings; "Walk Away Renee" by the Left Banke; and "Bus Stop" by the Hollies.

Nineteen sixty-six was surely a year of excitement and earth-shaking news events. Russia and America made their first soft landings on the moon. Fourteen people died at the University of Texas when a crazed sniper shot forty-four people. At the first Super Bowl, the Green Bay Packers defeated the Kansas City Chiefs. The Baltimore Orioles took the Los Angeles Dodgers in the World Series. The NBA championship once again went to the Boston Celtics. *A Man for All Seasons* was named Best Picture of the Year over *Alfie; The Russians Are Coming, The Russians Are Coming; The Sand Pebbles;* and *Who's Afraid of Virginia Woolf?* The country went Bat-crazy with a fad spawned by the *Batman* TV series, similar to the Davy Crockett craze some eleven years earlier. Along with the caped crusader, television offered *Star Trek, The Monkees, Mission: Impossible,* and the soap opera *Dark Shadows,* featuring the friendly neighborhood vampire, Barnabas Collins.

It was 1966—the twelfth year of rock and roll.

FOLK-ROCK

"The brightest new sounds heard through all the racket of rock and roll...Despite the surprising fact that every chord is in tune and every lyric in good taste, *The Kingston Trio at Large* is now the best-selling L.P. in the country."
—*Life* magazine, August 3, 1959.

The pop music establishment was up in arms over rock and roll. It wasn't a question of musical taste or morality, it was a matter of money. ASCAP, Tin Pan Alley's songwriters' protection society, felt its monopolistic grip on American music threatened. ASCAP refused to recognize rock-and-roll songs or songwriters. This triggered the emergence of ASCAP's powerful rival, Broadcast Music, Inc. (BMI), which warmly embraced the music and its authors. The music establishment hoped that rock and roll was just a passing fad, and they were eagerly on the lookout for any new fad to replace it. So when a clean-cut group called the Kingston Trio had a hit in 1958 with a resurrected folk tune, "Tom Dooley," those who had prayed for the demise of rock and roll jumped on the folk bandwagon head first.

"Tom Dooley," with its clean, crisp singing and strumming guitar, was one of the biggest records of 1958. At a time when gold records were very rare, "Tom Dooley" went gold, hitting number 1 in November 1958 and staying on the charts for nearly five months. This traditional American folk ballad from 1868 was about a Civil War veteran, Tom Dula, who was hanged for the murder of his cheating sweetheart, Laura Foster. "Tom Dooley" not only introduced the Kingston Trio, it ushered in the folk-music revival of the late fifties.

The Kingston Trio—Dave Guard, Bob Shane, and Nick Reynolds—started out singing folk music for free beers at Stanford University in 1957. With their button-down shirts and close-cropped hair, the Trio captured the collegiate image of the fifties. They wanted a name for the group that would sound both Ivy League and calypso. They decided on "Kingston."

The Kingston Trio felt that rock and roll was for high school teens, while folk music belonged to young adults seriously pursuing higher education. Their view may have been narrow and elitist, but it did make them a lot of money.

The trio made their professional debut in 1957 at the Purple Onion in San Francisco for the princely sum of sixty dollars a week each. In 1959, however, they spent a total of 278 days on the road, making considerably more than sixty dollars a week. The Kingston Trio was also one of the first groups to sell a lot of albums. The "long-playing" phonograph record was introduced in 1948, but it wasn't until 1958 with the introduction of stereo that most people would even consider buying a record player that could play albums. By July 1960 the Kingston Trio accounted for twelve percent of all of Capitol Records' album sales.

In 1959 the Kingston Trio followed the success of "Tom Dooley" with "M.T.A.," a novelty song about a fellow doomed to ride the Boston subways forever because he didn't have a nickel for the transfer. In July 1959 the Trio took "A Worried Man" all the way to the top twenty. With their easy-listening ballads, these urban folksingers gave folk music a patina of seriousness. Each song had a story to tell and a message. In time, folk's message would take on a more sociopolitical dimension. Joan Baez, Bob Dylan, Judy Collins, and Peter, Paul and Mary were all influenced by the Kingston Trio, but they came to believe that music should be used to change the world. The Kingston Trio were tagged crude commercialists for their lack of relevancy by many later humorless folkies. Few rock critics of the sixties

The Kingston Trio at San Francisco's Hungry i. *(Courtesy of Dick Clark)*

recognized them as a group whose main purpose was to entertain, not to preach, and who opened the college campuses to the folk revival that would set the stage for the turbulence of the late sixties. Dave Guard, sympathetic to the value of authentic folk music, was stung by the charges and left the group in 1961.

Dave's place was taken by John Stewart, a singer from San Diego who had written a couple of tunes for the Trio. The Kingston Trio recorded a classic antiwar folk tune, "Where Have All the Flowers Gone?" in the spring of 1962, followed by "Scotch and Soda" and "Greenback Dollar" in 1963. By 1964 there were already younger, hipper, and more political folksingers on the horizon. The Kingston Trio's time had just about passed.

Peter, Paul and Mary grabbed the Kingston Trio's mantle as the most popular folksingers in 1962 with their top-ten version of Pete Seeger's "If I Had a Hammer." Peter Yarrow, Paul Stookey, and Mary Travers helped to bring Bob Dylan's music to public attention when they took his "Blowin' in the Wind" to number 2 in the summer of 1963 and climbed to number 9 with his "Don't Think Twice (It's All Right)" in October 1963. The trio had formed in 1961 and played all the Greenwich Village hotspots. It was there they were discovered by Albert Grossman, the man who was managing young Bob Dylan. Peter, Paul and Mary went on to international fame with pure folk and folk-protest songs that included such material as Woody Guthrie's "This Land Is Your Land," "Lemon Tree," "Go Tell It On the Mountain," and John Denver's "Leaving on a Jet Plane." Their biggest hit was "Puff the Magic Dragon," a children's fantasy song, erroneously rumored to have been written about a certain hallucinogenic drug.

The success of Peter, Paul and Mary's "If I had a Hammer" in 1962 did for Pete Seeger what their "Blowin' in the Wind" did later for Bob Dylan. Seeger, who more than any other composer/performer deserves the title of "Father of Folk-Protest Music," began his career in the late 1940s as a lead singer for the Weavers. For the group he wrote such tunes as "Goodnight Irene" and "Kisses Sweeter than Wine." But his folk-protest status emerged with two songs that are already legendary in the field—"Where Have All the Flowers Gone?" and "We Shall Overcome," the latter of which would be adopted as the theme song of the black civil rights movement of the 1960s.

One of Seeger's earliest comrades in music was Phil Ochs, who rose out of the East Village folk scene in the early sixties with a highly political antiwar attitude. Ochs' classic contribution to the genre was the antiestablishment "I Ain't Marching Anymore." Ochs' success in the sixties faded in the seventies as activism gave way to apathy. He tried changing his approach by dressing in a gold lamé suit for a Carnegie Hall concert and by playing Buddy Holly's and Elvis' music. But the crowd didn't buy it and booed him offstage. In 1976 Phil Ochs committed suicide.

By the mid- to late 1960s folk-rock and the protest song were at their peak. The nation, the college campuses, the concert-goers, and the record-buying public were into the music and its performers. Joan Baez had popularized Pete Seeger's "We Shall Overcome" in the Freedom March of 1963 in Washington, D.C. She rose from outside agitator in Berkeley in 1964 to the queen of folk-rock. One of her contributions to rock-and-roll history was her public introduction of Bob Dylan at her concerts. She

Peter, Paul and Mary.

Joan Baez.

exposed him to massive audiences and the rest is history.

Buffy Sainte-Marie was another early folk-rocker whose song "The Universal Soldier" became a classic protest song with commercialized versions recorded by Donovan and Glen Campbell.

Judy Collins became the most enduring, most popular of all female folk-rock singers, to this day drawing crowds to her concerts and releasing strong-selling albums. Collins, the "Judy" of the Crosby, Stills and Nash tune, "Suite: Judy Blue Eyes," recorded the protest songs of Bob Dylan, Phil Ochs, and Tom Paxton, and brought well-deserved recognition to composers/performers of folk-rock such as Joni Mitchell, Leonard Cohen, and even Randy Newman. Judy's version of Joni Mitchell's "Both Sides Now" proved to be one of the biggest non-Dylan folk-rock hits of the era. Mitchell went on to an enormously popular career in her own right, yet still wrote songs for others, including "Willy" and "Woodstock" for Crosby, Stills, Nash and Young.

Women composers of the folk-rock era provided the core of material and overall achieved much more far-reaching success than the male songwriters, Dylan aside. Janis Ian's 1967 hit, "Society's Child," was written and recorded by her at the age of fifteen. It dealt with the social acceptance and problems of interracial love. Laura Nyro debuted at the 1967 Monterey Pop Festival and went on to gain fame as the songwriter of "Stoned Soul Picnic," "Sweet Blindness," "Wedding Bell Blues," "Eli's Coming," "Stoney End," and "And When I Die." Eventually she got back to performing her own material in concert.

Judy Collins. (Francesco Scavullo)

Tim Hardin, Tom Paxton, Arlo Guthrie, and Leonard Cohen represented some of the best music from the male songwriters/performers of folk-rock. Hardin gained recognition at the 1966 Newport Folk Festival and composed the smash "If I Were a Carpenter" which would become a hit for both Bobby Darin and the Four Tops. He died unexpectedly in January 1981. Tom Paxton's moment in the sun came with a critically acclaimed performance at the 1969 Isle of Wight Festival, but his career was rooted in the Village of the mid-sixties with Dylan. Paxton's work was filled with heavy folk protest as well as ballads and some satiric songs. Arlo Guthrie, on the other hand, was far more commercial. The son of the famed folksinger Woody Guthrie (whose life was immortalized on celluloid in United Artists' *Bound for Glory,* which was nominated for an Academy Award as Best Picture of 1976) was heralded for his folksong story of "Alice's Restaurant," which also became a major motion picture and starred Arlo in the lead. "Alice's Restaurant" was Arlo's own story of a crazy string of events that happened to him in the mid-sixties, including his bout with his friendly neighborhood draft board. Drawing attention at the 1967 Newport Folk Festival and peaking at Woodstock, Arlo complemented his "Alice's Restaurant" success with hit versions of "Comin' Into Los Angeles," "The Motorcycle Song," and Steve Goodman's "The City of New Orleans." For Canadian-born Leonard Cohen, his

Joni Mitchell takes the stage.

song "Suzanne," which was recorded by Judy Collins, brought him the career boost that would propel him all the way into the 1980s as a consistent, respected folk-rock artist.

Besides all the antiestablishment, antiwar folk music which caused the resurgence of this musical form, there also appeared a backlash folk movement that represented the establishment's retort to those who were "subverting" it.

By 1965 the Vietnam War was still a "popular" war. The minority viewpoint, however, was often expressed in the lyrics and music of folk-rock, and protest songs were making new inroads onto the singles and album charts. Peter, Paul and Mary and Bob Dylan led the new wave of singer/songwriters whose thought-provoking, controversial songs rallied a generation of young activists. Perhaps the biggest hit was "The Eve of Destruction" by the former lead singer of the New Christy Minstrels, Barry McGuire. Banned by many radio stations for being un-

Leonard Cohen.

189

American and reviled by conservatives throughout the country, the song prompted a right-wing response from the Spokesmen in a song cleverly called "The Dawn of Correction" and from Staff Sergeant Barry Sadler of the Green Berets, America's supersquad of the Vietnam War.

Back in 1962 Sadler had played in a local New Mexico rock-and-roll band. The jungles of Vietnam, however, were not conducive to a musical career. After falling into a Vietcong trap and lancing his leg on a poisoned spear, Sadler was sent back home. While recuperating, he wrote a song about the war and approached a music publisher with it. The publisher liked the tune and brought in a friend to rewrite some of the lyrics. That friend was Robin Moore, whose blockbuster novel *The Green Berets* was the book of the year. The new Sadler-Moore alliance also resulted in Sadler's posing for the Green Beret photo on the cover of the paperback version of Moore's novel. Before long they not only had the book of the year, they had the number-1 song of the year as well. Then the John Wayne motion-picture adaptation of the book utilized "The Ballad of the Green Berets" as the theme song. It was a reflection of hardline America. "Ballad of the Green Berets" buried "The Eve of Destruction" at the time. But in just a few more years rock and roll would become an integral part of the antiwar movement, and right-wing songs like Shelby Singleton's "The Battle Hymn of Lt. Calley" and Merle Haggard's "Okie from Muskogee" (both of which were really country-styled) would be few and far between.

Over the years there have been countless singers and groups who touched on folk-rock: Gordon Lightfoot ("Early Morning Rain," "If You Could Read My Mind," "The Wreck of the Edmund Fitzgerald"); Harry Chapin ("The Cat's in the Cradle"); Country Joe and the Fish ("Fixin' to Die Rag," "Fish Cheer"); John Sebastian; the Byrds; John Denver; the Beatles ("Revolution"); John Lennon ("Give Peace a Chance"); Crosby, Stills, Nash and Young ("Ohio," "Almost Cut My Hair," "Long Time Gone"); Earth Opera ("American Eagle Tragedy"); Creedence Clearwater Revival ("Fortunate Son"); the Temptations ("Ball of Confusion"); the Jefferson Airplane; the Mothers of Invention; and the Rolling Stones. By the end of the sixties the social consciousness spawned by folk-rock had become an important fixture in the world of rock.

Harry Chapin, whose story songs included the hits "Taxi," "W.O.L.D.," and "Cat's in the Cradle." *(Jeffrey Mayer)*

Raspy-voiced Rod McKuen, who started out as a rock and roller in the movie *Rock, Pretty Baby* in 1957 and damaged his vocal cords in 1962 doing one-night stands to promote his twist single "Oliver Twist."

Richie Havens, the angry folksinger from Brooklyn, was a regular at the Fillmores East and West in the late sixties and was one of the featured performers at Woodstock. Havens' best-known songs include "Freedom," "Handsome Johnny," Dylan's "Just Like a Woman," and George Harrison's "Here Comes the Sun."

Melanie Safka of Red Bank, New Jersey, better-known simply as Melanie, was the princess of folk-rock's peace-and-love brigade in the late sixties and early seventies. Taking their cue from her hit "Candles in the Rain," audiences marked Melanie's concerts by holding candles in the darkened arenas. Melanie's husky voice added charm to songs such as "Peace Will Come," "Any Guy," "Beautiful People," "Look What They've Done to My Song, Ma," and her number-1 hit in early 1972, "Brand New Key."

GARY LEWIS AND THE PLAYBOYS

It is not true that Gary Lewis' most significant contribution to rock and roll was that he and his father, comedian Jerry Lewis, were the only father and son team ever to host NBC's *Hullabaloo.* Gary wanted to make a career of rock and roll, but he wanted to do it on his own, rather than as Jerry Lewis' son. He organized a group with Dave Costell, Dave Walker, and Al Ramsey, and booked his first big gig at Disneyland without his parents' knowledge. They developed their own unique style that was an Americanized version of the British sound, and became one of the few American groups to survive and even prosper during the peak years of the British invasion from 1964 through 1966.

In fact Dick Clark recalls the Caravan of Stars tour that headlined Gary Lewis and the Playboys. Catering to popular tastes at the time, the opening act was the Yardbirds.

Al Kooper, former saxophonist for the Royal Teens ("Short Shorts"), who later founded both the Blues Project and Blood, Sweat and Tears, had just written a song for Bobby Vee. Bobby said it was not his kind of song and rejected it. "This Diamond Ring" found its way to Liberty Records, where they were searching for material for their latest group, Gary Lewis and the Playboys. Leon Russell arranged the tune that established Gary and the group as hitmakers, and "This Diamond Ring" eventually became one of the best-selling singles of the decade.

Gary and the Playboys attribute their success to the fact that they didn't look to fifties groups like the Belmonts or the Drifters, but to the Beatles and the Dave Clark Five, for their inspiration. Under the creative guidance of Leon Russell, who arranged, produced, and occasionally played for the group, Gary Lewis and the Playboys had two years worth of hits, including "Count Me In" (1965), "She's Just my Style" (1965), "Everybody Loves a Clown" (1965), "Save Your Heart for Me" (1965), and "Sure Gonna Miss Her" (1966). They even managed to find their way into a beach-party movie, *Swinging Summer.*

The end of the group came when Uncle Sam drafted Gary and sent him to Korea. By the time he was out of the service, his market was gone, his group had scattered, and his recording contract had expired. Today Gary has a new group. If he can manage to get a new recording contract, he will be attempting a very rare rock-and-roll achievement—a successful comeback.

THE MAMAS AND THE PAPAS

It wasn't folk music. It was too electric and had too much of a beat and a rock-and-roll attitude to be folk. But it wasn't raucous enough to be real rock and roll. What it was, was masterful—a little pop, a little vaudeville, a little folk, and a little rock. You had to call it "good-time music," and for three years in the mid-sixties, the Mamas and the Papas made some of the sweetest good-time music you would ever want to hear.

Hip and in tune with the times without quite being psychedelic, they were budding media darlings. Looking either like a hungry folksinger or a hippy businessman, depending on the season, John Phillips was an intelligent songwriter and the energetic center for the group. Cass Elliot was the big, bountiful earth mother with the powerful, crystal-clear voice. Michelle Gilliam Phillips was the perfect counterpart to Cass, both in harmony and physical appearance. Michelle was a long, lean blonde with the striking looks of a fashion model and an aura of sensuality. Denny Doherty looked like a laughing Irishman with a voice that must have come from heaven. Their dress was considered quite strange at the time, and their TV debut on *American Bandstand* was almost cancelled by the *Bandstand* staff because of it. But when they started to sing "California Dreamin'," everyone was impressed. Backed by some of the finest California musicians and produced by the intelligent and sometimes visionary Lou Adler, the Mamas and the Papas' intricate, weaving harmonies created the most distinctive sound of the era.

John Phillips, the son of a career marine officer, was born on the marine camp at Parris Island, South Carolina, in 1935. After bouncing in and out of a couple of colleges, John earned an appointment to the U.S. Naval Academy at Annapolis. But in 1957 he gave up his naval career for Greenwich Village and the life of a folksinger, eventually joining an up-and-coming trio called the Journeymen. John's first marriage soured, although it did give him a daughter, Mackenzie, named after his close friend from the Journeymen, Scott McKenzie. Starting in the late seventies, Mackenzie Phillips would star on TV's *One Day at a Time.* In 1962 John fell in love with a beautiful blonde from California who had come to New York to be a model. That year Holly Michelle Gilliam became John's second wife and an unofficial fourth member of the Journeymen.

About the same time Cassandra Elliot was also singing in Greenwich Village with a folk group called the Big Three. Cass grew up in the well-to-do suburbs of Washington, D.C. Her parents wanted to send her to Swarthmore College, but Cass preferred show business, so she hitchhiked to New York in 1961. She

auditioned for a number of Broadway musicals, appeared in a traveling satrical revue, and won a part in the touring company of *The Music Man.* Cass then became a member of the Big Three in those heady days when Bob Dylan first moved to Greenwich Village and revitalized the folk scene. But Cass soon left the group and joined Zal Yanovsky, Denny Doherty (fresh from the Canadian folk group the Halifax Three), and Paul MacDowell to form the Mugwumps. In the close-knit Greenwich Village folk community John, Michelle, Cass, and Denny knew of each other's work and became friends.

The Journeymen broke up in late 1963, and John began looking for a new situation. When the Mugwumps split up after Zal Yanovsky joined John Sebastian to form what eventually became the Lovin' Spoonful, Cass and Denny became interested in Phillips' plans. John, Michelle, and Denny headed to the Virgin Islands to sort out their futures. Cass later followed the others to the islands, working as a waitress. They decided to form a group there and lived together in communal splendor on a street called Creeque Alley, working out their music. However, after eight months the governor of the Virgin Islands personally invited the four musicians to leave the Caribbean. Tanned and well rehearsed, the group headed for California in 1965 to seek their fame and fortune.

In Los Angeles John met folk-rocker Barry McGuire, who was just about to hit the bigtime with "Eve of Destruction." McGuire introduced the group to his producer, Lou Adler, who owned Dunhill Records. He worked out a deal with the group and put them in the recording studio in late 1965. John, Denny, Michelle, and Cass were ready to put out a record, but they had no name for the group. It so happened that whenever John or Denny called out to one of the girls, they would yell "Hey, Mama!" When the Dunhill publicity people asked them what they wanted to be called, John and Denny said that the girls were "the mamas." Cass and Michelle figured that if they were "the mamas," then Denny and John should be "the papas." The name was adopted.

"California Dreamin'," a reverential ode to the West Coast told from the perspective of a depressing winter afternoon in the East, was the Mamas and the Papas' first release. It gradually wafted up the charts, starting in January and arriving at the number-4 position in mid-March. Their second single didn't take quite so long to make it. "Monday, Monday" sold 160,000 copies the first day out, hit the top ten in three weeks, and was the number-1 record for three weeks in May. Their first album, *If You Can Believe Your Eyes and Ears,* which featured Cass' vaudevillian salute to John Lennon, "I

Call Your Name," and a version of "Do You Wanna Dance," sold three million copies in its first year.

The Mamas and the Papas were always willing to try something new. In 1967 they were the subject of an ABC-TV documentary on the making of a hit record, showing millions of people for the first time the arduous practice of recording and rerecording vocal tracks, the blending of separately recorded instrumental and vocal tracks, and the technical tricks of the recording studio. They featured songs by Rodgers and Hart on two of their albums. They used a nostalgic ricky-ticky arrangement on John Phillips' "Words of Love," a top-five hit in December 1966. They even dared to do a jazzy Lambert, Hendricks and Ross vocal on "Once Was the Time I Thought." Perhaps their most daring move was to become an integral part of the first major rock festival, the Monterey Pop Festival, in the summer of 1967, with John Phillips and Lou Adler lining up the acts and financing the film.

Unfortunately, the magic left The Mamas and the Papas almost as quickly as it began. They reached number 2 with a remake of "Dedicated to the One I Love" in April 1967 and number 5 with the witty, autobiographical "Creeque Alley" in June 1967, but the haunting "Twelve Thirty" only climbed to number 20 in September. In 1966, Michelle and John broke up briefly, and Michelle left the group for a while. By the end of 1967, though, the marriage had fallen apart, with Michelle leaving John for his old friend, actor Dennis Hopper. The hunger that spurred John's songwriting was usurped by money and success, so he moved on to work in film production. The Mamas and the Papas had disintegrated by the end of 1967.

Mama Cass had a successful solo career for a while, placing "Dream a Little Dream of Me," "It's Getting Better," and "Make Your Own Kind of Music" on the charts. She teamed up with the Electric Flag on an unreleased album and Dave Mason of Traffic on an album called *Dave Mason and Cass Elliot* that made a slight splash in 1971. John wrote "San Francisco (Be Sure to Wear Flowers in Your Hair)" for Scott McKenzie in 1967 and had a minor hit of his own with "Mississippi" in 1970. In need of money, the Mamas and the Papas made a disastrous comeback album in 1971. Then Cass died of a heart attack in 1974. (Her last TV appearance was on Dick Clark's *Get It Together*.) Michelle moved in with Warren Beatty for a while and launched a new career as an actress, costarring with Rudolph Nureyev in the forgettable movie *Valentino*. John returned to film, finally encountering severe problems with the law over possession and sale of drugs, and Denny never got his solo career off the ground, keeping a low profile since the demise of the Mamas and the Papas. By 1981 John was touring the TV talk-show circuit with daughter MacKenzie, when he announced the formation of a new Mamas and the Papas that would include MacKenzie and Denny Doherty.

The Lovin' Spoonful interviewed by *Prom Magazine* at the Chase Hotel in St. Louis on December 4, 1966. John Sebastian is at far right. *(Courtesy of Julian H. Miller II)*

THE LOVIN' SPOONFUL

His father was well known for his classical harmonica skills. His mother worked as an administrator at Carnegie Hall. This is hardly the sort of background that spawns a rock-and-roll career. But when John Sebastian enrolled at New York University, he fell under the influence of Greenwich Village and the folk-blues scene that was burgeoning in the early sixties.

With guitar in hand and harmonica in mouth, John joined the Even Dozen Jug Band, which later became the Jim Kweskin Jug Band. The highlight of his early career came at Gerde's Folk City in the Village when he was asked to play the harmonica for Bob Dylan. But John's career didn't suddenly skyrocket. He cut a record with Felix Pappalardi (later of Mountain) and Eric Jacobsen (later the producer/manager of the Spoonful) under the name Pooh and the Heffalumps. John Sebastian then moved on to the equally unknown Mugwumps. The name of the group may have been silly, but the roster was impressive: Denny Doherty, Zal Yanovsky, John Sebastian, and Cass Elliot. As detailed in the Mamas and the Papas' autobiographical hit, "Creeque Alley," Cass and Denny left to form the Mamas and the Papas while John and Zal launched the Lovin' Spoonful, taking their name from a line in Mississippi John Hurt's "Coffee Blues."

Steve Boone on bass and Joe Butler on drums completed the Spoonful's lineup just in time for their first gig at the Village hotspot the Nite Owl. The club's owner is said to have been horrified by the group's debut. He told them to go find some place to practice—a lot! They holed up in the basement of the nearby Albert Hotel, where they polished their act for two months. By August of 1965 the Spoonful were packing them in at the Nite Owl. They became a "must-see" in New York. But as they were still unable to land a recording contract, manager Eric Jacobsen put up the last of his savings to get them studio time to cut "Do You Believe in Magic?" The tape went to Kama Sutra Records, and the Spoonful soon had their contract. The song became a national hit and was followed onto the charts by "You Didn't Have to Be So Nice" in the fall, which convinced critics that the Spoonful wasn't a flash in the pan. Superstar status came in 1966 with their first national number-1 song, "Daydream," written and sung by John Sebastian.

Nineteen sixty-six was the year of the Spoonful. A triumphant tour of Europe brought them international fame as "Daydream" went gold and their follow-up single, "Did You Ever Have to Make Up Your Mind?" was on the charts. A rocking portrait of urban life, "Summer in the City," sold over a million in the U.S. alone, monopolizing the number-1 spot for three weeks. They wisely promoted their record sales with frequent appearances on Dick Clark's *Where The Action Is* at this time. "Rain on the Roof" and "Nashville Cats" capped their year of hits. Unfortunately The Lovin' Spoonful would only have two more top-twenty hits, "Darling, Be Home Soon" and "Six O'Clock," before a controversial drug bust would shake up the group.

In July 1967 Zal left the group for a solo career. John did the same in 1968, and the Spoonful was soon officially disbanded. Sebastian scored the successful Broadway show *Jimmy Shine,* which starred Dustin Hoffman. In 1969 he appeared at Woodstock, then disappeared from the limelight for several years. His comeback debut was on *American Bandstand* in 1976. Sebastian had the number-1 hit in the land in March of that year with "Welcome Back," the theme song of the TV hit *Welcome Back, Kotter.*

Sometimes criticized for never maturing musically, the Spoonful still stand out for their well-written and spirited tunes. Whether using washboards and banjos or jackhammers and car horns, the Spoonful projected a naive freshness that entertained all but the most cynical.

THE FOUR TOPS

Few of us can imagine how Levi Stubbs, Abdul "Duke" Fakir, Renaldo Benson, and Lawrence Payton must have felt at the beginning of the summer of 1964. After ten years in the music business, they were still on the bottom rungs of the ladder of success. But by August of 1964 these four musical veterans were destined to climb that ladder to the top of the charts.

Levi, Duke, Lawrence, and Renaldo first met at a 1954 high school party in Detroit. They each sang with different local bands, but when they combined their talents at that party, their harmony was so sweet they decided to become a team. As the Four Aims, they quickly got a gig at a small nightclub in Flint, Michigan. Soon they were making the rounds on the Michigan club circuit. In 1956 a representative from Chess Records heard them and signed them to their first recording contract. After changing the group's name to the Four Tops, Chess released their first single, "Kiss Me Baby," which barely made a dent on even the regional record charts. Chess then sent the Four Tops packing. Over the next seven years the Tops passed from Red Top Records to Riverside Records to Columbia Records. Although the group developed professionalism, class, and expertise during this time, they just couldn't land a hit record.

In 1960 the discouraged Four Tops ran into an old friend from Detroit, an ex-auto worker who was starting his own record label. They were too busy making the rounds at the established record companies to sign up with a new label, but their friend made them a standing offer to record for him whenever they were ready. After their failure at Columbia in 1963, the Four Tops decided it was time to call their old friend, Berry Gordy. The Four Tops were soon part of Gordy's growing Motown empire, joining the Miracles, Martha and the Vandellas, and Marvin Gaye.

Gordy signed the Tops to Motown's experimental jazz label, Workshop, where they cut the jazz-flavored album *Breaking Through.* But jazz fans didn't buy it, and the album did not break through. But unlike the other recording companies, Motown didn't give up on the group after one shot. Gordy sent the Four Tops on a long national tour, opening for the old pro Billy Eckstine. While on the tour, Eckstine gave them some musical pointers and instructions in offstage behavior and onstage attire (a standard part of Motown schooling). The Four Tops returned to Detroit in early 1964 as a highly professional, polished outfit. Berry Gordy decided to make the Four Tops a mainstream soul group and move them from Workshop to Motown proper. Ten years of struggle were about to end in an "overnight" success.

In the spring of 1964 Gordy put the Four Tops under the wing of one of his production teams, Eddie Holland, Brian Holland, and Lamont Dozier, who were already working with the Supremes. An infectious beat, satin-smooth production, and crisp Holland, Dozier and Holland lyrics typified the highly popular Motown sound. During the summer of 1964 Holland, Dozier, and Holland turned their magic on the Four Tops.

In August 1964 the Four Tops recorded a song written by their producers entitled "Baby I Need Your Loving." Levi Stubbs' gutsy lead vocal powered it into the top fifteen, selling over a million copies worldwide. Their first smash after ten years of trying was hailed as a masterpiece by some brilliant newcomers to soul. "I Can't Help Myself (Sugar Pie, Honey Bunch)," another Holland, Dozier, and Holland song, was number 1 for two weeks in May 1965. In July Columbia Records dusted off an old Tops cut, "Ain't That Love," and released it as a single to cash

The Four Tops.

in on the group's newfound popularity. But when Motown caught wind of Columbia's ploy, they virtually remade "I Can't Help Myself" into "The Same Old Song," and released the record in three days, totally burying the Columbia single.

The Four Tops opened 1966 with "Shake Me, Wake Me," followed by "Loving You Is Sweeter Than Ever." Then "Reach Out, I'll Be There" rocketed to number 1 in October 1966 on the strength of the gritty, explosive lead vocal of Levi, the tight harmonies of Duke, Larry, and Renaldo, and the impeccable production of Holland, Dozier, and Holland. The Tops also gave a dramatic, soulful edge to "Standing in the Shadows of Love," riding it to number 6 in December 1966.

If the Four Tops were hot in the studio, they were a disciplined volcano on stage. Like their stablemates at Motown, the Temptations, The Tops could dance as well as they could sing. Their well-rehearsed moves blended well with their frantic, anguished, but always polished songs of love. Holland, Dozier, and Holland took the Four Tops up the charts three times in 1967 with "Bernadette," "Seven Rooms of Gloom," and "I'll Turn to Stone." But in 1968 Holland, Dozier, and Holland left Motown to form their own record company after a dispute with the Motown management. The Four Tops were then paired with several of Motown's staff producers resulting in less successful pop tunes like "Walk Away Renee" and "Still Waters Run Deep." Unfortunately, with the departure of Holland, Dozier, and Holland, their guiding light was gone.

The Tops left Motown in 1972 to sign with ABC Records. They recorded a couple of million sellers for ABC in 1973, "Keeper of the Castle" and "Ain't No Woman Like the One I Got," but the fire was now gone from Levi's voice and the group began to sound more like the Mills Brothers than the soulful Four Tops of the mid-sixties. Twenty-six years after they first sang together at that high school party, Levi, Renaldo, Lawrence, and Abdul now sing their oldies in supper clubs and resort-hotel lounges around America.

The Sound of 1966

SIMON AND GARFUNKEL

When the White Rabbit met the Cheshire Cat at a rehearsal of *Alice in Wonderland* at P.S. 164 in Forest Hills, New York, in the early fifties, a long and productive friendship between Paul Simon and Arthur Garfunkel began. Drawn together by a mutual interest in music, they would sing popular songs as well as Simon originals with Paul playing his guitar. They both became big fans of WINS disc jockey Alan Freed, who was introducing rock and roll to New York at the time.

Inspired by the Everly Brothers, Paul and Art cut a demo record at a midtown Manhattan recording studio with big hopes of rock-and-roll success. As fate would have it, an executive from Big Records was scheduled to have the same studio next. While waiting, the exec listened to the boys and liked what he heard. He signed them, and they released their first single, "Hey Schoolgirl," in 1957, billed as "Tom and Jerry." The song sold over one hundred thousand copies and just barely made the top forty. It wasn't a lot, but it was enough to get them booked on Dick Clark's Thanksgiving TV show.

When their follow-up singles "Don't Say Goodbye" and "Surrender, Please Surrender" failed to make the charts, Paul and Art went their separate ways. Art went to N.Y.U. and Columbia for degrees in math and architecture, respectively. Paul attended N.Y.U. and Queens College, majoring in English Literature and Music. Neither abandoned his singing, though. Art recorded a few songs for Warwick Records as Artie Garr. Paul did some work with Carole King, among others, writing, producing, and performing under the name of Jerry Landis. He also joined the immortal Tico and the Triumphs in 1961 for a song called "Motorcycle," which edged onto the charts for one big week.

With neither Simon nor Garfunkel able to make it alone, they decided, in 1964, to work together again. Their first big date was at Gerde's Folk City, which led to more work at other Village coffeehouses. In time they were signed by Columbia Records and recorded their first L.P., which featured a stark acoustic-guitar number called "Sounds of Silence." Shortly thereafter, Paul left for England to work on his songbook and Art later joined him during a vacation from school. While they were out of the country, "Sounds of Silence" started to get a lot of airplay in Florida. Columbia thought that if they could turn it into a Byrds-style rock song similar to "Mr. Tambourine Man," it would have some commercial

The casual Paul Simon.

The formal Art Garfunkel.

potential. They performed surgery and added electric guitars, bass, and drums to the song—without telling Paul and Art. They then released the tune as a single. Ironically, this song deals with the breakdown of communication. Simon and Garfunkel returned to America to find a quite different "Sounds of Silence" in the number-1 spot in January of 1966, and Simon was soon hailed as the new songwriter/poet for an alienated generation.

Wednesday Morning, 3 A.M., Simon and Garfunkel's first album, featured six Paul Simon songs and a few Dylan tunes. While Paul contributed the songs, Art contributed the strong, angelic voice reminiscent of a church-choir soloist. *Sounds of Silence* was their second album, followed by *Parsley, Sage, Rosemary and Thyme.* Their singles of this era included "Scarborough Fair," "Homeward Bound," "Dangling Conversation," "I Am a Rock," and "A Hazy Shade of Winter."

The poetic *Bookends* was Simon and Garfunkel's fourth album, released in 1967. The following year they did the soundtrack for *The Graduate,* one of the biggest-grossing motion pictures of the decade. Their single from the film, "Mrs. Robinson," contained verses not used in the soundtrack. It was number 1 for four weeks and won the Grammy Award for best pop performance by a vocal group in 1968. At this time the duo had five albums on the charts, including *The Graduate* soundtrack at number 1 and *Bookends* at number 2.

"Bridge over Troubled Water," Simon and Garfunkel's biggest single from their biggest album of the same name, was also their last as a duo. Art became more interested in acting than in music. He worked on the film *Catch-22* during the recording of this album, to Paul's chagrin. The single was number 1 for six weeks in 1970 and sold over two million copies as the best-selling record of the year; It won Grammy Awards for Song of the Year and Best Contemporary Song. Worldwide sales surpassed five million. The L.P. was number 1 for ten weeks in the U.S. and for thirty-five weeks in England, remaining on the charts there for an unbelievable 285 weeks. It was the best-selling album of 1970, and within five years it surpassed the ten million mark in worldwide sales. The album won three Grammy Awards and yielded another hit single, "Cecilia." Nevertheless, Simon and Garfunkel decided to split. In 1971 Art appeared with Jack Nicholson in the film *Carnal Knowledge.* However, it took Paul until 1973 to get his solo career on track. "Loves Me Like a Rock" from his second album was his first solo million seller. In December 1975 he hit again with "50 Ways to Leave Your Lover" from his fourth solo album. Meanwhile, Art returned to music, recording his own solo album, *Angel Clare.*

The pair reunited in 1972 for a benefit concert for George McGovern. They recorded "My Little Town" together in 1975, their first hit as a duo in almost five years. In 1978 Paul and James Taylor joined Art on his version of Sam Cooke's "Wonderful World."

Simon and Garfunkel were trendsetters. They had *the* sound of 1966 and came back even hotter in 1970. Simon and Garfunkel juggled intricate harmonies with a polished yet relaxed style. Their lyrics jarred an entire generation of young people. In the late sixties and early seventies they reached out to an alienated youth culture with their musical poems of loneliness. Moreover, their beautiful vocals affected and pleased listeners of all ages, an accomplishment in itself, with elegance, clarity, and honesty.

1967

Nineteen sixty-seven was the year of love. In May, Scott McKenzie beckoned people to San Francisco and advised them to wear some flowers in their hair. By June the Haight-Ashbury section of that city was awash with "flower power" as kids from all over the country gathered by the Golden Gate Bridge to turn on, tune in, and drop out. FM underground radio was born. And a summer of love was made complete with the peace, music, and good vibes of the first major rock festival, Monterey Pop.

But not everything was peace, love, and understanding in 1967. Israel and its Arab neighbors fought their third war in nineteen years, in which Israel scored a decisive victory and Moshe Dayan was proclaimed a hero. Racial riots shook Detroit, Newark, and Birmingham, turning the summer of love into the long, hot summer. Red China exploded its first hydrogen bomb. More American troops were sent to Vietnam.

In the Heat of the Night walked away with the Oscar for Best Picture. On television Sally Field floated around as the Flying Nun, and Sergeant Joe Friday (dum-de-dum-dum) was back with *Dragnet* after an eight-year absence. Sunday nights brought controversy, satire, and music with *The Smothers Brothers Comedy Hour,* and Raymond Burr as *Ironsides* patroled San Francisco in his wheelchair, but didn't wear any flowers.

In 1967 Music Explosion gave us "Little Bit o' Soul." But there was also "Soul Man" by Sam and Dave, "Sweet Soul Music" by Arthur Conley, and the Soul Survivors' "Expressway to Your Heart." There was blue-eyed soul with Mitch Ryder's "Sock It to Me, Baby" and the Spencer Davis Group's "Gimme Some Lovin'." The Buckinghams gave us "Kind of a Drag," which it was not. The top ten for 1967 contained "The Letter" by the Box Tops, "Ode to Billie Joe" by Bobbie Gentry, "To Sir with Love" by Lulu, "Windy" by the Association, "Light My Fire" by the Doors, "I'm a Believer" by the Monkees, "Somethin' Stupid" by Nancy Sinatra and Frank Sinatra, "Groovin' " by the Young Rascals, "Happy Together" by the Turtles, and "Can't Take My Eyes off You" by Frankie Valli.

In sports, Carl Yastrzemski won baseball's Triple Crown, but the St. Louis Cardinals nipped Yaz's Boston Red Sox in the World Series anyway. The World Boxing Association stripped Muhammad Ali of his heavyweight crown for refusing to be drafted into the Army. The San Francisco Warriors were beaten by the Philadelphia 76ers for the NBA crown and the Green Bay Packers crushed the Oakland Raiders in Super Bowl II. But after all, in 1967 San Francisco did have the Jefferson Airplane and *Rolling Stone* magazine.

It was 1967—the thirteenth year of rock and roll.

THE YOUNG RASCALS

The biggest event in New York City in August 1965 was the Beatles concert at Shea Stadium. Over fifty-six thousand screaming fans converged on Flushing, Queens, the night of August sixteenth to see John, Paul, George, and Ringo. When they got to Shea Stadium there was a cryptic message on the giant electric scoreboard in center field—"The Rascals are here." Who the hell were the Rascals? they all thought. A few days earlier Sid Bernstein, the promoter behind the Beatles concert at Shea, was taken, against his better judgment, to the Barge, a nightclub in Southampton, Long Island. Bernstein was shanghaied into listening to the Barge's house band, four young men dressed in knickers, Eton collars, and short ties, who looked like rejects from an *Our Gang* comedy. Bernstein was uninterested in the band until they started playing the most riveting, foot-stomping "blue-eyed" R & B Bernstein had ever heard. The day after that Beatles concert, Bernstein became the Young Rascals' manager. Within a month he had set off a bidding war among the major record labels, and the Young Rascals signed a contract with Atlantic Records. Now Bernstein could legitimately proclaim, "The Rascals are here."

The Young Rascals were Felix Cavaliere, Dino Danelli, Eddie Brigati, and Gene Cornish. Felix grew up in Pelham, New York, a mostly Italian and black working-class community. He learned classical piano, but listened to R & B. He was the only white member of the Stereos, a street-corner singing group that hit the bottom of the charts in 1961 with "I Really Love You." Felix left the Stereos to go to Syracuse University, with all intentions of becoming a doctor. In two years he was back in New York City looking for work as a musician.

Dino Danelli learned to play drums as a kid in Jersey City, just across the Hudson River from Manhattan. A fierce jazz drummer, Dino turned professional at age fifteen to tour with the Lionel

Hampton band. When his gig with Hampton was over, Dino wandered down to New Orleans, where he tuned in to rhythm and blues. In 1963 Dino headed back for New York City to work as an R & B session musician. While playing with a pickup band at the Choo Choo Club in Garfield, New Jersey, later that year, Dino met Eddie Brigati. Eddie, whose older brother, David, had played with one of the titans of the twist, Joey Dee and the Starlighters, was a seventeen-year-old wise guy who was trying to make it as a soul singer.

In early 1964 Felix and Dino both joined Sandy Scott and Her Scotties. After a quick tour of Las Vegas, both Dino and Felix had had enough of the Scotties and started looking for something else. Felix then played organ with Joey Dee and the Starlighters at the Peppermint Lounge in Manhattan. Joey Dee soon brought in a new lead singer, Eddie Brigati, and a new guitarist from Canada, Gene Cornish, whose group had broken up, leaving him stranded in New York. By the end of 1964 Felix, Eddie and Gene were chafing at the bit doing the twist every night at the Peppermint Lounge. They decided to form their own group, adding their old friend Dino on the drums. They spent the winter working on their act. In February 1965 the Young Rascals made their debut in Garfield, New Jersey, at the good old Choo Choo Club. By July they had moved to the Barge in Southampton, where Sid Bernstein found them.

The Young Rascals' first single was "I Ain't Gonna Eat Out My Heart Anymore," a blue-eyed soul rocker that climbed to number 52 on the charts in early 1966. Their next record, "Good Lovin'," a remake of the Olympics' 1965 record, started off as an embarrassment for the Rascals. They didn't like the mix on the record, so they began denying that it was theirs—but only until it hit number 1 in May 1966. The Young Rascals became the rage in New York, playing discotheques such as Harlow's and inspiring hundreds of white soul bands in the metropolitan area.

They started 1967 with a top-twenty hit, "I've Been Lonely Too Long," and an official change in the group's name to simply the Rascals. In the spring, Felix sang the lead on a jazzy, laid-back number about taking it easy on a Sunday afternoon called "Groovin'," which became one of the biggest singles of 1967. It was number 1 for two weeks in May and two weeks in June, staying nine weeks in the top ten. "Groovin'" marked a change in the Rascals' style. While they had started out as a gutsy, rough-and-tumble white R & B group, the Rascals became more introspective after "Groovin'." As Felix and Dino got more involved with Swami Satchidananda's Integral Yoga Institute, the Rascals felt that every single had to have some deeper meaning. "How Can I Be Sure" was a hauntingly beautiful ballad, light-years away from the Rascals' earlier sound. "It's Wonderful," an embarrassing psychedelic montage released in December 1967, was an attempt to prove that they were as hip as the Beatles and the Jefferson Airplane.

In 1968 the Rascals sat down to redo "Groovin'" and came up with the dreamy "Beautiful Morning," which climbed to number 3 on the charts. After the Rascals were run out of Fort Pierce, Florida, by a bunch of rednecks because of their long hair, Eddie and Felix wrote the angry anthem, "People Got to Be Free." This became the Rascals' biggest record, spending two months in the top ten and five weeks in the number-1 slot. The group practiced what they preached, too. After the Fort Pierce incident, the Rascals announced that they would not appear on any show that didn't include at least one black act. Many Rascals concerts were canceled as a result, and the group even turned down an appearance on *The Ed Sullivan Show* because of alleged "racist policies."

Unfortunately the group's star was on the decline after 1969. Their music had become too personal, too jazz-oriented, and too free-form to attract a large following. In 1970 Eddie Brigati left the group because he wasn't satisfied with the direction his music was taking. In 1971 the Rascals left Atlantic Records for Columbia. Then Gene Cornish quit. Cavaliere and Danelli added three new members—Buzzy Feiten, Robert Popwell, and Ann Sutton—but the Rascals' two Columbia albums were mere exercises in self-indulgence. In the summer of 1972 the Rascals disintegrated.

Following the demise of the Rascals, Felix Cavaliere furthered his involvement in Eastern religion while producing records for Laura Nyro and the feminist rock group Deadly Nightshade and recording three solo albums on his own. Dino Danelli and Gene Cornish began the band Bulldog in 1972, but had little success with it. In 1978 Danelli and Cornish joined forces with Wally Bryson, formerly of the Raspberries, to form Fotomaker. Fotomaker hit with the single "Where Have You Been All My Life," but their album was disappointing. These former members of one of the great rock bands of the sixties were never able to recapture the chemistry that had brought them so much success and made so much memorable rock and roll.

ARETHA FRANKLIN

Nineteen sixty-seven was the year of the "long hot summer," when the ghettos of Detroit and Newark exploded in anger and frustration, and frightened store owners scrawled "soul brother" on their doors to dissuade looters. H. Rap Brown, Huey Newton, Eldridge Cleaver, SNCC, the Young Lords, and the Black Panthers all declared that black was beautiful in 1967. Their watchwords were black power and black pride. And Soul Sister Number One in 1967 was Lady Soul—Aretha Franklin.

Aretha Franklin was the essence of soul music. While Motown offered homogenized soul—filtered, distilled, and prettily packaged—Aretha let the hurt and the blues show. She left all the rough edges in her music. Motown was Diana Ross with her little-girl voice pouting "Where Did Our Love Go?" But Aretha was rough, earthy, raw, and demanding "Respect." From 1967 on Aretha Franklin was the standard by which all other female singers were judged.

Aretha was born in Detroit in 1942 and grew up in the same neighborhood as Diana Ross. Aretha's father, Reverend C. L. Franklin, was the flashy, custom-tailored pastor of the 4,500 member New Bethel Baptist Church. The high-living Reverend Franklin had recorded some seventy albums of gospel sermons and was considered an important figure on the black Gospel-music circuit. The Franklins' home entertained the biggest names in gospel, and Aretha learned music by singing with Mahalia Jackson, Clara Ward, and James Cleveland in her daddy's living room. Aretha's mother deserted her family when Aretha was six. Four years later her mother died, and the great Mahalia Jackson came to fill the void in Aretha's life as her confidante.

When she was twelve Aretha began soloing in her father's choir. At fourteen she dropped out of school and toured the country by car as a featured performer in her father's evangelical show. Out on tour as a teen-ager she saw the seamier side of show business—the ten-hour car rides, the drinking, the partying, and the carrying on—and as a result Aretha grew up fast. By the time she turned eighteen she had moved to New York to try her hand at pop music and already had two children. Aretha had packed more hard living into her eighteen years than most people ever do in a lifetime.

In 1960 Aretha's manager, Jo King, tried to turn a shy, fat, untutored girl into a recording artist. King arranged an audition for Aretha with John Hammond. Hammond, who had recorded Bessie Smith, nurtured Billie Holiday, discovered Bob Dylan, and would later sign Bruce Springsteen, was very impressed with

Lady Soul—Aretha Franklin.

Aretha and got her a contract with Columbia Records. But in 1960 Columbia was run by Mitch Miller, a man who despised rock music. Columbia wanted to turn this fervent young Gospel singer into another Leslie Uggams, forcing her to do pop classics and show tunes with big orchestral arrangements. During this time Aretha's personal life was a mess. She was racked by self-hatred, plagued by unlucky love affairs, and obsessed with guilt stemming from her turbulent teen years. Aretha eventually withdrew. She began to dread recording sessions as she tottered on the edge of a breakdown. Her Columbia albums were commercial failures, and by 1966 she was ninety thousand dollars in debt to Columbia. If anybody ever had the right to sing the blues, it was Aretha Franklin.

In 1962 Aretha married Ted White, who then became her manager. After Aretha's six unsuccessful albums with Columbia, White secured a contract with Atlantic Records, the premier R & B label. At the end of 1966 Atlantic assigned its top production unit— Jerry Wexler, Tom Dowd, and Arif Mardin—to its newest artist. Wexler, an Atlantic vice-president, had produced Ray Charles' "I Got a Woman" in 1955 and "What'd I Say" in 1959, two monumental records in Charles' career. Wexler had worked with artists ranging from Clyde McPhatter and Solomon Burke to the Young Rascals. He took one look at the insecure singer whose gospel roots Columbia had tried to erase and knew immediately that he had to get her out of New York. Wexler took Aretha down to Rick Hall's Fury Studios in Muscle Shoals, Alabama. He brought in King Curtis and some down-home session musicians, sat her in front of a piano, and let her wail. Six years of musical frustration and pent-up emotions were unleashed at that legendary recording session that put Muscle Shoals on the map. What came out of it was the album *I Never Loved a Man (The Way I Love You)*. Full of fire, grit, and raw-edged soul, it was the first of many outstanding records and the beginning of amazing commercial success for Aretha.

The title cut of this first Atlantic album, "I Never Loved a Man (The Way I Love You)," was released as a single in March 1967 and ended up number 9 on the charts, earning Aretha her first of eight consecutive gold records. Next, Aretha took Otis Redding's "Respect" and topped the charts in June 1967, turning "sock it to me" into the phrase of the hour. "Baby, I Love You," Carole King's "A Natural Woman," "Chain of Fools," "(Sweet Sweet Baby) Since You've Been Gone" (written by Aretha and Ted White), "The House That Jack Built," and Burt Bacharach's "I Say a Little Prayer" all reached the top ten on the strength of Aretha's sanctified soul-shouting. She won two Grammys in 1967, was named the Best Vocalist of

1967 by *Billboard* magazine, and made the cover of *Time* magazine in 1968. For a year and a half Aretha was the queen of the music world. Then in the middle of 1968, the bubble burst.

Her sometimes rocky marriage to Ted White finally collapsed in the summer of 1968. *Time* magazine reported that Aretha had been roughed up in public by her husband. Aretha's father, Reverend Franklin, made it known that he hated Ted White. Moreover, the pressures of constant touring and the strains of success were just too much for the marriage. Aretha fell apart, avoiding recording sessions and missing live performances. She drifted into a semiretirement that lasted for a year and a half.

By the time Aretha reemerged in 1970, her taste in music and the tastes of her audience had changed. Nineteen sixty-seven's halcyon days of soul were now a distant memory. Eldridge Cleaver was in exile, H. Rap Brown was in jail, and the 1967 riots had left Newark and Detroit crippled and scarred. LBJ and his Great Society were replaced in the White House by Richard Nixon and his call for "law and order." Times had changed. Aretha drifted back into pop music and flirted with the celebrity pop scene. She even did comedy skits on the Flip Wilson Show. Having lost a great deal of weight, she displayed her new figure in transparent body stockings and wrapped herself in slinky gowns and minks. But the new Aretha Franklin has not yet been able to produce new hits.

The Association. (Courtesy of Dick Clark)

THE ASSOCIATION

In the early sixties Terry Kirkman played in a thirteen-member group called the Men, with Brian Cole (bass), Ted Bluechel, Jr. (drums), and Russ Giguere (guitar). That band only lasted eight months. Then Terry (keyboard and woodwinds) and Gary Alexander (guitar) formed the Association with former Men Ted, Russ, and Brian, adding only Jim Yester for his rhythm guitar and excellent tenor voice.

After months of rehearsing, the band made its debut in November 1965 at a nightclub theater called the Ice House in Pasadena, California. From there they landed gigs at Disneyland and on the college circuit. The Association developed a solid reputation and were soon snapped up by a local label, Davon Records. Their first release was Dylan's "One Too Many Mornings," in early 1966, which never got off the ground. But their next record, "Along Comes Mary" (June 1966), was a top-ten hit. The record did so well that Davon made a profit selling it and all future Association releases to a larger company, Valiant Records. The popularity of "Along Comes Mary" was attributed to its unique melody, delicate harmonies, and controversial lyrics. "Mary," it seems, referred to marijuana.

At the end of the summer, the Association entered the mainstream of pop with the beautiful ballad "Cherish." This August 1966 release written by Terry Kirkman was number 1 for three weeks, sold over a million copies in two months, and was the number-1 record of 1966 by many estimates. Furthermore, in many radio-station polls of the all-time top five hundred songs, "Cherish" has placed first.

The Association quickly became a top concert attraction with their clean-cut and wholesome image. They took their concerts very seriously, often warming up for two to three hours at a show, to hone their unique harmonies, which weren't created by studio wizardry alone. They could produce those thrilling sounds live, which ensured them success in concert once the hits stopped coming. Their late 1966 release "Pandora's Golden Heebie Jeebies" was a psychedelic forerunner to the many surreal tunes just around the corner—but it wasn't what the public wanted yet. The Association then burned up the charts in 1967 with three traditional pop tunes. "No Fair at All" started the ball rolling in February 1967. By the time of their next release Valiant had been purchased by Warner Bros. "Windy," written by nineteen-year-old Ruthann Friedman, was released in May 1967. It was number 1 for four weeks, giving the Association their second million seller. Released in August 1967, "Never My Love" sold a million copies by November and climbed to number 1 in the process. The group finished out the year with "Requiem for the Masses," an antiwar tune, in September 1967.

The first of many personnel changes occurred in 1967. Gary Alexander was replaced by Larry Ramos, a former member of the New Christy Minstrels. Eventually Russ Giguere was replaced by Richard Thompson, and Brian Cole died accidentally in 1972 of drug poisoning. Still the band went on, with "Everything That Touches You" in February 1968, "Time For Livin'" in May, and "Six Man Band" in August. In March 1969 they released the title song from the Paramount motion picture *Goodbye, Columbus,* and thanks to very strong sales in England, they had their fourth million seller. By 1970 the group had sold a phenomenal twelve million records, but the new decade yielded no chart action for the group. Unwilling to throw in the towel, they never stopped touring. In the spring of 1975 they signed with RCA Records, but had no recording successes. A complete personnel change then left the group far from the original sound that had produced the rock classic "Cherish." In 1981 they regrouped with all of the original members except Brian Cole.

THE TURTLES

In the wake of Bob Dylan's rock success, the Turtles—Howard Kaylan, Mark Volman, Al Nichol, Chuck Portz, Jim Turner, and Don Murray—found an obscure Dylan song and took "It Ain't Me, Babe" to the top ten. In search of a suitable follow-up, the Turtles were offered several tunes by P. F. Sloan, who was later the driving force behind the Grass Roots. The Turtles turned down Sloan's first offer and took "Let Me Be" instead, which made it to number 29 in the fall of 1965. But the song they turned down, "Eve of Destruction," became a number-1 hit for Barry McGuire and was the biggest protest song of the folk-rock era.

Of course, the Turtles were never really cut out to be folk-rockers. They were too bright, too funny, and too weird. For the Turtles' first appearance on *The Ed Sullivan Show,* lead singer Howard Kaylan made a lasting impression by wearing a turtleneck sweater *and* a tie. The Turtles just couldn't take the gloom-and-doom pretensions of folk-rock seriously. They gave it up after "Let Me Be," and, led by the clean, soaring vocals of Kaylan and Volman, turned out some of rock's best singles over the succeeding three years.

In 1963 Howard Kaylan, Al Nichol, and a few other friends formed a band called the Nightriders. They played surf music, which was the craze in Southern California at the time. While still juniors in high school in L.A., the Nightriders played local dances and even appeared on local TV. In late 1963 Mark Volman, a fledgling saxophone player and vocalist, and bass player Chuck Portz joined the group, now known as the Crossfires. The Crossfires cut a few records for some local record companies—"Fiberglass Jungle" for Capco and "One Potato, Two Potato" for Lucky Token—before changing from their surf sound to a British Invasion sound, then to folk-rock. After playing small L.A. rock clubs for a year, the Crossfires auditioned for L.A. disc jockey Reb Foster, who became their manager and made the group the house band at his Reblaire Club in Redondo Beach. Foster contacted a new record company, White Whale Records, which agreed to sign the Crossfires on the condition that they change their name. As the Turtles, the group gave White Whale a hit with the company's very first release, "It Ain't Me, Babe."

As 1966 began, the Turtles' old friend, P. F. Sloan, brought them a new song. Sloan had written a follow-up to the Vogues' "You're the One," but the Vogues had turned it down. The Turtles recorded the Vogues' reject and went gold with "You Baby," a cheerful song with a strong melody and a great lead vocal by Kaylan. Young, brash, and overconfident, the Turtles decided they could have hits with any style of music. They wrote and released a psychedelic rock raga, the morbid "Grim Reaper of Love," as the follow-up to "You Baby," and were amazed when radio stations ignored it. "Grim Reaper" was so bad that radio stations shunned all the Turtles' music for the next year.

But the stations couldn't ignore the Turtles' March 1967 release. "Happy Together" became *the* song for lovers in 1967. It had everything a hit song could ask for—superb, building production, a dash of horns, imaginative vocals, and great lyrics. This was the first of four consecutive Turtles' hits written by New Yorkers Gary Bonner and Alan Gordon, whose own group, the Magicians, had just dissolved. With the slick production of Joe Wissert (a regular dancer on *American Bandstand* in the early days in Philadelphia and later the production wizard of Boz Scaggs' *Silk Degrees* album in 1976), the Turtles took Bonner and Gordon's "She'd Rather Be With Me" into the top five. The Wissert/Bonner-Gordon/ Turtles combination hit again with "You Know What I Mean" and "She's My Girl," making 1967 a golden year for the Turtles.

But 1968 was the beginning of the end for the

Turtles. Volman and Kaylan, the core of the group, grew increasingly weird. The Turtles delved into psychedelia, recording countless wild and unintelligible tracks for unreleased albums. Kaylan and Volman wrote songs for and helped produce the Turtles' *Battle of the Bands* album, which satirized the entire rock scene with imaginery groups such as Yusef and the Udder People, Atomic Enchilada, and the Fabulous Dawgs. When White Whale Records blasted the Turtles for their latest flop single, "Sound Asleep," and told Kaylan and Volman to start writing Turtles' hits, Howie and Mark became incensed and decided to write a stinging parody of a Turtles' hit. This intended satire, "Elenore," became the Turtles' biggest hit in over a year. Volman and Kaylan threw every cliché in the book into "Elenore," coupled it with "Happy Together" style melody, and wound up tongue-in-cheek in the top five. A haunting version of the Byrds' "You Showed Me" (credited to Nature's Children on *Battle of the Bands*) was the Turtles' last big hit, in February 1969. At war with their record label and with each other, the Turtles disintegrated in early 1970 amid a flurry of lawsuits.

Mark Volman and Howie Kaylan joined Frank Zappa's Mothers of Invention in late 1970. Unable to use the name the "Turtles" because of a pending lawsuit, Howie and Mark borrowed the names of two of the Turtles' road managers and became "The Phlorescent Leech and Eddie," later shortened to just Flo and Eddie. They recorded four albums with the Mothers, then went off on their own in 1972. Volman and Kaylan never recaptured the widespread appeal of the Turtles, but as Flo and Eddie they remain the supreme jesters of rock. Most recently they supplied the backup vocals for Bruce Springsteen's 1981 hit single "Hungry Heart."

Mike Nesmith. *(Courtesy of Julian H. Miller II)*

Mickey Dolenz. *(Courtesy of Julian H. Miller II)*

Peter Tork. *(Courtesy of Julian H. Miller II)*

Davy Jones. *(Courtesy of Julian H. Miller II)*

THE MONKEES

In 1965 Bob Rafelson and Bert Schneider came up with a great idea for a TV show. The biggest sensation in the world was rock and roll. Whenever a big rock group appeared on a TV variety show, ratings soared. So they decided to give a rock group a regular TV series and run their own half-hour version of the Beatles' *A Hard Day's Night* every week. It was the perfect plan. The kids would get to see a rock group on TV every week, the TV network would get its ratings, and with such exposure, the group would be able to sell more than a few records.

Schneider and Rafelson first considered building the show around the Lovin' Spoonful. They were good-looking, outgoing guys with their pleasant candy-striped T-shirts. Moreover, they had just had a smash hit, "Do You Believe in Magic?" But Rafelson and Schneider decided that there were just too many problems with using a real rock group. First of all, they were musicians, not actors. Second, with a new show every week, you needed a hit record every week, and no group could write hits that fast. Finally, no matter what existing group they got, they just wouldn't be the Beatles. Such a mystique as the Beatles had couldn't be built up around an existing group. Therefore, on September 8, 1965, Rafelson and Schneider ran an ad in the *Hollywood Reporter,* asking for "four insane boys, aged 17 to 21" to be part of a mod, long-haired rock-and-roll group for a TV series.

They got 437 responses to their ad. Candidates came in all shapes, sizes, colors and nationalities. Some came with musical talent, some without. Rafelson and Schneider knew what they were looking for—four guys with stage presence, screen appeal, and the sort of personalities that would interact with one another naturally. Musical talent was secondary, since those problems could always be fixed in the recording studio. Rafelson and Schneider passed up Denny Hutton, later of Three Dog Night, and Stephen

Stills before choosing David Jones, Mickey Dolenz, Mike Nesmith, and Peter Tork to be the Monkees.

Mickey Dolenz had a wacky sense of humor and a good voice. He had also been a child actor, chasing Bimbo the elephant in *Circus Boy* for three years on TV in the mid-fifties. Since he couldn't play a musical instrument, the producers told him to sit behind the drums. He could learn to play them later.

Davy Jones was to be the Monkees' answer to Paul McCartney and to Peter Noone of Herman's Hermits. He was five-three with the kind of cute looks that would send teen-age hearts aflutter. Furthermore, he had an English accent and was also an actor. He had played the Artful Dodger in the Broadway musical *Oliver* and Sam Weller in *Pickwick.* Davy could sing, but he couldn't play an instrument either, so they gave him a tambourine.

To Rafelson and Schneider, Peter Tork was an amalgam of two of the Beatles. He seemed to have Ringo's looks and George's personality. Why the producers wanted those two qualities is anybody's guess. Born Peter Thorkelson, Pete was the son of a professor of economics at the University of Connecticut. Pete had gone to college to become a teacher, but poor grades helped turn him toward folksinging. While playing with the Phoenix Singers in a Greenwich Village coffeehouse he got the call to join the Monkees.

Robert Michael Nesmith was the most polished musician of the bunch. Mike's family had inherited some land in Texas and decided to settle on it. The estate turned out to be right smack in the middle of a black ghetto, Farmer's Branch, just outside of Dallas, so Mike grew up listening to the likes of B. B. King and Jimmy Reed. He joined the Air Force in 1960, but it wasn't until 1962, when he entered college in San Antonio, that he began to play the guitar. Mike eventually played folk clubs around San Antonio, then traveled the country and even did some session work for Stax/Volt Records in Memphis before heading out to California. "Wool Hat," as he was called, performed and wrote in California before becoming a Monkee. He also wrote a song called "Different Drum" for a group called the Stone Poneys, who featured a then unknown lead singer, Linda Ronstadt.

With the group finally chosen, the next step for the Monkees was the music. For this, the producers turned to the "Man with the Golden Ear," Don Kirshner, and Lester Sill, a music veteran who had been partners with pioneer rock producers Phil Spector, Jerry Leiber, and Mike Stoller. Kirshner was the guru of rock and roll in New York City. His publishing company housed the cream of rock's songwriters: Neil Sedaka, Carole King, Neil Diamond, Jeff Barry, and Ellie Greenwich. Kirshner put Tommy Boyce and Bobby Hart, two of his young staff writers, to work producing the Monkees and commissioned songs from Carole King, Neil Diamond, and David Gates, as well as Boyce and Hart. He then hired the Candy Store Prophets, a group of superb L.A. studio musicians, to play behind the Monkees. He knew the musical quality was good, perhaps the best money could buy. He was now ready to let the television show sell the records.

At the Beatles' August 1966 concert at Shea Stadium in New York, flyers were handed out that advertised a "great new group, the Monkees," who would have their own show on NBC in the fall. On August 16, 1966, six weeks before the series went on the air, the Monkees' first single, "Last Train to Clarksville," was released. The song was Boyce and Hart's answer to the Beatles' "Ticket to Ride," and it turned out to be just as successful. Pushed by the TV show, "Last Train" sold two million copies and climbed to number 1 in November 1966. *The Monkees,* their debut album, went gold in five weeks, selling 3,200,000 copies in three months and over five million by the end of 1967. The Monkees were the successful product of marketing genius.

The Monkees did turn out some excellent music. Their second single, "I'm a Believer," was a monster smash, spending seven weeks in the number-1 spot and the first three months of 1967 in the top ten. The record's success eventually convinced its author, Neil Diamond, to try his hand at a singing career. Diamond also wrote their follow-up, "A Little Bit Me, A Little Bit You," which became the Monkees' third gold single and peaked at number 2 on the charts. In

the summer of 1967 the Monkees had a two-sided hit, "Pleasant Valley Sunday," a mild critique of suburbia that hit number 3, backed by "Words," which reached number 11. The Monkees climbed back to number 1 for four weeks at the end of 1967 with "Daydream Believer," a soft, swaying ballad written by ex-Kingston Trio member John Stewart. The Monkees hit the top five once more in 1968 with the sizzling Boyce and Hart tune "Valleri."

The Monkees may have been manufactured, but they weren't happy about being manipulated. Their record company, Colgems, tried to keep it a secret that the Monkees didn't play their own instruments on record. By this time they could play, but they couldn't reproduce their superbly crafted singles in concert. Mike Nesmith called a press conference at which he disclosed that Colgems wouldn't allow the group to play on record. The Monkees were then allowed to play their own music, starting with *Headquarters.*

The Monkees also used their power and money to help new talent. Mickey Dolenz heard Jimi Hendrix in London in 1967 and invited him to open the Monkees' summer tour in America. The wild psychedelic feedback and outlandish stage show of Hendrix' act did not mesh with the Monkees' bubblegum image. Jimi bowed out before the tour ended, saying he was too ill to perform. However, this tour did bring the self-exiled Hendrix back home. The Monkees put up the money to buy equipment for Three Dog Night, paving the way for that group's success in the seventies. Also, *Easy Rider,* the generation's most important counterculture film, was financed by the Monkees.

By the end of 1968 the crazy antics and experimental film techniques of the Monkees' TV show had become stale to popular audiences, and the series was canceled, living on only in syndication. Peter Tork split after the Monkees' movie *Head* flopped. The Monkees worked as a trio for a while, but disbanded when Mike Nesmith decided to pursue a country-rock career. Mike had a couple of hits with "Joanne" and "Silver Moon," which established him as a respected, noncommercial figure in rock. Mickey and David tried a comeback in 1975, teaming up with Tommy Boyce and Bobby Hart, but the public wouldn't buy it. Dolenz continued to work in Hollywood, doing voiceovers for Saturday-morning cartoons. In 1976 he appeared with the star of *Deep Throat* in *Linda Lovelace for President.*

DONOVAN

Born in Glasgow, Scotland, Donovan P. Leitch was a major musical influence throughout Great Britain and the United States during the second half of the 1960s. Like Dylan, he wore an oversize denim cap and played a harmonica that rested on a stand around his neck. In the beginning he frequented the British television rock program *Ready Steady Go,* which aided him in his quest to become a major star in Great Britain. Initially, however, his music remained relatively unknown in the United States.

Donovan was introduced to American audiences on Dick Clark's *Where the Action Is.* And though Clark got Donovan his work permit here, he still abandoned the Caravan of Stars in the middle of the tour. Nonetheless, his first American single, "Catch the Wind," found its way to number 23 in 1965. British folk-rock took a giant leap forward with the growing popularity of Donovan. His second single, "Sunshine Superman," hit number 1 in 1966 and remained on top of the charts for thirteen weeks.

The popular acid-rock hoax of smoking bananas was the subject of Donovan's "Mellow Yellow," a song that featured backup vocals by Paul McCartney and wound up in the number-2 slot nationally. Donovan soon put a soft shroud of psychedelia over his basic folk-rock style. His lyrics grew more abstract, incorporating his feelings about meditation and mysticism at a time when gurus and transcendental meditation were the fads. Yet the rock-and-roll audiences supported Donovan, occasionally hailing him as one of the great musical maharishis. "Epistle to Dippy" (1967), the calypso beat of "There Is a Mountain" (1967), the very poetic "Wear Your Love Like Heaven" (1967), the love ballad "Jennifer Juniper" (1968), the hard rock "Hurdy Gurdy Man" (1968), the mournfully romantic "Lalena" (1968), "Atlantis" (1969), and the lyrical gobbledygook performed with the Jeff Beck Group, "Barabajagal" (1969), are among his big hits of the sixties.

Unable to repeat his recording successes in the seventies, he turned to the motion-picture industry as an actor and a soundtrack composer. He appeared in *If It's Tuesday, This Must Be Belgium* and *The Umbrellas of Cherbourg.* His music was featured in *Brother Sun, Sister Moon* and *The Pied Piper.*

In 1979 Donovan returned to popular music with a new album entitled *H.M.S. Donovan,* which reflected much of his old style with renewed energy. The release of the album prompted a national tour, opening the show for Yes. Accompanied by Ronnie Leahy (keyboards) and Colin Allen (drums), both of whom have played with such stars as Alvin Lee, Jack Bruce, and David Essex, Donovan is prepared to find a new audience for his music in the eighties.

Donovan (far left) and his band in the mid-seventies.

The original Jefferson Airplane.

THE JEFFERSON AIRPLANE

If artists are the mirrors of their time, then there is probably no better reflection of the social and political changes of the mid-sixties than the Jefferson Airplane. It was all there in the music: experimentation with drugs, the cries of rebellion, flower power, head shops, love-ins, dropping out, freaking out, hallucinations, incense, flowing vibes, and conflicts with the old guard.

The Jefferson Airplane started when Marty Balin (né Martin Buchwald) received financial backing to start a club in San Francisco called the Matrix. In addition to being a "folkie," Balin was a painter, sculptor, and amateur architect. His art decorated the club, and he built the stage himself. But the club needed a band, so Marty brought in two members from his folk group—Paul Kantner on guitar and Signe Toly on vocals. Next he invited his friend Jorma Kaukonen to play lead guitar and Jack Casady from Washington, D.C., to play bass. Balin asked guitarist Skip Spence to be their drummer because he looked like one! Their name is said to have come from Jorma's folk-club stage name—Blind Thomas Jefferson Airplane. But another story has it that Balin saw the name written on a bathroom wall. In either case the Airplane made its debut at the Matrix on August 13, 1965. They were the only act on the bill and just about the only show in town at the time. After a few months at the Matrix many record companies started making offers. An A & R man from RCA Records came through with the highest bid (which reportedly included an advance of twenty-five thousand dollars), and the deal was signed.

In September, 1966 the debut album, *The Jefferson Airplane Takes Off,* was released. Marty Balin's songs and vocals were featured because vocalist Signe was having a baby and had to leave the band. Spence, who had never felt comfortable behind the drums, left at the same time to play guitar with Moby Grape and was replaced by Spencer Dryden.

Previously, the Jefferson Airplane had occasionally shared the bill with a band called the Great Society. With Signe gone, the Great Society's vocalist, Grace Slick, was enticed to switch bands. Grace was an ex-model, the daughter of an investment banker, and a former undergraduate at New York's fashionable and expensive Finch College. Not only did she bring her raspy, leathery soprano and her provocative, slinky presence to the Airplane, she also brought two songs that she'd written and performed with the Society, "Somebody to Love" and "White Rabbit." Both songs appeared on the Airplane's second L.P., *Surrealistic Pillow,* which was released in February 1967. By early April the band had its first single on the charts with "Somebody to Love." "White Rabbit," which debuted on *American Bandstand,* was released as a single in June and also scrambled up the charts. The so-called Frisco sound had finally risen to national prominence.

The Jefferson Airplane then went on tour, pioneering the use of psychedelic light shows and bizarre concert-promotion posters. Whether playing for free in Golden Gate Park or putting on wild shows at the Fillmore East, the Airplane soared with the dancing vocal duets of Slick and Balin and the raw power of Casady's bass. In short, the Airplane created an environment that could not be captured on vinyl.

The 1967 summer of love came and went, and San Francisco's Haight-Ashbury scene turned sour and violent, but the Airplane kept flying with a series of popular L.P.'s: *After Bathing at Baxter's* (January 1968), *Crown of Creation* (September 1968), the live album *Bless Its Pointed Little Head* (March 1969), and *Volunteers* (November 1969). Balin's leadership role was now eroding, with Kantner and Slick's singing and songwriting dominance. Balin was also criticized by Jorma and Jack for his romantic ballads, which they didn't care for. With their L.P.'s already showing the signs of friction, with different

The successor to the Jefferson Airplane—the Jefferson Starship (from left: Pete Sears, Craig Chaquico, Grace Slick, Paul Kantner, David Freiberg, Marty Balin, and John Barbata).

tracks favoring various factions of the band, it came as no shock when Balin left the group in the spring of 1971. In 1970 Jack and Jorma had already formed a folk and blues subgroup, Hot Tuna, and signed a separate contract with RCA while still in the Airplane. That same year Grace and Paul started putting out L.P.'s of their own with the assistance of Bay Area star musicians like Jerry Garcia and David Crosby. Their unity was fractured, and the quality of Jefferson Airplane's music took a nosedive. *Bark* in 1971 and *Long John Silver* in 1972, both released on the Airplane's own RCA-distributed Grunt label, were not enthusiastically received. By 1974 it was all over, but out of the ashes rose the Jefferson Starship with Slick, Kantner, Craig Chaquico, David Freiberg (formerly of Quicksilver Messenger Service), John Barbata (former drummer with the Turtles and later with Crosby, Stills, Nash and Young), and Pete Sears (from Rod Stewart's contingent). The band's first L.P. was *Dragon Fly* (1974), which led to Marty Balin's return on their second album *Red Octopus* (1975). The

record went double platinum, reaching the number-1 slot four separate times.

Gone now were the revolutionary politics and the counterculture anthems of the Jefferson Airplane. The Starship sang songs of love. Their *Spitfire* L.P. hit the charts and was followed by their March 1978 L.P., *Earth,* which sold a million copies in one month. The singles "Ride The Tiger" (1974), "Miracles" (1975), "Play On Love" (1975), "With Your Love" (1976), "Count on Me" (1978), and "Runaway" (1978) brought many new fans to the Starship who had never heard of the Jefferson Airplane. But Balin refused to commit himself to the band and wouldn't even sign a contract with RCA. He wasn't exactly wild about Slick either, but Grace had personal troubles of her own. In the fall of 1978 Grace had to quit the Starship because of an intestinal ailment. Her departure was presaged back in June when her illness forced the cancellation of a concert at a German festival where over twelve thousand people rioted as a result, trashing the stage and the group's equipment. Grace is still committed to RCA Records as a member of the Starship, and she is still having problems. Her return to the band is always a possibility, but as of November 1979 the new Starship had surfaced without either her or Balin, who suffered a brain hemorrhage at the end of October of 1979, yet made a miraculously swift recovery.

The L.P. *Freedom at Point Zero* (1979) hit the top twenty within three weeks of its release with Mickey Thomas on lead vocals, Aynsley Dunbar on drums, and Steve Schuster on horns. "Jane," the single from the album, entered the top twenty with a bullet after five weeks on the charts. The Jefferson Starship is alive and well and on the road doing concerts of both the old and new material. Jack and Jorma split from Hot Tuna and are now involved in separate new-wave bands.

Grace's sarcastic but potent songs; Marty's unique ability to sing love ballads that speak to the soul; Jorma's unpredictable guitar lines; the band's appearance at the Woodstock festival, where they excited the crowd with "morning maniac music"; the band's fight with Hell's Angels at the Altamont concert; Grace calling talk-show host Dick Cavett "Jim," only to have Cavett reply, "You've got to learn my name, Miss Joplin"; Casady's complicated, throbbing bass style; Grace living with Paul for six years and giving birth to their daughter China; the booze and the coke and the acid and the smoke that created a haze around the musicians and their audiences as well; the frequent and sometimes bitter quarrels with RCA Records—prove that these artists certainly reflected the times in which they played.

220

The Sound of 1967
THE DOORS

The summer of 1967 is a landmark in rock and roll. It was the summer of *Sgt. Pepper* and *Surrealistic Pillow,* the Monterey pop festival, and the first underground FM radio stations. It was the summer that kids wore flowers in their hair and took off for Haight-Ashbury. And it was also the summer of the Doors.

"Light My Fire" was the perfect song for 1967's new FM underground. While AM radio clung to the three-minute single, "Light My Fire" clocked in at six and a half minutes, which gave the Doors time to blend a musical brew of jazz, blues, and rock, giving the guitar, organ, and drums all a chance to solo. Jim Morrison's vocals held the promise of sexual excitement and mind-expanding drugs. On July 29, 1967, during that psychedelic summer of LSD and free love, "Light My Fire" became the number-1 song in America.

The Doors—Jim Morrison, Ray Manzarek, Robbie Krieger, and John Densmore—were formed in July 1965, when Morrison, then a film student at UCLA, ran into his old friend and fellow film student, Ray Manzarek, on the beach in Venice, California. Under the influence of LSD, Morrison, according to Manzarek, began "taking notes on a fantastic rock concert going on inside his head." When Manzarek heard his friend's drug-induced lyrics, their future in rock and roll flashed before his eyes. He knew it was time to put a band together.

Manzarek, who had studied classical piano at the Chicago Conservatory and blues in the bars on Chicago's South Side, was playing in a rock band, Rick and the Ravens, with his brothers, Rick and Jim. Rick and the Ravens had cut some singles for World-Pacific Records, a tiny L.A.-based company, but the records flopped, and the Ravens were reduced to playing Santa Monica bars for fifteen dollars a night. However, Rick and the Ravens still owed World-Pacific some records, so Ray called in Jim Morrison, borrowed drummer John Densmore from the Psychedelic Rangers, and convinced his brothers to record some of Morrison's tunes. In a marathon session Rick and the Ravens cut a demo of six Morrison songs in three hours. But Ray's brothers just couldn't understand Morrison's music, so they quit and took the band's name with them. After Ray discovered guitarist Robbie Krieger at a transcendental meditation meeting, the lineup of the new band was complete. All that was missing was a name. Morrison then read the band a passage from

Jim Morrison of the Doors. *(Photo by Edmund Teske)*

William Blake: "There are things that are known and things that are unknown; in between are doors." The Doors were born.

Morrison hawked the Doors' demo to all the record companies in L.A. Billy James, a talent scout for Columbia Records, was tantalized by the Doors' sound and signed them to a six-month contract. But when James left Columbia for Elektra Records, the Doors' only real supporter at the label was gone. Months passed and Columbia didn't even bother to assign a producer to the group. The Doors asked to be let out of their contract.

In late 1965 the still-developing Doors began playing at the London Fog Club on Sunset Strip in L.A. The Doors were slightly ahead of their time with their literary songs that focused on sex and death. But it was too much for the London Fog Club, and the Doors were fired in the spring of .1966. Rejected by almost every club on the Strip, the Doors were finally hired as the house band at the Whiskey A Go Go. Opening for "name" groups like the Turtles and Them, the Doors had a chance to expand their repertoire of original material. Morrison became less inhibited as a performer and developed a screaming, erotic, frenzied stage presence. As the summer of 1966 drew to a close, the Doors had gathered a core of loyal fans. In October 1966, after a small bidding-war, Elektra Records—a label trying desperately to make the move from folk to rock—signed the Doors to a contract and turned them loose on the world.

The Doors' first album was released in January 1967. It was not the psychedelia of reversed tapes and sitar music like the Beatles' "Strawberry Fields Forever," or the coy drug allusions of the Jefferson Airplane's "White Rabbit." The instrumentation was simple, direct, and powerful—Densmore's jazz-influenced drumming, Manzarek's blues-tinged organ, and Krieger's distant guitar. Even more important than the sound was the fury of the Doors' message. Their lyrics explored ritual murder and incest in "The End," drug use and surrealistic eroticism in "The Crystal Ship," violence and rebellion in "Break on Through." "Light My Fire," Robbie Krieger's ode to smoldering sexual passion, was the key to the Doors' commercial success.

The follow-up album, *Strange Days*, released in September 1967, was similar in style and tone to the Doors' first album. The eleven-and-a-half-minute epic of the first album, "The End," had a counterpart in the eleven-minute "When the Music's Over" on *Strange Days*. The sensuality of "Soul Kitchen" became the swagger of "Love Me Two Times." The Doors themselves admitted that the second album wasn't as good as the first. After having a lifetime to prepare for their first album, they'd had only a few weeks to turn out *Strange Days*, with the added pressure of being heralded as rock's new saviors by some fans and critics.

Morrison, the son of a career Naval officer, tried to live up to his image of a rock star, but this image was full of paradoxes. With his dark, moody theatrics and revolutionary attitude, Morrison was the darling of the underground. At the same time, his pout, long curls, and leather pants made him the sweetheart of *Seventeen* magazine. He was both an acid-rock poet and a top-forty pop star. Unable to cope with the paradox of his life, Morrison turned to alcohol. Once, in a drunken stupor, he walked a fifteen-inch-wide ledge atop an office building in Beverly Hills. He fell out of windows. As he pushed his body to the brink, he began pushing the Doors stage act to the brink as well.

In concert, Morrison's bizarre behavior included raping his microphone stand, leading a lamb to symbolic slaughter, leaping into the audience, and collapsing onstage. In December 1967 the police interrupted Morrison and a girl in his dressing room before a concert in New Haven, Connecticut, and Morrison then went berserk on stage. He threw his mike stand into the audience, spat at the police who were standing in front of the stage, and sang about his being maced by the cops backstage. The police stopped the show and arrested Morrison onstage, charging him with an "indecent and immoral exhibition." The charge didn't stick, but thanks to extensive media coverage, future Doors' concerts became tense three-way affairs between the performers, the police, and the audience. Thanks to Morrison, they violated a concert curfew in Asbury Park, New Jersey, while other concerts in Arizona and on Long Island ended in riots. Finally, in March 1969, Morrison went onstage drunk at the Dinner Key Auditorium in Miami and proceeded to botch up a song. He raved in anger from the stage, and the audience began to boo and taunt the fallen idol. Morrison felt that they wanted to see his soul exposed. He gave them the next best thing and was arrested for "lewd and lascivious behavior in public, exposing his private parts, and simulating masturbation and oral copulation." Morrison was ultimately cleared of the felony charges, but was found guilty of indecent exposure and public profanity. Morrison immediately appealed his conviction on constitutional grounds, but the Doors were now considered too dangerous to book in concert.

For two years after the Miami incident the Doors were largely ignored by underground and pop audiences alike. A fine album *Morrison Hotel/Hard Rock Cafe,* featuring some of the Doors' most searing rock and roll, achieved almost instant obscurity in 1970. Nineteen seventy's *Absolutely Live* album was soon buried in the record-store budget bins.

In 1971 the Doors went back to work one more time. Morrison didn't like recording at Elektra's studios, so a studio was built in the basement of the Doors' offices. In this basement studio the Doors were reborn. Manzarek's keyboard work became a vital part of the group's sound again. With the burden of rock idolatry off their shoulders, Morrison and Krieger wrote crisp, fiery songs with the kind of vivid imagery that hadn't been seen since their 1968 album *Waiting for the Sun.* After he finished his love song to Los Angeles, "L.A. Woman," Morrison said good-bye to his friends and went to Paris for a rest. The *L.A. Woman* album resurrected the Doors. The single "Love Her Madly" climbed to number 9 in May 1971, their first top-ten hit since "Touch Me" in February 1969. "Riders on the Storm," with Morrison's raspy whisper and a keyboard solo by Manzarek that evoked an eerie picture of a thunderstorm on a dark night, was the Doors' most enduring song since "Light My Fire." *L.A. Woman* put the Doors back in the rock limelight, but for Jim Morrison, it came too late. On July 3, 1971, Morrison got up to take an early-morning bath in his Paris apartment. Later that morning his wife Pamela found him dead in the bathtub with a smile on his face.

For all intents and purposes the story of the Doors ended with the death of Jim Morrison. Krieger, Manzarek, and Densmore were all fine musicians, but Morrison embodied the spirit and the soul of the Doors. With Robbie Krieger singing lead, the remaining Doors released a surprisingly good single, "Tightrope Ride," in December 1971, but without the smoldering sensuality and fire of Jim Morrison there was no commercial success and the Doors drifted into oblivion. Seven years after his death, Manzarek, Krieger, and Densmore rejoined forces in the studio to record a musical bed for a long-lost tape of erotic poetry Morrison had recorded in 1970. The result, *An American Prayer,* seemed like a voice beckoning from the grave.

Was it a voice from the grave, or was Morrison still alive? Many clung to the notion that Morrison had not really died. No one had seen the body before Jim Morrison was reportedly laid to rest in Père-Lachaise cemetery in Paris, and there had been a suspicious delay in reporting his death. The more romantic created the rumor that Morrison was tired of the rock scene and the notoriety and wanted out, so he convinced the world of his death in order to live in peace and anonymity in either Paris or the Louisiana bayous. When a record by the Phantom sounding eerily like Jim Morrison surfaced on some FM stations in the late seventies, the story that he had faked his death won over some more converts. The rumor grew even stronger in 1980 with the publication of *No One Here Gets Out Alive,* a controversial biography that topped the best-seller list. In truth, it really doesn't matter whether Jim Morrison succumbed to his rock life-style in 1971 or simply dropped out of sight to live a simpler life. The music of Jim Morrison lives through the Doors—and that is enough.

The years 1979 to 1981 marked a building renaissance of interest in the Doors. Instigated by the use of Doors music on the soundtrack of Francis Ford Coppola's *Apocalypse Now* and fired by the stunning success of Jerry Hopkins' and Daniel Sugarman's best-selling book *No One Here Gets Out Alive,* Doors' albums sales skyrocketed again. At least two television/motion-picture projects about the group were being planned in 1980, and a group of Doors imitators began traveling the country following the trend set by a rash of Elvis imitators in previous years. The public refuses to let go. In 1980, nine years after Morrison's death, the Doors sold more copies of every one of their albums than in any year since their original releases.

1968

Nineteen sixty-seven had the summer of love, but 1968 had bad karma. In January, North Korea seized the U.S.S. *Pueblo* and held its eighty-three crew members as spies. The Vietcong launched its Tet offensive on South Vietnam. Gene McCarthy, a political dove, challenged the hawkish President Lyndon Johnson for the Democratic presidential nomination, but LBJ announced in March that he wouldn't seek re-nomination. Then Robert Kennedy threw his hat into the ring, but after winning the California primary in June, Kennedy was assassinated by Sirhan Sirhan. Just two months earlier civil rights leader Martin Luther King, Jr., had been gunned down in Memphis. That summer the streets of Chicago erupted with rioting and violence during the Democratic convention, where Vice-President Hubert Humphrey won the nomination. In the meantime, the Soviet Union crushed the liberal regime in Czechoslovakia, sending in tanks and troops to restore hard-line communism. Just one week before the American presidential election the Vietnam peace talks began in Paris with arguments over the shape of the negotiating table. But the peace talks came too late to help Hubert Humphrey, who was edged out by Richard Nixon for the Presidency.

At the Winter Olympics in Grenoble, France, the world marveled at the skiing exploits of Jean-Claude Killy, but at Mexico City's Summer Olympics, the world saw black American athletes raise their gloved fists in protest over racism in America. Pitcher "Fat" Mickey Lolich won three games as Detroit came from behind to beat the St. Louis Cardinals in the World Series. The Celtics topped the Los Angeles Lakers for the NBA championship. And Joe Namath engineered the biggest sports miracle of the year as the New York Jets upset the Baltimore Colts in Super Bowl III.

Oliver won the Oscar for Best Picture over *The Lion in Winter; Romeo and Juliet; Rachel, Rachel;* and *Funny Girl.* On television, Pete, Linc, and Julie joined Captain Greer for the first time on *The Mod Squad,* and Jack Lord started chasing crooks around the islands on *Hawaii Five-O. "Sock it to me!" "Here comes the Judge!"* Goldie Hawn, Joanne Worley, and Arte Johnson would all soon become part of the American way of life as *Rowan and Martin's Laugh-In* premiered. And Dick Clark helped bring rock and roll back to afternoon television with *Happening '68,* starring Paul Revere and the Raiders.

Rock and roll was a mixed bag in 1968. Psychedelic music like the Vanilla Fudge's "You Keep Me Hanging On" and Deep Purple's "Hush" battled the bubblegum ditties like "Yummy, Yummy, Yummy" by the Ohio Express for radio airplay. The Box Tops scored with "Cry Like a

Baby." Several songs about women found their way onto the charts in 1968, such as the Buckinghams' "Susan," Bobby Goldsboro's "Honey," Simon and Garfunkel's "Mrs. Robinson," and John Fred and His Playboy Band's "Judy in Disguise." Then there was Mary Hopkins' reminiscing in "Those Were the Days." The top ten for 1968 lined up like this: "Hey Jude" by the Beatles, "(Sittin' On) The Dock of the Bay" by Otis Redding, "This Guy's in Love with You" by Herb Alpert, "Honey" by Bobby Goldsboro, "People Got to Be Free" by the Rascals, "Sunshine of Your Love" by Cream, "The Good, the Bad, and the Ugly" by Hugo Montenegro, "Mrs. Robinson" by Simon and Garfunkel, "Love Is Blue (L'Amour est bleu)" by Paul Mauriat, and "Tighten Up" by Archie Bell and the Drells. It was 1968—the fourteenth year of rock and roll.

THE GRATEFUL DEAD

After Jerry Garcia was thrown out of the Army in 1959, he picked up his guitar and joined fellow guitarist Robert Hunter, who would later become the Dead's nonperforming songwriter, in a local folk group. But these folk gigs were less than satisfactory to Garcia. On New Year's Eve, 1964, at a Palo Alto party, Garcia and Hunter joined forces with Ron "Pig Pen" McKernan, a keyboard- and harmonica-playing vocalist who at the time was a janitor at the music store where Garcia had been giving banjo lessons. That night they also met guitarist Bob Weir. Together they formed Mother McCree's Uptown Jug Champions, trading in their acoustic instruments for electric ones. With the addition of drummer Bill Kreutzmann, whose roots were in rhythm and blues, and bassist Phil Lesh, a trumpet player who learned to play bass guitar in two weeks just to get the job, the group soon became known as the Warlocks and moved deeper into rock.

In early 1965 a state hospital in the Palo Alto area was conducting human experiments with hallucinogenic drugs, a practice that was still legal at the time. Robert Hunter volunteered along with author Ken Kesey. Before long the whole group was participating in "acid tests"—LSD parties with music supplied by the Warlocks. A year of heavier electric music followed for the group. But in February 1966 the Warlocks disappeared from the music scene after a threat of legal action from an older group with the same name. Legend has it that Garcia opened a dictionary and turned to two different pages at random. He pointed to the word "grateful" on one page and the word "dead" on another, and the Grateful Dead were born.

In June of 1966 the Dead moved to 710 Ashbury Street in the Haight-Ashbury district of San Francisco, the center of the blooming counterculture that would eventually be classified as "hippie." The Dead were the people's band, and they played for free at a local place called the Family Dog. When word started to spread about the group's incredible sound, five record companies responded with contract offers. Yet the Dead refused all of them until Warner Records promised them artistic control.

Warner released their first album, *The Grateful Dead,* in March 1967. Later that year the group rose to national prominence through their performance at the Monterey Pop Festival. *Anthem of the Sun* (August 1968) and *Aoxomoxoa* (June 1969) followed, but by this time Warner wanted some hit singles from the group. The Dead reacted in horror and reminded Warner that they weren't a singles group. They were primarily a performing group, the kings of the psychedelic circuit, attracting a cult of followers who called themselves "deadheads." The Dead gave six-hour marathon concert experiences, weaving one long song into the next, often playing nonstop for over an hour. Audiences described their happenings as "cosmic." Their main problem, however, was their inability to capture the crackling energy of their musical marathon magic on vinyl.

Woodstock happened that summer and the Dead were there. Later that year they planned on being part of the free Altamont concert with the Rolling Stones, but the murder and the mayhem that took place there prevented the Dead from performing. However, in early 1970 Warner released the group's first nonstudio album, *Live Dead.* This double L.P. finally captured what their concerts were all about and featured incredible renditions of their standards "Dark Star," "St. Stephen," and "Turn on Your Lovelight."

In spite of the release of *Live Dead,* 1970 wasn't a great year for the group. Mismanagement left them deep in debt, and their second drug bust put them deeper in trouble with the law. Frenzied touring and two quick L.P.'s, *Workingman's Dead* and *American Beauty,* helped bail them out. The former album was

The Grateful Dead.

churned out in a record-breaking nine days. The latter took a little longer and contained two of their most popular songs, "Sugar Magnolia" and "Truckin'."

Pig Pen became seriously ill in 1971 and had to be replaced for a while by Keith Godchaux. Meanwhile, offshoot bands from the Dead family were forming, most notably the New Riders of the Purple Sage, which initially featured Garcia on pedal steel. In 1972 Keith Godchaux's wife, Donna, was added to the Dead as a vocalist. The next year the heavily imbibing Pig Pen died of a liver ailment. Yet even after Pig Pen's death, the Dead continued with their concert appearances and album releases. Garcia and friends went on to start their own record company and expanded their musical horizons. By October 1974 the band had decided to take an indefinite break from performing and departed with a grand farewell concert at San Francisco's Winterland.

In the history of rock and roll few comebacks are triumphant. But the Dead came back strong with the feature film *The Grateful Dead Movie,* released in June 1977, which captured the 1974 Winterland farewell concert. After the collapse of their record company, they signed with Arista and released *Terrapin Station,* as well as individual solo efforts by Garcia and Weir. In 1979 the group underwent personnel changes, but the music itself didn't change, and really hasn't changed substantially since 1968. Interestingly, they managed to outlast their competition by attracting diehard fans. Although their critics have labeled them burned-out hippies, the Dead move into the eighties intact as serious musicians with a strong commitment to the quality of their sound.

Jerry Garcia of the Grateful Dead. *(John Wooding)*

JIMI HENDRIX

James Marshall Hendrix, the electric wizard of rock guitar, was raised in a middle-class section of Seattle, Washington. Jimi's mother died when he was ten, and he was raised by his father, a landscape gardener and saxophone player. Seeing how interested his son was in learning to play guitar, Mr. Hendrix swapped his sax for an acoustic guitar for Jimi. The boy was entranced by it and learned how to play by listening to the radio and to his dad's extensive rhythm-and-blues record collection.

By his teen-age years, Jimi had an electric guitar and was playing with several neighborhood rock bands. But his new rock-and-roll career ended when he was kicked out of Garfield High School. Jimi claimed that his expulsion was the result of his holding hands with a white girl in art class. Those who knew him at the time said it was simply a case of poor grades and boredom with his studies. In any case, Jimi enlisted in the armed services and found himself in the 101st Airborne Division at the age of seventeen. After injuring his back in a paratroop jump, he received his discharge.

Jimi then traveled to Nashville and found work as a sideman for the Isley Brothers. Next he joined a tour that starred B. B. King, Sam Cooke, Solomon Burke, and Chuck Jackson. On the road in Missouri he missed the tour bus and was stranded. At this point, he realized that in his present situation he wasn't fulfilling himself as a musician, so he never bothered to rejoin the tour. Instead, he made his way to Atlanta and got a job touring with Little Richard for almost a year. Seeing Richard's flamboyance onstage, then listening to his religious rap backstage, Jimi began to doubt the sincerity of his boss. One version of the story goes that Jimi told Richard that he would believe his line about serving God only after he saw Richard take the diamonds off his fingers and throw them into the river. The gems promptly splashed into the water.

Little Richard's tour ended on the West Coast, and Jimi moved on to perform with Ike and Tina Turner for a while, followed by stints in New York with King Curtis and Joey Dee. After three years of playing backup, Hendrix formed his own band called Jimmy James and the Blue Flames. Appearing regularly on the Greenwich Village club circuit, they were finally heard at the Cafe Wha by Chas Chandler, the original bass player for the Animals, who was now a producer and manager. Chandler and his partner, Michael Seffrey, signed Jimi and convinced him to tour England without the Blue Flames.

After auditions in England, Jimi and his managers selected a fast drummer, Mitch Mitchell, and a thin, spunky bass player, Noel Redding, to form one of the first power trios of rock—the Experience. Chandler knew that American blues were still popular at London clubs like Blaises and Bay O'Nails, and the act soon caught on. The trio was garbed in the wildest Carnaby Street fashions with ruffles, silk scarves, velvet vests, and jewels topped off with frizzy Afro haircuts. The real attraction, however, was Jimi's developing charisma and his growing sense of theater. He moaned and writhed with grace, attacked his guitar furiously and then intimately (some said "obscenely"), and created an atmosphere of brutal, deafening mayhem on stage. All those years of playing second fiddle were behind him now. Jimi was out front, and soon the entire world would recognize him.

The Jimi Hendrix Experience's first single was a new version of the classic "Hey Joe." With a boost from their appearance on the British TV rock show *Ready Steady Go,* the record shot up to number 4 in England. Chandler concentrated on manipulating the media with strategically planned photo and publicity releases, image shading, and on coaching Jimi in how to be deliberately outspoken and unconventional in interviews. Chandler claims that

231

Young Jimi Hendrix.

the legendary guitar-smashing on stage started by accident when Jimi was pulled off the stage by excited fans at a concert in Munich. He leaped back onstage, throwing his guitar ahead of him. It landed hard, cracking and breaking the strings. Mad as hell, Jimi began smashing everything in sight. The German audience was stunned. They loved it.

"Purple Haze" and "The Wind Cries Mary" followed "Hey Joe" as hit singles in England. Finally, word of this new sensation started to drift back to the U.S. Paul McCartney suggested that the organizers of the June 1967 Monterey Pop Festival book the Experience. They did, and Jimi's performance was almost mythic. Never before had such thundering volume and violent distortion come so savagely from an amplifier. But what really electrified the crowd was Jimi's physical relationship with his guitar. He caressed it with his lips, played it with his teeth, courted it with his pelvic thrusts, and stroked it between his legs. As a finale, he doused the instrument with lighter fluid and let it burn.

While Jimi's notoriety was mushrooming, Chandler booked the Experience as the opening act on the Monkees' first tour. Later that summer Hendrix left this tour. Unfortunately, the preteens who devoured the Monkees bubblegum music weren't ready for the theatrics of Hendrix. The mismatch forced the Experience to drop out of the tour with Jimi claiming an illness as their reason. But the contrast between the mild Monkees and the wild pyrotechnics of the Experience gained Hendrix some valuable publicity.

By the end of the summer of 1967 Hendrix had signed with Warner Records, which released "Purple Haze" in August and "Foxy Lady" in December. Jimi's first L.P., *Are You Experienced,* came out in September 1967, and the follow-up L.P., *Axis: Bold as Love,* was released in March 1968. Jimi's audience built slowly, but by August 1968 *Are You Experienced* was number 10 and *Axis* was number 16. The band then took to the road, crisscrossing the country, roaring in great psychedelic decibels.

In late 1968, amidst management hassles and personality problems with the Experience, Jimi dissolved the group. Hendrix then produced his own L.P., *Electric Lady Land,* which was released in August. It was Jimi's first number-1 record. Both *Billboard* and *Rolling Stone* named Hendrix 1968's artist of the year.

In 1969 Jimi formed the Band of Gypsies with army buddy Bill Cox on bass and Buddy Miles on drums. But they, too, broke up after a few short months. Jimi then assembled a new crew of musicians and appeared at the Woodstock festival that summer. But the pressures were building up inside Jimi. He felt trapped inside his image—as if he were just a product. He was no longer challenged by his fellow musicians or pleased by his audiences. By 1970 his shows became lackluster and mechanical. At this time, he also had serious run-ins with the police in Sweden and Canada.

Preoccupied with building his Electric Lady recording studio in New York City, Jimi only took time out to appear at the Isle of Wight concert in August 1970. When it was over he headed for London. On September 18, 1970, after taking barbiturates, Jimi suffocated on his own vomit while unconscious. At the age of twenty-seven Hendrix was dead from what was probably an accidental overdose. Jimi didn't exactly shy away from drugs, but it's doubtful that he committed suicide. After his death many old previously discarded tracks were repackaged and marketed as Hendrix L.P.'s, but none of them had the old magic. Hendrix was an innovator. Fuzz, feedback, phasing, wah-wah, and tremolo were squeezed out of his guitar, and many of his sounds remain mysteries to the masters of today's electronic music. Offstage, he tended to be shy and introverted, but when he strapped on his guitar, Hendrix was a rock-and-roll legend. And he still is.

CREAM

Eric Clapton (born Eric Patrick Clapp) came from an English working-class background. He gave up a career as a stained-glass-window designer to concentrate on blues guitar. Influenced by artists such as Muddy Waters, B. B. King, Albert King, and Elmore James, Eric lent his growing skills to several local teen-age bands, including Casey and the Engineers, Power House, and the Roosters. Eric's real breakthrough came in 1963 when he joined the Yardbirds ("For Your Love," "A Heartful Of Soul," "I'm a Man") just in time for the first British invasion on the American rock-and-roll scene.

At the end of 1964 Clapton left the Yardbirds and was replaced by Jeff Beck. Eric felt that the band had become far too commercial for a blues purist like himself. He was a construction worker for a while before joining John Mayall's Blues Breakers. Before long Eric's flashy guitar playing gained him cult status in England. Rock-and-roll graffiti of the day proclaimed, "Clapton is God."

Ginger Baker (born Peter Baker in England) also came from a working-class background. His first passion was jazz drumming, and by his teens he was playing with the jazz bands of Terry Lightfoot and Mr. Acker Bilk. When Ginger moved onto Alexis Korner's Blues Incorporated in the early sixties, he became friendly with the Scottish bass player, Jack Bruce. Bruce, who had worked with Manfred Mann, joined Baker in defecting from Korner's group to the Graham Bond Organization. There they stayed until 1966 when agent Robert Stigwood matched them with Eric Clapton. The three agreed to work together under the name Cream, and Stigwood produced their first British hit single, "Wrapping Paper."

In January 1967 Cream debuted in America with the release of their first album, *Fresh Cream.* The album turned gold, and yielded one single, "I Feel Free." Cream really took off in 1968 as their second album, *Disraeli Gears,* quickly climbed onto the

charts and stayed there for the entire year. Produced by Felix Pappalardi (later of Mountain), the album transcended the blues orientation of *Fresh Cream* and placed them in the vanguard of progressive rock. "Strange Brew," "Tales of Brave Ulysses," and "Sunshine of Your Love" were all singles from *Disraeli Gears.* The latter single was first released in January 1968, but only found success after its rerelease six months later. By that summer it had become a favorite with the growing legions of underground FM radio stations. The outrageous wah-wah guitar, catchy bass line, and surrealistic lyrics captured a market. More importantly, they proved to both the record and radio industries that it was no longer just the singles that were propelling bands to the top. Albums, concerts, and word of mouth were equally important to a band's success now. "You gotta see 'em onstage!" said their fans. Led by the legendary speed drumming of Baker, Cream was explosive in concert. The guitar work of Clapton and Bruce was second only to Hendrix's magic. Their audiences were always convinced that they had just seen the ultimate band, the most talented and loudest in existence. This reputation was reinforced by the June 1968 release of Cream's third album, *Wheels of Fire,* a two-disc set—one recorded live and the other recorded in the studio. The L.P. went platinum and featured the gold single "White Room" (October 1968) written by Ginger Baker and Jack Bruce.

By the end of 1968 Cream was the top new band in America. Then, without warning, the band announced that they would go their separate ways after a farewell tour, which concluded at London's Albert Hall on November 26, 1968. At the start of 1969 one last Cream album was released, aptly titled *Goodbye.* Shortly thereafter, rumors of the real reasons for the split-up began to leak out to the public.

Destructive egos allegedly led to musical duels onstage with each musician attempting to out-solo the others. Clapton blamed their problems on the strain of continuous touring. But whatever the reason, the supergroup was dead.

However, Robert Stigwood refused to lose one supergroup without creating a new one. From the ruins of Cream came Blind Faith. Clapton and Baker joined Traffic's Stevie Winwood and Rick Grech from a group called Family to produce an excellent album featuring the stirring "Well All Right." But Blind Faith came to a quick end as the same supergroup pressures that haunted Cream surfaced again. Clapton moved on to the group that had opened for Blind Faith on tour—Delaney and Bonnie and Friends. He played on their hit single "Never Ending Song of Love" before recording his first solo album. He soon formed Derek and the Dominoes with three ex-Delaney and Bonnie musicians and guitarist Duane Allman. In 1970 *Layla* was their L.P. and also the title of the hit single from the album. "Layla" was the nickname of Patti Harrison, wife of Beatle George and live-in lover of Eric after she separated from her husband. Unfortunately, the band split in 1972 when Clapton began his year-and-a-half battle with a heroin addiction.

Eric beat his heroin problem in 1974 and resurfaced with a new band and new studio album, *461 Ocean Boulevard.* A reggae-style single written by Bob Marley, "I Shot the Sheriff," hit number 1 for Eric that same year. Album successes followed with *There's One in Every Crowd, E. C. Was Here,* and *Slowhand.* His singles also continued to flow with "Hello Old Friend" (1976), "Lay Down Sally" (1978), and "Wonderful Tonight" (1978). He performed in the motion picture *Tommy* and played on the Beatles' "While My Guitar Gently Weeps," as well as with Steve Stills, George Harrison, and Aretha Franklin. The highlight of the seventies for Clapton may well have been his March 1979 marriage to Patti Harrison, where he played at the reception with a reunited Paul McCartney, Ringo Starr, and George Harrison. Clapton opened 1981 with his best single in years, the biting rocker "I Can't Stand It," but a long-standing ulcer problem knocked Eric out of commission, forcing him into the hospital and out of concert halls for a while.

Ginger Baker formed Ginger Baker's Air Force after Cream disbanded. It didn't fly very far, though, and Baker bailed out in time to start up the Baker-Gurvitz Army, which did about as well as his Air Force.

Jack Bruce released a few solo L.P.'s after leaving Cream. He also played with Tony Williams' Lifetime, then formed West, Bruce and Laing with two survivors from Mountain. Unfortunately for Jack, he never duplicated his earlier success.

Cream rose to the top of the rock-and-roll world in 1967 and 1968, liberating the music and introducing the free-form era of the extended instrumental solo. Many never forgave them for it; many more never forgot them for it.

Eric Clapton.

SLY AND THE FAMILY STONE

Sylvester Stewart was born in Dallas in 1944 and raised in the California factory·town of Vallejo. His family sang gospel together as the Stewart Four, and by the time Sly was four years old he was singing and recording with them. Before long he displayed as much talent playing guitar and drums as he did leading a street gang and participating in high school race riots.

By the time Sly was sixteen, he had enjoyed a mild success on the G & P label with the single "Long Time Away." He then went on to form a number of groups with his brother Fred. As the Stewart Brothers they recorded for Ensign; and as the Viscanes, they had a regional success with "Yellow River." Sly then enrolled in Vallejo Junior College to study music theory and composition. In 1964, at age nineteen, he became a record producer for the Autumn label, which was owned by the famous San Francisco radio personality Tom Donahue. Sly produced the Beau Brummels, who had national hits with "Laugh, Laugh" and "Just A Little," and produced and cowrote the successful "C'mon and Swim" for Bobby Freeman. He also produced the original version of "Somebody to Love" by Grace Slick and the Great Society.

During this period Sly also recorded his own work but was not satisfied with the results and would not release any of it. When producing became too impersonal for Sly, he enrolled in radio school. Three months later he was a disc jockey on KSOL in San Francisco—the number-two black station in the market. His radio show revealed a dynamic emerging performer. His rap was fast and streetwise, and he added his favorite tunes by the Beatles and Dylan to the playlist of soul artists. His ratings were good enough to keep him on the air. DJ Sly never lost touch with the music scene and promoted the short-lived Stoners in 1966. That experience reintroduced him to an old high school friend named Cynthia Robinson, a trumpet player. Together they assembled the

Family Stone with Sly's sister, Rose Stone; brother Fred Stone; cousins Jerry and Gregg; Cynthia's cousin Larry Graham, whose bass guitar playing and bass vocalizing would become a trademark of the band. The group was a liberal's delight—men, women, blacks, and whites performing equally and enthusiastically. They dressed with flair, though Sly was always the most outrageous. The band grooved to its freewheeling mixture of rock, jazz, and blues. Their club appearances and Loadstone label recordings began to draw more and more attention.

In 1967 the band signed with Epic Records, a major label. With the release of their first album, *A Whole New Thing,* in October 1967, the entire country could hear this new sound called "psychedelic soul." Sly was a master in the recording studio as well as a virtuoso on a dozen instruments. With Sly at the helm the band created a sound that was as alive as it was different. Voices and instruments were blended and alternated with genius. Flash and innovation were their guidelines.

"Dance to the Music" was their first single, released in November of 1967, and their first hit. In March the L.P. of the same name was released, followed in July by their third album, *Life,* which included the single "M'Lady." The November 1968 single "Everyday People," which was number 1 for four weeks, appeared on their fourth L.P., *Stand* (April 1969), along with the single, "Stand." A major boost to the group's career was their thunderous reception at the Woodstock Festival. The feature film of Woodstock shows them exciting over four hundred thousand people with their show-stopping version of "I Want to Take You Higher." Indeed, Sly took a whole generation of rock freaks higher. His hits kept coming with "Hot Fun in the Summertime" in 1969 and "Thank You Falettinme Be Mice Elf Agin" in 1970. In November 1970 a *Greatest Hits* album was released by Epic, which climbed to the number-1 spot and sold a million copies in less than two months.

Unfortunately, Sly was also developing a well-deserved reputation as a concert no-show. Sometimes he would appear hours late and so stoned that he couldn't remember what song he had just performed. According to his personal manager at the time, twenty-six out of eighty 1970 engagements had to be cancelled and eight others went on hours later than originally scheduled. By 1971 very few promoters in the U.S. would work with Sly Stone. While the group was still recording, no new material was released. Rumors of breakups, dope misuse, and lawsuits were common. Some said the Black Panthers were wooing Sly, and this political interference was tearing the band apart. Their no-show in Grant Park in Chicago caused a riot. Finally, after two years of erratic concertizing and ugly gossip, Sly and the Family Stone released their long-delayed album *There's a Riot Going On.* The reactions to this pessimistic, dark, and disturbing record were almost unanimously unfavorable. Sly had used the album to bare his soul, confessing his identity crisis and his contempt for the demands of his audience. His audience apparently couldn't care less about his problems. However, the L.P.'s three singles—"A Family Affair," a number-1 song for four weeks (1971); "Runnin' Away" (1972); and "Smiling" (1972)—carried it to the number-1 slot on the album charts.

Dick Clark took a big risk when he invited the long-idle Sly to be one of the hosts of *The American Music Awards* on *live* television. Sly proved his worst critics wrong when he did show up for the awards *on time,* albeit visibly sedated.

In 1973 Sly and the Family Stone released the album *Fresh* and the gold single "If You Want Me to Stay." Longing to regain the past glory, they set out on their first tour in two years. By this time two original members of the group had quit and had been replaced. An incredible publicity stunt was deemed necessary to recapture Sly's fame. In 1974 Sly was married onstage at Madison Square Garden in New York, possibly the only way he could have filled the Garden at this time. But their popularity began to wane again. Sly and the Family Stone produced a horde of uneventful L.P.'s: *Small Talk* (1974), *High Energy* (1975), and *High on You* (1975). In 1977 Epic Records, Sly's company for ten years, dropped the group after two years of inactivity. They did release *Ten Years Too Soon* in 1979, featuring his old hits remixed for the disco market. But the album had little impact. Warner Records then signed Sly later that year and released his L.P. *Back on the Right Track.* Unfortunately, he wasn't, and the record went nowhere.

Nothing can detract from Sly's role as a major

Sylvester Stewart, the leader of Sly and the Family Stone.

force in the social music that followed the 1973 release of *Riot,* which influenced the preaching and philosophizing of artists like the new Temptations and the O'Jays. Sly obliterated racial and sexual demarcations with his thoroughly integrated band and shattered musical conventions by encouraging his band to experiment with wild dynamics and complex vocals. Some called it radical soul, distorted soul, or freaky soul. But change was the "constant" that created what Sly called the "first fusion of psychedelia and rhythm and blues."

The Beau Brummels, an early San Francisco band with a British sound, produced by Sly Stone. The Beau Brummels hit big with "Laugh Laugh" and "Just a Little" in 1965.

TOMMY JAMES AND THE SHONDELLS

In 1960 Tommy Jackson was a twelve-year-old kid from Niles, Michigan. While most kids in his seventh-grade class were trading baseball cards, reading comic books, and watching *77 Sunset Strip* on television, Tommy was fronting a rock-and-roll band that played at school hops, local bars, and the American Legion hall. But who would have guessed that a song Tommy recorded as a twelve-year-old in 1960 would become the number-1 song in the nation in 1966, bringing Tommy the rock-and-roll stardom that he had just about given up on?

Tommy Jackson learned to play guitar when he was nine. In 1960 he put together his first band, the Shondells, named after rock singer Troy Shondell. At this time, Tommy took the stage name Tommy James. Jack Douglas, a disc jockey at local radio station WNIL, heard the Shondells and invited the group to cut a record in the radio station's studio. Tommy and the Shondells recorded a song they had heard in the local bars, a repetitive but catchy tune called "Hanky Panky." Jack Douglas liked what he heard and started his own label, Snap Records, so he could release the disc regionally. He played the hell out of "Hanky Panky" on his radio show, and it became a local hit. Douglas, however, was fired from WNIL for plugging the record, and it was soon back to the seventh grade and the American Legion hall for Tommy James.

In 1966, while sorting through a stack of throwaway records, a disc jockey at KDKA in Pittsburgh found an old copy of "Hanky Panky" by Tommy James and the Shondells and played it on his show. Immediately KDKA's telephone lines lit up. Within a week "Hanky Panky" was the most requested song in Pittsburgh, and within ten days there were orders for eighty thousand copies of the record in that city alone. Tommy James and the Shondells were the biggest thing since U.S. Steel moved to town, but no one knew a thing about them.

By 1966 Tommy had graduated from high school, and the original Shondells had long gone their separate ways. Tommy had played blues with Motown's Junior Walker in Detroit and jazz in some small clubs in Chicago. He was making fifteen dollars a night playing rock in local bars in Michigan when he received a puzzling phone call from a promoter in western Pennsylvania. Tommy dropped everything to headline in Pittsburgh for three thousand dollars a night. The amazing success of the record in Pittsburgh led to its sale to Roulette Records. Overnight Tommy James and the defunct Shondells, who had not played together since junior high, had the number-1 hit in America with a six-year-old record made before Tommy's voice had changed.

With this kind of success, Tommy James could have easily been just another one-shot artist. But fate had given Tommy his chance, and he wasn't about to let it slip away. With years of experience under his belt and new Shondells at his side, Tommy James decided to give Roulette Records and the rest of the rock-and-roll world a run for its money.

In February 1967 the group reappeared with a thumping guitar and a heavy back-beat on the penultimate teen-age song, "I Think We're Alone Now." With lyrics about suspicious parents, racing heartbeats, and aching teen-age lust, "I Think We're Alone Now" captured the sweaty side of teen-age romances in parked cars and drive-ins all over America. Not only was it a standard for every high school rock band in 1967, it was also rerecorded in 1979 by both the Rubinoos and Lene Lovitch for a new generation of sweaty teen-agers.

Tommy hit the charts consistently in 1967 and 1968 with "Mirage," "Gettin' Together," and "Mony Mony." But the Shondells' sound was ripped off, simplified, and generally exploited by saccharine wonders like the 1910 Fruitgum Company and the Ohio Express. Tommy James was tagged a bubblegum artist, and he didn't like it one bit. Making an abrupt switch, he moved from the fringes of bubblegum to the frontiers of psychedelia—without losing his commercial appeal. In December 1968 his "Crimson and Clover" exploded onto the scene. With its fluttering tremolo vocal, "Crimson and Clover" seemed to be about drugs or sex. But even after listening to it over and over, it was difficult to figure out what Tommy James meant. Some radio stations decided to ban the record just in case, but it didn't matter. "Crimson and Clover" hit number 1 on February 1, 1969.

Now Tommy was on a roll. "Sweet Cherry Wine" followed "Crimson and Clover" to the top ten. "Crystal Blue Persuasion," with its slightly more obvious lyrics about drugs, sat in the top ten for nine weeks, cresting at number 2 for three weeks in July 1969. Though not as big a hit, "Ball of Fire" broke through the top twenty in the autumn. The band was at its peak in 1969, playing as many as five one-night stands a week.

Unfortunately, it all came crashing down for Tommy James early in 1970. Tommy's infatuation with drug lyrics was no accident. In February 1970 Tommy James finally collapsed onstage in Montgomery, Alabama. He tottered on the edge between life and death with one doctor actually pronouncing him dead at one point. But Tommy James cheated death. He hung on, but was incapable of functioning. He had to be moved to his upstate New York farm, where he vegetated for almost a year.

Tommy's recovery was slow, but he fought back. Initially he was deathly afraid of the recording studio, but he eventually started his comeback by producing "Tighter and Tighter" in 1971 for a group named (appropriately enough) Alive and Kicking. With his confidence back, Tommy took the plunge and made his comeback as a solo artist with the 1971 hit "Dragging the Line." The next nine years were largely uneventful, but by 1980 Tommy had come full circle, appearing again on *American Bandstand* with a new hit, "Three Times in Love."

The Sound of 1968

OTIS REDDING

In the spring of 1963, Macon, Georgia's Johnny Jenkins and the Pinetoppers had an audition and a recording session in Memphis, Tennessee, with Stax records. Johnny had his valet/chauffeur drive the band to Memphis. As the Pinetoppers went through their paces in the studio, the valet, who was really just a shy country boy, sat quietly in the corner. He would willingly run out to get lunch or a six-pack for the group, occasionally mentioning to no one in particular that he could sing, too. When the recording session was over, the valet finally got up the nerve to ask if he could cut a song. The producer, Steve Cropper, and the Stax session band, Booker T. and the M.G.'s, had put in a long, hard day working with Johnny Jenkins, but they decided to stay and give the kid a chance. He started to sing a Little Richard song with Richard's voice and inflections down cold. Jim Stewart, the head of Stax Records, was in the studio. He told the valet that the last thing the world needed was another Little Richard. Stewart suggested that he try a slow song, and the valet started singing a song he had written years before, "These Arms of Mine." They didn't exactly flip over the song, but Stewart decided to record and release it anyway. "These Arms of Mine" slowly found its audience, first locally, then nationwide, eventually selling over 750,000 copies. Stax Records had found a star in that shy valet—Otis Redding.

The son of a Baptist minister, Otis was born in Dawson, Georgia, in 1941. When he was a youngster his family moved to Macon, Georgia, where Otis began singing in the church choir. In the mid-fifties, a local boy from Macon, Little Richard Penniman, had hit the big time in the music business. Little Richard was an idol to young Otis, inspiring him to make singing his career. Otis entered local talent contests and he often walked off the stage a winner. In 1960 Otis cut a Little Richard-styled number, "Shout Bamalama," for Bethlehem records, but the record didn't sell. Otis then began working for Johnny Jenkins and the Pinetoppers, primarily as a driver and valet, but occasionally as a singer, traveling the southern college fraternity circuit. When Otis was given his chance at Stax, he made the best of it. Johnny Jenkins, on the other hand, drifted off into obscurity.

In the fall of 1963 Otis was back in Memphis cutting an album for Stax with producer Steve Cropper. Redding's style was a mixture of several influences, primarily Little Richard and Sam Cooke. Although capable of

Little Richard rave-ups, he could also give emotional readings of slow, sad, and tender ballads like "Pain in My Heart," the title track of his first L.P., which was later covered by the Rolling Stones. Three singles in 1965 solidified Redding's position as a soul artist: two slow, aching songs of lost love, "Mr. Pitiful" and "I've Been Loving You Too Long," and the classic soul shaker "Respect." "Respect" hit number 35 on the national charts in November 1965, but Otis was still unknown in the white community. It wasn't until Aretha Franklin took "Respect" to number 1 in 1967 that the general public knew who Otis Redding was.

Otis wasn't getting the kind of pop radio airplay necessary to make him a star, so Stax decided that he should record the Rolling Stones hit "Satisfaction." Because Otis didn't know the song, Steve Cropper brought a copy of the Stones' 45 to the studio. When nobody could figure out Mick Jagger's lyrics, Otis decided to sing it his way. Redding's version was so different, a rumor started to circulate that Otis originally wrote "Satisfaction" and sold it to the Stones for fifty dollars. Although it helped him cross over to a white market, Otis later admitted that he never really wanted to cut the record because the song just didn't feel right to him.

The pieces began to fall into place for Otis Redding in 1967. He opened the year by putting a powerful ballad on the charts, "Try a Little Tenderness." He then formed his own record company, Jotis, and his own music publishing firm, Redwal. His protégé, Arthur Conley, had a gold record and number-2 hit with "Sweet Soul Music," which was cowritten by Otis, Conley, and Sam Cooke.

He made several appearances on Dick Clark's *Where the Action Is* in 1967. Otis also traveled to Europe on the Hit the Road, Stax tour, where he mesmerized crowds in Britain and France. In the fall of 1967 England's *Melody Maker* magazine named Otis the top singer of 1967, ending Elvis Presley's eight-year reign with that title. That summer Otis had performed at one A.M. before an exhausted crowd at the Monterey Pop Festival. Otis stirred them with his intense, emotional expressiveness.

Having broken through to a white audience, Redding became the uncrowned king of Stax/Volt Records with his blend of blues, gospel, and pop that enabled the label to compete with the majors. In December Otis found it necessary to purchase a twin-engine Beechcraft airplane to make his busy touring schedule a little easier.

On December 7, 1967, Otis was in Memphis recording "(Sittin' On) The Dock of the Bay," a song he had written with Steve Cropper. "Dock of the Bay" was a laid-back soul ballad that was to be Redding's next single. But Otis never lived to hear it. On his way to a concert in Madison, Wisconsin, on December 10, his plane crashed into the icy waters of Lake Monona, four miles from the Madison Airport. Otis, his valet, the pilot, and four members of his backup group, the Bar-Kays, died at the bottom of that frozen lake. A month after his death Stax released "The Dock of the Bay." The record shot to number 1 and stayed there for four weeks. It was the first posthumous number-1 hit in the history of recorded music. "(Sittin' On) The Dock of the Bay" was Otis' biggest record, selling over two million copies. In 1968 Redding won two Grammy Awards, Best Male Rhythm and Blues Vocal Performance and Best Rhythm and Blues Song. "(Sittin'

Otis Redding.

On) The Dock of the Bay" was the sound of 1968. Unfortunately, Otis Redding never got to enjoy his greatest success.

1969

On July 20, 1969, Neil Armstrong and Buzz Aldrin fulfilled one of man's greatest dreams, becoming the first men to land on the moon. It was an awe-inspiring event, but a miracle almost as big took place in New York City. The Mets—the amazing, inept, lovable laughingstocks of baseball—stunned the nation by clawing their way past Leo Durocher's Chicago Cubs to the top of the National League, then crushing the Baltimore Orioles in the World Series to become the World Champions of baseball.

Less inspiring were the teargas bombs that exploded in Berkeley as students battled the state of California over People's Park. Four hundred miles down the coast in Los Angeles, Charles Manson's "family" slaughtered actress Sharon Tate in the brutal Tate–La Bianca murders. In Massachusetts, Senator Edward Kennedy accidentally drove his car off a bridge at Chappaquiddick, killing Mary Jo Kopechne and marring his political future. The Who's rock opera *Tommy* set FM radio on its ear in the early summer. In October a Vietnam War moratorium was called, and massive demonstrations across the United States called for an end to the war in Southeast Asia. In August at Max Yasgur's farm in Bethel, New York, a half-million children of rock and roll convened to celebrate rock music at Woodstock.

Dustin Hoffman's performance as Ratso Rizzo earned *Midnight Cowboy* the Oscar for Best Picture of the Year. On television, *Marcus Welby, M.D.* and *Medical Center* picked up Drs. Casey and Kildare's caseloads. *The Music Scene,* an updated version of *Your Hit Parade,* with David Steinberg and Lily Tomlin, flopped, but *This Is Tom Jones,* starring the swivel-hipped singing Welshman, was a success in the ratings. And speaking of successes, the Boston Celtics won their eleventh NBA championship in thirteen years, driving past the Los Angeles Lakers, and the Kansas City Chiefs humiliated the Minnesota Vikings in Super Bowl IV.

In 1969 the second of two films produced by Dick Clark was released. The first, *Psychout* (1968), starred an unknown Jack Nicholson and was scored with contemporary music by the Strawberry Alarm Clock, the Seeds, and other psychedelic groups. *The Savage Seven,* a motorcycle movie, featured a score by the Iron Butterfly. The nucleus of that production crew went on to do the film *Easy Rider* in later years.

In music, 1969 brought singles as diverse as Marvin Gaye's "Too Busy Thinking 'Bout My Baby," the Isley Brothers' "It's Your Thing—Do Whatcha Wanna Do," Judy Collins' "Both Sides Now," the Lettermen's "Hurt So Bad," and the Foundations' "Build Me Up, Buttercup." Garrett

Scott and Steam, a group of studio musicians from Connecticut, offered the year's most meaningful lyrics in "Na Na Hey Hey Kiss Him Goodbye." Zager and Evans emerged from Kansas City with their apocalyptic hit about the absolute destruction of the human race, "In the Year 2525," which was number 1 in the nation for six consecutive weeks in the summer. But on the seventh week "In the Year 2525" fell from the charts, and Zager and Evans were never heard from again.

The top ten of 1969 panned out this way: "Sugar Sugar" by the Archies, "Aquarius/Let the Sunshine In" by the Fifth Dimension, "I'll Never Fall in Love Again" by Tom Jones, "Honky Tonk Women" by the Rolling Stones, "Dizzy" by Tommy Roe, "Everyday People" by Sly and the Family Stone, "I Can't Get Next to You" by the Temptations, "Hot Fun in the Summertime" by Sly and the Family Stone, "Build Me Up, Buttercup" by the Foundations, and "Crimson and Clover" by Tommy James and The Shondells.

It was 1969—the fifteenth year of rock and roll.

JANIS JOPLIN

As a teen-ager in Texas, Janis patterned her singing on the great blues singers like Bessie Smith. An ugly duckling who dressed like a bohemian to conceal her weight, Janis soon became an outcast in her high school. In her early twenties she began traveling the country, singing for a pittance at colleges and local bars. This tough, often harsh life-style served to alienate her more and more. Perhaps the last straw for Janis was when she was voted the "ugliest man on campus" at the University of Texas. She fled Texas and made her way to the flowering hippie community in San Francisco. But an ugly bout with drugs sent her back home to recover. However, San Francisco was not through with Janis.

Chet Helms was the resident guru of San Francisco's acid-rock community. He heard Janis sing in San Francisco and liked her. He told one of the local rock groups, Big Brother and the Holding Company, to follow the Jefferson Airplane's lead and hire a female lead vocalist. They agreed, and Helms sent his friend Travis Rivers to track down Janis in Texas and bring her back. Later Joplin claimed that she was conned into returning to San Francisco because "the guy was such a good ball."

Though Janis had never sung with electric instruments and drums, there was soul and magic in the room when she started singing with Big Brother. A recording contract with Mainstream Records yielded an album and two singles, but it was 1967's Monterey Pop Festival that brought the group to its first real recognition and appreciation. Janis stopped the show with the gravelly, growling voice that erupted from her soul. She thundered and screamed her lyrics into the microphone while leaping and shaking her body. Her sexual undulations wrapped her plain features with an eroticism that electrified the audience.

After Monterey Pop, Big Brother and the Holding Company were approached by Bob Dylan's manager, Albert Grossman. He added the group to his clientele and obtained a contract with Columbia Records for them. *Cheap Thrills* was their first Columbia album, released in 1968 with an illustrated cover by famed San Francisco underground cartoonist Robert Crumb. Sales quickly topped the million-dollar mark, and the single "Piece of My Heart" hit the top ten, soon followed by the popular "Ball and Chain."

Janis soon became the queen of acid rock, going out of her way to live up to the image. She was uninhibited, with a choice vocabulary lined with four-letter words. Her pleasures included downing quarts of Southern Comfort and taking assorted drugs. But behind the facade was a lonely, insecure woman. In her own words, "Onstage I make love to twenty-five thousand people, then I go home alone."

In 1969, after associates and critics told her that the musical limitations of Big Brother and the Holding Company were holding her back, Janis split from the group. At the time, she claimed the group wouldn't rehearse or learn new material. The group never hid their bitterness toward her after the split, feeling that they were abandoned after they helped make her a superstar. After their final concert with Janis in December 1968, she put together a fairly anonymous backup band and set out on her new solo career. Big Brother and the Holding Company, however, lasted only a short while without Janis.

I Got Dem Ol' Kozmic Blues Again Mama (1969) was her first solo album. It gave her the hit single "Try." Unfortunately, Janis had developed a heavy heroin habit by this time and fled to Brazil to kick it. Although her life seemed to be looking up with her plans to marry her old friend Country Joe MacDonald, upon her return to America she fell back into her former addiction. On October 4, 1970, Janis Joplin's body was found at Hollywood's Landmark Motor Hotel. With fresh puncture marks in her arm plus alcohol and morphine in her bloodstream, the

Janis Joplin.

coroner ruled her death an accidental overdose. Her body was cremated; the remains scattered along the California coastline.

In 1971 Columbia released *Pearl* posthumously. Recorded shortly before her death, the album was an immediate hit, featuring her classic rendition of Kris Kristofferson's "Me and Bobby McGee." Through the mid-seventies Columbia continued to issue previously unreleased and repackaged Joplin material.

THE WHO

The Who in 1965.

Peter Townshend simply hated his nose. In his British schoolboy years his outsized honker made him the object of easy and frequent ridicule. He felt alone, ugly, unwanted. Someday, he vowed, it would be different. He'd be famous. He'd see his face, nose and all, on every newspaper and billboard in the country! Rock legends are founded on such dreams of teenage revenge, and Peter Townshend's revenge led to one of the biggest and most enduring legends in rock—the incomparable Who.

In the early sixties a young Townshend grabbed onto rock and roll as an outlet for his frustrations. He joined his schoolmate John Entwistle in the Detours,

248

a band fronted by apprentice juvenile delinquent Roger Daltrey. Together with drummer Doug Sanden, they hit western London's school-dance and rock-club circuit.

When Peter realized that he'd never be a guitar virtuoso, he masked his lack of precision skills with a grab bag of flashy visual tricks. One minute he'd use his guitar like a machine gun, mowing down the audience. The next minute he'd attack his strings with vicious windmill-like swoops. He'd leap and twist his body in midair, throwing himself about the stage like a holy roller in the grip of rock-and-roll fever. Daltrey followed suit, swinging his mike like a lasso and strutting around in circles like a caged beast. It was strong stuff for the early sixties, but it gained the band, who were now called the Who, a following among London's growing mod cult.

Then manager Peter Meaden entered the picture, eager to use the band to exploit those young mods. Meaden dressed the band in trendy mod clothing, changed their name to the High Numbers (mod slang for uppers), sacked drummer Sanden for being on the wrong side of thirty, hustled a record deal with Fontana, and even found time to write their first single in 1964, "I'm the Face." None of this brought the band fame and fortune. It did, however, bring them a rather unusual drummer.

Most sources agree that Keith Moon just appeared out of nowhere one day, drunkenly demanding a tryout with the band. During his audition he played like a speed-crazed spasmodic, flailing wildly at the drum kit, and breaking the bass drum pedal, which wasn't even his. He was hired on the spot.

The group's anarchy onstage escalated to a new threshold of mania at the Railway Tavern. One of Townshend's leaps that night sent the neck of his guitar crashing through the pub's low ceiling. The crowd went wild, so Peter poked a few more holes in the ceiling with his now defunct instrument. The crowd loved it. Without hesitation Townshend whipped off his guitar and smashed it to smithereens across the stage. The audience was his.

Within days guitar slaughter became a regular part of the act. Keith was only too happy to add his drum kit to the carnage, and Roger wasn't far behind. Only John Entwistle abstained, standing aside stoically. But his reserve amid all the destruction only added to the lunacy. Guitars were smashed through amps. Mikes and cymbals crashed to the ground. It was the most spectacular finish a live rock show ever had. And it was also expensive!

Nonetheless, it paid off. One of those early Railway dates attracted aspiring film director Kit Lambert. Flabbergasted by their display, he dragged his partner, Chris Stamp, to see the band. Eventually their plans of making films were forgotten. Lambert and Stamp signed the band to a new management contract, rechristened them the Who, and prepared to set them on the world.

Through the tireless efforts of their new managers, the Who landed an extended run at London's influential Marquee Club, where their following grew by leaps and bounds. Lambert and Stamp also strong-armed the press into covering this bright, brash band with the penchant for "auto-destruction" (as they called their nightly demolition). By 1965 the Who were riding the crest of the mod wave, ready to record again.

Their first records were produced by Shel Talmy, an American expatriate fresh from his success with the Kinks, which is probably why the Who's first two singles sounded so much like the early Kinks. Both "I Can't Explain" and "Anyway, Anyhow, Anywhere" were built around simple but powerful chord progressions, punctuated by sharp, staccato stabs of percussion. For their third single Townshend was ready to break new ground. The result was a rock-and-roll revelation, the loud, wild, and out-of-control "My Generation." Over the din of the instruments, Daltrey stuttered like a mod on too many amphetamines, spitting out his rage at parents, teachers, and anyone else in his way. The record seemed to explode with Moon's nonstop frenzy, the wail of guitar distortion and feedback, and the continuous refrain "Talkin' 'bout my generation." Suddenly the song was over, leaving you breathless and exhilarated. For the growing youth culture on both sides of the Atlantic, "My Generation" would become an anthem. But not just yet.

Despite four excellent follow-ups ("A Legal Matter," "Substitute," "The Kids Are Alright," and "I'm a Boy"), which helped to establish them as one of England's biggest groups, the Who were still unknown in America. Some blamed their American label for their lack of support. Indeed, Decca had at first assumed that "My Generation" was a damaged recording. All that feedback and noise couldn't have been intentional, they thought. But the label that still thought Brenda Lee was where it was at in 1966 wasn't the only reason for the Who's trouble in the States. The band had never performed in America and their live show had been crucial to building their audience in Britain.

The Who entered 1967 determined to change their luck in America. The year started promisingly with the slightly softer sound of "Happy Jack," which finally broke onto American radio playlists, pushing all the way to number 24. They followed it with an album that drew critical praise, particularly for "A Quick One," an extended piece that Townshend called

Peter Townshend.

Roger Daltrey.

John Entwistle.

250

Moon the Loon—the late Keith Moon.

Keith Moon's replacement—Kenney Jones.

a "mini-opera." In June they stole the show at the Monterey Pop Festival. On a national tour produced by Dick Clark, they opened for Herman's Hermits as they enjoyed their first (and only) top-ten success that summer with "I Can See For Miles." It remains the quintessential Who single, propelled by Moon's frenetic drumming and the huge, bone-crushing chords of Townshend's guitar, capturing all the energy and exuberance that the Who could lavish on their music.

But it still wasn't enough to secure lasting fame for the group. In 1968 "Call Me Lightning" and "Magic Bus" failed to match the success of "I Can See for Miles." Their third album, *The Who Sell Out,* was a brilliant parody of pop radio, complete with jingles and ads that unfortunately was either misconstrued or lost in the avalanche of concept albums that followed the Beatles' *Sgt. Pepper.* By the end of the year the group was back in Britain, broke, and on the verge of splitting up.

Then things started to happen in 1969. "Pinball Wizard" was released in March. Fans took notice that the band was in classic form, but fewer people noticed that under the group's name on the label of the 45 was this strange little note: "Taken from the rock opera *Tommy.*" And before long everyone was paying attention to that little deaf, dumb, and blind boy named Tommy.

Not since *Sgt. Pepper* had an album captured America the way *Tommy* did. It became a favorite with the emerging album-oriented FM stations. Countless newspaper and magazine articles analyzed and scrutinized *Tommy* for its musical and cultural significance. The London Symphony recorded an orchestrated version of *Tommy,* featuring famous guest rock vocalists. The Who's album sales soared. After all those years of hard work in obscurity, the Who became "overnight" stars in America.

Tommy contained some of the Who's best material to date: "I'm Free," "Christmas," and the breathtaking finale of "See Me, Feel Me." Capitalizing on the album's amazing popularity, the Who barnstormed the country, playing the opera in its entirety on an S.R.O. tour that included a landmark performance at Woodstock. That tour, combined with their appearance in the film *Woodstock* and the subsequent release of the exquisitely raw *Live at Leeds* album, firmly established the Who as rock's premier live act.

Who's Next, released in 1972, proved that the Who were not one-album wonders. The long-awaited studio follow-up to *Tommy* showed that they had grown stronger. Townshend was maturing as a composer. He began to emphasize his concerns about becoming an aging rock and roller until it became almost an all-consuming issue for him. It was

an interesting counter to his earlier music, and nowhere is the point more evident than in the comparison of his 1972 song "Won't Get Fooled Again" to the 1965 song "My Generation." In *Who's Next,* Townshend looked back on his past disdainfully in "Baba O'Riley," regretfully in "Behind Blue Eyes," and sardonically in "Won't Get Fooled Again." The group responded with truly inspired performances that were equal to their material.

The Who's tours and record releases grew less frequent in the mid-seventies. The singles started to sound a little lackluster, and "The Seeker," "Join Together," and "The Relay," were met with top forty apathy. They puttered around with solo albums, Daltrey's first effort giving exposure to a then unknown songwriter named Leo Sayer. There was also some vague talk of film projects, and Moon actually took parts in the rock movies *Stardust* and Frank Zappa's *200 Motels.*

The group released another ambitious double album, *Quadrophenia,* in October 1973. It was to be Townshend's ultimate achievement. Not just another rock opera, *Quadrophenia* attempted to capture the flavor of the early sixties as seen through the eyes of a young mod. It was a rock symphony with several recurring themes. The Who played the finest music of their careers on this album. But despite their musical virtuosity, the overall concept of *Quadrophenia* was fuzzy. The plot was difficult to follow. It lacked *Tommy's* cast of colorful characters. Therefore *Quadrophenia* was panned by most critics. But it didn't matter. The public bought it anyway.

However, the tour that followed *Quadrophenia* almost killed the band. Wondering whether his life as a grown-up rock star wasn't an unnatural contradiction, Townshend became moody and withdrawn. The band sounded stale on stage. Tempers flared, and old rivalries were renewed. After starring in *Tommy: The Movie,* Daltrey toyed with the notion of quitting the group and becoming a movie star, but the dismal failure of *Lisztomania* snuffed that idea. In the meantime Entwistle was anxious to be on the road, so he formed his own band, first known as Rigor Mortis, then as Ox. When Townshend and Daltrey attacked each other in exaggerated newspaper stories, most observers felt that the band had reached the end of the line.

But somehow they stuck together, released *The Who by Numbers* (a sly reference to the High Numbers of old), and went back on the road. This album and the ensuing tour marked their return to the basics. Although the lyrics were dominated by Townshend's preoccupation with aging and the emptiness of stardom, *The Who by Numbers* featured music that was clean, hard, and solid. On a U.S. tour the band gradually caught fire. First playing several smaller towns that they had missed on previous tours, they inspired a contagious enthusiasm. The old brilliance returned, and the Who emerged from that tour revitalized and recommitted to the future.

The songs didn't come quickly anymore, however. It took Townshend two years to assemble the album *Who Are You?* During that time Keith Moon's longtime love affair with drugs, booze, and good living (he once nailed all the furniture in a hotel room to the ceiling) had taken its toll. In 1978, shortly after the release of *Who Are You?*, Keith Moon died of an overdose at age thirty-one in the same Mayfair flat where Mama Cass died in 1974. Although not exactly unexpected, Keith's death was a great loss. Despite Keith's reputation for driving cars into swimming pools and trashing hotel rooms, his reputation as a drummer was unchallenged. For thirteen years he was the standard by which other rock drummers were measured. Now a line from "My Generation" came back to haunt the Who—"Hope I die before I get old!"

Oddly, Keith's timing couldn't have been better for the album. *Who Are You?* had taken off fast, giving the band their best shot at a hit single in years with the title track. The band was also readying two film projects: *The Kids Are Alright,* a documentary pastiche of past Who concerts and TV appearances, and a film version of *Quadrophenia.* Entwistle, Daltrey, and Townshend decided to stay together. Said Townshend, "We want the spirit of the group—to which Keith contributed so much—to go on." Kenny Jones, former drummer for the Faces, was chosen as Keith's replacement. After their debut performance in London, the Who's new lineup headed to the States, looking for the strength and purpose they had gained on the road before.

Before Moon's death the Who had been together without personnel changes longer than any other band in rock history. They were far from the best of friends. They often fought both onstage and off. But they were originators and survivors, weathering every shift in musical style without significantly altering their own. They made their name playing pure rock and roll and probably will keep on rocking for a long, long time.

CREEDENCE CLEARWATER REVIVAL

In the Spring of 1964, John Fogerty sat down with his older brother, Tom, and some old school buddies, Stu Cook and Doug Clifford, to watch a show on San Francisco's educational TV station. The show, "The Anatomy of a Hit Record," was all about the making of the instrumental hit "Cast Your Fate to the Wind." The boys, who had been playing around the Bay Area as the Blue Velvets, had written four instrumentals of their own and thought maybe the record company could use some of their music. In March 1964 the Blue Velvets knocked at the door of Fantasy Records in San Francisco. And after only five years, two name changes, and thousands of hours playing music in studios, basements, small clubs, and halls, the Fogerty boys, Cook, and Clifford became an overnight success when "Proud Mary" chugged up the charts to become one of the biggest records of 1969.

Creedence Clearwater Revival had its real beginnings when John Fogerty cut school to watch the World Series and play his guitar. John began to cut school more and more as he became more skilled on the guitar. He was eventually tossed out of St. Mary's High in tenth grade for missing so much school and wound up in high school in El Cerrito on the San Francisco Bay, where he hooked up with Stu Cook and Doug "Cosmo" Clifford and formed a band that started playing junior high sock hops and Boys' Club dances in late 1959. The boys asked John's older brother, Tom, to join them, and the Blue Velvets were born.

The group started hanging around recording studios all around the Bay Area. John put in over 5,000 hours in recording studios while still in high school. He became a studio musician, playing as a sideman on polka albums, country and western sides, and wherever else he was needed. By the time they knocked on Fantasy Records' door in 1964, the Blue Velvets had logged some 2,000 hours in the studio, backing several local singers in recording sessions

and even cutting a few records of their own. Even more important, the group learned how to get the sound they wanted from a recording studio.

In March 1964 Fantasy Records asked the Blue Velvets to cut a demo for them. Months dragged on with no word from the record company. John journeyed north to Portland, which was an early sixties' rock mecca that had spawned the Kingsmen and Paul Revere and the Raiders, to play rock and roll. With a family and a full-time job, Tom was about ready to give up on the rock scene. Stu was being forced to go to college by his parents, while Doug was busy bouncing in and out of different colleges. Then at last, in December 1964, Fantasy released the Blue Velvets' single. They finally had a record out. Then the Blue Velvets looked at the label. Fantasy had changed the group's name to the Golliwogs to cash in on the mania for British bands. The boys finally had a record contract, but they were also stuck with a name that made them the laughingstock of San Francisco.

The Golliwogs had a minor local hit with "Brown-Eyed Girl," but in truth the Golliwogs couldn't really play musical instruments. Stu Cook knew only three notes on bass. Tom Fogerty could play only one string on his guitar. When they performed live, they were really just a lead singer and a drummer. In the studio, John Fogerty filled in on all the other instruments and used his studio skills to produce a finished record. The Golliwogs spent the next three years paying some heavy dues, learning their craft and mastering their instruments while playing countless bars, VFW halls, and battles of the bands in Northern California.

The big change came for the group in October 1967. John Fogerty was working at Fantasy as a shipping clerk when he became good friends with Saul Zaentz, a sales representative for the company. Zaentz soon bought Fantasy Records and asked the

Golliwogs to stay on, giving them new equipment and a new name—Creedence Clearwater Revival. He then asked John Fogerty to produce an album for his group.

Knowing that they wanted to play clean, straight-forward rock and roll, Fogerty and the group picked two rock-and-roll chestnuts—"Susie Q," a 1957 rocker by Dale Hawkins, and "I Put a Spell on You," the signature song of one of the wild men of early rock, Screamin' Jay Hawkins. With these two songs they produced good, hard-driving rock and roll filtered through the psychedelia of San Francisco. The key to their sound was John Fogerty's distinctive voice, flavored with a little grit, a little blues, a little Fats Domino, and a whole lot of Little Richard. With the help of an underground radio strike in San Francisco, Creedence got an abnormal amount of airplay on San Francisco's new progressive rock station before their album was even released. On the strength of their sales in San Francisco, Bill Drake, then the reigning mogul of top-forty radio in America, picked "Susie Q" to be played on all his stations across the country. Creedence soon made

Creedence Clearwater Revival (from left: Stu Cook, Tom Fogerty, brother John Fogerty, and Doug Clifford).

the crossover from FM underground to AM top forty and were on their way to the first of seven platinum albums.

In 1969 and 1970 Creedence was the best-selling rock band in America. They followed up "Spell" with "Proud Mary" from the *Bayou Country* album and they were off and running. Six more two-sided singles struck gold in 1969 and 1970. "Bad Moon Rising," "Born on a Bayou," "Green River," and "Run through the Jungle" all had the mysterious ambiance of the Bayou swamps that John Fogerty had never seen. However, Creedence wasn't just Cajun music and the good-time hand-clapping sounds of "Down on the Corner" and "Lookin' Out My Back Door." They were also capable of poignant ballads like "Who'll Stop the Rain" and "Have You Ever Seen the Rain?" Moreover, "Don't Look Now," "Fortunate Son," and "Bootleg" made some serious statements about responsibility, privilege, and lusting after the unattainable.

255

Creedence had a real desire to entertain and a true concern for their fans. They once stayed up most of the night to reshoot an *American Bandstand* spot that had been accidentally erased. But despite all their efforts, Creedence couldn't completely win over their critics because they were considered a singles group in an era of albums. They were the voice of reason in a time of political and musical extremism. They lacked stylish flamboyance and chafed under the criticism that their music wasn't artistic and had nothing to say.

Tom Fogerty left the band because of artistic differences in 1971 after the album *Pendulum* was released. The group embarked on a worldwide tour as a trio, but Cook and Clifford grew increasingly hostile, seeing Creedence as merely a front for spotlighting John Fogerty. Their hit single output slowed with this dissent. John, the writer and lead singer on all of Creedence's hits, then agreed to share the singing, songwriting, and production chores with Cook and Clifford. The result was the album *Mardi Gras,* which has been called "Fogerty's

Revenge." Neither Cook nor Clifford could write, produce, or sing nearly as well as John Fogerty. Finally, in October 1972, thirteen years after they had started playing together as a band, Fogerty, Cook, and Clifford went their separate ways.

Tom Fogerty had a brief solo career after he split from Creedence, while Cook and Clifford became studio musicians, surfacing again for a short time with the Don Harrison Band in the late seventies. Following the demise of Creedence, John recorded a solo album of country and bluegrass tunes, *The Blue Ridge Rangers,* on which he played all the instruments and sang all the vocal parts. John had two hit singles from that album, "Jambalaya" and "Hearts of Stone." They were the last big hits John Fogerty had. After a dispute with Saul Zaentz, he left Fantasy for Asylum Records. A second solo album came out in 1975, but even though it had some fine music in the Creedence vein, such as "Rockin' All Over the World," it was largely ignored. Fogerty kept trying, but on his own he could not repeat the successes he had scored with Creedence Clearwater Revival.

THE FIFTH DIMENSION

As a child, Marilyn McCoo migrated to Los Angeles from New Jersey with her family. She sang from the time she was in elementary school and got her first break on Arthur Godfrey's television show *Talent Scouts.* While a teen-ager, Marilyn began to work as a fashion model, eventually winning the Grand Talent Award in the Miss Bronze California pageant. She was photographed by her friend Lamonte McLemore, who had sold some of his other work to *Life* and *Ebony* magazines. Lamonte, who was also a singer, joined Marilyn and two other friends in forming a vocal group, The Hi-Fi's. Ray Charles discovered them, produced their first single, "Lonesome Mood," and took them on tour. A short time later they disbanded, and Marilyn returned to UCLA to complete her studies. Her interest in music, however, did not fade, and she and Lamonte formed a new singing group. This time they asked their friend Florence LaRue (another winner in the Miss Bronze Grand Talent Pageant) to join them. Although initially she preferred to keep her teaching job, she was eventually persuaded to accept the offer. After they had invited their old friend Ron Townson to join, they needed just one more voice to complete the group.

Billy Davis, Jr., had sung gospel for many years. His dream of becoming a professional baseball player was supplanted by his stronger desire to record music. After serving in the United States Army in Germany, he returned home to St. Louis to open a night club where he could perform and promote other groups. His own group, The St. Louis Gospel Singers, recorded spiritual songs, but Billy began to long for something different. About this time he received a telephone call from his cousin in L.A., Lamonte McLemore, who invited him to complete his new singing group, the Versatiles.

In 1966 the Versatiles auditioned for Marc Gordon, the former head of Motown in Los Angeles. He agreed to manage them and brought them to the attention of Johnny Rivers, who signed them to his new Soul City Records.

Rivers, whose real name is Johnny Ramistella, came out of Louisiana, but his sound was pure Nashville. He was good enough to attract the attention of Alan Freed, who got him his first recording contract and suggested that he change his name to Johnny Rivers. His next big break came when he secured a performing contract with the L.A. talent showplace the Wiskey A Go Go and proceeded to turn the place upside down with his energetic, rousing show. Rivers became the hottest act in town, and the "in crowd" flocked to the club to see him.

The electricity of his personal appearances was carried over into the recording studio. With Chuck Berry's "Memphis" in 1964 Johnny hung on to the tip of the top forty. He bucked the encroaching British invasion and had big hits with "Mountain of Love" (1964), "Midnight Special" (1965), "Seventh Son" (1965), "Poor Side of Town" (1966), "Secret Agent Man" (1966), "Tracks of My Tears" (1967), and "Baby I Need Your Loving" (1967). Of these songs, "Midnight Special" and "Secret Agent Man" gained additional fame as TV theme songs.

By the end of 1966 Rivers had charted a new direction for his career. He became the owner of Soul City Records with hopes of developing his own talent while also producing other artists. The first group he signed was the Versatiles, whose sound he felt was a Motown-style imitation. Their previous two records, "Bye Bye Baby" and "Easy to Say," had gone nowhere. It was Rivers who then reshaped their sound, introduced them to the songs of Jim Webb, and changed their name to the Fifth Dimension. "Go Where You Wanna Go," a song originally recorded by the Mamas and the Papas, was the Fifth Dimension's first hit in February 1967, edging up to number 16 on the charts. The Fifth Dimension became specialists in pop melodies with smooth, soaring harmonies and a

Billy Davis, Jr., and Marilyn McCoo.

258

little jazz thrown in for good measure. Their style soon proved to be a sensation.

In 1967 Jim Webb planned to coproduce a movie about a balloon trip, but the project never got off the ground, so Webb offered the title song of his aborted movie to the Fifth Dimension. "Up, Up and Away" made stars of both the Fifth Dimension and Jimmy Webb. It skyrocketed to number 7 during the summer of 1967 and won an astounding five Grammy awards for Record of the Year, Song of the Year, Best Performance by a Vocal Group, Best Contemporary Pop Vocal Performance by a Group, and Best Contemporary Recording. "Up, Up and Away" also gave Jim Webb's career a big boost as recording artists now clamored to record Webb songs. Some of Webb's greatest successes include "By the Time I Get to Phoenix" and "Galveston," recorded by Glen Campbell; "MacArthur Park" by Richard Harris; and "The Worst That Could Happen" by the Brooklyn Bridge.

The Fifth Dimension struck gold in 1968 with two songs by New York's cult singer/songwriter Laura Nyro. "Stoned Soul Picnic" was a stoned soul smash, settling in the top ten for seven weeks in July and August and reaching number 3. "Sweet Blindness," a cosmic drinking song, made it to number 13 in November. Then, in 1969, their version of "Aquarius/Let the Sunshine In" from the hit Broadway musical *Hair* spent six weeks in the number-1 slot and eleven weeks in the top ten. "Aquarius/Let the Sunshine In" also inspired an avalanche of hit records taken from *Hair,* including "Easy to Be Hard" by Three Dog Night, "Good Morning Starshine" by Oliver, "Be In/Where Do I Go" by the Happenings, and a godawful version of "Hair" by the Cowsills.

The Fifth Dimension followed up "Aquarius/Let the Sunshine In" with "Wedding Bell Blues," another number-1 song. Around this time manager Marc Gordon married Florence LaRue, and Billy Davis, Jr., tied the knot with Marilyn McCoo. In 1970 the Fifth Dimension released "One Less Bell to Answer" just before Florence temporarily left the group to have a baby. With Flo back in the fold, the group had another top-ten hit, "(Last Night) I Didn't Get to Sleep at All" in the summer of 1972. But the group's sound was now becoming much lighter and much less dynamic. As they leaned toward easy listening, the Fifth Dimension began having trouble selling records.

In 1975, after almost ten years of recording with the group, Billy Davis, Jr., and Marilyn McCoo left the band to become a duo. Their first single was "Love Hangover," but unfortunately Diana Ross heard it, quickly covered it, and beat McCoo and Davis to the punch for the hit record. However, their second single, "You Don't Have to Be a Star (To Be in My Show)," became a number-1 hit and won them a Grammy in 1977 for Best R&B Vocal Performance by a Duo. Their first album, *I Hope We Get to Love in Time,* received a Gold certification from the recording industry. Their success continued as CBS television signed them in 1977 for the short-lived *The Marilyn McCoo and Bill Davis, Jr. Show,* and their second album, *The Two of Us,* also became a hit. Today they continue to perform together at clubs and hotel resorts.

THE ARCHIES AND THE SOUND OF BUBBLEGUM MUSIC

After the individual egos of the Monkees botched up that great money-making enterprise, Don Kirshner contemplated the possibilities of a group that could repeat *and* improve on the success of the Monkees. Wouldn't it be great to have a group with no egos, he thought. Better yet, a group with no people at all to get in the way of the hit records! Kirshner wanted a singing group that wasn't really a singing group at all. And when he got his wish, that group had the biggest record of the summer of 1969. In fact, it was one of the biggest records in rock history. In that summer of Woodstock and the rock opera *Tommy,* the biggest record by far belonged to a "phantom" group of anonymous studio musicians dubbing in the music for a Saturday-morning cartoon show. The record was "Sugar Sugar" by the Archies.

Behind the cartoon images of Archie, Jughead, Betty, and Veronica were musical supervisor Don Kirshner, producer Jeff Barry, singer Ron Dante, and a group of Kirshner's studio musicians. With cartoon characters up front, the group might not be able to tour, but there was no chance that Jughead would ever threaten to quit the group.

Ron Dante was the voice of the Archies. Dante started out in the business by replacing Tony Orlando as a demo singer for Don Kirshner in the early sixties. Dante recorded thousands of songs that Kirshner's songwriters cranked out so that big-name singers who couldn't read music could hear how the song was supposed to sound. He was also a studio singer who did backup vocals for groups like Jay and the Americans and the McCoys, as well as one of the most popular jingle singers in New York, lending his uncredited talents to countless commercials. Moreover, he was the mastermind of the Detergents, the group that had parodied the Shangri-Las in 1965 with "Leader of the Laundromat," and fronted his own "phantom" group, the Cuff Links, who scored

with the bubblegum hit "Tracy" in 1969. Through the magic of overdubbing, Ron Dante did virtually all of the vocals for the Archies. Not only was he Archie and Jughead, he was Betty and Veronica, too.

"Sugar Sugar" was a tasty confection with an infectious beat. It had a good-time sound with solid production that captivated top-forty radio stations from Boston to San Diego, although progressive rock stations would have nothing to do with it. Jeff Barry, who had worked in the studio with early rock's premier producers Leiber and Stoller and with his wife, Ellie Greenwich, had written some of the best rock to come out of New York, produced "Sugar Sugar." The record's quality sound set it apart from the other bubblegum records of the day. "Sugar Sugar" spent an amazing twelve weeks in the top 3 spots on the singles charts—four weeks of that in the number-1 position. The competition on the charts included the Beatles, the Rolling Stones, and Elvis Presley, but the Archies won hands down.

Bubblegum music was meant for children. Just as early rock and roll had been aimed at the newly prosperous teen-agers of 1955, bubblegum zeroed in on the new group in town with money—prepubescent adolescents. By the mid-sixties preteens had too much money to be ignored as a significant market.

The preteen market was considered unsophisticated by the bubblegum moguls, so bubblegum biggies, people like Neil Bogart of Buddah Records (later head of Casablanca Records), insisted that bubblegum lyrics had to be simple and repetitive. Thus America was treated to such classics as "Chewy, Chewy" and "Yummy, Yummy, Yummy" by the Ohio Express. With Kiss' pseudoviolence and Alice Cooper's nightmare theatrics still half a decade away, bubblegum boldly faced the burning issues of preteen concern in "1, 2, 3, Redlight," "May I Take a Giant Step," and "Simon Says" by the 1910 Fruitgum

Company. The squeaky-clean sexual-fantasy Bobby Sherman ("Easy Come, Easy Go") was presented to the bubblegum crowd's budding Lolitas—little girls who knew that sex was just around the corner, but were still too young to cross the street without permission.

But while bubblegum music may have been wholesome, it certainly wasn't nutritious. From the first bubblegum hit, the Chordettes' "Lollipop" in 1958, to the Lemon Pipers "Green Tambourine," like most sugary treats, bubblegum rotted the mind. Fortunately for Ron Dante, he graduated from the saccharine mania of the Archies to produce Broadway's *Ain't Misbehavin'* and *They're Playing Our Song.*

The Sound of 1969

BLOOD, SWEAT AND TEARS

The story of Blood, Sweat and Tears begins with Al Kooper. He started his professional music career with the Royal Teens, whose single "Short Shorts" was a rage in 1958. More than just an accomplished guitarist and organist, Kooper also had the songwriting skills that produced Gene Pitney's "I Must Be Seeing Things" and Gary Lewis and the Playboys' "This Diamond Ring." His big break, however, was his involvement with Bob Dylan's *Highway 61 Revisited.* At the right place at the right time, he was called upon to do some inventive organ playing on "Like a Rolling Stone."

Now into electric folk and blues, Kooper's groundbreaking studio sessions in New York led to the formation of the Blues Project with Tommy Flanders, Danny Kalb, Roy Blumenfeld, Andy Kulberg, Artie Traum, and Steve Katz. From their modest beginnings backing up Chuck Berry in concert, the Blues Project became the leaders of blues/rock in the mid- to late sixties. Unfortunately, the group had their share of problems. After Flanders departed, a struggle started over the direction of their music. By the summer of 1967 a surplus of ideas and vocal personalities led to their breakup. Al saw the breakup as his opportunity to put together his dream band, which would include brass and possibly even symphonic orchestration. The only problem was that Al was broke.

If Al's dream band was to become a reality, he had to raise money. His friends Judy Collins and Paul Simon put on benefit concerts for him at New York's Café Au Go Go, where Kooper himself would perform with a pickup band made up of Steve Katz, Jim Fielder (formerly of Buffalo Springfield and the Mothers of Invention), and Bobby Columby (former drummer for Odetta). These concerts were all smashes, but after all the bills were paid and every businessman got his due percentage, Al was left with a mere five hundred dollars. The dream seemed to be over until Katz, Fielder, and Columby prodded Al into forming his dream band with them. Actually, Al didn't want Katz, considering him only a fair guitarist. But with no other alternatives at this point, he agreed to lead the group provided that he alone could set policy and determine their material. The deal was made, and soon Fred Lipsius, Randy Brecker, Jerry Weiss, and Dick Halligan were added to the group. Kooper pitched the band to Columbia's Clive Davis and landed a recording contract. Now all they needed was a name.

Blood, Sweat and Tears.

In the autumn of 1967 at the Café Au Go Go an amazing all-night jam session took place, featuring Al, B. B. King, and Jimi Hendrix. When the lights were turned on the next morning Al was shocked to see that the keyboard on his organ was caked with blood. He had cut his hand without realizing it and had been bleeding most of the night as he played. The organ was a mess, but it inspired the name of the group. Adding this blood to the dripping sweat of an energetic performance and the tears that accompanied the mere five-hundred-dollar profit of his otherwise successful benefit concerts, Blood, Sweat and Tears had its name.

David Clayton-Thomas of Blood, Sweat and Tears.

BS&T's first album, *Child Is Father to the Man,* is frequently cited as one of the great rock albums. It contained rock's first overture and underture; an old Gene Pitney song originally written for him by Randy Newman entitled "Just One Smile"; Harry Nilsson's "Without Her," and "Meagan's Gypsy Eyes," which was sung by Steve Katz, who tugged up and down on his Adam's apple to simulate a trembling wah-wah effect.

In time the blood and tears began to roll again as Columby and Katz protested Kooper's unyielding control over the group. Al had to remind them of their deal—it was *his* group. Feeling that Katz was holding the group back from new musical heights, Kooper then tried to gather the necessary strength to oust him. But they all refused to let Katz go. Needless to say, Katz was furious. The group began to crumble. Brecker announced his departure. Weiss and Kooper got into a verbal fight onstage at a New York City concert in 1968. Columby and Katz demanded a new lead singer to replace Al. Kooper's dream band had become a nightmare, so he left.

Al went on to produce for Columbia Records, masterminding *Super Session,* with Mike Bloomfield and Stephen Stills; *Kooper Session* with Shuggie Otis, the fourteen-year-old guitar whiz and son of rhythm-and-blues great Johnny Otis; and his own solo album *I Stand Alone,* which could actually pass for *Child Is Father to the Man—Volume Two.*

Meanwhile, the Kooperless Blood, Sweat and Tears, now with Lew Soloff, Chuck Winfield, Jerry Hyman, and the lead voice of Canada's David Clayton-Thomas, went on to superstar status with *Blood, Sweat and Tears,* 1969's album of the year. With surplus Kooper material as well as new works, they put together an L.P. that contained three top-ten singles: "You've Made Me So Very Happy" (1969), cowritten by Berry Gordy; "Spinning Wheel" (1969); and Laura Nyro's "And When I Die" (1969). In 1970 *Blood, Sweat and Tears III* joined the first two albums in the gold category and produced three more hit singles: Carole King's "Hi-De-Ho" (1970), "Lucretia MacEvil" (1970), and "Go Down Gambling" (1971).

BS&T continued to be active throughout the seventies. Clayton-Thomas made a brief attempt at a solo career without much luck before returning to the group. Kooper continued to produce, having great success with the southern group Lynyrd Skynyrd (whose career eventually ended in a plane crash). Nevertheless, Kooper and BS&T reintroduced the brass section to rock and roll and paved the way for Chicago, the Ides of March, Chase, and many other such bands.

1970

The Vietnam War came home to America in 1970. Following President Nixon's announcement of the invasion of Cambodia, antiwar demonstrations erupted on college campuses all over the country. On May 4, Ohio National Guardsmen opened fire on protesters at Kent State, killing four students. On that same day two students were shot and killed during demonstrations at Jackson State College in Mississippi. In June antiwar radicals bombed the physics building at the University of Wisconsin, demolishing it and killing a graduate student. The circuslike trial of the Chicago Seven in 1970 pitted Judge Julius Hoffman against Abbie Hoffman, Tom Hayden, and a bound and gagged Bobby Seale. It concluded with the jury finding the Chicago Seven guilty. In the meantime, Lieutenant William Calley was charged with the My Lai massacre in Vietnam.

Patton won the Oscar for Best Picture over *Love Story, Airport, Five Easy Pieces*, and *M*A*S*H,* but George C. Scott, protesting such competition among actors, refused to accept his Academy Award for Best Actor in *Patton.* Muhammad Ali returned to boxing after a forty-two-month exile, scoring a TKO over Jerry Quarry. The Baltimore Orioles knocked off Cincinnati's Big Red Machine in the World Series. In the first year of the AFL-NFL merger, the Baltimore Colts defeated the Dallas Cowboys in Super Bowl V. And the Knicks brought the NBA championship to New York.

On television, *Sesame Street* started its long residence on public TV. Lou Grant, Ted Baxter, and Rhoda Morgenstern were introduced on the premiere of *The Mary Tyler Moore Show.* TV also created clones of the Cowsills for *The Partridge Family,* which turned David Cassidy into a teenybopper idol. And 1970 was the year ABC teamed "Dandy" Don Meredith with Howard Cosell as pro football moved to Monday Night.

Following the long-awaited release of the *Let It Be* album, the Beatles split up in May amid a flurry of lawsuits and hard feelings. Janis Joplin and Jimi Hendrix fell victim to drug-related deaths within weeks of each other. The Kinks made a comeback in the summer with their ambiguous lovesong about Lola, "who walks like a woman but talks like a man." The Hollies turned the Boys' Town slogan "He Ain't Heavy, He's My Brother" into a hit. Edwin Starr recorded a protest song for Motown called "War." Beset by defections and internal turmoil, Motown gave a white, heavy-metal band their own record label, and Rare Earth responded with "Get Ready." Badfinger hit the charts with "Come and Get It," written by Paul McCartney for the film *The Magic Christian.* Tony Orlando gave up his record-executive position to return to the spotlight, hitting the charts with "Candida." "Venus" by the Dutch group Shocking Blue, "Mississippi Queen" by Leslie West and Mountain, "Green-Eyed Lady" by Sugarloaf, and "Ride Captain Ride" by the Blues Image all added a dash of pure rock and roll to the 1970 music scene.

The top ten records for 1970 were "Bridge over Troubled Water" by Simon and Garfunkel, "American Woman/No Sugar Tonight" by the Guess Who, "(They Long to Be) Close to You" by the Carpenters, "Raindrops Keep Fallin' On My Head" by B. J. Thomas, "Let It Be" by the Beatles, "Ain't No Mountain High Enough" by Diana Ross, "I'll Be There" by the Jackson 5, "War" by Edwin Starr, "Get Ready" by Rare Earth, and "Band of Gold" by Freda Payne.

It was 1970—the sixteenth year of rock and roll.

The only group in the book to be booted out of Disneyland was none other than the Carpenters. Fired for looking like hippies, Karen and Richard Carpenter retaliated by adding former Mouseketeer Chubby O'Brien to their backup band. This brother-and-sister team recorded hit after pop hit throughout the first half of the seventies, including "Close to You," "We've Only Just Begun," "Rainy Days and Mondays," "Hurting Each Other," "Yesterday Once More," and "Top of the World."

After recording for over twenty years, the king of the blues finally got a top-twenty hit in 1970. Riley "Blues Boy" King—better known as B.B. King—hit the charts in 1970 with "The Thrill Is Gone." A sharecropper from Indianola, Mississippi, B.B. moved to Memphis in 1947 and became a disc jockey on WDIA radio. With his guitar, Lucille, B.B. King influenced a generation of British musicians including Eric Clapton.

CROSBY, STILLS, NASH AND YOUNG

In 1966, in the middle of an L.A. traffic jam, Steve Stills and Richie Furay noticed a hearse with Ontario plates ahead of them. Richie recognized the driver as Canadian folkie Neil Young. They stopped to talk and before long agreed to form a band, taking their name from a steamroller manufacturer—Buffalo Springfield.

The Buffalo Springfield's reputation spread quickly, and they were signed by Atlantic late in 1966. Aided by the success of their first national hit, Steve Stills' "For What It's Worth," their first L.P. received an unusual amount of attention in 1967. Unfortunately, conflicts of ego began to plague the band; and to complicate matters, their bass player, Bruce Palmer, was busted for possession of pot and deported to Canada. Jim Fielder of the Mothers of Invention took his place but was eventually removed after several disputes with Stills. Jim Messina then took over on bass. After constant feuding with Stills, Neil Young quit the band just before they were scheduled to play at the Monterey Pop Festival in 1967. Dave Crosby of the Byrds volunteered to fill in for Young that night. He loved the gig and briefly considered joining the Springfield, before deciding to stick with the Byrds at least for the time being. The aloof Young eventually returned to the Springfield, but the band was dissolving. Stills and Young didn't even want to be in the same studio together. Finally, in May 1968, the Buffalo Springfield played their final gig.

Jim and Richie went on to form the successful country rock band Poco. Jim later hit the top again as part of the duo of Loggins and Messina. Neil Young released a string of solo L.P.'s, starting with *Neil Young* (1968) and *Everybody Knows This Is Nowhere* with Crazy Horse (1967). In May 1969 Columbia Records issued *Super Session* by Steve Stills, Michael Bloomfield, and Al Kooper.

Meanwhile Graham Nash wound up in L.A. with the Hollies, where he made friends with Cass Elliot. One day Cass dragged him to Joni Mitchell's house, where he met Stills and Crosby, both of whom had left their bands by now. Nash wasn't happy with the pop direction that the Hollies had been taking. They had rejected his songs "Marrakesh Express" and "Lady of the Island," and were about to record an all-Dylan album, which he found distasteful. Nash eventually made up his mind about his future, and in late 1968 the leader of the Hollies quit to form a band with Stills and Crosby.

Crosby, Stills, and Nash started recording in California in the spring of 1969. By June their first album, *Crosby, Stills and Nash,* was ready. In just one year it sold over two million copies, and the group won a Grammy as Best New Artists of 1969. However, they didn't tour until Neil Young joined the band later that summer. After their first live performance in August in L.A., they appeared at the Woodstock Festival and were "scared shitless," in Stills' words.

Their first L.P. yielded two hits, Nash's "Marrakesh Express" (July 1969) and Stills' "Suite: Judy Blue Eyes" (October 1969). Orders for their next L.P. reached two million, an unprecedented advance for Atlantic. After *Deja Vu* was finally released in March 1970 under the adjusted name of Crosby, Stills, Nash and Young, it sold two million copies in two weeks, became the number-1 album for four weeks, stayed on the album charts for sixty-five weeks, sold over four million copies worldwide, and yielded two singles, both written by Nash: "Teach Your Children" (June 1969) and "Our House" (September 1970). *Deja Vu* was the number-1 L.P. of 1970. "Woodstock" (March 1970), written by Joni Mitchell, and "Ohio" (June 1970), written by Neil Young, also became hit singles, and the group was beginning to be referred to as "the American Beatles." But like the Beatles, they broke up after their summer 1970 tour in order to explore their individual musical horizons.

Stephen Stills (left) and David Crosby. *(Robert Wexler)*

David Crosby (left) and Graham Nash. *(Robert Wexler)*

Neil Young.

After the breakup, Steve Stills recorded his first solo album, which included his hit single "Love the One You're With." In 1971 his second solo L.P. was followed by *Four-Way Street,* a live Crosby, Stills, Nash and Young album. In 1972 Stills formed Manassas while Crosby and Nash were making records on their own. Neil Young took the spotlight, however, with his million-selling *After the Goldrush* in 1970, followed by his two-million-selling *Harvest,* which was considered the top album of the year by many. From that album came the gold single "Heart of Gold," which was released in December 1971.

Crosby, Stills, Nash and Young reunited in the summer of 1974 and toured the U.S. and England. Following that tour, plans to record a new album were announced, but nothing ever materialized. Neil was content to concentrate on his own L.P.'s, which included *Tonight's the Night* (1975), *American Stars 'n Bars* (1977), *Comes a Time* (1978), *Rust Never Sleeps* (1979), and *Live Rust* (1979). In the meantime, Stills switched to Columbia and released a string of his own solo L.P.'s while Nash and Crosby worked together, making records and live appearances. At one Nash and Crosby show Stills showed up to sing a few tunes with his old partners. The feeling was right, and this led to a reunion of Crosby, Stills and Nash and the L.P. *CSN.* The album went platinum, and its singles, Nash's "Just a Song before I Go" and Stills' "Dark Star," were well received.

In 1976 Stills and Young toured together and released an L.P., *Long May You Run.* Then suddenly, without explanation, Young left the tour, notifying Stills of his decision by telegram. In September 1979 Nash helped to organize the Musicians United for Safe Energy concerts at New York's Madison Square Garden. For the occasion, Crosby, Stills and Nash regrouped and appeared at an outdoor rally in Manhattan's Battery Park as well as at the Garden. Their performance was captured on Asylum's triple album of the *No Nukes* event.

Crosby, Stills, Nash and Young's light, acoustic sound, soaring harmonies, immaculate studio production, and talented arrangements were artistically refreshing as well as highly commercial. They've earned their place in the pantheon of supergroups.

SANTANA

Santana (Carlos Santana is fifth from left).

Carlos Santana was born in 1947 in Mexico. His father played violin, an instrument that Carlos worked on until his dad bought him an electric guitar and an amplifier. After finishing high school, he started to play in small bars and clubs in the red-light district of Tijuana. In 1966 Carlos moved to San Francisco, where the psychedelic counterculture had already established itself. By early 1967, Santana had put together a band consisting of Gregg Rolie on keyboards, Jose Chepito Areas on percussion, Michael Carabello on percussion, David Brown on bass, Michael Shrieve on drums, and Carlos himself on lead guitar and vocals. They were called the Santana Blues Band.

The concept of Latin blues appealed to rock promoter Bill Graham. Graham, who had become hooked on Latin music while working as a waiter in the Catskills, took Santana under his wing and hired them to play his halls, The Fillmore West and The Fillmore East. In 1968 the band became a hot attraction. Several record companies offered them recording contracts, and they signed with Columbia Records. Their first record was the L.P. *Santana,* which was released shortly after their exciting performance at the Woodstock Festival. That highly charged set gave many in the audience their first exposure to congas, timbales, maracas, and the dynamic, dazzling force of Latin rhythms. They were featured in the *Woodstock* film, performing "Soul Sacrifice." The film and its soundtrack album turned many more people on to their intensity and vitality.

Within the year the *Santana* L.P. had sold two million copies. It was a top-ten album for twenty-eight weeks, went gold, and stayed on the best-seller charts for 108 weeks. In addition the L.P. contained two hit singles, "Jingo" (October 1969) and "Evil Ways" (January 1970). In 1970 they released their second L.P., *Abraxas,* which climbed to number 1 and yielded two successful singles: "Black Magic Woman," an old Fleetwood Mac song (November 1970), and "Oye Como Va" (February 1971). *Santana 3* was released in October 1971, turning gold instantly and claiming the number-1 slot for five weeks in the U.S. This album contained the February 1972 hit single "No One to Depend On."

By 1972, management, personal, and drug problems forced changes in the band's membership. Despite all the changes, Carlos always remained in command. However, Carlos was still insecure about his musical abilities. The pressures of success combined with his rock-star life-style led to a heavy drug dependence. Carlos nearly burned out before fellow guitarist John McLaughlin brought him to the spiritual teachings of Sri Chimnoy, a guru from Ceylon. This religious experience possibly saved Carlos from joining the growing list of rock casualties and certainly supplied him with the inner resolve to regain his confidence and build his guitar skills.

For the next four years Carlos branched off in the direction of jazz-rock fusion. In addition to recording with his own group (*Welcome, Borboletta,* and *Lotus*), Carlos collaborated with McLaughlin on *Love Devotion Surrender* (1973) and with Alice Coltrane on *Illuminations* (1973). His U.S. sales dropped noticeably in response to this new direction, but European and Japanese reaction was extremely favorable.

It was not until 1976 that Santana reestablished their musical rapport with American audiences by returning to Latin rock with *Amigos.* As the albums continued, so did the rapid turnover of the group's musicians. The *Moonflower* L.P. gave the band their first top-twenty hit in five years. In 1978 the L.P. *Inner Secrets* provided the singles "Well All Right," originally done by Buddy Holly, and "She's Not There," the old Zombies hit of 1965. Santana celebrated its tenth anniversary with Columbia in 1979 with the release of the album *Marathon.*

Santana will be long remembered for having brought Latin influences—South American psychedelia—to hard rock.

JOE COCKER

John Robert Cocker was born in 1944 in Sheffield, England. He attended Sheffield Central Technical Trade School, where he studied to become a plumber. As a youngster Cocker spent hours listening to Ray Charles, and by the time he was fifteen he was playing drums and harmonica in a band called the Cavaliers. Two years later they became Vance Arnold and the Avengers, featuring Joe as their lead vocalist.

In 1964 a representative from British Decca picked Joe out of the group and signed him to a solo recording contract. But his first release was a bomb, and a frustrated Joe returned to plumbing. In time, he grew bored with plumbing and put together a band. Dubbed the Grease Band, they were Chris Stainton on keyboards, Henry McCullough (later a member of Wings) on guitar, Alan Spenner on bass, and Bruce Rowlands on drums. The group were playing their British soul music in northern England when record producer Denny Cordell heard them. Eventually they cut and released "Marjorine," a moderate hit. However, an appearance at the Windsor Jazz and Blues Festival and the release of their next single, "With a Little Help from My Friends," boosted Cocker and his band to the top. Their slow version of the Beatles tune raced to number 1 in England. When released in the U.S. on A&M Records in November 1968, it became a top-ten hit. The L.P. of the same name followed in June 1969, featuring the additional talents of Jimmy Page, Albert Lee, and Stevie Winwood, who supplied Cocker with his next hit single, an old Traffic song called "Feeling Alright" (June 1969).

Cocker's success in the U.S. can be attributed to Dee Anthony, who caught Cocker's act at the Marquee Club in London one night and soon became his manager. Dee's constant efforts brought Cocker and the band fame in the U.S. In August 1969 they converted half a million people into fans at the Woodstock festival. Cocker also had a prominent segment in the film of the festival, and America was finally able to witness Joe's strange stage mannerisms. He was spastic, staggering precariously around the stage with his fingers flailing away at an imaginary guitar, his eyes popping out of their sockets and lips contorted in agony. Twitching, flinching, shaking, jerking, and quivering—you name it and Cocker had it. His strange behavior, however, was redeemed by his big, funky, soulful voice and his subtle phrasing. The pain in his raw vocals was genuine enough to make his entire stage show work.

Joe Cocker.

Leon Russell and his wife, Mary. Leon helped put together Joe Cocker's Mad Dogs and Englishmen tour in 1970, making sure to take a moment in the spotlight during each concert, and when the tour ended, Leon had become a star in his own right. A singer, songwriter, studio musician, and record producer, Leon has worked with the likes of Ricky Nelson, Gary Lewis and the Playboys, and David Gates and Bread.

During the recording of his second album, Cocker met keyboard player, singer, and song-writer Leon Russell, who agreed to supervise Joe's studio work. Cocker's hit singles from these sessions were the Russell tune "Delta Lady" (October 1969), followed by another Beatles tune, "She Came in through the Bathroom Window" (December 1969). After touring the U.S., recording here, and finally appearing on *The Ed Sullivan Show,* Cocker went back to England to rest. By March Joe had decided to dump most of the Grease Band, believing them to be loyal but erratic musicians.

Cocker returned to the U.S. when Anthony committed him to an extensive American tour. Still weary and now without a band, Joe had to depend on Leon Russell, who assembled ten musicians and started rehearsals in just one day. Leon organized what became an incredible fifty-seven-day, sixty-five-performance American tour called Mad Dogs and Englishmen. The group included musicians, their families, roadies, and a few others just along for the ride. The tour yielded a successful motion-picture feature in 1971, as well as a hit L.P. Meanwhile, Cocker had been high on the charts with the old Box Tops song "The Letter" (April 1970) and "Cry Me a River" (October 1970), which went gold. Unfortunately, the Mad Dogs tour left Joe emotionally and physically devastated.

The tour gave Leon Russell enormous exposure, and as a result his career skyrocketed, while Cocker vanished from the scene after his single "High Time We Went" (May 1971) became a top-ten hit. But Cocker had become a burn-out. In 1972 he managed to resurface with a band called Concert. When American reviews were unfavorable, the group moved on to Australia, where Cocker was busted for possession of pot. After resisting arrest, Cocker was hit with an assortment of other charges. Joe faded from sight again after the release of the December 1972 single "Woman to Woman."

In January 1975 Cocker returned once again with the moving hit ballad "You Are So Beautiful," penned by Billy Preston. By the late seventies, however, fame had slipped through his fingers once more. Joe's 1978 L.P. *Luxury You Can Afford* created barely a ripple.

THE GUESS WHO

Chad Allan and Randy Bachman formed Allan and the Silvertones in 1959 while they were still in high school in Winnipeg, Manitoba. After playing high school dances and hops, Allan and the Silvertones graduated to playing clubs as the Expressions. After entering college, Chad decided to rename the group again, this time choosing the Guess Who. With Chad singing lead, the group had two Canadian hits, "Tossin' and Turnin' " and "Shakin' All Over."

Then, in 1965, Chad gave up the frivolous world of rock and roll when he decided to return to the University of Manitoba to work on a master's degree in psychology. Randy Bachman inherited the leadership of the Guess Who from Chad. While searching through a bin of 45's in Winnipeg one day, he met eighteen-year-old Burton Cummings, Jr., an avid record collector and The Guess Who's next lead singer. With Randy on lead guitar, Burton singing lead and playing keyboards, Garry Peterson on drums and Jim Kale on bass, the regrouped Guess Who went back to playing clubs and developed quite a local reputation for themselves. By 1967 they had their own weekly TV show *Where It's At* on the Canadian Broadcasting Company network, and had become the biggest group in Canada. However, Cummings put their Canadian success into perspective when he admitted, "You just gotta realize that there's maybe seven acts in the entire country you can hear more than once without throwing up. All you have to do is form a band and you're automatically one of the top five groups in Canada."

With Cummings and Bachman sharing the writing chores, the Guess Who had nineteen hit singles in Canada between 1967 and 1968, but try as they might, they just couldn't make it in the United States. Finally, in late 1968 they broke the ice in the U.S. with a monster hit, "These Eyes." At the urging of the groups' Canadian producer, Jack Richardson (who later produced Alice Cooper's *Muscle of Love*

album), RCA records signed the Guess Who in January 1969, and "These Eyes," a ballad featuring Cummings' silken voice and electric piano, climbed to number 6 on the American charts.

Bachman and Cummings wasted no time writing hits for their American neighbors. "Laughing," a medium-tempo ballad, and "Undun," a jazzy portrait of a troubled lady, was their two-sided gold record (through airplay or sales requests, each side individually sold over a million copies), which remained on the charts from July to the last week of 1969. Nineteen seventy brought the Guess Who's first certified American rocker, "No Time (Left for You)," a nasty song that was highlighted by Randy Bachman's buzz-saw guitar work. They also had one of 1970's biggest hits in April with "American Woman." While many thought the song was an indictment of America's involvement in the Vietnam War, the song was actually the group's anthem to Canadian nationalism, criticizing close-minded American attitudes toward Canadian culture. "American Woman" went number 1, but it was the last hit Burton Cummings and Randy Bachman would have together.

Problems started when Randy Bachman got married, converted to Mormonism, and began to preach the Mormons' morality of abstinence to the band. The other members of the group had grown accustomed to the rock-and-roll life-style and resented Bachman's sudden holier-than-thou attitude. The band also felt that he was manipulating them for his own gain. In the summer of 1970 Bachman refused to tour with the Guess Who, claiming that he had a gall bladder problem that kept him from traveling. The group toured with a replacement, but when they arrived in New York to play the Fillmore East, they were stunned to find that Randy had been in town to negotiate a contract for a solo album. Bachman was promptly thrown out of the group.

The Guess Who permanently replaced Bachman

with two guitarists, Kurt Winter and Greg Leskiw, but they still had their most distinctive asset, Burton Cummings' fire-and-ice voice. In the last half of 1970 they attacked the record charts with renewed vigor on a song that Kurt Winter had written for his old group, Brother, called "Hand Me Down World." It became a top-twenty hit. "Share the Land," which was attacked from some quarters for its socialist outlook, climbed into the top ten at year's end. But by 1971 it became apparent that without the strength of Randy Bachman the Guess Who were finding it increasingly difficult to get on the charts. Between "Rain Dance" in August 1971 and "Clap for the Wolfman," a tribute to Wolfman Jack, in August 1974, they did not have any records in the top twenty. The latter proved to be the Guess Who's swan song. In September 1975, after a seventy-five-city North American tour and a number of personnel changes, the Guess Who split up for good.

After his forced departure from the Guess Who, Randy Bachman cut an unsuccessful solo album, *Axe,* in late 1970. He then looked up his old friend Guess Who charter member Chad Allan. In 1971 they formed Brave Belt with Fred Turner and Randy's brother, Robbie Bachman. Chad left after the first album. With the second album's failure to set the world on fire, the group added a third Bachman brother, Tim, and changed its name to Bachman-Turner Overdrive. BTO was a heavy-metal boogie band with their 1974-75 hits "Let It Ride," "Taking Care of Business," "You Ain't Seen Nothing Yet," and "Roll on Down the Highway." With every member of the group weighing over 250 pounds each, BTO were truly rock heavyweights.

Bachman-Turner Overdrive. This version of BTO featured (from left) Robbie Bachman, Blair Thornton, C. F. Turner, and Jim Clench.

THE JACKSON 5

In late 1969 Motown Records was in trouble. Its top production team, Eddie Holland, Lamont Dozier, and Brian Holland, left the company in a dispute over back royalties. Without the Holland-Dozier-Holland golden touch, some of Motown's biggest acts, including the Supremes, the Four Tops, and Martha and the Vandellas, found it nearly impossible to hit the charts. Then David Ruffin walked out on the Temptations in 1968, leaving that group in search of a new direction as well as a new lead singer. Diana Ross had split from the Supremes and was now concentrating on Las Vegas and Hollywood. Smokey Robinson had grown tired of performing, now preferring to sit behind a desk in Motown's executive suite. What the label needed in 1970 was a shot in the arm. What Motown got was the biggest-selling singles group of 1970—the Jackson 5.

Back in the fifties Papa Joe Jackson had played guitar with the Falcons, an R & B group from Chicago, but in the sixties he worked as a crane operator in Gary, Indiana. He was disturbed by the conditions he saw in Gary. Kids were dropping out of school, playing with dope and leading dead-end lives. Joe vowed that his children would have a better life. He believed that music would be their way out of Gary. With nine children it was tough, but Joe managed to save up enough to buy secondhand musical instruments for his brood. Joe and his wife, Katherine, made sure each child learned at least one instrument and practiced it every day after school. After a while the five oldest boys—Sigmund Esco ("Jackie"), Toriano Adaryll ("Tito"), Jermaine, Marlon, and Michael—began to sing and dance together as a group for their own enjoyment. In 1967 Tito thought the five brothers should turn professional, and the Jackson 5 were born.

With nine-year-old Michael and oldest brother Jackie singing lead, Tito and Jermaine playing guitar and bass, Marlon doing backup vocals, and father Joe acting as business manager, the Jackson 5 played all over the Indiana club, college, and fraternity scene. A blazing whirlwind of singing and dancing talent led by the little dynamo, Michael, the Jackson 5 made Indiana sit up and take notice. Often, after turning in an electrifying performance at a fraternity party, little Michael would fall asleep in a chair as the party went on past his bedtime. After they played at a campaign benefit for Gary mayor Richard Hatcher, the mayor introduced the group to Diana Ross, who then told Motown chieftain Berry Gordy about them. Motown recognized their talent and signed them to a contract in the autumn of 1969.

Gordy assigned the Jackson 5 to the production unit called "the Corporation"—Freddie Perrin, Fonso Mizell, Deke Richards and Gordy himself. "The Corporation" wrote their songs, produced their records, and directed the group's career.

The Jackson 5's first single, "I Want You Back," was the best record Motown had put out in years. With its exciting dance beat and Michael's dynamic lead vocal, "I Want You Back" sold two million copies in six weeks, climbed to number 1 in January 1970, and spent nine weeks in the top ten. "The Corporation" decided to market the group for the teen-age and preteen audience. The Jackson 5's second single, "ABC," soared to the number-1 spot in April. The schoolboy charm of "The Love You Save," a clever wordplay on traffic safety warnings, took that single to the top of the charts in July. Their follow-up, "I'll Be There," was their biggest record yet, with five weeks in the number-1 position and three months in the top ten. It was the third biggest-selling single of 1970. All in all their records spent thirty-eight weeks in the top ten and an amazing ten weeks in the number-1 slot in 1970.

Nineteen seventy-one started with a number-1 hit, "Mama's Pearl." Their next record was a ballad, "Never Can Say Goodbye," written by Clifton Davis

The Jacksons (Michael Jackson seated second from left).

(who later starred in TV's *That's My Mama*). It sold over 1,200,000 copies just five days after its release and shot to the top of the charts. The group's first six singles were all number-1 hits and gold records, selling over sixteen million copies in all. They conquered television with their top-rated special, *Goin' Back to Indiana,* which led to a Jackson 5 animated-cartoon series on Saturday mornings. In late 1971 Motown began to push Michael's solo career, and the youngest member of the Jackson 5 had three top-five hits in the next year with "Got to Be There," a remake of Bobby Day's "Rockin' Robin," and a love song to a rat, the title song of the movie *Ben.* Brother Jermaine also had a solo act. He hit the top ten in early 1973 with "Daddy's Home," a song originally done by Shep and the Limelites in 1961.

Then came trouble. The ultimate white bread group, the Osmond Brothers, returned in 1971 to challenge the Jacksons for the prepubescent market. In place of funky professional Michael Jackson, the Osmonds served up soulless Donny Osmond, complete with his purple socks and toothy smile. Motown fought back by aiming the Jackson 5 at younger audiences, but record sales slipped as a result. Interestingly, Dick Clark was asked to manage tours for both the Jacksons and the Osmonds—simultaneously. He booked them at the same theaters on consecutive nights, and neither group ever had less than a sellout. But even though the Jackson 5 hit number 1 again in 1974 with "Dancing Machine," it was the beginning of a three-year downhill slide. Jermaine, who had married Berry Gordy's daughter, Hazel, in 1973, remained loyal to Motown, but the rest of the Jacksons moved to Epic Records in 1976 with youngest brother Randy taking Jermaine's place in the group. When Motown claimed the rights to the "Jackson 5" name, the group decided to call themselves simply the Jacksons.

Epic paired the Jacksons with producers Kenny Gamble and Leon Huff, then the hottest producers in the business with their successful "Sound of Philadelphia" (The O'Jays, MFSB, the Three Degrees). However, in three years with Gamble and Huff, the best the Jacksons could score was a minor hit, "Enjoy Yourself." In 1979 they began producing and writing their own material, finding their way back to the charts with the sophisticated disco sound of "Shake Your Body."

It seemed as if Michael Jackson had been transformed overnight from a chubby eleven-year-old into a tall, lean, sexy man of twenty-one. His "Rock With You" was a number-1 single in 1979. Michael, who starred in the film version of *The Wiz,* has a good chance of becoming one of the leading singing sex symbols of the eighties.

THE BAND

Robbie Robertson, Levon Helm, Rick Danko, Garth Hudson, and Richard Manuel were the band. They were the band that backed Ronnie Hawkins. They were the band that backed their own Levon Helm. They were the band that backed Bob Dylan. And only then were they *The Band.*

In the late fifties and early sixties Ronnie Hawkins was a rockabilly/country-western singer playing the clubs and dives of the South. As his sound dipped

The Band (from left: Garth Hudson, Levon Helm, Richard Manuel, Robbie Robertson, and Rick Danko).

more and more into rhythm and blues and stronger rock-and-roll influences, he recruited the right kind of background musicians for his group, the Hawks. Switching his home ground to Canada, he was led to

279

Bob Dylan and The Band (from left: Danko, Robertson, Hudson, and Dylan).

four Canadians: guitarist Robertson, bassist Danko, pianist Manuel, and organist Hudson. Added to his local Arkansas drummer, Levon Helm, the group was destined to overshadow its leader. Together they learned musical teamwork and how best to mesh their respective sounds and styles. Unlike most groups of those years, they never had ego conflicts that could threaten to break them up. When they did break away from Hawkins in 1963, they broke away as a group. As Levon and the Hawks, they played their way north, out of the redneck-infested southern backroads.

Gradually the group earned the respect of the music world with their consistently strong performances. In 1965 they were brought to the attention of Bob Dylan. Dylan drove down the Jersey shore in 1965 to Somers Point, where he heard the Hawks play at Tony Mart's Bar. When he invited them to play behind him at two upcoming big gigs, the boys were hesitant; they questioned his ability to fill a large amphitheater. As a result, only Robbie and Levon showed up for the first gig, which was the now-famous Bob Dylan Forest Hills concert of 1965. When they saw his drawing power, they summoned the others for the performance at the Hollywood Bowl. The results were good enough in Dylan's eyes to make him hire the band for his tour of England.

On the road they became The Band, and drew recognition in a positive light as master musicians and in a negative light as the underlying cause (according to Dylan's folk fans) of Dylan's sellout to commercialism—his defection from folk to rock. Working with Dylan they often played to sellout crowds and lots of angry booing. After Dylan's 1966 motorcycle accident The Band worked with him in his seclusion, then turned their attention toward preparing for their own career. The product of that preparation was a 1968 debut album called *Music from Big Pink*. In an attempt to classify the work, critics and fans came up with labels as varied as rock, country rock, rhythm and blues, rockabilly, folk rock, and any combination thereof. It certainly was their own music, however, and the group was no longer relegated to the background as they had been for so long on albums like Dylan's *Blonde on Blonde*. In 1969, The Band premiered in concert at Bill Graham's Winterland in San Francisco and then set out touring, something they had been used to doing for the past seven-plus years.

Music from Big Pink went gold and was critically claimed as a classic rock-and-roll album. They followed it up with 1969's *The Band* and accomplished what few rock stars have been able to do—follow up a huge, successful first album with a second that is just as critically acclaimed and just as good a seller as the first. This album brought the public's attention to a Robbie Robertson composition, "The Night They Drove Old Dixie Down," a song that would be covered as a hit by Joan Baez. The Band even managed to break onto the singles charts with their countrified rock tune "Up on Cripple Creek." That famous Band country sound was urbanized in their third album, *Stage Fright*, a departure from their previous product.

The road continued to bring the group some of its biggest rewards musically: In 1969 it was their intense performance at the Woodstock Festival; in 1974 it was touring the United States again with Bob Dylan; and in 1976, following nearly sixteen years on the road and dwindling success with their albums, The Band's farewell performance at the place where they started, Bill Graham's Winterland.

The last Band concert, held on Thanksgiving, 1976, was billed as "The Last Waltz." It produced a hit soundtrack album from the film of the event. Director Martin Scorcese put together what has been called the best rock-concert film ever photographed. The United Artists release captured the end of an era and one of The Band's best moments. It also preserved on celluloid the performances of the guest stars who dropped by to sing and jam: Bob Dylan, Ronnie Hawkins, Eric Clapton, Van Morrison, Joni Mitchell, Paul Butterfield, Neil Young, Neil Diamond, Dr. John, Muddy Waters, Ron Wood, Ringo Starr, Steve Stills, and many others. Since The Band's breakup Robbie Robertson has made his way into acting, appearing in the Lorimer Production of *Carny*, which failed to set the box office on fire. Levon Helm has fared better in filmdom, acting in the award-winning picture *Coal Miner's Daughter*.

The Sound of 1970
CHICAGO

One night as Dick Clark's Caravan of Stars cruised down the highway on the tour bus, Dick found himself sitting next to a young bass player of the backup band for the Caravan. The kid told Dick how exhilarated he felt to be on the road. Dick told him he was kidding himself. Most of the money was back down the road with the promoter. Years later when the two met again, the ex-bassplayer told Dick that it was on that night on the bus that he decided to become a record producer.

James William Guercio left the Caravan tour to produce and write liner notes for a band from Chicago called the Buckinghams. Under James' guidance they had hits like "Kind of a Drag" (1966), "Don't You Care" (1967), and "Susan" (1967). When James left the Buckinghams to join Frank Zappa's Mothers of Invention as lead guitarist, the Buckinghams' hits stopped. After the Mothers, Guercio went on the road with Chad and Jeremy. One night he received a call from Al Kooper, who wanted James to produce a Blues Project record and possibly work with a big brass rock band that Kooper was trying to put together. Guercio laughed at Al's suggestion that Kooper would be the first in rock to have a band like this. James told Al he had friends back in Chicago already getting such a band off the ground. James didn't do the Blues Project or Kooper's brass band— Blood, Sweat and Tears. However, after BS&T's first L.P., Kooper left, and Guercio was called upon to produce their second album. James did most of the charts and rearranged many of the tunes for that record that became one of rock's biggest-selling albums and yielded three hit singles.

When Al Kooper's big dream rock-group with horns, Blood, Sweat and Tears, was still on the drawing board, a big brass rock band was already playing in Chicago, and they were starving. Audiences in the clubs and bars of the Midwest were very unreceptive to the sound. The nucleus of this band, Danny Seraphine (drums), Walt Parazaider (woodwinds), and Terry Kath (guitar) first met in the early sixties at an audition for a local Chicago group called the Executives. They later added Lee Loughnane (trumpet) and James Pankow (trombone) to the band. When Robert Lamm was brought in on keyboards and Peter Cetera was recruited to play bass, the band was complete.

In 1967 they called themselves the Missing Links, and wore sharkskin suits and greasy pompadours. When that didn't work for them, they became the Big Thing, minus the suits and hairstyles. But despite their efforts they had reached a dead end in the Midwest by 1968. So when producer James Guercio invited them to L.A. to develop their sound, the band eagerly made the journey. Guercio, who was still associated with Columbia Records, eventually landed the band a contract. They took his suggestion and changed their name to Chicago Transit Authority. Soon they toured the West Coast, first with Janis Joplin, then with Jimi Hendrix.

Their first L.P., *Chicago Transit Authority,* released in April 1969, was a double album—something unheard of for a new group. It contained long songs with complicated arrangements more suitable for FM underground radio than pop AM radio. Furthermore, rock fans were shocked by the blast of brass. This album and the single "Questions 67 and 68" (August 1969) were not immediately successful. Then, taking some advice from Dick Clark, Chicago began to make television appearances to promote their record sales. Dick Clark then produced several television specials for them. The additional exposure gained from their tours and the top-ten success of their next single, "Make Me Smile" (April 1970), brought public attention back to their debut L.P., which went on to become one of the top ten albums of 1970 and stayed on the charts for 148 weeks.

The list of Chicago's albums and singles reads like a record salesman's dream. *Chicago II,* which introduced their new shortened name, Chicago, was another double-disc set released in May 1970. Sitting in the top ten for thirty-one weeks, the album went gold and yielded the singles "Make Me Smile," "25 or 6 to 4" (July 1970), and "Color My World" (June 1971). Their next hit, "Does Anybody Really Know What Time It Is?" was released as a single in November 1970. *Chicago III,* released in January 1971, continued the double-record gold tradition and contained the singles "Free" (February 1971) and "Lowdown" (May 1971). Three months later, *Chicago IV* came out. This was a quadruple record set recorded live at Carnegie Hall, containing thirty-seven songs, a giant poster of the group, and voter registration charts intended to encourage youth participation in the 1972 presidential elections. It was the first four-record set ever released by a rock group, and many critics called it an overindulgent rip-off. The band must have taken notice; *Chicago V,* a single disc, was issued in July 1972. It was their fifth gold album in a row and featured "Saturday in the Park" (August 1972). In June 1973, *Chicago VI* became the number-1 album for three weeks and stayed on the charts for five more. It included the number-1 single "Just You 'n' Me" (September 1973). March 1974 brought *Chicago VII,* which went gold that same month and shot to number 1. *Chicago VIII* was an instant gold album in 1975 with its popular single "Harry Truman" (February 1975). *Chicago IX,* a greatest-hits album, was released in December 1975 and was number 1 for eight weeks. *Chicago X* (September 1976) and *Chicago XI* (November 1977) both went platinum on the days they were shipped, the latter containing the hit single, "Baby, What a Big Surprise" (September 1977).

In January 1978 lead guitarist Terry Kath, an avid gun collector, played Russian roulette and lost. The police listed his death as accidental. Donnie Dacus replaced him on guitar as the band bounced back in September with the L.P. *Hot Streets,* the first of their albums to be co-produced by the group. By 1979 their first eleven L.P.'s had all gone platinum, generating over $160 million in sales. In September of that year Chicago released *Chicago XIII.* Surprisingly, it didn't sell as well as their previous discs. After ten long years, some say the party may well be over. Chicago is the original faceless supergroup. They are one of the most successful bands of the seventies, but they promote no recognizable personality. Nonetheless, they go down in rock-and-roll history as an international phenomenon that has utilized keen musicianship to create a popular combination of soul, jazz, and the forties big-band sound.

1971

In 1971 the voting age was lowered to eighteen. Twelve thousand people were arrested in a May Day Vietnam War protest in Washington, D.C. The Pentagon Papers were published. Idi Amin took over in Uganda. And Palisades Park, the New Jersey amusement park immortalized in a song recorded by Freddie Cannon and written by Chuck Barris, closed its doors for good.

Nineteen seventy-one saw *The French Connection* win the Oscar for Best Picture of the Year, and in television it was also the year Archie Bunker came into our lives. CBS was desperate for a "second season" replacement series in January, so they took a chance on *All in the Family,* a show that ABC had already turned down. The show's ratings were dismal at first, but word of mouth spread fast. People just couldn't believe what *All in the Family* was getting away with. Bigotry, religion, politics, and sex—all of TV's taboos—were now fodder for TV comedy. After Archie, Edith, Gloria and Meathead, television was never the same again.

On March 8 Muhammad Ali stepped into the ring at New York's Madison Square Garden for his first historic battle with Joe Frazier. After fifteen rounds of superb boxing, Frazier walked out of the ring the winner and still champion. In other sports, seven-foot three-inch Lew Alcindor changed his name to Kareem Abdul-Jabbar and led the Milwaukee Bucks to the NBA championship in his rookie season. The Dallas Cowboys thrashed the Miami Dolphins to win Super Bowl VI. Roberto Clemente and Steve Blass led the Pittsburgh Pirates to a World Series victory over the Baltimore Orioles.

In 1971 rock could be artsy, as in "Lucky Man" by Emerson, Lake and Palmer, or just plain stupid, as in "Chick-a-Boom" by Daddy Dewdrop. Ike and Tina Turner were "nice and rough" in their version of "Proud Mary," while Isaac Hayes was warm and mellow with "The Theme From *Shaft."* The Buoys offered a tasteless song about cannibalism called "Timothy," while rock gourmands feasted on "Have You Seen Her?" a tasty soul number by the Chi-Lites. All in all, rock was a grab bag in 1971, with Melanie's "Brand New Key," Coven's "One Tin Soldier," Van Morrison's "Domino," Cher's "Gypsies, Tramps and Thieves," and the Osmonds' "One Bad Apple." The top ten in 1971 settled in like this: "Maggie May/Reason To Believe" by Rod Stewart, "Joy to the World" by Three Dog Night, "One Bad Apple" by the Osmonds, "It's Too Late/I Feel the Earth Move" by Carole King, "How Can You Mend a Broken Heart" by the Bee Gees, "Indian Reservation" by Paul Revere and the Raiders, "Knock Three

Times" by Dawn, "Go Away Little Girl" by Donny Osmond, "Take Me Home, Country Roads" by John Denver with Fat City, and "Just My Imagination (Running Away with Me)" by the Temptations.

It was 1971—the seventeenth year of rock and roll.

Van Morrison fronted Them, a rock group from Northern Ireland who made the charts in the mid-sixties with raucous versions of "Here Comes the Night" and "Gloria." A solo effect, "Brown-eyed Girl," reached number 10 in 1967. Van the Man then moved toward a jazzier, mellower sound, and the result was the classic album *Moondance* in 1968. Morrison had his greatest success in the singles market in 1971 with "Domino," "Blue Money," and "Wild Night," followed by "Tupelo Honey" and "Jackie Wilson Said" in 1972.

A former keyboard player for Otis Redding, cowriter of some of
Sam and Dave's biggest hits ("Hold On, I'm Comin'," "Soul Man"),
and a staff producer for Stax/Volt records, Isaac Hayes had one
of the biggest records of 1971 with the "Theme from *Shaft.*"

Three Dog Night.

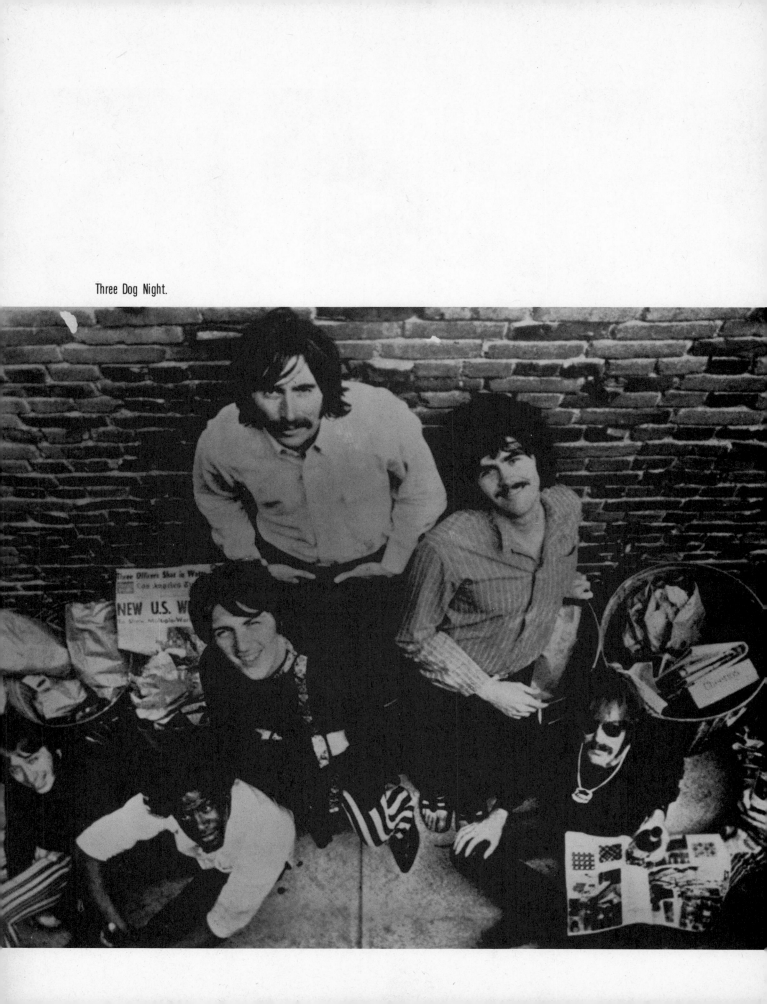

THREE DOG NIGHT

Three-part harmony was the key to the success of Danny Hutton, Chuck Negron, and Cory Wells, who were collectively known as Three Dog Night. Each had floated from group to group for years before making it together. Hutton had a few solo flops with "Roses and Rainbows" (1965), "Big Bright Eyes" (1965), and "Funny How Love Can Be" (1966) before he met Cory Wells, a member of an obscure band called the Enemies, who had bombed with "Hey Joe" (1966), "Too Much Monkey Business" (1966), and "Mo-Jo Woman" (1966). Around this time, Chuck Negron was with the lackluster Rondells. The three vocalists got together and decided that it would be a good idea to find a backup band of musicians, so they recruited Mike Allsup (guitar), Joe Schermie (bass), Floyd Sneed (drums), and Jim Greenspoon (keyboards).

Now all they needed was a name. As it happened, Danny's girl friend came to the rescue while browsing through an old *National Geographic.* "Three dog night" was an Australian colloquialism that referred to the temperature. If the night was somewhat cold, a man slept with one dog for heat. If it was quite cold, he slept with two dogs. But if it was frigid, then it was a "three-dog night."

The group was playing California bars and clubs before they came to the attention of ABC Records. Gabriel Mekler, who was also managing Steppenwolf, took Three Dog Night under his wing. He decided that their image should be pure and their material simple and harmonious. Their first single, "Nobody"

(1968), went straight down the tubes, but "Try a Little Tenderness" (1969), an Otis Redding classic, took them straight up the charts. Next Harry Nilsson's "One" turned gold for Three Dog Night in 1970, obscuring Al Kooper's version of the song. Consecutive hits were released furiously now with "Easy to Be Hard" from Broadway's *Hair;* Laura Nyro's "Eli's Coming," "Celebrate," Randy Newman's "Mama Told Me Not to Come," "One Man Band," Hoyt Axton's "Joy to the World," and "An Old Fashioned Love Song," all going gold in 1970 and 1971.

The Three Dog Night were just as good live as they were on vinyl. *Captured Live at the Forum* actually did capture the energy of their concerts and was one of the better live albums of 1971. Originally Three Dog Night toured as the opening act for Steppenwolf, but their audiences' wild reactions coupled with their increasing collection of hits convinced ABC and concert promoters to let them tour as headliners. Touring constantly, they only took out enough time to rush through one album and allow Chuck to recuperate from a car accident in 1971.

After B.W. Stevenson's "Shambala" in 1974, Three Dog Night vanished from the charts. Perhaps if the group had been permitted to evolve and grow, they would have kept pace with the public's changing tastes. Today the three principals have gone their own ways.

CAT STEVENS

Stephen Demetri Georgiou was born in July 1948 in London to a Swedish mother and a Cypriot father. Although his family exposed him to music at an early age, his dream was to become a famous painter. At the age of sixteen he enrolled in art school, where he became influenced by folk music. Because he spent most of his time learning the guitar, he was dismissed from art school.

Stephen played some local clubs, but he concentrated on his song-writing, hounding agents and publishing houses with his material. One of the many demo tapes he circulated eventually won him a contract with British Decca. In 1966, at the age of seventeen, he had his first hit, "I Love My Dog." That was followed in 1967 by his European hit, "Matthew and Son." This record received a good deal of progressive radio airplay in America, breaking open a new market for his work. Hitting the road, he toured England, Belgium, and France with Engelbert Humperdinck and Jimi Hendrix.

In 1968 Cat had a falling-out with his record company over their imposition of what he considered commercialism on his work, and the company agreed to release him from his contract. But by the fall, overwork, drinking, smoking, and career anxieties left him discouraged and exhausted. Cat had developed a severe case of tuberculosis that put him in a hospital for well over a year. This illness and his recuperation from it were the catalysts for the development of Cat's unique singing/songwriting style. As he studied metaphysics, practiced yoga, and searched out a "knowledge of self," he continued to write songs.

Stevens was back in 1970 with the L.P. *Mona Bone Jakon,* which created renewed interest in his electric folk-rock style. By early 1971 his next album, *Tea for the Tillerman,* was a smash on the charts, and his single "Wild World" (February 1971) was also quite successful. Later that year Stevens struck again with *Teaser and the Firecat,* which contained three hit singles: "Moon Shadow" (June 1971), a song inspired by a night Cat spent alone on the coast of Spain, dancing and singing on the rocks as the waves crashed in the bright moonlight; "Peace Train" (September 1971); and "Morning Has Broken" (April 1971). The single "Lady D'Arbanville," a big hit in France and England during the summer of 1970, was about a girl friend who left him for Mick Jagger.

In 1972 the L.P. *Catch Bull at Four* was released as Cat was completing a successful tour of the U.S. However, his 1973 *Foreigner* album did not sell well. His intriguing lyrical vagueness had become pretentious and obscure. Yet Cat rebounded in 1974 with *Buddah and the Chocolate Box,* its single "Oh Very Young," and his version of an old Sam Cooke tune, "Another Saturday Night." His *Greatest Hits* album (1975) went gold and was followed by the L.P. *Numbers* (1975). In 1977, *Izitso* went gold shortly after its release, documenting his renewed strength in the rock market. His 1979 album, *Back to Earth,* made a respectable showing on the charts, but the glory days of Cat Stevens were clearly gone. Nonetheless, Stevens will be remembered for creating some enchanting melodies, cleverly exploiting calypso funk, and producing bright arrangements that effectively showcased his tunes and his stylish vocal phrasing.

Cat Stevens.

JAMES TAYLOR

James Taylor was born in March 1948 to an upper-class family in Chapel Hill, North Carolina. His father was the dean of the University of North Carolina Medical School, and his mother was a soprano and teacher at the New England Conservatory of Music. By 1953 the family was spending its summers on Martha's Vineyard, where young James took cello and guitar lessons. James and his musically inclined siblings—Alex, Kate, Livingston, and Hugh—would often give what their mom called kitchen concerts.

Influenced by the Vineyard area folk scene and Alex's collection of blues records, James and Alex formed a group, the Fabulous Corsayers. The band basically played R & B standards for proms and fraternity parties at the university. James also performed with his brother Liv, playing jug band music at hootenannies.

In the fall of 1965 seventeen-year-old James Taylor entered the McLean Psychiatric Hospital in Belmont, Massachusetts, with acute depression, which he'd developed in his senior year at his high school academy. It was here that James first started to write songs seriously. He later described his experiences there in "Knocking 'Round the Zoo," a tune that was on his first L.P. Perhaps not coincidentally, brother Liv and sister Kate eventually entered McLean. After nine months James discharged himself, and in the fall of 1966, moved to New York City.

While settling down in New York, he formed a band called the Flying Machine with his childhood friend, Danny Kortchmar. They played regularly on the Greenwich Village club circuit, and James began to take heroin at about this time. He became a junkie, and that ended the Flying Machine. James then left for London, planning on playing his way through Europe. It didn't work out that way, though. His inability to get work permits kept him in England, where he cut a demo tape and auditioned for several record companies. He heard that Peter Asher, the newly appointed head producer of the Beatles' new Apple record label, was auditioning new artists. Taylor got his phone number from Kortchmar, who used to back Asher's old act, Peter and Gordon. Both Peter and Paul McCartney were impressed by James, and James became one of the first "outside" acts signed by Apple.

Taylor and Asher began working on James' first album in early 1968. Unfortunately, Apple's newest artist was by now into what were called "speedballs," mixtures of smack and meth. Somehow the album was cut. Titled *James Taylor,* the L.P. received some critical praise but only moderate sales. When Apple started to fail, Taylor fell into a state of nervous and physical exhaustion. At the end of 1968 he returned to the U.S. and admitted himself into Austin Riggs, another mental institution in Massachusetts, with hopes of kicking his heroin habit. Asher, who now lived in the U.S., had become a good friend of Taylor, and agreed to act as his manager. When Taylor was discharged after five months, Asher obtained a contract with Warner Brothers Records for him, and they set to work on a new L.P.

Sweet Baby James was released in March 1970. Containing the hit single, "Fire and Rain" (September 1970), the album was a huge success, eventually selling over three million copies and making Taylor a star. Like many of his songs, "Fire and Rain" was autobiographical, offering some insight into the artist's psychological condition. The song dealt with a friend who had killed herself and with his attempts to kick his heroin habit in the institution.

In November 1970 Apple released the single "Carolina in my Mind" from his first L.P. It featured Paul McCartney on bass and George Harrison on harmonies. The single "Country Road" (February 1971) kept the ball rolling for James. That same month William Bender, *Time* magazine's music critic, attended a Taylor concert at New York's Philharmonic

Sweet Baby James Taylor.

Hall and wrote an in-depth article about him. James had the rare honor of being on the cover of *Time.* His tours then started to sell out consistently, and in June 1971 he released the first of his singles to go gold, "You've Got a Friend." The tune had been written by Carole King, who had recorded it earlier in the year on her "Tapestry" album. Taylor introduced audiences to King, taking her on his tours as his opening act. This million-selling single from his L.P. *Mud Slide Slim* won him a 1971 Grammy Award for Best Pop Vocal Performance by a Male and Carole the 1971 Grammy Song of the Year Award.

Although romantically involved with Joni Mitchell at one time, James married Carly Simon in November 1972. Carly's December 1972 single "You're So Vain" skyrocketed, while James' late 1972 L.P. *One Man Dog* was his worst seller to date. That year, Taylor made his acting debut in the motion picture *Two Lane Blacktop,* indicating that he would stop recording.

In 1974, nevertheless, a new Taylor album, *Walking Man,* was released. Taylor and Simon teamed up on "Mockingbird" in 1974 and this single turned gold. *Gorilla,* his sixth L.P., contained two hit singles, "How Sweet It Is" (June 1975) and "Mexico" (October 1975), and featured vocals by Carly, Randy

Newman, Graham Nash, and David Crosby. The spirit of joy that pervaded this album suggested that Taylor might have finally licked his long-standing drug problem. James' 1976 *Greatest Hits* L.P. went platinum. While his *In the Pocket* album did very little, 1977's *JT* went platinum and provided the hit single "Handy Man."

In early 1978 James cut the nerve in his hand that controls the left index finger. This temporarily stopped his guitar playing and kept him off the road for nearly two years. In 1979 his *Flag* L.P. didn't sell well, but he finally went back out on tour. In September 1979 James and Carly participated in the Musicians United for Safe Energy (MUSE) concerts at Madison Square Garden in New York City. He occasionally performs on TV, most recently on NBC's *Saturday Night Live.* James and Carly's tempestuous marriage weathered a number of highly publicized separations and reconciliations in 1980.

James' success opened up formerly closed doors for three of his siblings in the rock-music field. Older brother Alex released two albums, *Alex Taylor* and *Dinnertime;* sister Kate released one album, *Sister Kate;* and James' very talented brother Livingston Taylor had three quality L.P.s, *Livingston Taylor, Liv,* and *Over the Rainbow.*

The Sound of 1971

CAROLE KING

Carole Klein was born in 1941 in New York City. By the age of four she was singing and taking piano lessons from her mother, who wanted her to be an actress. In high school Carole formed a vocal quartet called the Co-Sines. Carole wrote songs for this group, which performed at local school dances. She later attended Queens College with the intention of becoming an elementary school teacher. In 1958 she met Queens College chemistry major and aspiring lyricist Gerry Goffin. She also met Paul Simon, another Queens College student. At that time, Paul and Carole cut some rather unsuccessful demos together.

In 1958 Don Kirshner and Al Nevins formed Aldon Music. With the old masters and hacks of Tin Pan Alley unwilling to write for rock-and-roll artists, Kirshner and Nevins hired Barry Mann, Cynthia Weil, Bobby Darin, Neil Diamond, and Neil Sedaka to capture the youth market by creating songs in the pop format.

In late 1958 Carole made some singles for ABC Paramount and RCA that went nowhere. Then, in October 1959, her single "Oh! Neil" on the Alpine label brought her some attention. "Oh! Neil" was her answer to her neighbor Neil Sedaka's hit about her—"Oh! Carol." Kirshner was present at her recording session and was very impressed by her feel for the piano. After graduating, Gerry and Carole were married and soon went to work for Aldon Music. Carole's musical talent complemented Gerry's lyrical skills well. Their first hit was "Will You Still Love Me Tomorrow?," recorded by the Shirelles in 1960. A list of their songs reads like an *American Bandstand* silver-dollar survey: "Take Good Care of My Baby" for Bobby Vee, "The Loco-Motion" for Little Eva, "Up on the Roof" for the Drifters, "Chains" for the Cookies, "Go Away Little Girl" for Steve Lawrence, "I'm Into Something Good" for Herman's Hermits, "Pleasant Valley Sunday" for the Monkees, "One Fine Day" for the Chiffons, "A Natural Woman" for Aretha Franklin, "Point of No Return" for Gene McDaniels, "Don't Bring Me Down" for the Animals, and "Goin' Back" for the Byrds. And this is just a partial list! They were a prolific, expressive, and brilliant writing team. Indeed, from the formation of Aldon until 1965, the company dominated American pop; clearly, Carole King and Gerry Goffin were the jewels of the crown.

Goffin and King made it their practice to cut demos of their songs to give artists an idea of how a song should sound. King's demos were done so well that they were often exactly duplicated by the artist on the record. In August 1962 Kirshner formed Dimension Records and asked Goffin and King to do most of the label's writing and producing. Their first record on Dimension was sung by Eva Boyd, the couple's teen-aged babysitter. Turning her into "Little Eva," they gave her a hit with "The Loco-Motion." The three backup singers on that song then had their own hit on Dimension as the Cookies, with Goffin and King's "Chains." Carole released three singles of her own on Dimension, most notably "It Might As Well Rain until September" (August 1962).

Aldon and Dimension were eventually sold to Screen Gems, and by 1965 the era of the "Brill Building sound" had come to an end. The British

Carole King.

invasion of the mid-sixties established a trend for groups to write their own songs. In 1966 Goffin and King formed the unsuccessful Tomorrow label. By 1968 Carole had separated from Goffin and moved to L.A. She formed a group called the City with Danny Kortchmar on guitar and Charles Larkey on bass, whom she later married. They released one L.P., *The City,* then broke up. With encouragement from Lou Adler of Ode Records, Carole recorded a solo L.P., *Writer,* which brought her critical acclaim in 1970. However, she was still relatively unknown to record buyers and concertgoers. No one suspected that her next record, *Tapestry,* would be number 1 for fifteen weeks, remaining on the charts for an unprecedented 292 weeks. *Tapestry* was the biggest-selling L.P. in history by a female artist, selling twelve million copies by the end of 1973. It was the first recording to be awarded a Gold Tape Cartridge (1971). It was also the Grammy winner for the Best Album of the Year (1971) and the Album of the Decade, netting Carole another Grammy in 1971 for Best Pop Vocal Performance (Female). The gold single "It's Too Late" (May 1971) from *Tapestry* was number 1 for five weeks, quickly sold a million copies, and won a Grammy for Record of the Year (1971). Carole received yet another Grammy for Song of the Year (1971) with "You've Got a Friend," also on *Tapestry.* However, this song was made a big hit by her friend James Taylor, who had introduced her to his audiences on his 1971 tour. *Tapestry* also contained the hit single "So Far Away" (August 1971).

Carole King Music was her December 1971 follow-up to *Tapestry,* and simply had to be a letdown by comparison. Still, it sold over 1,300,000 upon release, was number 1 for three weeks, and went platinum, eventually selling well over two million copies. In October 1972 Carole released *Rhymes and Reasons,* which was number 1 for two weeks, turned gold, and yielded the single "Been To Canaan" (November 1972). Her June 1973 L.P., *Fantasy,* hit number 1, turned gold, and contained two singles: "You Light Up My Life" (July 1973) and "Corazon" (October 1973). In the mid-seventies she released the L.P.'s *Wrap Around Joy* and *Really Rosie,* her score for the 1976 Maurice Sendak animated TV show of the same name. Carole's final L.P. on Ode was 1976's *Thoroughbred,* which contained the single "Only Love Is Real."

In early 1977 she switched record companies and signed a long-term contract with Capitol Records. Carole also started to record and tour with a club band from Boulder, Colorado, called Navarro. By the summer their *Simple Things* was released on her own record label, Avatar, which was handled by Capitol. But the critics labeled the record banal and flat. In the fall of '78 Carol released the L.P. *Welcome Home,* which included the single "Main Street Saturday Night." Unfortunately, sales were minimal. Carole came back strong in 1980 with a remake of her tune written for the Chiffons, "One Fine Day."

The sensitive and sentimental songs that Carole King created over the years will live on in her own as well as in other singers' versions. With a career that spans three decades, she has helped to make rock what it is today. Now she is watching her daughter, Louise Goffin, pursue her own singing career in rock and roll.

1972

Nineteen seventy-two was an ominous presidential election year. Governor George Wallace, one of the leading candidates for the Democratic nomination, was shot by Arthur Bremer and paralyzed for life. Dark-horse Senator George McGovern won the Democratic nomination, naming Senator Thomas Eagleton his running mate. When it was revealed that Eagleton had undergone electroshock therapy, McGovern quickly replaced him with Sargent Shriver. Nixon then crushed McGovern in the election, carrying every state but Massachusetts and the District of Columbia. And on June 17, five men were apprehended in a "third-rate burglary" at the Democratic National Headquarters in Washington's Watergate complex.

This was also an Olympic year. At the Munich summer games Mark Spitz, the American swimmer, won seven gold medals, but his achievements were overshadowed by a Palestinian terrorist raid on the Olympic village in which eleven Israeli athletes were held hostage and murdered. Perhaps the most unlikely sports event of 1972 occurred in Reykjavik, Iceland, where Bobby Fischer of the U.S. bested the Soviet Union's Boris Spassky for the World Chess Championship. The Oakland A's knocked off the Cincinnati Reds in the World Series. The L.A. Lakers polished off the N.Y. Knicks for the NBA crown, and the Miami Dolphins capped a perfect 17–0 season by drubbing the Washington Redskins in the Super Bowl.

Two TV favorites, *M*A*S*H* and *Columbo,* debuted in 1972. In the year that the film *The Godfather* made audiences offers that couldn't be refused and was judged Best Picture of the Year, Chuck Berry had his very first number-1 hit with the naughty "My Ding-a-Ling." In another blast from rock-and-roll's past, Elvis Presley shot back into the number-1 seat in November with "Burning Love." Roberta Flack and Donny Hathaway asked, "Where Is the Love?" Billy Preston offered his instrumental "Outa Space." In 1972 the Staple Singers had "I'll Take You There," the Raspberries did "Go All the Way," America recorded "A Horse with No Name," and Looking Glass gave us the mellow "Brandy." The 1972 top ten looked like this: "Alone Again (Naturally)" by Gilbert O'Sullivan, "First Time Ever I Saw Your Face" by Roberta Flack, "American Pie" by Don McLean, "Without You" by Nilsson, "Lean on Me" by Bill Withers, "I Gotcha" by Joe Tex, "Baby Don't Get Hooked on Me" by Mac Davis, "Brand New Key" by Melanie, "Daddy Don't You Walk So Fast" by Wayne Newton, and "Candy Man" by Sammy Davis, Jr.

It was 1972—the eighteenth year of rock and roll.

A member of the Memphis Backstreet Boys and the Roadrunners before he was even fifteen, Brooklyn-born Neil Diamond had music in his blood. A 1963 single "Clown Town" didn't go anywhere, so Neil became a songwriter and demo singer in New York. After writing "I'm a Believer" for the Monkees, Neil had the confidence to try a singing career again. Neil's long string of hits proves that he was one of the most important singer/songwriters of the era: "Solitary Man," "Cherry, Cherry" (a hit twice), "Kentucky Woman," "Holly Holy," "Cracklin' Rosie," "Sweet Caroline," "I Am, I Said," and "Song Sung Blue."

Helen Reddy made the long journey from Australia to *American Bandstand* and became one of the top-selling female artists in the process. Helen beat out 1,358 contestants in an Australian TV talent contest to win a trip to New York, but the Big Apple wasn't ready for Reddy in 1966. Helen met her husband, agent Jeff Wald, at a party. After three years and moves to Chicago and Los Angeles, Jeff finally landed his wife a record contract in 1969. In 1972 Helen had the first of her many number-1 songs, "I Am Woman," which became an anthem for the women's lib movement. Some of Helen's other hits include "Delta Dawn," "Leave Me Alone (Ruby Red Dress)," "Keep On Singing," and "Angie Baby." *(Courtesy of Dick Clark)*

Rock eccentric Harry Nilsson scored big in 1972 with the singles "Without You" and "Coconut" and the albums *Nilsson Schmilsson* and *Son of Schmilsson*. Nilsson, who to this date has never performed live in public, also traded licks on albums with George Harrison and Ringo Starr and recorded a memorably bad album with John Lennon, *Pussycats*.

CARLY SIMON

(Pam Frank)

Carly Simon was born in New York to a family rich both monetarily and musically. Her father was one of the founders of the book publishing company Simon and Schuster as well as a classical pianist. One of Carly's uncles was a jazz critic and another claimed to have discovered Dinah Shore. Carly's older sister, Joanna, had pursued a career as an opera singer.

But despite her musical heritage, little Carly first made her mark on the baseball diamonds as an unofficial mascot of the Brooklyn Dodgers. At Sarah Lawrence College in 1963–64 Carly joined her sister Lucy to form a folksinging duo, the Simon Sisters. Bookings at the Bitter End in New York's East Village brought them significant attention, and they were eventually signed by Kapp Records. In April 1964 they had a minor local hit with "Winkin, Blinkin and Nod." Shortly thereafter, however, Lucy got married and Carly was forced to go solo.

In 1966 Carly met Albert Grossman, manager for Bob Dylan and Peter, Paul, and Mary. He saw her as a female Dylan and scheduled a recording session for her at Columbia (Dylan's label) with Bob Johnston (Dylan's producer), Robbie Robertson, and Rick Danko (Dylan's sidemen), using material composed by Dylan for the session. But after Carly and Albert had some differences of opinion, the music was canned and never reached the public.

Three years passed during which Carly briefly sang with a New York rock band called Elephant's Memory. After Carly left the group, they hooked up with John Lennon and Yoko Ono while she tried writing commercials for an ad agency. Her singing-career prospects were looking grim before her demo luckily found its way to Jac Holzman at Elektra. Word quickly spread that Elektra had found a female Mick Jagger. With a boost from her hit single "That's The Way I've Always Heard It Should Be," her first album, entitled *Carly Simon,* sold over half a million copies in 1971. She was soon on the road and debuted at L.A.'s Troubadour Club, opening for Cat Stevens. Although audiences were responsive and enthusiastic, Carly began to dislike performing in public. She revealed that she felt too vulnerable on stage,

overwhelmed by the energy of the crowd. Nevertheless, by the end of the year she had won the Grammy Award for Best New Artist of 1971.

Early in 1972 her second album was released and was propelled to the top of the charts with the aid of the album's hit single, "Anticipation." In November she married folk-rocker James Taylor. Her third album, *No Secrets,* hit the stores in December and shot to number 1, where it stayed for six weeks, selling over two million copies. Her single from the L.P., "You're So Vain," leaped to number 1 for three weeks, rapidly selling a million copies. The entire country seemed eager to guess the identity of the lover referred to in the song. Carly claimed that it was a composite of several people. Mick Jagger, the leading contender, had sat in on the song, which incited rumors that Carly had tricked him into singing about himself. Other contenders were Warren Beatty, Kris Kristofferson, Cat Stevens, and her own Sweet Baby James Taylor.

Hotcakes was Carly's fourth album, recorded while she was pregnant. It turned instant gold in 1974 with its two smash singles: "Mockingbird," the old Inez Fox hit sung as a duo with James, and "Haven't Got Time for the Pain." In 1975 her *Playing Possum* yielded the single hit "Attitude Dancing" and was followed in 1976 by *Another Passenger* in 1976, "Nobody Does It Better" (the hit single from the James Bond film *The Spy Who Loved Me*) in 1977, "You Belong to Me" in 1978, *Boys in the Trees* in 1978, *Spy* in 1979, and the hit single "Jessie" in 1980. In 1977 she overcame her stagefright to perform for two unannounced nights at New York's Other End. As a result she decided to tour in 1978 for the first time in six years.

Today, despite a sometimes stormy marriage, Carly and James spend most of their time with their two children on Martha's Vineyard, where Carly owns a disco called the Hot Tin Roof. Her singles and albums continue to sell well and draw raves for her powerful, emotional voice and sensitive songwriting talent.

THE MOODY BLUES

On January 11, 1965, the rock variety show *Hullabaloo* premiered on NBC-TV. A special part of the program was "Brian Epstein's London," a satellite transmission from England in which the Beatles' manager presented Britain's hitmakers. Naturally, many people expected Epstein to kick off his first segment with the Beatles, but unfortunately for the millions who tuned in to see John, Paul, George, and Ringo, Epstein presented his new group, the Moody Blues, singing "Go Now." Although this was a big hit in its own right, many disappointed viewers turned off their sets. It would be three years before the Moody Blues would have another American audience.

The Moody Blues started in 1964 in Birmingham, England. With Denny Laine on guitar and lead vocal, Clint Warwick on bass, Ray Thomas on wind instruments, Mike Pinder on keyboards, and Graeme Edge on drums, the Moody Blues played a commercial brand of R & B on the Birmingham club circuit. When the quintet graduated to the Marquee Club in London, they were signed by manager Brian Epstein, who got them a record contract with British Decca. The Moody Blues' first single, "Lose Your Money," did lose money for Decca, but their follow-up, "Go Now," featuring Denny Laine's plaintive vocal and Mike Pinder's rocking piano, became an international success, selling over a million copies worldwide and reaching the number-1 spot in Britain in February, 1965.

The Moody Blues then joined the Beatles' fabulously successful 1965 world tour. But in 1966 management problems developed as the Beatles and drugs took up more and more of Brian Epstein's time, leaving less for the Moody Blues. Eventually Denny Laine and Clint Warwick abandoned ship, Laine later joining Paul McCartney and Wings in 1971.

Although Justin Hayward and John Lodge soon replaced Laine and Warwick in the group, the Moody Blues hit their lowest point in 1966. Without Denny Laine's vocals, the hits ceased, and the band was reduced to playing small cabarets. The future looked bleak, so the band journeyed to Belgium in 1967 and spent three months at a retreat, sorting out their musical plans. They returned to England with a renewed sense of purpose and decided that they were going to make the kind of music they wanted and let the business chips fall where they might.

With producer Tony Clarke, the Moody Blues began to work on their first album since 1965, an experimental collaboration with the London Festival Orchestra. Until this time, no rock group had ever worked as closely with classical musicians. The result was the lush harmonies of the 1968 album *Days of Future Passed.* The music swirled and swooped with a wondrous, ethereal orchestrated majesty. The Moody Blues poured all of their emotions into the album and even broke down in tears while recording the cut "Nights in White Satin." *Days of Future Passed* was a great success, selling a million copies, reaching number 3 on the U.S. album charts, and staying high on the charts for fifty weeks.

When the Moody Blues recorded their next album, *In Search of the Lost Chord,* they didn't need an outside orchestra, since they now could play over thirty instruments themselves. On *Lost Chord,* the band continued to use the mellotron, an electronic keyboard instrument that became their trademark with its celestial wall of sound. *Lost Chord* contained the single "Ride My See-saw" and the track "Legend of a Mind," which opened with the infamous lyrics "Timothy Leary's dead..."

With *Lost Chord,* the Moody Blues touched a responsive chord with a large, mostly collegiate audience in America. The group repeated its cosmic message of love and understanding in their subsequent albums. With *On The Threshold of a Dream* (1969), *To Our Children's Children* (1970), *A Question of Balance* (1970), and *Every Good Boy*

The Moody Blues.

Deserves Favor (1971), the message grew more clichéd and more pretentious.

In 1972, their seventh album, *Seventh Sojourn,* had advance American sales of 1.5 million and climbed to the top of the album charts. The band toured the United States twice in 1972, concertizing for their fanatical American fans. After these tours revived interest in their classic song "Nights in White Satin," it was rereleased as a single and became the Moody Blues' biggest-selling single ever, reaching number 1 on the American charts nearly five years after it was initially released. The 1968 album *Days of Future Passed,* which contained that single, was resurrected and reached number 1 on the album charts in the autumn, staying at the top of the charts all the way into 1973. "I'm Just a Singer (In a Rock and Roll Band)," a fast-paced single that was their denial of any messianic role, was released in February 1973 and also nestled in the top ten.

Without formally disbanding, the Moody Blues stopped playing together in 1974. Although they remained together in the village of Cobham to run their record company, Threshold, as well as their record shops, they each actively pursued other careers. Hayward and Lodge recorded together as the Blue Jays. Edge teamed up with Adrian Gurvitz on *Kick Off Your Muddy Boots.* Thomas recorded *From Mighty Oaks,* while Pinder did *The Promise.* All in all, some eight mediocre splinter albums came out of this period, proving that the whole of the Moody Blues was greater than the sum of its parts. The group's 1977 success, *Caught Live Plus Five,* a live recording of a 1969 concert with five previously unreleased studio recordings, convinced the Moody Blues to make a comeback. In June 1978 the reunited Moody Blues released the album *Octave,* which eventually went platinum. It could never have met the expectations of the band's dedicated following, and the Moody Blues' comeback was considered an overall disappointment.

Denny Laine, an original member of the Moody Blues, then a member of Wings.

BREAD

Nineteen seventy-two was a big year for soft rock. *Time* magazine's cover story on James Taylor called soft rock the wave of the future. The Carpenters, Cat Stevens, the Moody Blues, Helen Reddy, and John Denver were constantly making the charts with sounds that were light-years away from the driving beat of Chuck Berry, Little Richard, and Bill Haley. One of the most popular soft rock bands was Bread.

Born in Tulsa, Oklahoma, in 1940, David Gates began to show his musical prowess at an early age, learning to play the violin when he was four years old and taking up the piano at five. By the time he reached high school, David was an accomplished musician. He formed a musical group at Will Rogers High School, and as a favor to his girl friend, he let her brother, Leon Russell, join the band. David's band became the big thing in Tulsa, backing visiting artists who came to town, including early rock and rollers Chuck Berry, Carl Perkins, and Johnny Burnette.

By the early sixties David Gates had outgrown Tulsa. Looking for bigger challenges, David was drawn to Hollywood by glowing reports from his old high school chum Leon Russell, who was there working with Ricky Nelson. David left college and headed west, determined to break into the L.A. music scene. He started out playing clubs, then landed some jobs as a studio musician. Because of his formal musical training, David found it easy to move up the musical ladder and soon became an arranger. He arranged the music for an Elvis Presley movie, as well as Glenn Yarborough's stirring 1965 hit "Baby, the Rain Must Fall." He also worked on sessions with Glen Campbell, Merle Haggard, and Duane Eddy. A one-man musical machine, David wrote "Popsicles and Icicles," a number-3 hit for the Murmaids in 1964, and "Saturday's Child" for the Monkees' first album in 1966. Branching out in the mid-sixties, he produced such diverse talents

as Pat Boone and Frank Zappa's protégé, Captain Beefheart.

In 1968 Robb Royer and Jim Griffin were writing songs and performing with Pleasure Faire, a gentle California rock band that recorded for UNI Records. Pleasure Faire was about to cut an album at Leon Russell's Skyhill Studio and wanted Leon himself to produce the record. But Russell was no longer interested in producing pop music and turned down the offer. He did, however, recommend old friend David Gates. Griffin, Royer, and Gates hit it off immediately, and by October 1968 they decided to write and record for themselves as Bread.

In 1969 the group signed a recording contract with Elektra Records and entered the studio to produce their first album themselves. David, Jim, and Robb were all multitalented musicians and created a full, rich sound through overdubbing. But their debut album *Bread* just didn't make it commercially. They decided to give it one more try, agreeing to disband if they were not successful. In the meantime Robb and Jim were commissioned to write a song for fifteen hundred dollars for the film *Lovers and Other Strangers.* Feeling that their work might not be accepted by the film community because of their rock backgrounds, Jim and Robb adopted pseudonyms. As Robb Wilson and Arthur James, they wrote "For All We Know." The Carpenters took their song to the top of the charts, and Robb and Jim won an Academy Award for Best Song with it.

With Oscar in hand, Jim and Robb rejoined David in their attempt to make Bread work. Adding the drums of Mike Botts, a former jazz session-man, Bread turned out their last-chance album, *On the Water,* a soft, clean, and precise commercial collection with a strong acoustic flavor. Bread's well-blended harmonies and soothing songs about bittersweet love appealed to young housewives who had grown up watching **American Bandstand.** "Make It with You," featuring David Gates' soft lead vocal, went all the way to number 1 in the summer of 1970. "It Don't Matter to Me," a ballad about a shattered love affair, moved up the charts in September 1970. In March 1971 the saccharine "If" became a million seller. About this time Robb Royer decided to leave Bread for a screenwriting career. He was replaced by Larry Knechtel, a respected West Coast studio musician who had worked with Simon and Garfunkel, the Mamas and the Papas, the Byrds, and Phil Spector. With Larry they continued to make gold records like "Baby I'm a Want You" in October 1971.

In early 1972 "Everything I Own" reached number 5. Bread surprised their audiences in the summer of 1972 with the heavier rhythm of "Guitar Man." But "Sweet Surrender" was another overly sweet, laid-back love song that hit for them.

By 1973 their music had grown stale. In late 1973, Gates, Griffin, Botts, and Knechtel disbanded the group. David Gates told *Cashbox* magazine at the time, "When you make an album and it's not as good as the previous one, then it's time to quit. None of us wanted a downhill ride."

David Gates of Bread. *(David Alexander)*

DON McLEAN

Sometimes, all an artist gets is one moment in the sun. One chance to make his contribution, to create his masterpiece, and then he is never heard from again. Rock and roll is littered with the remains of one-shot artists who had but a fleeting minute in the spotlight—Zager and Evans, Robin Luke, Ron Holden, Laurie London. Although Don McLean seems to fall into this category, he was not really a one-shot artist. He has had the opportunity to record some seven albums, and he has had a few singles on the charts. But Don McLean produced one rock masterpiece that put him among rock's greats—"American Pie," the biggest record in 1972.

Don McLean was a troubadour, a singing minstrel from Westchester. He became a folksinger after he graduated from school in 1963. As a wandering balladeer traveling New York State, McLean became known as the Hudson River Troubadour and hooked up with legendary folk singer Pete Seeger. After traveling and writing songs for some time, Don thought it was time to record. Unfortunately, the record companies did not agree, and it took Don two years to land a contract with a small record company for the album *Tapestry*. United Artists bought out McLean's contract, as they moved to capture a share of the rock market. It was now late 1971, and the moment was right for Don McLean's masterwork.

Don McLean dedicated "American Pie" to Buddy Holly, his inspiration. As a thirteen-year-old, McLean was shaken and moved to tears on February 3, 1959, the day Buddy Holly's plane crashed. In the song, he calls it "the day the music died," and it is the starting point of McLean's personal odyssey through rock and roll, a long rollicking song flavored with both religious allegory and musical allusion.

In "American Pie," McLean scanned the innocent days of early rock and roll when the music was more powerful than any religion to a true rock-and-roll believer. "The Book of Love," "Lonely Teenager," and "A White Sportcoat and a Pink Carnation" all made McLean's personal hit parade. Slow dancing at the school sock-hop was his primary image of love and desire in those early years of rock.

The song then moved to 1964 and "the jester," Bob Dylan. Dylan, the brooding loner who spoke for everyman, replaced Elvis as McLean's musical savior. According to McLean, Dylan stole "the King's" crown, but the Beatles lurked on the sidelines, practicing their music in the park.

McLean then skipped to 1967 and used a football metaphor to focus on the new rock generation. After Dylan's motorcycle accident the Byrds, who had recorded Dylan's "Mr. Tambourine Man," carried the ball in Dylan's absence. But in the psychedelia of 1967, the Beatles' *Sgt. Pepper's Lonely Hearts Club Band* recaptured their lead in the world of rock.

Although 1969 was the year of Woodstock and the first men on the moon, McLean's vision of rock that year was dark and troubled. He saw rock as symbolized by Altamont and the satanic majesty of Mick Jagger. The Hell's Angels knife that killed a young black at Altamont also cut into McLean's rock-and-roll heart. He sought to regain that piece of his heart from "A girl who sang the blues," but Janis Joplin died of a drug overdose. Then concert halls like the Fillmores began to close because of the avarice of the performers and the ugliness of the audiences. It was 1971, and the music had died for Don McLean.

"American Pie" was a musical tour de force. It ran eight minutes, weaving mysteries and revealing truths about rock and its effect on a generation. Despite its length radio stations clamored to play the record. "American Pie" was the number-1 song in America for five weeks and the number-3 song of the year in 1972.

McLean followed "American Pie" with his tribute to the artist Van Gogh, "Vincent," and a song about the spinning life of a rock star, "Driedel." Both were moderate successes, but nothing in comparison to "American Pie." McLean's later albums were full of folk-flavored, sometimes heavy-handed music and just didn't make much of a dent in the United States. For all intents and purposes it seemed that "American Pie" was the day the music died for Don McLean. Songwriters Charles Gimbel and Norman Fox saw Don McLean perform "American Pie" in concert and they wrote a song about him. Roberta Flack recorded the tune, and Don McLean was immortalized in "Killing Me Softly," the Grammy winner as Best Record of 1973.

Nine full years after "American Pie" was released, Don McLean found himself back on the charts. Don cut an achingly beautiful rendition of Roy Orbison's "Cryin'" and settled in for a long run in the top ten in the spring of 1981. The music hadn't died for Don McLean after all.

Don McLean. (Susan Ravich)

FRANK ZAPPA AND THE MOTHERS OF INVENTION

Today, the middle-class mothers of America can breathe easy. Frank Zappa, the man who threatened to envelop their children in psychedelia and who epitomized hippiedom in the sixties, is now past forty and may be considered no longer dangerous to society. But during those rebellious sixties, he was not only shaking up middle-class mothers, he was shaking up rock-and-roll music.

Frank Zappa's musical roots took soil in rhythm and blues as a guitarist for such forgotten high school groups as the Blackouts and Joe Perrino and the Mellotones. Fittingly, rock's leading crazy man of the decade formed the earliest version of the Mothers of Invention in a town called Cucamonga, California. Called "the Muthers," this group began experimenting with rock and roll and rhythm & blues about the time of the birth of Beatlemania in the U.S.

Life, however, was not without its problems for Zappa. He had been entrapped by the law and brought up on charges dealing with an allegedly obscene film he was hired to make and wound up spending ten days in the hoosegow. This misadventure helped push him from the secure hamlet of Cucamonga to the Sunset Strip in Los Angeles. There Zappa joined up with a group called The Soul Giants. After their new member took control, influencing the music and look of the group, the Soul Giants were transformed into the second version of the Muthers, this group using the less flagrant spelling "Mothers."

The Mothers found work in early 1965 at the attention-attracting showcase known as the Whiskey A Go Go. It was a strange time socially as well as musically, as the earliest rumblings of the peace movement were echoing with the explosive civil rights movement; young dropouts and runaways were merging into a society and spawning a growing drug culture; and the music world began to pick up the reins of the Beatles and Bob Dylan, taking rock and roll into what seemed at the time "brave new worlds." Frank Zappa and the Mothers rose to the foreground of this burgeoning counterculture's music world. They became the rock spokesmen for the new underground. Zappa's rebellion against California middle-class society and its values echoed that of his young audience. It manifested itself in his work and in his appearance, which became more and more bizarre from a mid-sixties establishment perspective. His hair length and garb were actually the badges of those among the young who had come to be labeled "hippies"—kids who had "freaked out" (a term that Zappa would one day adopt for an album title). His act was becoming just as bizarre. Onstage the Mothers might examine vegetables, wear gas masks, insult G.I.'s in the audience, or perform "Dead Air," where they would drop their instruments and revel in silence.

By 1965 the Mothers were becoming one of L.A.'s hit underground groups. It was while performing at the Whiskey A Go Go that they were approached by Dylan producer Tom Wilson. Wilson brought them to the attention of MGM Records and the Mothers wound up with a recording contract—and a new name. The MGM brass were concerned that somebody somewhere would view the name "Mothers" as only half a word. In what could only be considered a blow against everything the Mothers represented, MGM went ahead and changed the group's name on the records to "The Mothers of Invention," after the old adage.

Freak Out was the first album engineered by Zappa for the group. Released in 1966, the L.P. was a free-form mixture of what would become for many psychedelic or acid rock: craziness, lyrics for the counterculture, and the detailed adventures of one of rock's greatest heroines—Suzy Creamcheese. The title of the album accurately describes the contents. But *Freak Out* was only the beginning; it was followed by *Absolutely Free* (the first album ever to

be launched by a massive ad campaign in the pages of Marvel and DC comic books) and the amazing parody of the Beatles' *Sgt. Pepper's Lonely Hearts Club Band* album, *We're Only in It for the Money.* Zappa continued his attack on society and its values, and the records continued to sell.

Over the years there have been some three dozen members of the ever-changing Mothers of Invention. And at times Zappa went off by himself to do his own thing. His first solo attempt, *Lumpy Gravy,* in 1968, was an experiment in a melting-pot recording of classical music and rock. It was back to the group for *Cruising with Ruben and the Jets,* another experiment, this time creating a 1958 New York doo-wop sound. The liner notes and photographs printed on the album were designed to convince the buyer that this L.P. was sung by a real throwback group called Ruben and the Jets. The highpoint of the album was "Cheap Thrills" ("In the back of my car"), which was written by and had all the instruments, vocals, and mixes done by Zappa himself. The Mothers' next album, *Uncle Meat,* marked a return to the underground, hard-rock sound of earlier days.

Among the Mothers' most flamboyant accomplishments were their stage shows. In a combination of rock concert and guerrilla theater, the Mothers created some of the wildest, funniest, strangest moments any audience had ever seen. A legendary incident took place one night in New York when Zappa had some U.S. Marines ripping apart and bayonetting dolls on stage. Equally strange was Zappa's entrée into theatrical motion pictures. United Artists turned him loose in 1971 and the result was *200 Motels,* starring Ringo Starr as the world's tallest dwarf. The soundtrack album did better than the film.

Forget necessity. Frank Zappa is *the* Mother of Invention.

Burnt Weenie Sandwich, a somewhat autobiographical Mothers L.P., was the last of the line. In 1969 Zappa disbanded the group. Because of all the experimentation, they had been traveling with a huge number of musicians and road men and the expense was outweighing the box-office receipts. Record sales had dwindled. After the breakup Zappa's attention was fixed on solo efforts like *Hot Rats* and *Chunga's Revenge,* which led to a string of L.P.'s, most recently 1979's *Martian Love Secrets.* He also turned to producing records, including ones for high school friend Don Van Vliet, giving him his first break by recording him and rechristening him Captain Beefheart. Although the Mothers disbanded in 1969, Zappa regrouped them from time to time for tours and resulting live albums. The live albums and collections of old tracks were the predominant material representing the Mothers on the record racks of the seventies. What was most amazing was that Frank Zappa was becoming commercial—almost pop-oriented. In 1974 Zappa had a single hit in the top ten. In true Zappa fashion, however, the song (from his *Apostrophe* L.P.) was entitled "Don't Eat the Yellow Snow."

Zappa is still a part of rock and roll in the 1980s. His album, *Sheik Yerbouti,* with Zappa on the cover in Arabian garb, was a devastating parody of disco music; and in 1980 he released his rock film *Baby Snakes.* Whether his future lies in Las Vegas, rebellious rock, rhythm and blues, or some new, experimental musical ground, Zappa will always be a rock-and-roll figure to contend with.

The Sound of 1972

ALICE COOPER

The crowd roars as the arena is plunged into darkness. As the macabre baroque stage is spotlighted, the band blasts off at full throttle. Centerstage is enveloped in a multicolored fog. Out of the mist, his face in white greasepaint, his eyes etched in black with black painted fangs emerging from his mouth, bursts Alice Cooper, the personification of a rock-and-roll nightmare. For the next eighty minutes Cooper, his malevolent sneer framed by his long, stringy black hair, would gruesomely bludgeon and hatchet baby dolls, fondle an armless and legless female mannequin, sexually molest a giant tooth with a toothbrush, dance lasciviously with a live boa constrictor, and end up beheaded by a giant guillotine, as he and his band filled the arena with songs such as "Dead Babies," "Sick Things," and "I Love the Dead." Welcome to Alice Cooper's 1973 Billion Dollar Babies tour, one of the biggest-grossing tours in rock history.

In 1972 Alice Cooper had the most fascinating stage show in all of rock and roll. While most bands were content to play standing still on a bare stage, Alice Cooper brought theater into rock and roll. Gigantic, elaborate sets, costume changes, magic tricks, and dazzling visual and lighting effects were all part of the Alice Cooper stage show. With his manager, Shep Gordon, Alice Cooper's concerts became the biggest thing to hit the hinterlands after his initial debut at the outdoor Three Rivers Stadium, which was produced by Dick Clark. Playing towns like Utica, New York; Toledo, Ohio; and Greensboro, North Carolina, the Alice Cooper show was a tour de force of violence, sex, and death. Over one million people paid to see Alice Cooper in concert in 1973.

Alice would speak the unspeakable, flaunting horrible fantasies in the faces of his fans. Cooper mutilated baby dolls, killed Santa Claus, and died in the electric chair every night on stage. Kids got flashy glitter, a bizarre spectacle, and a swift kick in the libido, all for the price of a concert ticket.

Rock's king of evil and perversity was the son of a preacher, born in Detroit and raised in Phoenix, Arizona. Alice answered to the name Vincent Furnier in those days. Vince was the class cut-up and a member of the high-school track team. He and four of his teammates, Mike Bruce, Glen Buxton, Neal Smith, and Dennis Dunaway, were asked to sing rock-and-roll parodies at an awards dinner for the track team. After the dinner, they decided to become a rock-and-roll band. Upon graduation

Vince, Neal, and Glen enrolled as art-and-design majors at Glendale Community College, but after playing locally as the Earwigs, the Spiders, and Nazz, they had rock-and-roll fever. The group moved to California in 1967 to hit the bigtime.

One of about five thousand striving bands in Los Angeles, Vince and the band decided that the best way to attract attention was to be bizarre. Calling himself Alice Cooper, Vince painted his face while the band dressed in unisex and women's clothes. Shep Gordon, a young New York businessman with a burning desire to manage a rock group, heard about the group from a salesgirl at a boutique—Neal Smith's younger sister, Cindy. Shep went to see the band that night at the Cheetah, where the

A rare shot of Alice Cooper without makeup.

310

Welcome to his nightmare—Alice Cooper.

crowd jeered, hooted, and ran for the exits. Shep felt that any group that could elicit such a negative response had the makings of rock-and-roll stars. He became the band's manager that night.

Shep had his work cut out for him. Musically they were just a run-of-the-mill rock band. Shep decided to highlight Alice and build up the band's reputation through outrageous publicity. While Shep planted stories that Alice Cooper killed live chickens onstage and drank the blood, the band cut two albums, *Pretties for You* and *Easy Action,* for Frank Zappa's Straight Records. In 1970 the group left Straight and L.A. and moved to Detroit, the home of such outrageous rockers as the MC5, Ted Nugent, and Iggy and the Stooges. In early 1971 the group recorded the album *Love It to Death,* and by the spring the single "Eighteen" had become a teen-age anthem and a top-twenty hit. As Cooper's lyrics became more outrageous, Shep Gordon found it easier to get publicity. By the summer of 1972 "School's Out" had become a top-ten smash, and Alice Cooper was established as a symbol of hatred for parents all over America. The more parents protested, the more perverted Cooper's stage show became, drawing more and more teenagers to see the man called Alice.

The elaborately packaged *Billion Dollar Babies* and *Muscle of Love* albums followed *School's Out* and became part of Alice Cooper's Grand Guignol stage act. But by 1974 Alice was becoming increasingly weary of his violent image. Cooper was never really a rock revolutionary or violent musical messiah, and he was uncomfortable with his role. Cooper, a TV addict, longed to be a guest on *The Hollywood Squares,* play golf with Johnny Carson, and break into the movies. The rest of the band was uncomfortable with Alice's ambitions. In late 1974 their differences became irreconcilable, and Alice and the band went their separate ways.

By the end of 1974 much of Alice's appeal had vanished. The dead-babies routine had grown boring to both Alice and his audiences, and the teenie boppers who had thrilled to Cooper's perversities were now grown up and into other things. In the mid-seventies Alice finally succumbed to his liquid diet of a case of Budweiser and a quart of V.O. a day and eventually had himself institutionalized and confessed to being rock's most celebrated alcoholic. After drying out, Alice tried a number of image changes, including a Bogart-type tough guy and a defender of women's rights. Although Alice still hits the charts occasionally ("Only Women Bleed," "I Never Cry"), other groups have bettered Cooper's theatrical act. But don't cry for Alice—he finally got to open in Las Vegas and appear on the *Hollywood Squares.*

1973

Nineteen seventy-three started off on an auspicious note in January. In a landmark decision the Supreme Court legalized abortion. On January 27, just days after Lyndon Johnson died, North Vietnam, South Vietnam, the Vietcong, and the United States signed the Paris peace accords, bringing the Vietnam War to an end. Then, as 1973 wore on, the American public became more and more absorbed in the continuing soap opera of Watergate. In May, President Nixon went on national television to accept the resignations of H. R. Haldeman and John Ehrlichman and to fire John Dean. Dean then talked to Sam Ervin's Senate Watergate committee, which was the best TV series of 1973. In September, Egypt and Syria launched a surprise attack on Israel, inciting the Yom Kippur War. When Israel emerged victorious again, the Arabs levied an oil embargo on the United States, forcing Americans to sit on gas lines for the first time. In 1973 Spiro Agnew resigned from the vice-presidency in disgrace after pleading *nolo contendere* to charges of income-tax evasion and accepting bribes while he was the governor of Maryland. When Watergate started to get too hot in October, Nixon ordered the "Saturday Night Massacre," firing Watergate special prosecutor Archibald Cox and Deputy Attorney General William Ruckelshaus and accepting the resignation of Attorney General Elliot Richardson. But this was only the beginning for Nixon and Watergate.

It was a big year in sports as Secretariat became the first horse in twenty-five years to win the Triple Crown. O. J. Simpson set the NFL record for a single season by rushing for 2,003 yards—and then ran through airports for Hertz Rent-a-Car. Larry Csonka and Jim Kiick took the Miami Dolphins to a victory over the Minnesota Vikings in Super Bowl VIII. The fussin' and fightin' Oakland A's knocked off the New York Mets in the World Series, as the great Willie Mays retired from baseball. The Knicks edged the Lakers for the laurels in the NBA, while George Foreman knocked out Joe Frazier to capture the heavyweight title.

Paul Newman and Robert Redford proved to be an unbeatable team as *The Sting* walked off with the Academy Award for Best Picture, although Linda Blair's antics made *The Exorcist* the biggest box-office smash of 1973. Lucille Ball ended her reign on TV, just as *Kojak* and *The Six Million Dollar Man* began theirs. And George Lucas' sensational film *American Graffiti* asked, "Where were you in '62?" and inspired a rock-and-roll revival.

In 1973 separate presentations by both Dick Clark and Don Kirshner resulted in the new late-night ninety-minute TV show, *In Concert.*

Dr. Hook and the Medicine Show finally made the cover of *Rolling Stone* in 1973, helped by the gold record of the same name. Discovered by *Playboy* magazine cartoonist and songwriter Shel Silverstein, Dr. Hook played a rock group in the Dustin Hoffman movie *Who Is Harry Kellerman and Why Is He Saying Those Terrible Things About Me?* in 1971, before first assaulting the charts with "Sylvia's Mother" in 1972. Dr. Hook (from left: Jance Garfat, Bill Francis, Rik Elswit, Ray Sawyer, Bob "Willard" Henke, John Wolters, and Dennis Locorriere) overcame bankruptcy to achieve success recording suggestive humorous songs like "Only Sixteen," "A Little Bit More," "Sharing the Night Together," and "When You're in Love with a Beautiful Woman (It's Hard)."

In rock and roll Dr. Hook and the Medicine Show got their wish for stardom with "The Cover of ***Rolling Stone***," while Dr. John hit with "Right Place, Wrong Time." Loggins and Messina offered their spirited "Your Mama Don't Dance," and Lou Reed released his ultracool "Walk on the Wild Side." With his Rod Stewart imitation Ian Lloyd of Stories took "Brother Louie" to the top of the charts. The O'Jays rode the Philadelphia soul sound to the top ten with "Love Train." The Isley Brothers returned with "That Lady," and Sweet arrived with "Little Willy," while Stealers Wheel showed up with "Stuck in the Middle with You." The ten top records of 1973 were "Bad, Bad Leroy Brown" by Jim Croce, "Tie a Yellow Ribbon (Round The Old Oak Tree)" by Tony Orlando and Dawn, "Killing Me Softly with His Song" by Roberta Flack, "You're So Vain" by Carly Simon, "My Love" by Paul McCartney and Wings, "Let's Get It On" by Marvin Gaye, "Why Me" by Kris Kristofferson, "Will It Go Round in Circles" by Billy Preston, "Crocodile Rock" by Elton John, and "Touch Me in the Morning" by Diana Ross.

It was 1973—the nineteenth year of rock and roll.

BEATLES REPRISE

Together as the Beatles, they were masters of the rock world. After the breakup in 1970, the Fab Four struggled for acclaim as individual rock artists. By 1973 they had succeeded—to a point—and Lennon, McCartney, Harrison, and Starr all found themselves back on the charts.

Ringo Starr. Before the Beatles disbanded in April 1970, Ringo released his first album, *Sentimental Journey,* amid great fanfare. Ringo sang traditional pop tunes that predated rock and roll, but he didn't sing any of them particularly well. On the strength of his name, the album reached number 22 on the charts. Unfortunately, Ringo's name was the only strength this album had. Undeterred, Ringo headed for Nashville to cut a country-and-western album, *Beaucoups of Blues.* Backed by some of Nashville's finest session men, *Beaucoups of Blues* was musically more successful than his first venture, but commercially it sank without a trace.

George Harrison then produced two singles for Ringo in 1971 and 1972. "It Don't Come Easy," with George's ringing guitar work and Ringo's nasal vocal, was a number-3 hit in June 1971. "Back Off Boogaloo," a full-tilt boogie with nonsense lyrics, shot to number 9 in the spring of 1972.

Nineteen seventy-three brought a very pleasant surprise from Ringo—the delightful *Ringo* album, produced by Richard Perry. It featured songs written by John Lennon ("I'm the Greatest"), Paul McCartney ("Six O' Clock"), George Harrison ("Sunshine Life for Me," "Photograph"), and Richard Starkey himself ("Oh My My," "Devil Woman"). Moreover, his ex-mates even sang and played on the album, though not together. "Photograph" and "You're Sixteen" became number-1 singles, and the thumping dance tune "Oh My My" peaked at number 5.

Perry and Ringo collaborated again on *Goodnight Vienna* in 1974, with songs composed by Lennon

Ringo Starr.

("Goodnight Vienna"), Elton John and Bernie Taupin ("Snookeroo"), and Harry Nilsson ("Easy for Me"). Lennon actually let his hair down and had a good time on Ringo's albums, something he wouldn't allow on his own records.

When Richard Perry moved on to other projects, Ringo's solo career seemed to falter. Despite some fine tunes, his albums after 1975 received little attention. His 1978 *Bad Boy* album was virtually ignored by American radio stations, despite the fact that it was promoted by a TV special on NBC. In 1981 Ringo brought his acting talents to the screen in a silent comedy called *Caveman.* Ringo married his *Caveman* co-star, the beautiful actress Barbara

315

Bach, whose previous claim to fame was a co-starring role in the James Bond film *The Spy Who Loved Me.*

George Harrison. George had specialized in noise on his two prebreakup solo albums, *Electronic Sounds* and *Wonderwall,* and so his first album after the split, the three-record set *All Things Must Pass,* came as a great surprise. George's mysticism was just right for late 1970. "My Sweet Lord," which sounded an awful lot like the Chiffons' "He's So Fine" wrapped in a sari of zen, dominated the singles charts in December 1970, resting at number 1 for five weeks. "What Is Life," more philosophical mumbo-jumbo, hit number 9 in March 1971, and George was hailed as the real talent of the Beatles.

George championed the cause of Bangla Desh, the former Bengal region of East Pakistan that was devastated by famine and war in its struggle for independence. He put together a star-studded benefit concert for Bangla Desh at Madison Square Garden in New York on August 1, 1971, featuring Bob Dylan, Ringo, Leon Russell, Eric Clapton, and Billy Preston, among others. The concert was the highpoint of George's career. However, George's single, "Bangla Desh," showed that he had a long way to go with his lyrics.

George chastised rock fans with his "Living in the Material World," while he collected his millions and traveled the Grand Prix auto-racing circuit. The repetitious "Give Me Love (Give Me Peace on Earth)" reached number 1 for a week in June 1973, which said something about American tastes at the time. George's next few albums—*Dark Horse, Extra Texture, 33 1/3,* and *George Harrison*—were generally lackluster, although there were a couple of tasty tracks like "You," "This Song" (his sarcastic comment on the "He's So Fine"/"My Sweet Lord" plagiarism trial), and "Crackerbox Palace." George also took part in the Rutles' spoof of the Fab Four, "All You Need Is Cash," and financed Monty Python's film *Life of Brian.*

Paul McCartney. After the Beatles split, Paul was victimized by bad press, self-doubts, and his musical association with his wife, the former Linda Eastman. His career nearly ended at this time.

The *McCartney* album in 1970 was sloppy and too long, but it did have a few bright spots like "Maybe I'm Amazed" and "Junk." It seems that what Paul really wanted to do was tend to his farm and family. *Ram* in 1971 was brutalized by the rock press, but "Backseat of My Car" and "Monkberry Moon Delight" were musical delights, and "Uncle Albert/Admiral Halsey" reached number 3 on the American charts and won a Grammy.

George Harrison.

Paul McCartney.

Backed for the first time by Wings (whose only constant members were his wife, Linda, and Denny Laine, formerly with the Moody Blues), Paul's next outing, *Wild Life,* was awful. At the time of Harrison's greatest triumphs and Lennon's canonization by *Rolling Stone,* Paul's future looked as dismal as *Wild Life* sounded. His March 1972 single, "Give Ireland Back to the Irish," was derided as McCartney's "Bangla Desh." Nothing Paul did seemed to come out right—until his December 1972 single, the rocking "Hi, Hi, Hi," backed by the reggae-inspired "C Moon." Then "My Love," a sugar-coated love song, won the scorn of rock critics and the praise of record buyers as it became the number-1 single in the spring of 1973. The uneven album *Red Rose Speedway* did contain an excellent tune, "Big Barn Bed."

However, if Paul's solo career had produced nothing but *Band on the Run,* it would have been more than enough. *Band on the Run,* the finest album of 1974, was made under trying circumstances, to say the least. After Paul decided to record at Ginger Baker's studio in Lagos, Nigeria, Henry McCullough and Denny Seiwell decided to quit Wings. Paul used unfriendly Nigerian musicians who were suspicious and fearful that Paul would rip off their music. But McCartney didn't have to borrow from anybody for *Band on the Run,* his most solid, disciplined effort with no weak tracks anywhere in sight. Paul masterfully shifted tempos and textures throughout the album, using a synthesizer to fill out the sound on cuts like "Mamunia." The abstract tribute to Picasso, "Drink to Me," inspired by Picasso's dying words, was Paul's response to a challenge from actor Dustin Hoffman to write a song about the artist's death. Paul garnered three hit singles from the album, "Helen Wheels" (which reached number 7), "Jet," (another number 7 hit), and "Band on the Run" (number 1), receiving critical acclaim for the first time since the Beatles parted.

With melodies and hooks galore, Paul turned out some excellent singles over the next few years, but he couldn't resist loading up his albums with filler. The single "Junior's Farm" had obscure lyrics and a solid rock beat that took it to the top five in January 1975. His next album, *Venus And Mars,* was recorded in New Orleans after a mysterious session in Nashville came up empty. "Listen to What the Man Said" was dopey, but it went to number 1 anyway. "Venus and Mars/Rock Show" only reached number 14, but it did encourage Paul to organize his own rock show, the Wings Over America tour in the summer of 1976. The album that preceded the tour, *At the Speed of Sound,* attempted to highlight the talents of Wings, but the singing of Joe English, Jimmy

McCulloch, and Mrs. McCartney left something to be desired.

In 1977 Paul wrote a Scottish drinking song, "Mull of Kintyre," which became the biggest single in British history. America, however, wasn't in the market for a tap-room ditty, so the single was less successful on this side of the Atlantic. Nineteen seventy-eight's *London Town* album had only one notable song, "With a Little Luck." Nevertheless, Columbia Records made Paul the biggest offer in recording history to get him over to their label, and Paul cut a disco single, "Goodnight Tonight," and another uneven album, *Back to the Egg,* in 1979. After his celebrated drug bust in Japan in January 1980, Paul decided it was time to cut a solo album. The *McCartney II* album soared up the charts without Wings in the summer of 1980 and yielded a top-ten smash single, "Coming Up." But for all his shortcomings, Paul has proven to be the most enduring of all the four Beatles, as his melodies consistently attract record buyers.

John Lennon. John was always touted as the most intellectual of the Fab Four. He was raucous, troubled, and a bit rebellious in his Hamburg days, but manager Brian Epstein cleaned him up and kept him pretty much in line in the Beatlemania era. John had fancied himself an artist since his early days at the Liverpool Art Institute, but with the death of Epstein in 1967, John's concept of "artist" began to change. In 1968 he met avant-garde artist Yoko Ono at an art exhibit, where she handed him a card with the word "Breathe" printed on it. John and Yoko soon became a pair and began taking part in bizarre media events like bed-ins for peace and the news conference given inside a big white bag where they claimed "bagism" was the ultimate in human communication. With Yoko at his side, John put together the eerie sound effects conglomeration entitled "Revolution #9" for the Beatles' *White Album* in 1968. If "Revolution #9" was bizarre, avant-garde aural art, his first three albums with Yoko—*Two Virgins, Life with the Lions,* and *The Wedding Album*—were unlistenable. Experimentation in "noises" replaced the expressions of music found in John's Beatles songs. The only distinguishing feature among these three records was the full-frontal nude portrait of John and Yoko on the cover of *Two Virgins.* With the Plastic Ono Band in 1969, Lennon cut "Give Peace a Chance," which became an instant anthem for the antiwar movement and has since become a universal chant for peace. John then released a blistering antidrug song, "Cold Turkey," which featured the powerful guitar work of Eric

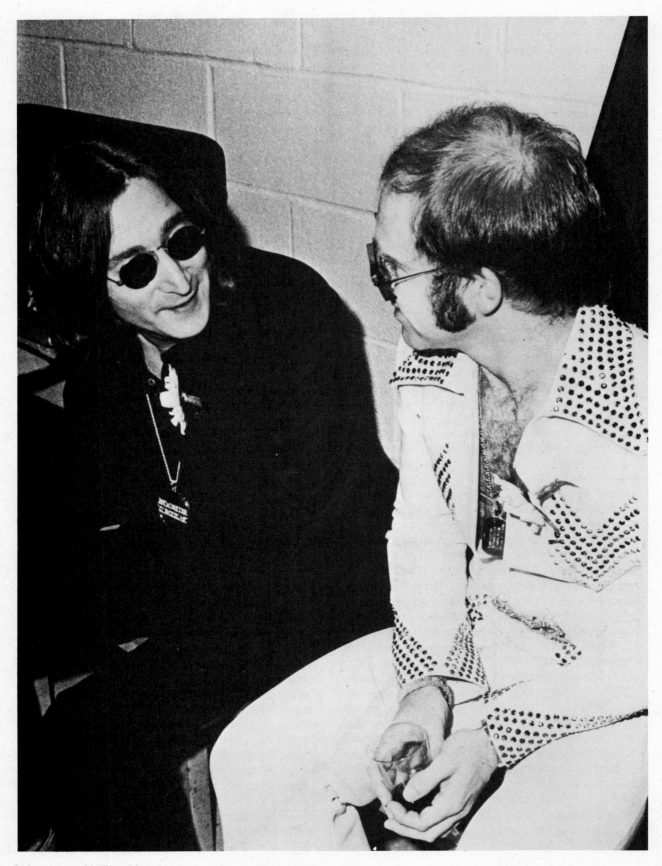

John Lennon with Elton John. *(Courtesy of Dick Clark)*

Clapton. "Instant Karma," with its rousing chorus of "we all shine on," was one of John's best singles, climbing all the way to number 3 in early 1970. Yoko continued to record the B-sides to his singles. Featuring her discordant yowling, the song "Don't Worry Kyoko (Mummy's Only Looking for a Hand in the Snow)," the flip side to "Cold Turkey," was viewed by many as a musical abomination. Lennon thought it was the best rock-and-roll record of all time.

John's first solo album, *John Lennon/Plastic Ono Band,* was an experiment in primal-scream therapy that reflected John's own personal evolvement. It was sparse, bitter, painful, and revealing, but it just wasn't good music often enough. Nevertheless, the rock press deified John as an artist for his politics, his music, and his lyrics.

One of the major events in rock in 1971 was the release of the album *Imagine,* which was hailed by fans as the second coming of John Lennon. The title cut was Lennon's attempt to deflate myths as he sang that there were no Beatles, no property, no God. With its simple instrumentation and powerful message, "Imagine" was Lennon's most enduring solo single and reached number 3 on the charts. *Imagine* also featured a bitter attack on Paul McCartney, "How do You Sleep?" telling Paul "the only thing you done was Yesterday." For good measure, John threw in a photo of him holding a pig that suspiciously resembled the cover of Paul's *Ram* album. The album also contained "Oh Yoko!" a pleasant, childlike sing-song about his love.

John and Yoko now humorlessly took up every chic radical cause you could imagine—"Power to the People," "Woman Is the Nigger of the World," "Attica," and "The Luck of the Irish." His 1972 *Some Time in New York City* album was a politicized bore that got little radio airplay. But if his music was turning people off, his fight to remain in the United States, after a marijuana bust in England, won him wide support.

In 1973 John and Yoko's marriage was on the rocks, but John's music began to improve. *Mind Games* was still a little too hip and egocentric, but the melodic title cut made the top twenty in November 1973. Yoko and John separated in 1974, and without Yoko's influence Lennon created his most listenable music in years. *Walls and Bridges* yielded two hit singles: the danceable "Whatever Gets You Through the Night," a number-1 song that also featured Elton John, and the beautifully haunting "No. 9 Dream," which placed in at number 9.

In 1974 John released the long-delayed *Rock 'n' Roll*—a good-time album of old rock favorites like "Ain't That A Shame," "Be Bop A Lula," and two Berry numbers, including "You Can't Catch Me." *Rock 'n' Roll* not only fulfilled his legal obligations, it also gave John a hit single with his version of Ben E. King's "Stand By Me."

In 1975 John won his battle to stay in the United States and released a greatest-hits collection, *Shaved Fish,* which contained his Christmas message, "Happy X-mas (War is Over)," a song that received considerable airplay each Christmas season through the years. John and Yoko then reconciled, and they had a baby son, Sean. John retired from recording for the next five years, turning his business affairs over to Yoko while he devoted his time to raising Sean. Finally, in November 1980, John released his first album in six years, *Double Fantasy.* John seemed to have regained his sense of humor and sense of perspective as well. "(Just Like) Starting Over" was a happy, well-produced shot of rock-and-roll complete with a doo-wop chorus. John described his life since his retirement in the poignant "Watching the Wheels." *Double Fantasy* was a joyous event for rock fans not only because it brought back John Lennon after too long an absence, but because it brought back the most together John Lennon the rock world had seen in years.

On the night of December 8, 1980, returning home from recording guitar tracks for Yoko's song "Walking On Thin Ice," John Lennon was senselessly gunned down in front of his apartment building, the Dakota, in New York City. Five bullets felled the former leader of the Beatles, one of the greatest songwriters of the rock generation. The world mourned his death with a sorrow that had barely been witnessed since the assassination of John F. Kennedy.

John Lennon was a wit, a pundit, a pacifist, a philanthropist, an honest man who believed passionately in causes; but most of all, he was an artist, and rock music was his art. As Dick Clark said after Lennon's death: "John Lennon was the most unique of the Beatles. They were all talented and all made significant contributions to rock and roll, but if there was a genius in the Beatles, it was John. It was a crime that his music was denied us so long during his retirement. It was a tragedy that his music was silenced forever by a gunman's bullet after he had come back to us."

JIM CROCE

Jim Croce's desire to be a songwriter/musician was nurtured during his years at Villanova University in the early sixties. Two of his college chums, Tommy West (who later formed Cashman and West) and Timmy Hauser (who later led the Manhattan Transfer), had sung together in a nineteen fifties doo-wop group called the Criterions, whose biggest hit was a love ballad entitled "I Remain Truly Yours." By the time they all reached college, however, they were into folk music.

Upon his graduation from college Jim took to the road and worked at several jobs ranging from teacher to truck driver to construction worker. In fact his music career nearly ended on a construction site before it had even begun. He accidentally smashed his finger on the job, putting his chances of ever playing the guitar again in jeopardy. Fortunately Croce devised his own unique picking style that allowed him to keep playing. As he wandered through America and Mexico he wrote songs about the people and places he encountered. These songs later became some of his greatest hits: 1972's "You Don't Mess Around with Jim," 1973's "Bad Bad Leroy Brown," and 1974's "Workin' at the Car Wash Blues."

Croce was far from an overnight success in the music world. He persevered despite many frustrating years and several career setbacks. He did whatever odd jobs he could get, refusing to give up his songwriting. After his marriage to Ingrid, a talented songwriter in her own right, she assisted him in writing a number of his tunes. The ceremony, by the way, took place at her parents' Philadelphia home, the former residence of Dick Clark. Then, in 1972, Jim finally had his first hit, "You Don't Mess Around with Jim." Produced by his old friends Tommy West and Terry Cashman, Jim began turning out successful albums and singles. Now on top of the charts, he began packing them in on tour. He proved that he was capable of writing sensitive love songs as well as his famous "character" songs with 1974's "I'll Have to Say I Love You in a Song" and 1973's hauntingly prophetic "Time in a Bottle."

Jim Croce's career was soaring at the end of the summer of 1973. For a long time he had wanted to take a break from the endless world of touring in order to get back home to his wife, young son, and a new baby on the way. But the bookings didn't cease. With top-ten hits and gold albums he was a sensation in concert, particularly on college campuses. Then, on September 20, with the end of the tour finally within his grasp, his plane crashed en route from a show at Northwest Louisiana State University to Sherman, Texas. Croce's career was cut tragically short. Posthumously released singles and albums continued to reign over the charts.

By 1981 Ingrid Croce returned to songwriting and prepared to move on to a new life as a solo artist singing her own original material. At the same time, Jim and Ingrid's son, Adrian, was honing his guitar and piano skills for his own eventual music career.

THE ALLMAN BROTHERS BAND

Southern Fried Boogie was one of the big sounds of the seventies. It was just good old-fashioned straight-forward down-home rock and roll with a touch of blues and a dash of country, and it was a refreshing change in an era of glitter, flamboyance, and theatrics. Bands like Lynyrd Skynyrd, The Marshall Tucker Band, and the Charlie Daniels Band preferred to appear unadorned in concert as they whipped through sets of blistering, aggressive rock. Many people found this southern sound boring and lacking in innovation. Others reveled in displays of technical virtuosity, swore by the white man's boogie music, and swore at its detractors. Whatever side of the argument you were on, in 1973 the leading exponent of southern-fried boogie was the Allman Brothers Band.

In 1947 one-year-old Howard Duane Allman's younger brother Gregory was born in Nashville, Tennessee. After their father died in 1959, their mother gathered up the family and moved to Daytona Beach, Florida. The brothers liked to stay up late at night listening to far-off radio stations that played rhythm and blues. They would sneak across to the black side of town to buy blues records. One Christmas, Gregg received a guitar and Duane got a motorcycle. After smashing up the Harley, Duane figured it would be safer if he learned to play the guitar, too.

In 1961 the brothers formed their first band, the Y-Teens, and played at school dances and the Boys' Club. By 1963 they had joined the House Rockers. In St. Louis in 1967, Duane and Gregg put together the Allman Joys and found success on the southern honky-tonk circuit. The Allman Joys even cut a single for Dial Records, a psychedelic version of Willie Dixon's old blues number "Spoonful."

After the Allman Joys broke up, the Allman boys tried their luck in Los Angeles, joining three Alabama musicians to form Hourglass. They were signed to a recording contract by Liberty Records but had no artistic freedom. Liberty told the band what to play, and Hourglass cranked out two bland, emotionless albums. In April 1968 Duane and Gregg went to Muscle Shoals, Alabama, to play some material they liked. The Allmans sent a tape of these sessions to the Liberty kingpins in L.A., but Liberty rejected them. Hourglass then dissolved in disgust, and the Allmans headed back to Florida.

In 1968 Duane and Gregg briefly teamed up with the 31st of February, a band that had been founded by Butch Trucks, a drummer at Florida State University. Gregg eventually flew back to Los Angeles, hoping to get another group together, while Duane was called back to Muscle Shoals to do some session work for Rick Hall, the owner and operator of Fame Studios. Hall remembered Duane from his earlier Muscle Shoals sessions and arranged for him to play guitar on a recording date with Wilson Pickett. At the session Duane suggested to Wilson that he do the Beatles' "Hey Jude." Before Pickett had a chance to say no, Duane was playing the tune on his guitar. Pickett tried a vocal and liked the idea. Released as a single in December 1968, it sold over a million copies. Duane was invited to stay on in Muscle Shoals, where he did studio work for the likes of Aretha Franklin, King Curtis, Arthur Conley, and Clarence Carter.

In the spring of 1969 during a visit to Jacksonville, Florida, Duane jammed with Butch Trucks and two members of a band known as Second Coming, Dickey Betts and Berry Oakley, who was a former sideman with Tommy Roe. After a weekend of playing together, it became obvious that this was the band they had all been looking for. Duane summoned brother Gregg back from the West Coast to sing and play organ and brought in a second drummer, Jai Johanny Johanson a.k.a. Jaimoe, an R & B session drummer. Duane then sought out Otis Redding's old manager, Phil Walden, to handle the group. As the

The Allman Brothers Band.

band spent the summer of 1969 rehearsing, Walden formed Capricorn Records and signed the Allman Brothers Band to a recording contract.

The Allman Brothers Band recorded their first album in New York City. While *The Allman Brothers Band* album was praised by the critics, the group headed out on the road. They played concerts for the next two years, developing a solid contingent of ardent fans. Duane also continued his session work on the side, earning a well-deserved reputation for his contributions to Derek and the Dominoes' "Layla" and Boz Scaggs' "Loan Me a Dime," as well as his work on albums by John Hammond, Laura Nyro, and Delaney and Bonnie.

In October 1969 the Allman Brothers Band released their second album, *Idlewild South,* to disappointing sales. The Allmans' first two albums were good, but they lacked the awesome power of their live performances. So in March of 1971 the group recorded their third album live at the Fillmore East in New York. The double disc, *At the Fillmore East,* was released in July 1971 and became the band's first gold record. The Allmans' reputation spread like wildfire now. With Oakley's thunderous bass, the climbing call-and-response guitar solos of Duane and Dickey, and Gregg's growling vocals and inventive organ, this album caught the Allman Brothers at their artistic peak on their classic versions of "Statesboro Blues," "You Don't Love Me," "In Memory of Elizabeth Reed," and the ominous "Whipping Post."

The Allmans played their fifth Fillmore East engagement on June 25–27, 1971, the final weekend before Bill Graham closed his New York concert hall. The Allmans played until dawn on the last night that the Fillmore was open to the public. The band then toured until September 1971, before moving down to Miami to begin their fourth album. Three tracks were completed when the band decided to take their first real vacation in two and a half years. It was on his vacation in Macon, Georgia, that Duane swerved on his motorcycle to avoid an oncoming truck. His bike skidded and fell, crushing him to death. On October 29, 1971, at the age of twenty-four, Duane Allman was dead.

The band regrouped under Gregg for an upcoming tour starting in late November 1971, knowing that it was what Duane would have wanted. In December they completed the album that they had begun with Duane, *Eat a Peach.* It was a double record set, featuring Duane on three sides. A mixture of live and studio cuts, it sold well over a million copies, going platinum and climbing into the top five on the album charts. *Eat a Peach* also yielded three singles: "Ain't

An Allman Brothers spinoff—Dickey Betts (seated front) and Great Southern.

Wastin' Time No More," "Melissa," and "One Way Out."

Then tragedy struck the Allman Brothers Band again. On November 11, 1972, thirteen months after the death of Duane Allman, Berry Oakley's motorcycle collided with a city bus in Macon. He died less than three blocks away from the site of Duane's fatal accident. Without Duane Allman and Berry Oakley the Allman Brothers Band was only a shadow of its former self. But ironically, the band found their greatest popularity after the loss of their two founding members. In July 1973 the Allman Brothers Band coheadlined the bill with The Band and the Grateful Dead at Watkins Glen, the biggest rock concert in history, with an audience of over six hundred thousand. Their August 1973 album *Brothers and Sisters* sold over two million copies and yielded the number-1 single, "Ramblin' Man."

By the end of 1975, however, the members of this "family" band were at each other's throats. Chuck Leavell, who joined the band after Duane's death, longed to move in a jazzier direction, while Dickey Betts refused to alter his country sound. Gregg Allman was a zombie, overindulging in booze, cocaine, heroin, and Cher Bono, to whom he was married for a short time. When Gregg testified against his former personal road manager, Scooter Herring, to avoid his own prosecution on drug-possession charges, the Allman Brothers Band angrily disintegrated. Then, in 1979, after finding out that they could not make it individually, Gregg, Betts, Jaimoe, and Trucks reformed the Allman Brothers in an attempt to cash in on their earlier success.

BETTE MIDLER

She was a most improbable star. Born in Paterson, New Jersey, she grew up as the only Jewish girl in the Samoan working-class district of Honolulu. Bette was valedictorian of her high school class, another rarity among show-business people. She worked as a pineapple canner in Hawaii, a go-go dancer in Union City, New Jersey, a typist at Columbia University, and a saleswoman in the glove department at Sterns' department store in New York. Approaching manager Aaron Russo, son of a Manhattan lingerie manufacturer and the former owner of Chicago's rock club the Kinetic Playground, Bette demanded "Make me a legend!" Russo met the challenge, and the legendary Divine Miss M was born.

The daughter of a star-struck housewife who named her three daughters after her Hollywood favorites, Judy Garland, Susan Hayward, and Bette Davis, Bette Midler was more than a bit stagestruck herself. She parlayed her earnings from a bit part in the movie *Hawaii* on a plane ticket to New York City. In 1966 Bette made a splash in Greenwich Village clubs, then found herself in the chorus of Broadway's *Fiddler on the Roof*, eventually moving up to play Tevye's eldest daughter, Tzeitel. After three years in that role Bette decided that *Fiddler on the Roof* was no longer "where it's at." She decided to concentrate on singing and in 1972 found herself performing before towel-clad gay audiences at New York's Continental Baths. Playing the Turkish baths, the rapier-tongued Miss Midler did a campy act, filled with flash, trash, devastating satire, and astonishing energy. The unpredictable, leering Divine Miss M became the rage of New York City.

Now the chanteuse of the chic, Bette burst upon the recording scene in 1973 after garnering national attention with her wild and often bizarre appearances with Johnny Carson on *The Tonight Show*. Bette released two gold albums that year, *The Divine Miss M* and *Bette Midler.* The first one featured singles that included a fourth remake of "Do You Wanna Dance." Her sultry, suggestive hit version was more than a mere invitation to boogaloo, as the previous treatments by Bobby Freeman, the Beach Boys, and the Mamas and the Papas had been. Bette followed "Do You Wanna Dance" with an old chestnut from the Andrews Sisters, triple-tracking her voice on "Boogie-Woogie Bugle Boy." Backed by her musical director, Barry Manilow, Bette had a grab bag of styles ranging from early sixties Ronettes to the big-band sound of the forties to the blues of the Roaring Twenties. Ms. Midler's manic flash and talent lit up the Broadway stage with a triumphant live show at the Palace Theatre in 1973 and garnered her a Grammy Award as the best new artist of the year. Part of that award was the result of the *Bette Midler* album, which was an intriguing mixture of rave-ups and ballads spanning three musical generations. The unfortunate thing about her studio-produced L.P.'s was that they just couldn't capture Bette's crazy stage energy. After sitting out 1974, her long-awaited album *Songs for the New Depression* was a major disappointment in the recession of late 1975.

Bette turned her career right around in 1976. Her *Bette Midler, Live at Last* album was a hit and included music from her precedent-shattering Home Box Office live show, which singlehandedly created strong consumer interest in cable television. Her prime-time network TV special followed and won the lady an Emmy to go with her Grammy Award. Broadway had not become immune to Miss M either. The ten-week engagement of her insane musical "tour de farce" *Clams on the Half Shell Revue* was S.R.O. all the way. Now Bette had a Tony Award to add to her collection.

Broken Blossom, Bette's fifth album, was sand-

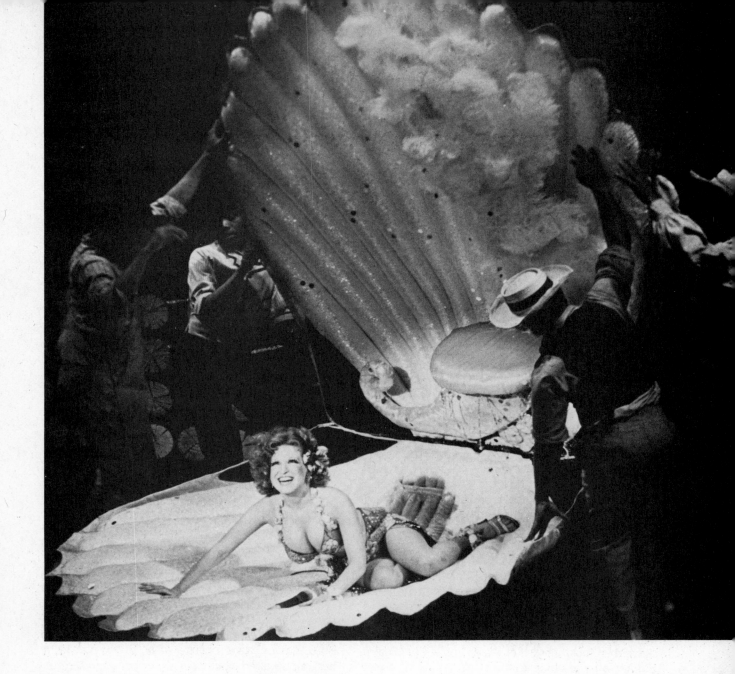

The Divine Ms. M on the half shell.

wiched in between tours of Europe, Asia, Australia, and Africa. Yet her stunning popularity transcended the recording industry. Her riveting performance as a self-destructive Janis Joplinesque rock singer in the film *The Rose* won unanimous critical acclaim in 1979, as well as an Academy Award nomination for Best Actress. In addition the film generated a number-1 record, "Theme from *The Rose*." Her second motion picture, *Divine Madness,* was a 1980 Ladd Company release that preserved her second Broadway revue on celluloid. The revue was an outrageous, funny, irreverent musical event that brought New York audiences to their feet night after night. As always, Bette was performing with her staggering Harlettes—backup singers whose ranks previously included such rock luminaries as Melissa Manchester. Her costumes and sets were as elaborate and hysterical as ever. The revue followed on the heels of a new L.P., *Thighs and Whispers,* a European tour, and the publication of her best-selling autobiography, *View from a Broad.* As the 1980s unfolded, the focus of Bette's career moved from that of recording and stage queen to that of potential Hollywood screen legend.

PINK FLOYD

At the start of 1973 many people in the music business were betting that Pink Floyd would never attract anything more than a cult following. They were just too weird! Their gloom-and-doom lyrics were depressing, and their spacey, atonal musical interludes were almost painful to listen to. By that spring, however, all bets were off. In one fell sweep, Pink Floyd jumped from cult band to international sensation with the release of *Dark Side of the Moon.*

Pink Floyd was a by-product of the psychedelic sixties, taking shape when Syd Barrett joined forces with Rick Wright, Nick Mason, and Roger Waters in 1965. Syd convinced them to dump the R & B material they were playing to experiment with a far stranger sound. Barrett named the group the Pink Floyd Sound, supposedly getting the idea from two American bluesmen—Pink Anderson and Floyd Council.

The group's early shows were among the first to incorporate the swirling lights and psychedelic mixed-media experiments that were the rage in the late sixties. Their inclination toward innovation attracted an audience among England's art-school crowd and brought them a record contract with Britain's huge EMI label.

Pink Floyd's reputation for the bizarre was established with their very first British single, "Arnold Layne," in March of 1967. The tune, written by Barrett, was simply a little ditty about a transvestite. Naturally, the song was banned by both the BBC *and* the offshore pirate radio stations. And just as naturally, the ban helped take the single into Britain's top ten. It was followed by *The Piper at the Gates of Dawn,* the group's first album, in August. Here Barrett's eccentric ballads were interspersed with long, chaotic sound collages.

At this time drugs were beginning to have a greater influence over Syd Barrett. Slowly but surely his sanity was slipping away. He moved back with his parents, so he could flip out in private. He struggled through Pink Floyd's first U.S. tour, but before the release of their second album, he was eased out of the group and replaced by an old friend of his from art school, David Gilmour.

With their captain of madness retired, Pink Floyd embarked upon a more methodical course. Although they were still into their space rock, *Saucerful of Secrets* showed that the band was capable of staying within the boundaries of recognizable rock.

With David Gilmour on guitar, Rick Wright on keyboards, Roger Waters on bass, and Nick Mason on drums, the band hummed along, releasing albums that delighted space cadets everywhere: *Ummagumma, Atom Heart Mother,* and a pair of sound-tracks for art films directed by Barbet Schroeder: *More* and *Obscured by Clouds.* The records were released in America by subsidiaries of Capitol, but the band's futuristic surrealism never gained them anything beyond a devoted group of hard-core crazies.

Things started to change, however, with 1971's *Meddle.* Their instrumental passages were not so choppy and cluttered here. The music had a smooth, spacey feel that was actually soothing. And despite their twisted lyrics, Pink Floyd's vocals were taking on a majestic pop feel that was reminiscent of the Moody Blues.

The band recorded their next album at the legendary Abbey Road studios. They recruited a young engineer named Alan Parsons, who later used his technical virtuosity in the studio to produce some of his own albums, *I, Robot* and *Tales of Mystery and Imagination,* which contain the decade's finest concept-album work. Parsons and the band spent nine months on their hypnotic exploration of the outer and inner space, *The Dark Side of the Moon.*

Premiered at the London Planetarium, *The Dark Side of the Moon* became the most popular album in

Pink Floyd (from left: Rick Wright, David Gilmour, Roger Waters, and Nick Mason).

the world within months. The band had always been big in Europe, but in America, where they were still practically unknown, the album shot to number 1, produced a surprising hit single with the superbly cynical "Money," and proceeded to hang on to the album charts until 1977—four years after its release! By the end of 1979 radio programmers almost unanimously named it the album of the decade.

Pink Floyd seemed to take it all in stride, though. True, they had shifted to the monetarily greener pastures of Columbia Records, but success had neither dampened their musical energy nor brightened their pessimistic world view. Nineteen seventy-five brought *Wish You Were Here,* which with the cut "Shine on You Crazy Diamond," was a loving tribute to the band's founder and spiritual mentor, Syd Barrett, who was then recording on his own again. *Wish You Were Here* also included a jaundiced look at the band's late-blooming success, "Have a Cigar," and the usual array of sonic nonsense. They closed the decade with *Animals* and *The Wall,* both continuations of the musical and lyrical themes of their earlier albums. *The Wall* soared into the upper reaches of the album charts in the early months of

1980, spurred on by a number-1 single, "Another Brick in the Wall." While the lyric "We don't need no education" became a teen anthem, it did prove that they could have used a remedial course in grammar.

Pink Floyd has become one of rock's most sought-after concert groups. Their touring baggage includes nearly eleven tons of sound-and-light equipment. The visuals of their stage show reflect their constant search for intriguing special effects. During their 1977 *Animals* tour, for example, huge inflatable creatures, such as a soft pig with glowing eyes, were sent hovering over the audience.

Pink Floyd is one of the rare bands who have combined wild experimentation with equally wild commercial success. Their use of feedback, reverb, echo, distortion, and phasing has helped to create a whole new vocabulary for musicians in the studio. Moreover, success has not changed their style or approach, as they continue to perform on rock's outer fringes.

The Sound of 1973
STEVIE WONDER

"People at school told me I couldn't make it, that I would end up making potholders."　　—STEVIE WONDER.

On May 13, 1950, a blind black baby named Steveland Morris was born in Saginaw, Michigan. Steveland was the third of six children, all of whom had different fathers. Times were hard in Saginaw, so Steveland's family moved to the housing projects of Detroit in 1953. However, life wasn't much easier in the Motor City. To keep warm in the winter, the family had to steal coal. But no matter how poor they were, Steveland's mother always found money for faith healers who claimed they could cure the boy's blindness.

Stevie's first real remembrance is that of listening to "Pledging My Love" by Johnny Ace, a 1955 R & B ballad by a tragic figure who killed himself on Christmas Eve, 1954, playing Russian roulette to impress a girl friend. Stevie started singing the R & B songs that he heard pouring out of the radios in the projects. Seeing that Stevie enjoyed music, a barber gave him a toy harmonica. Then, when Stevie was seven, a neighbor gave him an old upright piano, which he eventually mastered. Stevie played his toy drums until they fell apart, and was then given a real set of drums at a Lions Club Christmas party for blind children.

Ronnie White, one of Smokey Robinson's Miracles, was amazed by the little blind boy who played with his younger brother. But when White introduced him to the folks at Motown, the reception was less than enthusiastic. Stevie would stop at Motown every day after school and make a general pest of himself. He would play all of the instruments in the studios, pull practical jokes on the secretaries, and burst in on recording sessions, ruining more than a few potential hit records. Nevertheless, when the record execs heard him sing the songs he had written, they called him "the little boy wonder." In 1962 Berry Gordy, Jr., the head of Motown, signed the blind boy to a record contract, dubbing him "Little Stevie Wonder." Motown became his legal guardian, taking care of his education and charting the course of his career.

Unfortunately, when Motown put their new artist in the studio in late 1962, Stevie sounded more like Little Millie Small ("My Boy Lollipop," 1962) than the Little Stevie Wonder we all came to know. But Stevie was an irrepressible entertainer in front of a crowd—arms and head in motion, clapping, dancing, and playing the harmonica with a gospel fervor. So in 1963 Berry Gordy recorded the live Motown Revue, capturing Stevie Wonder's amazing live performance on tape. The result was a number-1 single, "Fingertips—(Part II)," and a number-1 album, *Little Stevie Wonder, the 12-Year-Old Genius.* It was the first time that a singer had the top single and the top album on the American charts at the same time.

For the next two years Motown found it difficult to sell Stevie's high-pitched immature voice. But when his voice deepened in late 1965, Wonder began an amazing string of hit records. Stevie Wonder's sixties singles were some of the best that Motown ever put out. "Uptight (Everything's Alright)" was a supercharged soul rocker that streaked up to number 3 in early 1966. Stevie followed it with Dylan's "Blowin' in the Wind" and "A Place in the Sun," two "message" songs that didn't really fit the Motown mold but were certainly portents of things to come. In the summer of 1967 seventeen-year-old Stevie soared back into the top ten for seven weeks with "I Was Made to Love Her," a bouncy soul tribute to teen-age love.

After "Shoo-Be-Do-Be-Doo-Da-Day," a Cajun-style Detroit boogie, Stevie Wonder fell into the pattern that ruined several Motown artists. Motown kept pushing its soul singers toward posh supper clubs and Las Vegas lounges. But as they reached out to middle-aged, middle-class audiences, their music had to be compromised and the results were usually artistic disasters. Stevie Wonder was no exception. At Motown's direction, Stevie turned out show tunes and limp ballads like "For Once in My Life," "My Cherie Amour," and "Yester-Me, Yester-You, Yesterday." By the middle of 1970 Wonder began rebelling against Motown's immovable bosses, who seemed so lacking in vision. After having been produced by Motown's various production teams for eight years, often given no say in the arrangements, Stevie produced his own album, *Signed, Sealed and Delivered,* in June 1970. Stevie finished his revolution in 1971 when he turned 21, collected the million dollars Motown had been holding in trust for him, and told Motown he was leaving the label and wanted to be released from his contract.

When Stevie left Motown, he mastered the electronic sounds of the Arp and Moog synthesizer, spent a quarter of a million dollars on studio time, and recorded some two hundred songs for future use. In 1972, Wonder and Motown got back together, after Stevie negotiated a 120-page contract granting him his own production company, greater royalties, control of his publishing rights, and complete artistic control—a new concept for Motown. The first album under this deal, *Music of my Mind,* released in early 1972, was only a moderate success, but it set the tone for a new, introspective, more mature Stevie Wonder.

Nineteen seventy-three was an incredible year for Stevie Wonder, starting with the release of the album *Talking Book* at the tail end of 1972. By January 1973 the single "Superstition," with its precise electronic keyboard work, tight horn section, and wailing vocal, wasted no time in rising to the top of the charts. In 1973 Stevie frequently appeared on television to transmit his excitement and energy to an ever-growing audience. As "Superstition" began to fade from the charts in March, Stevie released "You Are the Sunshine of My Life," a beautiful love song with a lilting Latin rhythm. It was the love song of 1973, climbing to number 1 in May and inspiring countless pop cover versions. That year Stevie won a Grammy for Best Male Pop Performance with "You Are the Sunshine of My Life," and two Grammy awards for Best Male R&B Performance and Best R & B Song with "Superstition."

Also in 1973 the Grammy for Best Album went to Stevie's next work, *Innervisions,* a masterpiece on which Wonder played virtually every instrument. Stevie's tendencies toward maudlin sentimentality and cosmic idealism were repressed here, as *Innervisions* balanced his ballads with some extremely tasty rock and roll. "Higher Ground," a number-3 single from that album, had a pulsing, circular, predisco beat and pointed lyrics about man's failings. "Living for the City," a number-7 record at the end of 1974, was a genuine tour de force. It followed the journey of an idealistic country boy from hard times in the South to his unjust arrest, conviction, and jailing in New York City for unknowingly holding drugs. "Living for the City" won a Grammy for Best R & B Song of 1974, one of Stevie's four Grammys that year. The third single from *Innervisions* was a satirical jab at supercool, streetwise blacks, "Don't You Worry 'bout a Thing."

After a concert in Winston-Salem, North Carolina, on August 6, 1973, the car Stevie was riding in collided with a logging truck. A log smashed through the windshield and struck the singer in the head. Stevie fell into a coma for ten days, suffering from a contusion of the brain. When he finally regained consciousness, he discovered he had lost another one of his senses in the accident—his sense of smell. Shaken by the experience, Stevie's zest for his work seemed to disappear as it took him longer and longer to complete each succeeding album.

Fulfillingness' First Finale had been almost completed before the accident, but was not released until the summer of 1974. The two singles from the album—"You Haven't Done Nothin'," an attack on Richard Nixon that climbed to number 1, and "Boogie On Reggae Woman"—were scintillating, but the rest of the album was tedious. In 1975 Stevie signed the biggest recording contract up to that time—thirteen million dollars for seven years. Still, it took him until the end of 1976 to release his next album, a two-record set titled *Songs in the Key of Life*. Again Stevie released great up-beat singles: the brilliant salute to Duke Ellington, "Sir Duke"; the tune for his baby daughter, Aisha, "Isn't She Lovely?" and an autobiographical piece about his rascally younger days, "I Wish." The awards kept coming, but his work was beginning to grow stale. By now Stevie had added six American music awards to his collection.

Wonder was then commissioned to write the soundtrack and score the film *The Secret Life of Plants.* Stevie Wonder may be extremely talented, but the idea of a blind man doing a movie soundtrack seemed almost ridiculous. Stevie had never seen a movie and could hardly be expected to know how to blend his music with visual images he could never experience. It took Wonder three years to finish the soundtrack, delaying the release of the movie for over two years. There was little excitement or anticipation surrounding the release of Stevie Wonder's first release in three years, because he had simply waited too long. Moreover, his "experimentation" on this work sounded too much like a rehash of the cut "Golden Lady" from the *Innervisions* album.

At the tail end of 1980, Stevie was back on the track with the release of *Hotter Than July.* The new album was lean, scintillating, and rhythmic, featuring Stevie's best, most disciplined work in years. The single "Master Blaster (Jammin')" was a hot, rocking reggae number that blasted its way to the upper reaches of the top forty. Stevie Wonder was back in a groove, promising to be a major force again in rock and roll in the eighties.

1974

Watergate continued to grip the nation in 1974. The Nixon White House tapes were finally made public, and "expletive deleted" became household words as America wondered about the infamous eighteen-minute gap. The House Judiciary Committee solemnly and cautiously went about the business of trying to remove a president from office. The "smoking gun" was the tape in which Nixon discussed a Watergate cover-up six days after the break-in. The House Judiciary Committee finally endorsed three articles of impeachment on July 30, and Nixon resigned on August 9, making Gerald Ford the new president. The specter of Watergate continued to haunt the country as Ford granted his former boss a "full, free, and absolute pardon" on September 8.

The story that rivaled Watergate in 1974 was the kidnapping of newspaper heiress Patty Hearst. On the night of February 5, Patty was abducted from her Berkeley apartment by members of the Symbionese Liberation Army. While Patty's father Randolph Hearst gave away millions of dollars worth of food in San Francisco to appease the revolutionaries, the SLA made Patty one of their own, renaming her Tania and including her in an armed bank robbery. A shoot-out in Los Angeles killed most of the SLA in May, but Patty Hearst had mysteriously vanished.

On television the Fonz burst onto the scene with *Happy Days,* a clone of the film *American Graffiti.* Nineteen seventy-four saw *Rhoda* spin off from *The Mary Tyler Moore Show,* and *Good Times* spring from *Maude,* giving us Jimmy Walker's famous phrase "Dy-no-mite!" Freddie Prinze in *Chico and the Man,* James Garner in *The Rockford Files,* Angie Dickinson in *Police Woman,* and Tony Orlando and Dawn all brightened up the TV screen in 1974. And Robert De Niro played young Don Vito Corleone in *The Godfather, Part II,* which won the Oscar for Best Picture over *Chinatown, Lenny, The Conversation,* and *The Towering Inferno.*

Hank Aaron hit his 715th home run in April, breaking Babe Ruth's record, while Lou Brock stole 118 bases in one season, shattering Maury Wills' record. In the World Series, Catfish Hunter led the Oakland A's to their third straight championship, this time over the Dodgers. Then, finding a loophole in his contract, Catfish became baseball's first free agent and jumped over to the New York Yankees. Muhammad Ali regained his heavyweight title by knocking out George Foreman in Zaire, Africa. The Steelers bested the Vikings in Super Bowl IX, and the Boston Celtics won the NBA Championship one more time.

Australian Olivia Newton-John had a super year in 1974 with "Let Me Be There," "If You Love Me (Let Me Know)," and "I Honestly Love You." The granddaughter of a Nobel prize-winning physicist, this 1959 winner of an Australian Hayley Mills look-alike contest hit the top ten again in 1975 with "Have You Never Been Mellow?" and "Please Mr. Please," before branching off into the movies to star in *Grease* and *Xanadu*. Hollywood didn't slow down the gold records, though, as Olivia topped the charts with "Hopelessly Devoted to You" from *Grease* and "Magic" from *Xanadu*.

Rock was the word in 1974. There was "Rock Your Baby," "Rock Me Gently," "Rock the Boat," and just plain "Rock On." The Philadelphia soul sound of producers Bell, Gamble, and Huff created such hits as "When Will I See You Again?" by the Three Degrees, "For the Love of Money" by the O'Jays, and "TSOP (The Sound of Philadelphia)" by MFSB, who had had a hit in 1968 with "The Horse" when they were known as Cliff Nobles and Co. Some folk artists hit it big in 1974: Joni Mitchell with "Help Me," Gordon Lightfoot with "Sundown," Harry Chapin with "Cat's in the Cradle," and Maria Muldaur with "Midnight at the Oasis." Australian Olivia Newton-John had three hits: "Let Me Be There," "If You Love Me, (Let Me Know)," and Peter Allen's ballad "I Honestly Love You." And as college kids took off their clothes to run around in the buff, Ray Stevens' "The Streak" out-stripped all competition on its way to number 1 in May.

The top ten of 1974 shaped up like this: "Bennie and the Jets" by Elton John, "Seasons in the Sun" by Terry Jacks, "The Way We Were" by Barbra Streisand, "Come and Get Your Love" by Redbone, "Love's Theme" by Love Unlimited Orchestra, "Dancing Machine" by the Jackson 5, "TSOP" by MFSB, "The Locomotion" by Grand Funk Railroad, "The Streak" by Ray Stevens, and "One Hell Of A Woman" by Mac Davis.

It was 1974—the twentieth year of rock and roll.

GLADYS KNIGHT AND THE PIPS

She could be as gritty and as soulful as Aretha Franklin. She could also be as cool, elegant, and poised as Diana Ross. With a pop ballad, her moving, powerful vocals rivaled Barbra Streisand's. Gladys Knight was the woman of the hour in 1974. But Gladys was no overnight sensation. By 1974, she had been singing professionally for twenty-two years.

Gladys was born in 1944 in Atlanta, Georgia. By the age of four she was singing with the Mount Moriah Baptist Church Choir, eventually becoming their featured soloist. She appeared on *Ted Mack's Original Amateur Hour* and won first prize three times. In 1952 Gladys won the *Amateur Hour's* National Grand Prize before she had reached her eighth birthday. As kids, Gladys, her brother Merald (also known as Bubba), her sister Brenda and her cousins William and Eleanor Guest would get together to harmonize on gospel hymns. At a family party in 1952 older cousin James "Pip" Wood heard the kids singing and encouraged them to form a group. James managed his younger cousins and arranged some appearances for them in the Atlanta area, mostly at school dances. The kids used James' nickname for their group name, billing themselves as the Pips. After a few years Brenda and Eleanor left the group. When another Knight cousin, Edward Patten, joined the group in 1958, the Pips had the lineup that would eventually yield eleven gold singles, five gold albums, and two plantinum records.

In 1961 Gladys and the Pips got their first chance to record. They took Johnny Otis' "Every Beat of My Heart," added Gladys' breathy lead vocal, and cut it for a local Atlanta label, Huntom Records. When the record started to get radio airplay in the Atlanta area, it sparked the interest of the national record companies. Bobby Robinson, the owner of Fury Records, was so impressed with the record that he had the Pips flown to New York immediately, where they rerecorded "Every Beat of My Heart" in just two

takes, duplicating their original version. Fury released their record in April 1961 under the name Gladys Knight and the Pips. "Every Beat of My Heart" became a number-1 smash on the rhythm-and-blues charts and eventually sold a million copies. But in the meantime Vee Jay Records purchased the rights to the original single from Huntom and released that version of "Every Beat of My Heart" nationwide, forcing the group's Vee Jay single to compete with their Fury single. Fury and Vee Jay went to court over the record, and Fury eventually won the exclusive rights to Gladys Knight and the Pips. However, the Pips may have been the real losers in that lawsuit, for though they followed up that record with an even bigger hit, "Letter Full of Tears," in early 1962, Fury Records went out of business. The group was left high and dry in New York, without Gladys, who returned to Atlanta with her husband to give birth to a baby.

By 1964 Gladys was back in New York performing and recording with the Pips. They played the soul circuit for several years, building a reputation while polishing their act and developing a routine of slick stage moves to accompany their smooth harmonies. In 1966 Gladys and the Pips signed with Motown, who put the group on their Soul label under the direction of Norman Whitfield, the producer of the Temptations. The Pips had some chart action in 1967 with "Take Me in Your Arms and Love Me" and "Everybody Needs Love," but it was their October 1967 single that really made it for the group. "I Heard It through the Grapevine," a raucous, up-beat soul stomper, hit number 2 on the national charts, became the first million seller for the Soul label, and led to an appearance on *The Ed Sullivan Show* and gigs at the Copa and other posh supperclubs. The Pips continued to make the charts with "The End of Our Road" (number 15 in 1968), "The Nitty Gritty" (number 19 in 1969), "Friendship Train" (number 17

Gladys Knight and the Pips. *(Courtesy of Dick Clark)*

OPPOSITE PAGE:

The Pips (from left: Merald Knight, William Guest, and Edward Patten).

in 1969), and "If I Were Your Woman" (number 7 in 1971). However, Motown never treated them as one of their top-line acts. Dissatisfied because they felt Motown wasn't paying enough attention to them, Gladys and the Pips let their Motown contract expire in March 1973 and switched their allegiance to Buddah Records.

Nineteen seventy-three proved to be a landmark year for Gladys Knight and the Pips. In January the group's last single for Motown, the soulful love song "Neither One of Us (Wants to Be the First to Say Good-bye)," had sales of over two million, reached the number-1 spot in America, and earned Gladys and the Pips a Grammy for Best Pop Vocal Performance. Motown must have had second thoughts about letting Gladys slip away, but it was too late. With Buddah, Gladys and the Pips released their best record ever in September, the sensational "Midnight Train to Georgia." With the Pips' great backup vocal complete with train whistles and Gladys passionate promise to stick with her man, "Midnight Train to Georgia" shot to number 1, selling two million records and winning the Pips another Grammy, this time for Best R & B Vocal Performance. On the strength of "Midnight Train to Georgia," "Neither One of Us," and "I've Got to Use My Imagination,"

their third million seller that year, Gladys Knight and the Pips were the biggest-selling recording group of 1973.

As 1974 began, Gladys Knight and the Pips were on a roll. "I've Got to Use My Imagination" was on a four-week run through the top ten. Their next single, the mellow love song "You're the Best Thing That Ever Happened to Me," lengthened the Pips' string of successes, landing at number 3 on the charts. Their first album for Buddah, *Imagination,* brought Gladys Knight a Grammy for Best Album by a Female Soul Artist. In May 1974 the group hit with their fourth consecutive gold record for Buddah, "On and On," a syncopated boogie written by Curtis Mayfield for the soundtrack of the movie *Claudine.*

After twenty-two years Gladys finally received the recognition she had been seeking. Gladys and the Pips hosted a summer variety series on NBC in 1975. On her own, Gladys starred in the movie *Pipe Dreams* in 1976, a romantic adventure set along the construction sites of the Alaskan pipeline. After Gladys and the Pips filed suit against Buddah Records for back royalties in 1978, they signed with Columbia Records. In 1980, Gladys Knight and the Pips were back in the recording studio, heading for their third successful decade.

JOHN DENVER

No one's music was more "mellow" than John Denver's folksy soft rock. Colorado seemed to be the place to be in the mid-seventies, so John made his home in Aspen, sang "Rocky Mountain High," and even took his stage name after passing through the Mile High City. With a face like a smile button, John Denver was floating energy, est, ecology, and "have a happy day" all in one. He was not only the best-selling recording artist in 1974; he *was* 1974.

John Denver was born John Henry Deutschendorf in Roswell, New Mexico, on December 31, 1943. His dad was a record-breaking aviator in the U.S. Air Force. As an "Air Force brat," John spent his childhood in Tucson, Arizona, Oklahoma, Japan, and Montgomery, Alabama, before settling in Fort Worth, Texas, for his high school years. This constant moving made it difficult for John to make new friends. In fact, it was his music that helped him overcome his shyness and relate to people. In the late fifties John drifted naturally toward folk music. In 1961 he entered college at Texas Tech in Lubbock, Texas, Buddy Holly's hometown. However, John was more affected by the music of Joan Baez, Peter, Paul and Mary, and the New Christie Minstrels. More interested in hootenannies than in architecture, Denver quit college in the middle of his junior year and headed to California to become a folksinger.

John found work as a draftsman in Los Angeles and sang folk music in his spare time. By 1965 he had become a regular at Leadbetter's, a folk club in L.A., and at the Lumbermill in Phoenix. When John heard that Chad Mitchell was leaving the Chad Mitchell Trio to pursue a solo career and that the Trio was looking for a replacement, John flew to New York to audition with 250 other singers. He got the job and sang with the Trio for four years. But in 1969 the other two original members of the group decided to split, leaving Denver with forty thousand dollars in Mitchell Trio debts and a threatened law suit by Chad Mitchell

for using his name. Denver convinced Mitchell to hold off on the lawsuit, so he could play concerts as the Chad Mitchell Trio to pay off the debt. With the forty thousand dollars paid, John headed for Aspen to begin his solo career.

In 1969 Peter, Paul and Mary recorded a Denver song, "Leaving on a Jet Plane," and had a number-1 hit with it. Still John had difficulty establishing his solo singing career. Denver recorded three unsuccessful albums for RCA Records, and the company considered dropping Denver's contract early in 1971. About this time Denver was playing with Bill and Terry Danhoff at the Cellar Door in Washington, D.C. One night after a gig John and the Danhoffs were involved in a minor traffic accident. Too keyed up to go to bed, they stayed up all night and wrote "Take Me Home, Country Roads." It became the first of seven top-ten records for Denver over the next four years, including four number-1 songs. RCA's patience was rewarded.

In the mid-seventies "mellow radio" became the rage, and John Denver's folksy homilies were tailor-made for this soft-rock format. Denver's call to abandon the city for the clean air and slower pace of the country became the staple of mellow, top-forty, and easy-listening stations. His message was so convincing that his reputation as an environmentalist was barely tarnished when it was discovered in 1979 that he was hoarding gasoline on his ranch. He went on to star in the movie *Oh, God* with George Burns, host a slew of top-rated TV specials, earn six gold albums, and play Lake Tahoe with Frank Sinatra. Unfortunately, by 1980 he had lost much of his audience, and his record sales today hardly reflect the fact that John Denver was once RCA's biggest-selling artist since Elvis.

OPPOSITE PAGE: John Denver.

338

JETHRO TULL

Jethro Tull is the brainchild of Ian Anderson, rock's premier flautist. To some, Anderson is one of rock's most gifted talents—a composer, producer, arranger, and performer of considerable stature. To others, he is an egotistical dictator whose narrow-minded musical manipulations strangled what was once one of rock's most ambitious experiments. In truth he's all that and more. Yet under his stern direction Jethro Tull has weathered personnel and stylistic changes and survived into the eighties, long after many of their "art rock" contemporaries have fallen by the wayside.

In the late sixties many bands journeyed into the uncharted regions of musical innovation. One such band was the John Evans Blues Band, who traveled from Blackpool to find success in London. Ultimately they broke up, but the group's flautist/guitarist, Ian Anderson, wasn't ready to give up. In less than a year he formed a band with Mick Abrahams on lead guitar, Glenn Cornick on bass, and Clive Bunker on drums. Their university-educated agent suggested that they adopt the name of an eighteenth-century British agriculturist. Figuring that they could always change it later, the band agreed and Jethro Tull was born. Incorporating elements of jazz, classical, and traditional British folk on a solid rock foundation, the band centered around Anderson's crude but effective flute work, which gave the band its distinctive sound.

In 1968 the band hit the British club circuit, eventually building a word-of-mouth reputation that led to a record deal with Chris Blackwell's Island Records and the release of their first album, *This Was.* The disc showcased a rocking style that they never repeated on record again. Mick Abrahams, the leading proponent of this hard-rock style, soon tangled with Anderson over the group's direction and became the first of many to be ejected from Jethro Tull. Abrahams was replaced by the more docile Martin Barre, who accompanied the band on their first tour of the U.S.

This Was sold surprisingly well on both sides of the Atlantic, and Jethro Tull became one of the early mainstays of album-oriented FM radio. *Stand Up* followed *This Was* in 1969, and *Benefit* followed that in 1970, and each album sold better than the last. Moreover, they succeeded without top-forty airplay.

Aqualung in 1971 firmly established their supremacy in rock's avant-garde. It was a witty concept album that dealt with the hypocrisy of organized religion. It was also Tull's first top-ten album.

More hirings and firings kept fans wondering who was still with the group. Barrie Barlow, Jeffrey Hammond-Hammond, and John Evans (formerly of the John Evans Blues Band) were in, while Glenn Cornick and Clive Bunker were out. By 1972 all of the original members save Anderson were gone, replaced by people who would conform to Ian's vision of what the band should be.

However, success bred excess. *Thick as a Brick* and *A Passion Play* were not divided into individual cuts, presenting entire sides of continuous music instead. The music was frequently overblown and self-important. The albums sounded, in effect, like one man's private bitch sessions.

Nineteen seventy-four's *War Child* was the last L.P. to have any of the early Tull fire. This was another concept album, dealing with the conflicts of the human condition. It contained one of the group's few hit singles, "Bungle in the Jungle," which, with *Thick as a Brick, A Passion Play,* and the *Living in the Past* compilation, represents Jethro Tull's height in terms of sales and popularity.

Beginning with *Minstrel in the Gallery* in 1975, the band's albums adopted the feel of old-English folk music, downplaying the electronics in favor of an acoustic sound. But with their popularity now waning, Ian Anderson and Jethro Tull may soon have to choose between artistic integrity and commercial survival.

GRAND FUNK RAILROAD

In 1971 Grand Funk was the most popular rock band in the United States. By 1976 ten of their albums had struck gold, and they had grossed sixty million dollars from record sales alone. Such success did not seem possible when Grand Funk started in Flint, Michigan. Drummer Don Brewer put together the Jazz Masters with Mark Farner, a former member of ? and the Mysterians. When local disc jockey Terry Knight was fired from his radio station, he convinced the Jazz Masters to hire him as their lead singer, enticing them with his music-industry connections. In 1966, as Terry Knight and the Pack, they were signed by the local Lucky Eleven label. They put out some marginally successful regional singles, but when Cameo-Parkway Records assumed Lucky Eleven's national distribution, the Pack broke into the top forty with their November 1966 remake of the Ben E. King hit "I (Who Have Nothing)." However, when the band found that they couldn't make the charts again, Knight and the Pack went their separate ways. Knight became a record producer, while Brewer, Farner, and bass player Mel Schacher continued on as the Fabulous Pack.

In February of 1969, the Pack found themselves stranded on Cape Cod when several promised gigs never materialized. They had to sell their equipment to get back home. Back in Flint, they asked Terry Knight for help. Terry agreed to manage them only if they would give him complete artistic and business control over the group. The band signed an agreement with Knight on May 1, 1969.

Knight first told lead vocalist Farner to shake his ass on stage, then he instructed the band to play LOUD. He changed their name to Grand Funk Railroad—a hip pun on the name of the turn-of-the-century rail line, The Grand Trunk Railroad. In the spring of 1969 Terry arranged some gigs for the band in upstate New York. At their very first concert in Buffalo a young lady who was overwhelmed by the performance took off her clothes and rushed the stage. However, the band's big break came with their July 4, 1969, appearance at the Atlanta Pop Festival, where Grand Funk brought a hundred thousand screaming people to their feet in 110-degree heat. This helped to land a contract for the group with Capitol Records.

In late 1969 Grand Funk Railroad released their first L.P., *On Time*, and their first single, "Time Machine." Though their critics showed no mercy, their fans sent the album to number 27 on the charts. Nineteen seventy brought the single "Closer to Home," a mellow departure from heavy metal that momentarily charmed Grand Funk's fiercest detractors and broke into the top twenty. Their second gold album, *Grand Funk*, soared to number 11 by early 1970, and their third album, *Closer to Home*, turned gold even faster. The more savage their reviews, the better the records sold. Although FM airplay of Funk was miniscule, their grand national tour swiftly sold out and they even outgrossed the Beatles at Shea Stadium. The 1970 double, *Grand Funk Live*, a recording of their set at the Atlanta Pop Festival in 1970, went gold immediately, with the largest advance order Capitol had had since the Beatles. It went to number 5 and sold over two million copies by the end of the year. Nineteen seventy-one brought the album *Survival*, which sold a million copies immediately. *E Pluribus Funk* shot to number 3 on the album charts with prerelease orders of over six million dollars. This first gold album on Grand Funk's own honorary label contained two singles, "Footstompin' Music" and "Upsetter."

Grand Funk was now one of the most successful American bands ever, but they were not happy with their situation. Mark Farner was writing most of the material, but Terry Knight called all the shots. Knight was Grand Funk's spokesman. The band wasn't allowed to talk to the press. Farner was tired of "balling" his guitar on stage, but Knight insisted. Their spirit of brotherhood began to vaporize. When they learned the actual size of Knight's percentage of their profits, they decided to dump him. In 1971 they charged him with misappropriating funds, and fraud. Terry fought back with a lawsuit for breach of contract. After months of legal wrangling, Grand Funk was finally free of their manager. After the success of *Mark, Don and Mel* (their last album with Knight at the helm) the band's confidence was renewed when the Knightless *Phoenix* album sold well in 1973.

In 1973 an old friend from Flint, Craig Frost, was added to the band on keyboards, and Grand Funk began working with producer Todd Rundgren. "We're an American Band," written by Don Brewer, was their first single to sell a million copies, climbing all the way to number 1 in September. They struck gold again and nestled in the number-1 spot for two weeks in May of 1974 with a brash remake of Little Eva's "The Loco-motion." With Rundgren now in control, Grand Funk surprised more than a few of their critics with their new-found vocal harmonies.

Although it reached the top twenty, *Shinin' On* was the beginning of the end for Grand Funk, as their audiences outgrew their heavy-metal panderings. By the end of the year, Grand Funk had recorded *All the Girls in the World Beware,* and record buyers stayed away in droves. The band decided to split up after the *Born to Die* album in 1976, but an offer to work with Frank Zappa made them stick it out for one more album, *Good Singin', Good Playin',* which Zappa produced. After this album Grand Funk Railroad, America's premiere lowbrow heavy-metal band, was finally derailed.

BARRY WHITE

He was a big bear of a black man, with heavily pomaded hair and a goatee. He looked like a cross between a hustler and a truck driver. But his voice was a deep, sensual growl, half singing, half mumbling the words to his lushly orchestrated songs. His music, which was suited for the disco *and* the bedroom, inspired the return of touch dancing, for love and sex were the matter of his songs. With four gold singles Barry White was the man to be reckoned with in 1974.

Barry was born in Galveston, Texas, on September 12, 1944, and moved with his family to East Los Angeles when he was six months old. He started playing the piano when he was five and sang with his church choir when he turned eight. By the time he was ten Barry was playing the organ and directing the choir. He joined a rhythm-and-blues quintet when he was sixteen. It was at this time that Barry took a long, hard look at his poor neighborhood and decided that he wanted something better. At seventeen Barry dropped out of high school to make his mark on the music world.

In 1963 Barry met an R & B duo, Bob and Earl, and wrote the music for their record "Harlem Shuffle," which climbed to number 44 in the early days of 1964. Bob and Earl split up when Earl Cosby decided to go solo, changing his name to Jackie Lee and taking Barry with him as his manager. In 1965 Barry wrote a dance song, and Jackie Lee took "The Duck" all the way to number 14 on the charts. Barry was then offered the chance to become a producer and head the artists-and-repertoire department for Bronco Records in 1967. Bronco Records did not last long, but Barry did earn a reputation for producing such hits as "I Feel Love Comin' On" for Felice Taylor. After Bronco Records folded, Barry became an independent producer. In 1968, he discovered three backup singers, Linda James, Glodean James, and Diane Taylor. He became their manager, renamed them Love Unlimited, and carefully nurtured their sound. By 1972 he felt they were ready, and wrote and produced "Walkin' in the Rain with the One I Love" for them. Barry himself was the deep voice on the telephone at the end of the record, which made it to the top ten.

Barry signed with 20th Century Records in 1973 and continued to write and produce lush albums and singles for Love Unlimited. White also put together a forty-one-piece orchestra, and although he could not read or write music, he arranged, composed, and conducted for his Love Unlimited Orchestra. They had a gigantic instrumental hit in early 1974 with "Love's Theme," earning Barry a Grammy nomination and the nickname "The Bronze Maestro."

In 1973, Barry decided to weave erotic, romantic fantasies for audiences who he felt were bored with the bitter reality presented in most songs. Barry turned out a series of sexy hit records as a solo artist. "I'm Gonna Love You Just a Little More Baby" struck gold, reaching number 3 in June 1973. Barry then moaned his way into the top ten to open 1974 with "Never, Never Gonna Give You Up," which was on the charts at the same time as "Love's Theme." With their steady beats and White's sophisticated rap, "Can't Get Enough Of Your Love, Babe" and "You're My First, My Last, My Everything," kept Barry in the upper reaches of the top forty from August 1974 through February 1975. However, by the middle of 1975 he had fallen off the disco summit. He continues to record and will no doubt recapture the golden touch that made 1974 such an incredibly successful year for Barry White.

The Sound of 1974

ELTON JOHN

Captain Fantastic—Elton John.

Elton John was more than just the sound of the year in 1974. In a way, he was the seventies. His success started with the decade, as his first U.S. release, *Elton John,* became a hit in 1970. Elton was a superstar by the middle years, but petered out as the decade closed. Nevertheless, he captured the hearts of an entire generation and mirrored the pop trends and tastes of the seventies with stylish perfection.

Elton John was born Reginald Dwight. Prior to his reincarnation as Elton, Reg played keyboards with Bluesology, a small combo who used to back artists like Long John Baldry and tour in Britain with U.S. stars like the Drifters. However, Reg soon grew tired of staying in the background. Splicing Long John Baldry's name with that of Baldry's sax man, Elton Dean, he changed his name in preparation for bigger things.

Answering an ad in the *New Musical Express,* he auditioned as a singer for Liberty Records. Totally unprepared, he was turned down flat. However, Liberty did suggest that Elton look up another rejected singer, Bernie Taupin. Bernie was primarily a lyricist, while Elton was primarily a composer. The two men set up a correspondence in which Bernie sent Elton his poems through the mail and Elton set them to music. It was only after Elton took some of their songs to the Beatles' early publishers, Dick James Music, who showed some interest in them, that he and Taupin met at a demo session.

They convinced James to hire them as full-time composers. The duo then spent many fruitless months trying to write hits for easy-listening stars of the day like Tom Jones. Realizing that they couldn't write easy-listening music, they decided to concentrate on the songs they'd like to record themselves. Eventually they did just that with "Lady Samantha," which they sold to Britain's DJM label. Surprisingly, the single did well enough to merit an album, and *Empty Sky* was released in Britain in 1969. Sales were sluggish, but a fair amount of radio play gave Elton and Bernie the chance to have another go at it in 1970.

Elton John was cut in ten days. While the British response to it was lukewarm, the album attracted the American label MCA. The disc quickly grabbed a toehold on the American charts and earned several favorable reviews.

MCA then pressured Elton to tour. After some initial resistance, Elton gave in and put together a band with Dee Murray on bass and Nigel Olsson, formerly of the Spencer Davis Group, on drums. Even Jeff Beck expressed an interest in joining the band. But after a few rehearsals it became apparent that Elton and the ex-Yardbird were headed in different musical directions, so Beck soon departed.

The band arrived in L.A. in August 1970 for a crucial one-week stand at the Troubadour. This hangout for critics and music-industry heavies has always been an important venue for breaking new acts. After Elton's debut album with its lush strings and flowery lyrics, most people were expecting an introspective singer/songwriter. What they got was a junior Jerry Lee Lewis who pounded the piano and carried on in high style. The Troubadour dates were a total triumph as the press eagerly spread the news of the new pop messiah. With such publicity *Elton John* climbed to number 4 in the album charts, while its single, "Your Song," warbled its way into the top ten.

After finishing the soundtrack to the movie *Friends,* Elton and Bernie turned to the Hollywood image of the American West for their next album. With songs like "Ballad of a Well-known Gun" and "Burn Down the Mission," *Tumbleweed Connection* continued the duo's association with producer Gus Dudgeon and Paul Buckmaster. Then *11-17-70,* an album recorded at a live radio broadcast, joined *Friends, Tumbleweed Connection,* and *Elton John* on the charts, giving Elton four L.P.'s in the top thirty, something only the Beatles had ever done. On his second U.S. tour Elton sold out larger and larger halls as the contrast between his timid appearance and his outrageous stage act delighted audiences from coast to coast.

Elton was a superstar now with hit records seemingly flowing in an endless, effortless stream. "Levon," "Rocket Man," and "Daniel" all took their places on the charts. Both he and Taupin felt that pop songs should be disposable, here one month and gone the next, so they wrote their tunes for the moment with Bernie providing clever bits of pop imagery that Elton then dressed up with the most irresistible melody hooks since Lennon and McCartney. Even their "throwaway" songs like "Honky Cat" or the rollicking "Crocodile Rock" provided the early seventies' top forty with its few really exciting moments.

Onstage, Elton combined the raucous style of Jerry Lee Lewis with the wardrobe of Liberace. His gaudy sequined outfits and surrealistic specs often generated more talk than his highly energetic music. Elton was now living out his wildest pop-star fantasies.

In 1973 Elton formed his own label, Rocket, but he had the good sense not to record for it. He felt that superstars who recorded on their own labels detracted from the label's other artists. Therefore, his October studio album, *Goodbye Yellow Brick Road,* was released on MCA. It became Elton's biggest seller, with cuts like "Funeral for a Friend" and "Candle in the Wind" getting airplay on the album-oriented radio stations and others like "Saturday Night's Alright for Fighting" and the title track continuing his string of top-ten singles. However, the album's biggest tune was the soul crossover "Bennie and the Jets," which peaked at number 1 in April 1974.

At this point everything Elton touched turned to platinum. "Pinball Wizard," his song from Ken Russell's film of the Who's *Tommy,* and an updated version of the Beatles' "Lucy in the Sky with Diamonds" sold just as well as his own compositions. *Caribou,* named for James William Guercio's recording studios in Colorado, went quadruple platinum, fueled by the radio-active monsters "Don't Let the Sun Go Down on Me" and "The Bitch Is Back." "Philadelphia Freedom," released in March 1975, was one of his biggest singles ever, selling over two million copies. The song centered around Billy Jean King's pro tennis team, but no one seemed to care. His farewell salute to his loud and brash early days was chronicled on *Captain Fantastic and the Brown Dirt Cowboy.* The quasiautobiographical nature of the lyrics, especially on "Someone Saved

My Life Tonight," gave his fans what they thought was a real peek into the life of their idol.

His next album, *Rock of the Westies,* was number 1 for five weeks. His duet with sometime protégée Kiki Dee, "Don't Go Breaking My Heart," was the sound of the summer of 1976. However, he had put so much of himself into his music that he was beginning to run dry. The records started sounding more slick and facile. The strain of performing also took its toll of Elton. Following his summer of 1976 tour, he announced his retirement and, after selling over eighty million albums, returned to England to serve as chairman of his local soccer club.

His retirement didn't last long, though. Elton was back a year later for six shows at London's Rainbow Theatre and a charity gig at the Empire Pool. Shortly thereafter he retired again and came back again with a major European tour in 1979. He then became the first major rock star to perform in the Soviet Union, where he delighted crowds by playing the Beatles' "Back in the U.S.S.R."

Unfortunately, his *Single Man* album in 1978 was a disappointment. *Victim of Love,* a pure disco album released in 1979, featured a revamped version of Chuck Berry's "Johnny B. Goode" and six thoroughly mediocre dance tunes, none of which was written by Elton. The album bombed, and most people never even knew that it had been released.

The cold shoulder that Elton has been getting from record buyers recently will certainly spur him on to new efforts such as his top-ten smash in the summer of 1980, "Little Jeannie." With an ego as big as his talent Elton John will surely bounce back in the eighties.

1975

"I think the disco thing started when the twist hit. That was when people went to what were formerly just drinking holes and began to dance—mostly to live music. I think of the Peppermint Lounge, where Joey Dee had the house band and Jimi Hendrix was a guitar player with that band in the twist era, back in 1962 and 1963. But it was all a live-band situation. They didn't start playing records until later, so discotheque was really a misnomer.

"The drummer and the bass player became the heroes because disco is just music with a very heavy beat. It's not listening music; it's dancing music. For a quarter of a century kids had been saying on *Bandstand,* 'I like the beat—it's easy to dance to.' And basically that's what disco was all about."

So says Dick Clark about the unbelievable dance craze that started to catch on in 1975—disco. That infectious dance beat became a worldwide phenomenon in 1975. We had the thumping beat of "That's The Way I Like It" by Florida's K.C. and the Sunshine Band. Munich, Germany, gave America the Eurodisco sound of the Silver Convention's "Fly, Robin, Fly." The Average White Band sent "Pick Up the Pieces" all the way from Scotland. The late Van McCoy and his Soul City Symphony from New Jersey created disco's most popular dance with "The Hustle."

However, music wasn't all disco in 1975. Graham Gouldman, Kevin Godley, Lol Creme, and Eric Stewart—those British rock veterans who were known collectively as 10cc—scrambled up the charts in the summer with the hauntingly ironic "I'm Not in Love." Minnie Riperton, formerly of Rotary Connection, struck gold in the spring with her chirping birds on "Lovin' You." Labelle had a hit with the scorching soul of "Lady Marmalade." The booming C.B. radio craze carried C. W. McCall to the number-1 slot with "Convoy." This year also produced the syrupy sentimentality of "Feelings" by Morris Albert. The top ten of 1975 shaped up like this: "Love Will Keep Us Together" by the Captain and Tennille; "Laughter in the Rain" by Neil Sedaka, "Philadelphia Freedom" by the Elton John Band, "Rhinestone Cowboy" by Glen Campbell, "Before the Next Teardrop Falls" by Freddy Fender, "Shining Star" by Earth, Wind and Fire, "My Eyes Adored You" by Frankie Valli, "Fame" by David Bowie, "Thank God I'm a Country Boy" by John Denver, and "One of These Nights" by the Eagles.

Outside the world of rock, Haldeman, Ehrlichman, Mitchell, and Mardian were found guilty of the Watergate coverup. North Vietnam seized Saigon, putting an end to sixteen years of fighting between North

Dick Clark with the Captain and Tennille, who had the number-1 record of 1975 with "Love Will Keep Us Together." Captain Daryl Dragon, whose father was the conductor for the Hollywood Bowl Symphony, was once a keyboard player for the Beach Boys. *(Courtesy of Dick Clark)*

Natalie Cole, Nat "King" Cole's daughter, made her first splash on the music scene in 1975 with "This Will Be." *(Vincent Frye)*

Minnie Riperton, formerly with Rotary Connection, filled the airwaves in the spring of 1975 with number-1 hit "Lovin' You." Minnie died of cancer in 1979. *(Charles Bush)*

British rock veterans 10cc (from left: Kevin Godley, Eric Stewart, Lol Creme, and Graham Gouldman) cracked the top ten in 1975 with "I'm Not in Love."

and South Vietnam. Cambodia captured the American merchant ship *Mayaguez,* and President Ford sent in the Navy and Marines to rescue her. In 1975 Ford himself survived two unsuccessful assassination attempts within seventeen days. On September 5, Patty Hearst was finally captured in San Francisco by the FBI after nineteen months on the run.

In sports, Ali decked Frazier after fourteen brutal rounds in "The Thrilla in Manila." The Cincinnati Reds and the Boston Red Sox took the World Series to seven classic games before Cincinnati came out on top. The Pittsburgh Steelers won Super Bowl X, their second in a row, defeating the Dallas Cowboys. And the teamwork of the Golden State Warriors brought the NBA crown to Oakland.

On the screen, *Jaws* broke all box-office records to date and cleared the beaches that summer. But *One Flew Over the Cuckoo's Nest* knocked off *Jaws, Nashville, Barry Lyndon,* and *Dog Day Afternoon* for the Academy Award for Best Picture. On TV, *The Jeffersons* moved on up while *Starsky and Hutch* moved on out. *Barney Miller* took command of the twelfth precinct, and Robert Blake upheld the law on *Baretta.*

It was 1975—the twenty-first year of rock and roll.

Gloria Gaynor copped the title Queen of Disco with her 1975 rendition of "Never Can Say Goodbye." Gloria was back on the charts in a big way in 1979 with "I Will Survive."

LINDA RONSTADT

In 1975 Linda Ronstadt made it to the top of the heap. She was acclaimed the top female vocalist in pop, rock, and country. With her coquettish sex-kitten charm and her membership in the Los Angeles inner circle of stardom, Linda became a media darling. But it had been a long, hard climb, for prior to 1975 Linda had been recording for eight years with little more than a cult following and no commercial success. In those days Linda had been dogged by insecurities about her singing, her appearance, and her career. But when she found a rigid musical formula, Linda Ronstadt became one of the most popular singers of the late seventies and one of the most predictable.

Linda was born in Tucson, Arizona, in 1946. She grew up with the sounds of Mexican mariachi music, her older sister's country-and-western records, and her father's Billie Holiday and Ella Fitzgerald discs, which he played around the house to wean her away from top-forty radio. In high school Linda was part of a singing trio with her older brother and sister. They made numerous local TV appearances in Tucson and even did some recording. She enrolled in the University of Arizona in 1964, but her old friend guitarist Bobby Kimmel convinced her to join him in California. After one semester Linda abandoned higher education for a higher calling—rock and roll.

In 1965 Linda's music was a mixture of country, folk and rock. In Los Angeles she and Kimmel found a kindred spirit in bass player Kenny Edwards, and the three formed the Stone Poneys. They had been playing the L.A. club circuit for a couple of years when one of their demo tapes convinced Capitol Records to sign the Stone Poneys to a recording contract. Their first album, *Stone Poneys,* released in early 1967, flopped. Then a song written by Monkee Mike Nesmith, "Different Drum," gave the Stone Poneys national exposure, climbing to number 13 on the charts in the fall of 1967. But the group was hard-pressed to produce a follow-up hit. By the end of 1968, with three unsuccessful albums, the group split up.

Linda stayed on with Capitol and released her first solo album in 1969, *Hand Sown, Home Grown.* A smorgasbord of country, folk, and pop, this was the first of many albums in which the ever-insecure Ms. Ronstadt let boyfriends decide the course of her musical career. Her second solo album, *Silk Purse,* which featured a cover photo of Linda sitting in a pig pen with a hog, contained her first hit single—the beautiful bittersweet ballad "Long, Long Time." In 1971 Linda successfully toured England and France, then returned to put together a new band with Glenn, Frey, Don Henley, and Randy Meisner. With Linda's encouragement, they would later go off on their own as the Eagles. She then turned out her third album, *Linda Ronstadt,* in 1972, but this album sold no better than had her previous efforts. Blaming the album's failure on Capitol's unwillingness to promote her properly, Linda angrily left Capitol in 1973 for David Geffen's new label, Asylum.

The move to Asylum was a step in the right direction. Asylum put a striking photo of Linda on the cover of her late 1973 album, *Don't Cry Now,* and the record made some headway in the record stores. Produced in part by her boyfriend at the time, J. D. Souther, *Don't Cry Now* was Linda's best album to date, although still somewhat uneven. It featured Eric Kaz' beautiful "Love Has No Pride," a rollicking hoedown version of "Silver Threads and Golden Needles," and Randy Newman's satiric "Sail Away." Although *Don't Cry Now* gained Linda a greater following, radio stations, particularly top-forty stations, stayed away from her music. Many program directors said in private that they liked Linda's music, but it wasn't commercial enough for airplay. Linda's next album, however, changed all that.

During most of 1974 Linda was tied up in a

Linda Ronstadt.

contract dispute between Asylum and Capitol. Capitol eventually won the right to one more Ronstadt album, and for this one, Linda chose a producer with whom she had no romantic attachments, Peter Asher of Peter and Gordon fame. Asher took a hard look at Linda's strengths and weaknesses. Linda possessed a clear, strong, supple voice; but since she didn't write her own music, she was at the mercy of her songwriters. Asher chose a varied assortment of commercial songs for Linda. The result was *Heart Like a Wheel*, which set the pattern for all her future albums with a soul classic here, a Buddy Holly song there, a few country tunes, and some tearful ballads. Her first single from the album, a driving version of Betty Everett's 1963 soul tune "You're No Good," took off like a shot and hit the number-1 spot in early 1975. "When Will I Be Loved," a countrified remake of the Everly Brothers hit, followed "You're No Good" up the charts in the spring. Linda's version of Buddy Holly's 1958 single "It Doesn't Matter Anymore" fanned the flames of a mounting Buddy Holly revival. Finally attaining commercial success after all those years, Linda rewarded Peter Asher by making him her manager, and they spent the next five years slavishly following the *Heart Like a Wheel* formula.

Whereas *Heart Like a Wheel* dug up some interesting, relatively unknown oldies, Linda's succeeding albums took on some of rock's biggest hits; and Ronstadt could only suffer by comparison. Linda struck gold with both "Heat Wave" and "Tracks of My Tears" in late 1975, but it was obvious that she didn't have the soul of Martha Reeves or Smokey Robinson. Her obligatory Buddy Holly tributes, "That'll Be the Day" in 1976 and "It's So Easy" in 1977, grew tiresome after a while. Her versions of Chuck Berry's "Back in the U.S.A." and the Rolling Stones' "Tumbling

Dice" simply didn't have the zest of the originals. Linda didn't even wait for the acetate to dry before covering Elvis Costello's "Alison," and she proved that she couldn't hold a candle to Elvis' sparsely produced original.

Despite these shortcomings Linda Ronstadt became a star. Her on-again, off-again romance with California's Zen governor, Jerry Brown, gave her front-page publicity. Her lovely face regularly graced the covers of *Time, Rolling Stone,* and *People* magazines. As America read about her jogging and her weightlifting, she sold millions of records. Though Linda Ronstadt didn't make it to the White House with Jerry Brown in 1980, she is already the first lady of rock to her many fans, who don't seem to mind her predictability.

At first glance, 1980 seemed to usher in a new Linda Ronstadt—the punk Linda Ronstadt. Her hair was cropped short and spiky and she dressed in punk fashions of pink and black. She even recorded three songs by the L.A. new-wave group the Cretones and three more by Elvis Costello on her new album, *Mad Love.* But although Linda actually rocked out on a few cuts, most notably "Mad Love" and "How Do I Make You," her hit single was a syrupy remake of Little Anthony and the Imperials' 1965 tearjerker "Hurt So Bad." Then in the summer of 1980 Linda abandoned Los Angeles and punk rock for New York City and Gilbert and Sullivan operettas. Linda joined teen heartthrob Rex Smith on Broadway in Joseph Papp's production of *The Pirates of Penzance.* While Linda was acclaimed more for her singing than for her acting, she charmed the New York press, and *The Pirates of Penzance* was assured of a long, successful run. While a long-anticipated album grouping her with Dolly Parton and Emmy Lou Harris remained stalled, Broadway provided a new avenue for Linda Ronstadt's talents in the eighties.

THE DOOBIE BROTHERS

In the early seventies, drummer John Hartman, guitarist Tom Johnston, and bassist David Shogren began playing dates around California as Pud. On one of those early dates they shared the bill with a young bluegrass picker named Pat Simmons, who soon joined them when he learned of their fondness for a certain illicit weed. In fact, they were christened the Doobie Brothers (a "doobie" being the northern Californian slang term for "joint") by a friend because of their predilection for that herb.

The Doobies were then hired as house band at the Château Liberté, a biker hangout in the Santa Cruz Mountains. Playing for sixty dollars a night, the band developed a churning guitar style that pleased the local Hell's Angels. Although the band weren't bikers themselves, they projected a tough image to keep from getting their tails kicked in too often.

While working at that club, the band sent a demo tape to Warner Brothers production ace Lenny Waronker. He and fellow producer Ted Templeman (formerly of Harper's Bizarre) liked the tape and went out to see the band. As a result of their interest Warners soon had the Doobies under contract and in the studio with Templeman, cutting their first album, *The Doobie Brothers*, in early 1972. However, the public failed to share Warner's enthusiasm; the album went nowhere. Sadly, it was back to the bikers and the Château Liberté. Shogren became discouraged and split. He was replaced by Tiran Porter, an old bandmate of Simmons. Mike Hossack was then added as a second drummer. After a few months with the bikers the band was ready to take another stab at the record business.

When the Doobies were told that they needed a hit single in order to succeed, Tom Johnston simply went home one day and wrote one. In thirty minutes, he wrote both the words and the music to "Listen to the Music." When it was combined with Templeman's smooth, seamless production, it became one of the biggest singles in the history of Warner Brothers. *Toulouse Street,* the album that included "Listen to the Music," quickly went gold and wound up spending 103 weeks on the charts.

The Doobies worked hard on the road, playing straightforward rock 150 to 200 nights a year. Their third album, *The Captain and Me,* featured that rocking style through Templeman's beautifully understated production, an increased use of synthesizers, and a lot of magnificent hard-driving guitar work. The singles "Long Train Running" and "China Grove" from that album helped it into the top ten in 1973.

By now the strain of constant touring was beginning to show. While recording their fourth album, *What Were Once Vices Are Now Habits,* Mike Hossack abruptly quit the band. He was replaced by drummer Keith Knudson. On this record the Memphis Horns, Little Feat's Bill Payne, and Steely Dan's Jeff Baxter dropped by the studio to lend a hand. However, after an impressive start, *What Were Once Vices* stalled. The lack of a strong single was blamed. Several cuts were released without much success. Then, late in 1974, they released an uncharacteristically laid-back tune from that album that had been penned by the ole country picker Pat Simmons. "Black Water" became the fastest-breaking single in Warner's history, staying on the charts for twenty weeks and lifting the album to platinum status in early 1975.

With the release of their fifth album, *Stampede,* Jeff "Skunk" Baxter became a full-time member. Baxter had become dissatisfied with Steely Dan when they decided to stop performing live. The Doobie Brothers now embarked upon a thirty-eight-city tour to promote the album. But on that tour Johnston collapsed with a bleeding ulcer and was forced to leave the band for a while. Baxter suggested that they hire another disgruntled Steely Dan member, Mike McDonald, to finish the tour. With only two days

The ever-changing Doobie Brothers (from left: Keith Knudsen, Bobby LaKind, John Hartman, Tiran Porter, Michael McDonald, Jeff "Skunk" Baxter, and Patrick Simmons).

of rehearsal the Johnstonless Doobies were called back for three encores in New Orleans. As a reward for a job well done McDonald was asked to stay on.

While Johnston was still recovering, the band headed back to the studio. Without their chief songwriter, they were short on material. When McDonald was asked if he had any songs that he wanted to record, he responded with the album's two biggest tunes, "Takin' It to the Streets" (the L.P.'s title cut) and "It Keeps You Runnin'," which was later a hit for Carly Simon.

The album was a lot mellower than the group's previous releases, and that distressed Tom Johnston. He considered himself a rocker in the tradition of Little Richard and James Brown. His contribution to this album had been reduced to just one song. Moreover, Baxter and McDonald were moving the Doobies in the direction of Steely Dan. It was simply too much for him to take. During the recording of *Livin' on the Fault Line,* Johnston walked out on the band he had helped to found.

The Doobies did not look back, though. "Little Darling (I Need You)" and "Echoes of Love" went to the top of the charts. *Livin' on the Fault Line* recovered from a shaky start and made a respectable showing through 1977 and into 1978. Johnston's chunky guitar lines were now replaced by the streamlined flow of McDonald's keyboard-dominated style.

In December 1978 *Minute by Minute* was far and away the tightest, most technically mature recording the Doobies had ever made. McDonald was now totally out front (though Templeman was still at the helm in the studio). His compositions "What a Fool Believes" (cowritten with Kenny Loggins) and the title cut, with its subtle, infectious chorus, were two of the main reasons *Rolling Stone* named it the number-1 album of 1979.

Success did not stabilize the band any, as upheaval had become a way of life for the Doobies. In February of 1979 Baxter fought with McDonald and left. Then John Hartman quit. Three new members—Chet McCracker, John McFee, and Cornelius Bumpus— were pressed into service just in time for the September MUSE concert at Madison Square Garden in New York.

Today only Pat Simmons remains from the Doobies' wild and wooly days as a California biker band. Who can say how long he may last? The only thing that is certain is that while the Doobie Brothers stay together, they'll continue to make some of the most interesting and professional music being produced in America—and that will be enough for the band's legion of fans.

DAVID BOWIE

One of rock's most enigmatic performers had his most successful year in 1975. Always the artiste, transcending explanation and offering none, David Bowie had previously played all the rock-and-roll roles, from orange-haired spaceman to bisexual bopper. His career had gone through many changes but his 1975 change stunned even the veteran Bowie watchers. In 1975 David Bowie became the Thin White Duke, the Philadelphia soulman, discoing his way into the hearts of America.

Bowie was born David Jones in London in 1947. As a boy David was once astonished to see his otherwise straitlaced cousin dancing her heart out to Elvis' "Hound Dog." He had never seen anyone so moved, and he knew then that he wanted to taste the awesome power of that music. He immersed himself in jazz, blues, and R & B and learned to play the guitar. By the late sixties David was working as a commercial artist while also writing and recording with various pop bands in and around London.

Change soon became the key to his career. After working as David Jones and the Lower Third, David temporarily abandoned music for the mysticism of Eastern religion. He then switched courses again, performing with a mime troupe. Returning to music, he changed his name from David Jones to David Bowie to avoid any confusion with Davy Jones of the Monkees. He released an almost traditional pop album in 1967, *The World of David Bowie,* on which he crooned the minor British hit "Love You Till Tuesday."

Bowie made a greater impact in 1969 with the album *Man of Words, Man of Music* and the single "Space Oddity." The single featured weird echo effects and Bowie's spacey, emotionless, monotonic vocals, which set a mood of alienation. Released to coincide with the first moonwalk, "Space Oddity" hit it big in England in the summer of 1969, but floundered in America until its reissue in 1973. In 1970 Bowie's apocalyptic vision, *The Man Who Sold the World,* was well received among the avant-garde, but did not break through to a wider audience. However, Bowie was beginning to build a reputation.

Hunky Dory in 1971 was a collection of clever pop songs showcasing Bowie's unique talent for weaving a lyric. It was an ambitious yet very accessible record, dealing with a variety of subjects ranging from Dylan and Warhol to fatherhood. On *Hunky Dory,* Bowie worked with the band that would eventually become known as the Spiders from Mars—Mick Ronson, Woody Woodmansey, and Trevor Bolder. Bowie's stuttering anthem "Changes" was released as a single in America in April 1972, but never climbed past number 72 on the charts. *Hunky Dory* did win praise, however, and a growing audience eagerly anticipated his next release.

The Rise and Fall of Ziggy Stardust and the Spiders from Mars was a remarkable album that brought Bowie to the attention of the general public in America. Of course, Bowie was hard to ignore at this time, with his electric orange hair, silver lamé jumpsuit, and his declared bisexuality. Although married and with a son, Zowie Bowie, David announced that he had met his wife, Angie, through a mutual lover.

Ziggy Stardust was one of the first successful concept albums. It was a portrait of the ultimate rock star, reputedly based on Jimi Hendrix. *Ziggy Stardust* contained outstanding tracks like "Five Years," "Moonage Daydream," and "Rock 'n' Roll Suicide," and was the final word on glitter rock.

As *Ziggy Stardust* made its way up the album charts, Bowie and the Spiders from Mars embarked on their first tour of the United States. It was a triumph. Bowie played the role of Ziggy to the hilt with his space-age costumes, elaborate staging, and outstanding support from the Spiders. Bowie also produced the ex-leader of the defunct Velvet Under-

David Bowie.

ground, Lou Reed, on his *Transformer* album, and wrote and produced the glitter theme song for Mott the Hoople, "All the Young Dudes."

Bowie followed up his masterpiece with *Aladdin Sane* in the spring of 1973. With *Aladdin Sane* Bowie moved into a hard-rock vein, disappointing some of his more arty followers. The album featured "The Jean Genie," "Panic in Detroit," and his version of the Rolling Stones' "Let's Spend the Night Together." In late 1973 *Pin-Ups* was Bowie's tribute to the rock music he'd grown up with in the mid-sixties, with his versions of Them's "Here Comes the Night" and the Yardbirds' "Shapes of Things." It was an intriguing oldies collection, but ultimately disappointing, as Bowie's versions never measured up to the originals.

After another retirement from music and the breakup of the Spiders from Mars, Bowie returned in 1974 with *Diamond Dogs* and the single "Rebel Rebel." This was an album of futuristic rock once again, with Bowie playing all of the guitar parts as well as saxophone and keyboards. In May 1974 he launched a three-month concert extravaganza, the 1980 Floor Show, in which he used every stage prop imaginable. *David Live* was his two-record live album, recorded at the Tower Theater in Philadelphia; but, unfortunately, it didn't capture the real excitement of a Bowie performance. Nevertheless this album gave his audience a clue to Bowie's next change.

In 1975 Bowie became enchanted with black R & B music and traveled to Philadelphia's Sigma Sound Studios, the home of the "Sound of Philadelphia." Using Sigma's top session men, Bowie recorded the album *Young Americans.* The title track was a disco tour de force with honking saxophones, lyrics that commented on the American scene, and Bowie's wailing blues cry, "Ain't there one damn song that can make me break down and cry?" "Young Americans" entered the top twenty. But his next single, "Fame," a cynical look at rock superstardom cowritten with John Lennon, went all the way to number 1 for two weeks on the singles charts and earned Bowie a gold record.

The Thin White Duke followed up his remarkable commercial success of 1975 with another "plastic soul" album, *Station to Station.* This was one of Bowie's most enjoyable albums, with its impeccable musicianship and slick production. "Golden Years," a jazzy, atonal Frank Zappa–like 45, stayed on the singles charts for five months, making it to number 11. "TVC 15" was another Bowie trip into the future that blazed a path between white soul and electronic music.

Bowie abruptly switched directions again in 1977. He teamed up with Brian Eno of Roxy Music to do three avant-garde albums of instrumental electronic experimental music. The first two albums of this trilogy, *Low* and *Heroes,* were bizarre and inaccessible. In 1979 Bowie inched back toward more conventional rock with the third part of this series, *Lodger.* Nineteen eighty brought another stunning change in Bowie's career as he turned up on Broadway in the award-winning play "The Elephant Man." Always the supreme actor among rock stars, Bowie won accolades for his portrayal of John Merrick, the hideously deformed but always human sideshow attraction in Victorian England. His change of direction with "The Elephant Man" only proves that even though we may never know where Bowie is going next, we do know that he will never stay there for very long.

THE EAGLES

The Eagles (from left: Glenn Frey, Don Felder, Don Henley, John Walsh, and Timothy B. Schmit). *(Lorrie Sullivan)*

Named for our national bird, the Eagles merged two American musical forms, country and rock, into a potent blend of pop that cuts across all musical barriers. The mixture of musical styles worked well for them as every one of their albums has soared near the top of the charts. No other American band has come close to matching their success or longevity. And it all started with Linda Ronstadt, who put together the nucleus of the group—Don Henley, Glenn Frey, and Randy Meisner—as her backup band in 1971.

Glenn Frey came to L.A. from Detroit, where he used to hang out with local rock star Bob Seger. On his first day in town he met J. D. Souther, and they soon formed an acoustic duo called Longbranch

Pennywhistle. However, because success was not right around the corner for them, they were forced to move into the sixty-dollar-a-month apartment of another struggling musician named Jackson Browne.

Don Henley came west from a small town in Texas where he played drums with his old boyhood band, Shiloh. The group had managed to land a record deal with the tiny Amos label, but their releases all flopped. Don would drown his sorrows at the Troubadour Club, and it was there that he met Frey, who was also floundering while under contract to Amos.

Randy Meisner had a somewhat easier time of it. He left Nebraska for California to play in a group called the Poor. The band's high point was opening concerts for Buffalo Springfield. When the Springfield's Jim Messina and Richie Furay split to form Poco, they brought Randy along as bass player. After a year with Poco he backed up Rick Nelson for a while as a member of the Stone Canyon Band. But in 1971 Meisner found himself just hanging around L.A. with Frey and Henley.

Linda Ronstadt had originally asked only Glenn and Don to join her band, but they soon convinced her that she needed Meisner as well. When Bernie Leadon, one of Linda's former sidemen, drunkenly took the stage one night and began jamming with Glenn, Don, and Randy, he was added to the band. Linda's manager at the time, John Boylan, was very enthusiastic about the quartet. He wanted them to stay behind Linda, but the boys had already decided to strike out on their own. So with Linda's blessing, the four secluded themselves and began rehearsing their own material.

After their third rehearsal Glenn and Don appointed themselves leaders. Their rules were simple. Only the best material and musicians would be welcome in the band. Their goals were respect, fame, and money—but not necessarily in that order. After just three weeks of rehearsal Glenn and Don approached Asylum Records' president, David Geffen, for a contract. Frey's old roommate and Asylum artist Jackson Browne helped break Geffen down, and a deal was drawn up.

With $125,000 from Asylum, they took off for a four-week stint at Aspen, Colorado's Gallery Bar to tighten up the act. Then it was on to London to record their first L.P. Glyn Johns, who had made records with the Who, the Stones, and Steve Miller, produced this album. For the occasion Jackson Browne coauthored a tune with Frey which they planned to use as their first single release.

When that tune, "Take It Easy," was released in June of 1972, the Eagles were off and running. With their next couple of albums the band developed a reputation as a laid-back singles band. "Take It Easy," "Witchy Woman," "Peaceful, Easy Feeling," and "Tequila Sunrise" were all in that same mold.

When the Eagles began to resent the laid-back image, they dumped producer Johns in favor of Bill Szymczyk. Looking for a harder sound, the group had been impressed when their manager Irving Azoff played them an L.P. that Szymczyk had produced for Joe Walsh. With *On the Border* Szymczyk got the rougher mix that the band wanted. Tunes like "Already Gone" and "James Dean" displayed more rock-and-roll chops than most people thought the band had. Around this time guitarist Don Felder joined the band, swelling their ranks to five.

In 1975 *One of These Nights,* Szymczyk's second production for the Eagles, established the group as America's foremost musicmakers. It featured their Grammy Award-winning "Lyin' Eyes," a cheatin' song that focused on the desperation of the wayward wife rather than that of the abandoned husband. "Lyin' Eyes" was later joined at the top of the charts by "Take It to the Limit" and the album's title cut.

It is common for successful bands to fall into a rut and lose their musical vitality. But the Eagles were lucky. Following *One of These Nights,* Bernie Leadon left and was replaced by former James Gang great Joe Walsh. Walsh added the perverse sense of humor and the hard-rock sensibility that made *Hotel California* the Eagles' most successful album to date. This album stripped the Day-Glo patina from the California mystique, a revealing decadent scene. "Life in the Fast Lane," the title of their hit from the album, became an instant catch phrase for the shallow, selfish "me generation" of the late seventies.

In 1977 Randy Meisner left the band to spend more time with his family. Ironically, he was replaced by Tim Schmidt, who had previously replaced him in Poco.

The Eagles spent most of 1977 and 1978 on tour. Although they were a top draw, the group was often accused of being dreadfully dull on stage. Frey and Henley's slavish devotion to perfection robbed their concerts of any spontaneity. Except for Walsh, the crowd pleaser, the band hardly ever moved onstage. Their concerts were about as exciting as listening to their records at home.

The Long Run in 1979 continued the band's gradual metamorphosis from barefoot country boys to big-city rockers. It also continued their unbroken string of successful albums. That success, however, is no accident. Under the leadership of Frey and Henley, the Eagles have always exercised a caution and control that is seldom seen in the emotional, erratic world of rock. And they will doubtlessly continue their long run into the eighties.

362

THE BAY CITY ROLLERS

In 1975 the rock-and-roll hype machine was working overtime for a British group that was heading for America. It was said that they would top the phenomenal success of the Beatles. The publicity people at Arista Records laid it on thick. Rollermania was in the air. British teen-agers were dressing head to toe in Bay City Roller tartan, and teen-age girls were fainting and screaming at Roller concerts. With three straight number-1 hits in Britain and a hit BBC TV series, the Bay City Rollers were ready to take on America.

America watched and listened for the Bay City Rollers, and perhaps that was their downfall. With every move the Rollers made, they were compared with the Beatles, and the Rollers just weren't in the Beatles' league. Indeed, there was a crowd at the airport when the Rollers landed in New York, but it was nothing like the one that had greeted the Beatles' arrival eleven years earlier. At their press conferences reporters found that the novelty of the Rollers' heavy Scottish accents was no substitute for the style and wit of a John Lennon. Howard Cosell featured the Bay City Rollers on his *Saturday Night* variety show. On their first American television appearance they proved that they were a somewhat personable bubblegum group. But as it turned out, Cosell's show was canceled in thirteen weeks, and Rollermania didn't last much longer.

The Bay City Rollers started in 1967 when Alan and Derek Longmuir formed the Saxons in Edinburgh, Scotland. In 1969 the Saxons hooked up with manager Tam Paton and changed their name by randomly sticking a pin in a map of the United States that landed on Bay City, Michigan. Despite their new name the Bay City Rollers still loaded trucks by day while playing Edinburgh bars for fifteen dollars a night. In 1971 Dick Leahy, the head of the teenybopper-oriented Bell Records, was stuck between plane flights in Edinburgh. Killing time at the Top Storey Club, he caught the Rollers' act and signed them to a record contract as a result.

The Longmuir brothers added Eric Faulkner and Les McKeown to the group in 1972, the year that saw the Rollers' first single, "Keep on Dancin'," reach number 9 on the British charts after five months of ceaseless promotion. The Rollers won a song contest on Radio Luxembourg with "Mañana," but the record stiffed in Britain. The Rollers then offered "Saturday Night," but British teens still weren't buying. After the Rollers added Stuart "Woody" Wood on guitar in 1974, Rollermania finally burst onto the British scene. "Summerlove Sensation," "All of Me Loves All of You," and "Bye Bye Baby" all went to number 1 in Britain. However, unlike the Beatles, the Rollers did not write their own songs. While the Rollers did appeal to British teen-age girls, they demonstrated no particular talents that set them apart from the rock-and-roll crowd.

Now managed by the Beatles' old promoter, Sid Bernstein, the Rollers invaded America in 1975. Even though they hit the number-1 spot with their old British flop "Saturday Night," the Rollers found that America already had its own bunch of teen idols. Donny Osmond, David Cassidy, and the Partridge Family were all homegrown, clean-cut bubblegum artists who made young teen-age girls shriek but let their parents rest easy at night. Moreover, Donny Osmond and David Cassidy were featured on network TV programs, and up-and-coming heartthrobs such as David's younger brother Shaun Cassidy and Leif Garrett were ready to pick up the bubblegum slack in the U.S.

As time passed, the Rollers found it difficult to maintain their innocent image. Les McKeown was involved in a car accident that killed an elderly pedestrian. Alan Longmuir, one of the Rollers' founding fathers, attempted suicide and finally left the group in April 1976. Eric Faulkner succumbed to

the pressure of Rollermania and took an overdose of sleeping pills in an unsuccessful suicide attempt. With the group in disarray, the Bay City Rollers did manage to hit the charts with two fine singles: the brilliant upbeat "Rock and Roll Love Letter" and their rollicking remake of a Dusty Springfield classic, "I Only Want to Be with You." However, by the end of 1976 Rollermania was just a memory. The Bay City Rollers proved that it would take much more than a good press agent to dethrone the Beatles.

The Bay City Rollers (from Left: Eric Faulkner, Derek Longmuir, Stuart "Woody" Wood, and Les McKeown).

Dick Clark with teen heartthrob Leif Garrett. (Courtesy of Dick Clark)

BELOW:
The Osmond Brothers with a bearded Dick Clark on *American Bandstand.* (Courtesy of Dick Clark)

The Sound of 1975

LED ZEPPELIN

Heavy metal, the lewd, pulsating rhythms played at a volume loud enough to make your ears bleed, has become one of rock's most enduring subgenres. Part of its popularity is due to the ease with which garage bands can imitate it. Bands from Aerosmith to Kiss have peddled their cosmic thunderings with an astonishingly high rate of success. But whether one loves or loathes it, all must agree that heavy metal started with Led Zeppelin.

With nine albums released, Led Zeppelin have never failed to make the top ten. In fact, all but three have gone to number 1. And one even entered the charts at number 1 in its first week of release! Since their very first American tour, they have consistently played to S.R.O. crowds at record-breaking concerts all over the world. Their thick, fuzzy slabs of guitar work and sledgehammer drumming have spawned an army of imitators. However, no one has even come close to dethroning them. In an era when "superstar" has become an overused term, it is really the only adjective that can describe them adequately.

The Zeppelin is led by ex-Yardbird Jimmy Page. Page's early career was spent working in British recording studios, where he lent his guitar licks to records by the Rolling Stones, Donovan, and the Who. He was then signed up to play bass with the Yardbirds, but he was soon moved up to second lead. When Jeff Beck left the group, Page assumed full responsibilities on lead guitar. But the band broke up in 1968, leaving him with their name and some unfulfilled concert obligations. Page chose to meet those commitments with a new group of Yardbirds. He enlisted bass player John Paul Jones, whom he knew from Donovan's "Hurdy Gurdy Man" sessions. From Birmingham's Band of Joy he hired vocalist Robert Plant and drummer John Bonham. It was apparent from the beginning that calling the band the New Yardbirds would be very misleading, so when the Who's Keith Moon jokingly described the band's sound by nicknaming them "Led Zeppelin," the name stuck.

October of 1968 found the quartet rehearsing in London while their manager, former pro wrestler Peter Grant, flew to America to get his boys a deal with a record label. Atlantic signed them without ever seeing or hearing them. Grant returned to England, hustled his band into a studio, and one week later had *Led Zeppelin* in the can. This album contained the same basic elements that Led Zeppelin have included on

Led Zeppelin (from left: John Paul Jones, the late John Bonham, Robert Plant, and Jimmy Page).

every subsequent L.P.—old blues riffs with a psychedelic flair, Jones' fat-bottom bass, Bonham's thunderous drums, and the piercing wails of Robert Plant.

Despite their American record contract the band was unknown in Britain and couldn't get any bookings. Therefore they went to the States, started opening concerts for other groups, and methodically blew the headliners off the stage. The Zep's wall of amplifiers and crude stage behavior were well received by concert goers.

Within months their first album was in America's top ten—even without a hit single to push it, something unheard of at the time. *Led Zeppelin* was the first real indication of the growing dominance of the album over the single. *Led Zeppelin II,* released nine months later, repeated the success of the debut album. This time, however, there was a single, the classic "Whole Lotta Love," which became a top-five hit worldwide and introduced the band back home in Britain. *Zep II* was the fastest-selling album in Atlantic Records' history. The band's concert fee was promptly raised to twenty-five thousand dollars a night. In just one year they had gone from relative unknowns to one of the biggest bands in rock.

Through the seventies the band continued to release albums that sold in the multimillions. *Led Zeppelin IV,* released in 1971, contained a song that became their all-time classic, potentially the song of the decade, and certainly the most requested record that radio has ever seen—"Stairway to Heaven." The song starts quietly with Plant and an acoustic guitar, builds slowly to a truly apocalyptic climax, then ends with a whimper. The strength of that song helped *Led Zeppelin IV* stay on the charts for 212 weeks.

Like many superbands, Led Zeppelin formed their own label, Swan Song, in 1974. But unlike most bands the Zep actually found some fine talent to record on it, most notably Bad Company. Led Zeppelin's own debut on their own label was also their first double album, 1975's *Physical Graffiti.* Here they demonstrated why they were able to maintain their supremacy over all challengers. Page's production gave the band a big booming sound, while his guitar took the group into uncharted territories. The urgently mystical aura of *Graffiti*'s "Kashmir" is only one example of Page's genius. By the end of 1975 manager Grant was declaring Led Zeppelin the most popular band in the world. Few could argue.

In 1975 Robert Plant was in a car accident that halted their live appearances until 1977 as they waited for Plant to recover. To fill the void, Led Zeppelin released a concert film, *The Song Remains the Same,* in 1976. Not unexpectedly, the two-record soundtrack stormed its way to number 2 before the year was out. The band also released their seventh studio album, *Presence,* that year.

Their return to the concert stage in 1977 was not an unqualified success, however. More fans than tickets destroyed more than a few stadium ticket-offices, and promoters had to resort to mail-order sales to combat the stampedes. There were also crowd-control problems at their concerts. An outdoor show in Tampa had been billed as a rain-or-shine event, so despite a slight downpour, the band took to the stage. But after a few numbers they walked off without a word to the audience and retreated to their hotel, leaving the promoter to explain to over fifty thousand Zeppelin fans that the show was over. A riot followed, leaving fifty injured, nineteen arrested, and the Tampa Stadium off limits to rock shows for three years. A Zep concert in Houston resulted in a half-million dollars in damages. That awesome tour finally ground to a halt on July twenty-sixth when Robert Plant learned that his six-year-old son had died of complications from a virus.

The Zep then lay low, biding their time until the waning moments of the decade. Their relative inactivity had people wondering if the band still had it in them. Filled with the same pile-driver rock their fans had come to expect, *In through the Out Door* proved that they did. At the end of rock's first twenty-five years, this album shot to number 1 upon release and proved that Led Zeppelin was still the heaviest metal on earth.

Led Zeppelin's outlook for the future plummeted like a lead balloon in the summer of 1980 with the death of their drummer, John Bonham. "Bonzo" Bonham, notorious for his free spirit and partying life-style, became yet another rock and roller to fall victim to alcohol and drugs. Rather than replace Bonham, Led Zeppelin announced in late 1980 that they would disband, amid rumors that Jimmy Page planned to team up with Eric Clapton and Jeff Beck and reform the Yardbirds.

Ann and Nancy Wilson led their hard-rocking group Heart on its first assault on the charts in 1976 with "Crazy on You" and "Magic Man." (From left to right: Michael Derosier, Howard Leese, Roger Fisher, Ann Wilson, Steve Fossen and Nancy Wilson.)

Leo Sayer.

1976

Nineteen seventy-six was the year of the Bicentennial, and America celebrated with parades, festivals, the procession of the tall ships, and the election of Jimmy Carter. On July 4, Israeli commandos staged the raid on Entebbe, freeing a hijacked Air France jet. Two of the worst earthquakes in history left 23,000 dead in Guatemala and 655,000 dead in T'ang-shan, China. While lame duck President Ford ordered Americans to get swine flu shots, the mysterious legionnaires' disease spread in Philadelphia.

Skater Dorothy Hamill captured the hearts of America during the Winter Olympics, while the incredible Nadia Comaneci of Rumania achieved gymnastic perfection at the Summer Olympics in Montreal. The Cincinnati Reds destroyed the New York Yankees in four games in the World Series, and Kenny Stabler and the Oakland Raiders ripped the Minnesota Vikings in Super Bowl XI. And the Boston Celtics won the NBA Championship again.

Farrah Fawcett-Majors was the TV sensation of 1976 on *Charlie's Angels.* Louise Lasser became *Mary Hartman, Mary Hartman* every weeknight on the year's most talked-about show. Those pearly dental wonders, Donny and Marie Osmond, premiered on ABC. *Laverne and Shirley, Alice,* and *One Day at a Time* all featured women on their own. In film, Sylvester Stallone's *Rocky* conquered *Taxi Driver, All the President's Men, Network,* and *Bound for Glory* for the Oscar for Best Picture.

As Leo Sayer sang "You Make Me Feel Like Dancing," everybody hustled to Vicki Sue Robinson's "Turn the Beat Around," K.C. and the Sunshine Band's "Shake Your Booty," and Maxine Nightingale's "Right Back Where We Started From." Heart's Wilson sisters sang about their "Magic Man," Gary Wright offered "Dream Weaver," and Boston's heavy-metal roar gave "More Than a Feeling." Nazareth wailed "Love Hurts" while the Sylvers gave us "Boogie Fever." But the sickest song of the year had to be "Disco Duck" by Rick Dees and His Cast of Idiots.

In 1976 the top ten singles included: "Don't Go Breaking My Heart" by Elton John and Kiki Dee, "Silly Love Songs" by Wings, "December, 1963 (Oh, What a Night)" by the Four Seasons, "Disco Lady" by Johnnie Taylor, "Play That Funky Music" by Wild Cherry, "Kiss and Say Goodbye" by the Manhattans, "50 Ways to Leave Your Lover" by Paul Simon, "A Fifth of Beethoven" by Walter Murphy and Big Apple Band, "Love Is Alive" by Gary Wright, and "Love Machine Pt. 1" by the Miracles.

It was 1976—the twenty-second year of rock and roll.

KISS

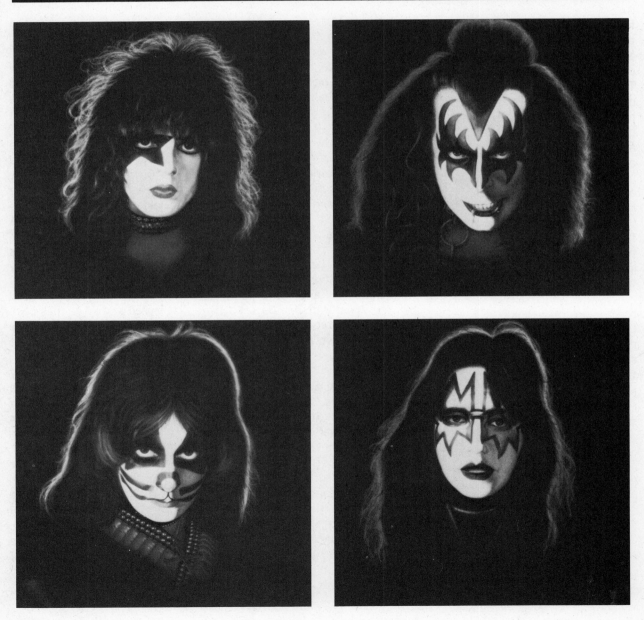

In 1972 Stanley Eisen and Eugene Klein, two bright, street-wise Jewish kids from New York City, sat down to plan their futures. Eisen's background was in marketing, advertising, and commercial art. Klein, who had a degree in journalism from the City University of New York, had worked at various times as a teacher at P.S. 75 in Manhattan, a proofreader for the Bowker Publishing Company, and an editorial assistant for *Vogue* magazine. Eisen and Klein both had grown up with rock and roll and even played a little guitar. Klein was a big comic-book fan, collecting Marvel Comics and publishing a collectors' magazine. They now wanted to find a way to turn their interests into a money-making enterprise. They knew that there was a lot of money to be made in rock and roll if only an untapped market could be found. Klein knew from his teaching experience that there was no rock group in 1972 that had a direct appeal for kids. The Beatles were from an entirely different era. Mick Jagger was an over-thirty jetsetter. The Osmond Brothers really appealed to parents more than to kids. Kids from ages nine to fourteen had the money to spend on albums, concerts, and merchandise, but no one was playing for them. Stan and Gene had their market; now they had to figure out what to do with it.

They decided to form a rock band and follow the old axiom: "If the parents hate it, the kids will love it." Parents hated Elvis Presley, the Beatles, and Alice Cooper; and the kids, looking for stars of their own, flocked to them in droves. Heavy-metal rock would fit the bill for two reasons, they thought: Parents loathed the sound, and you didn't have to be a virtuoso to play power chords. So far, so good.

However, sound alone wasn't enough. Eisen and Klein knew that their band would need an image. David Bowie and the New York Dolls had found a niche in the rock market with glitter and costumes, and Alice Cooper had incorporated greasepaint and theatrics into his highly successful rock act. So why not do them one better? A comic-book superhero rock band! Give the band a mystique. Mask them in secret identities and don't allow them to be seen without their masks. Then take Alice Cooper's concept of rock-and-roll theater and create a really spectacular stage show. Stanley Eisen, the son of a Queens furniture-store owner, changed his name to Paul Stanley, and Eugene Klein, a former Yeshiva

student, became Gene Simmons. They picked up their guitars, and Kiss was about to come to life.

Simmons and Stanley then read a classified ad in *Rolling Stone*, "Drummer willing to do anything to make it," and they soon had their drummer—Peter Crisscoula, a short, thirtyish drummer from Brooklyn who was playing weddings and bar mitzvahs and who had even recorded with a defunct group called Chelsea. Peter Crisscoula became Peter Criss. Now the group needed another guitarist, and Gene, Paul, and Peter held hundreds of auditions until they came up with Paul Frehley, an ex-street fighter from The Bronx who had been thrown out of two high schools, dropped out of a third, and had had his face smashed in with a bottle in a barroom brawl. Paul Frehley was dubbed Ace Frehley, and the band was now complete.

Through trial and error the costumes and characters of Kiss gradually evolved. After opening at the Coventry in Queens, New York, on January 30, 1973, as a rather effeminate glitter band, Kiss adopted black leather, silver, chrome, and lots of stage makeup to create distinct comic-book-type characters. Peter Criss became a whiskered, bandoliered cat. Ace Frehley was transformed into "Space Ace" the Spaceman, firing his guitar into the audience while perched on his eight-inch silver platform boots. Gene Simmons metamorphosed into the bat-lizard, an evil reptile with a long, menacing tongue. Paul Stanley became the sex symbol for the group with his pouting ruby lips, black star painted over one eye, and exposed hairy chest. In August 1973 Bill Aucoin, the producer of a syndicated TV rock show called *Flipside,* caught Kiss' act at the Hotel Diplomat in New York and offered to become their manager. Kiss agreed to accept him on condition that he would get them a recording contract within two weeks. Aucoin managed to do it, and Neil Bogart, formerly the king of bubblegum music at Buddah Records, signed Kiss as the first recording act for his new label, Casablanca.

After recording their first album, *Kiss,* a collection of hard-driving, eardrum-pounding heavy-metal songs, Kiss took their act on the road. They made their debut on Dick Clark's *In Concert,* with flashpots of lights, twelve-foot-high neon letters that spelled KISS, snow machines, and stroboscopic police lights before a backdrop of gothic-castle ruins. Peter Criss levitated twenty feet above the audience behind his drums. Ace Frehley's guitar exploded like a rocket, bursting into flames on stage. Gene Simmons spat fire and blood at the audience, standing defiantly on his silver-and-red gargoyle boots. Their stage show reeked with pseudoviolence and theatricality. Not only did it attract the teenybopper crowds, it helped mask the mediocrity of the musical talents.

Concerts were very important to Kiss. They

The four faces of Kiss (clockwise from top left: Paul Stanley, Gene Simmons, Peter Criss, Ace Frehley). *(Courtesy of Casablanca Record and Filmworks. Copyright 1978 Aucoin Management, Inc., by agreement with Kiss)*

371

received very little radio airplay, so they had to sell themselves and their albums through live appearances—a long, slow way for a band to make it. Kiss was constantly on the road, sometimes seven nights a week. However, the group soon led the Kiss Army, their loyal fans who bought the albums, attended the concerts, and believed in the Kiss myth. The more Kiss was attacked, the more loyal the Kiss Army became. In 1976 Kiss gave their legions an anthem: "I Want to Rock and Roll All Night and Party Every Day."

Once Kiss was established as a concert attraction, the music became almost secondary. They were a strange phenomenon, for without radio airplay, Kiss albums—*Alive, Destroyer, Rock and Roll Over*— went gold or even platinum. By 1976 the most important part of the Kiss empire was merchandising. The group's goal at their concerts was to sell five dollars' worth of Kiss merchandise—T-shirts, programs, dolls—to every member of the audience. A sellout concert at Madison Square Garden could gross up to an additional one hundred thousand dollars in merchandise sales. The Kiss phenomenon also moved into other media. Marvel Comics published Kiss Comics which were printed with ink mixed with the group's own blood to spur sales. A made-for-TV movie, *Kiss Meets the Phantom,* was aired on NBC in 1978. Gene Simmons moved in with Cher Bono Allman and later, Diana Ross, and made the cover of *People* magazine. The merchandising of Kiss was so successful that the group was able to purchase an industrial park in Cincinnati as an investment.

By 1979, however, Kiss had begun to fade despite the fact that the quality of the music had actually improved. "Back in the New York Groove" from Ace Frehley's solo album—one of the four Kiss solo albums simultaneously released in December 1978— was potent, catchy rock and roll. Their summer of 1979 single, "I Was Made for Loving You," was a heady blend of heavy metal and disco that actually made the playlists on many top-forty, progressive, and disco radio stations. But while the group improved, their record sales slipped. Kiss became a victim of their own marketing theory. Their initial preteen audience grew up and grew out of Kiss. Every rock generation needs its own band, and to the up-coming crop of potential recruits for the Kiss Army, Kiss was now old news, their older brother's band.

ABBA

What is the biggest corporation in Sweden? Volvo? SAAB? Vita Herring? No, it is ABBA, "the largest-selling group in the history of recorded music." ABBA is paid for their record and song royalties in tangible goods, like shoes from Poland and wheat from Australia. They have therefore become the biggest exporter and most profitable business concern in Sweden. Now, who was the best pop group of the mid-seventies? The answer to that is always debatable, but ABBA wouldn't be a bad choice.

ABBA's melodies are not just catchy, they're positively addicting. ABBA's production is their strongest attribute. It is full-bodied, exquisitely woven, and richly laden with well-placed saxophones and exotic rhythm instruments, but never overpowering. Furthermore, for all their commercial success, ABBA isn't locked into one formula. On the contrary, ABBA is amazingly versatile, presenting reggae on "Tropical Loveland," disco on "Dancing Queen," fifties rock and roll on "I Do, I Do, I Do, I Do, I Do," European folk melodies on "Chiquitita," Gilbert and Sullivan-style operetta on "The Girl with the Golden Hair," and pure pop in "Mamma Mia." Agnetha and Annifrid's soaring vocals and harmonies with their slight teasing accents are the perfect vehicles for Benny and Bjorn's songwriting and production. If there is one serious fault with ABBA, it is Benny and Bjorn's lyrics, which can be inane and sometimes embarrassing, as in "When I Kissed the Teacher." However, this may be due to the fact that Swedes Benny and Bjorn do all their writing in English. But most importantly, ABBA's music is not the pretentious meanderings of art rock, the nonmusical theatricality of glitter rock, or the political mouthings of folk rock. It is three-minute doses of pure fun.

Bjorn Ulvaeus was a member of the folksinging Hootenanny Singers when he met Benny Andersson, the songwriter and organist for a Swedish rock band called the Hep Stars. After some drinking and discussion at a party in Vastervik in 1966, Bjorn and Benny decided to work on some songs together. Bjorn joined the Hep Stars for one concert tour, but Benny and Bjorn found that they couldn't write together seriously until the Hep Stars disbanded in 1969. Within two years Bjorn and Benny became two of the best-known songwriters in Sweden, turning out hit songs for Swedish pop stars and scoring many Swedish films.

In the autumn of 1970 Bjorn met Agnetha Faltskog and Benny met Annifrid Lyngstad. Agnetha began her singing career with a dance band at age fifteen, and by 1967 she was a successful recording star. Annifrid first sang on the stage when she was ten years old and eventually had her own orchestra, TV show, and successful solo career before she met Benny. The four first performed together as the Festfolk Quartet in November 1970. By July 1971 Benny had moved in with Annifrid, and Bjorn had married Agnetha.

That summer Benny and Bjorn were made producers at Stig Anderson's Polar Records in Stockholm. Benny and Bjorn recorded "She's My Kind of Girl" in 1972 with the girls singing backup vocals on the disc. A Japanese music executive passing through Paris heard the record and bought the publishing rights. "She's My Kind of Girl" became a big hit in Japan, and Benny and Bjorn were asked to take part in the competitive Tokyo Song Festival in November 1972. Frida and Agnetha joined the boys in Tokyo, helping out on their winning entry, "Santa Rosa." On their next single, "People Need Love," Frida and Agnetha received equal billing with Bjorn and Benny. The foursome finally decided to establish themselves as a group in 1973, taking the name ABBA from the initials of their first names. To gain a wider appeal, ABBA decided to write and record their music in English.

In 1973 Benny and Bjorn entered the internation-

ABBA. (From left: Benny, Agnetha, Frida, and Bjorn.)

ally televised Eurovision Song Contest. Benny, Bjorn, and Stig Anderson joined forces with Neil Sedaka and Phil Cody to write "Ring, Ring" for the contest. Strangely, "Ring, Ring" never made it past the first round, losing out in the Swedish Song Contest. Nevertheless, it did become a number-1 selling record all over Europe. ABBA decided to try the contest again in 1974, this time putting together an elaborately staged presentation to accompany their song "Waterloo." It won the Grand Prize in the Eurovision contest, reached number 6 in the United States, and climbed to number 1 in Sweden, Britain, Norway, Holland, Denmark, and Belgium, selling over five million records worldwide. "Honey Honey," a smooth and happy medium-tempo pop tune, barely cracked the top forty in America, peaking at number 34 in October 1974, but it became ABBA's second million seller in Europe.

Through elaborate lip-synched videotape productions ABBA proceeded to become the number-1 group in all the world except the United States, selling zillions of records. ABBA's second album, *ABBA,* sold four million copies in Britain before it was released, and the four singles from the album sold over a million each. Their rocker "S.O.S." climbed to number 10 in America and sold four million in Europe alone. "I Do, I Do, I Do, I Do, I Do" was an echo of the late fifties that captured the sound of Connie Francis and sold over two and a half million copies. "Mamma Mia," "So Long," and "Fernando," which sounded like a South American revolutionary folk song, all earned more precious metal for the group. *ABBA's Greatest Hits* album repackaged all their million sellers with some of their earlier material and sold over six million copies worldwide in 1976. The *Arrival* album in 1976 featured three more big hits: ABBA's first number-1 hit in America, "Dancing

Queen"; the beautiful ballad "Knowing Me, Knowing You"; and "Money, Money, Money."

In 1977 "Take a Chance on Me," with its a cappella opening, was the perfect summer song; and "The Name of the Game," a ballad with a good beat and lush harmonies, was another richly produced hit. But *ABBA, the Album* was sorely lacking in upbeat tunes, and the group began to wallow in the pretentiousness of their autobiographical "minimusical," "The Girl with the Golden Hair." Many rock critics raved over the new album, praising the group's "growth" and "sophistication." It also proved the group's least successful venture in America.

But ABBA was not ready to abandon their commercial sense for good reviews. Benny and Bjorn labored for close to two years in their state-of-the-art recording studio in Stockholm, and their hard work was rewarded when "Does Your Mother Know," a great rocker about jailbait, climbed the singles charts in the summer of 1979. *Voulez-Vous* marked a return to rock and roll for ABBA, with catchy tunes like "Kisses of Fire," "If It Wasn't for the Nights," "As Good As New," and the title cut, a searing song about a pick-up at a disco. In September 1979 the group made its long-awaited first concert tour of North America, playing to packed houses. Nineteen eighty-one brought the long-awaited album *Super Trooper* and a top-five hit single in America, a touching ballad about divorce called "The Winner Takes It All." ABBA secured their place as one of the world's great rock groups with their ability to put a smile on the face of rock and roll.

374

BOZ SCAGGS

Boz Scaggs almost became the lead singer of the Who in 1964. As usual, the Who were fighting. This time, Entwistle, Townshend, and Moon agreed that Daltrey was out and Scaggs would be his replacement. Unfortunately for Boz, "My Generation," a single the Who had cut several months earlier, suddenly took off and started to climb the charts in Britain. Daltrey's stuttering voice on the record saved him from being tossed out of the group, as concert promoters demanded the Who with their stammering lead singer. A contrite Roger was brought back into the fold. Poor Boz would have to wait twelve long years before he would see superstar success with his *Silk Degrees* album.

William Royce ("Boz") Scaggs went to England in 1964 from the University of Texas, where he had transferred from the University of Wisconsin. Boz was put on probation at Wisconsin for spending too much time playing in a blues band fronted by his old high school friend Steve Miller. However, in Texas, Boz joined another rock band, and they left for England at the onset of the British invasion.

Taking a band to England in 1964 was a little like driving the wrong way up a one-way street. The competition was overwhelming and cutthroat. Scaggs' band, the Wigs, fell apart shortly after they arrived, leaving Boz temporarily stranded.

After his brief romance with the Who, Scaggs bummed around Europe and India for a while, singing in the streets. He found some time to do a little recording in Stockholm, which was released on an album called *Boz* and distributed throughout Europe on the Polydor label with mild success.

In 1967 Scaggs hightailed it back home after receiving an invitation from Steve Miller to join a new band that Steve had just formed in San Francisco. Boz joined the Steve Miller Band just as the summer of love was winding to a close, playing rhythm guitar and contributing some of his own compositions to the

group's first two albums, *Children of the Future* and *Sailor.* However, he began to fight with Miller, so after the release of *Sailor* Boz bade farewell to the Miller Band.

Choosing a musical direction proved more difficult than Boz had anticipated. Jann Wenner, Boz' neighbor and the publisher of *Rolling Stone,* wanted to take a stab at producing an album with him. It seemed like a good idea to Scaggs so he let Wenner take him to Muscle Shoals, Alabama, where they cut some tunes for Atlantic Records in 1969. Duane Allman, then a session man in Muscle Shoals, contributed some of his best licks ever to Boz' bluesy "Loan Me a Dime" on that album. Nevertheless, Scaggs failed to make a dent in the charts despite the phenomenal airplay the record received in California. Boz was then quickly dropped from Atlantic. Columbia Records picked him up about a year later. Of his first four Columbia albums, though, only *Slow Dancer* broke the top one hundred, reaching number 81 on the charts. Although a critics' favorite and a star in California, his blues-flavored R & B style seemed hopelessly out of step with the rest of the country.

But then came *Silk Degrees* in 1976. It seemed to burst onto the scene from nowhere, rocketing to triple platinum and yielding four hit singles in the process. Boz received five Grammy nominations that year and copped a statuette for Best R & B Song of 1976 with "Lowdown." Scaggs was finally in the right place at the right time with *Silk Degrees.* Disco was just beginning to peak and the album's basic R & B with a doubled-up drum track was great dance music. The laid-back funk and trashy talk of "Lowdown" became the number-1 favorite at the discos, which in turn spurred sales of the album. Scaggs' pop leanings and past history with Steve Miller gained him access to both top forty and album-oriented radio stations. That resulted in widespread airplay for "It's Over," "Lido Shuffle," and "What Can I Say," all of which pushed the album into the stratosphere.

Another reason for the success of *Silk Degrees* was Boz' voice. Whether he was lazily slurring his way through a smooth ballad or pumping up a catchy dance number, Boz could capture his audiences with his crooning. His strength was in phrasing, communicating emotion through his songs. His thin, reedy voice never overpowered you. It charmed.

The man behind *Silk Degrees* was David Paich. Playing keyboards, arranging, and cowriting several of the record's tunes with Scaggs, Paich was the catalyst who was able to highlight and complement Boz' talents. However, Paich wasn't around for the next album, *Down Two, Then Left.* He had formed Toto with some of the *Silk Degrees* session men, and their first album was a textbook for aspiring pop arrangers. But Paich was sorely missed on *Down Two,* which sounded a little too much like a careful reworking of *Silk Degrees* with light, bouncy rhythms sweetened with just the right amount of strings and horns. But although it lacked the earlier disc's spontaneity, it sold over a million copies on the strength of Boz' reputation. The singles "Hard Times" and "Hollywood" from that album never really caught on, though.

Boz came back strong in the summer of 1980 with the album *Middleman.* While never quite able to scale the heights of Scaggs' masterpiece, *Silk Degrees, Middleman* had a power and charm all its own. Not everyone was charmed by *Middleman,* however; The *Los Angeles Times* refused to run an ad for the disc because of the allegedly sexist album cover. Nonetheless, "JoJo," a powerful rocker, became a top-ten single. "Love Look What You've Done To Me," a poignant cut from the soundtrack of *Urban Cowboy,* powered its way to the top in the fall of 1980; and following the release of a *Greatest Hits* package, Boz Scaggs found himself back on the charts—where he always belonged.

ELECTRIC LIGHT ORCHESTRA

The Electric Light Orchestra was originally supposed to be a rock-and-roll chamber ensemble, fusing basic rock with the subtler qualities of classical music in order to apply avant-garde concepts to a pop format. By 1976, however, ELO had become a slick money-making machine that cranked out hit after mainstream hit. A rock chamber ensemble had evolved into a rock corporation.

ELO is an offshoot of the Move, a band from Birmingham, England, that had a long string of hits in Britain but never penetrated the American market. In 1971 Move helmsmen Carl Wayne and Roy Wood announced their plans to create rock's first orchestra. The nucleus of the Move would be joined by strings, oboes, and bassoons, all as full-time band members. Unfortunately, Wayne and Wood immediately quarreled over the direction of the new group, and Wayne eventually left to pursue a short-lived career as a cabaret singer.

Wood then recruited another Birmingham musician, Jeff Lynne, to join the orchestra. Lynne had been leading his own group, the Idle Race, who had received a fair amount of critical acclaim for combining their Beatles-based style with heavy classical influence. Having had formal musical training, Lynne was quite excited about this new group, the Electric Light Orchestra, and soon he, Wood, and Move drummer Bev Bevan eagerly went to work on their debut album.

While they were working on that album, they financed themselves by releasing two brilliant albums as the Move, *Looking On* and *Message from the Country,* as well as a splendid two-sided single that featured Roy Wood's "California Man" (which Cheap Trick later reheated for their third L.P.) and its too-long-for-top-forty flip side, Jeff Lynne's "Do Ya."

Unfortunately, ELO's first effort, *No Answer,* met with a rather cool reception in 1972. It had some promising moments, but most of it was bogged down with weepy vocals and scratchy, ham-fisted strings. Wood had insisted on playing many of the instruments himself, even some that he had never played before. Eventually he was fighting over the group's direction again, only this time with Lynne. These differences were resolved when Wood split and took horn and keyboard player Bill Hunt with him. Bevan and Lynne now had to map out a new course for the group. First, they decided to establish the band in the United States rather than in Britain. Second, they decided to split their responsibilities, with Lynne supervising the music and the more outgoing Bevan handling their public relations. Both proved to be wise decisions.

Lynne wanted a band that could reproduce their albums faithfully in concert, so he swelled ELO's lineup to seven, adding Richard Tandy on keyboards, Mike de Alberquerque on bass, and London Symphony Orchestra defectors Mike Edwards, Colin Walker, and Wilf Gibson to his string section. Their first album together, *Electric Light Orchestra II,* was a vast improvement over *No Answer* and laid the foundation for the ELO sound. Tandy's synthesizer created a Phil Spector–like "wall of sound" and added a futuristic quality that transcended the band's chamber-music origins. But more importantly, this ELO could rock. Their bold blend of Ludwig Van and Chuck Berry on "Roll Over Beethoven" defined their approach and set the tone for the L.P. It also gave ELO their first taste of FM airplay in America.

To support this album and the subsequent release of *On the Third Day,* they crisscrossed the country for a back-breaking series of one-night stands and even found time for their American TV debut on *American Bandstand.* Like Grand Funk and Kiss, ELO got around the dearth of radio airplay by taking their music directly to the people, who liked what they heard. The group sounded bigger and richer than any other previous rock-and-roll stage show,

The Electric Light Orchestra (from left: Hugh McDowell, Richard Tandy, Bev Bevan, Melvyn Gale, Jeff Lynne, Mik Kaminski, and Kelly Groucutt).

roaring through Bach one moment, the Beatles the next. With the addition of violinist Mik Kaminski, who whirled and cavorted onstage like some bizarre character out of Dickens, ELO concerts were even more spectacular.

On the Third Day sold even better than *ELO II,* and their single, "Showdown," became a regional hit in the South, threatening to go national. After their tour with Three Dog Night the band finally went over the top with *Eldorado* in 1974. For this album Lynne pulled out all the stops. He augmented the band with a choir and a brass section and ran the album's cuts together to create what he called a "rock symphony." To make sure the album stood out in the record racks, he put Dorothy's ruby shoes from the movie *The Wizard of Oz* on the cover.

Musically *Eldorado* was reminiscent of the dream-like pop that the Beatles had produced on *Sgt. Pepper.* In fact, Lynne's voice even sounded like John Lennon's at times. Lyrically, the album was a frothy concoction of mythical mumbo-jumbo and obscure romantic allusions. Nevertheless the album slid up the charts to number 16, while its single, the wistful "Can't Get It Out of My Head," crossed over from the rock charts to the M.O.R. (Middle of the Road) charts, exposing the band's music to a wider market.

Having finally secured success, ELO did what a lot of bands did in the seventies—they played it safe. *Face the Music* was almost a carbon copy of *Eldorado.* The vocals were mixed a *bit* hotter, the music was a *little* rawer, and the strings a *bit* more lush; but basically the sound was the same. With a gargantuan potential on one side and the high mortality rate of rock acts on the other, ELO were not about to take any risks. As predictable as it was, *Face the Music* was money in the bank. It became the group's first gold album and yielded three monstrously successful singles: "Evil Woman," "Strange Magic," and "Nightrider."

To celebrate ELO's new superstar status, their label, United Artists, released a special collection of their early hot tracks called *Olé ELO* in 1976 for radio station use only. However, demand for the record was so strong that UA quickly pressed the album for general release to satiate the band's growing cadre of admirers.

ELO's studio release for 1976, *A New World Record,* was everything you'd come to expect from ELO and nothing more. They had their formula down pat from the opening instrumental passage to the standard rock/classical fusions such as "Rockaria." The Move's "Do Ya" was redone in a gimmicky slowed-down version. But the big innovation of the album wasn't in the music at all. It was the unveiling of the band's corporate logo on the cover. Soon it was plastered on everything from T-shirts to belt buckles.

A trendy spaceship cover graced ELO's seventh studio album, *Out of the Blue,* in 1977. It went platinum immediately and contributed still more songs to the ELO hit parade. But there was still no sign of any further musical development or variation from the formula. Except for the somewhat ambitious "Concerto for a Rainy Day," *Out of the Blue* was just more of the same old stuff. In 1979 ELO went to CBS and released *Discovery,* yet another pleasant-sounding formula album. With two smash singles, "Shine a Little Love" and the rocking "Don't Bring Me Down," *Discovery* had no trouble turning platinum.

Today ELO, with their laser light show, remain a top concert draw. They sound so big and so full on stage that you'd swear seven people couldn't possibly make all that music. In fact, the band frequently relies on prerecorded tapes of additional instruments and voices to augment their live performances. But their fans don't seem to mind at all, for their stage show more than makes up for the minor deceptions of ELO in concert.

BOB SEGER

Bob Seger and the Silver Bullet Band (from left: Drew Abbott, Robyn Robbins, Alto Reed, Bob Seger, Chris Campbell, and Charlie Allen Martin).

In the mid-seventies rock and roll started to remember a lot of the talented performers it had previously overlooked. One by one they came forward— Fleetwood Mac, Boz Scaggs, Steve Miller, Ted Nugent. But no one was more deserving than Robert Clark Seger, though getting rock and roll to recognize him took fifteen years.

In Detroit, Bob Seger had been a big star ever since his first group, the Last Heard, released "East

Side Story" in 1965. Detroit's urban rockers loved his follow-up, "Persecution Smith." His "Heavy Music" became an anthem around the Motor City.

Seger's records sold well in Detroit for three reasons. First, he was a local boy. Second, he shared that city's legendary "no nonsense" attitude toward rock and roll as exemplified by Mitch Ryder in the sixties and Ted Nugent today. Third, and most importantly, Bob was (and still is) managed by Punch Andrews, who owned Detroit's Palladium and Hideout labels and who knew so very well how to work that city's rock market. Nationally, however, it was a different story, because Seger's records were distributed by the Cameo-Parkway label, and they were too busy going broke to spend any time promoting records.

After Cameo-Parkway went under, Seger was picked up by Capitol. His first single for Capitol, "2 + 2 = ?" was a hard-rocking antiwar song, but it was released before antiwar songs came into fashion. At that time, not even the Doors could get their protest song "Universal Soldier" on the radio. So for his follow-up Bob laid off politics and offered the masculine swagger of "Ramblin' Gamblin' Man," which gave him a top twenty smash in the summer of 1968.

Bob's band eventually became a problem for him. The Bob Seger System, as they were known in those days, was run democratically, basically because of Seger's lack of self-confidence. However, too many band members making crucial musical decisions nearly killed his career. On his albums *Noah* and *Mongrel,* the band sounded fragmented. Onstage they were erratic. Seger then dumped the System and decided to go it alone. In an abrupt change of style he went acoustic on *Brand New Morning,* but the softer sound wasn't appealing, and he was lucky his Detroit fans didn't drop him for good after that fiasco. He returned to hard rock and roll on his next two albums, *Smokin' O.P.'s* and *Back in '72.* He was now with Warner Brothers. Each sold well enough in the Detroit area alone to guarantee his continued existence as a recording artist. Nevertheless, outside the Midwest Seger was a virtual unknown.

Seger finally had to take charge of his own records. He stopped jumping on bandwagons and started to cut his own songs. For *Bob Seger Seven* he put together a band that was willing to follow his direction. It was a good start, but it wasn't enough. The album helped spread his fame in the Midwest, but it just didn't click with the rest of the country. Fortunately, the band did, and they stayed on with Seger, dubbing themselves the Silver Bullet Band.

It was 1975 and Bob was playing some of his ballads for Glenn Frey of the Eagles. These songs were a new direction for Bob—softer, more introspective. Frey was knocked out by them and encouraged Seger to take a chance on releasing them. He did release *Beautiful Loser,* and it scarcely sold better than *Seven.* But it did catch the ears of the critics and brought Seger's songwriting talents some long-overdue praise. Unmotivated and bogged down in the studio, the band stalled for time by releasing a double album recorded live at Detroit's Lobo Hall. *Live Bullet* was Seger's breakthrough record. The four sides presented Seger's past efforts as a "greatest hits" package of sorts, featuring only his best songs and no filler. *Live Bullet* gave him a national audience for the first time since 1968 and established the Silver Bullet Band as one of rock's hottest live shows.

In the meantime Seger finished his long-delayed studio effort, *Night Moves,* released in 1976. The opening track set the mood for the entire album. "Rock and Roll Never Forgets," with its raucous beat, searing vocal, and hard look at the aging of the rock-and-roll generation, invoked the spirit of rock's founding fathers. The rest of the album alternated between more rocking bone-crushers and some sophisticated ballads.

The rock generation was growing older, and the album touched something sympathetic inside them. *Night Moves* became a staple on album-oriented stations around the country. Three hit singles— "Night Moves," "Rock and Roll Never Forgets," and "The Fire Down Below"—from that album landed in the top twenty. On the road Seger was met with S.R.O. crowds and thunderous ovations.

In 1978 Seger repeated the success of *Night Moves* with the release of *Stranger in Town.* The Silver Bullet Band shared the instrumental chores with the Muscle Shoals Rhythm Section here, and once again the songs were a potent mixture of tough, nasty rockers and gentle, vulnerable ballads. Seger spent more time recording *Stranger in Town* than he had on any of his previous albums, and the care showed. The up-tempo tunes like "Hollywood Nights" and "Old Time Rock and Roll" mingled well with the slow tunes like "We Got Tonite" and "The Famous Final Scene." This combination made pure platinum, for Seger's songs were aimed at older rock and rollers as well as teen-agers. Over half the cuts of this album were released as singles, and all met with incredible success. Seger once again posed his favorite question, "Is there rock after thirty?" in his 1980 album *Against the Wind.* As both the title cut and the album stormed up the charts, Bob Seger showed rock and rollers everywhere how to grow old gracefully and keep on rockin'.

Peter Frampton. *(Courtesy of A&M Records.*
Copyright 1977 Bandana Mdse., Inc.)

The Sound of 1976

PETER FRAMPTON

Although his boyish good looks and innocent appearance led some people to believe that he was a novice, by 1976 Peter Frampton was already a grizzled veteran of the rock-and-roll wars. Frampton got his first guitar when he was eight years old. Inspired by British pop star Cliff Richard and French jazz guitar virtuoso Django Reinhardt, Peter played guitar with various groups while still in his early teens. In 1966, Peter turned professional when he was sixteen years old, by joining the Herd, a British teenybop band. The Herd had a few hits in Britain and a small cult following, but were better known as teen idols than as talented musicians. Before the Herd broke up two years later, Peter had been tagged "The Face of '68," giving him his first taste of pop star adulation.

In 1969 Frampton formed Humble Pie with Steve Marriott, the former vocalist and rhythm guitarist of the Small Faces, drummer Jerry Shirley, and bassist Greg Ridley. After cutting two albums and touring America, the group returned to England to find that their record label, Immediate, had folded. The band then hired Dee Anthony to manage them and straighten out their affairs. Anthony, who had started out in 1951 as Tony Bennett's manager, was handling some of the best-known performers in rock by 1970, including Joe Cocker, the J. Geils Band, and Emerson, Lake and Palmer, through his firm, Bandana Enterprises. He soon swung a deal for Humble Pie with A&M records, and the band was off.

Humble Pie was a loud, aggressive band fronted by Steve Marriot, whose white R & B posturings made for some legendary concerts. The band released *Rock On* in 1971, a heavy rock album that was their most successful both artistically and commercially. However, they had serious musical differences of opinion, and eventually Frampton felt that he could not work with the band any longer. Peter split in 1971 after their blockbuster live album, *Rockin' at the Fillmore,* and Humble Pie replaced him with Dave "Clem" Clempson.

With his reputation as one of rock's premier guitarists, Frampton tried his hand at session work before seeking a solo career. Peter made a name for himself by playing on George Harrison's *All Things Must Pass,* Nilsson's *Son Of Schmilsson,* and John Entwistle's *Whistle Rhymes.* In 1972 Peter started to work on his first solo album and with some help from Ringo Starr, Billy Preston, and Nicky Hopkins, he turned out *Winds*

Of Change. Yet despite some critical acclaim, the album flopped, and Frampton was still an unknown.

Peter decided to build his reputation on the road, so in 1973 he put together Frampton's Camel and toured almost constantly for the next three years. The *Frampton's Camel* album dealt with the breakup of Peter's marriage, but it won little sympathy from the record-buying public. His next album and its title single, "Somethin's Happening," bombed, even though it was well received by the critics. Still, he had built a growing and dedicated following through his concerts, and his fourth solo album, *Frampton,* finally broke through, although modestly, onto the charts in late 1975.

A&M realized that Peter's greatest successes had been in concert, so it was only logical to cut a live album of his best tunes. *Frampton Comes Alive,* sort of a live greatest-hits package, far surpassed A&M's wildest expectations. Released in January 1976, the album was at the top of the charts by March. After sitting in the top five for a few months, *Frampton Comes Alive* roared back to number 1 in June and stayed there for an unprecedented seventeen weeks. In 1976 he had three monster hit singles from that live double album: "Show Me the Way," "Do You Feel Like We Do," and "Baby, I Love Your Way."

Unfortunately, Peter waited too long to release his follow-up to *Frampton Comes Alive.* When *I'm In You* finally came out at the end of 1977, its formulated attempt to cash in on "easy listening" rock was a major disappointment. The title track was a dreary love song. Peter offered a horribly limp version of Stevie Wonder's "Signed, Sealed, Delivered (I'm Yours)." His next mistake was in appearing in one of the biggest film fiascos of the seventies, Robert Stigwood's *Sgt. Pepper's Lonely Hearts Club Band.* After two straight box-office smashes, *Saturday Night Fever* and *Grease,* Stigwood figured that joining the hottest names in rock— Frampton and the Bee Gees—with the Beatles' "Sgt. Pepper" could not miss. Well, it did miss, because neither Frampton nor the Bee Gees could act, the film's plot was inane, and no one could top the Beatles' original versions of that material. This dismal movie proved to be an unwelcome setback to Peter's career.

To make matters worse, he was involved in a horrible car crash while vacationing in the Bahamas in 1978. Peter was flown to New York for special treatment and spent the next few months recuperating. When he resurfaced in 1979, he was sued unsuccessfully in a "palimony" case by his longtime girl friend, Penny McCall.

Though Peter no longer plays to S.R.O. crowds, he has the distinction of being one of the very few rock stars to have remained genuinely gracious before, during, and after his stint at the top. This alone should reserve him a seat in the rock-and-roll pantheon.

1977

"May the force be with you" became the catch-phrase of 1977, and Ben "Obi-Wan" Kenobe, Luke Skywalker, Darth Vader, R2-D2, and C3PO were the superstars of the year, as the film *Star Wars* smashed all box-office records. Kids of all ages cheered when the rebel alliance struck a blow against the empire; however, *Annie Hall* struck a blow against *Star Wars, Close Encounters of the Third Kind, The Turning Point,* and *Julia* when it snatched the Oscar for Best Picture of the year.

On television, the descendants of Kunta Kinte enthralled audiences every night for a week with *Roots,* the entertaining black history lesson that cemented ABC's position as the top TV network. In 1977 ABC also presented the jiggle of Suzanne Somers on *Three's Company,* the outrageous comedy of *Soap,* and the cruises of *The Love Boat. Lou Grant* moved from a TV station in Minneapolis to a newspaper in Los Angeles and became one of the best dramas on television. Nineteen seventy-seven was also the twenty-fifth birthday of *American Bandstand.*

Bandstand celebrated its anniversary with a new crop of hits like Jimmy Buffett's laid back, ironic "Margaritaville." The blue-eyed R & B of Darryl Hall and John Oates had a nasty edge on "Rich Girl," while Pablo Cruise rocked with "Watcha Gonna Do?" and Marvin Gaye crooned "Got to Give It Up."

The top ten singles of 1977 were "Tonight's the Night (Gonna Be Alright)" by Rod Stewart, "Best of My Love" by the Emotions, "I Just Want to Be Your Everything" by Andy Gibb, "Love Theme from *A Star Is Born*" by Barbra Streisand, "I Like Dreamin' " by Kenny Nolan, "Angel in Your Arms" by Hot, "Don't Leave Me This Way" by Thelma Houston, "(Your Love Has Lifted Me) Higher and Higher" by Rita Coolidge, "Torn Between Two Lovers" by Mary MacGregor, and "Undercover Angel" by Alan O'Day.

In sports, international superstar Pele and the Cosmos created soccer fever in America. Seattle Slew was the horse-racing sensation, winning the Triple Crown. Macrobiotic Bill Walton took the Portland Trail Blazers to the top of the NBA, while the "Orange Crush" of the Denver Broncos proved no match for the Dallas Cowboys in Super Bowl XII. The New York Yankees won their first World Series in fifteen years, knocking off the Los Angeles Dodgers.

Nineteen seventy-seven saw the worst plane crash in history as two jumbo jets collided in the Canary Islands, killing 582 people. Lightning turned off the power in New York City on July 13, creating a major blackout that led to looting sprees in some areas of the city. The maniacal murderer Son of Sam paralyzed New York City with fear for the entire year. The Concorde supersonic jet made its first controversial landing in the United States, and the Alaskan pipeline started to flow oil in 1977. Egyptian President Anwar el-Sadat made a historic visit to Israel in November, moving the two countries closer to a lasting peace. Anita Bryant, born-again Christian, singer, and spokeswoman for Florida orange juice, declared war on homosexuals. And on August 15, Elvis Presley, the king of rock and roll, died in Memphis.

It was 1977—the twenty-third year of rock and roll.

Daryl Hall and John Oates.

ROD STEWART

With his shaggy blond mane, satin pants, and shirt open to the waist, strutting and prancing onstage, he is the quintessence of a rock star in concert. When he and his mates—each with a bottle of whiskey in one hand and a mug of beer in the other—trash hotel suites and the first-class sections of transcontinental aircraft, he is merely acting the way rock and rollers are expected to act. With his love life splashed across the front pages—Britt Ekland this month, actor George Hamilton's ex-wife the next—he is living up to the public's fantasy image of a rock star's life-style. He is Rod Stewart—the very image of rock and roll in the seventies.

Although he claims to be from Scotland, Rod Stewart was born and bred in North London. He attended the same secondary school as the Kinks' Ray and Dave Davies, where he learned to play a little guitar and harmonica. As a teen-ager he sang along with his favorite records by Elvis, Eddie Cochran, and his main man, Sam Cooke.

He left school to embark upon a musical career. When he couldn't feed himself as a musician, Rod took a variety of odd jobs, including gravedigging. He also played the English equivalent of semipro soccer for a while. But despite his love for soccer, he preferred his music, so he wandered around Spain and Italy, singing folk songs. At this time Rod learned to play banjo from his mentor, Wizz Jones, the English folk legend. Charged with vagrancy in Spain, Rod was eventually put on a plane back to England.

Rod's first professional gig was with the British blues band Jimmy Powell and the Dimensions, but the association was brief. Rod was a big fan of the popular British blues artists of the time, especially Alexis Korner and Cyril Davies. Long John Baldry, who launched the careers of a number of rock stars, including Elton John, discovered the raspy-voiced Stewart and hired him in 1965 for his R & B band, Long John Baldry and the Hoochie Coochie Men.

When the Hoochie Coochie Men broke up, Baldry put together a high-powered R & B ensemble called Steam Packet and invited Rod, Brian Auger, and Julie Driscoll to join him. Musical differences between Rod and Auger splintered Steam Packet, and Rod left in a huff to join Shotgun Express, a similar band that included Mick Fleetwood and Peter Green, who would later form Fleetwood Mac. Shotgun Express was wracked with problems from the very beginning and soon disintegrated. Once again Rod was out of work.

By 1968 Rod's reputation as a lead singer had grown considerably, and famed guitarist Jeff Beck asked Rod to join his brand-new quartet, along with Ron Wood on bass and Mick Waller on drums. With such personnel the Jeff Beck Group promised to be a very exciting unit. Rod's hoarse vocals were unique, and his phrasing was exceptional. Originally a lead guitarist, Ron Wood switched to bass just for the chance to join Beck and company. The rhythm section of Waller and Wood proved to be the perfect complement to Beck's guitar and Rod's voice.

The Jeff Beck Group toured the United States in the spring of 1968. They were a smash, getting rave reviews from the critics and standing ovations at such notable rock halls as the Fillmores East and West. Although a standout, Stewart still was not a fully developed front man. *Truth,* the Beck Group's first album, released in 1968, was a fine debut with a mixture of innovative new versions of rock classics and newly penned tunes such as "Let Me Love You" and "Rock My Plimsoul." The album was both a commercial and a critical success, but as the Jeff Beck Group prepared to begin work on their follow-up L.P., Rod signed a solo contract with Mercury Records, claiming that it would not interfere with the band's activities.

At this time Rod Stewart and Ron Wood became the best of friends, so when Beck decided to replace Wood and Mick Waller, a restless Rod, who had never gotten along well with Beck, quit. Ronnie Wood returned to playing lead guitar with the Small Faces, who'd had a big hit with their single "Itchycoo Park" and *Ogden's Nut Gone Flake,* the first album ever with a round record jacket. The Small Faces had just lost their lead vocalist-guitarist Steve Marriott, and the remaining members—Ronnie Lane, Ian Mac-Lagan, and Kenney Jones—wanted to continue as a band. Ronnie Wood filled their guitarist slot, but they still needed a singer, so Rod was asked to consider the position. He accepted the offer in 1970.

The "new" Faces (they dropped the "Small") recorded their debut album for Warner Bros. *First Step* was generally considered uneven, but it did have some flashes of brilliance. Their second L.P., *Long Player,* was more varied and featured a great version of Paul McCartney's "Maybe I'm Amazed." The Faces, who were known for their rapport with their fans, were always a very entertaining band in concert, despite the fact that they were sometimes sloppy and off-key. They were certainly one of the most colorful bands on the rock scene with their satin suits, tartan scarves, and "Rod the Mod's" spiky shag haircut. With Rod kicking soccer balls into the audience, wiggling his behind, and playing off the other members of the band, the Faces put on a good-time rock-and-roll show. Yet despite their success in concert, the Faces' albums—*A Nod Is As Good As a Wink to a Blind Horse, Ooh La La*—were never huge successes on the charts and were greeted with mixed reviews. Finally, in 1975, with Rod's solo career in full swing and Ron Wood joining the Rolling Stones, the Faces disintegrated.

Rod Stewart's simultaneous solo career took some time to get off the ground. His first solo effort, *The Rod Stewart Album,* which included "Handbags And Gladrags," "Man Of Constant Sorrow," and "An Old Rain Coat Won't Ever Let You Down," was moving, but it did not move from the record racks. His second album, *Gasoline Alley,* was one of his most consistent works, displaying his talent as an interpreter of other people's songs, such as Dylan's "Only a Hobo" and Elton John and Bernie Taupin's "Country Comfort." Unfortunately, *Gasoline Alley* sold little better than the first album had. What Rod needed was a hit single.

"Maggie May" finally made Rod Stewart's career, sweeping out of the blue to the top of the singles charts for three weeks in October 1971. A rousing rocker about a bedroom dilemma, "Maggie May" set the tone for other Stewart singles about women he'd rather not see when he woke up in the morning— "Stay with Me" and "You Wear It Well." His albums of 1971 and 1972—*Every Picture Tells a Story* and *Never a Dull Moment*—moved easily from ballads to window rattlers, and both went gold. His next album, *Smiler,* was delayed because of bickering between record labels over recording rights, and when it finally was released in late 1974, Stewart fans wished it had never been released at all; it was sloppy and lacked inspiration. In 1975 Stewart moved to Hollywood and recorded *Atlantic Crossing* with some of the top American session men, like Steve Cropper and Duck Dunn. However, this album was such a disaster that many felt that Rod was washed up in rock and roll.

Rod bounced back with a vengeance, though. The single "Tonight's the Night"—Stewart's seduction of the innocent—was number 1 for eight weeks in 1976. And current girl friend Britt Ekland's cooing in French didn't hurt record sales one bit. "The First Cut Is the Deepest" followed "Tonight's the Night" right up the charts. "The Killing of Georgie," the ballad of the senseless murder of a homosexual friend, showed another side of Rod's music and earned him FM airplay. After Britt and Rod's nasty parting, 1977's *Foot Loose and Fancy Free* presented a couple of autobiographical pieces. "You're in My Heart," a romantic lovesong on that album, became a big chart success for Rod. By 1979 Rod had gotten over Britt and had married Alana Hamilton, settling into a more sedate life-style. Rod then crossed over into disco, recording one of the biggest hits of early 1979, "Do Ya Think I'm Sexy?" Rod was also the highlight of the Year of the Child concert at the United Nations, crooning "If you want my body..." and strutting his stuff on the floor of the Security Council. With Rod Stewart at the U.N., rock and roll had surely come a long way.

Rod Stewart.

STEVE MILLER BAND

Steve's career started in Texas, where he learned electric guitar from the man who made it famous—Les Paul. Les and his wife, Mary Ford, were friends of Steve's family, as were Charlie Mingus and T-Bone Walker. By age twelve Miller knew his instrument well enough to form his first group, The Marksmen, with young Boz Scaggs. They played their raw mixture of rock and blues throughout Texas and Oklahoma.

Miller left Texas to attend the University of Wisconsin at Madison, intending to major in comparative literature. Proust, Tolstoy, and Faulkner never interested him as much as his guitar did, though, and it wasn't long before his studies started taking a back seat to his music. By the time Scaggs arrived in Madison a year later, Miller was in a band called Knight Train, playing frat parties dressed in matching gold lamé vests and doing little dance routines to accompany their numbers. But the strain of being a singer, guitarist, choreographer, and scholar eventually proved to be too much for Steve, so he left the university to spend some time abroad.

After a year in Copenhagen, Miller returned to the States and headed for the electric blues scene that was shaping up around Chicago in the mid-sixties. There he jammed with black masters like Muddy Waters, Otis Rush, Buddy Guy, and Junior Wells, as well as some of the young white boys who were aping them, like Paul Butterfield, Mike Bloomfield, and Barry Goldberg. Miller tried to form a band with Goldberg, who was then fronting his own World War III Blues Band, but nothing came of their plans.

Steve then stuck a flower in his hair and headed for San Francisco in November 1966. The psychedelic craze was just getting under way in San Francisco, and there were literally hundreds of groups in town itching to break onto the national scene. Miller took one look at the competition and decided that his old college chums could blow them all away. A phone call

back to Wisconsin brought the Steve Miller Blues Band to the West Coast for their San Francisco debut at the Matrix. Paul Butterfield suggested that Steve drop the "Blues" from the band's name to keep his musical options open for the future. It was a piece of advice that the Butterfield Blues Band never took.

By January of 1967 the Steve Miller Band was one of the regular bands at the Fillmore's archrival, the Avalon Ballroom. Their unique blend of Chicago blues and gutsy rock earned them an invitation to the Monterey Pop Festival in June. Steve's band got their first taste of recording shortly thereafter, backing up Chuck Berry on his *Live at the Fillmore* album.

At this time record scouts were all over the Bay Area searching for "flower power" groups. The spaced-out love children were easy pickings for the record companies, naively signing whatever contract they were offered. But not Steve. When Capitol showed an interest in his band, he held out for fifty thousand dollars up front plus a royalty rate that was three times the industry average. Miller's trend-setting contract also gave him the right to choose when and where his albums would be recorded. That clause alone broke the stranglehold of label-owned studios on artists and marked the beginning of the end for inferior staff producers, who were arbitrarily assigned to bands.

A letter from Miller brought Boz Scaggs back to the group in time for their first album. Steve chose to record it in England with Glyn Johns at the controls. Since Miller had already put the album together in demo form, *Children of the Future* was completed in record time. Capitol gave the disc strong promotional support just as the band was starting a major European tour in May 1968.

The lack of American concerts could have been the reason for *Children*'s disappointing sales. But whatever the reason, the band was back in the studio five months later. By this time, Scaggs and Miller were

Steve Miller. *(David Stahl)*

feuding. At one point they just refused to show up at each other's sessions. Nevertheless, they plowed ahead and finished the album. *Sailor* sold significantly better than *Children of the Future* and produced one of the first classics of album-oriented radio, the satirical, bluesy "Living in the U.S.A." However, it was clear that Boz Scaggs' emerging talent needed more room to grow, so he left the Miller Band shortly after the album was completed.

More albums followed: *Brave New World, Your Saving Grace, Number 5, Rock Love,* and *Recall the Beginning...Journey from Eden.* Sales were strong enough to continue Miller's recording contracts but not strong enough to achieve his dream of independent wealth. Steve Miller changed the band's personnel frequently. Curley Cooke, Tim Davis, Ben Sidran, Lonnie Turner, and many others came and went over the next few years. Perhaps the trouble was with Miller himself. He couldn't seem to decide who he was. On *Sailor* he was the "Gangster of Love." On *New World* he became the "Space Cowboy." Then on *Rock Love,* he declared, "The Gangster's Back!" No artist since Bo Diddley had spent so much time singing about himself.

In 1973 Miller finally came clean on his eighth studio album, admitting that he was really "The Joker." Steve's candid confession earned him his first gold single. The album of the same name went platinum but the rest of the cuts were not nearly as

provocative or interesting as the title track. Miller then decided to take a short hiatus from recording.

He returned in 1976 with *Fly Like an Eagle,* which soared through the summer on the strength of its two top singles, "Take the Money and Run" and "Rock'n Me." Many album-oriented FM radio stations featured the rest of the album's cuts. Steve Miller's superstar status was now confirmed.

Miller's next album, *Book of Dreams,* became his biggest L.P. ever almost upon release. It sold four million copies and remained high on the charts for sixteen months. But that hardly seemed surprising. Miller often borrowed riffs for fun and profit, and he had the good sense to borrow from the best. At times "Jet Airliner" reminded you of Cream's "Crossroads," and the opening lyrics of "Winter Time" sounded like someone trying to remember the words to "California Dreamin'."

As a fitting tribute to his transition from blues band to jukebox, Steve closed out the seventies with a greatest-hits package. They were all there: "Jet Airliner," "Jungle Love," and the rest—all bright, bouncy, big-beat numbers. It's the kind of stuff Miller does best: flashy chunks of guitar, a few cosmic noodlings on the synthesizer—sort of a junk food for the ear served up piping hot for your consumption.

STEELY DAN

Apparently no one ever clued in Donald Fagen and Walter Becker to the ground rules of rock and roll at Bard College in upstate New York in 1967. Otherwise they might have given up their quest for a successful jazz-rock fusion before they'd even started. Their initial bands, like the Bad Rock Group (allegedly featuring Chevy Chase on drums) made little headway. Between 1970 and 1972 they had to play backup for Jay and the Americans while trying to peddle their songs to music publishers around New York.

Their first break came when a friend, producer Gary Katz, was offered a position with ABC/Dunhill on the West Coast. Katz agreed to accept only if Fagen and Becker were hired as staff songwriters. ABC agreed, and the three headed for L.A. Gary convinced Fagen and Becker that the easiest way to get their songs recorded was to form a band and do it themselves. They sent for Denny Dias, who had played in one of their early college bands, while Gary found two East Coast session men, Jeff Baxter (a former member of Boston's ill-fated Ultimate Spinach) and Jim Hodder. Becker and Baxter handled the guitar chores, Dias took the bass spot, Hodder the drums, and Fagen played keyboards and sang. And though most top-forty programmers never realized it, the band took its name from a steam-powered dildo in William Burroughs' *Naked Lunch.* The band thought it sounded provocative, enigmatic, and intriguing.

Provocative, enigmatic, and intriguing is a pretty accurate description of their first album, *Can't Buy a Thrill,* which was released in 1972. Donald Fagen's vocals were distant and dispassionate, yet somehow his flat, nasal whine enhanced the pessimistic weirdness of his songs. Katz's pristine production showcased the unusually effective hooks, making big hits out of "Do It Again" and "Reeling In the Years." Elliot Randall's blistering guitar work on the latter began

what became a Steely Dan tradition of featuring guest appearances by brilliant studio musicians on their records. All in all, it was a remarkable album from a band that had yet to play their first live date.

When album sales took off, the group went on a mad dash from coast to coast, often playing dives with little or no rehearsal. To call this tour haphazard and unorganized would be kind. It was such a disaster that their manager, who didn't care for Fagen's voice, forced David Palmer into the lineup for added vocal punch.

Somehow they survived and returned to L.A. to begin work on their follow-up L.P. Once they were safely inside the studio, Palmer was sacked. From now on Donald Fagen was Steely Dan's only lead singer. With that out of the way, the band settled down to record *Countdown to Ecstasy.* The group exploded their early "singles band" image with longer, more complex cuts like "Show Biz Kids" and "My Old School." But without a hit single to promote the album, it never had a chance, topping off at a rather disappointing number 35 in the charts.

A few more concerts followed in 1974 with the addition of Mike McDonald on keyboards. However, the bad taste of that first tour lingered. Fagen and Becker preferred to remain in the studio, polishing and reworking their songs until every note and nuance was perfect. Of course, those two could make ends meet without touring, for if the albums sold well, they had their songwriting royalties as well as their share of the performer's take. But for the rest of the group the lack of touring was a hardship. One by one they quit. Baxter and McDonald went to the Doobie Brothers; Dias and Hodder to parts unknown.

Pretzel Logic brought Steely Dan back to the radio with "Rikki Don't Lose That Number." Again, the Katz production was immaculate, the hooks were fresh, and the oblique lyrics had fans and disc jockeys alike wondering what "that number" was (a song? a

phone number? a joint?). *Pretzel Logic* went gold and firmly established the band's witty but weird reputation.

Steely Dan was now solely a creature of the studio, and Fagen and Becker could realize a lifelong dream. They could record their songs with the finest studio talent available, drawing on the best musicians rock and jazz had to offer. Artists like Wayne Shorter, Tom Scott, and Larry Carlton were brought in to execute Becker and Fagen's increasingly challenging charts. Because credit on Steely Dan albums was always sparse, fans delighted in trying to figure out exactly who was playing what.

Hits seemed to follow effortlessly, generating both top-forty and FM airplay. *Katy Lied,* their fourth album, begat the superbly cynical "Black Friday."

Steely Dan—Donald Fagen (left) and Walter Becker.

Royal Scam in 1976 yielded "Kid Charlemagne" and "The Fez." *Aja,* released a year later, was the biggest Steely Dan album of all, featuring "Peg," "Deacon Blues," "Josie," "Black Cow," and the title track. So strong was the band's appeal that even when the movie *FM* bombed in 1978, their recording of the title track still became a hit.

Steely Dan has proved that musical integrity doesn't always have to take a back seat to commercial considerations and that selling records doesn't have to mean selling out. Perhaps this is the final contradiction in a band that seems to thrive on them.

393

BARRY MANILOW

Barry Manilow. *(Lee Gurst)*

Barry Manilow was born in Brooklyn in 1946. Doo-wop music was king in New York when Barry was growing up and kids sang rock and roll in five-part harmony on their stoops. In the fifties there was a street-corner symphony on every block. Moreover,

Broadway was just a subway ride away, and Barry saw musicals like *The King and I, My Fair Lady, Carousel,* and *The Most Happy Fella.* Barry's mother was a fan of the big-band music of the forties, and Barry's stepfather introduced him to the jazz sounds of Gerry Mulligan and Count Basie. This varied musical background is one of the reasons Barry Manilow can serve up such a smorgasbord of musical delights today.

Barry started to play the accordion when he was seven and switched to piano when he turned thirteen. However, music was only a sideline for the young Mr. Manilow until one year as an advertising major at City College in New York changed his mind about his hobby, and he transferred to the New York College of Music. Barry soon transferred again to the prestigious Juilliard School of Music.

While attending Juilliard, Barry took a job in the mailroom at CBS to help pay his bills. There he met a director who was interested in turning a melodrama, *The Drunkard,* into a musical. When he learned that Manilow was going to Juilliard, the director asked Barry to arrange a few songs in the public domain for the drama. Barry knew opportunity knocking when he heard it, so instead of adapting a few old songs, Barry composed an entire original score. Manilow's musical version of *The Drunkard* ran for eight years off-Broadway.

The talent hidden in the mailroom had been discovered. In 1967 Manilow became the musical director of a talent show on WCBS-TV in New York. Ed Sullivan then hired him as the musical conductor for his production company. Barry composed a new theme for *The Late Show* to replace the classic "The Syncopated Clock." At the end of 1969 Manilow left CBS to put together an act with a female singer, "Jeanne and Barry." Together they paid their dues playing motel lounges, second-rate clubs, and piano bars, before settling in for two years as the opening act at Upstairs at the Downstairs, a New York City nightclub.

In his spare time Barry wrote commercial jingles, and by the early seventies he was Madison Avenue's Golden Boy, the undisputed master of the jingle. Barry wrote the jingle for State Farm Insurance, ("Like a good neighbor, State Farm is there"). He sang solo on "You deserve a break today" for McDonald's. Barry wrote, arranged, and sang jingles for all kinds of products. Anytime, day or night, television viewers could hear Manilow singing the praises of Band-Aids, Dr. Pepper, or Stridex. Then, at a recording session for a Kentucky Fried Chicken commercial in 1972, Barry made an acquaintance that changed his life.

When the casting call went out for singers for the Kentucky Fried Chicken jingle, Ron Dante, the voice of the Archies, the Cufflinks, and the Detergents, was hired. Between "Finger-lickin' good" takes, Manilow and Dante became friends. When Barry found out that Dante was a record producer, he asked him to listen to some of his original compositions. Dante was floored. They soon rented a recording studio, and Dante produced a master tape of Manilow material that he tried to sell to a variety of record companies. While waiting for a record contract to come through, Dante convinced Barry to take a fill-in job as the house pianist at a gay hangout, the Continental Baths, where he found himself backing Bette Midler. Bette soon became the rage of New York, and Barry became Bette's musical director, arranger, and pianist.

Still waiting for a recording contract, Manilow accepted an offer to coproduce and arrange Bette Midler's first album, *The Divine Miss M.* After winning a Grammy for his work on that record, Barry signed with Bell Records in 1973. Bell, however, was in a state of flux, about to become Arista Records with Clive Davis at the helm, and Manilow's first album, produced by Ron Dante, was lost in the shuffle. Barry then accompanied Bette Midler on her 1973 tour, and the Divine Miss M convinced the still-unknown Mr. Manilow to open her second act by singing three of his own originals. After producing Bette's second album, Barry took off in early 1974 on a solo concert tour, the highlight of which was a medley of his commercial jingles.

Arista had not given up on Manilow, though, and they invited him to try his luck on a second album. In November 1974 *Barry Manilow II* was released. Shortly thereafter, Barry made his television debut on *American Bandstand,* singing "Mandy," the single from that album. On January 11, 1975, it was the number-1 song in the nation. The public finally had discovered Barry Manilow.

Thanks to his broad musical background, honed by his years of writing commercial jingles, Barry Manilow had an ear for what the public wanted to hear. Manilow and his backup group, Lady Flash, followed "Mandy" up the charts with the explosively uptempo hit "It's A Miracle." In the summer of 1975 Arista plucked a single from Manilow's first album, and Barry's variation on a Chopin étude, "Could It Be Magic," became the number-7 song nationwide, climbing to number 1 in many cities. Barry then took a song written by ex-Beach Boy Bruce Johnston, gave the ballad an inspirational treatment, and made "I Write the Songs," one of the top-selling records of 1976. Barry hit the charts consistently in 1976 and 1977 with "Tryin' to Get the Feeling Again," "This One's for You," "Weekend in New England," and "Looks Like We Made It," a series of love songs that avoided being saccharine only because of Manilow's commercial touch and Ron Dante's lively production. Barry finally got out of his sentimental rut in 1978 with a bouncy disco whodunit, "Copacabana (At the Copa)." Also to his credit are the lyrics to "Bandstand Boogie" and the lyrical recording of the song, the *American Bandstand* theme, which was originally written by the Les Elgart Orchestra. Manilow has consistently struck the heartstrings of record-buyers and, though often criticized, has maintained his spot at the top of the charts.

The Sound of 1977

FLEETWOOD MAC

Nineteen seventy-six was the year that America surrendered to what can only be called a Fleetwood Mac Attack. It began slowly with the release of *Fleetwood Mac,* the tenth album from a band whose nine previous efforts had gained them little more than a cult following. The album gathered strength through the fall and winter of 1975 as its simple, straight-ahead sound sent it crashing through the boundaries that normally separated top forty, progressive, and middle-of-the-road music. Finally its full fury broke loose in 1976, sweeping across America like a musical tornado.

Fleetwood Mac sold over four million copies that year. Its success was simply one more unlikely event in the band's extremely unlikely history.

The group began during the British blues revival of the late sixties, the principal members coming from John Mayall's Blues Breakers, whose alumni include Eric Clapton, Jack Bruce, and Mick Taylor, among others. In 1967 guitarist Peter Green, bassist John McVie, and drummer Mick Fleetwood left the Blues Breakers to form a new band that they hoped would preserve the "purity" of the blues, since they felt Mayall had sold his musical soul for commercial acceptability.

Initially they called themselves Peter Green's Fleetwood Mac (Mac being short for McVie). With the addition of Jeremy Spencer on guitar, they were off and running, playing rock venues such as London's Marquee Club. Their association with Mayall had already given them a notoriety of sorts, and it wasn't too long before they had enough of a following to release their first album, *Fleetwood Mac,* on Britain's Blue Horizon label in 1968.

Fleetwood Mac's manager, Clifford David, introduced the band to another guitarist, Danny Kirwan, who joined them in time for *English Rose,* their second album. Behind an outrageous cover photo of Mick Fleetwood in comic drag was a tight, well-thought-out collection of early Fleetwood Mac classics, including Peter Green's "Black Magic Woman" and the group's British instrumental hit "Albatross." Green's guitar licks were so tasty on this album that when Santana covered "Black Magic Woman" a year later, Carlos lifted Peter's solo almost note for note. The group then toured the U.S. in 1968 and again in 1969, when another Peter Green tune, "Oh Well," almost cracked the American charts. However, even after it was hastily added to the already-recorded *Then*

Fleetwood Mac (from left: Lindsey Buckingham, Christine McVie, Mick Fleetwood, Stevie Nicks, and John McVie).

Play On album, Fleetwood Mac was still hard pressed to find an audience in America.

Then personnel problems afflicted the group. After Green mixed equal doses of acid and religion, he suddenly left the group in mid-tour to pursue a "Christian" life-style of menial labor, which included a brief stint as a gravedigger. A similar thing happened to Jeremy Spencer about a year later. Spencer simply failed to show up for a gig at L.A.'s Whiskey A Go Go one night. When he returned three days later with a blissed-out grin and a haircut, he announced that he was withdrawing from the band to follow the Children of God. Before anybody could talk him out of it, he was gone.

In the meantime Christine Perfect had been moving the band in a new, pop-oriented direction. Christine had replaced Green as lead singer, coming from another British blues band, Chicken Shack. Her ability to play keyboards and compose were valuable assets to the band. She also happened to be married to John McVie.

Fleetwood Mac's slow drift toward pop began on *Kiln House* in 1970. It continued when Californian Bob Welch replaced Jeremy Spencer. On the next four albums, *Future Games, Bare Trees, Penguins,* and *Mystery to Me,* Welch and Christine McVie traded vocals and songwriting chores. His songs "Sentimental Lady" on *Bare Trees* and "Hypnotized" on *Mystery to Me* rank among the band's best work from this period.

Just when things seemed to be settling down, Danny Kirwan walked out in 1972. Then his replacement, Robert Weston, was fired a year later after he was discovered with Fleetwood's wife. After all that, the band learned that there was another Fleetwood Mac on the road playing their songs. The bogus Fleetwood Mac had been assembled by their manager, Clifford Davis, who claimed to have sole ownership of the name. Davis was promptly fired, and a court battle over the name ensued. Mick and John were ultimately granted legal custody of their own last names, and the imposters were forced out of business.

After the trial Fleetwood Mac moved their base of operations to Los Angeles. They also took over their own management, and most of those duties fell squarely on the shoulders of six-foot-six Mick Fleetwood, who seemed to enjoy the role. The rest of the band were now free to work on their ninth album, *Heroes Are Hard to Find.* But despite heavy touring to back the album, it reached no higher than the mid-thirties on the charts. By 1975 Bob Welch had quit, and the band had to hang out its old "Help Wanted" sign again.

Mick Fleetwood remembered a tape he had heard when he was shopping for recording studios for the band's next album. Producer Keith Olsen had played Fleetwood a demo he'd cut with a pop-rock duo, which

Christine McVie.

Mick Fleetwood.

398

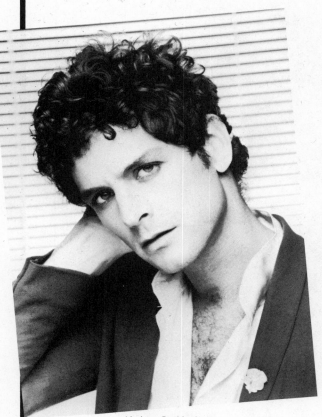

Lindsey Buckingham.

Stevie Nicks.

John McVie.

An ex-member of Fleetwood Mac who made it on his own—Bob Welch. *(Olivier Ferrand)*

was later released on Polydor. Olsen's production was impressive, but Mick was more impressed with the duo, Lindsey Buckingham and Stevie Nicks. Fleetwood soon contacted the couple.

When Buckingham and Nicks went to see Fleetwood, they were hoping the drummer would grant them an audition. To their surprise, Mick wasn't interested in an audition. He just wanted to know if Buckingham and Nicks were interested in joining Fleetwood Mac. Flabbergasted, they stammered out their approval. It was a union made in rock-and-roll heaven.

Lindsey Buckingham met Stevie (née Stephanie) Nicks when they played together in an acid-rock ensemble called Fritz. The band's collective agreement to keep their hands off Stevie kept their relationship strictly platonic for three and a half years. After Fritz split up, Stevie and Lindsey fell together on- and offstage. After two years of sporadic touring and their Polydor album, which sold zilch everywhere except Birmingham, Alabama, they were still looking for that one big break. That break came with Mick's offer. For Fleetwood Mac, they proved to be the missing ingredient that made the *Fleetwood Mac* magic. This was a back-to-the-basics kind of album without heavy-handed strings or synthesizers, self-indulgent guitar solos, or overly obvious "concept" packaging. Instead, using only guitar, keyboard, bass, and drums, it demonstrated a diversity and depth enhanced by the three distinctly different personalities who shared the singing and songwriting tasks. Buckingham's guitar work was lean, muscular, and to the point—very reminiscent of Harrison's early work with the Beatles. Christine McVie's sadder but wiser vocals complemented Stevie Nicks' coquettish sex-kitten purrs. And it was all backed by perhaps the best rhythm section in rock—McVie and Fleetwood.

Warners was caught flat-footed by the initial response to the album. After nine mediocre sellers, no one expected this kind of reaction. The label was finally coerced into releasing Christine's "Over My Head" as a single. But still skeptical, they had Buckingham overdub a more strident guitar track onto the song's opening. Whether the new opening made a great difference or not, "Over My Head" had no trouble gliding up to number 16. Stevie's ode to a Welsh witch, "Rhiannon," soon eclipsed "Over My Head" on the charts. A third single, "Say You Love Me," followed "Rhiannon." There seemed to be no end in sight.

Onstage the band was electric. Buckingham and Nicks added the element of showmanship that had been lacking from the band. Draped in chiffon, Stevie would spin in circles, building her songs to a frenetic climax with Lindsey's guitar leaning in at just the right moments, crackling with erotic intensity. For a full six months they barnstormed the cow palaces and stadiums of America, holding crowds spellbound with their virtuosity.

Curious fans went to the record bins digging for old Fleetwood Mac albums. This meant additional royalty payments, which didn't please Peter Green, who was angered when the checks arrived in the mail. He wanted nothing to do with Fleetwood Mac or his sordid rock-and-roll past, so he went to his accountant and explained, at gunpoint, that the payments simply had to stop! Green was swiftly and unceremoniously committed to a mental institution.

But this was the least of the band's worries. John and Christine McVie weren't speaking, having ended a seven-year marriage. Buckingham and Nicks soon followed suit. Fleetwood and his wife were already in divorce court. Then, to top it all off, Warner Bros. started breathing down their necks for a follow-up album.

However, the group had been through too much to throw it all away because of personal problems. During 1976, as the million-dollar melodrama that had become their lives held their audience captive, Fleetwood Mac struggled fitfully to produce another album. And the fact that all three songwriters could write only painfully autobiographical material about shattered love affairs didn't make their work any easier. But the torment added a certain edge, an emotional intensity that is impossible to counterfeit. As a result, *Rumours* was an even bigger smash than *Fleetwood Mac,* previously the best-selling album in Warner's history. This time the singles preceded the album. "Go Your Own Way," "Dreams," "Don't Stop," and "You Make Loving Fun" all hit the upper reaches of the charts.

In the meantime Bob Welch returned to rock, signing Mick Fleetwood as his manager and refurbishing the old Mac classic "Sentimental Lady" to launch his *Ebony Eyes* album. Stevie Nicks lent her voice to several hit singles by other artists: Walter Egan's "Magnet and Steel," Kenny Loggins' "Whenever I Call You Friend," and John Stewart's "Gold."

With all their successes the band still refused to play it safe. While most superstars are content to make carbon copies of their monster albums ad infinitum, Fleetwood Mac gambled on musical expansion. Almost a year and a half in the making, *Tusk* was released in October of 1979. The group displayed three diverging styles on this double album— Buckingham's stark Buddy Hollyesque rockers, Christine McVie's soft sentimental songs, and Stevie Nicks' hypnotic, intensely personal poems. This combination was a lot for listeners to handle, and the record received generally mixed reviews. The title track, a rave-up recorded with the USC Trojan marching band, went top ten. The album also went number 1, but *Tusk* didn't match the sales of its two illustrious predecessors. However, the band could put up with that. After everything Fleetwood Mac had been through, sales of only a few million wasn't that hard to take.

1978

In November, Representative Leo Ryan of California flew to the small South American country of Guyana to investigate expatriate Reverend Jim Jones and his People's Temple. Ryan and three newsmen were ambushed and killed at a Guyana airstrip by members of Jones' cult. Then, as Jim Jones preached the gospel of mass suicide, 911 of his followers obeyed his orders and drank a cyanide punch, wiping out the entire community. The world was stunned.

However, 1978 was not without its good news. On September 17, after thirteen days of intense negotiations at the Camp David summit, Israel and Egypt signed a peace treaty, ending thirty years of conflict and hatred. The world's first "test-tube" baby, Louise Brown, was born in England on July 26. And as the U.S. Senate voted to return the control of the Panama Canal to Panama, the people of California voted on Proposition 13, firing the first salvo in a nationwide tax revolt.

On television, *Mork and Mindy* debuted, and the comic genius of Robin Williams made him an overnight superstar. The wild antics of DJ Dr. Johnny Fever were overshadowed by Loni Anderson's figure on *WKRP in Cincinnati.* In 1978, *Taxi,* with Judd Hirsch and Andy Kaufman, picked up its first fare on ABC. *Holocaust,* a searing four-part drama about the Nazi extermination of the Jews, had a worldwide impact when it was aired in April. And NBC briefly attempted to bring back the variety show with *Dick Clark's Live Wednesday.*

Although *Superman: The Movie* turned Christopher Reeve into the Man of Steel, *The Deer Hunter* wrested the Best Picture Oscar from *Coming Home, Interiors, Heaven Can Wait,* and *Midnight Express.*

Some other men of steel, the Pittsburgh Steelers, flattened the Dallas Cowboys to win Super Bowl XIII. Leon Spinks, the boxer with the Ipana smile, took the heavyweight title from Muhammad Ali in February, but Ali "whupped" Leon in the return match in September. Affirmed became the third horse in six years to win racing's Triple Crown. The Washington Bullets grabbed the NBA title, nipping the Seattle Supersonics. In baseball the Yankees staged a remarkable comeback, climbing from fourteen games behind to beat the Boston Red Sox for the American League pennant, then defeating the Los Angeles Dodgers in the World Series, four games to two.

In rock and roll Elvis Costello gave the quote of the year to *Newsweek:* "Take a band like Boston. They may sell nine million records, but they're about as exciting as a plate of tripe. Rock and roll is about sex, and they might as well be eunuchs. They're just a wet dream for an accountant."

Nevertheless, Boston's single "Don't Look Back" must have given their accountant some thrills. While Chuck Mangione offered his mellow "Feel So Good," Devo displayed the wave of the future with their android version of "Satisfaction." 10cc took up reggae on "Dreadlock Holiday." Bonnie Tyler, whose vocal cord injury made her sound like Rod Stewart, wailed "It's a Heartache." The Bee Gees' production helped Frankie Valli's "Grease," Samantha Sang's "Emotion," and Yvonne Elliman's "If I Can't Have You" soar to the top of the charts, while the Bee Gees and baby brother Andy Gibb grabbed five of the top ten songs of the year. Nineteen seventy-eight's top ten broke down this way: "Night Fever" by the Bee Gees, "Shadow Dancing" by Andy Gibb, "Stayin' Alive" by the Bee Gees, "You Light Up My Life" by Debby Boone, "Kiss You All Over" by Exile, "Three Times a Lady" by the Commodores, "How Deep Is Your Love" by the Bee Gees, "Love Is Thicker Than Water" by Andy Gibb, "Baby Come Back" by Player, and "Boogie Oogie Oogie" by A Taste of Honey.

It was 1978—the twenty-fourth year of rock and roll.

Devo, hailing from Akron, Ohio, gave rock a look at the future in 1978 with their android version of "Satisfaction."

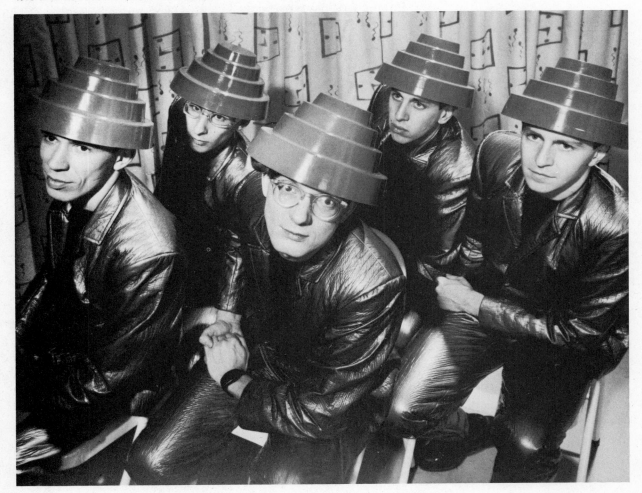

The Patti Smith Group. Patti, the Poet Princess of Punk, scored high on the charts in 1978 with "Because the Night," a song she cowrote with Bruce Springsteen.

One of the biggest singles of 1978 was "Boogie Oogie Oogie" by A Taste of Honey (from left: Don Johnson, Hazel Payne, Perry Kibble, and Janice Johnson).

Bruce Springsteen at the Capitol Theater in Passaic, New Jersey.
(John Wooding)

BRUCE SPRINGSTEEN

Born on September 23, 1949, in Freehold, New Jersey, Bruce Springsteen had a normal Catholic childhood until he was thirteen, when a cousin showed him how to play the songs he had heard on the radio with a guitar. Bruce's dream of being a baseball player was instantly replaced by an uncontrollable lust to be a rock and roller. He began to imitate many of his favorites, such as the Beach Boys, the Chiffons, the Shirelles, and Gary "U.S." Bonds. Except for a brief gardening job and a short stint at Ocean County Community College, Springsteen never wavered from the rock-and-roll path after graduating from high school.

Having been rejected for military duty for "reasons of weirdness," Bruce was certain that rock and roll was his destiny.

He played with a series of local bands at dances, fraternity parties, and bars. From the early Castiles to the locally popular Steel Mill, Bruce displayed a special spark in his guitar playing and an amazing intensity on stage, throwing himself completely into his music. For a while Bruce was part of the zany Dr. Zoom and the Sonic Boom, a mixture of psychedelic music and theater that included a staged game of Monopoly. Then he formed the ten-piece Bruce Springsteen Band. Finally, when he turned twenty-one in 1970, Bruce decided to become an acoustic solo performer. At this time, he often hit the folk clubs in New York and spent a lot of time with a colorful cast of lowlifes on the boardwalks of the Jersey shore. As the fall of 1971 rolled around, Bruce's career was still in limbo. Nevertheless, his faith in the power of the music remained constant.

At the suggestion of his manager, Bruce went to see Mike Appel, a slick management executive, to see if he could make him a star. Appel didn't feel that Bruce had enough polish, so he told him to keep playing and writing for a while, then to come back and see him. After a trip to Mexico and California,

where his father worked as a bus driver, Bruce returned to the East Coast and signed with Appel in March 1972. Springsteen signed publishing, recording, and management deals with Appel without paying much attention to the details. His main concern was the music, and in Mike Appel Bruce had found a true believer. Appel was convinced that this scruffy kid from the Jersey shore was a major talent.

Mike brought Bruce to Columbia executive John Hammond, Sr., the man who had signed Billie Holiday, Aretha Franklin, and Bob Dylan. Bruce was embarrassed as Appel raved to Hammond about the superstar in their midst. Appel openly questioned whether Hammond had just been lucky with his other discoveries and if he really did have an ear for quality. When the tidal wave of hype subsided, Bruce played "Hard to Be a Saint in the City," and despite Appel, Hammond signed Bruce. Hammond later explained that someone so talented only comes around once every ten years, at best, and Bruce was more developed than Dylan had been at the time of his signing.

With little technical background Appel and Springsteen produced Bruce's first album, *Greetings from Asbury Park, N.J.,* which was released in January 1973. Columbia's promotion department presented Springsteen as "the new Dylan," but to no avail. Sales were low, under fifty thousand. Nevertheless, Columbia was still behind Bruce, for reviews of the first album, which included unique tunes like "Spirit in the Night," had been highly favorable. Meanwhile, Bruce took to the road again, opening his shows with a solo acoustic set before bringing out his ever-changing road band. Bruce's appearance at the Columbia Records convention in the summer of 1973, however, was a disaster, and Hammond's selection of Springsteen was openly jeered.

For his next album Bruce wanted a harder rock sound, while Columbia encouraged him to pursue the

Dylan folk route. Bruce formed the E Street Band with some of the musicians who had played on *Greetings from Asbury Park*—David Sancious on keyboards, Gary Tallent on bass, Danny Federici on organ, Vini Lopez on drums, and Clarence Clemons on saxophone. In the fall of '73 *The Wild, the Innocent, and the E Street Shuffle* was released. The reviews of the album were even better than the last, but its sales were lower. Appel wrote letters to radio stations asking what the hell it took to get airplay. Behind Appel's harsh manner was justifiable frustration, for the album contained true rock classics like "Rosalita" and the romantic ballad "Sandy." But disc jockeys had been turned off by the severe hype, so airplay was negligible. While Columbia considered dropping him, Bruce did the only thing he could do—he took his music to the people.

After a disastrous attempt to open a show for the group Chicago, Springsteen decided that it would be to his advantage to headline clubs, where the atmosphere was more controllable. In 1973 and early 1974 Bruce gradually developed a hard-core following in cities like Austin, New York, Cleveland, Philly, and Phoenix. One show was all it took to turn a skeptic into a fanatic. The Springsteen cult was especially strong in Boston, where rock critic Jon Landau wrote a glowing review of a Springsteen performance. The review was posted in the window of the Cambridge bar where Bruce was playing in April 1974. Jon happened to be there when Bruce was reading it, and they soon became friends. That review contained Landau's now-classic statement, "I have seen rock and roll future and its name is Bruce Springsteen." Since Landau was also the influential record editor of *Rolling Stone,* Columbia used the review to push Bruce's second album. Personally, Bruce didn't care for this promo overkill. Anyway, people still were not rushing to purchase his records.

Bruce and his band were at their lowest point now, working for peanuts. However, Landau's review did strengthen Bruce's inner drive at a crucial moment. John Hammond was still supportive of Bruce, but Columbia pressured him for a commercial single to break his third and possibly last album. In May 1974, Bruce went to work on a last-ditch effort to make that single. After months of agonizing toil in the studio, the amazing "Born to Run" was sent out for industry reaction. Word came back that it was not top-forty material, that it was too long and definitely not a hit. Undaunted, Bruce had "Born to Run," with its spectacular wall-of-sound production, sent to stations in the cities where most of his fans were. The response was tremendous. They wanted more.

Bruce then went back to work on the rest of the album, but progress was slow. Jon Landau reentered

The Boss. *(John Wooding)*

the scene, pointing out production problems that Bruce had not seen. Landau had previously produced The MC5 and Livingston Taylor, and he felt that he could help translate the elusive sounds in Bruce's head onto tape. Landau convinced Appel to switch the recording to the better-equipped Record Plant in New York. Since the recording of this album had only been sputtering along with Appel in charge, Bruce now asked Landau to coproduce it. In April 1975 Jon started to work for Bruce. In the meantime Sancious left the band to pursue his own career, and after many auditions Roy Bittan was added to the band on keyboards. Bruce also felt that he needed a steadier drummer, so "Mighty" Max Weinberg was hired for the E Street Band. Many grueling sessions with engineer Jimmy Iovine took place as the band struggled to capture that elusive early-sixties Phil Spector sound. Bruce was determined to make the perfect rock record, even if it meant that the versatile Roy Bittan would have to double-track

Danny Federici's organ parts as well as his own. Finally, in September 1975, the album *Born to Run* was released, and, amazingly, on October 27 Bruce was on the cover of both *Newsweek* and *Time*. A Springsteen backlash then peaked as cynics who had never seen him perform claimed that Bruce was overrated and nothing more than the product of hype. Bruce himself felt that his control over his life and his career were slipping away. Fame had become an obstacle for him.

The turning point in Bruce's career was his Bottom Line club concerts in New York in 1975. On the opening night, the house was packed with music-industry tastemakers, many of them out for blood or at least a little bruising. But Bruce and the E Street Band blew the crowd away. They were jolted by Bruce's flair, his timing, his command of moods, and his miraculous vigor. He danced and strutted all over the stage with his funky grace for over two hours while the band played for their professional lives. The audience could sense the special chemistry that pulsated between Bruce and the black giant with the sax, Clarence Clemons. Masterpieces like "Jungleland" and "Backstreets" were enacted with urgency and spine-tingling fanfare. Each night of that gig, audiences were smashed in the gut by rock and roll, and a live radio broadcast of one of the concerts spread the message: Springsteen was the real item. The album that contained classics like "Thunder Road," "Tenth Avenue Freeze-out," and the single "Born to Run" zoomed to number 3 on the charts, going gold in six weeks. Bruce became the hottest concert attraction in the country.

Appel, who had stuck by Bruce in the lean years, now grew concerned about Landau's increasing influence with Springsteen, especially since the financial struggle was now becoming a financial bonanza. With money finally coming in, the outrageous nature of Bruce's contracts with Appel came to light. The royalty structure was ridiculously unbalanced in Appel's favor. Tension built. Then, in May 1976, Appel tried to attach the proceeds from a series of Springsteen's shows until he was paid his commission. In July Bruce filed a massive breach of contract suit against Appel in U.S. district court, asking for one million dollars in damages and permanent dissolution of any prior agreements with Appel, who Bruce claimed had "wholly failed and neglected to administer" his financial affairs properly. Bruce pointed out that Appel was demanding the unconscionable commission of fifty percent of all weekly earnings over fifteen thousand dollars. Appel countered with an injunction that barred Landau and Springsteen from entering a recording studio together, claiming piracy on Landau's part. He then filed a suit

charging that Springsteen had illegally broken his contract. After ten months of legal battling, the two parties settled on May 28, 1977. Appel claimed total victory because he retained the right to share in the profits from the first three albums. Bruce, however, won control of his entire catalogue of songs, the right to pick his own producer, and most importantly, his complete freedom from Appel. What he did lose was time. Originally he had wanted to start work on his fourth album in June 1976, but recording had been prohibited until June 1977, at which time he and Landau went back to work. It took ten months to make, but when *Darkness on the Edge of Town* was released in June 1978, it shot right into the top ten with a bullet. The album was shipped gold and soon turned platinum with solid FM airplay. Bruce was, indeed, the Boss.

A major concert tour began in May 1978, and the band was truly inspired. Pianist Roy "The Professor" Bittan was dazzlingly delicate. Tallent and Weinberg were now one of the most powerful rhythm sections in rock. "Miami" Steve Van Zandt traded zinging guitar leads with Springsteen. Federici's organ added a grand texture to the band's overwhelming sound, and the Kahuna—Clarence Clemons, a former member of James Brown's Famous Flames—blew his sax with soulful brilliance. Bruce himself was up to his old tricks, leaping into the audience, milking every climax to the point of exhaustion, playing encore after encore every night, giving a hundred percent and then some. Running through the highlights of the *Darkness* L.P., tunes like "Prove It All Night," "Badlands," "Racing in the Street," and "The Promised Land," Bruce dealt with heavy themes of despair, pain, desperation, and guilt with an underlying message of salvation, dignity, and hope. The usually three-hours-long shows achieved Bruce's goal. Call it magic, call it a miracle. His fans will tell you that his concerts are the ultimate rock experience.

Other rock stars have scored chart successes with Bruce's songs. Manfred Mann had a number-1 smash in 1977 with Bruce's "Blinded by the Light," then hit again with "Spirit in the Night." Patti Smith cracked the top ten in 1978 with the Springsteen composition "Because the Night." The Pointer Sisters ushered in 1979 by scorching the top ten with Bruce's tune "Fire." Southside Johnny and the Asbury Jukes featured Springsteen songs on their first three albums with production help from E Streeter "Miami" Steve Van Zandt.

In September 1979 Bruce made his only concert appearance of the year at Madison Square Garden's MUSE antinuclear concerts. A recording of this concert was the first live Springsteen officially put on vinyl. The triple record set, *No Nukes,* was released in December 1979, and prominently features Springsteen performing his Mitch Ryder medley.

The breathless anticipation of Springsteen's fans was rewarded in October 1980 with the release of the Boss' long-awaited fifth album, *The River.* Once again Bruce covered familiar turf with lyrics about highways, cars, and girls, but this time the familiar landscape also became a metaphor for the changing times. The album's title track is a touching ballad about a couple who leaves high school to get married because of an impending pregnancy and shares the meaning in their lives by walking by the river. "Sherry Darling" is a rousing rocker with the feel of a live recording and the taste of the city streets. With its potent rhythm and the backing vocals of Flo and Eddie, "Hungry Heart" became Bruce's first single ever to break into the top ten. In the closing months of 1980, Bruce took the E Street Band back out on the road and won over legions of true believers with incredible four-hour performances. Thanks to the public's awesome response to *The River* and "Hungry Heart" and the rousing reception European crowds gave his first tour of the Continent, Bruce Springsteen finally crossed over from cult curiosity to full-fledged superstardom in 1981. Make no mistake about it. The Boss was back—to stay!

BILLY JOEL

Like Sylvester Stallone's Rocky Balboa, Billy Joel is a fighter. He's short, stocky, and solid, with a nose that's a genuine souvenir of his juvenile boxing career. Billy even ran with a gang during his schooldays. No doubt about it: Billy Joel is a real fighter. For seven years he fought for control of his music and his career. When he finally had his shot, Billy went in swinging and landed a knockout punch in 1978 with his fifth solo album, *The Stranger.*

It could have turned out differently, though. Billy was almost condemned to a normal childhood. Like many middle-class fathers in the fifties, Howard Joel fled the city and moved his family out to the suburbs. In the Joels' case it was Levittown, Long Island, one of the biggest and tackiest suburban developments in America. However, when Billy was seven, his father returned to his birthplace in Europe, abandoning Billy, his sister, Judy, and their mother. The family's standard of living plummeted. With little money for outside entertainment, Billy occupied his time reading. He particularly liked books on history and classic works of American literature.

Billy's piano lessons began at age four, but he eventually grew bored with the classics. He preferred the driving beat of soul music and the melodies of his idols, the Beatles. Young Billy couldn't resist the temptation to add a bit of boogie-woogie to his Bach every now and then. However, this classical training would later serve him well as a composer.

During his high school years, he hung around rock clubs and recording studios in New York City. In fact he spent so much time there that he never graduated. But to Joel, it was worth it. He sat in on some sessions with producer Shadow Morton, the Phil Spector clone who recorded some of the true masterpieces of teen-age angst with the Shangri-Las. At the time, Billy wanted the experience, and he was willing to work for nothing.

In the late sixties he put a group together called the Hassles and somehow managed to land a contract with United Artists Records. They recorded two albums, *The Hassles,* which brings a stiff price on the collector's market today, and *Hour of the Wolf,* which was and is just a stiff. The band broke up soon after the release of the second L.P., and Joel and Hassle drummer John Small formed a two-man band, recording one album with Epic. After a brief gig as a rock critic, Billy finally went solo and recorded *Cold Spring Harbor* in 1971.

Unfortunately, the tape decks they had used in recording were defective, and they didn't realize it until the records came back from the pressing plant with all the tracks recorded at the wrong speed. Paramount Records released it anyway and shoved Billy out on the road with a second-rate backup band that the company threw together for him. Naturally the album flopped, and further recording efforts were foiled by a binding agreement that Billy had signed with Artie Ripp's Family Productions.

Disgusted with the record business, Billy Joel simply dropped out of sight. Taking the name Billy Martin (Martin was Joel's middle name), he started tickling the ivories along the L.A. bar circuit. Alcohol helped blot out some of the bitterness, but his deepest wounds still festered. The saccharine character of his early optimistic songs soon gave way to a sly, biting cynicism.

Family Productions finally let Billy off the hook in 1973, and he soon started work on a new solo album for Columbia Records. There was one catch, though. All of Joel's subsequent releases would be required to carry the Family Productions logo no matter who actually produced it.

His first release on Columbia, *Piano Man,* was produced by his manager, Michael Stewart. Stewart was determined to cast Billy as a macho Elton John. Elton was at his peak then, and Stewart highlighted Joel's piano on every song, adding Elton John touches to songs like "Ain't No Crime" and "Billy the Kid." Approaching his work as a songwriter, Billy thought more stylistic variety was in order. Their differences were shelved, though, when the album's bittersweet title tune started to climb the charts. Columbia promptly proclaimed 1974 the Year of Billy Joel.

Regrettably, the Stewart-produced follow-up, *Street-life Serenade,* did not produce a single to match "Piano Man," and the album stalled at number 35. This was unfortunate, for the cut "The Entertainer" was one of the few honest looks behind the tinsel and glitter of the contemporary rock scene. People in the industry thought it was a backhanded slap at the "biz" by an ungrateful kid who'd been lucky enough to score big his first time out. Moreover, his stinging portrayal of rock audiences as fickle lynch mobs didn't win him many points with potential fans.

Once again bitterness and suspicion crept back into his life. A dispute with his manager over the use of the road band on future recordings (Billy wanted to use them; Stewart did not) led to a parting of the ways. Sick of L.A., Billy and his wife, Elizabeth, returned to New York, settling in Highland Falls.

Joel produced his next album himself. Although the songwriting on this album showed strong signs of growth, particularly on "New York State of Mind" and "Say Goodbye to Hollywood," the production was weak and uneven. Commercially, *Turnstiles* was a disaster, elbowing its way no higher than number 122 in 1976. Now mired in contractual and financial problems, Joel jokingly suggested to his wife that she take over his career management. She did and with a vengeance.

First, Elizabeth got Billy a larger slice of his record and concert profits, which freed him to concentrate on his music. More importantly, she introduced him to Paul Simon's producer, Phil Ramone. Ramone loved Billy's touring band, and the two established an immediate rapport. Ramone was used to taping in a casual atmosphere, encouraging musicians to get involved with their music. With Ramone at the board, Billy could relax and get into his songs as he never had before.

To thank his wife, he wrote a special song for her and presented it on her birthday in 1977. Appropriately that song, "Just the Way You Are," became Billy Joel's first smash hit. The album it came from, *The Stranger,* soon followed it up the charts and stayed there for over a year, yielding the hits "Movin' Out," "Only the Good Die Young," and "She's Always a Woman." Joel had achieved his goal, which was to do what the Beatles had done—make an album with absolutely no filler. He and producer Ramone deftly shifted tempos and textures on *The Stranger* while never straying too far from mainstream pop. Even on

the coldly dispassionate title track, Billy was able to reveal the heart of a true romantic.

After *The Stranger,* the struggle was over for Billy Joel. He toured the nation's biggest arenas, living up to his reputation as a hardworking, exciting performer. *52nd Street,* which was released at the end of 1978, out-performed *The Stranger.* "My Life," another one of Billy's anthems to independence, continued his string of successful singles. Billy Joel may have entered 1978 as "The Stranger," but he left it a star.

Billy's star was in full ascent in 1980. While some critics threw stones at his *Glass Houses* L.P., the public immediately fell in love with it. "Just the Way You Are" had left Joel with a tag as a pop lightweight, but Billy showed his hard-rocking side on *Glass Houses,* which won him that year's Grammy for Best Rock Vocal Performance by a Male. The album blasted its way to the top of the charts on the strength of two monster singles: the nasty, driving "You May Be Right," and the biting, brilliant "It's Still Rock 'n' Roll to Me." Success hadn't spoiled Billy Joel; aiming his rock at the music's glass houses, Billy Joel was still a fighter.

MEAT LOAF

Marvin Lee Aday was born in September 1947 in Dallas, Texas, to a family of gospel singers. His high school football coach gave him the nickname "Meat Loaf" when the young six-foot-two-inch 260-pound Marvin accidentally stepped on the coach's foot. Marvin left his salesman father and hymn-singer mother in 1966 for the glitter of Los Angeles. He decided to use the name Meat Loaf so that his future endeavors wouldn't embarrass his religious parents.

For three years Meat played with a West Coast band called Popcorn Blizzard, touring with such acts as the Who, Iggy Pop, and Ted Nugent. In 1969 he auditioned in California for the road-show version of the musical *Hair.* He got the part and traveled from city to city until the tour left him in Detroit, Michigan, where he decided to stop. There Loaf teamed up with a soul singer named Stoney and released an album on Motown, making Meat one of the few whites ever to record for Motown. Although they opened concerts for acts like Rare Earth and Alice Cooper, Meat Loaf and Stoney weren't exactly a blazing success. Meat soon longed for the glamor of the theater again, so he headed for New York City.

In early 1973 Meat Loaf landed a part in the Broadway production of *Rainbow.* Later in that year he auditioned for a rock musical called *More Than You Deserve,* a Joseph Papp production that had been scored by Jim Steinman. Jim had grown up in both California and New York, and his diverse upbringing showed in his music. *Dream Engine,* a musical he created in his senior year at Amherst College, was produced in New York shortly after he graduated. Steinman's songs were grand, glorious, and theatrical. When he heard Meat Loaf audition for *More Than You Deserve,* he knew that he had finally found the kind of majestic singer that he needed for his operatic rock epics.

More Than You Deserve didn't make a big splash on Broadway. When it folded, Jim and Meat Loaf found themselves working together again on the *National Lampoon* show. Meat and Jim eventually began to rehearse Steinman's songs seriously. They rehearsed for a full year in New York, usually with just voice and piano. The tunes were rocking theatrical tributes to hot and horny teen-age love, propelled by Meat's dynamic ability to project passion, lust, and frustration.

Meat Loaf then sang behind Ted Nugent on his 1976 platinum album for Epic, *Free for All.* Signing for a bit part in the low-budget film *The Rocky Horror Picture Show,* he played Eddie, a crazy biker who is eventually eaten for dinner. Back in New York the extremely talented rock gadfly Todd Rundgren heard one of Steinman and Meat's rehearsals and agreed to produce and play guitar on their projected album. A record deal was negotiated with RCA, but when the label refused to include Todd in the package, Jim and Meat backed out of the deal. The three decided not to delay the project any longer and began work on their album with some production money from Rundgren's Bearsville label and Rundgren himself. Warner Bros. Records eventually agreed to release the projected album, but made no commitments to promote it. Dissatisfied with that deal, their manager, David Sonenberg, took the tapes to Cleveland International, a production company formed in early 1977 by Steve Popovich, formerly of Epic Records, and Stan Snyder and Sam Lederman, formerly of Columbia Records. Cleveland International bought the record and successfully pitched it to Epic for distribution. In September 1977 *Bat Out of Hell* was finally released with Todd producing and playing guitar and Steinman writing and arranging all the songs.

With its grotesque cover painted by comic book artist Richard Corbin, *Bat Out of Hell* sold two hundred thousand copies within three months—impressive sales figures for a debut album. *The*

Mr. Loaf and Jim Steinman.

Rocky Horror Picture Show's intense cult following aided Meat Loaf's sales. Loaf and Steinman hit the road with a seven-piece band, playing over 170 dates in the next eleven months. Epic Records put together a rigorous promotional campaign for *Bat Out of Hell.* While most promotion campaigns last about a month, Loaf and Steinman stayed on the road, enduring a grueling full year of promotion.

Bat Out of Hell was a sweeping, grandiose album filled with teen-age anthems meant for high school kids. On his first big hit, "Two Out of Three Ain't Bad," Meat Loaf told his girl that he wanted and needed her but that he would never love her. The public wanted, needed, and loved the single, pushing it into the top ten in March 1978. "Paradise by the Dashboard Light" was an 8½-minute suite about a moment of teen-age passion and the price Meat Loaf had to pay for his lust. Phil Rizzuto, the voice of the New York Yankees, unwittingly provided the song's double-entendre play-by-play. Phil received letters of outrage from ministers and priests but graciously accepted a platinum record from Meat Loaf in a

ceremony before a home game at Yankee Stadium. One of the biggest surprises of the summer of 1978 was the enormous amount of airplay "Paradise" was getting on AM radio. In the meantime, "You Took the Words Right Out of My Mouth," a classic rock-and-roll beach song complete with a Phil Spector wall of sound, and "All Revved Up with No Place to Go," a blistering teen-age rocker about boredom and passion, became FM radio favorites. By the end of 1978 the album had sold over five million copies worldwide, including two million outside the United States.

Research revealed that two out of three Meat Loaf records were purchased by females. It might be hard to imagine that this gargantuan figure of a man could arouse erotic fantasies in teen-age girls, but when Meat Loaf took the stage in tuxedo and ruffled shirt, he performed like a man possessed. He could easily whip a crowd into a frenzy with such stage moves as his flying somersault. In fact Meat Loaf was so frenetic that he often needed oxygen after his performances. In the spring of 1978 he actually catapulted himself off the end of a six-foot stage at

415

the Ottawa Civic Center, spraining his knee and tearing a ligament. Fortunately, he didn't land on anybody.

His second album was originally scheduled for the spring of 1979. It was postponed until the summer, but no album ever appeared because Meat claimed he had developed a vocal problem on the long tour. His voice "went crazy," he said. With only half the vocals on the new album completed, Meat Loaf regretted that he couldn't sing anymore. Epic tried hypnotists and psychologists on their heavyweight rock star, but nothing worked. On the first album he had worked closely with Jim Steinman, but on this project Steinman wrote the songs without Meat Loaf's input, and Mr. Loaf just couldn't manage to get out the words. The instrumental tracks and backup vocals were all finished, and even Todd Rundgren was waiting patiently in the studio, but Meat Loaf was vocally impotent.

After appearing in a non-singing role in the 1980 rock-and-roll film *Roadie,* Meat Loaf proclaimed that not only his second album, but a new third album, was on its way to the record stores. But his patient fans kept waiting and waiting with only the sounds of *Bat Out of Hell* to comfort them. Maybe, as Meat Loaf might have said, "one out of three ain't bad."

EARTH, WIND AND FIRE

Maurice White, the founder, mastermind, and producer of Earth, Wind and Fire, was born in December 1941 in Chicago. By the age of six Maurice was singing gospel. At age twelve he started playing drums. In high school he played in a school band led by Booker T. Jones, who later became the leader of the MG's. Maurice went on to the Chicago Conservatory of Music, where he studied percussion, piano, and composition while still playing in local clubs whenever possible. His next job was as a session drummer for Motown, cutting tracks for their best groups, including the Supremes, the Four Tops, and the Temptations. Very often White did not know which groups used his instrumental tracks until he heard the songs on the radio. Tired of Motown, Maurice became the staff drummer at Chess Records in Chicago, working with the Impressions, Billy Stewart, and Muddy Waters. When jazz great John Coltrane came to Chicago and his regular drummer became ill, White filled in for a week, and that gig changed Maurice White's life. Coltrane, a deeply spiritual man, moved Maurice with his philosophical concerns. Coltrane taught Maurice that art could have a positive effect on the way people related to their problems and their goals.

Mindful of that wisdom, Maurice landed a job with the Ramsey Lewis Trio in 1966. While touring with this group, he yearned to form a band that could uplift spirits as well as entertain. In 1970 White formed the first Earth, Wind and Fire, taking the band's name from three of the four primal elements. Maurice omitted the fourth element, water, because there were no water signs in his astrological chart. Based in L.A., this first incarnation of the group signed with Warner Bros. and released the L.P. *Earth, Wind and Fire* in 1970, which was followed the next year by the album *The Need of Love.* At this time Earth, Wind and Fire also recorded the soundtrack for Melvin Van Peebles' film *Sweet Sweetback's Baadasssss Song.*

In 1972 White disbanded this group, which didn't seem to match his vision and immediately formed a new Earth, Wind and Fire, bringing in younger musicians like Ronnie Laws, Ronald Bautista, and Jessica Cleaves from the Friends of Distinction. The new band signed with Columbia and in 1972 released *Last Days and Time,* which included the cut "Power." On the next album, *Head to the Sky,* Laws and Bautista were replaced by guitarists Al McKay and Johnny Graham, and horn player Andrew Woolfolk. The title single was a popular soul hit that sang the praises of positive thinking. In 1974, after Cleaves left the band, the group journeyed to Colorado to record their next album, *Open Our Eyes,* at James Guercio's Caribou Ranch. Released in March 1974, it contained the single "Mighty Mighty," with its driving horns and chorus of "yeows"—an Earth, Wind and Fire trademark. In September the band released the single "Devotion," a popular ballad that showed the group's smoother side. In early 1975 the youngest White brother, Fred, joined the band on drums and percussion, completing the lineup that would carry Earth, Wind and Fire to superstardom. Maurice and Philip Bailey now handled the lead vocals, Brother Verdine White played bass, McKay and Graham took care of the guitars, Larry Dunn played keyboards, Ralph Johnson was their second drummer, and Woolfolk played wind instruments.

That's the Way of the World was released in July 1975. It shot up to number 1 for a four-week stay, handily selling a million copies. The album was originally conceived as the soundtrack for the movie of the same name, which finally came out two years later. This movie contained Earth, Wind and Fire's first film appearance, in which they portrayed a rock-and-soul band. The album yielded the monster

Earth, Wind and Fire. Maurice White stands at center. *(Courtesy of Columbia Records. Copyright Bruce W. Talamon)*

million-selling single "Shining Star," which shot to number 1 in May 1975 and won Earth, Wind and Fire a Grammy that year for Best R & B Performance by a Vocal Group. "That's the Way of the World" also won a Rock Award for Best R & B Single of 1975.

Earth, Wind and Fire became a very popular concert attraction, selling out halls all over the country with their flashy, exotic stage shows. Never content merely to repeat their hits note for note, Earth, Wind and Fire constantly experimented in concert, even drifting into jazz improvisation. With

their explosions and funky choreography, Earth, Wind and Fire radiated pure energy. Later in 1975 this spirit was captured live on three sides of their double album *Gratitude.* The fourth side contained new studio material, including the million-selling singles "Sing a Song" and "Can't Hide Love." The LP went double platinum, and Earth, Wind and Fire was voted the Favorite R & B Group in the American Music Awards' balloting in 1975.

The group's 1976 *Spirit* album was dedicated to longtime friend and coproducer Charles Stepney, who had died just before the record was finished. From this album came yet another gold single, "Getaway." This album cover featured the Pyramids, and the band now dressed in pure white as their disco-funk evolved into cosmic awareness. Their double platinum album *All in All* contained mystical cover graphics that were reproduced on their stage sets for their 1977 American tour. Even if one did not care for their sermonizing, the band was so visually intriguing and musically exciting that it was very easy to ignore the lyrics that dealt with infinity and brotherhood. *All in All* sold over two million copies in just a few weeks and launched two successful singles: "Serpentine Fire" in the fall of 1977 and "Fantasy" in March 1978.

In 1978 Earth, Wind and Fire appeared in the Robert Stigwood film *Sgt. Pepper's Lonely Hearts Club Band* with headliners Peter Frampton and the Bee Gees. *Sgt. Pepper* was a cinematic disaster, and the soundtrack didn't fare much better. However, Earth, Wind and Fire's version of the Beatles' classic "Gotta Get You into My Life," the sole original interpretation in the movie, was the only cut from the soundtrack to go gold. Nineteen seventy-eight also brought *The Best of Earth, Wind and Fire—Volume I,* the group's first release on ARC Records, a division of Columbia of which Maurice White was president. This L.P. contained the smash top-ten single "September." By the end of 1978, Earth, Wind and Fire had seven gold L.P.'s, of which five were platinum and four double platinum, and four gold singles.

In May 1979, *I Am* broke into the top five on the album charts. It contained two top-ten singles, the mellow ballad "After the Love Has Gone" and the syncopated disco smash "Boogie Wonderland," which featured the Emotions. (The trio had been signed to Columbia by Maurice. White also became the Emotions' producer, scoring big with their 1977 hit "Best of My Love"). Earth, Wind and Fire received five Grammy Award nominations for 1979, including Record of the Year and Best R & B Vocal Performance for "Boogie Wonderland" and have won four American Music Awards to date.

Their 1979 U.S. tour was made with sixteen performers—the regular group of nine, a four-man horn section, and a chorus of three women. Their stage show was as wild as ever, pulling out every theatrical trick in the book, with their drummer spinning complete circles, myriad costume changes, and band members magically vanishing into thin air. However, Earth, Wind and Fire's real strength is their musical virtuosity. Their ability to blend rock, jazz, African rhythms, soul, and Chicago blues into a precise commercial sound has made Earth, Wind and Fire one of the seventies' premier acts. Whether the band is punching out intricate, driving rhythms or gliding along on a lush vocal harmony, Maurice White's production is immaculate. Maurice's cosmic philosophy may not be everybody's cup of tea, but his efforts have still made Earth, Wind and Fire one of the funkiest, most sophisticated groups in rock's twenty-five–year history.

THE VILLAGE PEOPLE

Just as rock and roll sprang from the R & B of the black community in the late forties, disco started in the clubs of the latest minority groups to gain visibility and recognition in America, gays and Latins. Before it came to be identified with John Travolta and Studio 54, disco burgeoned on the dance floors of gay bars and Latino discotheques, gradually adopting the dress, style, and movements of these two groups. By 1978 disco had gained wide acceptance. However, except for a handful of artists like Gloria Gaynor and Donna Summer, disco was relatively faceless and nameless. But disco received six strong personalities that year—a wailing traffic cop, a GI in jungle camouflage, a musical midnight cowboy, a wild Indian in feathered headdress and bells, a chain-wielding biker in studded leather, and a hardhat construction worker with mirrored shades and a screwdriver thrust between his teeth. Not only did disco get its identity, but America got a tongue placed firmly inside its cheek. Otherwise known as Victor Willis, Alex Briley, Randy Jones, Felipe Rose, Glenn Hughes, and David "Scar" Hodo, these guys were the macho men of disco—the Village People.

The Village People were created in early 1977 by French composer/producer Jacques Morali to appeal specifically to gays. At the time, disco was happening in gay bars and discotheques. Morali knew that even without radio airplay a record could sell big in just the discos, so he set out to conquer the gay market, which still had no singing group to call its own.

When Morali saw Felipe Rose dancing in a Greenwich Village gay bar in his Indian costume, he had a brainstorm. Morali envisioned a group made up of strong American male stereotypes, a group that would appeal to the growing gay sense of macho, a group that could capture the mystique of the American male to the delight of gay and straight audiences alike.

With executive producer Pete Belolo, Morali wrote songs about the most notorious gay communities in America—Greenwich Village, San Francisco, Hollywood, and Fire Island—then took his concept to the recording studio. The songs were not blatantly gay, but they could lend themselves easily to a gay interpretation. Using studio musicians for the music and models for the album cover, the first Village People record, entitled *Village People,* was released and sold a hundred thousand copies on the strength of disco play alone. Morali's concept obviously worked, but the Village People needed real members if they were to break out of the discos.

Morali kept his nucleus of studio musicians—lead singer Victor Willis, soldier Alex Briley, and Indian Felipe Rose. The group was to be built around Willis, who had a strong, distinctive, R & B-style voice as well as theater experience in musicals such as *The Wiz.* The Frenchman conducted some two hundred auditions to fill his roster. He found leatherman Glenn Hughes in a tollbooth in the Brooklyn-Battery Tunnel, cowboy Randy Jones in the Agnes DeMille Dance Company, and construction worker David Hodo in the unemployment line. The all-singing, all-dancing, all-American Village People were now ready.

Morali sent the group on a tour for seasoning and exposure in order to get their music played on the radio. The Village People put on their fantastic show in discos from coast to coast. They were so exciting that one woman actually went backstage and chased the leatherman with a whip.

Victor Willis began to write lyrics for the group,

OPPOSITE PAGE:

Dick Clark and the Village People (top row, from left: Randy Jones, Glenn Hughes, Alex Briley, and Victor Willis; bottom row front, from left: Felipe Rose, Jacques Morali, Dick Clark, and David "Scar" Hodo). *(Courtesy of Dick Clark. Copyright 1978 Wren Photography)*

playing up to the gay audience's fantasies while keeping their image tongue in cheek for the straight audiences. This careful blend of self-parody, humor, and strong musical hooks won over the nation. "Macho Man" came out in February 1978 and soon became the gay national anthem *and* a pop smash as well.

Willis found the right formula on the Village People's next album, *Cruisin'*. The YMCA was said to have everything for young men to enjoy, and the Village People picked up on that national organization for their next hit. To those who knew the group's image, the thought of the Village People wrapped in towels in the Y's steam room was a howl. To those who knew nothing of the group, the infectious beat was enough. Senior citizens even spelled out the letters Y-M-C-A with their bodies while dancing to the beat poolside in Miami. When the group was scheduled to perform "YMCA" on Dick Clark's *Live Wednesday* program, the Y threatened to sue them. Dick ignored the threat, and the next day the San Francisco YMCA contacted the group about making it their theme song. Twelve million records were sold worldwide. The Village People even rode on a float in Macy's Thanksgiving Day parade—just like Santa Claus.

The group followed up "YMCA" with a tribute to our fighting men at sea, "In the Navy." The Village People serving in a submarine was a mind-boggling concept. Victor even abandoned the police force to become a lead-singing naval commander. The Village People went on a nationwide tour, featuring a Busby Berkeley-type naval frigate on stage complete with firing cannons and flying confetti.

The Village People were the toast of the pop music world. They were a constant sellout attraction on tour. Their albums were shipped platinum. Then, during the summer of 1979, Victor Willis quit. Victor was the soul of the group, their distinctive lead singer and lyric writer. It was Willis who gave the songs their wit and the singing its bite. The Village People recruited a new cop, Ray Simpson, the brother of Valerie Simpson of Ashford and Simpson, and the group's former percussionist. Ray was the spitting image of Victor Willis in uniform. Now the Village People began to share the lead-singing chores among Ray, David "Scar" Hodo, and Alex Briley.

A more serious problem for the Village People may prove to be the decline of disco and the full-fledged return of rock and roll in the 1980s. As 1979 drew to a close, discos were being converted into rock clubs, and the Village People sang "Rock and Roll Is Back Again" on their *Live and Sleazy* album. The dismal failure of *Can't Stop The Music,* a film that starred the Village People and Valerie Perrine, proved a further setback. Whether disco's macho men can successfully make the move to rock and roll in the eighties remains to be seen.

JACKSON BROWNE

Born in West Germany, Jackson Browne entered the American rock music scene in 1967 as a songwriter. His poetic form of rock music quickly attracted the attention of material-seeking performers such as Johnny Rivers, Nico, Tom Rush, Joan Baez, Joe Cocker, the Dirt Band, the Jackson 5, and the Eagles.

By 1971 Jackson Browne's songs and his own rendition of them at local Los Angeles clubs brought him recognition as a talented performer and led to a contract with Asylum Records. That same year his first L.P., entitled *Jackson Browne,* moved up the ranks into hit status as more and more of the record-buying public began to acknowledge him as the composer of many of the songs that had been popularized by other singers and groups.

Jackson Browne was followed by two more successful albums, *For Everyman* and *Late for the Sky.* Now quickly solidifying himself as a major rock figure and often being compared to the likes of Bob Dylan, Browne began exploring new, original material. Unlike the songs on his debut album, the new tunes had not been interpreted by other artists first. They were his songs, sung as he had envisioned them, and were the definitive versions. No longer was it Jackson Browne doing Tom Rush doing Jackson Browne.

His popularity soaring, Browne took time off in 1975 and 1976 to turn his attention to something new—producing. Warren Zevon's first album was also the first of many producing ventures for Browne. When the producing stint was over, Browne was able to divert all of his time and effort into his fourth album, one that would gain recognition as his greatest work and become one of the the classic L.P.'s of rock and roll's first twenty-five years—*The Pretender.* It was while Browne was hard at work on *The Pretender* that a scarring tragedy occurred. His wife committed suicide by overdosing on sleeping pills, leaving Browne alone with his very young son, Ethan.

As a result of his wife's death the rock poet's work became ever more infused with images and themes of love, death, and rebirth. If not blatant before, his structuring of his albums in a narrative, sequential form became more pronounced. On the *The Pretender* L.P. itself he confronted his wife's death and poured himself out through his song "Sleep's Dark and Silent Gate."

There was no further record production from Jackson Browne for two years after that gold album was released. His career became more oriented to live performing. His fifth L.P., *Running on Empty,* was in fact recorded live. Released in 1978, this work featured much music by Browne that had previously gone unrecorded by him or anyone else. Perhaps the most interesting thing about it was the theme—the album unravels a tale of life on the road, experiences of touring with a rock-and-roll band from the first bus ride to the standing ovation in concert. This high-energy disc is a "rockumentary" of life on the road by the minstrel who was there to capture the experiences in song.

After producing more albums by other artists, Jackson Browne returned in 1980 with his sixth L.P., *Hold Out,* which garnered generally strong, but some mixed, reactions. One of the cuts on the album apparently frightened off a number of fans and critics alike, who assumed that the bizarre "Disco Apocalypse" was a move by Browne to sell out to commercialism. Most people, however, recognized it as the parody it was. Browne began working on the tune in 1976 at a time when he was truly taken by the disco sound. It wasn't long after that when Francis Ford Coppola invited him to the Philippines, where he was shooting *Apocalypse Now.* Browne thought he was being summoned to work on the epic. Actually, Coppola was just looking for someone interesting to talk to in that neck of the woods! Somehow, this incident, Browne's early interest in disco, and his knack for complex, poetic songs merged into 1980's "Disco Apocalypse," for better or worse.

Nineteen eighty also brought a new life to Jackson Browne in the form of a new love, Lynne Sweeney—with marriage already in the planning stages. In addition Browne began to turn his talents to the new vista of filmmaking. He is at work on a new project, partnered with young screenwriter Jeffrey Fiskin, who recently completed *Pursuit*, the story of everybody's favorite hijacker, J. D. Cooper, for Polygram Pictures. Jackson made his film debut in *No Nukes*,

the documentary film about the series of antinuclear rock concerts in New York that Browne helped organize in late 1979. Undoubtedly the future holds more tours and songs by one of rock music's leading poets, as well as more timeless albums.

Jackson Browne. *(Randee St. Nicholas)*

THE BEE GEES

In 1978 *Saturday Night Fever* struck rock and roll. Twenty-five million copies of that movie's soundtrack album were sold—more than the sales of the previous top three all-time best-selling albums combined. (Those three were *Tapestry* by Carole King, *Rumours* by Fleetwood Mac, and *Inna Gadda Da Vida* by Iron Butterfly.) *Saturday Night Fever* was number 1 on the album charts for twenty-four consecutive weeks, an incredible feat for a double album with a list price of over ten dollars. From November 23, 1977, through May 6, 1978, the Bee Gees always had at least one of the top three singles. For five weeks in March and April the Bee Gees held down both the number 1 and the number 2 positions. For one glorious week they were able to claim that they had a hand in five of the records in the top ten. The Bee Gees virtually owned 1978 much the way Elvis had stolen 1956 and the Beatles had dominated 1964. But they were not newcomers to the rock scene. By the time *Saturday Night Fever* was released, the Brothers Gibb had been performing together for twenty-one years.

Like the mythical Phoenix the Bee Gees rose from the ashes of a shattered career to climb rock's summit a second time.

The Bee Gees made their performing debut in December 1956 at the Gaumont Theater in Manchester, England, where lip-synching to hit records between movies was the rage. Ten-year-old Barry Gibb and his seven-year-old twin brothers, Robin and Maurice, had practiced all week with Barry's real guitar and Robin's and Maurice's homemade replicas. When they finally took the stage at the Saturday matinee, disaster struck. The sound man at the theater broke their record. But the Gibb Brothers hesitated for only a moment and quickly broke into three-part harmony. The theater manager promised them bus fare home if they would sing at his Odeon Theater as well. Their careers were born.

In 1957 The Gibb family moved to Australia, partly because times were tough for their bandleader father and partly to keep the mischievous boys out of reform school. The brothers debuted in Australia at a racetrack in Brisbane, singing between the races. They quickly graduated to nightclubs and became the darlings of Australia, not unlike America's Osmond Brothers.

Unfortunately, the Bee Gees recorded ten flop singles in a row in Australia. They couldn't even buy a hit record, although they did try: They figured that if they sold just 400 records in one week, they could break into Australia's top forty. They begged and borrowed two hundred dollars, then sent it to the six members of their fan club to go on a Bee Gees record-buying spree. For their efforts, "Wine and Women" hit number 35 on the charts. When they finally realized that they couldn't make it down under, the Bee Gees decided to go back to England to seek success. Ironically, on the day they left for England their single "Spicks and Specks" became the number-1 song in Australia.

Before leaving Australia the Brothers Gibb took on drummer Colin Petersen and guitarist Vince Melouney. Considering a name change to "Rupert's World," they mailed tapes of their songs to all the management firms in England. At NEMS, the Beatles' company, Brian Epstein and his lieutenant, Robert Stigwood, decided to listen to a few unsolicited tapes for the hell of it. Impressed with the Bee Gees tape, a hungover Robert Stigwood arranged an audition for the band at the Seville Theater in London, where the concert scenes in *A Hard Day's Night* were filmed. Looking for a group to rival Epstein's, Stigwood signed the Bee Gees to a five-year contract and then cranked up his hype machine.

"New York Mining Disaster 1941" was sent to radio stations in America without a label. The sound was similar to some of the Beatles' haunting Sgt. Pepper work. In 1967 DJ Murray the K, who was once known as the fifth Beatle, was the guru of the newly born FM underground radio movement in New York. He announced to his audience that "New York Mining Disaster" was by the Beatles, recording as the Bee Gees. Robert Stigwood's strategy worked, and Barry, Robin, and Maurice received their first notice in America.

The Bee Gees made an instant impact on America with their Edwardian outfits and their distinctive sound, a close three-part harmony led by Robin's trembling vibrato. In 1967, a year of classic albums, their album *Bee Gees 1st* was a semiclassic. "To Love Somebody," a song Barry and Robin wrote with Otis Redding in mind, was a powerful, soulful hit. However, early on the Bee Gees found themselves in a musical rut. Every single from "I've Gotta Get a Message to You" to "I Started A Joke" was achingly slow and full of images of misery and suffering. One of their tours of America was cut short when Robin was allegedly hospitalized for nervous exhaustion. In truth, Robin was suffering from an acute case of slow ticket sales. Vince Melouney then suddenly quit the group. The Bee Gees had begun to self-destruct.

In the late sixties the personal lives of the Bee Gees fell into disarray. Robin became convinced that he was the true talent of the Bee Gees, so he opted for a solo career. Barry and Maurice had to have their older sister, Leslie, fill in for Robin on a TV show. Soon they were at each other's throats, battling each other in court. Colin Petersen joined in the fray, claiming sole right to the name the Bee Gees, which is short for Brothers Gibb. A judge threw Colin's claim out of court, and Colin sheepishly left the scattered ruins of the Bee Gees.

The battle among the brothers raged for two years before business pressures and their newly developed maturity brought them back together in 1971. They released "Lonely Days," their biggest record in

Robin, Barry, and Maurice Gibb—the Bee Gees.

America up to that time. "How Can You Mend a Broken Heart" then became their first number-1 song in the United States. However, these new songs were as gloomy as the old ones. Their albums *Trafalgar* and *Life in a Tin Can* were big losers. When they recorded *A Kick in the Head Is Worth Eight in the Pants* in 1973, Atlantic Records refused to release it. In desperation Robert Stigwood asked Arif Mardin, a respected rhythm-and-blues producer, to produce the next Bee Gees album, *Mr. Natural,* but even with Mardin's expertise the album stiffed. Of the three singles released from *Mr. Natural,* the best one peaked at number 90 on the top forty. By 1974 they were reduced to playing third-rate nightclubs in the north of England as an oldies act.

Atlantic Records had given up on the Bee Gees, but Arif Mardin convinced them to give the Bee Gees one last chance to record. In 1975 Arif sent the brothers to Miami's famous R & B recording studio, Criteria. He made the Bee Gees listen to the radio to find out what was really going on in the top-forty music scene. Arif demanded complete control over this last-chance album so that he could try to pull some soul out of one of the whitest and whiniest bands in rock. When Arif was called away for a week, he told the Bee Gees to try to write some songs in a new direction. Barry was struck by the "chucka-chucka-chucka" beat as he was driving over a bridge one day. This "chucka-chucka- chucka" became "Jive Talkin'," and the Bee Gees finally had a new sound.

The Bee Gees were soon to capture American audiences. Like a master surgeon in the studio, Arif Mardin worked on Barry Gibb and came up with a screaming, soulful falsetto. The *Main Course* album yielded the hit singles "Jive Talkin'," "Nights on Broadway," and "Fanny," and Mardin had brought the group back to life.

When Stigwood moved his label to Polygram at the end of 1975, Atlantic Records refused to let their staff producer Mardin work with the Bee Gees. Fearing that their new-found success was in jeopardy, the Gibb brothers quickly found Richard Perry, one of the best-known producers of the seventies, who had produced the likes of Ringo, Barbra Streisand, and Harry Nilsson. However, this association lasted less than three weeks, for Mardin convinced the Bee Gees that they had learned their lessons well on *Main Course* and were ready to produce themselves. Unable to read or write music themselves, the Bee Gees put together a production team with Karl Richardson and Albhy Galuten, who had a special talent for expressing the Bee Gees' musical ideas to professional musicians and who were also engineering wizards to boot. They got the sound they wanted and sent America to the dance floor with "Love So Right" and "You Should Be Dancin'." Although the Bee Gees called their music R & B, the rest of the world called it disco.

In 1977 the Gibb Brothers flew to Paris and the Château D'Herouville to mix their live album and start work on a new studio L.P. Stigwood called the brothers in Paris to ask them to write four songs for a movie that he was producing about the New York disco scene. With just the basic plot of the film the Bee Gees put together the music for *Saturday Night Fever* in less than a week.

As 1978 began, the Bee Gees dominated the music world as no group had since the Beatles. "How Deep Is Your Love," "Stayin' Alive," and "Night Fever" were consecutive number-1 singles. The Bee Gees also wrote and produced "If I Can't Have You" for Yvonne Elliman, which became the film's fourth number-1 song. They wrote and produced "I Just Wanna Be Your Everything" for younger brother Andy Gibb, and he soon joined his brothers at the top of the charts. Samantha Sang, a previously unknown singer from Australia, cut "Emotion" with the Bee Gees, and she, too, reached number 1. Barry Gibb wrote the title cut for Stigwood's film version of the Broadway musical about the fifties, *Grease,* and Frankie Valli took it to the top spot.

Twelve years younger than Barry and nine years younger than Robin and Maurice, Andy Gibb wasn't even in his teens when the Bee Gees had their first successes. Andy became a musical force in the late seventies on the strength of hits such as "(Love Is) Thicker Than Water," "(Our Love) Don't Throw It All Away," "Shadow Dancing," and the top-selling song of 1978, "I Just Wanna Be Your Everything"—all written and produced with the help of his older brothers. The Bee Gees weren't just standing by idly watching Andy's rise to the top. A powerfully produced single, "Tragedy," and two romantic songs, "Too Much Heaven" and "Love You Inside Out," kept the Brothers Gibb well supplied with platinum records in 1979, while two albums, *Spirits Having Flown* and *Bee Gees Greatest,* sold in the multimillions. All in all it was an unbelievable string of successes for a group that had faced the end of its recording career in 1975. Nineteen seventy-eight truly belonged to the Bee Gees.

1979

Nineteen seventy-nine was a turning point for rock and roll. When the year started, disco was the king of popular music. Disco radio stations flourished in many large cities. Old-line rock stars like the Beach Boys, Rod Stewart, the Kinks, and Paul McCartney and Wings hopped on the bandwagon, recording disco cuts. Disco monopolized the singles charts for the first six months of 1979. Even *Rolling Stone* magazine dedicated an entire issue to the disco craze in April.

Frustrated rock fans just couldn't see disco for what it actually was— another offshoot of rock and roll. In condemning disco, these bitter rockers sounded like anti-rock parents of the fifties, with their complaints that the music was unimaginative and monotonous. Nevertheless, people wanted to dance. Therefore rock went back to its roots and picked up the beat. Whether they called it power pop, or new wave, or disco-rock, rock and roll became dance music again. By the end of 1979 disco had been absorbed into rock and roll and was no longer a threat.

With all this change, music was vibrant and varied in 1979. There was the fresh pop sound of Nick Lowe's "Cruel to Be Kind." Dire Straits did the Dylanesque "Sultans of Swing," and band member Mark Knoffler went on to play on Dylan's *Slow Train Comin'*. "Chuck E's in Love" was a jazzy excursion from newcomer Rickie Lee Jones. Suzi Quatro and Chris Norman became the punk Sonny and Cher with "Stumblin' In." Supertramp topped the charts in the early summer with "The Logical Song," while the Little River Band came out of Australia with "Lady" and "Lonesome Loser." The suggestive Dr. Hook sang "When You're in Love with a Beautiful Woman, It's Hard." Amii Stewart did a supersyncopated disco remake of Eddie Floyd's "Knock on Wood," and the Pointer Sisters recorded a sizzling version of Bruce Springsteen's "Fire." Hot Chocolate summed up the scene in 1979 with "Every 1's a Winner."

The top ten singles for 1979 included: "My Sharona" by the Knack, "Le Freak" by Chic, "Bad Girls" by Donna Summer, "Do Ya Think I'm Sexy" by Rod Stewart, "I Will Survive" by Gloria Gaynor, "YMCA" by the Village People, "Hot Stuff" by Donna Summer, "Ring My Bell" by Anita Ward, "Sad Eyes" by Robert John, and "Reunited" by Peaches and Herb.

In sports, Willie Stargell and the Pittsburgh Pirates adopted "We Are Family" by Sister Sledge as their theme song and conquered the Baltimore Orioles in the World Series. Those who bet on the Los Angeles Rams in Super Bowl XIV could have taken "What a Fool Believes" by the Doobie Brothers as their theme, for in 1979 the Pittsburgh Steelers grabbed their fourth Super Bowl title in six years. In basketball, the

430

Britain's Dire Straits broke onto the scene in 1979 with their Dylanesque "Sultans of Swing."

Australian hit-makers, the Little River Band (back row, left to right: David Briggs, Glenn Shorrock, George McArdle, Graham Goble; forefront from left: Beeb Birtles and Derek Pellicci). Little River Band made their first big splash in America in 1978 with "Help Is on the Way" and "Happy Anniversary." LRB stayed "radioactive" in 1979 with the top-ten smashes "Reminiscing," "Lady," and "Lonesome Loser."

Rickie Lee Jones—a runaway from Chicago who found peace and stardom in Los Angeles, thanks in part to her hit single "Chuck E's in Love."

431

Seattle Supersonics snatched the NBA title away from the Washington Bullets.

In the movies, *Kramer vs. Kramer* won the Oscar over *All That Jazz,* Francis Ford Coppola's Vietnam War epic *Apocalypse Now, Norma Rae,* and the year's sleeper, *Breaking Away.* In 1979, television offered the bigger-than-life soap opera *Dallas,* the hillbilly antics of *The Dukes of Hazzard,* and the inane realism of *Real People.* It was also the year of TV's most expensive night, February 11. *Gone With the Wind, One Flew over the Cuckoo's Nest*—two Academy Award–winning movies— were beaten in the ratings game by Dick Clark's film, *Elvis—The King of Rock and Roll.*

The real-life theme song of 1979 should have been the Bee Gees' "Tragedy." The nuclear power plant at Three Mile Island spewed radioactive steam into the air around Harrisburg, Pennsylvania, threatening a meltdown in March. As Skylab crashed to earth, gold prices skyrocketed, reaching eight hundred dollars an ounce by January 1980. An American Airlines DC-10 crashed in Chicago on May 25, killing 275 passengers and grounding all DC-10's for the summer. Chrysler was in such a bad way that it needed a government handout in December to stay in business.

But the biggest tragedy of 1979 came from the Persian Gulf. On January 16, the Shah of Iran was overthrown, leading to the creation of an Islamic state headed by the fanatical religious leader Ayatollah Khomeini. The turmoil in Iran caused a gasoline shortage in America, and gas-station lines became a way of life. Gasoline prices doubled in just one year. Then, in November, Iranian "students" stormed the U.S. Embassy in Tehran, seizing fifty-two American hostages. While Iranian leaders turned a deaf ear to American and U.N. negotiators, world peace was further threatened in the last week of 1979 by the Soviet invasion of Iran's neighbor, Afghanistan.

It was 1979—the twenty-fifth year of rock and roll.

ELVIS COSTELLO

"Rock and roll is the lowest form of life known to man."—ELVIS COSTELLO

Pop music came back with a vengence in 1979 as power pop and Elvis Costello was its avenging angel. This form blended the simplicity of punk and the strong commercial melodies of pop with clean production and sophisticated lyrics that bristled with satire, irony, and frustration. Elvis Costello was the angriest of 1979's power pop musicians because he loathed the overblown artistic pretenses of rock. He was bored by the incessant high-powered drone of the heavy-metal groups and put off by the artistic arrogance of punk. Costello thought that rock audiences had been put to sleep by ten years of "artsy" rock, so he aimed his nasty lyrics right at the jugular.

Elvis was born Declan Patrick McManus in London in 1955. His father, Ross McManus, had been a singer with the Joe Loss Orchestra. Declan was a lonely, frustrated teen-ager. One of his few pleasures was listening to rock and roll on the radio in bed under the sheets late at night. Short, awkward, bowlegged, and bespectacled, Declan became obsessed with his fumbling sexuality. He eventually tried to channel his frustrations and his love of rock by working as a roadie for the ill-fated English pub-rock group, Brinsley Schwartz.

After Brinsley Schwartz fell apart in February 1975, Declan got a job as a computer operator for a London cosmetics firm. He soon grew to hate that job. At age nineteen he married and was a father at age twenty-one. All the while he was determined to become a recording artist. Hauling his guitar with him, he would make the rounds of the London record companies, singing to executives in their offices. The record execs were simply bewildered by the odd-looking chap. The humiliation of daily rejection soured Declan. One day in 1976 Declan ran into his old mate

Elvis Costello.

433

An important British rocker in the Elvis Costello mold—Graham Parker, who records with the Rumour. *(John Wooding)*

Costello's producer and a power pop star in his own right—"The Jesus of Cool," Nick Lowe.

from Brinsley Schwartz, Nick Lowe, in the subway. Lowe suggested that his disillusioned friend try his luck at Jake Riviera's Stiff Records. In time Riviera did sign Declan, became his manager, and put him in the studio with Nick Lowe producing. Riviera also renamed him Elvis Costello, reasoning that this generation was ready for its own Elvis.

Elvis cut his first album, *My Aim Is True,* in just four six-hour recording sessions spread over a six-month period in 1977. Using a small crude demo studio to record the album, Elvis achieved a spare, lean texture. Costello's early sound reminds some of Bruce Springsteen, but his unsentimental, searing honesty and venom are uniquely Elvis. Costello's importance rests in his lyrics. They cut through the pap better than those of anyone else in rock. His next two albums, *This Year's Model* and *Armed Forces,* which featured his backup band, the Attractions, were more richly produced by Lowe to give Elvis a fuller, more commercial sound. American FM stations picked up on Elvis, turning him into something of a cult figure—just what he didn't want to be.

"I don't want to be a cult figure," he said. "I could be a cult figure very, very easily. I know the things I would have to do to make myself an acceptable cult figure. I've read the right magazines. I have the right albums. I'm not interested in that. I want to make records that get on the radio all the time." Elvis longed for AM top-forty recognition. He was obsessed with the fact that he'd never had a hit single in America. He'd come close with "Alison," a sterling love song from his first album. Released at the end of 1977, "Alison" was played on RKO Radio's chain of top-forty stations, sparking interest in Costello's first album but never really breaking through on its own. Linda Ronstadt recorded a version of "Alison" in 1978 on her *Living in the U.S.A.* album and had a hit with it. Elvis came close to having a hit again in 1979 with "Oliver's Army," a jaunty rocker about mercenary soldiers, but his use of the word "nigger" in the song turned off too many radio stations. It was not the last time that word would get Elvis Costello in trouble.

In March 1979, while on an extended American tour, Elvis entered a bar in Columbus, Ohio, after a concert date. In the same bar were Bonnie Bramlett, Stephen Stills, and their entourage—exactly the kind of "pompous" rock stars Costello couldn't stand. Half drunk and itching for trouble, Elvis began to taunt Stills and Bramlett, berating America, calling James Brown "a jive-ass nigger" and shouting that Ray Charles was "nothing but a blind, ignorant nigger." The well-publicized brawl that followed boosted ticket sales on his sagging tour, but alienated many rock fans. However, one couldn't help feeling that Costello, who was a headliner at a Rock Against Racism concert in Britain in 1978, was playing a role for the press.

Costello and his manager, Jake Riviera, seem to enjoy manipulating Elvis' image. Elvis Costello the angry young lout. Elvis Costello the rock star who won't talk to the press or discuss his past. Elvis Costello, who insults his audience in concert, plays short sets, and deliberately turns on a high-pitched screech just to clear the theater. However, it remains to be seen whether this man with the contrived looks of a wimpy Buddy Holly and a passion to be the new king of rock can forget about his image and concentrate on his music.

Elvis adopted a new low-profile image in 1980, but hung on to his lean, mean brand of rock and roll. He decided to give his fans value for their dollars and recorded twenty—count 'em, twenty—songs for his album *Get Happy.* The music on *Get Happy* sounded familiar—it seems as if Costello had borrowed popular riffs from the entire rock spectrum. While he didn't exactly put away his venom, his lyrics pointed to a more mature Elvis. Paradoxically, *Get Happy* showed a sadder but wiser Costello. While the album wasn't the smash hit he was looking for, maybe it was a step in the right direction for the new wave's wayward son, Elvis Costello.

Blondie (from left: Gary Valentine, Clement Burke, Deborah Harry, Chris Stein, and Jimmy Destri).

BLONDIE

Deborah Ann Harry is *not* Blondie—she's one member of the group called Blondie. But take away her seductive presence, her sardonic vocals, and her bleached blond glamor, and what do you have left? A tight but unremarkable band. Sex sells. Little Deborah knew that when she made her singing debut in sixth grade, soloing on "I Love You Truly." So though Blondie is the band, perhaps Deborah Harry really *is* Blondie.

Born in Miami in the mid-forties, Deborah was raised in Hawthorne, New Jersey. As a teen-ager, Deborah was attracted to the progressive energy of New York's art and rock cultures. She moved to Manhattan after high school and tried anything that was considered hip at the time. She joined a folk-rock group, Wind in the Willows, when folk rock was in. While writing and painting, Deborah took a job as a beautician and later became a Playboy Bunny. For a time she ran with Andy Warhol's crowd and slipped into her heroin phase at this time. Ironically, she also worked as a barmaid at Max's Kansas City, an underground nightclub to which she would eventually return as a star.

In the mid-seventies Deborah hooked up with the Stilettos, a campy female glitter trio who played in Manhattan punk clubs like CBGB's. Shortly after she started singing with the Stilettos, guitarist Chris Stein joined the band, and they soon became very close. When the Stilettos closed up shop, Harry and Stein decided to form a new band with Jimmy Destri on keyboards, Gary Valentine on bass, and, on drums, Stein's high school buddy from New Jersey, Clem Burke, whose uncle, by the way, once drummed for Joey Dee. Deborah and Chris, the only members with any real professional rock experience, led the crew that became Blondie in 1975.

Blondie's sound was a lively sixties' pop style influenced by some of the great forgotten groups of that era like the Knickerbockers ("Lies"), the Cryan'

Shames ("Sugar and Spice"), and the McCoys ("Hang On Sloopy"). Their sound enticed producer Richard Gottehrer, who had played in one of those forgotten bands, the Strangeloves ("I Want Candy," 1965; "Night Time," 1966), and had produced "Hang On Sloopy" for the McCoys and "My Boyfriend's Back" for the Angels. Gottehrer liked the band's petulant stance, Harry's provocative but trashy looks, and the kooky lyrics that raised Blondie a step or two above the rest of New York's punk bands. Gottehrer lined up the band with a small New York label owned by Larry Uttal, Private Stock, and coproduced Blondie's first single, "X Offender." The single didn't sell, but Uttal gave them the go-ahead for an album, figuring that this New York phenomenon was a good bet. That first album released in 1976, *Blondie,* featured such deathless classics as "The Attack of the Giant Ants," "Rip Her to Shreds," and "Kung Fu Girls." It did not take the country by storm.

After a tour of England in May 1977 and a swing opening for Iggy Pop and David Bowie, Blondie became something of a sensation in Europe. Strangely enough, Europeans saw Deborah Harry as the typical American girl-next-door. Gary Valentine left Blondie in a huff in July 1977, complaining that he couldn't keep his artistic integrity intact with the group. Stein, the Rasputin of the group, known as such for his undisputed leadership of the group and for the complete control he had over Deborah, quickly replaced him with another old friend from New Jersey, Frank Infante. Stein thought the band should cash in on Deborah's vacuous allure, so an album of tongue-in-cheek eroticism, *Plastic Letters,* was released in late 1977. When Deborah sang Blondie's remake of Randy and the Rainbows' 1963 hit "Denise," she sang it partly in French—it had been transformed into a love song for a young Frenchman named Denis. It was smart-ass rock and roll with a lively pop beat, but Private Stock just couldn't give

Blondie the promotion they deserved. In September 1977 Blondie's management bought out their contract with Private Stock for half a million dollars, and Blondie signed up with Chrysalis Records.

After a five-month tour of Europe, Australia, Thailand, and Japan, Blondie went to work on their next album with producer Michael Chapman. With Nicky Chinn, Chapman had produced a string of highly commercial, mindless pop and rock smashes in England in the early seventies for artists like the Sweet and Suzi Quatro. Now working alone in Los Angeles, Chapman moved Blondie in his relentlessly commercial direction, but preserved the group's avant-garde aura. The result was *Parallel Lines,* which was released in September 1978. *Parallel Lines* was a time bomb just waiting to explode. Although its first single, a supercharged rave-up of Buddy Holly's "I'm Gonna Love You Too," fell on deaf ears and the follow-up, "Hanging on the Telephone," was a big hit only in Europe, the disco single, "Heart of Glass," hit big in the early spring of 1979. With its Eurodisco "popcorn" production, a bass line Chris Stein lifted from the James Bond *Goldfinger* soundtrack, and irresistible vocals by Deborah Harry, "Heart of Glass" charmed new wavers, disco jet-setters, and rock fans alike. It was the number-1 single in the nation in April. *Parallel Lines* went platinum on the strength of "Heart of Glass."

Blondie was the first commercial triumph for new wave in America, and Deborah Harry became the media's newest darling. Even though the band was often hostile with the press, Deborah's photogenic face appeared everywhere from teen-age fan magazines and *Rolling Stone* to *People* and *Penthouse.* Putting their sleazy new-wave days behind them, Blondie cultivated a new international, clever, trendy image. Deborah was presented as a jet-setting airhead, making the scene at Studio 54 and discoing with Wilt "The Stilt" Chamberlain in L.A. Deborah, the most striking female rock star since Linda Ronstadt, was suddenly inundated with movie offers. She appeared in the low-budget epic *Union City* and the star-studded *Roadie* with Alice Cooper, Meat Loaf, and Art Carney.

In the fall of 1979 Blondie released *Eat to the Beat.* Deborah's eerie, zombielike vocals had a bit more emotion and passion on this new album, which featured Blondie's usual kinky, ironic, snide lyrics and Mike Chapman's golden production. *Eat to the Beat* was also rock's first full-length video cassette album, presenting dramatic images, close-ups of Deborah, and shots of the band in concert to go with the album's twelve tracks. "Dreaming," the album's first single, bounced into the top twenty by the year's end. "The Hardest Part," "Union City Blue," and "Accidents Never Happen" (Blondie's answer to Elvis Costello's "Accidents Will Happen"), were also on *Eat to the Beat.*

After *Eat to the Beat* Blondie signed up to sing the theme song to the movie *American Gigolo,* entitled "Call Me." Written and produced by Giorgio Moroder, one of the masterminds behind Donna Summer's career, "Call Me" was a rousing blend of disco and power pop, burying everything in its path on its way to a long stay in the number-1 slot in the spring of 1980. While the group was divided between casting their fortunes with Mike Chapman or Giorgio Moroder, Deborah Harry decided to cash in as the commercial spokeswoman for Gloria Vanderbilt jeans.

Mike Chapman won the battle to remain Blondie's producer, and in November 1980 the group released their new epic, *AutoAmerican.* Deftly produced by Chapman, the new album had a variety and range that was lacking in *Eat to the Beat.* Sounding like a reggae band in Tijuana, Blondie scored with the infectious rhythm of "The Tide Is High," which streaked its way up the singles chart at the close of 1980. Blondie made it back-to-back number-1 smashes when their hilarious parody of disco-rap records, "Rapture," featuring a gluttonous man from Mars, topped the charts. In 1981 Deborah sang the title track for the offbeat film *Polyester,* which starred Tab Hunter and everyone's favorite transvestite, Divine. Chris Stein composed the music.

Blondie's tight power-pop sound, laden with tasty hooks, made for snappy, lively rock and roll. Their melodies are elusively sweet, their harmonies pleasantly spacey, and their lyrics sardonically humorous. There is every indication that they will continue to grace the airwaves through the eighties.

OPPOSITE PAGE:

Cheap Trick (from left: Rick Neilsen, Tom Petersson, Robin Zander, and Bun E. Carlos). *(Jim Houghton)*

CHEAP TRICK

They are, after all, rock and roll's answer to Japanese horror movies. Cheap Trick is like a gross larger-than-life cartoon. It's no surprise that Cheap Trick is Japan's favorite band. Like a Japanese monster movie, Cheap Trick is carefully costumed and marketed. In fact, despite some stiff competition, Cheap Trick may be rock's most contrived group of 1979. To gain publicity the band tried to create an exotic past for themselves. They were billed as "the band with no past." Then they spread rumors that they were originally from Europe and Venezuela. The next rumor was that Cheap Trick were American exiles.

The truth of the matter is that all the members of Cheap Trick—Rick Neilsen, Robin Zander, Bun E. Carlos, and Tom Petersson—hail from Rockford, Illinois. Based in Madison, Wisconsin, they spent years playing bars in Wisconsin and northern Illinois, paying their rock-and-roll dues.

With his rubber face, big eyes, bowtie, baseball cap, and idiotic grin, Rick Neilsen is the Huntz Hall of rock and roll. Neilsen is the group's buffoon, playing three guitars simultaneously onstage, throwing countless guitar picks into the audience, and constantly mugging. In fact Rick is the most calculating of the bunch. Success is his passion, and he'll play his fool's role to the hilt to make it. His wild, windmill guitar chords are reminiscent of the Who's Peter Townshend's. Not only do they make for good visuals, they cover up any deficiencies in Rick's musical ability. As the songwriter and cofounder of the group, he is the acknowledged leader of Cheap Trick.

It is the bass playing of Tom Petersson, the handsome sex symbol of the group, that cements Cheap Trick's sound and allows Neilsen to carry on onstage. Tom played with Neilsen in a group called Fuse in 1966. (Fuse, incidentally, was supposed to be Otis Redding's opening act in Madison on the night his plane crashed in 1967.) Fuse cut a few singles and an unsuccessful album for Epic Records before Tom and Rick split for England. In 1969 Neilsen met Todd Rundgren, then with Nazz, in London. When Rick and Tom returned to America, they traveled to Philadelphia to look up Rundgren and found that Nazz had disintegrated. Ex-Nazz members Thom Mooney and Robert "Stewkey" Antoni joined up with Rick and Tom, but Mooney left their aggregation a few months later. Heading back to Rockford to find a new drummer, Rick and Tom came up with Bun E. Carlos.

Overweight and jowly, with his tie loosened and a cigarette dangling from his lower lip, Bun E. Carlos has the look of a disheveled malevolent South American coffee-bean trader. The last thing he looks like is a rock-and-roll drummer. He is really Brad Carlson, prominent Rockford record collector and the son of a roofer. In high school Brad played with a local

band called the Pagans. After college and some traveling in Europe he returned to Rockford to join his father's roofing empire. Neilsen and Petersson saved Brad from a lifetime of roofing and siding when they formed the band Sick Man of Europe with "Stewkey" Antoni. When Antoni didn't pan out, Sick Man of Europe found itself in need of a lead singer. Their hunt led them to Robin Zander.

Zander, the youngest member of the band, was born in Rockford in 1953 and grew up just outside the city limits. He quit school at sixteen and headed for Scotland. Upon returning to the States, Robin supported himself by doing impressions of rock singers at a resort in Wisconsin Dells, a vacation area outside of Madison. He made a name for himself with his repertoire of rock voices. When Sick Man of Europe first asked him to join their ranks, Robin told them that he preferred Wisconsin Dells. Sick Man wouldn't take no for an answer, though. In 1974 Zander hopped on board, and the band changed its name to Cheap Trick. Robin is the cute blonde counterpoint to the tall, dark, and sexy Petersson. For his character in Cheap Trick, Zander wears a three-piece suit, adopting an image similar to Roxy Music's Bryan Ferry. Robin also resembles a home-grown version of David Bowie's Thin White Duke.

After playing bars and opening concerts for two years, Cheap Trick signed with Epic Records in 1976. Their first album, *Cheap Trick,* produced by Aerosmith's producer, Jack Douglas, was an excursion into heavy metal. It did not set the world on fire. On their second album, *In Color,* Cheap Trick switched producers and concentrated on melody instead of volume, but the public still wasn't buying. A clever publicity campaign that compared Cheap Trick with the Beatles didn't help their third album, *Heaven Tonight,* which also stiffed.

Although they made little headway in America, Cheap Trick became the hottest rock band in Japan. Cheap Trick was the ideal band for Japanese society. The Japanese elders don't exactly welcome rock and roll, but they are willing to tolerate Cheap Trick. They consider the group cute and nonthreatening without the pseudoviolent, antisocial, drug-crazed posturings of the likes of Alice Cooper or Kiss. Also, Japanese girls fell for Cheap Trick in a big way. Robin, Tom, Rick, and Bun became idols in the Far East.

On their tour of Japan in April 1978 Cheap Trick recorded a live album intended for their Japanese audience only. The group felt that the quality of the recording was not good enough for an American release. *Live at Budokan* was really a Cheap Trick greatest-hits album that presented all the excitement of their stage show. While Neilsen may not have written enough solid songs to carry any one of Cheap

Trick's studio albums, there were certainly enough good, weird tunes like the melodic "I Want You to Want Me" and the sardonic rocker "Surrender" to fill a live album. The music was so good on *Live at Budokan* that Americans started buying the Japanese imports. Epic was caught with its pants down, but *Live at Budokan* was quickly rushed into production in America and eventually went platinum. "I Want You to Want Me" was released as a single and shot into the top ten. America suddenly recognized Cheap Trick.

Cheap Trick had a new studio album ready for release when *Live at Budokan* broke, but Epic decided to sit on it until *Budokan* peaked. By the time *Dream Police* was finally released, though, in the fall of 1979, the band's situation had changed. Cheap Trick now had to at least match *Live at Budokan,* and *Dream Police* was an unfortunate disappointment. In 1980 Cheap Trick hooked up with the Beatles' former producer George Martin for the album *All Shook Up. All Shook Up* opened by finally completing the last chord of *Sgt. Pepper's* "A Day in the Life" and then roared into a flashy rocker, "Stop This Game." Unfortunately the rest of the album came up empty. Once again Neilsen didn't have enough good material to flesh out an album, but don't write them off just yet. Cheap Trick may eventually have enough good material to do *Budokan, Volume Two.* Stay tuned.

THE CARS

The story of the Cars starts not in Detroit but in Baltimore with Ric Ocasek. Ric grew up in a tough Baltimore neighborhood and ran with some of the local youth gangs as a kid. By the time he reached fifth grade he had already been kicked out of school and was playing a guitar that his grandmother had given him. Ric somehow managed to get into college, dropping in and out of Antioch College and Bowling Green University. At this time Ric started writing songs and formed a number of bands just so he could hear his songs played.

In 1970 Ric met Ben Orr at a jam session. Ben was trained as a percussionist, but had learned to play guitar and bass in numerous bands in Ohio. He had quit high school in order to write songs and do session work, performing and producing. Eventually he landed a gig with the house band on a TV rock-and-dance show in Cleveland. Of all his talents it was Ben's distinctive voice that impressed Ric Ocasek most.

In Ohio, Ric and Ben played as a duo and in various groups, doing rock, folk, and even country, but never finding the success they were seeking. In 1972 they headed for Boston and that area's thousands of college students. In Boston, Ben and Ric became part of a folk trio called Milkwood and actually put out an album, *Milkwood,* in 1972. At these Milkwood sessions they met the multitalented Greg Hawkes, who joined them in a short-lived band called Richard and the Rabbits. Hawkes moved on to a local country-rock group called Orphan, then hooked up with comedian Martin Mull and his Fabulous Furniture back in the days when Mull toured with a sofa, a loveseat, and an easy chair.

For Ric and Ben it was a succession of odd jobs in many odd bands until they formed Cap'n Swing in 1976 with southpaw guitarist Elliot Easton, who had studied at the Berkeley School of Music in Boston. When WBCN-FM disc jockey Maxanne Sartori began playing Cap'n Swing's demo tapes, the band started getting favorable press. But a series of disastrous performances in New York told Ocasek and Orr that it was time for some remodeling. Easton was asked to stay on, and Hawkes was offered the keyboard slot after his stint with Mull. With the addition of drummer David Robinson, who was a founding member of the avant-garde Modern Lovers and a member of Boston punk band DMZ, the Cars were ready to roll.

The Cars made their debut on New Year's Eve, 1976, at Pease Air Force Base in New Hampshire. They were now precise and marketable. For the next three months they played regular club dates at the Rat, Boston's premier new-wave club, and eventually opened and then headlined at the Paradise, Boston's leading rock emporium at the time. With the Cars opening concerts for Bob Seger, the J. Geils Band, Nils Lofgren, and Foreigner, they became Boston's most talked-about new band. During the summer of 1977 a Cars demo tape was so heavily requested on Boston's progressive rock radio stations that the record industry couldn't help but notice. The cut "Just What I Needed" received so much airplay in Boston that it was listed in the national trade papers even though it wasn't available on record. Record companies began courting the Cars and Elektra signed the band to a contract in November 1977.

The Cars traveled to London in February 1978 to record their first album with producer Roy Thomas Baker, who was well-known for his work with Queen. Taking only twelve days to record and nine days to mix, *The Cars* was released to an unsuspecting public in May 1978. The halting vocal of "Just What I Needed" was followed up the charts by "My Best Friend's Girl," a breathless tribute to an ex-girlfriend. The Cars' blend of pop, rock, and new wave, with their chunky rhythms, crisp arrangements, and urgent, ironic lyrics, earned them a platinum album and a Grammy nomination for Best New Artists of 1978. The band won widespread popular support by cutting through the sharp musical divisions of the late seventies and combining early and contemporary rock influences in a sparse, witty package.

The Cars released their follow-up album, *Candy-O,* in the early summer of 1979. Using producer Baker again, the band completed *Candy-O* in just sixteen days. Drummer Dave Robinson brought famed pin-up artist Vargas out of retirement to paint their album cover of a scantily clad woman provoca-tively reclining on a car. *Candy-O* yielded one superb single, "Let's Go," a throbbing number about a hot seventeen-year-old girl. Even though *Candy-O* went platinum in August 1979, the album was somewhat disappointing. The group seemed remote on this album, showing signs of stiffness, predictability, and an enigmatic glibness. The group will have to add a touch of freshness and vitality to the futuristic flash of *The Cars* and *Candy-O* if they are to ride the road to success in the 1980s.

The Cars (from left: Ric Ocasek, Greg Hawkes, David Robinson, Benjamin Orr, and Elliot Easton). *(Jeff Albertson)*

443

THE KNACK

Once upon a time rock and roll was fun. Rock and roll was teen-age music about teen-age problems. It was Chuck Berry itching to get out of class in "School Days," the Beach Boys' girl friend who was grounded when her daddy took the T-bird away in "Fun, Fun, Fun," and the Beatles checking out the action at a dance in "I Saw Her Standing There." The music made you feel good because it talked right to you. But somewhere along the line it all became a big industry, and rock critics, not fans, became the tastemakers. The music now dealt with itself rather than with the people who listened to it. Rock became George Harrison bitching about his taxes in "Taxman," and The Who fretting over writer's block in "Guitar and Pen." What rock needed was a good airing out. In 1979 the music finally got its needed breath of fresh air—the Knack.

The Knack are Doug Fieger, Berton Averre, Bruce Gary, and Prescott Niles. They play hot, nasty, commercial teen-age rock and roll, songs often about wanting sex and not getting it. The Knack does not do Art. They do teen-age songs about teen-age girls. Their return to the basics brought the Knack the best-selling single of 1979, "My Sharona," and the fastest-selling debut album since *Meet the Beatles.* That may sound easy, but it took Doug Fieger eight years to get a record company to even listen.

The tale of the Knack starts with Doug Fieger, who went to L.A. in 1971 from Detroit with the soft-rock band Sky, determined to make it in the music biz. Sky split up after two albums, leaving Fieger in L.A. without fame or fortune. Doug was anxious to play his commercial pop songs for teen-age audiences, but the record moguls just weren't buying. In 1974 he met Berton Averre, and they eventually recorded a demo that included Doug's songs "Good Girls Don't" and "That's What the Little Girls Do." Record execs scoffed at them, calling their efforts "novelty songs" that would never sell. Doug then headed to

Germany to play bass for a high-tech electronic band called Triumvirate. He returned to the States to do an album with the Sunset Bombers, but still no one would let him play his kind of rock and roll. In 1978 Doug, Berton, and old friend and popular session drummer Bruce Gary cut some more demos. Again the record companies turned them down, but Doug, Bruce, and Berton knew that their sound was right. They decided to play the L.A. club scene to make a name for themselves and then let the record companies come to them. Inviting New York bass player Prescott Niles to join them, the Knack was ready to rock.

The Knack's aim was to make rock and roll that made you feel good, and they were certainly making little girls in Southern California feel just that. A group of Beverly Hills high school girls began to follow the band around, calling themselves the Knackettes. With a decided passion for young girls, the Knack dated the Knackettes, and soon Fieger and Averre were writing songs about their Lolitas, most notably Doug's sometime flame, Sharona Alperin. But little girls weren't the only ones turned on to the Knack. The group became the hottest act on Sunset Strip; rock stars like Bruce Springsteen, Stephen Stills, Eddie Money, Tom Petty, and Ray Manzarek would frequently jam with them at club dates. Sure enough, the record companies picked up the scent and started flashing recording contracts. But Fieger said he wouldn't go for the biggest contract; he wanted the band to sign with the label that "felt the best." Fieger declared, "When I first saw the Beatles, I didn't just want to be a musician—I wanted to be a *Beatle,* a big star." Therefore the Knack went with the label that made them feel most like the Beatles, Capitol Records, who even resurrected their Beatle-era logo for the group.

Doug Fieger had waited eight years to put his songs on wax, so the Knack was ready to start

recording immediately. With the hottest producer of 1979, Mike Chapman, who had produced Blondie and Suzi Quatro, among others, the Knack entered the recording studio in April and walked out eleven days later with *Get the Knack.* Deciding not to use overdubs or studio gimmickry, the band turned out the finished version of "My Sharona" in just three hours—less time than it takes some bands just to set up in the studio. While it had cost over $460,000 for drum tracks alone on Fleetwood Mac's *Tusk* L.P., the Knack did their entire album for $18,000.

Featuring some of the crispest, most exciting, and most listenable rock and roll of the year, *Get the Knack* was a refreshing event in the summer of 1979. "My Sharona," their first single, took off like a rocket. The record was distinguished by Bruce Gary's solid beat and some super guitar work. With Roger Daltrey's "My Generation" stutter, Fieger sang a smirking tribute to his high school honey with lyrics like "I always get it up for the touch of the younger kind," making "My Sharona" teen-age rock and roll at its best.

With its Beatle-ish "I Should've Known Better" harmonica opening, "Good Girls Don't" was the second Knack single to scramble up the charts. Even though AM radio made the Knack replace the words "sitting on your face" with "put you in your place," they couldn't change the sweaty, humping flavor of the song. Capitol wanted to release "(She's So) Selfish"— by far the nastiest and most up-front cut

The Knack (from left: Bruce Gary, Doug Fieger, Prescott Niles, and Berton Averre). *(Courtesy of Capitol Records. Photo: Randee St. Nicholas. Copyright 1979 Capitol Records, Inc.)*

on the album—as a single in time for the Christmas record sales. Good taste would demand they cut out the most scatological references. The Knack refused to cut up another single and vetoed the release, to Capitol's chagrin.

In February 1980 the Knack released their second album, *But the Little Girls Understand,* the title of which was taken from the Doors' (and Willie Dixon's) "Back Door Man." It featured a tribute to the Phil Spector wall of sound, "The Feeling I Get"; an Elvis-type rockabilly number, "Tell Me You're Mine"; and a "Sharona" sound-alike single, "Baby Talks Dirty." It was a surprisingly good second effort, but the rock press, turned off by the Knack's contrived image, panned *But the Little Girls Understand.* At a conference where he was discussing the large sums of money it takes to produce a rock album, Knack producer Mike Chapman was asked what *But the Little Girls Understand* had cost. Chapman quipped, with deadly accuracy, "my reputation."

The Knack are experts on the Beatles, but they take offense when they are called Beatle imitators. Perhaps Berton Averre put it best: "Asking a new band if they're trying to be like the Beatles is like asking a rookie outfielder if he's trying to be like Babe Ruth. The answer is an obvious yes."

445

The Sound of 1979

DONNA SUMMER

La Donna Andrea Gaines always thought that she was something special when she was growing up in Roxbury, Massachusetts. Even the neighborhood shopkeepers felt that she would be rich and famous one day, so they often extended credit to her. One of seven children born to a butcher and his schoolteacher wife, La Donna wasn't allowed to solo in her church choir. Nevertheless, she knew that she had a powerful voice and that she would make it out of the ghetto. She was determined to become a real-life urban Cinderella.

At sixteen La Donna became the lead singer in a rock band called Crow, playing regularly at Boston's Psychedelic Supermarket. But as the only woman and the only black in the band, she felt intimidated. The pressures of the psychedelic rock scene led La Donna to the reckless lifestyle of her idol, Janis Joplin, with almost uncontrollable drug use and two hundred high school truancy notices. Dropping out of school in 1968, two months short of graduation, she gave up drugs cold turkey and landed a part in the European touring company of *Hair.* In late 1968 she moved from Roxbury to Munich.

Donna became well-known as a comedienne in Europe. She sang with the Vienna Folk Opera, where she met her husband, Austrian actor Helmut Sommer. While appearing in productions such as *Showboat, Porgy and Bess,* and *Godspell,* she also sang backup at Munich's Musicland Studios, where she got her first taste of the developing Eurodisco sound. At Musicland, Donna found not one but two Prince Charmings, record producers Giorgio Moroder and Pete Bellotte.

In the mid-seventies Donna was the clean-cut American girl, singing European hits. Just for a kick, in 1975 Donna cut "Love to Love You Baby" in her comic style. It didn't work. Moroder then challenged her to dramatize the song. "Don't sing," he said, "whisper and groan." In response Summer simulated twenty-two orgasms on a sixteen-minute, fifty-second record. He then sold the three-minute record to Neil Bogart, head of Casablanca, who agreed to release it. The record came out—and failed. Three months later Bogart played the record at a party. The machine got stuck and the record kept playing over and over. Everyone danced and loved it! Bogart realized the record needed to be much longer. He called Bellotte and asked him to rerecord it, making it twenty minutes long. Although the three–minute single didn't have any impact, this version of Donna's ecstatic moaning over Moroder and Bellotte's disco production sent shivers through American discos. Casablanca head Neil Bogart would soon give disco a sex goddess.

With her daughter, Mimi, Donna returned to America in 1975, divorced. At this time she was unable to cope with her new sexy identity. While Casablanca pictured her as Cleopatra and Marilyn Monroe on her seductive album covers, Donna Summer, the product of a straitlaced, churchgoing family, suffered from ulcers and temporary amnesia, and flirted with a nervous breakdown. Donna pulled herself together only to find that she had been branded a musical automaton. With her second gold single, "I Feel Love," the critics claimed that anyone could have had a hit with Moroder and Bellotte's synthesized production behind them. Although Donna struck a chord with the disco audience, the critics were slaying her.

Donna had expanded her musical horizons by 1977. Her *I Remember Yesterday* album explored the nostalgic swing-boogie sound of Dr. Buzzard's Savannah Band's "Cherchez la Femme." Her next album, *Once Upon a Time,* was a disco opera based on her own urban Cinderella fairy tale. Donna's version of "MacArthur Park Suite" breathed new life into the old Jim Webb-Richard Harris song about a lost recipe and the cake that washed away in the rain. In 1978 she was featured in the Casablanca-Motown disco movie *Thank God It's Friday,* singing "Last Dance." In the same way Lee Andrews and the Hearts' "Goodnight Sweetheart" had closed sock hops in the fifties and the Drifters' "Save the Last Dance for Me" had ended dances in the sixties, "Last Dance" was the ultimate disco finale in the late seventies. She was now dating Bruce Sudano, a member of Brooklyn Dreams, the disco-rock opening act on her 1978 tour. As 1979 approached, with the support of Sudano, Moroder, and Bellotte, Donna Summer vowed that she would no longer be just the queen of disco, but the princess of pop and rock as well.

The year opened with "Last Dance" winning the Oscar for Best Song of the Year, the Academy of Motion Picture Arts and Sciences apparently atoning for its 1978 snub of *Saturday Night Fever.* Donna started off the year with the gold single "Heaven Knows," a sizzling duet with Brooklyn Dreams' Bean Esposito. After a dispute with Casablanca, Donna Summer took more control of her career and collaborated on half the songs on *Bad Girls,* making a definite move toward rock. *Bad Girls* became a platinum triumph for Donna.

"Hot Stuff" scorched the airwaves in the late spring as the best single of 1979. Jeff Baxter, formerly of the Doobie Brothers and Steely Dan, provided the fiery guitar work as Donna pleaded for a lover to bring back home. The record transcended classification as even staunchly antidisco rock stations found themselves playing "Hot Stuff." Donna then accomplished a feat achieved only twice before in rock history. Like the Beatles in 1964 and the Bee Gees in 1978, Donna Summer had the top two records on the charts in the same week in July 1979 as the hook-laden, beeping, and tooting of "Bad Girls" chased "Hot Stuff" up the top ten. For a month "Hot Stuff" and "Bad Girls" remained two of the three top-selling records in the world.

The *Bad Girls* album jacket, which was designed by Donna, portrayed her as a hooker, her manager and Mrs. Neil Bogart (the wife of the president of the record company) as "bad girls," and producer Giorgio Moroder as her pimp. This was her answer to those who claimed that she prostituted her talent to accommodate her producer's vision. With *Bad Girls* Donna told the world that she knew what she was doing. *Bad Girls* was the biggest-selling album of early 1979, yielding three number-1 singles: "Dim All the Lights" as well as "Hot Stuff" and "Bad Girls."

Claiming that it was the only thing she'd ever really wanted to do, Donna hosted *American Bandstand* in 1979, the only person other than Dick Clark to do that since the early fifties.

Donna survived the sudden decline of disco, having caught a serious dose of rock and roll from her boyfriend Sudano. As the fall approached, she teamed up with Barbra Streisand on "Enough Is Enough." Although the two did battle during the recording session, Streisand introduced Summer to the pop world, while Donna allowed Barbra to flirt with disco. Together they had a number-1 hit record.

Donna Summer ended 1979 as hot as she began it. Her double-disc greatest-hits album, *On the Radio,* was the top-selling album in November and December, and the single "On the Radio" was added to her growing string of gold records. Donna Summer had survived disco to become the top female singer in the business. In 1979 Summer lasted all year long.

In 1980 Summer and Bogart had a split and they are presently involved in a lawsuit involving not only Neil Bogart but his wife, Joyce, who was Summer's manager. Summer has announced she is now a born-again Christian and has released her new album with David Geffen Records.

Donna Summer on Dick Clark's *Live Wednesday.* (Courtesy of Dick Clark)

1980

Tensions increased throughout the world in 1980. Despite an aborted rescue attempt in April in which eight American soldiers died, fifty-two Americans remained the hostages of Iranian militants for the entire year. A border war between Iran and Iraq flared, but did nothing to speed the release of the kidnapped Americans. Despite worldwide protest, the Russians continued to occupy Afghanistan in 1980. Worker revolts in Poland led to the formation of free trade unions and a clamoring by Poles for even greater freedoms. This led Russia to send troops to the borders of Poland in December, and the threat of invasion hung in the air.

After what seemed like an endless campaign, Ronald Reagan swept past incumbent Jimmy Carter and independent John Anderson to win the Presidency. The Republicans won control of the Senate for the first time since 1954. As interest rates soared to new highs, Mount St. Helens blew its top in the first volcanic eruption in America in this century. While the Midwest and South were scorched by a killer heatwave, Voyager I sent home dazzling color photos of Saturn.

The United States beamed with glory as the U.S. hockey team defeated the heavily favored Russian squad and swept to a gold medal in the Winter Olympics at Lake Placid, New York. Eric Heiden was another American golden boy, winning five gold medals in speed skating. The United States boycotted the Summer Olympics in Moscow to protest the Soviet invasion of Afghanistan. In other sports, the Philadelphia Phillies held off George Brett and the Kansas City Royals to win their first World Series in 97 years. Magic Johnson led the Los Angeles Lakers to the NBA championship, while the Oakland Raiders bested the Philadelphia Eagles in Super Bowl XV.

On television, the question of the year was, Who shot J.R.? as *Dallas* climbed to the top of the ratings. The spectacle of the miniseries *Shōgun* came in the same year that the tube offered *That's Incredible* and endless designer jeans commercials. On the silver screen, *The Empire Strikes Back* continued the *Star Wars* saga while *Ordinary People* and *Raging Bull* earned deserved honors. And in December the Academy of Television Arts and Sciences presented a special award to Dick Clark to commemorate his thirtieth year in television.

Rock and roll was marked with tragedy on December 8 when John Lennon, one of rock's greatest musicians, was murdered in New York City. John's death brought the greatest mass spontaneous outpouring of grief since John F. Kennedy was assassinated in 1963 as thousands flocked to the streets to pay their last respects to the former Beatle.

Perhaps as a final tribute to John, *Double Fantasy,* his first album in six years, became the best-selling L.P. in the country.

Rock wasn't all tragedy in 1980. Christopher Cross made his debut with two smashes, "Ride Like the Wind" and "Sailing." Second-generation rocker Rocky Burnette, Johnny Burnette's son and Dorsey Burnette's nephew, sizzled the airwaves during the summer with "Tired of Toein' the Line." Nineteen eighty's hottest new female singer had to be Pat Benatar, who sang the super-charged "Hit Me With Your Best Shot." Air Supply sailed out of Australia with two top-forty favorites, "Lost in Love" and "All Out of Love." Jazzy George Benson pleaded "Give Me the Night" and the S.O.S. Band urged "Take Your Time (Do It Right)." While Devo sang "Whip It," Stephanie Mills cooed "Never Knew Love Like This Before." Queen and their lead singer from Zanzibar, Freddie Mercury, may have summed it all up with "A Crazy Little Thing Called Love."

The top ten of 1980 shaped up this way: "Another One Bites the Dust" by Queen, "Call Me" by Blondie, "Funky Town" by Lipps, Inc., "It's Still Rock 'n' Roll to Me" by Billy Joel, "Another Brick in the Wall" by Pink Floyd, "Working My Way Back to You" by the Spinners, "Rock With You" by Michael Jackson, "A Woman in Love" by Barbra Streisand, "Upside Down" by Diana Ross, and "Fame" by Irene Cara.

It was 1980—the first year of the second quarter–century of rock and roll.

THE FUTURE

Perhaps the most frequent question Dick Clark is asked concerns the likelihood of the coming of another musical messiah like Elvis Presley or the Beatles—an act whose sound is so revolutionary that it will radically change the direction of rock and roll. Dick has some strong ideas on this hope for a rock savior.

"If you're waiting for that musical messiah, it's not going to happen. Today's sophistication in musical taste and the dividing of the market have made the music business the biggest it has ever been, and it'll only get bigger as audiences become more divided and more sophisticated. I don't foresee masses of people embracing an Elvis Presley or a Beatles ever again. True, some embraced Elton John, some embraced Peter Frampton, and some embraced the Bee Gees, but they were not the super idols. If you're waiting for another super idol, I don't think he, she, or they will happen in our lifetimes."

American Bandstand is perhaps the only rock-and-roll "constant," the only common experience shared by rock and rollers in 1955, 1965, 1975, and today. We asked Dick Clark what rock's second twenty-five years will hold for him and the show:

"I'm now shooting to keep the *Bandstand* on for thirty years. It appears we'll do that, because it's enjoying wonderful ratings. As for my life, every two to three years I sit down and try to figure out what things I haven't done. I see a lot more films in my future, and hopefully many will be musically oriented. Some day I'd like to go back in the record business. I will always continue to think of crazy things to do. Part of the fun of my life at this point is doing things I haven't done and making as much money out of it as I can, because I enjoy making money. It gives me the joy of recognition I never have gotten in the performing end of my life. People who talk for a living don't get standing ovations or a lot of applause. You just do it and make it look easy, and if you make it look easy enough, you're good at it."

Dick Clark must be good at it, because he's made it look easy for the past twenty-five years.

But what will happen to rock and roll itself? One of the hardest things anyone can do is predict the future of rock and roll successfully. Just ask the guy with that warehouse full of Bay City Rollers T-shirts. Anybody who has lived through the changes in rock, from rockabilly to the British invasion to acid rock to bubblegum to glitter rock to disco to new wave, will probably think twice before gazing into any crystal balls.

But there are a couple of movements to be on the lookout for as we head into the eighties.

Good, danceable rock and roll is back, this time around going by the name of power pop. Rock and roll started out in 1955 because kids wanted to feel that beat and dance, dance, dance. After twenty-five years kids still want to know if rock has a good beat and you can dance to it. Where kids were once dancing to Bill Haley, the Diamonds, and Chubby Checker, now they're moving to the beat of Blondie, Styx, and the Police. Power pop grew out of punk rock and new wave, and as power pop grows, some of those sounds will fill the radio airwaves of the eighties, sounds like the Talking Heads, The B-52's, Graham Parker, and the Police.

Rock and roll runs in cycles, and one sound all poised and ready to make a comeback in the eighties is the Motown sound of the mid-sixties. Motown slowed down in the seventies as its early stars grew older, its best producers left the company fold, and audiences began looking for messages and relevancy in its rock and roll. In the 1980s kids want to dance again, and the Motown sound was always some of rock's best dance music. In 1979 Bonnie Pointer's "Heaven Must Have Sent You" seemed like a medley of Motown's greatest hits all rolled into one record. Motown veterans Smokey Robinson and Michael Jackson opened the new decade perched high in the top ten.

The former leader of the First Edition ("Just Dropped in to See What Condition My Condition Was In"), Kenny Rogers shifted over to country when it seemed rock abandoned him in 1971. Kenny became the success story of 1980 when he crossed over from country to pop and even rock, with smashes like "The Gambler," "She Believes in Me," "Coward of the County," and his duet with Kim Carnes, "Don't Fall in Love with a Dreamer."

For years, ever since Jimmy Cliff's movie *The Harder They Fall,* people have been waiting for the Jamaican sound of reggae to be the next rock-and-roll craze. In the mid-seventies Bob Marley and Toots and the Maytals had their day in the sun. By the end of the seventies reggae and its Jamaican cousin, ska, had become the fastest-rising sound in Britain.

But whether rock in the eighties turns to reggae, power pop, cosmic funk, or something else entirely new, one thing is certain. Rock and roll will grow and evolve, keeping a finger on the pulse of young America. Rock and roll's first generation danced to the sounds of the Platters' "Only You" at their proms in 1955. In 1979 their kids rocked to the sounds of The Knack's "My Sharona" on their prom nights. Who knows what *their* kids—rock and roll's grandchildren—will be dancing to when they graduate in 2005.

The Spinners were the hottest soul group in the country in 1980 with their versions of "Workin' My Way Back to You" and "Cupid/I Loved You for a Long Time." The Spinners were originally a spinoff from Harvey and the Moonglows in 1960 and they spent many years recording in relative obscurity for Motown (Stevie Wonder was one of their producers), with their first big hit coming in 1970—"It's a Shame." The Spinners abandoned Motown for Philadelphia soul and ran off an impressive string of hits in the mid-seventies—"I'll Be Around," "Could It Be I'm Falling in Love," "One of a Kind (Love Affair)," "Mighty Love," "Rubber Band Man," "Games People Play," and "Then Came You" (with Dionne Warwick). The Spinners are, from left to right, Pervis Jackson, Billy Henderson, Henry Fambrough, John Edwards, and Bobby Smith.

454

Reggae had its roots in the Jamaican sounds of calypso and ska. The distinctive reggae beat was picked up by many rock artists in the seventies, including Paul McCartney ("C Moon"), Paul Simon ("Mother and Child Reunion"), Eric Clapton ("I Shot the Sheriff," written by Bob Marley), and Loggins and Messina ("Vahevella"). The 1972 film *The Harder They Come*, starring Jimmy Cliff and featuring the music of Cliff, Desmond Dekker, and Toots and the Maytals, helped popularize reggae in America. The leading reggae artist is the late Rastafarian Bob Marley, who could neither read nor write, but whose songs earned him the title the Poet of Reggae.

British new-wave group the Clash (from left: Mick Jones, Paul Simonon, Joe Strummer, and Nicky "Topper" Headon), whose album *London Calling* was a chart-topper in early 1980. *(Mike Putland/Retna)*

Detroit's Chrissie Hynde and her British group the Pretenders were a sensation in the summer of 1980 with songs like "Brass in Pocket (I'm Special)" from *The Pretenders* album. The group are (from left) Pete Farndon, Chrissie Hynde, Martin Chambers, and James Honeyman Scott.

The B-52's flew out of Georgia with some strange outfits, strange hairdos, and even stranger new-wave sounds like "Rock Lobster."

A favorite of the New York new-wave crowd, with songs such as "Psycho Killer" and "Take Me to the River"—Talking Heads. The members are (from left) Chris Frantz, Jerry Harrison, David Byrne, and Martina Weymouth. *(Ron Pownall)*

INDEX

McGuire, Barry, 166, 189, 194
McKay, Al, 417
McKennan, Ron "Pig Pen," 228, 230
McKeown, Les, 363
McLaughlin, John, 272
McLaughlin, Ollie, 107
McLean, Don, 305-6
McLenore, Lamonte, 257
McManus, Ross, 433
McNally, John, 153
McPhatter, Clyde, 64
McVie, Christine Perfect, 397, 401, 402
McVie, John, 396ff., 401
Maffei, Frank, 52
Maguire, Lee, 148
Majewski, Hank, 121
Mamas and the Papas, 193-95
Manilow, Barry, 325
Mann, Barry, 294, 394-95
Mann, Manfred, 150, 409
Manuel, Richard, 174, 279, 280
Manzarek, Ray, 221ff.
Marcucci, Bob, 71, 72
Mardin, Arif, 207, 428
Marley, Bob, 456
Marriott, Steve, 383, 388
Marsden, Freddy, 148
Marsden, Gerry, 148
Martin, George, 158, 159, 163
Martino, Al, 71
Marvelettes, the, 134, 135
Mason, Dave, 195
Mason, Nick, 327
Massi, Nick, 121, 122
Mastrangelo, Carlo, 51
Mastrangelo, Johnny, 68
Mauldin, Joe, 50, 55
Mayall, John, 234, 396
Mayfield, Curtis, 116, 337
Meaden, Peter, 249
Meat Loaf, 414-16
Meisner, Randy, 353, 361, 362
Mekler, Gabriel, 289
Melcher, Terry, 166
Melouney, Vince, 426
Messina, Jim, 268, 362
Midler, Bette, 325-26, 394
Miles, Buddy, 233
Miller, Mitch, 207, 231
Miller, Steve, 375-76, 390-91
Miracles, the, 133-34, 135
Mitchell, Chad, 166, 338
Mitchell, Mike, 132
Mizell, Fonso, 277
Monkees, the, 215-16, 303
Montgomery, Bob, 49
Moody Blues, 301-2
Moon, Keith, 249ff., 375-76
Mooney, Thom, 440

Moore, Johnny, 80, 81
Moore, Pete, 133
Moore, Robin, 190
Moore, Scotty, 32
Moore, Thomas, 157, 158
Moroder, Giorgio, 438, 446ff.
Morrison, Jim, 221-25
Morton, George "Shadow," 144, 412
Most, Mickie, 177
Mothers of Invention, 208, 213, 282
Motown, 133-35. *See also* specific groups
Mugwumps, the, 197
Murray, Dee, 346
Murray, Don, 212

Nader, Richard, 19, 28, 69, 83, 102
Nash, Graham, 151, 268-70, 293
Nash, Johnny, 116
Nathan, Syd, 171
Neal, Bob, 32
Negron, Chuck, 289
Negroni, Joe, 26
Neilsen, Rick, 440
Nelson, Nate, 23
Nelson, Ricky, 102-3, 362
Nesmith, Mike, 215-16
Nevins, Al, 98, 294
Newman, Randy, 293
Nichol, Al, 212
Nicks, Stevie, 400-1, 402
Niles, Preston, 444
1910 Fruitgum Company, 260-61
Noone, Peter, 177
Norman, Ben, 53
Norris, Dale, 53
Novelty records, 56-58
Nugent, Ted, 414
Nunn, Bobby, 62
Nyro, Laura, 188, 205

Oakley, Berry, 322, 324
Ocasek, Ric, 442
Ochs, Phil, 186
Oldham, Andrew Loog, 179
Olsen, Keith, 398-400
Olsson, Nigel, 346
Ono, Yoko, 162, 163, 300, 317, 319
Orbison, Roy, 84-85
Orr, Ben, 442
Otis, Johnny, 14, 64
Otis, Shuggie, 265
Osmond, Donny, 278, 363
Osmond Brothers, 278

Page, Jimmy, 273, 365, 367
Paich, David, 376
Palmer, Bruce, 268
Palmer, David, 392
Pankow, James, 282
Pappalardi, Felix, 197, 234
Parazaider, Walt, 282
Parker, Colonel, Tom, 32, 33
Parris, Fred, 28
Parsons, Alan, 327
Parsons, Gram, 167
Paton, Tam, 363
Paul, Les, 390
Paxton, Tom, 189
Payne, Shari, 147
Payton, Denis, 155
Payton, Lawrence, 198, 199
Peeples, Lewis, 28
Pender, Mike, 153
Perkins, Carl, 29
Perkins, Clayton, 29
Perkins, Jay, 29
Perrin, Freddie, 134, 277
Perry, Richard, 315, 428
Peter and Gordon, 149
Peter, Paul and Mary, 186, 338
Petersen, Colin, 426
Peterson, Gary, 275
Peterson, Ray, 144
Peterson, Sylvia, 125-26
Peterson, Tom, 440
Petty, Norman, 50, 51
Phillips, Michelle, 194-95
Phillips, John, 194-95
Phillips, Sam, 29, 32, 36-37, 85
Pickett, Bobby "Boris," 57
Pickett, Wilson, 67, 322
Pinder, Mike, 301, 302
Pink Floyd, 327-28
Pitney, Gene, 113
Plant, Robert, 365ff.
Plastic Ono Band, 317
Platters, the, 22-23
Playmates, the, 57
Pointer, Bonnie, 453
Poole, Brian, 149, 155
Popovich, Steve, 414
Popwell, Robert, 205
Porter, Tiran, 356
Portz, Chuck, 212
Presley, Elvis, 29, 30-34, 85
Price, Alan, 151
Price, Lloyd, 24, 66-67

Quaife, Peter, 153

MICHAEL USLAN grew up in the area of Asbury Park, New Jersey. At Indiana University he taught the first accredited college course on comic books in the country, ran an oldies rock-and-roll radio show called "Bloomington Bandstand," and earned his A.B., M.S., and J.D. In 1976 Michael joined United Artists Corporation as an attorney in motion-picture production. He now devotes his time to writing books and producing motion pictures. His latest films include *Swamp Thing,* a 1930s-styled monster movie for United Artists and Avco-Embassy and a new version of *Batman* for Polygram Pictures and Warner Bros. Michael lives in Cedar Grove, New Jersey, with his wife, Nancy, and son, David.

BRUCE SOLOMON grew up in Jersey City and attended the University of Wisconsin, where he developed a career as a disc jockey and campus trivia expert. Bruce received his law degree at Rutgers University School of Law and simultaneously began writing a series of successful books of trivia, most notably *The Rock 'n' Roll Trivia Quiz Book.* While continuing his work in entertainment and corporate law, he is a producer of television and syndicated radio programs. Bruce resides with his wife, Leah, in Elizabeth, New Jersey.